Communications
in Computer and Information Science   318

T0297869

Nils Aschenbruck   Peter Martini
Michael Meier   Jens Tölle (Eds.)

Future Security

7th Security Research Conference
Future Security 2012
Bonn, Germany, September 4-6, 2012
Proceedings

 Springer

Volume Editors

Nils Aschenbruck
University of Osnabrück
Institute of Computer Science
Osnabrück, Germany
E-mail: nils.aschenbruck@uos.de

Peter Martini
Fraunhofer FKIE
Wachtberg, Germany
E-mail: peter.martini@fkie.fraunhofer.de

Michael Meier
University of Bonn
Institute of Computer Science 4
Bonn, Germany
E-mail: mm@cs.uni-bonn.de

Jens Tölle
Fraunhofer FKIE
Wachtberg, Germany
E-mail: jens.toelle@fkie.fraunhofer.de

ISSN 1865-0929   e-ISSN 1865-0937
ISBN 978-3-642-33160-2   e-ISBN 978-3-642-33161-9
DOI 10.1007/978-3-642-33161-9
Springer Heidelberg Dordrecht London New York

Library of Congress Control Number: 2012945558

CR Subject Classification (1998): K.6.5, H.4, K.4.4, K.5.1, J.1, J.2, I.4.8, C.2.4, J.4

Typesetting: Camera-ready by author, data conversion by Scientific Publishing Services, Chennai, India

Printed on acid-free paper

Springer is part of Springer Science+Business Media (www.springer.com)

Foreword of the Conference Chair

Welcome to the proceedings of the 7th Future Security Research Conference 2012 held in Bonn, Germany.

The Fraunhofer Group for Defense and Security has established a successful conference series in the emerging field of security research. After conferences in the cities of Karlsruhe and Berlin, the 2012 edition went to Bonn, the former capital of Germany. The conference was held in the World Conference Center Bonn in the former premises of the Bundestag, the German parliament – a perfect venue for bringing together decision makers, public authorities, industry, and scientists to discuss new ways of protecting both our freedom and our open society. Numerous presentations were held in the former plenary hall of the Bundestag. The foyer and additional rooms were used for special interest group meetings, poster presentations, and exhibitions.

The conference program offered several keynote speeches, panels, and many scientific presentations. The scientific papers accompanying the presentations are included in this book. All the papers were reviewed according to tough scientific standards. They provide a broad overview over the state of the art in security research.

My sincere thanks go to the Program Committee, in particular to the Program Co-chairs Nils Aschenbruck, University of Osnabrück, and Michael Meier, University of Bonn, for orchestrating the review process and arranging the scientific program; to Jens Tölle, Fraunhofer FKIE, for handling the publication process and spending hours on making these proceedings look the way you, the reader, expect publications to look in this series by Springer; and to Hans Peter Stuch, Fraunhofer FKIE, for taking care of the local arrangements.

Most of all, I thank the authors for providing us with their scientific results, ideas, and reflections on security issues. We know that there is a wide range of conferences held all over the world and we very much appreciate the authors choosing Future Security as the conference for presenting their work.

Peter Martini

Foreword of the Program Chairs

Welcome to the proceedings of the 7th Future Security Research Conference. It was our privilege to coordinate the review process and to put together a high-quality technical program.

Research in the area of security in the future is very important. The challenges concerning security in the future are miscellaneous, broad, and often fuzzy. We were proud to present a program that covered many important areas of future security research.

Future Security 2012 received 137 submissions (papers, short papers, and posters) from authors from 19 countries on four continents. Out of 61 submitted full papers, 24 full papers presenting novel perspectives and research results within the scope of the conference were selected for presentation at the conference and publication in these proceedings (39%). In addition, short papers and posters presenting preliminary or interim results were selected to complement the program.

The Future Security Program Committee members as well as the external reviewers did a wonderful job to ensure that Future Security had a strong and solid technical program. Based on the paper reviews, the papers were selected for the conference. In our opinion, these papers were the most interesting and thought-provoking. We are very confident that these excellent papers will trigger interesting discussions. Accepted papers were revised by the authors before publication. The revisions have not been checked for correctness, and the authors bear full responsibility for the contents of their papers.

The conference program comprised new theoretical and practical approaches and results from research as well as experience reports on the topics of urban security, supply chain and critical infrastructure security, security situational awareness, crisis management, sensor technologies, social, psychological and political aspects, cloud and law, cybercrime, industrial espionage, border security, detection of hazardous materials, food chain security, user, sensor and system aspects of public security, aviation security, and ergonomic aspects.

We warmly thank all those who contributed to the program of the conference, especially the authors, the invited speakers and panelists, as well as the members of Future Security Program Committee and the additional reviewers. We hope that you will enjoy reading the papers of Future Security 2012 as much as we did, and that the conference will promote further research interests and activities in the important area future security as previous editions already have done.

Nils Aschenbruck
Michael Meier

Organization

Program Committee

Oliver Ambacher	Fraunhofer IAF
Achim Bachem	Forschungszentrum Jülich GmbH
Bernd Becker	Albert-Ludwigs-Universität Freiburg
Jürgen Beyerer	Fraunhofer IOSB
Peter Boßdorf	Report Verlag GmbH
Adam S. Cumming	Defence Science & Technology Laboratory, UK
Eckhart Curtius	Bundesministerium für Bildung und Forschung (BMBF)
Armin Dirks	Bundesministerium der Verteidigung (BMVg)
Bert Don	TNO Defence, Security and Safety
Claudia Eckert	Fraunhofer AISEC
Peter Elsner	Fraunhofer ICT
Joachim Ender	Fraunhofer FHR
Sabine Groth	Ministerium für Innovation, Wissenschaft und Forschung NRW
Karsten Heidrich	Deutsche Bank AG
Albert Heuberger	Fraunhofer IIS
Wolfgang Jans	BWB FWG
Rüdiger Klein	Fraunhofer IAIS
Andreas Könen	Bundesamt für Sicherheit in der Informationstechnik (BSI)
Rainer Krug	Bundesministerium der Verteidigung (BMVg)
Tobias Leismann	Fraunhofer VVS
Monika Lieberam	Bundesanstalt Technisches Hilfswerk (THW)
Peter Martini	Fraunhofer FKIE
William Robertson	Northeastern University, Boston
Christopher Schlick	Fraunhofer FKIE
Viola Schmid	Technische Universität Darmstadt
Françoise Simonet	CEA Commissariat à l'Energie Atomique
Birgitta Sticher	Hochschule für Wirtschaft und Recht, Berlin
Jürgen Stock	Bundeskriminalamt
Maurus Tacke	Fraunhofer IOSB
Klaus Thoma	Fraunhofer EMI
Thomas Tschersich	Deutsche Telekom AG
Markus Ullmann	Bundesamt für Sicherheit in der Informationstechnik (BSI)
Norbert Weber	Bundesministerium der Verteidigung (BMVg)
Karin Wey	VDI Technologiezentrum GmbH
Uwe Wiemken	Fraunhofer INT

Table of Contents

Crisis Management

Security for Critical Infrastructure And Urban Areas

Sensor Technology

Social, Psychological and Political Aspects

Cyber Defense and Information Security

Maritime and Border Security

Detection of Hazardous Materials

Food Chain Security

Aviation Security

Ergonomic Aspects

Measurement Concept
for Security in Mass Transportation

Jan-Peter Nicklas, Nadine Schlüter, and Petra Winzer

Research Group of Product Safety and Quality Engineering, University of Wuppertal, Germany
{nicklas,schluete,winzer}@uni-wuppertal.de

Abstract. In order to reduce endangerments in the field of mass transportation systems, new technologies and methods for a customer- and situation-oriented approach are needed. This paper outlines a concept to better understand the customers´ reasons and their effects on the sense of security as well as a system that can offer permanent updated information on the security sensations of customers related to real situations.

Keywords: security feelings, mass transportation, permanent survey, measurement concept, multi-criteria analysis.

1   Introduction

The security of customers in the field of bus transportation are difficult to fulfill because of the grown infrastructures as well as security methods that were only adjusted over the time instead of redesigned in regarding new circumstances and requirements (on e.g. law, norms, customer acceptance). [1]

There is a need for developing new methods that offer security for critical infrastructures. Furthermore these methods – using already existing and / or new technologies - need to detect and identify situations that are felt as endangerments by customers on a parameter-based and automatic level. Only this way can offer a possibility for process owners to take preventative actions. The missing of such a systematic approach is a major problem in detecting dangerous situations in an early stage in mass transportation. [2]

Furthermore we know the factors influencing the customers´ security feelings in mass transportation, but do not know the meaning of each factor and their correlation. [3]

2   Approach

The approach to solve above mentioned problems is based on two different methodical strategies and their integration in an interdisciplinary approach. On the one hand there is a systematical differentiation of **data**[1] (recorded data / sensor components, cameras, survey data / touchscreens, applications, QR-codes) and the processing of

---

[1] Definition data: Data consist of a combination of characters that are ordered by a ascertained rule. [9].

N. Aschenbruck et al. (Eds.): Future Security 2012, CCIS 318, pp. 1–4, 2012.

data to **information**[2] (in the system backend), respectively information output (e.g. displays). On the other hand selected scenarios, sensors and information outputs are designed customer- and process-oriented. In the following the last mentioned approach should be explained in more detail.

Customer- and Process-Oriented Approach

In order to consider each situation, scenario, sensor components, factors, measurement concepts and indicators, a customer- and process-oriented approach for measuring customer satisfaction is chosen – the Generic Customer Satisfaction Measurement (GCSM). [4] This method is based on the customer relevant processes that are detected by a Service Blueprinting. [5-6]

In the beginning customer relevant processes and services – in this case travelling by bus – are detected. At the linking points of customer and business processes – so called contact points [7] – the enlisted services are itemized. [8] For each service and its attributes performances indicators (like security at the bus platform) are developed so that the performance can be measured.

The gathering of performance data consists of two separated measuring systems: one system for an objective detecting of the services and one for the subjective detecting of customer feelings with reference to the indicators of the service performance. The interlinking of those data adds up to the customer opinion respectively the security feeling in dependency on the really generated (security-) services.

The detection of the trust into the used technology as well as the collection of subjective data is carried out by surveys. Those surveys are supported by touchscreens, mobile phone applications and QR-codes.

The analysis of gathered measurement and survey data that is carried out in a system-backend is based on the performance cluster[3] of GCSM. This performance cluster links customer processes, influences on the customer and customer survey results with each other in accordance to an applied logic. This logic must be able to offer a multi-criteria analysis, because influences can affect each other respectively the customers´ feelings and sensations in different ways. The logic has to be able to identify the impact of each influence factor as a fragment of the whole customer sensation.

3   Results

The basic concept for combining objective and subjective data, customer voice data as well as trust and acceptance-surveys has already been developed. [3, 9] Yet, more research on sensors, their combination with survey-tools for detecting security feelings and an incident-related data output has to be carried out in order to realize an operational measurement system in busses.

This includes the development of a multi-criteria logic that analyzes the correlations of several influences on the security feeling of bus travelers. Only after

---

[2] Definition information: Information is a combined, interpretable amount of data that is set into context. [10].

[3] Definition performance cluster: Database for handling performance data of a system.

completing theses mile steps a test of the master system "e-security Guide" can be accomplished.

In practice this requires a bus to be equipped with sensors for objective measurements while touch-screens are installed in the passenger areas. The equipment set up is connected to a mobile data processing unit. In addition to the touch-screens survey applications and QR-codes should enable the customer to evaluate situations. The system-backend processes the received data and provides derived information on the security feelings of mass transportation customers to e.g. a disponent. The equipment as well as the handling of information is designed in a user and customer oriented way. The considerable value of this approach is the evaluation of a situation by the customer himself by using touch-screens, mobile applications and QR-codes. Security is no longer evaluated by a third party but actively affected by the customer.

Every component of the e-Security Guide (sensors, data handling, data processing, survey equipment) should be designed and developed on a modular basis to allow a transfer to other application areas. This assures the use of e-security Guide in other scenarios. So this new system is not only a new technology- and security-standard for busses but also for the whole mass transportation system.

4 Outlook

One main challenge is to combine the different approaches of a customer integrated security system. Different kinds of scientific disciplines like sensor technology, survey methods, acceptance measurements and regulatory frameworks have to be linked with each other in order to create a common system that offers customer oriented security concepts. This includes the integration of experts for multi-criteria analysis. The linking of performances, influences, security parameters and process workflows demands the development of an empirical data analysis so that it becomes possible to understand the reasons and the effects of dangerous situations in the field of mass transportation.

References

1. Reinkober, N. (Hrsg.): VeRSiert - Sicherheit im ÖPNV bei Großveranstaltungen; Vernetzung von Verkehrsunternehmen, Einsatzkräften, Veranstaltern und Fahrgästen des ÖPNV.1., Auflage, EAN: 9783863422318 (2011)
2. Schlüter, N., Schulze-Bramey, U., Winzer, P.: Die sozialwissenschaftlichen Dimensionen beim Schutz von Verkehrsinfrastrukturen. In: Fähnrich, K.-P., Franczyk, B. (Hrsg.) Tagungsband Informatik 2010 - Service Science- Neue Perspektiven für die Informatik, Band 1, Leipzig, September 29-October 01 (2010) ISBN 978-88579-269-7
3. Sicherheitsbedürfnisse als Bestandteil von Servicequalität im ÖPNV - Das Problem der Messung von Sicherheit bei großen Menschenmassen. In: Winzer, P. (Hrsg.): Entwicklungen im Wuppertaler Generic-Management-Konzept. Berichte zum Generic-Management. Band: 1, S.51–S.62. Shaker Verlag, Aachen (2010) ISBN 978-3-8322-9356-7
4. Zeithaml, V.A., Bitner, M.J., Gremler, D.D.: Service Marketing. Integrating Customer Focus Across the Firm, vol. 5. Mc Graw Hill, New York (2009)

5. Kleinaltenkamp, M.: Service-Blueprinting - Nicht ohne einen Kunden. Ein Instrument zur Steigerung der Effektivität und der Effizienz von Dienstleistungsprozessen. Technischer Vertrieb, Heft 2, S.33–S.39 (1999)
6. Lovelock, C., Wirtz, J.: Services Marketing. People, Technology, vol. 5. Strategy Pearson, Aufl. (2006)
7. Vogt, E., Fiedrich, S.: Mehr vom Kunden wissen – sichert langfristigen Unternehmenserfolg. In: Winzer, P. (Hrsg.) Berichte zum Generic Management: Generic Management und Möglichkeiten der Stakeholderintegration. Band: 1/2006, pp. 61–66. Shaker Verlag, Aachen (2006)
8. Renn, O.: Technikakzeptanz: Lehren und Rückschlüsse der Akzeptanzforschung für die Bewältigung des technischen Wandels. In: Technikfolgenabschätzung Theorie und Praxis (TaTuP), vol. 14(3), pp. 29–38 (2005)
9. Braunholz, H.: Werkzeugentwicklung für informationsflussorientierte Prozessmodelle. Shaker Verlag, Aachen (2006)
10. Rehäuser, J., Krcmar, H.: Wissensmanagement im Unternehmen. In: Schreyögg, G., Conrad, P. (Hrsg.) Managementforschung 6: Wissensmanagement, pp. S.1–S.40. De Gruyter, Berlin (1996)

Improved Emergency Management
by a Loosely Coupled Logistic System

Dirk Thorleuchter[1], Joachim Schulze[1], and Dirk Van den Poel[2]

[1] Fraunhofer INT, Appelsgarten 2, D-53879 Euskirchen, Germany
{dirk.Thorleuchter,joachim.schulze}@int.fraunhofer.de
[2] Ghent University, Faculty of Economics and Business Administration, B-9000 Gent,
Tweekerkenstraat 2, Belgium
dirk.vandenpoel@ugent.be
http://www.crm.UGent.be

Abstract. We investigate a robust and intelligent logistic system for emergency management where existing commercial logistic systems are loosely coupled with logistic systems of emergency management organizations and armed forces. This system is used to supply the population in case of a disaster where a high impact of environmental conditions on logistics can be seen. Very important are robustness as the ability of a logistic system to remain effective under these conditions and intelligent behavior for automated ad-hoc decisions facing unforeseen events. Scenario technique, roadmapping, as well as surveys are used as qualitative methodologies to identify current weaknesses in emergency management logistics and to forecast future development of loosely coupled logistic systems. Text mining and web mining analysis as quantitative methodologies are used to improve forecasting. As a result, options are proposed for governmental organizations and companies to enable such a loosely coupled logistic system within the next 20 years.

Keywords: Roadmap, Scenario, Logistic, Emergency Management.

1 Introduction

After the terrorist attacks of 11 September 2001, it could be seen that a large impact of such attacks on the global economy and on individual sectors e.g. on logistics take place. In general, a supply chain is vulnerable concerning terrorism (destroying of goods), crime (theft of goods) [1], and natural disasters (e.g., earthquakes, tsunamis, hurricanes) [2]. Further aspects - among others - are the damage / destruction of existing infrastructure for the transportation of goods or the means of transportation and the cyber attack on information and communication systems needed for supply chain management [3]. Thus, beside well-known factors in logistics (transportation, inventory, warehousing, material handling, packaging, and integration of information) supply chain security has becomes a more and more important factor [4], [5].

Emergency management is the process of protecting population, critical infrastructures etc. from hazard risks as occurred by natural and artificial disasters. Literature

N. Aschenbruck et al. (Eds.): Future Security 2012, CCIS 318, pp. 5–8, 2012.

shows challenges of logistics in emergency management [6]: A challenge is that the flow of relief services and information is directed from relief distribution centers to a specific point of destination in affected areas where it is difficult to operate because of the environmental conditions. A further challenge is the time aspect. The timeliness of relief supply distribution is hard to control (e.g. considering a critical 3-day period following a disaster). Further, in emergency situations communications challenges occur as well as operational un-certainties (i.e., controlling the inventory of supplies ready for transport). Last, the occurrence of information gap is a challenge because information immediately following a disaster normally is decentralized distributed and it may not be as accurate as needed.

National governments are responsible for emergency management however the governmental capacities in logistics have been reduced significantly (e.g. see the current structure reform of the federal armed forces in Germany). The support of the population can only be implemented as a loosely coupled system where the logistic capacities of emergency management organizations and armed forces on one hand and the - additionally purchased - commercial logistic capacities on the other hand worked together [7].

Thus, this work investigates a loosely coupled logistic system for emergency management that consists of commercial logistic systems and of logistic systems of emergency management organizations and armed forces. Whereas this system is used to supply the population in case of a disaster, unforeseen events often appear that lead to changes in the environmental conditions. Facing these events, the loosely coupled logistic system has to be the ability to remain effective (robustness). An intelligent behavior for automated ad-hoc decisions is also needed.

2   Methodology

The aim of this study is to enable a loosely coupled logistic system for emergency management. We use a methodology that consists of five steps. The first step is to identify scenarios by use of scenario technique [8-11]. A specific scenario is selected considering the occurrence of terrorism attacks and natural disasters in Germany that represents the environment of a logistic system.

Based on the first step, the second step identifies the requirements for a future loosely coupled logistic system. Information about the current situation and about the possible future of such a coupled logistic system is collected. This is done in a qualitative way by human experts. A literature review is done, expert workshops are organized and surveys have been done to get experts opinions about the requirements.

The third step is to evaluate the collected information to improve forecast accuracy. This is done by use of quantitative text and web mining methods. Descriptions about the possible future of the coupled logistic system are analyzed automatically. We use text mining methods (e.g. tokenization, case conversion, part-of-speech tagging, stop word filtering, stemming, term weights) to identify keywords [12-14]. Based on the keywords, multi-occurrences are identified that are multiple terms that occur more frequently together than it would be expected by chance within a specific term distance [15], [16]. Human experts select relevant multi-occurrences that represent requirements of a future coupled logistic system. Search queries are built based on the relevant multi-occurrences. To consider worldwide available information where web pages are formulized in different languages, the search queries are translated to several languages. A web mining approach based on Google search advanced programming interface (API) is used to identify relevant documents in the internet [17]. For each document, keywords are identified that occur together with the corresponding multi-occurrences within a specific term distance. We translate the keywords to the target language (English) by use of Goolge translate API. They are compared to keywords from further retrieved documents to identify their above-chance frequent occurrence. As a result, new multi-occurrences are identified that are related to relevant requirements of a future coupled logistic system.

In the fourth step, human experts analyses the new multi-occurrences for each requirement. As a result, some requirements are modified. The fifth step is to create a system roadmap [18] that contains a time table for realizing the modified requirements and outlines the recommendations for government and companies.

3   Recommendations from the Roadmap

The created system roadmap shows detailed recommendations for different time steps. The expected year where results should be implemented is mentioned in parentheses. Below, the results are summarized in short notes:

An improvement of the logistical capacities of governmental organizations specifically in those kinds of equipments that are not available in commercial logistics is suggested (2020). An improvement in robustness of commercial logistic systems enables them to operate under difficult environment conditions as expected in emergency situations (2030). An improved cooperation and coordination between governmental organization and companies in logistics is also suggested (2020) as well as the creation of standardized interfaces and of general conditions for legal aspects where much organizational and legal work is to do by governmental organizations to enable cooperation and coordination (2015-2020). A further kind of recommendation focuses on the goods that reach from a more robust water and energy supply (2025) to the introduction of new decentralized stockpiling approaches (2015). Further recommendation concern the creation of emergency management plans for different scenarios (2015) and an increased research and development (e.g. through research funding) (as from now) as well as an increased investment in the technologies 'Future Internet / Internet of Things', 'Cloud Computing', 'Agent based open-loop controller', 'Fleet management', 'Identification', 'Location Determination', 'Artificial Intelligence', and 'IT Security'. Overall, this system roadmap - based on a preselected scenario - shows that such a loosely coupled logistic system for emergency management is not realizable at present time in Germany. However, such a system is realizable within the next 20 years. Estimations about the future of logistics can be received in good quality by human experts. Further, quantitative methods are a good mean to reduce the uncertainty in the qualitative estimations and to increase its accuracy.

References

1. Lee, H.L., Whang, S.: Higher supply chain security with lower cost: Lessons from total quality management. Int. J. Prod. Econ. 96(3), 289–300 (2005)
2. Flotzinger, C., Hofmann-Prokopczy, H., Starkl, F.: Logistik 2030 – Zukunftsszenarien für eine nachhaltige Standortentwicklung in Österreich. FH OÖ, Steyr, Austria (2008)
3. Von der Gracht, H., Däneke, E., Micic, P., Darkow, I.L., Jahn, C.: Zukunft der Logistik-Dienstleistungsbranche in Deutschland. Media Group GmbH, Hamburg (2008)
4. Pfohl, H.C., Wimmer, T. (eds.): Robuste und sichere Logistiksysteme. DVV Media Group GmbH, Hamburg (2008)
5. Plotzki, S.: Trends im Global Supply Chain Management, p. 39. VDM Verlag Dr. Müller, Saarbrücken (2007)
6. Sheu, J.B.: Challenges of emergency logistics management. Transp. Res.: Part E: Logist. Transp. Rev. 43(6), 655–659 (2007)
7. Hale, T., Moberg, C.R.: Improving supply chain disaster preparedness: A decision process for secure site location. Int. J. Phys. Distrib. Logist. Manag. 35(3), 195–207 (2005)
8. Geschka, H.: Die Szenariotechnik in der strategischen Unternehmensplanung. In: Hahn, D. (ed.) Strategische Unternehmensplanung, pp. 518–545. Physica, Würzburg (1999)
9. Thorleuchter, D., Van den Poel, D.: Rapid Scenario Generation with Generic Systems. In: International Conference on Management Sciences and Information Technology 2012. Lecture Notes in Information Technology. IERI, Delaware (in press, 2012)
10. Thorleuchter, D., Weck, G., Van den Poel, D.: Usability Based Modeling for Advanced IT-Security – An Electronic Engineering Approach. In: Jin, D., Lin, S. (eds.) Advances in Mechanical and Electronic Engineering. LNEE, vol. 177, pp. 615–619. Springer, Heidelberg (2012)
11. Thorleuchter, D., Weck, G., Van den Poel, D.: Granular Deleting in Multi Level Security Models – An Electronic Engineering Approach. In: Jin, D., Lin, S. (eds.) Advances in Mechanical and Electronic Engineering. LNEE, vol. 177, pp. 609–614. Springer, Heidelberg (2012)
12. Thorleuchter, D., Van den Poel, D., Prinzie, A.: Analyzing existing customers' websites to improve the customer acquisition process as well as the profitability prediction in B-to-B marketing. Expert Syst. Appl. 39(3), 2597–2605 (2012)
13. Thorleuchter, D., Herberz, S., Van den Poel, D.: Mining Social Behavior Ideas of Przewalski Horses. In: Wu, Y. (ed.) Advances in Computer, Communication, Control and Automation. LNEE, vol. 121, pp. 649–656. Springer, Heidelberg (2011)
14. Thorleuchter, D., Van den Poel, D.: Using NMF for Analyzing War Logs. In: Aschenbruck, N., et al. (eds.) Future Security 2012. CCIS, vol. 318, pp. 73–76. Springer, Heidelberg (2012)
15. Thorleuchter, D., Van den Poel, D.: Extraction of Ideas from Microsystems Technology. In: Jin, D., Lin, S. (eds.) Advances in CSIE, Vol. 1. AISC, vol. 168, pp. 563–568. Springer, Heidelberg (2012)
16. Thorleuchter, D., Van den Poel, D.: Predicting E-Commerce Company Success by Mining the Text of Its Publicly-Accessible Website. Expert Syst. Appl. (in press, 2012)
17. Thorleuchter, D., Van den Poel, D.: Using Webcrawling of Publicly-Available Websites to Assess E-Commerce Relationships. In: Annual SRII Global Conference 2012, IEEE Press, New York (in press, 2012)
18. Laube, T., Abele, T.: Technologie-Roadmap: Strategisches und taktisches Technologiemanagement. Ein Leitfaden. Fraunhofer IPA edition, Stuttgart (2005)

Monitoring Security and Safety of Assets in Supply Chains

Ganna Monakova[1], Cristina Severin[2], Achim D. Brucker[1],
Ulrich Flegel[3], and Andreas Schaad[1]

[1] SAP Research, Vincenz-Priessnitz-Str. 1, 76131 Karlsruhe, Germany
{fganna.monakova,achim.brucker,andreas.schaad}@sap.com
[2] esciris gmbh, Max-Eyth-Str. 38, 71088 Holzgerlingen
cristina.severin@esciris.de
[3] HFT Stuttgart, Schellingstr. 24, 70174 Stuttgart, Germany
ulrich.flegel@hft-stuttgart.de

Abstract. In the today's world of the global economy supply chains become more and more complicated. Widely distributed supply chains open more possibilities for attacks on both IT as well physical level. The potential threats can span over multiple supply chains. For example, if the same truck is used to transport chemicals and then the same truck is used to transport food, a contamination threat arises that neither of the supply chains can detect when analysed independently. In this paper, we present a tool-supported framework that extends modelling and execution of supply chains processes with specification, execution and monitoring of the security and safety constraints that are used to protect supply chain assets. The tool allows to detect not only threats scoped to a single supply chain, but cross-cutting threats that can only be detected through analysis of the whole system.

Keywords: Supply Chain Security, Monitoring, Resource modelling.

1   Introduction

Security, safety, and compliance of a supply chain process and involved assets are critical to any organisation. Especially all supply chain participants want to be sure that assets sent to another party are treated correctly and that assets received from another party can be trusted. For example, supply chain partners not only want to ensure that the purchase order data and the payment data are correct, but also that the ordered goods have been treated according to various requirements. To obtain such an assurance, partners need to get a proof that the asset will be treated in a certain way, e.g., it will be ensured that the temperature and packaging of the ordered goods is correct. As many enterprises need to comply to regulations such as the European Food Safety regulations (e.g., see Regulation (EC) No. 882/2004 of the European Parliament and of the Council of 29 April 2004 and related documents), there is a strong demand to specify and communicate security and safety requirements on the level of the supply chain models. In this way, each of the supply chain participants will be

N. Aschenbruck et al. (Eds.): Future Security 2012, CCIS 318, pp. 9–20, 2012.
© Springer-Verlag Berlin Heidelberg 2012

able to explicitly specify taken security and safety measures to other partners. Documenting such requirements as part of the supply chain model can also be used as contract specification between supply chain participants. During the execution of a supply chain, the compliance with the specified security and safety requirements needs to be monitored and certified.

In addition to the threats related to a single supply chain, there are a number of threats that occur when different supply chains come together. For example, product cross-contamination can occur when incompatible goods belonging to different supply chains are stored in the same area. This means, that in addition to the threats scoped to a single supply chain, threats that span across multiple supply chains must be considered. We refer to such threats as *contextual* threats, emphasising that a specific issue only becomes a threat when the environmental and logical contexts of a supply chain execution are considered.

Together with retailers, freight carriers, and food manufactures, we identified the following objectives that must be supported by a framework for business level specification of the security and safety constraints:

- *Security and Safety Awareness:* a supply chain participant should be aware of security and safety threats for the assets used in a supply chain.
- *Security and Safety Visibility:* a supply chain partner should be able to communicate security and safety requirements as well as taken measures through visual representations or annotations.
- *Security and Safety Consistency:* requirements should be fulfilled in a consistent way.
- *Security and Safety Provability:* it should be possible to prove fulfillment of specified requirements.

To address these requirements, we developed an approach for modelling and monitoring security and safety requirements. In contrast to previous work [7] that presented the general approach, in this paper we concentrate on the modelling and detection of security and safety threats scoped to a single supply chain, as well threats related to the relationships between different supply chains.

2   Motivating Example

According to [4], approximately one-third of all fresh fruit and vegetables produced worldwide is lost before it reaches consumers. In [5] the authors state that sometimes the losses and wastage of the food may even reach 50 percent between field and fork. Incorrect harvesting, transport, storage and packaging play an important role in these losses.

To demonstrate the developed approach we consider two initially independent supply chains, one that orders and delivers ice cream, and another one that orders and delivers toxic chemicals. Figure 1 presents the simplified model of the ice cream supply chain involving three parties: *Retailer* sends an order to *Production* in the *Order* activity; Producer dispatches the required amount of the product (*Dispatch* activity) and uses *Logistic* partner to deliver it (*Transport* sub-process) to *Retailer*. There are two data objects modeled in the process: *PurchaseOrder* object contains all information required to make an order, including required amount of the product and the delivery destination; *IceCream* data object represents the actual physical good that is passed between the supply chain participants.

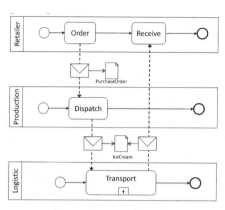

Fig. 1. A supply chain process

PurchaseOrder contains sensitive information and must be protected against tampering. For instance, the *Production* wants to be sure that the requested amount and the destination address have not been changed by an unauthorised party. *Retailer* wants to be sure that *IceCream* has been handled in a correct manner, e.g., temperature of the product was always in the region of -26 °C to -25 °C and that there was no unauthorised access to the product during transportation to ensure that product was not deliberately contaminated.

The second supply chain has the same basic structure: it has a *Retailer* who orders chemicals from a *Production* unit. The chemicals are delivered through a *Logistic* partner. Similar to the first supply chain it contains two assets: *PurchaseOrder* and *Chemical*. While *PurchaseOrder* in this case has the same threats as in the previous supply chain, *Chemical* has a threat of being exposed, e.g., through evaporation.

In addition, when considering both of the supply chains, there is a potential threat of ice cream contamination through the toxic chemicals if at any point in time the ice cream will either be stored too close to the chemicals, or the same truck will be used first for the transportation of the chemicals, and then for the ice cream.

With respect to the four objectives we identified, the desired outcome in our example is as follows: support during supply chain design with identification of the potential threats that span over multiple supply chains for the *Purchase-Order*, *IceCream* and *Chemical* assets to achieve *security awareness*; automated help in identification of countermeasures for the identified threats to achieve *consistency* in applying security controls; suitable tools for visualisation of the security measures taken to protect assets for *security visibility* and *provability* on the design level; extension of the execution environment to allow monitoring and execution of security measures to achieve *provability* of the taken measures during runtime.

3   Proposed Approach

Ensuring the safety and security of assets in supply chains requires special support both at design and at runtime (see Figure 2). At design time, we need to

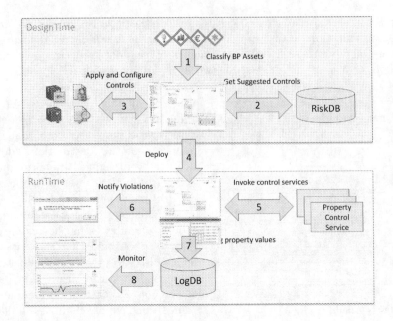

Fig. 2. Approach in prototypical implementation

specify the security requirements and, moreover, we need to apply and config-
ure the necessary controls. The selection of necessary controls is supported by
a specific risk database (RiskDB). At runtime, the compliance to the specified
security and safety requirements is monitored and violations are reported. On
the modelling level, the three main concepts of our approach are *Asset*, *Threat*,
and *Control*. An asset has potential threats, while controls can countermeasure
these threats. The role of the rest of the model is to help identify which threats
are applicable to which asset and which controls can be used to countermeasure
identified threats. The following describes the main steps of our approach:

1. *Asset identification*: In this step we analyse what are the assets used in a
   supply chain that we want to protect. We identified two types of assets:
   a *logical asset* is data that contains certain sensitive information, such as
   purchase order details or credit card number, while a *physical asset* is a real
   world object that is used in the supply chain. Any asset can be described by
   a set of *properties* it possesses. Thereby any logical asset can be described
   by a set of the same properties, such as *signature*, *content* and *encryption*
   properties. Similar, any physical asset can be described by the set of the
   same properties, such as *temperature*, *location* and *size*.
2. *Threat modelling*: Different threats are applicable to different assets depending on asset classification. Thereby it is not sufficient to only distinguish
   between logical and physical assets. For example, two logical assets can have
   different threats: the first logical asset might contain *private* information
   about a customer with a threat of information disclosure, while another logical asset might contain *financial* data, which has a threat of unauthorised

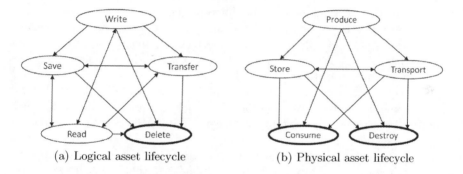

Physical Asset		Logical Asset	
Deep-frozen		Private	
Light-sensitive		Financial	
Explosive		Legal	
Poisonous		Confidential	
Radioactive		Audit-relevant	

Physical Asset		Logical Asset	
Light		Signature	
Temperature		Encryption	
Concussion		Audit-Controls	
Pressure		Privacy-Policies	
Location		Separation of Duties	

(a) Tags for assets   (b) Controls for assets

Fig. 3. Tags and controls for logical and physical assets

(a) Logical asset lifecycle   (b) Physical asset lifecycle

Fig. 4. Action lifecycles for physical and logical assets

modification. Similar, a *frozen* physical asset might have a threat of being defrozen, while a *fragile* physical asset has a threat of being broken. To allow supply chain designer to classify different assets, a concept of *tag* has been introduced. A tag attached to an asset identifies a certain characteristic or classification of this asset. 3(a) shows an example set of tags that can be used to classify logical and physical assets. An asset can be a subject to a number of actions. Figure 4 shows the action based lifecycles for logical and physical assets where bold lines denote the final actions performed on an asset[1]. Each action in the asset lifecycle bears different threats depending on asset classification. For example, the *Read* action on *financial* data bears a threat of consuming incorrect or maliciously modified information, while the *Consume* action on *food* bears a threat of consuming contaminated products. RiskDB (see Figure 2) stores a set of rules that relates asset classifications defined by the asset tags to the potential threats depending on the actions performed on this asset.

---

[1] We assume that a data object can only be written once: if a data object is modified then the old data object is deleted and a new data object is created.

3. *Control identification*: After the potential threats for each activity and each asset have been identified, we need to specify countermeasures to protect assets from these threats. The RiskDB contains rules that map different threats to the possible countermeasures, also called controls, that can be applied to prevent, detect or react to the threat occurrences. For example, if an activity writes a data object, then it might need to sign it to protect the data from unauthorised modification and to ensure non-repudiation of the *financial* data. If an activity stores data, then it might need to encrypt the data before saving it to protect the *confidential* data. Similar, if an activity transports a physical asset, it has to apply controls with regard to the transportation regulations for the given object depending on the asset classification defined by the tags, e.g. *flammable*, *explosive*, or *deep-frozen* goods.

   Controls can be divided into three main categories based on their execution point with respect to the threat occurrence. We will use the threat of food contamination to demonstrate the difference between these categories:
   - *Preventive controls* are controls that are applied to prevent a certain threat. For example, ensuring correct storage conditions, such as low temperature and clean storage areas, are some of the preventive measures that can be taken to avoid food contamination.
   - *Detective controls* are used to identify occurrence of a threat. For example, laboratory examination can detect contamination of a product, while evaluation of the temperature sensor data allows to detect incorrect storage conditions.
   - *Reactive controls* are used to recover from a violation. For example, if contamination of a product has been detected, then product recall must be initiated. In case of a high temperature detection an emergency refrigerator can be started.

   When a threat is scoped to a single supply chain, such as for example melting of the ice cream, all of the control types can be realised locally to the execution of the supply chain. However, when we consider contextual threats, such as product cross-contamination, detective controls become more complicated. In general, there are four stages to a detective control:
   (a) *Signalling*. At this stage all events related to the threat are collected. For example, to detect cross-contamination we require location information, such as GPS data, related to the position of ice cream and toxic chemical.
   (b) *Evaluation*. At this stage the collected events are evaluated according to the rules that identify threat occurrence. In our example we would see that the goods are located too close to each other.
   (c) *Notification* After a violation has been detected, the responsible party is notified at this stage. In our example the retailer who ordered the ice cream must be notified. In addition other participants and legal authorities can be notified as well.
   (d) *Reaction*. After a violation notification has been received, reactive actions can be taken to recover the fault. If cross-contamination has been

detected before the ice cream reached the retailer, the retailer might decline the order. Otherwise all contaminated ice cream must be destroyed. In case of contextual threats signalling is implemented locally on each supply chain, while evaluation of the produced events must happen on the external component that can combine events coming from differnt supply chains.

4 Implementation

Our approach is supported by a prototype: To demonstrate design concepts we extended Windows Workflow Foundation (WF 4.0) with the supply chain modelling capabilities. We introduced assets, tags and control modelling blocks that enable specification of security and safety in the supply chains.

4.1 Workflow Design

Windows Workflow Foundation uses variables to represent data used in a business process. The variables are defined in a variable tab and are not visible in the designer. To advocate security awareness, we extended existing workflow modelling constructs with two visual elements for logical and physical assets. We added an asset (or variable) panel to the business process, which contains all assets used in the process. To add a new asset (variable) to the process, the user needs to drag & drop the corresponding visual element into the asset panel of the workflow.

To enable asset classification we provide a tag toolbar: the user can drag & drop the corresponding tag from the toolbar onto the visual asset specification being present in the asset panel. By combining different tags, a user can specify different characteristics of an asset.

Figure 5 shows a screenshot of the ice cream supply chain process modeled using our tool. It contains two variables that can be seen in the right panel: an *IceCream* variable annotated with a *DeepFrozen* and *LighSensitive* tags, and a *PurchaseOrder* variable annotated with *Financial* and *AuditRelevant* tags.

Figure 5 shows four activities: *Order*, *Dispatch*, *Transport*, and *Receive*. The *Order* activity outputs *PurchaseOrder*, which is then passed as an input argument to the *Dispatch* activity. The *Dispatch* activity then outputs *IceCream*, which is passed to the *Transport* activity and then through the *Transport* activity to the *Receive* activity. Depending on the argument type (In, Out or InOut), we can see different types of control points available for each asset in each activity. This allows the user to define input state controls on the incoming asset states (*PurchaseOrder* in *Dispatch* activity) output controls on outgoing asset states (*PurchaseOrder* in *Order* activity), and internal controls on data that exists all the way through activity execution (*IceCream* in *Transport* activity).

To identify controls required to countermeasure potential threats, we developed a Risk Database (RiskDB). The RiskDB stores relations between asset tags, threats these tags imply for different activities, and controls that should be applied to such assets in each activity. When a user annotates an asset with a

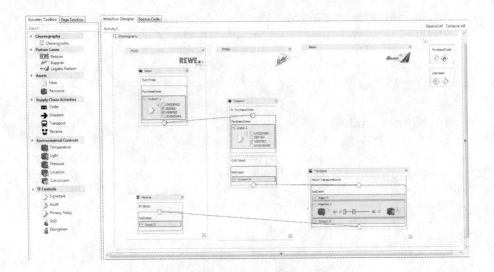

Fig. 5. Design of the supply chain process

new tag, a query is sent to the RiskDB that selects the potential threats for the current asset classification and each activity that uses this asset, as well as applicable protection measurements (controls) for each identified threat . After this the tool checks if the controls are already present in the model and if not, shows an error with the information about missing controls. This enforces the user to model secure processes with respect to the rules stored in the RiskDB. The rules in RiskDB reflect expert knowledge with respect to each asset classification.

To enable control specification, we provide a control toolbar. To identify at which point of activity execution a control must be applied, the user needs to drop a control into the corresponding container. In Figure 5 we can see an output signature control applied to the *PurchaseOrder* variable in *Order* activity. This control specifies that the data must be signed when it leaves this activity. In the *Dispatch* activity we can see an example incoming state control, that states that the *PurchaseOrder* signature property must be in state *verified* to be used by this activity. In the *Transport* activity the internal temperature and light controls are applied. The controls specify that the *IceCream* temperature must be between -50 °C and -25 °C and the light must be under $200lm$. Additional controls could be added as input and output controls. In general, any number of controls can be applied to each asset in each activity at any control point.

Design time extensions of the workflow foundation provides security visibility and awareness by providing tag and control toolbars, security awareness and consistency through connection to the RiskDB that consistently applies the same rules in similar situations and notifies violations if any controls are missing, and security provability on design level by showing that there are no missing controls in the model with respect to the RiskDB rules.

4.2 Workflow Execution and Monitoring

To enable execution of the extensions, the visual assets have been mapped to the variables and passed as arguments into the corresponding activities. Incoming state controls and outgoing state controls are enforced by the workflow engine— it invokes property related control services to verify that the asset properties are in a correct states. If a violation is detected it either suspends the workflow, reschedules the failed activity, or executes any other specificly defined reactive process. The internal controls on the other side can be viewed as the require- ments on the activity implementation with regard to the asset handling. Each control knows the property it targets. When a control is scheduled, it invokes the corresponding property control service. Such a service can be an internal implementation, such as automatic signature implementation, but can also be a remote service, such as sensor control that monitors resource temperature. In general, all property-specific actions are done by the property control services. This allows for a general model of the controls in the business process: a business process control knows the asset it needs to control, the property it targets, the service that can evaluate the state of this property, the point in time when the state needs to be evaluated, and the states that are allowed at the evaluation time point. The property control service knows how to determine the current state of the resource and how to modify the state, but it is unaware of the business related semantics or the valid states of this property. At the specified execution point, the control asks a property service to evaluate the current state of an asset, logs results into the *LogDB* (see Figure 2), compares it with the set of valid states and notifies the user, if the state is invalid.

All input controls scoped to an activity are evaluated before this activity starts its execution. If any violations are detected during these checks, the pro- cess terminates. After each activity execution, all output controls scoped to these activity are evaluated, and, if any violations are detected, the activity is reiter- ated[2] until all assets have the valid property states. For the internal controls, monitors are triggered at the beginning of the activity execution and stopped when activity completes. Monitors observe, evaluate and log the states of the cor- responding properties during the activity execution with the specified frequency. Collected evidence can then be used to prove fulfillment of the specified restric- tions. If a violation of an internal control is detected during activity execution, business process partners are notified.

Figure 6 shows an example monitoring screenshot taken during the simulation of the *Transport* activity in the supply chain process. On the right side we can see a chart representing the values logged by the internal temperature and light controls. Traffic light symbol in the top right corner of the light monitor is red (top circle of the traffic light), signalling that a violation has been detected. To compare, the traffic light of the temperature monitor is green (bottom circle of the traffic light), which shows that the temperature is in the valid region. At the

---

[2] Process termination and activity reiteration have been implemented as examples of the possible reactions to the control violations. In general, any customer-defined actions ca be used as reactions to the detected violations.

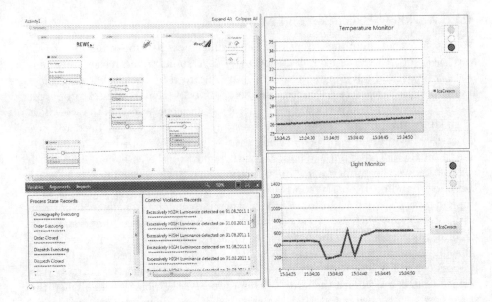

Fig. 6. Execution of the supply chain process

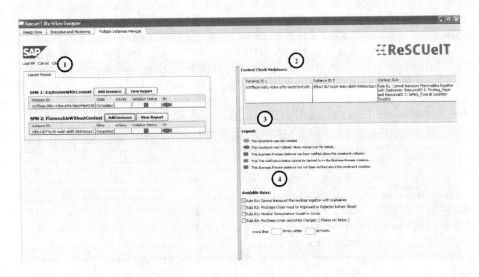

Fig. 7. Detection of contextual threat occurrences

bottom left of the screen we can see the tracking information about the current state of the process execution and logged violations, while the currently active activity is highlighted on the top left part of the screen.

Figure 7 shows a screenshot of the contextual dashboard. To detect contextual threats we evaluate events coming from different supply chains using a complex event processing engine. The screenshot in Figure 7 displays the state of two running process instances in (1) with respect to the rules activated in (4). In the top left corner (1) it can be seen that rule R_1 that forbids transportation of incompatible goods has been violated, which in our implementation is signalled through the red circle in R_1 column. The *Violation Status* column visualises whether the corresponding supply chain instance has been notified about the violation(status green) or not (status red). In our scenario only the first supply chain has been notified, while the second one does not know about it at the current point in time. The table at (2) gives details about the rule violations and impacted supply chains, while (3) explains the legend.

5   Related Work

There is a large body of literature, e.g., [10,1,6] that motivate the need for improving the process visualisation to enhance the understanding of the processes in general. It is well known that workflows and business processes are security critical. For example, in [3] the authors present workflow related security goals and study their possible assignment to main categories of business process elements such as agents, roles, artifacts, and activities. Consequently, there are several work, e.g., [11,12,2,9] that suggest domain-specific extensions of a process modelling language for expressing safety or security properties, only a few, namely [12,2], use these extensions for monitoring or enforcing the specified properties at runtime. From those, [2] is the closest to our work: the authors of [2] present a tool-supported approach for modelling security properties on the business process level and to generate both security configurations for standardised security infrastructures as well as specific security controls for a business process execution engine. Still, this work does not discuss physical assets and, moreover, does not integrate a risk database.

6   Conclusion and Future Work

We presented an approach allowing business users to easily specify security and safety requirements of supply chains. The compliance to these requirements is monitored during the execution of the processes. Overall, this transfers the well known model-driven software development paradigm to workflow management systems that can execute the abstract process models directly.

   Our prototype has been developed in the context of a German funded project RescueIT that develops techniques for security- and safety-critical supply chains. This prototype has been showcased at various trade fairs and received positive feedback from the different parties involved in such supply chains. We found that even a non IT audience easily understands the visualisation of security constraints (e.g., a signature symbol on a purchase order) as well as safety constraints (e.g., a temperature symbol on the purchased good).

Further work also includes the integration of business process constraint visualisation and analysis techniques. For example, [8] presents 3D visualisation approach that allows the analysis of business process constraints and dependencies between different process dimensions. Integrating such analysis and visualisation frameworks into our prototype would provide an integrated toolchain for business experts for modelling, analysing, and executing security-critical and safety-critical supply chains or business processes in a way that guarantees the monitoring and enforcement of the security and safety requirements.

Acknowledgments. The research leading to these results has received funding from the German "Federal Ministry of Education and Research" in the context of the project "RescueIT".

References

1. Bobrik, R., Bauer, T., Reichert, M.: Proviado – Personalized and Configurable Visualizations of Business Processes. In: Bauknecht, K., Pröll, B., Werthner, H. (eds.) EC-Web 2006. LNCS, vol. 4082, pp. 61–71. Springer, Heidelberg (2006)
2. Brucker, A.D., Hang, I., Lückemeyer, G., Ruparel, R.: SecureBPMN: Modeling and enforcing access control requirements in business processes. In: SACMAT. ACM Press (2012)
3. Herrmann, P., Herrmann, G.: Security requirement analysis of business processes 6, 305–335 (2006)
4. Kader, A.: Increasing food availability by reducing postharvest losses of fresh produce. In: V International Postharvest Symposium. International Society for Horticulutral Science (2005)
5. Lundqvist, J., de Fraiture, C., Molden, D.: Saving water: From field to fork – curbing losses and wastage in the food chain. In: SIWI Policy Brief (2008)
6. Mendling, J., Recker, J.: Towards systematic usage of labels and icons in business process models. In: 13th International Workshop on Exploring Modeling Methods for Systems Analysis and Design (2008)
7. Monakova, G., Brucker, A.D., Schaad, A.: Security and safety of assets in business processes. In: ACM Symposium on Applied Computing (SAC). ACM Press (2012)
8. Monakova, G., Leymann, F.: Workflow art: a framework for multidimensional workflow analysis. In: Enterprise Information Systems (2012)
9. Mülle, J., von Stackelberg, S., Böhm, K.: A security language for BPMN process models. Technical report, University Karlsruhe, KIT (2011)
10. Rinderle, S., Bobrik, R., Reichert, M., Bauer, T.: Business process visualization - use cases, challenges, solutions. In: ICEIS (3), pp. 204–211 (2006)
11. Rodríguez, A., Fernández-Medina, E., Piattini, M.: A bpmn extension for the modeling of security requirements in business processes. IEICE - Trans. Inf. Syst. E90-D, 745–752 (2007)
12. Wolter, C., Menzel, M., Schaad, A., Miseldine, P., Meinel, C.: Model-driven business process security requirement specification. Journal of Systems Architecture 55(4), 211–223 (2009)

Standards for the Protection of Transport Infrastructures

Norbert Siegel[1] and Simone Wurster[2]

[1] DIN Deutsches Institut für Normung e. V., Berlin
[2] Technische Universität Berlin, Berlin, Germany

Abstract. Standards and specifications are important instruments for opening up new markets. Furthermore, carrying out standardization at an early stage in development supports the development of new products and services because it improves communication between the various developers by providing standard definitions of interfaces or a uniform terminology. The joint project "INFRANORM" of DIN, the German Institute for Standardization and the Berlin University of Technology (TU Berlin) will help introduce standardization for the protection of transport infrastructures, an area in which standards and specifications are currently lacking. Several DIN Specifications on the subject are being drawn up and are or will soon be published.

Keywords: Standardization, DIN Specifications, transport infrastructures.

1 Stimulating the Security Market through Standardization

To take full advantage of the potentials of the market for civil security technologies and related services, standards and specifications are needed at both European and global level. To stimulate lead markets for security-related technologies and services in Germany, standards and specifications can provide the following means of support [1]:

- knowledge and technology transfer,
- networking the relevant stakeholders,
- fostering innovative demand,
- innovation-enhancing regulatory frameworks,
- intensifying competition,
- increasing exportability.

DIN, the German Institute for Standardization, offers stakeholders a platform for the development of standards as a service to industry, the state and society as a whole.

DIN's "R&D Phase Standardization" section provides strategic services for putting research results into practice with economic success. R&D Phase Standardization is a platform for developing standards that allow innovative technologies to be implemented as marketable products, processes and services.

In addition to formal, full consensus based standardization, there is a process for drawing up informal specifications which is called "consortial standardization". In this process DIN helps consortia draw up common, widely acknowledged

N. Aschenbruck et al. (Eds.): Future Security 2012, CCIS 318, pp. 21–24, 2012.

specifications for their innovations. The results of the consortial standardization process are called "DIN SPEC", for "DIN Specification".

2   R&D Phase Standardization for the Protection of Transport Infrastructures – The INFRANORM Project

INFRANORM is a joint project of the German Institute for Standardization (DIN) and the Berlin University of Technology (TU Berlin) and is funded by the German Federal Ministry of Education and Research (BMBF). The project will run from March 2010 to February 2013 and its aim is to initiate the development of standards and specifications on the protection of transport infrastructures.

INFRANORM is collaborating with ten project consortia founded to improve the protection of airports, train stations, ports, railways, bridges and tunnels. The consortia sponsored by the BMBF are referred to (in most cases) by their acronyms: AISIS, SKRIBT, ORGAMIR, SinoVE Management, VeRSiert, Critical Parts, VESPER, V-SICMA, FluSs and SiVe. The ten consortia comprise a total of approximately 80 partners. INFRANORM also has contact with numerous other stakeholders in this field. Besides the early development of specifications standardization guidelines for research projects will be drawn up.

The following DIN Specifications are in preparation or will be published soon:

DIN SPEC 91282:
Terminology for the Security Management of Transport Infrastructures
To ensure a common language that can be used by all those involved in the security management of transport structures, the specification clearly defines and classifies key terms in this area.

Beginning with the more general definitions found in relevant laws, directives and standards, the terms will then be more precisely defined within the context of transport infrastructures; thus the definitions may deviate from those used in other subject areas.

This DIN Specification is already published.

DIN SPEC 91284:
Principles of Microscopic Evacuation Analysis
For buildings intended to be used by a large number of persons, it is recommended that evacuation analyses be carried out in addition to maintaining the permissible escape route lengths and the required widths of emergency exits specified in building regulations. Modern computer-assisted methods for such analyses often present a challenge for building authorities. Standardized criteria are particularly needed for the scenarios and parameters used in calculating escape routes.

The objective of this DIN Specification is to specify the goals, terminology and procedures for microscopic evacuation simulations, and to make these accessible to a wide group of users. Safety-relevant quantities are not specified in this document.

However, it describes a method for carrying out evacuation simulations. The precise definition of parameter values or acceptance criteria will be left to the user.

DIN SPEC 91284 is available already.

DIN SPEC 91285:
Holistic Description of Security Processes
Security processes involve a great number of man-machine interfaces, that is, steps which are not fully automated but which have to be performed by the security staff with or without the aid of technical devices. For example, the primary purpose of passenger control at airports is to stop passengers from carrying forbidden objects into the security area of the airport and onto the airplane. Detectors for metallic objects and explosives are used for this purpose. However, the decision as to whether an alert is serious and whether suitable measures are to be initiated is taken by the security staff - the final decision is thus made by humans.

The specification will define descriptive elements which allow quality criteria to be established for the interface between processes or between individual process steps to take into account the man-machine interface.

DIN SPEC 91287:
Data Interchange between Civil Protection Information Systems
In order to properly respond to large-scale emergencies, a number of participants working across departments, organizations and even systems must work hand in hand. Because most information in such cases is exchanged by means of direct verbal communication, by telephone or other communication devices, or via liaison officers, such communication is never completely free of errors, is often lossy, and is complicated and time-consuming because numerous persons and organizations are involved.

Coupling information systems to all the organizations involved would make it possible to transmit a large amount of information directly from system to system. This is of course known before new information systems are established. For this reason proprietary data interfaces, which are sometimes quite complicated, are developed to allow the systems to exchange information. The time and effort needed to implement and maintain product updates is reduced by the DIN SPEC 91287 communications standard for exchanging information among information systems used in operative civil protection systems.

DIN SPEC 91287 is already published.

3   Project "PreparedNET"

Logistics hubs (referred to in Germany as Güterverkehrszentren) play an important role in ensuring a smooth supply of goods. Thus these centers form a critical infrastructure linking various means of transportation (e.g. road or rail) as well as different actors. The project "PreparedNET" addresses the problem of reinstating emergency operations as soon as possible after a harmful incident such as an act of terrorism. DIN is investigating how standardization results can best be designed for practical application.

The results of this investigation will be used to develop a DIN Specification which will be made available to a large circle of users. Work on the development of DIN SPEC 91291 "Emergency concept for sensitive logistics hubs – Configuration, simulation and implementation" has already begun.

Reference

1. Blind, K.: Deutschlands Standardisierungsstrategien hin zum Leitmarkt: Potenziale und Herausforderungen. In: Stober, R. (ed.) Jahrbuch des Sicherheitsgewerberechts 2007, Hamburg, pp. 183–212 (2008)

Security in Supply Chains in the Scope of Surface Transport of Goods by Secure Information Patterns on the Freight – Trans4Goods

Hagen Borstell[1], Liu Cao[1], Klaus Richter[1], and Christian Schäfer[2]

[1] Fraunhofer-Institut für Fabrikbetrieb und – automatisierung IFF,
Sandtorstr. 22, 39106 Magdeburg
klaus.richter@iff.fraunhofer.de
[2] T-Systems Multimedia Solutions GmbH, Riesaer Str. 5, 01129 Dresden
Christian.Schaefer@t-systems-mms.com

Abstract. Situations in which the civil supply of goods is threatened or affected by attacks, natural catastrophes, major accidents or criminal activities are increasing. Furthermore the unique identification of goods as well as the traceability up to the manufacturer gain in importance. Currently, the question is how to get more security in the flow of commodity in a feasible manner, without constraining them with additional inspections. Therefore the partners of the joint research project "Trans4Goods - Security in supply chains in the scope of surface transport of goods by secure information patterns on the freight" ("www.trans4goods.org") determine feasible approaches.

Referring to a pharmaceutical supply chain, an IT-system concept shall be developed bundling capture and communication systems in a web portal solution. Additionally, local AutoID-data carriers (currently: 2D-Codes, RFID) which are attached to goods, packaging and carrier are examined as new technological solution for tracking security relevant data electronically in real-time concerning dimension and weight, means of transportation, temperature, location as well as the method of control. To assure data integrity and thus prevent manipulation suitable encryption methods are researched.

Innovative depth image sensor concepts are tested on the level of freight, whose measured data alone or in combination with the data of the AutoID carrier from the different object levels allow a station history related analysis of the data model.

Keywords: Security, Supply Chain, Information Pattern, RFID EPC, Signature, Depth Image Sensor, Pharmaceutical Goods.

1 Initial Situation

The security of logistic activities respectively the implementation of security requirements is based on current information about the good and the segments in the logistic chain. The knowledge about the location, the condition and the applicable security guidelines (logistic security, civil security) of the good is relevant. Nowadays these

N. Aschenbruck et al. (Eds.): Future Security 2012, CCIS 318, pp. 25–28, 2012.
© Springer-Verlag Berlin Heidelberg 2012

information are often not continuously available which can cause interruptions in complex logistic chains. Therefor the aim of Trans4Goods is to increase security of surface transports by an improved traceability of the movement of goods. Referring to the pharmaceutical logistic chain the goals are:

— Fulfilment of the highest demands on protection against forgery
— Unique identification of goods and prevention of plagiarism
— Detection of damage
— Aggravation of theft
— Traceability of goods
— Decrease of failure costs
— Increase in efficiency of logistic processes

2   Approach

2.1   IT System Concept

Due to the global context of the project the system conception was based on the manufacturer independent GS1 EPCglobal-standard-framework which supports the global widespread GS1-standards [1, 2]. Hence a system is developed composed of standardized but extendable system components, interfaces and data models. The standard compliant management of logistic event data which conduces to the traceability of goods is enriched by security relevant good and control attributes that are protected against manipulations by means of digital signatures.

Goal of the planned system is the inter-organisational consistent reconstruction and analysis of the current supply chain in real-time as well as their user defined visualization in a central web-portal considering the advanced good and control attributes. Thereby the responsible supply chain participant is informed about security relevant incidences by different communication channels like e-mail or text message.

The increased amount of data that is expected due to capturing of detailed data about controls and goods may reach terabytes within a few weeks. This constitutes a challenge, especially concerning near real-time alerting. Particularly for real-time analysis of historical data the application of traditional relational databases is considered to be a disadvantage. Due to this circumstance the highly scalable, distributed, column-oriented Apache HBase database which is based on the BigTable-concept [3] has been adopted in the concept. The database is designed for analysis but can also respond to random access queries in real-time. In addition to the low latency times and a high performance of parallelized analysis via MapReduce the chosen, distributed database also provides various auto-failover mechanisms, which secure the availability of the database as well as the durability of the data. Test series could already prove that the distributed database is also continuously available throughout several server failures while keeping constant data throughput.

Currently a prototypal test system based on the IT-system concept made of certified Open Source components is built. On this basis a real pharmaceutical supply chain will be simulated using the concepts from chapter 2.2 and chapter 2.3.

2.2   Signature Based Labelling of Freight

For the verification of the authenticity of the freight label digital signatures shall be applied to avoid forgery of the contained data and therefore prevent criminal actions like contraband, piracy and attacks in the supply chain. For that purpose special RFID-tags will validate scans in which they are involved by creating signatures or checksums. Since also bulk scanning should be possible to prevent a slowdown of the delivery process UHF-Tags are used to achieve reading ranges for a practicable and efficient application in the supply chain. In this context passive UHF-tags are used to provide an economic solution even when labelling occurs on a low freight hierarchy level.

Based on this a security concept is currently developed which shall allow the validation of the authenticity of the secured objects, the integrity of the data stored on the transponder and the secure identification as well as the traceability of goods in the supply chain. The security concept mainly contains

— Protecting confidentiality by encryption as well as ensuring the integrity by cryptographic checksums [4, 5] so-called Message Authentication Codes (MACs),
— Writing of an electronic signature calculated by the reader (from the content of the transponder) onto the transponder as well as
— Calculating an electronic signature directly by the transponder [6].

Furthermore, also the cost efficiency as well as the scalability of the suggested cryptographic solutions will be considered to enable adjustments on different application and security levels. In addition, the possibility of a hybrid multi-tag accretion for labelling of valuable objects is researched.

The developed concept for encryption and data integrity shall be refined and exemplarily realized on a RFID-Tag.

2.3   Depth Image of Freight as a Security Characteristic

To support supply chain supervision on freight level, besides AutoID read-processes, depth image sensors are applied as exclusive control element or in connection with RFID technology. The freight offers specific characteristics like volume, colour settings or geometrical form (Fig. 1). In combination with further sensor sources, that provide data for the current temperature or the weight as well as the data from the freight reading, data could be captured along the supply chain from which conclusions about manipulation of the transport can be drawn. On an arbitrary station of the chain it is possible to access previous data records from the central database. Those records are compared to the current data locally. Reference data for the depth image scan or additional good properties can be given with the cargo via AutoID-Data-Carriers which enable a local (partial) comparison of the data, even if the central web portal is not available. On this basis, decisions can be made quicker than today, whether a good is free of manipulation, and secure. Additionally the result will be documented locally and centrally.

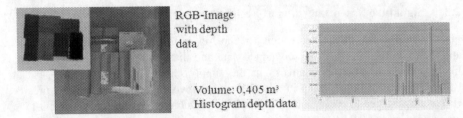

RGB-Image
with depth
data

Volume: 0,405 m³
Histogram depth data

Fig. 1. Packet structure of a palette with depth image sensor. Fraunhofer IFF.

3   Conclusion and Future Work

The concepts and solutions described above will be examined on the basis of a real supply chain at the end of 2012/ at the beginning of 2013. Thereby novel, signature based, passive UHF-Tags based on RFID will come into operation as well as depth image information of freight will be processed.

Additionally, the development of the so-called GS1 Discovery Service Standard will be followed up in the belonging task force. The standard being in development specifies concepts that allow a reconstruction of the supply chain only for authorized users based on fine-grained authorization concepts.

Furthermore, options which allow on-demand usage of external IT-infrastructure for the single components of the IT-system shall be evaluated in the future. In consequence of low setup and maintenance expenses this should encourage the spread of the aimed system. This spread is crucial since a supply chain can only be reconstructed and supervised cross-company without a gap, when all business partners operate the system or at least an EPCglobal compliant system.

References

[1] EPCglobal, The EPCglobal Architecture Framework, EPCglobal Final Version 1.4 (2010)
[2] EPCglobal, EPC Information Services (EPCIS), EPCIS Specification Version 1.0.1 (2007)
[3] Chang, F., Dean, J., Ghemawat, S., et al.: Bigtable: A Distributed Storage System for Structured Data. ACM Transactions on Computer Systems (TOCS) 26, Article No.: 4 (2008)
[4] Aigner, M., Plos, T., Feldhofer, M., et al.: Building Radio frequency IDentification for the Global Environment (BRIDGE). Report on first part of the security WP: Tag security, D4.2.1 (2007)
[5] Chae, H.-J., Yeager, D.-J., Smith, J.-R., et al.: Maximalist Cryptography and Computation on the WISP UHF RFID Tag, University of Massachusetts, Amherst. Intel Research Seattle, Seattle (2007)
[6] Pendl, C., Pelnar, M., Hutter, M.: Elliptic Curve Cryptography on the WISP UHF RFID Tag. In: Institute for Applied Information Processing and Communications (IAIK) (2011)

A Process for Secure Supply Chain Evaluation

Maria Akbulatova and Matthias Winkler

SAP Research, Dresden, Germany
{maria.akbulatova,matthias.winkler}@sap.com

Abstract. To improve the security of international supply chains, we present a semi-automatic approach for evaluating tracking information and transport data to assess the risks posed by sea freight containers.

1 Introduction

The secure transport of goods within international supply chains is important for countries around the globe. The manipulation of e.g. sea freight containers poses severe risks. Not only the smuggling of illegal goods and substances or counterfeit products harm people and companies but also the usage of containers as a means for attacking supply chain infrastructure. Several legislations were initiated with the goal to secure supply chains. Examples are the US National Strategy For Global Supply Chain Security [1] and the H.R.1 law [2].

Within the ECSIT project [1] we investigate how to secure supply chains and how different container inspection technologies (e.g. x-ray) can help with that. As part of that work we present a semi-automatic approach for container risk assessment, which can be executed e.g. by customs and border personnel. While several research projects investigate the capturing of security relevant information, we describe how this data can be used for security assessment and how this evaluation can be integrated into the supply chain processes. In Chapter 2 we describe related projects and discuss in how far our work extends the state of the art. In Chapter 3 we present our approach for semi-automatic risk assessment and a first demonstrator based on which we plan to evaluate the approach. We conclude this paper with an outlook on future steps.

2 Related Work

A common problem in supply chain management is ensuring the security of the overall process. Several projects have been initiated to address this challenge. One example is the SMART-CM project [4] which aims to provide a platform for a secure and streamlined supply chain management process. The platform consists of three layers: an information gateway for information collection from different sources, a visibility tool for logistics operators and value added services using the data for optimization.

---

[1] ECSIT project web page: http://www.isl.org/projects/ecsit/

N. Aschenbruck et al. (Eds.): Future Security 2012, CCIS 318, pp. 29–32, 2012.

The INTEGRITY project [5] tried to solve the same problem as SMART-CM by developing the Shared Intermodal Container Information System (SICIS). This platform matches logistical data with security data, e.g. from electronic seals or other container security devices, and provides it to authorized supply chain participants.

Although these two projects share similar goals with our work, they do not support container risk evaluation processes like we propose. Furthermore, ECSIT explores the application of additional technologies (e.g. 2D/3D container scan and radioactivity measurement) as part of the container risk evaluation.

The CASSANDRA project is a continuation of the INTEGRITY and SMART-CM projects and aims at designing and implementing a new approach to risk assessment based on information obtained from the whole supply chain [6]. However, at the time of writing this paper, no solution has been published.

3   Secure Supply Chain Evaluation

Securing supply chains is important for collaboration of the supply chain partners as well as the proper functioning of the overall infrastructure. While no complete security can be achieved it is important to make manipulation of infrastructure more difficult and increase chances for the detection of issues before problems arise. The work presented in this paper aims at supporting the latter aspect.

We aim to evaluate our work based on an international beverage transport use case. Beer is produced in Germany, loaded into a container and transported to the US in three steps: pre-carriage via truck from the factory to the port, main carriage via container ship to the USA, and on-carriage via truck to the destination. Transport data is captured during loading and transport and is used for security risk assessment when the container enters the terminal in Germany, i.e before it is sent to another country.

3.1   The Process

The process of container risk evaluation (Fig. 1) starts with the automatic capturing of relevant security data. Information about the supplier, buyer, partner certifications, etc. is first gathered when the container is packed by the supplier. This information is partly contained in the Importer Security Filing [3]. All collected data is automatically checked for completeness, compliance and against export prohibition lists. These steps are executed during the transport of the container to the last port before loading on a vessel to the USA.

As soon as the container arrives at the harbor entrance the system decides whether it must be sent for detailed inspection or may receive immediate clearance (green lane). The decision is made automatically based on the collected transport data and all incidents which occurred during the transport, e.g. unauthorized attempt to open the container seal. A container inspection may include x-ray container scanning, scanning for nuclear materials or manual inspection.

When information from a container inspection is available, the border personnel analyses it together with all security alerts. This can include checking

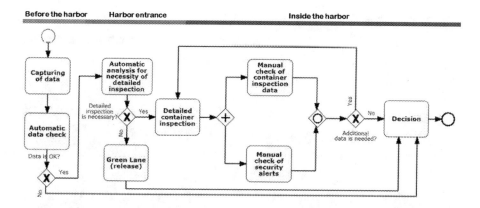

Fig. 1. Container security evaluation process

suspicious supply chain partners, seal logs, cargo descriptions etc. This process
can be repeated with additionally requested inspection data before a decision to
release or reject the container.

3.2   The CoRiAs Tool

A prototype of a container risk assessment (CoRiAs) tool was developed. The
application presents relevant container security data in a way which enables
automatic and manual analysis of security risks. The security related information
about the container is divided into several categories: **Cargo Details** - general
data about the cargo, supplier and buyer; **Cargo Route** - container route as
well as locations and times for stops during the transport; **Seal Log** - records all
attempts to open, close, and change the container seal, along with the responsible
institution; **Scan Result** - scan images and radioactivity measurements; **Case
Log** - recorded history of all system activities related to the container handling;
Documents - repository of available transport related documents.

In the case of security alerts the corresponding category is highlighted with a
red color making it easy for customs employees to analyze the level of risk. In Fig.
2 one can see a possible scenario which shows that evaluating the container risk
is easier when all relevant information is displayed together in corresponding
categories. For the Scan Result category (Fig. 2 right image) one can match
the cargo description provided by the Cargo Manifest with the scan image and
identify anything that is not listed. At the same time Cargo Route category
(Fig. 2 left image) allows the cross reference of actual route of the cargo with
system alerts after seal log analysis, as well as other detected alerts on the
corresponding leg of the route. In the example a deviation from the planned
route is detected. Alerts are shown in a table and highlighted on the map.

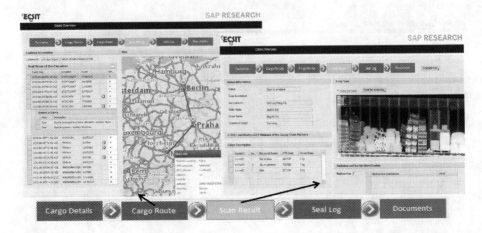

Fig. 2. CoRiAs tool: Cargo Route and Scan Result Views

4 Summary and Future Work

In this paper we outlined first results of our work on container security evaluation. We presented a semi-automatic evaluation approach and a first prototype
supporting the evaluation of security relevant container and supply chain data.

During the further progress of the project we aim to integrate the prototype
with a tool for collaboration and data exchange in the supply chain. Furthermore,
we plan to capture end user feedback and improve the process as well as the
tool. Finally, further work is required to evaluate which data can be used for
risk evaluation while protecting sensitive data.

References

1. The White House: National Strategy for Global Supply Chain Security (2012),
   http://www.whitehouse.gov/sites/default/files/national_strategy_for_
   global_supply_chain_security.pdf
2. 110th Congress: Implementing Recommendations of the 9/11 Commission Act of
   (2007), http://www.govtrack.us/congress/bills/110/hr1 (visited June 21, 2012)
3. US Customs Border Protection: Security Filing "10+2", http://www.cbp.gov/
   xp/cgov/trade/cargo_security/carriers/security_filing/ (visited June 21,
   2012)
4. SMART-CM: Container Security & Tracking Devices-Technical Specifications and
   Communication Standards. In: The European Committee for Standardization Workshop on Container Security & Tracking Devices, Brussels (2011)
5. Arendt, F., Meyer-Larsen, N., Mueller, R.: Supply Chain Predicability and Security.
   e-Freight Conference, Munich (2011)
6. Uronen, K., Hintsa, J.: CASSANDRA - Project Deliverable No. D1.1. Project page
   (2011), http://www.cassandra-project.eu

Unsupervised Techniques
for Audio Summarization
in Acoustic Environment Monitoring

David Damm, Dirk von Zeddelmann, and Frank Kurth

Fraunhofer FKIE, KOM Department
Neuenahrer Str. 20, 53343 Wachtberg, Germany
frank.kurth@fkie.fraunhofer.de
www.fkie.fraunhofer.de

Abstract. The detection of relevant audio events is a key task in various monitoring scenarios. Especially in the context of acoustic surveillance of real-life outdoor environments, there is a high demand on effectiveness and reliability of audio signal processing techniques. This paper summarizes key technology used for unsupervised audio summarization and shows how this technology is integrated into an innovative monitoring system.

1   Introduction

Heterogeneous sensor networks play an increasingly important role for surveillance and protection of critical infrastructures, major events, etc. Besides sensing classical modalities such as the visual or infrared, acoustic sensor data can provide important complementary information, especially on out-of-sight events or under conditions of low to no visibility. Supervised methods from the field of audio signal processing, such as voice activity detection (VAD) [2] and keyword spotting [6,3], have been succesfully applied to specific monitoring scenarios assuming homogeneous and time-invariant types of background noises. However, those methods rely on extensive training data, and, moreover, tend to fail or at least do not provide satisfactory results, if either extensive training is not possible or noise properties are unknown a priori. As outdoor audio recordings are a mixture of different superimposed audio sources, usually affected with heavy, unpredictable background noises, we propose an *unsupervised* approach that allows to model aspects of the expected background noises at an early stage, i. e., directly in the feature extraction process. The main contribution of this paper is to transfer a set of robust and unsupervised matching and detection techniques from the audio retrieval domain to the field of audio monitoring. In Sect. 2, we first introduce techniques for roughly detecting speech activity as well as for spotting sequences of words in monitoring recordings. On the one hand, our approach is inherently affected with a loss of precision regarding temporal resolution, e. g., an exact transcription of speech would be impossible. On the other hand, in the context of monitoring just a rough estimate of the period of audio

N. Aschenbruck et al. (Eds.): Future Security 2012, CCIS 318, pp. 33–36, 2012.

activity and the identification of speech fragments contained in the recording with some probability are perfectly adequate for many application scenarios. It turns out that the temporal roughness significantly improves detection rates under certain conditions with high amounts of noise, where more classical methods tend to fail. Additionally, a method for extracting *repeated* acoustic events turns out to be particularly powerful in the monitoring context. The utilization of an innovative type of acoustic sensor [1] allows us to incorporate localization information, hence further improving the accuracy of acoustical monitoring. The proposed techniques work largely unsupervised without training and require only a limited amount of adaptation to environmental conditions. In Sect. 3, we additionally show how these techniques can be integrated into an innovative multimodal monitoring system and illustrate how the incorporation of localization techniques can further enhance the system's capabilities.

2   Robust Audio Monitoring: Methods

The subsequently introduced signal processing techniques rely on a concept of audio feature extraction that considerably generalizes classical MFCC features known from speech processing, see [4]. Roughly speaking, features can be adapted to (a) the noise scenario and (b) the monitoring task at hand.

For the proposed VAD application, particularly designed FBCC-ENS features are used. The resulting features constitute a good representation of the local spectral properties of a signal. Because of the severe noise conditions in real acoustic channels, we suggest to apply additional postprocessing steps in the feature domain in order to enhance speech components and attenuate noise-like parts. Those steps mainly consist of filtering and averaging. In particular, initially a first-order highpass FIR filter is applied directly on the feature subbands, resulting in accentuating speech parts. By lowpass filtering the features afterwards, the influence of low frequency noise such as vehicular noise is partly rejected. Subsequently, the calculation of Hilbert envelopes of the filtered FBCC-ENS bands results in a coarse temporal shape of the 2D feature surface. By taking the mean of all resulting Hilbert envelopes, inter-band variations are compensated, such that remaining energy fluctuations are smoothed out over time. Finally, VAD is performed by applying a thresholding procedure to the resulting mean envelope.

Our basic approach for automatically detecting short sequences of words—in this context called *phrases*—in audio monitoring signals combines the technique of *audio matching* with HFCC-ENS features [7]. To this end, both the phrase (given in form of a short audio signal) and the monitoring signal are converted to feature sequences $q = (q_1, \ldots, q_M)$ and $d = (d_1, \ldots, d_N)$, where each of the q_i respectively d_j are feature vectors. Matching is then performed using a cross-correlation-like approach, where a similarity function $\Delta(n) := \frac{1}{M} \sum_{\ell=1}^{M} \langle q_\ell, d_{n-1+\ell} \rangle$ gives the similarity of phrase and monitoring signal at position n. Using normalized feature vectors, values of Δ in a range of $[0, 1]$ can be enforced. In order to be more flexible w. r. t. the typical non-linear variations in speaking tempo, in our monitoring scenario we replace the above correlation-based approach to calculate a cost function by a variant of subsequence DTW. Compared to classical keyword spotting [6,3], the proposed approach is particularly beneficial when the target phrase consists of at least 3–4 syllables. Advantages inherited from using the proposed HFCC-ENS features for this task are speaker and also gender independence.

To obtain the similarity of a short feature sequence q and a particular position of a longer sequence d, the similarity function Δ averages M local comparisons $\langle q_i, d_j \rangle$ of feature vectors q_i and d_j. In general, the similarity between two feature sequences $a := (a_1, \ldots, a_K)$ and $b := (b_1, \ldots, b_L)$ can be characterized by calculating a *similarity matrix* $S_{a,b} := (\langle a_i, b_j \rangle)_{1 \leq i \leq K, 1 \leq j \leq L}$ consisting of all pair-wise comparisons. To analyze the structure of an audio signal, the *self-similarity matrix* $S_a := S_{a,a}$ of the corresponding feature sequence a can be employed [5]. Diagonal-like trajectories in S_a indicate the presence of *repeated* audio events within the analyzed signal.

3   An Audio Monitoring System

In a case study, the proposed system was set up at Fraunhofer FKIE. In an experiment, different persons located at different distances to the sensor network were producing different types of verbal exclamations as well as various types of knocking sounds. Evaluations show that VAD, keyword spotting, and detection of repeated sounds work very robustly. However, the limited sensor range due to filter effects caused by the windshields will have to be considered in the future. To present the detection and localization results to the user in an intuitive and easy-to-browse way, a multimodal user interface (UI) has been developed. Fig. 1 shows an overview of the main components for user interaction. The system basically acts as an interactive audio player where selected audio streams recorded by the sensors may be played back. On the left side, the system displays the signal and spectrogram of the selected audio channel (top left) and a timetable-like overview of the detected audio events (bottom left). In this example, voice activity, detected keywords (here cries for help shouted in German), and repeated audio events are displayed. Repeated instances of the same sounds are displayed in the same color; in this example the repeated sound of knocking on a metal plate is shown in black color, repeated exclamations of the same sequences of words are shown in red, green, blue, and yellow colors, respectively. All of the visualizations are synchronized, indicated by a sliding cursor that moves during playback. By clicking on the detected audio events, playback can be continued from the corresponding temporal position. Localization information is presented in the right part of the UI, showing an areal map of the monitored area, where positions of acoustic sensors are indicated by red bullets. Detected and localized events are indicated by small blue crosshairs during playback. By using short intervals of display time, temporal trajectories like detected footsteps can be visualized as well. Additionally, small textboxes indicate labels specifying individual events. The whole UI works for real-time playback and in an offline-mode.

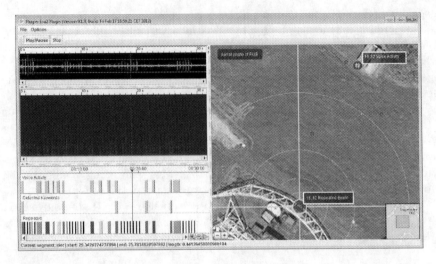

Fig. 1. User interface of the proposed monitoring system, showing input signal's waveform and spectrogram representation (top left), extracted audio events (bottom left), and localization information (right)

4 Conclusions and Future Work

A main focus of this paper was on adapting audio retrieval techniques for unsupervised acoustic monitoring. First case studies show how the proposed system benefits from suitable integration of detection and localization results obtained from data recorded by acoustic vector sensors. Besides more comprehensive evaluations, future work has to deal with mechanisms for more systematically combining outputs from different detectors. In this context, another issue will be how to exploit results obtained from a larger, spatially distributed sensor network.

References

1. de Bree, H.E., et al.: The μ-flown: the microflown: a novel device measuring acoustical flows. Sensors and Actuators A 54, 552–557 (1996)
2. Chen, S.H., Guido, R.C., Chen, S.H.: Voice activity detection in car environment using support vector machine and wavelet transform. In: Proc. IEEE ISMW (2007)
3. Keshet, J., Grangier, D., Bengio, S.: Discriminative keyword spotting. Speech Communication 51, 317–329 (2009)
4. Kurth, F., von Zeddelmann, D.: An Analysis of MFCC-like Parametric Audio Features for Keyphrase Spotting Applications. In: ITG-Fachtagung Sprachkommunikation, Bochum (2010)
5. Müller, M., Kurth, F.: Towards structural analysis of audio recordings in the presence of musical variations. EURASIP JASP 2007(89686) (2007)
6. Wilpon, J., Rabiner, L., Lee, C.H., Goldman, E.: Automatic recognition of keywords in unconstrained speech using hidden Markov models. IEEE TASSP 38(11) (1990)
7. von Zeddelmann, D., Kurth, F., Müller, M.: Perceptual audio features for unsupervised key-phrase detection. In: Proc. IEEE ICASSP (2010)

Integrating Persistent Surveillance Systems into ISR Architecture

Çağatay Soyer[1], Florian Segor[2], Barbara Essendorfer[2], and Wilmuth Müller[2]

[1] NATO Consultation, Command and Control Agency NC3A, The Hague, Netherlands
Cagatay.Soyer@nc3a.nato.int
[2] Fraunhofer Institute of Optronics, System Technologies and Image Exploitation IOSB,
Karlsruhe, Germany
{Florian.Segor,Barbara.Essendorfer,
Wilmuth.Mueller}@iosb.fraunhofer.de

Abstract. Persistent Surveillance is an increasingly important concept in today's conflicts due to the asymmetric and complex nature of threats. With the
proliferation of Persistent Surveillance Systems, NATO and its nations face a
new challenge to integrate these systems into their overall Intelligence, Surveillance, and Reconnaissance (ISR) architecture. The same can be observed for the
civil security domain. Persistent Surveillance Systems are widely used, but
without integrating them into an overall Surveillance and Reconnaissance
Architecture. This paper addresses the issue of integrating a Persistent
Surveillance System into a standards-based architecture enabling efficient dissemination, search and retrieval. In particular, specific features of Persistent
Surveillance Systems and current ISR architectures, potentially causing poor
and inefficient integration, are identified. Functional and technical requirements
and operating procedures are discussed as potential solutions to prevent these
adverse effects. An example system compliant with the NATO ISR Interoperability Architecture (NIIA) is considered to demonstrate applicability and effectiveness of proposed solutions in a perimeter surveillance scenario. The
proposed solutions, including the (I)SR Architecture are applicable also in the
civil security domain.

Keywords: Persistent Surveillance, ISR Architecture, Interoperability.

1   Introduction

Persistent Surveillance is a casual term without an agreed technical definition. When
the term is used in a military context, it is generally understood that the system can be
available or 'on station' on a continuous basis. In the civil security context, the term
Persitent Surveillance is not used yet, but there exists the mutual understanding that a
surveillance system is permanently available. Permanent availability requires not only
24/7 operation, but also an 'all weather' capability for the sensor payload and supporting elements. In this respect, it can be argued that ideal persistent surveillance (i.e.
100% availability) is a theoretical concept, which cannot be realized. In practice,
however, several systems and systems of systems come close enough to meeting this

N. Aschenbruck et al. (Eds.): Future Security 2012, CCIS 318, pp. 37–48, 2012.
© Springer-Verlag Berlin Heidelberg 2012

requirement. Current systems which are generally considered to be persistent include fixed surveillance cameras, aerostats, long endurance UAVs or teams of UAVs, unattended ground sensors for vibration, pressure, sound, chemical/biological/radiological agents and several types of intrusion detection systems.

In this paper, we primarily focus on video surveillance systems and imagery intelligence. However, other sensors are considered as complementary elements potentially co-existing with a video surveillance system, especially in a perimeter surveillance scenario. The key difference between imaging systems and other sensors is the significantly lower information content of the latter. For example, signals transmitted by vibration or acoustic sensors are usually processed and classified automatically in order to trigger an alert whereas a video stream requires human analysis.

In the next section we summarize the key features of ISR architectures using NATO ISR Interoperability Architecture (NIIA) as an example. In section 3, we identify the differences between a traditional ISR asset (such as a UAV system) and a Persistent Surveillance System, which make such systems a challenge for integration into ISR architectures. We propose potential solutions to the integration problem in Section 4. The proposed solutions are intended to be used both in military and civilian applications. In section 5, we discuss potential application in a perimeter surveillance scenario. The paper concludes with a summary and future directions.

2   ISR Architecture

For the military domain, NATO has defined an ISR Interoperability Architecture (NIIA) [1]. This architecture defines how reconnaissance and surveillance assets will achieve interoperability within coalition and NATO environments. A series of Standardization Agreements (STANAG) standardize the exchange of ISR data.

The STANAGs include amongst others:

- STANAG 3377, "Air Reconnaissance Intelligence Report Forms", which defines the standard reporting formats for intelligence reports (e.g. results of image exploitation processes) to operational users.
- STANAG 4545, "NATO Secondary Imagery Format (NSIF)", which establishes the format for exchange of electronic secondary imagery. Secondary imagery is sensor data that has been previously processed into a human interpretable picture.
- STANAG 4609, "NATO Digital Motion Imagery Standard", which intends to provide common methods for exchange of motion imagery (video) across systems within and among NATO nations. It includes guidance on uncompressed, compressed, and related motion imagery sampling structures; motion imagery time standards, motion imagery metadata standards, interconnections, and common language descriptions of motion imagery system parameters [2].
- STANAG 7085, "Interoperable Data Links for Imaging Systems", which establishes interoperability standards for imagery data links.
- STANAG 4586, "Standard Interfaces of UAV Control System for NATO UAV Interoperability", with the objective to facilitate communication between UCS and different Unmanned Aerial Vehicles (UAV) and their payloads as well as multiple Command, Control, Communications, Computers, and Intelligence (C4I) users.

Although not part of NATO ISR Interoperability Architecture, STANAG 4586 mandates the use of NIIA STANAGS for the Command and Control Interface (CCI) to enable interoperability of a UCS with other systems.

- STANAG 4559, "NATO Standard ISR Library Interface (NSILI)", which provides interoperability between NATO nations' reconnaissance databases and ISR product libraries by defining an interoperable interface to the ISR library systems (for more details see 4.3 and [4]).

The NIIA orients itself on the reconnaissance cycle (Figure 1). The reconnaissance cycle is a process, subdivided into five phases.

- Based on a Request for Information (RFI) by an operational user, a reconnaissance mission is tasked. The mission tasking identifies the area to be reconnoitered and further requirements set by the tasking agency.
- The aircrews prepare the flight plan to accomplish the mission.
- Subsequent to the flight preparations, the reconnaissance flight is performed.
- The reconnaissance flight mission is followed by the actual interpretation of the data collected during the flight.
- Upon completion of a mission, an exploitation report containing the results and answers to the RFI is prepared and forwarded to the tasking agency.

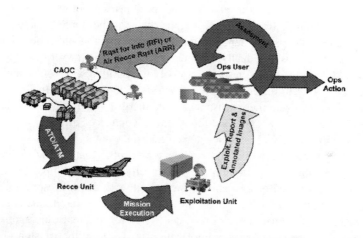

Fig. 1. The NATO Reconnaissance Cycle (from [1])

The reconnaissance cycle was designed with classical ISR assets in mind, and is not well suited for newer persistent capabilities like long endurance flight platforms, aerostats, mast-mounted long range sensors and unattended ground sensors, as well as small tactical UAVs with nowadays video and other sensing capabilities.

For the civil security domain a Surveillance Interoperability Architecture similar to NIIA does not exist.

3   Persistent Surveillance Challenge

In this section we identify key properties of Persistent Surveillance Systems that make them a challenge for integration into the overall ISR architecture. As mentioned above, video surveillance is our primary focus with other sensors considered as supporting elements providing either cueing or contextual information.

Using video as the primary sensor, coupled with other sensors, a persistent surveillance system is characterized through:

- Continuous streaming of large amounts of low relevance data
- High percentage of idle time
- Possibilities for automatic operation via cross-cuing and rule-based video analytics
- Multiple sensors in one system dynamically allocated by operator
- No pre-defined mission or collection plan
- Collection triggered by events either through human response or automatically
- Closed and highly dynamic tasking-collection loop.

In a typical persistent surveillance scenario, video sensors deliver a continuous stream of data which shall be monitored and exploited almost instantly. Relevant information, captured in appropriate video clips and extracted images as well as other sensor data shall be stored and disseminated to a higher headquarter. For an eventual forensic analysis at a later point in time, the data streams shall also be stored for a longer term. Furthermore, a persistent surveillance system does not comprise only one single video sensor, but multiple sensors, ideally mounted on platforms with various characteristics such as fixed platforms on masts or roofs of high buildings, aerostats, and mobile platforms, like UAVs in different sizes – from small multi-copters to large surveillance assets. The data from these sensors shall be merged and displayed in one single monitoring and control station, which also allows control of different sensors both manually and automatically, based on detected relevant events.

The system generates multiple video streams and other data, which is generally stored only for a short time period unless it is directly relevant or linked to an event. This data is not presented or available to the people with overall responsibility of a particular area or operation. When high-relevance video is captured, this is generally assessed locally by the operators and recorded for future reference or reporting purposes. In a developing situation, this information is also used by decision makers to guide the operators, who actively control the sensors, creating a local tasking-collection loop. A significant amount of contextual information about the event is used during these activities. Current standards for recorded imagery or clips do not contain this context and therefore the resulting sensor products become very difficult or impossible to interpret at a later time.

In addition to the event context, there are several possibilities for automatic operation in conjunction with other sensors used as triggers. These include alerting the operator, e.g. in case of a critical event, performing automatic video analysis or recording tasks and cross-cueing of different sensors used within one system. These automation parameters, cross-cueing rules and overall system architecture are not evident in recorded clips and imagery, contributing to the lack of contextual information and situational awareness.

In case of automatic video analysis (or video analytics), several algorithms are being developed, which enable detection and identification of humans, human actions and activities, vehicles, unattended objects, separation/merging events, intrusion/violation events, movement and trajectories [8]. Although some of these technologies are still at lower readiness levels, there is significant progress in specific applications. Developments in the field of video analytics are critical to dealing with high volumes of sensor data in Persistent Surveillance Systems. Current ISR architectures and standards do not readily capture results of video analytics and associate them with stored clips. As discussed in the next section, integration of Persistent Surveillance into current architectures will require solutions to associate automatic exploitation results with imagery, either directly or through further processing and mapping into existing metadata fields where possible.

The traditional reconnaissance cycle also fails to capture the highly dynamic nature of a persistent surveillance system, the need to react immediately on a critical event, and to cross-cue (automatically) other sensors or sensor platforms in near real-time. In a persistent surveillance environment, a sensor platform is triggered by events – a reaction of the human operator to some suspicious appearance or by other sensors. The tasking-collection-exploitation loop is therefore highly dynamic and it is a closed loop within the persistent surveillance cell. The only pre-defined mission or collection requirement within a collection plan is to task the persistent surveillance system to perform its mission.

4   Proposed Solution

Based on the requirements described in the previous section, solutions can be identified to facilitate the permanent use of surveillance systems, make them more reliable and improve the usefulness of the results. The proposed solution consists of both a new tasking-collection process and technical innovations.

In order to tackle the highly dynamic nature of a persistent surveillance system, a new tasking-collection process was defined (see Figure 2). The persistent surveillance system integrates all the sensors, sensor assets, and a local command & control station into one node, the Persistent Surveillance Cell (PSC). The Persistent Surveillance Cell is tasked by a Collection Planning System or a Command & Control Station of a higher headquarter only once, with the task to survey permanently a given area, an infrastructure, etc. The Persistent Surveillance Cell plans the sensor deployment autonomously, selecting dynamically the most appropriate sensors. Based on collected relevant data or critical events detected during its mission, a sensor re-deployment or tasking (deployment) of additional sensors under direct control of the PSC is performed. The higher headquarter and decision-makers are informed about critical events and may access relevant data, but sensor control authority remains within the PSC.

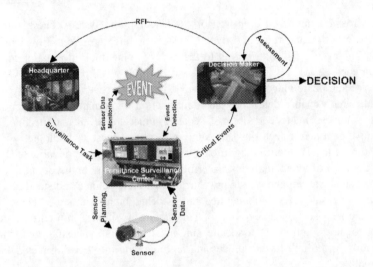

Fig. 2. Tasking-Collection Loop for Persistent Surveillance

The sensors and sensor assets are controlled and tasked by a control station, which provides the operator with

- Display of data stream from selected sensors and flipping through different streams
- Display of a map of the monitored area, showing also the sensor positions and their footprints, thus contributing to the operator's situational awareness
- Tools for tasking additional sensors, re-tasking sensors, and sensor-assets
- Tools for communicating with the higher headquarter
- Tools and algorithms for automatic video exploitation
- A storage and dissemination mechanism, allowing for interoperable exchange of relevant data with other PSCs or with higher headquarters.

4.1   Enhancing the Discovery of Useful Information

A persistent surveillance system, such as an aerostat, can produce large amounts of video data containing only small fragments of useful information. This information has to be identified during the evaluation of the real-time data stream, and tagged (marked) appropriately for dissemination to the higher headquarter as well as for later search and retrieval. Such tags, also called metadata, help to find the interesting data by other users or other systems which has to process the data.

Evaluating continuous streams of video data in real time manually is only possible with enormous effort on personnel. Using a combination of automated video exploitation algorithms and supporting sensors as triggers, the workload on the operator can be reduced drastically. The operator may still screen the video data, but he will be alerted about events that were not recognized by him.

Possible critical events are those, in which a change in the environment is detected. The change detection method is based on comparing current images with an original base image and calculating the differences between the two images. For example, a solid pan tilt camera can be trained on the surrounding terrain as part of its installation. This means it will record its environment and create an internal image of a "normal" situation. In operational use, this camera constantly matches the current environment to what was trained as "normal". If the camera (the algorithm) detects a deviation, extended algorithms can be used to process this further and alert the operator if the deviation is critical, or the operator is alerted immediately.

Additional sensors (vibration detection, magnetic sensors, passive infrared sensors) can be used to trigger the video sensors by cuing them to the corresponding location and by providing information for tagging the video stream. If the data is merged from several sensors and types of sensors it is possible to identify the cause of the disorder.

The operator is provided with an effective user interface, which allows him to quickly mark and tag the relevant video segments. In addition, the operator is supported by automatic clipping and tagging mechanisms, including metadata generation. STANAG 4609 (NATO Digital Motion Imagery Standard) [2] of the NIIA provides the possibility to add metadata to a video stream, but the offered metadata types are not tailored to persistent surveillance systems. Within a PSC additional metadata can be generated. Some examples of this metadata are as follows:

- Local Features: Pre-defined areas of interest, cultural and geographic features inside a fixed sensor's footprint can be used as metadata to provide additional information about the content of video clips.
- Periodic or Planned Activities: Video segments can be clipped and tagged automatically based on periodic or planned events such as patrols, force movements, shift changes and routine activities of the local population.
- Change Detection: Video segments can be marked and tagged based on the results of change detection as described in Section 4.1.
- Video Analytics and Cues: Cues from other sensors and built-in video analytics rules can be used to automatically clip and tag video segments. These include motion detection, intrusion detection, automatic target recognition and tracking.

4.2   Adding Operational Context

In addition to external events and sensor data processing, operational context plays an important role in understanding video content. One possibility to capture this information is for the operators to manually enter/select operating modes for their system such as "idle", "search", "track vehicle", "track human", etc. which can later be used as additional metadata attached to clips.

In an attempt to automate this process (at least partially), an additional inward directed analyzing component can detect the situation based on the behavior of the operator and draw conclusions about possibly important meta information.

For example during "search" the common operator behavior is "pan/tilt, zoom in, zoom out, pan/tilt, zoom in, zoom out, etc." Similarly during "track vehicle", the behavior is a smooth path aligned with roads with a relatively fixed field of view. Combined with data from a Geographic Information System (GIS), the current task can be detected automatically and confirmed by the operator.

Another interesting aspect is the possibility of strengthening the information by the use of semantic analysis. This way, linkages between data sets can be detected automatically. Because of the tags and metadata associated, the semantic analysis can draw conclusions on possible cross-connections and the unity of different information is recognized. For example, such connections can be made to previous mission reports or even chat logs.

The combination and data fusion of different sensors as mentioned earlier can also be done on a semantic basis. If the system can assign a spatial and temporal component to a detected event, identification of other affected sensors becomes possible and events in the past which might be related to the current event can be linked.

4.3   Storage and Dissemination

To be able to share information that was collected in one PSC with other PSCs and, more importantly, a higher headquarter, an adequate storage and dissemination architecture has to be defined and put in place [3]. A higher headquarter should be able to access relevant data from multiple PSCs, different organizations and different sources to enable situation awareness. As mentioned above it is of importance that surveillance information is tagged with specific metadata and can be discovered.

Standardized interfaces and data formats help to integrate information flexibly. The NIIA (see section 2) foresees STANAGs as a solution. For information sharing the Coalition Shared Data (CSD) concept based on STANAG 4559 [4] is of interest.

Here sensor systems store relevant surveillance data like images, videos, radar plots or surveillance reports on a local server (see Figure 3). Connected to the same network, exploitation systems are taking in a filtered set of the provided information (depending on the tasking) by querying or subscribing to metadata. By fusion and analysis they generate new additional information (e.g. reports) that is also stored on the data server(s). Situational awareness systems are able to display selected intelligence and can ask for additional information from sensors, exploitation or information systems to support decision makers. The concept foresees that each processing system can use internally proprietary formats. In this way each system can provide advanced mechanisms of data processing and exploitation with the full spectrum of information a sensor type provides. For dissemination purposes, the proprietary data formats are converted into standardized ones. In this way, other communities of interest (COIs) do not have to concentrate on specifics of the surveillance domain.

On a CSD server the data (sensor data, exploitation results) is stored together with the attached metadata. Within the metadata all relevant aspects of the product (depending on the domain) are defined and searchable. Those parameters could be for example: location, time, speed, size, friend/foe, weather condition, certainty of the info, and product type. An important aspect of the CSD concept is the ability to synchronize data over wide area networks. Here a server A connects to another server B and performs a subscription on all metadata or specific aspects (e.g. only video data). By this the information about all data is available in the full network. The original product data (e.g., images, video clips of possibly high data volume) is kept on the originating server. Only when a client connected to server A has analyzed the metadata and is actually interested in a product that resides on server B the specific data is transferred. Transferring only relevant high-volume data over the network saves bandwidth.

Fig. 3. Information sharing within a local architecture

The CSD concept is based on NATO STANAGs (see section 2). It has already been tested and fielded by different nations and system owners in exercises and military operations (e.g. [5], [6], [7]). However, this architecture was developed with a focus on classical ISR assets, such as surveillance aircraft. In order to adapt the CSD concept to other environments like the Persistent Surveillance scenario, the metadata model of the CSD can be extended as described in the previous sections. Specific attributes or new entities can be added and, if desired, access options can be defined by filtering through those attributes. In the process, the core of the data model is maintained and the server continues to be compatible with other CSDs.

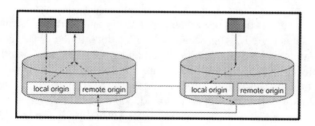

Fig. 4. Synchronization, single point of contact

Another aspect of adapting the CSD concept to the usage of "off the shelf" sensors or exploitation systems is to add an additional interface to the CSD. The STANAG 4559 demands CORBA based client-server interaction [4]. This is specific to the standard and therefore interoperability with civil systems is somewhat complicated. Currently work is performed to add an interface to the CSD that takes open standards like the Web Feature Service (WFS) by the Open Geospatial Consortium (OGC) into account. First tests are showing good results.

By the usage of open standard interfaces the CSD could be used by a wider community and in a civil security environment a lot easier than before. Through this and by extending the metadata to the requirements of the PSC domain the CSD concept recommends itself to be used as a means of data storage and dissemination among PSCs and higher headquarters.

5   Perimeter Surveillance Scenario

This section discusses the use of a system that allows persistent surveillance and threat analysis for an infrastructure with a permanently high threat potential and its integration into an existing (I)SR Architecture.

On this assumption it is basically irrelevant whether it is a civilian or military scenario because the main distinguishing features can be seen in the response to a perceived threat and not so much in their reconnaissance.

Let us consider the following scenario: we are in a property with a size of 200 x 200 meters. The perimeter is secured primarily by a two meter high fence to the outside. Within the site there are several buildings. The main command and control center is located inside one of the buildings. In addition there is a second control center (PSC) which oversees the use and control of the applied sensor network.

On the perimeter a permanent network of motion detectors, vibration sensors and various video cameras (IR, EO) is installed. Imaging sensors mounted on fixed platforms, like masts or roofs of high buildings provide a complete, persistent monitoring of the area. An aerostat serves as a long endurance supervision platform above the area, which provides an overview of the situation. In addition, there are several multi-copter drones on standby and can be used as needed for single spot reconnaissance.

Of great importance, however, are not only the sensor systems that are responsible for the provision of environmental data, but also the back-end systems which allow fusion of data and analysis at a high level. A permanent threat does not necessarily mean a permanent real danger. Due to the high idle times, the system must have certain intelligence to detect acute hazards independently and alert the operator.

Most of the data created in this scenario is video data. In the PSC, data is collected continuously and must be evaluated, managed and stored. The associated metadata to the video recordings e.g. footprint, time, or used sensor carriers have to be given special consideration because this information contribute significantly to situational awareness. As a very efficient way to keep video and metadata together, the PSC can provide its data on an external interface in the STANAG 4609 standard. The two data types (video and metadata) are packed into one combined data stream, which is then stored on a local CSD server. The local CSD server is connected with CSD servers in the main command and control center. Using STANAG 4609 for providing video data and a CSD server for storing and disseminating the data, the PSC is effectively integrated into an already existing ISR Architecture. Using the provided standards such as

STANAG 4609, as it has been done in this experiment, the exchange of information between the PSC and other nodes within the ISR Architecture is seamlessly possible.

Within a PSC the amount of generated data is very large and not all of this data ends in the CSD for further dissemination to headquarters. However, events that are recorded by the sensor network could remain entirely undetected and a subsequent review of the data will become necessary. Due to this, the collected data as well as sensor status data, including the dependencies between the employed sensors is stored persistently and tamper-proofed in the PSC. This provides the ability to replay a situation as it was recorded by all sensors in real time after the event took place. Undetected events or activities can thus be explained and analyzed retrospectively. In addition, the operator has the possibility to even retrospectively create CSD products.

In support of the operator, video analysis algorithms are used. These algorithms provide functionalities like video stabilization, super resolution, and are detecting and tracking moving objects such as people or vehicles in order to mark suspicious movements or identify potential threats. Artificial intelligence methods like a rule processing engine are used to detect and respond to certain events. Detected anomalies can then be reported and placed as a product into the CSD automatically.

If a sensor placed around the perimeter is triggered, some automated functions will be called. This allows recognizing that the sensor is located in an area that cannot be seen by a stationary camera. Therefore, an automatic command to the aerostat's camera platform is sent to align its payload to this position. The operator will be alerted by just the automatic response of the system. The IR sensor on the aerostat detects a nonspecific heat signature, but neither the software nor the operator is capable of identifying the target. After a brief observation, however, a movement is registered and the software recognizes that the anomaly is a human trespasser in the security zone. As a result an alarm is generated and the operator of the sensor network is provided with a feedback about the perceived threat. In addition, the reconnaissance results are automatically or semi-automatically stored in the CSD. The threat information is synchronized to the CSD in the main command and control center, where this data is accessed and further analysis is performed. In the absence of information about the intentions of the unidentified person a miniature unmanned air vehicle (multicopter UAV) is sent autonomously to the position with an optical sensor as payload. The UAV is manually maneuvered to get the best view on the localized threat. The result of this single spot reconnaissance is also streamed to the main command and control center. The PSC will switch back into the routine mode until the orders are changed or a new alarm occurs.

6   Conclusion and Future Work

Persistent Surveillance Systems present a challenge to ISR managers in military and civilian domains due to their differences from traditional sensor platforms. Current ISR processes and interoperability architectures designed around a tasking-collection-exploitation cycle do not necessarily apply to such systems, which continuously provide real-time video and other sensor data in border surveillance or perimeter protection applications. Furthermore, due to continuous and unstructured collection, a large percentage of collected data is not directly relevant to an event, making it difficult to exploit for intelligence purposes. As a result, sensor products from these systems are rarely available or useful to a wider group of users through a dissemination and exploitation network.

In this paper, we compared Persistent Surveillance Systems to traditional ISR assets and identified key differences that make them difficult to integrate into a classical ISR architecture such as NATO ISR Architecture or NIIA. We proposed manual and automated methods to associate relevant metadata and contextual information with imagery products from Persistent Surveillance Systems. Based on our experience with operational and research systems, we envisaged a scenario where these methods could significantly improve our ability to exploit sensor products at a later time. A key requirement in our approach was the ability to integrate with an existing ISR Architecture such as NIIA in a relatively short time, rather than to propose bespoke solutions. Therefore, the use of metadata fields in video and imagery STANAGs is proposed as the technical solution by which context information is captured, archived and discovered. However, new procedures and algorithms are required to generate additional metadata that is either not present or not exploited in current standards.

The next step in our research is to implement and demonstrate the proposed solutions in a real world system, which is already based on NIIA. For this purpose, an existing perimeter surveillance system will be used and modified as discussed in Sections 4 and 5 in order to assess its potential to achieve better utilization of continuous sensor feeds. Initial results from development of proposed methods as well as the implementation of NIIA in a perimeter surveillance application have been promising. If successful, these solutions can also be utilized to reduce analyst effort required for exploiting increasing volumes of imagery from traditional ISR assets.

References

1. NATO Intelligence, Surveillance, and Reconnaissance (ISR) Interoperability Architecture (NIIA). Allied Engineering Documentation Publication (AEDP)-2. Edition 1 (2005)
2. STANAG 4609 (Edition 3) – NATO Digital Motion Imagery Standard. Edition 3 (2009)
3. del Pozo, F., Dymock, A., Feldt, L., Hebrard, P., Sanfelice di Monteforte, F.: Maritime Surveillance in Support of CSDP. In: The Wise Pen Team final report to EDA steering board, European Defence Agency (2010)
4. STANAG 4559 (Edition 3) – NATO Standard ISR Library Interface. Edition 3 (2010)
5. SOBCAH. Surveillance of Borders, Coastlines and Harbors (2005), doi: ftp://ftp.cordis.europa.eu/pub/fp7/security/docs/sobcah_en.pdf
6. Stockfisch, D.: Common Shield 2008. TechDemo 2008/Harbor Protection Trials. Strategie & Technik (October 2008)
7. Trial Quest. Key NATO Reconnaissance Technology Passes Major Test, doi http://www.nato.int/docu/update/2007/12-december/e1210d.html
8. Ma, Y., Qian, G. (eds.): Intelligent Video Surveillance: Systems and Technology. CRC Press (2010)

Collaborative Mapping for Pedestrian Navigation in Security Applications

Maria Garcia Puyol, Martin Frassl, and Patrick Robertson

German Aerospace Center (DLR), Institute of Communications and Navigation,
Muenchnerstrasse 20, 82234 Wessling, Germany
{maria.garciapuyol,martin.frassl,patrick.robertson}@dlr.de
http://www.kn-s.dlr.de/indoornav/

Abstract. In rescue missions or law enforcement applications, accurate determination of every team member's position and providing this information on a map may significantly improve mutual situation awareness and potentially reduce the risk of accidentally harming a team member. Furthermore, it could help keep track of the areas that have been already visited, helping the coordination of the mission at hand.

Whereas in outdoors environments accurate positioning information can be obtained using a GNSS receivers, in indoor or underground environments GNSS signals are strongly disturbed and other means of localization must be called into play. Foot mounted inertial sensors or IMUs have been one of the proposed solutions, but their performance is prone to errors that grow over time. Only when the map of the environment is provided, can these IMUs perform with high accuracy. But building plans or maps of indoor and underground areas are often unavailable, outdated, incomplete and do not reflect furniture or other obstacles that also constraint the pedestrian's motion. How can a reliable map of an indoor environment be generated?

FootSLAM - Simultaneous Localization and Mapping for pedestrians - is a novel technique based on foot mounted IMUs that measure the pedestrian's steps while walking. These measurements can be used to generate a map of an environment while determining the pedestrian's location within that map. FootSLAM was recently extended to FeetSLAM, the multiuser scenario in which the maps obtained by two or more pedestrians are combined to generate a more extensive and accurate map of the environment.

In this paper we elaborate on different deployment scenarios for Foot-SLAM and its collaborative counterpart in security and emergency applications, yet to be experimentally validated.

Keywords: pedestrian navigation, indoor navigation, SLAM, FootSLAM, collaborative mapping.

1 Introduction: FootSLAM for Pedestrian Navigation

The problem of pedestrian navigation has received significant attention in the past few years and has been recognized as one of the most fundamental problems

N. Aschenbruck et al. (Eds.): Future Security 2012, CCIS 318, pp. 49–60, 2012.
© Springer-Verlag Berlin Heidelberg 2012

in the navigation community. Pedestrian navigation is the process by which the location of a pedestrian can be determined over time. This technique is especially important in security and emergency applications, where having precise and real-time knowledge of the location of all the persons involved, i.e. rescue teams and victims, plays a vital role in the success of any emergency operation.

Whereas in outdoor environments the problem can be addressed using satellite navigation receivers (e.g. GPS receivers), their performance is very much impaired in situations suffering from multipath propagation or in indoor and underground environments where the signal strength is not sufficient. This has led to the development of algorithms using other low-cost sensors that the pedestrian wears or carries. Foot mounted MEMS-based inertial sensors (IMUs) have been one of the proposed approaches but their performance suffers from unbounded error growth [1]. Nevertheless, when the environment constrains the movements of the pedestrian and these constraints (i.e. a map) are known, it has been shown that the error can be limited [2], thus allowing stable positioning in two and three dimensions even in the absence of other signals [3], [4].

Accurate positioning information using IMUs can only be obtained when the map of the environment is well-known. However, building plans or maps of indoor or underground areas are often unavailable, private, outdated, incomplete or inaccurate. Moreover, available indoor maps rarely reflect non-wall obstacles that also limit or channel pedestrian motion significantly. If we could rely on a technology that enabled pedestrians to generate a map of an environment while simultaneously providing his position within this map, many location based security applications could be developed.

To this end, FootSLAM - Simultaneous Localization and Mapping for pedestrians - was recently presented [2]. FootSLAM draws on the use of foot-mounted IMUs and builds on SLAM [5] for indoor and urban environments, whereby robots can generate a map of the environment and simultaneously locate themselves within that map. These robots are usually equipped with visual sensors such as laser scanners and cameras, whereas FootSLAM uses *only* the odometry - the noisy IMU-based measurements of a person's step vectors. Using a Rao-Blackwellized Particle Filter, FootSLAM searches over many different odometry error hypotheses finding one which best fits the previous pose history. Hypotheses in which the pedestrian revisits certain areas in the environment are rewarded and over time a reliable 2D map of essentially "walkable areas" is constructed. To help the convergence of the algorithm, FootSLAM allows the inclusion in its estimation process of other data sets obtained while walking in the same building. These data sets are used in the form of a *prior map*.

Real data from people walking within office environments at five locations have been used to validate the map building and relative localization abilities of FootSLAM [2], [10]. All calculations can be done in real-time. Figures 1 and 2 represent two of the scenarios. Figure 1 shows the FootSLAM map of a building in Vienna that presents a rather interesting layout. Figure 2 depicts two walks within an office building and the original building plan. On the image above, an extensive walk is depicted and the map encompasses almost all offices and other walkable areas. Below, the corresponding map of a shorter and less extensive walk is shown.

Fig. 1. FootSLAM map obtained from a walk in a building with an unusual layout

The approach can use other positioning techniques to anchor the map to a global coordinate frame. This can be a GNSS receiver, e.g. GPS, before and after entering a building, or WiFi stations with known positions (see also section 2.3 about sensor fusion), anchoring the map with reasonable position accuracy. Nevertheless, the use of such anchors is not a prerequisite for a valid map to emerge. When no anchor is used, the map has no global reference.

In this contribution we focus on FeetSLAM, the extension of FootSLAM to multiuser cases in which a group of pedestrians collaborate to generate a map of the environment while localizing themselves within that map. This approach is suitable to solve the problem that emergency, security and law enforcement operations often need to face, that is, the problem of having a team of pedestrians moving in an unknown environment and not knowing each other's relative positions.

The rest of this paper is organized as follows: Section 2 starts presenting Feet-SLAM as a solution for the problem of pedestrian collaborative mapping. Section 2.1 addresses the different applications for FeetSLAM in online and offline scenarios. Section 2.2 focuses on the possibilities to implement FeetSLAM using either a centralized or a decentralized approach. In Section 2.3, some sensor fusion solutions are proposed to address the generation of a combined map by the collaborating pedestrians and Section 2.4 illustrates how humans and robots can collaborate in the mapping task. Section 2.5 points out the main factors that affect the generation of an accurate combined map. Finally in Section 3, the main conclusions and outlook are presented.

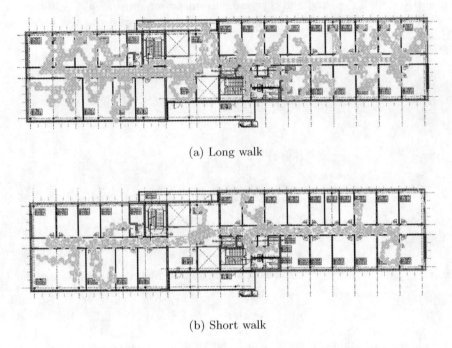

(a) Long walk

(b) Short walk

Fig. 2. Two examples of FootSLAM maps and building plan overlay for an office building. 2(a) shows the map obtained from a longer and more extensive walk than 2(b).

2 Collaborative Mapping of Indoor Areas

The state-of-the-art solutions for collaborative mapping of indoor areas draw on mobile robots that use on-board cameras and laser scanners to detect features in the environment and other robots to compute their relative position and pose [6], [7], [8]. There are also some hybrid solutions where humans and robots collaborate in the mapping task like [9], where the map is generated with the help of RFID tags. To our knowledge, the problem of real-time collaborative mapping by pedestrians using only inertial sensors has not been addressed yet.

FeetSLAM is a new technique [10] that addresses this problem. Following the concept of *crowdsourcing* [11], [12], in which sourcing tasks traditionally performed by specific individuals are delegated to a group of people or community, FeetSLAM relies on a group of pedestrians to undertake the mapping task. These pedestrians roam through accessible rooms and areas of different levels of a building collecting data by means of an IMU located on their foot or other forms of step measurement with different sensor arrangements. The data is processed by FootSLAM to obtain the individual maps and used in a combined fashion to generate a combined map. In order to do that, the FeetSLAM algorithm needs to find the transformations that place all the considered individual maps into the same coordinate system. Once the maps are located within the same coordinate system, their contributions are added to compose the combined map. This combined map can, in turn, be used as a prior map by another data set in another FootSLAM process, provided that data set and prior map are also placed within the same coordinate system. Note that in order to use a map as a prior for a given data set, the map must not contain any contributions from that data set. This is an important requirement that must be held in order to provide the data set with information from other walks while avoiding biasing it with its own contribution.

Collaborative mapping may be processed online in real-time or as an offline mapping process. FeetSLAM was recently implemented and tested in two different office environments in an offline fashion [10], that is, the data are first collected and then processed. Nevertheless, we expect the technique to be sped up to real-time capabilities over time, allowing online location-based services to develop. The next section introduces the main applications for online and offline FeetSLAM.

2.1   FeetSLAM Online and Offline Applications

An interesting *online* use case is the mapping of a building by multiple collaborating pedestrians with the objective of providing immediate map and position information to the other pedestrians or to external users at the time they walk through the building. Feasible scenarios for this use case in the security context are situations like the following:

– Rescue team coordination: A rescue team enters a building through the same or different entrances. Keeping track of the positions helps obtain a status about already visited areas and helps to find areas which have not been explored yet.
– Firefighters safety: Fire fighters operating under respiratory protection in a smoke-filled building are under extreme stress and high risk of hazardous situations. Knowing their exact locations and the shortest route to get there increases the safety during the operations. Figure 3 illustrates such a situation fire fighters often need to face.
– Law enforcement operations: Precise determination of the position of all agents involved in the mission and the knowledge of this position on a map can improve mutual situation awareness and potentially reduce the risk of accidentally harming a team member as well as help coordinate the team.
– Search for missing people in outdoor areas: In areas like deep forest, tunnels or canyons, the use of GNSS is prevented. FeetSLAM can be used to generate a map of the areas as they are visited by the search team and help speed up the search process, specially under bad weather conditions.

In these applications the real-time requirements are severe and usually no prior map data is available, or the map has significantly changed due to the event itself. Doors can be locked or walls might have been destroyed, opening new routes for movement.

Fig. 3. A team of firefighters undertakes a rescue operation under respiratory protection. The generation of a map of the environment they move in and knowing the position of the rest of the team members can be crucial for the success of the operation. Source: US Navy (Licence CC BY 2.0).

In *offline* applications we wish to derive a map that can be stored on a server or distributed to localization devices that use it to perform map-aided pedestrian dead reckoning. As more data is collected, the new walks can be incorporated and the maps be refined. Some examples of these offline applications are:

- Localization services for visually impaired people: FeetSLAM maps include information about the layout of the walls, the furniture and other obstacles and can be used by people with reading or vision disabilities, possibly through speech translation.
- Support to mobility-impaired people: These individuals might greatly benefit from FootSLAM maps in which the location of ramps and elevators can be indicated. Also, these maps can help find the shortest path to the destination, avoiding long detours that may cause more discomfort to the pedestrian with the walking disability.
- Intelligence services: Intelligence services can use FootSLAM to generate a map of buildings they are interested in. In this kind of applications, not depending on a external preinstalled infrastructure is a valuable characteristic.
- Evacuation routes: Evacuation routes for events with multitudinous attendance can be planed using FeetSLAM. In case of emergency, these routes can be sent to all the mobile terminals, avoiding locked doors and other obstacles. These applications are especially important in public buildings, airports, and any other buildings with high density of people. The maps can help make the crowd move in a coordinate manner and without colliding with each other, following a swarm behavior.

– Rapid response to accidents: A person among a multitudinous group of persons and located in a huge and complex building structure such as a museum, a football stadium or a concert hall, can be reached more quickly thanks to the knowledge of the map of the area, provided the person's location within this map is known. If such person had just suffered a critical incident (e.g. a heart attack), the time to locate him becomes crucial. Furthermore, determining the position of the closest defibrillator, which could also be indicated in the map, can increase the probabilities of saving the person [13].

This offline approach has been implemented in a centralized manner. The data collected by each pedestrian are uploaded to a central server where all the walks are processed in a combined fashion. The next section deepens in both centralized and decentralized approaches for FeetSLAM.

2.2   Centralized and Decentralized Approaches

Whereas offline FeetSLAM has been implemented using a central server, the online scenario is also suitable for a decentralized approach.

Centralized Approach: The pedestrians only exchange information with the server, but not with each other. The pedestrians can be involved in the combined map generation process in more or less degree:

– The pedestrians are responsible for collecting the odometry data. In this case, the pedestrians are only equipped with an IMU.
– The pedestrians can also generate their own FootSLAM map. To this end, the pedestrians must also carry a FootSLAM processor.
– The pedestrians can also generate the combined map using the information that they obtain from the server. In this scenario, the pedestrians need to be equipped with a FeetSLAM processor.

Likewise, the server can take on one of the following possibilities:

– The server takes all individual data sets or FootSLAM maps and is responsible for the generation of the combined map, which can be then distributed to the pedestrian's terminals.
– The server coordinates the information exchange, but the combined map is computed at each one of the pedestrian's terminal.

The more responsibilities the pedestrians have, the more robust the system is against a failure in the central server or in the communication links.

Decentralized Approach: The pedestrians exchange data directly with each other and compute their own individual map and their own version of the combined map. It is possible to exchange odometry data, individual FootSLAM maps or even the combined map. A synchronization system needs to be defined and the amount and order of data transmitted (e.g. the whole map obtained by each pedestrian, or only the last computed portion since the last transmission) has to be determined. This is especially important as the pedestrians are constantly moving and the time available for data transmission is limited to the time the two pedestrians are within communication range.

The communication can be done using a centralized network or a decentralized ad hoc network. If the FeetSLAM processing is done centrally, a connection to the central server has to be constantly available, either given implicitly through the centralized network, or through a multihop connection using the decentralized network. If both communication and processing is organized centrally, the system can still benefit from the decentralized network. Map information which has most relevance in the direct vicinity of a person can be exchanged with communication partners located in the vicinity. Communication bandwidth which would be needed to communicate with a central server can be saved. Nevertheless, operational teams are expected to have their own communication network which could be used to distribute maps.

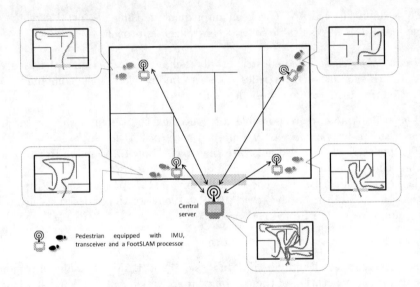

Fig. 4. Centralized FeetSLAM: Four pedestrians have entered the building through the main entrance. Each one of them is equipped with an IMU, a transceiver and in this case, a FootSLAM processor. All of them are able to generate a map of the areas they have visited, shown on their side. In this case, the central server is in charge of the generation and distribution of the combined map.

Figures 4 and 5 illustrate both of these alternatives for the online case. In the depicted cases, each pedestrian has direct access to her own individual map, but to be able to compute a combined map they need to communicate with the central server (centralized approach) or with the other pedestrians (decentralized approach) using the available network. The arrows indicate the possibility of communication between two pedestrians or a pedestrian and the central server.

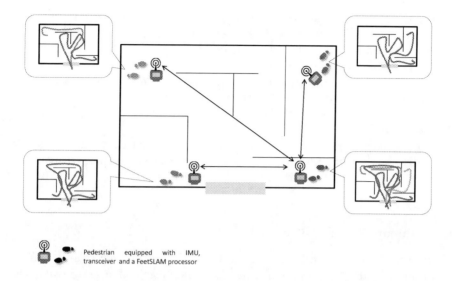

Pedestrian equipped with IMU, transceiver and a FeetSLAM processor

Fig. 5. Decentralized FeetSLAM: The four pedestrians have now access to the maps of some of the other pedestrians and are able to compute their own partial combined map. This map can be sent to the other pedestrians, helping all pedestrians have knowledge of the position of all the other pedestrians.

In any case, the pedestrians or the server in charge of the combination of the maps need to generate a table of contributing sources to avoid data sets using their own maps as priors. In that case, the map that arose from that specific data set can be subtracted from the combined map to obtain a fit prior map for the data set.

The main burden that FeetSLAM needs to face when computing a combined map is the need to transform the individual maps to place them within the same coordinate frame. The next section introduces some sensor fusion solutions to ease its time requirements.

2.3 Sensor Fusion Solutions

FootSLAM draws on the exclusive use of inertial sensors, but allows the integration of other sensors (sensor fusion) to help anchor the maps to a ground truth on the one hand, but also to increase their accuracy. This property can also be exploited by FeetSLAM to find the transformations that place all individual maps into the same coordinate system more quickly. The following approaches might be used:

– Use a GNSS receiver to anchor the map to a global coordinate system when possible (e.g. before entering the building). Due to GNSS inaccuracies, the individual maps still need to undergo transformation, but the area in which the transformation is searched can be drastically reduced, speeding up the combination process.

- Use the concept introduced by PlaceSLAM [14], whereby recognizable markers are used to help the FootSLAM algorithm converge. This could be markers already available in the environment, like WiFi or mobile network stations or optical features, or it could be markers which are manually placed in or around the building, e.g RFID tags or UWB stations, but whose position is known. Furthermore, if the position of another pedestrian or a potentially involved robot is known, this information can be used as a form of dynamic PlaceSLAM.
- Use the communication network through signal strength or time of arrival measurements between the pedestrians to get a rough distance estimation to support the needed transformation between their corresponding individual maps.

2.4   Human-Robot Collaborative Mapping

Hybrid solutions can also be used to face those cases in which the human intervention is partially prevented, such as a building in danger of collapsing, uncontrolled fire, hazardous materials, etc. In these scenarios, it can be useful to call robots into play. The robots can perform some parts of the exploration and undertake the mapping role. The following scenario is envisioned: The pedestrian performing the mapping task enters the building carrying a robot up until a point where the robot is set free. Then, the pedestrian exchanges his current location with the robot, who can start then performing his SLAM process, using visual sensors, PlaceSLAM or any available mapping and localization process. The robot can access and explore those areas where human life is threatened or where human access is not possible. Again, the whole process can be optionally anchored to a global coordinate system using a GPS receiver before entering the building. Figure 6 illustrates this idea.

2.5   Influence on the Collaborating Pedestrians

There exists a number of factors which have an influence on the mapping accuracy of FootSLAM, therefore affecting the resulting combined maps and the speed of the combination process:

- Number of users: the more users, the bigger the area that can be potentially mapped, but also the longer it takes to generate a combined map.
- Overlap of the areas visited by the pedestrians: overlap between the individual maps helps to find the best transformation between maps and also increases the convergence when using one as prior of the other.
- Duration of the walks (extension of the visited area and revisited area): the longer a walk lasts, the more the area is revisited (helping convergence) or the more area is explored (helping extensive mapping).
- Loop closure: closing loops helps the FootSLAM algorithm converge.
- Use of other sensors: The more sensors are used in the mapping and navigation process, the more accurate the maps are.

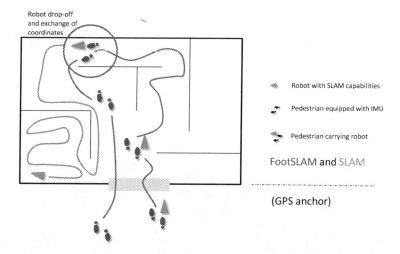

Robot drop-off and exchange of coordinates

Robot with SLAM capabilities

Pedestrian equipped with IMU

Pedestrian carrying robot

FootSLAM and SLAM

(GPS anchor)

Fig. 6. Example of human-robot collaborative mapping: A pedestrian carrying a robot enters the building from the outside world optionally anchoring her position to the global coordinate system using a GPS receiver. Once inside the building, the pedestrian uses FootSLAM to generate a map of the areas she visits and locate herself within it. She reaches a certain point where she drops the robot off, which starts performing SLAM using the last coordinates of the pedestrian as starting point. The pedestrian leaves the building and the robot continues mapping the building autonomously.

Thus, the collaborating pedestrians could be instructed or rewarded to walk for a longer time in certain areas, to close loops, to revisit areas, to flag some markers, to use other sensors, etc. so that a more extensive and accurate combined map is generated.

3   Conclusions and Further Work

In this paper FootSLAM and its collaborative version FeetSLAM have been proposed to address the navigation challenges that arise in indoor environments in which the use of GNSS is prevented and a map is usually not available. FootSLAM and FeetSLAM allow the generation of a map of an indoor or underground area that can be used by rescue and emergency teams to localize themselves. Awareness of the relative position of the team members helps the coordination of the mission at hand, increasing the chances of its success. This has been illustrated with different cases of use for the online and for the offline scenarios. Two approaches have been presented to implement FeetSLAM: a centralized and a decentralized approach and the use of other sensors or robots has been explored to increment robustness, performance and safety.

To experimentally validate the applicability of FeetSLAM to the different scenarios presented in this paper, further research needs to address online exchange of maps between the mapping agents or between the agents and a central server, that is, the definition of an ad-hoc network. Further work should also target the enhancement of the performance of the combined map generation and try to reduce its time demands. Likewise, the map generation abilities of FootSLAM in different kinds of environments or while the pedestrian runs, jumps, etc. is yet to be studied. Ongoing work is extending FootSLAM and FeetSLAM to three dimensions.

References

1. Foxlin, E.: Pedestrian tracking with shoe-mounted inertial sensors. IEEE Computer Graphics and Applications 25(6), 38–46 (2005)
2. Krach, B., Robertson, P., Angermann, M., Khider, M.: Inertial systems based joint mapping and positioning for pedestrian navigation. In: Proc. ION GNSS 2009, Savannah, Georgia, USA (2009)
3. Woodman, O., Harle, R.: Pedestrian localization for indoor environments. In: Proc. of the UbiComp 2008, Seoul, South Korea (2008)
4. Beauregard, S., Widyawan, K.M.: Indoor PDR performance enhancement using minimal map information and particle filters. In: Proc. of the IEEE/ION PLANS 2008, Monterey, USA (2008)
5. Durrant-Whyte, H., Bailey, T.: Simultaneous Localization and Mapping: Part I Tutorial. IEEE Robotics & Automation Magazine (2006)
6. Howard, A.: Multi-robot Simultaneous Localization and Mapping using Particle Filters. International Journal of Robotics Research 25(12) (2006)
7. León, A., Barea, R., Bergasa, L., López, E., Ocaña, M., Schleicher, D.: SLAM and Map Merging. Journal of Physical Agents 3(1) (2009)
8. Lee, H., Lee, S., Lee. S., Lee, T., Kim, D., Park, K., Lee, K., Lee, B.: Comparison and Analysis of Scan Matching Techniques for Cooperative-SLAM. In: 8th International Conference on Ubiquitous Robots and Ambient Intelligence (URAI), Songdo Conventia, Incheon, Korea (2011)
9. Kleiner, A., Dornhege, C., Dali, S.: Mapping disaster areas jointly: RFID-Coordinated SLAM by Humans and Robots. In: Proceedings of the 2007 IEEE International Workshop on Safety, Security and Rescue Robotics, Rome, Italy (2007)
10. Robertson, P., Garcia Puyol, M., Angermann, M.: Collaborative Pedestrian Mapping of Buildings Using Inertial Sensors and FootSLAM. In: ION GNSS 2011, Portland, Oregon, USA (2011)
11. Howe, J.: The Rise of Crowdsourcing. Wired 14(6) (2006)
12. Brabham, D.: Crowdsourcing as a Model for Problem Solving: An Introduction and Cases. Convergence: The International Journal of Research into New Media Technologies 14(1), 75–90 (2008)
13. Dao, T., Zhou, Y., Thill, J., Delmelle, E.: Spatio-temporal location modeling in a 3D indoor environment: the case of AEDs as emergency medical devices. International Journal of Geographical Information Science 26(3) (2012)
14. Robertson, P., Angermann, M., Khider, M.: Improving Simultaneous Localization and Mapping for Pedestrian Navigation and Automatic Mapping of Buildings by using Online Human-Based Feature Labeling. In: Proc. IEEE/ION PLANS 2010, Palm Springs, CA, USA (2010)

Image-Based Situation Assessment in Public Space

Hagen Borstell, Bernd Gebert, Liu Cao, Cathrin Plate, and Klaus Richter

Fraunhofer Institute for Factory Operation and Automation IFF,
Material Handling Engineering and Systems, Sandtorstr. 22, 39106 Magdeburg, Germany
{hagen.borstell,bernd.gebert,liu.cao,
cathrin.plate,klaus.richter}@iff.fraunhofer.de

Abstract. This paper describes various technical solutions related to image IP video surveillance systems in public spaces. Standard image processing procedures can compress event data, in this case people movements, and automatically capture it for aggregated processing in control center components for normal and emergency situations. Data from video sensors covering large areas may have to be fused. Reusable IT components, such as simulation models or scheduling systems, help various stakeholders perform their jobs based on a standard and unique base of data. Furthermore, new range imaging sensors or new visualization standards such as the virtual bird's-eye view improve surveillance of events in public spaces and thus support security staff.

Keywords: Video Surveillance, Virtual Bird's-eye-View, People Density, People Flow, Mesoscopic Simulation, Range Image Sensor.

1 Analysis of People Flows and Forecasting in Short Time Horizons

The Fraunhofer IFF developed technical solutions for the public zone of an airport terminal in the joint research project "FluSs - Airport Security System: Development of an Integrated Holistic Security Management Concept for Airport Infrastructures ". (Project Ref. No. 13N10048).

Important for national and international flows of passengers and cargo, airports impose special demands on the operation of cost effective safety technologies. A potential lies in the synergetic use of sensor infrastructures such as video surveillance with standard network cameras, in which the same data serve different evaluation functions or intended purposes. Imaging systems measure analysis values such as people density and flow direction or speed in real time [1]. The use of the results is subject to the intended application, which may be:

— airport security, distributing passengers in terminal areas and detecting blockages of escape routes by people,
— operational management, comparing manpower at check-in counters with waiting lines and detecting bottlenecks at entries and exits, and
— facility management, rerouting people flows away from construction and barriers and detecting blockages of entries and exits.

N. Aschenbruck et al. (Eds.): Future Security 2012, CCIS 318, pp. 61–64, 2012.

Video monitoring of passenger flows in airport terminals provides real time information on people flows, especially for security control centers. Deviations from the "normal flow" can be verified and validated messages or alarms can be generated for a control center in keeping with a company's policy, which alert staff to a changing situation in real time and thus facilitate much faster proactivity.

1.1   Measurement of People Density in a Space

The visualization of people density makes control center staff aware of anomalies or disturbances and supplements existing information options, such as images from single cameras or verbal information from staff patrolling a terminal. Furthermore, main flow directions or average speeds can be captured and visualized.

1.2   Mesoscopic Simulation in a Short Time Horizon

The actual people density values can serve as input for a mesoscopic simulation in a short time horizon, which runs through different scenarios in real time and, when required, forecasts people flows for the next sixty minutes. Since both pre-defined evacuation scenarios and operating modes can be simulated, this image-based situation assessment covers requirements of civil defense as well as aspects of process reliability. The results are available in seconds.

Mesoscopic simulation is based on a spatial model of the area under observation and interfaces to the sensor sources for counting or density estimation. The Fraunhofer IFF uses the MesoSim system as a tool [2]. Basically, the mesoscopic approach is intended to reproduce aggregated logistical flows. Rather than single flow objects, groups of flow objects are analyzed. Logistics processes can thus be reproduced by flows with piecewise constant intensities. This allows applying mechanisms of discrete rate simulation and model calculation in near-real time. Microscopic and macroscopic simulation models on the other hand require considerably more modelling and calculation [3].

2   The Virtual Bird's-eye View

Aerial and satellite as well as panoramic photography are classic methods for the generation of virtual views. Aerial images are assembled from individual, oblique, nearly parallel photographs, while panoramic images are assembled from non-oblique (but rotating) images. The images of both are aligned using image registration methods [3]. Google Street View and Microsoft Street Slide developed by Google and Microsoft respectively are new developments in this field [4]. Both systems enable the viewer to adopt virtual viewpoints based on 3-D panoramic pictures taken once.

The virtual bird's-eye view developed by the Fraunhofer IFF is a system that adopts a defined (bird's-eye) view of a defined space (plane) from a number of distributed cameras in real time. The defined view additionally acts as a metric cluster of all the connected sensors. Since object level views are not interpolated, only a small number of cameras are required and the system can be used in near-real time. Mathematically, a homographic image is used to implement the virtual bird's-eye view [5, 6, 7, 8].

In its final stage, the system constitutes a control center for the planning, coordination and monitoring of conditions and processes on premises for logistics operations. This enables security staff to act preemptively. The view of all events makes it possible to grasp a current situation quickly because the intuitive representation supports a situation assessment, thus reducing stressful situations induced by incomplete or unclear information from camera views of the premises. An example of a virtual bird's-eye view of premises for logistics operations measuring 300 m x 75 m with seven cameras mounted as high as 35 m, which are combined for a complete view, is pictured in Figure 1.

Fig. 1. Near-real time virtual bird's-eye view of the Hanse Terminal in Magdeburg (1 frame/sec.). [9] Fraunhofer IFF.

The virtual bird's-eye view of a public space from any number of camera views is a basic innovation for logistics and security-driven development of image processing algorithms to:

— reference objects with and without markers, e.g. people, equipment and freight, including location, position and movement [10],
— modify concepts and program libraries for motion analyses for logistics and security and
— may use non-photorealistic rendering (NPR) technologies.

3   Conclusion

The reliable technical solutions of people density measurement, mesoscopic simulation, virtual bird's-eye view and AO alarm increase the coverage of automatically monitored public spaces considerably at reasonable expense without violating the privacy of staff or other individuals. Benefits include:

— use of existing IP video infrastructure and inexpensive range imaging sensors,
— a scalable system,
— automatic detection of standard situations and deviations based on thresholds and reference patterns,
— forecasting of people flows in a short time horizon by mesoscopic simulation for proactivity,

64   H. Borstell et al.

– intuitive manual capture of an overall situation in a control center instead of numerous single camera images in different views,
– multiple use of identical data sources for different jobs and
– control center decision making support for different stakeholders.

The methods and specifications are transferrable to any location (airports, train stations, downtown areas, stadiums, etc.). The technical components are standard products and function with standard interfaces.

References

[1] Höferlin, M., Höferlin, B., Weiskopf, D.: Video visual analytics of tracked moving objects. In: Proceedings of 3rd Workshop on Behaviour Monitoring and Interpretation, pp. 59–64. Ghent University, Belgium (2009)
[2] Reggelin, T.: Mesoskopische Modellierung und Simulation logistischer Flusssysteme, Dissertation, Universität Otto-von-Guericke, Magdeburg (2010)
[3] Treiber, M., Hennecke, A., Helbing, D.: Congested traffic states in empirical observations and microscopic simulations. Physical Review E 62(2), 1805–1824 (2000)
[4] Szeliski, R.: Image Alignment and Stitching: A Tutorial. Microsoft TechReport MSR-TR-2004-92, Microsoft Research 2004 (2006)
[5] Kopf, J., Chen, B., Szeliski, R., Cohen, M.: Street Slide: Browsing Street Level Imagery. In: Hoppe, H. (ed.) ACM Transactions on Graphics (TOG) Proceedings of ACM SIGGRAPH 2010, vol. 29 (4), pp. 96(1)–96(8). ACM, New York (2010)
[6] Agarwal, A.C.: A Survey of Planar Homography Estimation Techniques. In: Jawahar, V., Narayanan, P.J. (eds.) IIIT Technical Report IIIT/TR/2005/12 (Juni 2005)
[7] Hayashi, K., Saito, H.: Synthesizing Free-Viewpoint Images from Multiple View Videos in Soccer Stadium. In: International Conference on Computer Graphics, Imaging and Visualization, pp. 220–225. IEEE Computer Society, Los Alamitos (2006)
[8] Wang, C., Zhao, L.: Intermediate View Synthesis Based on Adaptive BP Algorithm and View Interpolation. JCIT, 72–81 (2010)
[9] Hafen, Mehr: Effizienzsteigerung in Logistikknoten am Beispiel des Magdeburger Binnenhafens, Projektträger Investitionsbank Sachsen-Anhalt, FKZ 6060140101
[10] Borstell, H., Richter, K., Nykolaychuk, M.: Die Virtuelle Draufsicht für den Teamsport - Aggregation bildgebender Sensorquellen, 13, pp. 48-61. IAT Selbstverlag, Frühjahrsschule Informations- und Kommunikationstechnologien in der angewandten Trainingswissenschaft des IAT, Leipzig (April 2011)

DSO Cognitive Architecture in Mobile Surveillance

Gee Wah Ng, Yuan Sin Tan, Xuhong Xiao Xiao, and Rui Zhong Chan

Cognition and Fusion Laboratory,
DSO National Laboratories,
Singapore
{ngeewah,tyuansin,xxuhong,cruizhon}@dso.org.sg

Abstract. The paper presents the usage of a prototype DSO cognitive architecture (DSO-CA) for mobile surveillance. DSO-CA is able to bring to bear different types of knowledge to solve problems. It imbues mobile robots with intelligent capabilities like reasoning and adaptive path planning in dynamic environments, and achieves human-inspired object recognition. These intelligent robotic movements and object recognition capabilities can potentially be applied to mobile surveillance to enhance security situational awareness.

Keywords: Cognitive Architecture; Mobile Surveillance; Reasoning; Path Planning; Image Understanding.

1 Introduction

Surveillance for security purpose has attracted a lot of research and applications [1, 2]. In most applications, cameras are stationed at fixed positions and send images to humans or automatic monitoring systems to detect intrusions or malicious activities. This is static surveillance. With rapid advances in unmanned autonomous systems, mobile surveillance - surveillance systems installed on mobile robots or unmanned vehicles - will be more popular in time. Mobile surveillance is advantageous as it is active and can reach places we desire. It is applicable for places that require wide coverage but is difficult or impossible to install static cameras like hostile territories.

Robots doing mobile surveillance are challenged by intelligent navigation and image understanding. Intelligent navigation offers dynamically-determined routes for less vulnerable surveillance, watching over larger areas than static fixed areas. Total scene understanding [3] is needed to perceive the environment, identify targets and activities, despite being on the move. This paper presents our effort in using the DSO cognitive architecture (DSO-CA) to build a prototype mobile surveillance system to intelligently control the mobile platform while achieving total scene understanding.

2 DSO Cognitive Architecture

A cognitive architecture specifies a computational infrastructure that defines the various regions and functions working as a whole to produce human-like intelligence [4]. This architecture also defines the main connectivity and information flow between

N. Aschenbruck et al. (Eds.): Future Security 2012, CCIS 318, pp. 65–72, 2012.

various regions and functions. These functions and the connectivity between them in turn facilitate and provide implementation specifications for a variety of algorithms. There exist a number of excellent cognitive architectures but many have overlooked the importance of biological validity.

Drawing inspirations from various fields, for examples, neuroscience, psychology and biology, a top-level cognitive architecture was developed. Various key parts of the human brain and their functions are identified and included in the design. Some of the desired behaviors are set as design principles. The cognitive architecture also models information processing in the human brain. The human brain is able to process information in parallel and is able to bring to bear different types of knowledge, distributed throughout the brain, to solve a problem.   The top-level cognitive architecture design [5] is shown in Figure 1. Five core regions in the human brain, namely, Frontal Cortex, Perception, Limbic System, Association Cortex and Motor Cortex, are identified. Each of these five regions represents a class of functions in the brain. The corresponding classes of functions are Executive Functions, Perception, Affective Functions, Integrative Functions and Motor Control, respectively. In the next section, a description of a prototype cognitive system developed based on this design will be given.   This is followed by a discussion on how the cognitive system has been used to develop a prototype mobile surveillance system.

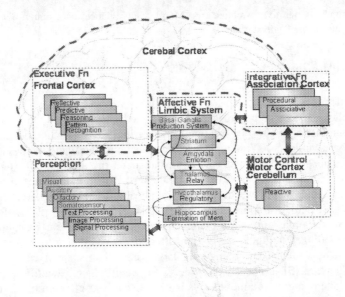

Fig. 1. Top-level Cognitive Architecture Design

3   Prototype Cognitive System

A prototype cognitive system (Figure 2) is developed based on the top-level design. Some functions from each of the five core regions are developed as modules which form the basic building blocks.

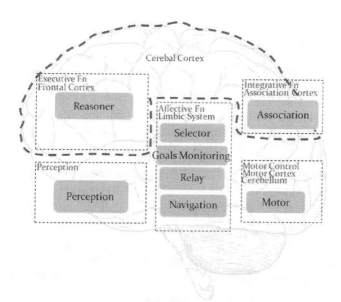

Fig. 2. Prototype Cognitive System

A module is the smallest functional unit of the computational architecture and provides a certain capability. A module is fully encapsulated, with its own knowledge base (distributed long term memory), internal representation schemes and inference methods. Thus a module can be treated like a black box. Other modules in the system do not have to know how it works internally. Each module communicates with other modules either directly or through the Relay (Thalamus) module. Since different modules may have different internal representation schemes, a potential communication problem among the modules may arise in the computational architecture. This problem can be solved by adopting a common representation scheme for all the outputs of the modules.

Modules that perform similar functions are grouped together into classes. For instance, the Perception class comprises of all modules that perform perceptual functions. The reason for grouping similar modules into classes is because different algorithms may be used to find the solution for different problem spaces. By having the concept of classes, each module in the same class can implement just one specific algorithm. This makes the code of each module smaller and easier to maintain. The modules in a class can have complementary, competitive or cooperative relationships. A meta-module for each class may be required to manage the outputs from the different modules within the class. The prototype system implements each module as an individual executable program. This is in concordance with the parallelism principle of the cognitive architecture.

3.1   Description

Perception Class: Modules belonging to the Perception class act as receivers to the external world. They take in raw inputs from the external world and process them into useful information. The processed information is then sent to the Relay module for distribution to the rest of the modules in the agent.

Motor Class: Modules in the Motor class are used to alter both the external environment and the internal state of the agent. These modules receive instructions from modules such as Selector and apply the necessary actions to the external environment or internal state of the agent.

Association Class: Association modules retrieve a list of plausible actions or states when presented with a situation picture. This list of actions or states is associated with the current decision or situation picture. The list is then sent back to the Relay module for further processing by other modules. The current implementation contains a module which builds upon a rule-based engine.

Reasoner Class: Reasoner modules analyze situations and propose actions. They are responsible for higher-level reasoning. Current implementation contains a Dynamic Reasoner module, which uses D'Brain [6] for its internal algorithm, and an Associative Reasoner, which is able to perform reasoning on any generic semantic network.

Selector Class: The role of Selector modules is to select an action or a decision from a list of proposed actions or decisions so as to reach the current goals or sub-goals. The current implementation contains a FALCON module [7] which enables reinforcement learning in the cognitive system. This will enable the Selector module to make better selections over time.

Relay Module: The Relay module distributes information to the relevant modules and maintains the current situation picture, in a form of working memory, for all the modules in the system. It functions like the Thalamus in the Limbic System. The current Relay module is able to combine information from different modules and distribute the information to the relevant modules, as well as route information according to some parallel pathways defined by a user-specified pathway configuration. The cognitive architecture also has the capability to learn pathways on its own.

Goals Monitoring Module: The purpose of the Goals Monitoring module is to produce appropriate sub-goals from the top-level goals and then monitor the current situation to check for status of these goals. The status of the goals can be used to update the other modules which may affect their processing of information.

Navigation Module: This module will contain a map representation of its surroundings and plan the path the mobile platform will take. It has to take into factors such as obstacles, covers, terrain and hostility of areas.

4   Prototype Mobile Surveillance System

4.1   Intelligent Reasoning and Path Planning

DSO-CA has been implemented on a physical robot with mounted camera as a prototype mobile surveillance system (Figure 3). It is capable of intelligent reasoning and adaptive path planning in large dynamic environments like the outdoor scenarios in Figure 4 and Figure 5. In such a scenario, a mobile surveillance system passing by a building's perimeter fence can move to another surveillance position (Figure 4). But seeing a suspicious person at the entrance, it is able to reason on its own and smartly moves to the other position via more tactical paths (Figure 5).

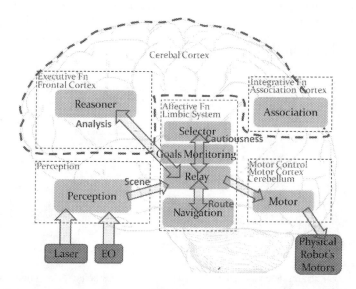

Fig. 3. Information flow in Prototype Cognitive System for intelligent reasoning and path planning

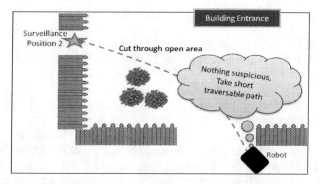

Fig. 4. No suspicious activity: Take Direct Path

In Figure 5, *Perception* detected a person at a building entrance but his activity/intention is not clear yet. *Reasoner* analyzes the situation with contextual information to reason that his behavior is suspicious; perhaps a potential illegal break-in. E.g., knowing the building occupiers are overseas translates to low possibility of anyone near it. Combining with perceptual observations like a toolbox beside him help increase the suspicion. *Reasoner* then proposes high-level action of moving tactically to surveillance position 2 for better view/confirmation and video record potential evidences without alerting him unnecessarily.

Selector then selects the robot's cautious level for movement, directly influencing *Navigation* in planning a specific path required. *Navigation* also considers its surroundings via influence mapping. Intending to stay out-of-sight from the suspect until position 2 is reached, surrounding objects giving good cover influences the robot to move near them and away from him. Additionally, in events of having time constrains, it will sacrifice stealth from cover for a faster/shorter path by automatically adjusting influences of the suspect and objects. *Motor* then executes low-level commands for the intelligent path planned via its physical motors.

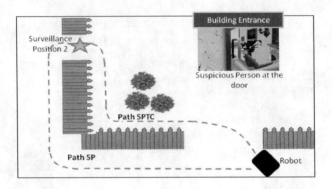

Fig. 5. Suspicious person detected: Take Path SP (most cautious behavior, minimal exposure); With time constrain, take Path SPTC (less cautious to avoid open area). High perimeter fences allow total cover while shorter bushes provide partial cover.

4.2   Human-Inspired Object Recognition

A complete mobile surveillance system also needs good image understanding. Humans do classification using other information as well, via object-based and context-based cortical mechanisms in the brain [8]. Such a human-inspired process is also implemented in DSO-CA (Figure 6) with two loops. The first loop involves initial classification, top-down facilitation and fine-grained classification. Initial classification takes place in *Perception* for early coarse-level classification of local image regions using popular classifiers like Support Vector Machines and Multiple Layer Perceptron.

Top-down facilitation takes place in *Reasoner* to resolve uncertainties of the initial classification through analysis of expert knowledge and contextual information. Image areas are also suggested for further attention. Fine-grained classification identifies more specific categories about interesting objects or objects of interest from some task requirement. When there are still uncertainties, the second loop - an object-based blending-feedback loop will be activated. A best-matched template will be retrieved from *Association* as visual feedback, blended with original target chip for another round of classification at *Perception*. This process models after the human visual recognition of adjusting perceived images with preconceived templates.

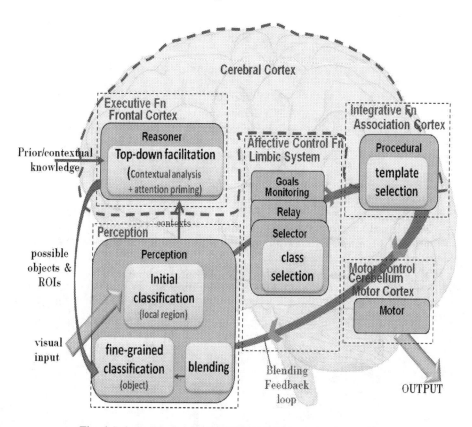

Fig. 6. Information flow in the DSO-CA for image understanding

5   Discussions and Conclusions

A cognitive architecture that models after human brain information processing is presented here. A prototype cognitive system with various modules has been developed based on this cognitive architecture. One key feature of the cognitive system is its ability to bring to bear different types of knowledge to solve problems. In mobile robotics, DSO-CA is able to imbue intelligent capabilities like reasoning and adaptive path planning in dynamic environments. In object recognition, DSO-CA is able to exploit bottom-up perceptual information, top-down contextual knowledge and visual feedback in a human-like way of utilizing different knowledge to recognize objects in images. Current results also show that incorporating contextual information and visual feedback in a human-like approach helps improve image classification performance.

The DSO-CA approaches to object classification and intelligent robotic movements can be combined and applied as a mobile surveillance system to enhance security situational awareness like in the outdoor scenarios presented. Such a system can be used as mobile patrol to exploit the flexibility of planning intelligent paths to cover large areas and provide intelligent surveillance. Future work includes activity learning to build on object classification and move towards a more holistic total scene understanding and thus better mobile surveillance.

References

[1] Hampupur, A., et al.: Smart Video Surveillance. IEEE Signal Processing Magazine, 38–51 (March 2005)

[2] Girgensohn, A., et al.: Dots: Support for Effective Video Surveillance. In: Proc. 15th International Conference on Multimedia, New York (2007)

[3] Li, L., Socher, R., Li, F.: Towards Total Scene Understanding: Classification, Annotation and Segmentation in an Automatic Framework. In: CVPR 2009 (2009)

[4] Newell, A.: Unified Theories of Cognition. Harvard University Press, Cambridge (1990)

[5] Ng, G.W., Tan, Y.S., Teow, L.N., Ng, K.H., Tan, K.H., Chan, R.Z.: A Cognitive Architecture for Knowledge Exploitation (2010)

[6] Ng, G.W., Ng, K.H., Tan, K.H., Goh, C.H.K.: The Ultimate Challenge of Commander's Decision Aids: The Cognition Based Dynamic Reasoning Machine. In: Proceeding of 25th Army Science Conference, Paper BO-05 (2006)

[7] Tan, A.-H., Carpenter, G.A., Grossberg, S.: Intelligence Through Interaction: Towards a Unified Theory for Learning. In: Liu, D., Fei, S., Hou, Z.-G., Zhang, H., Sun, C. (eds.) ISNN 2007. LNCS, vol. 4491, pp. 1094–1103. Springer, Heidelberg (2007)

[8] Fenske, M.J., Aminoff, E., Gronau, N., Bar, M.: Top-down facilitation of visual object recognition: Object-based and context-based contributions. Progress in Brain Research 155, 3–21 (2006)

Using NMF for Analyzing War Logs

Dirk Thorleuchter[1] and Dirk Van den Poel[2]

[1] Fraunhofer INT, Appelsgarten 2, D-53879 Euskirchen, Germany
`dirk.thorleuchter@int.fraunhofer.de`
[2] Ghent University, Faculty of Economics and Business Administration, B-9000 Gent,
Tweekerkenstraat 2, Belgium
`dirk.vandenpoel@ugent.be`
`http://www.crm.UGent.be`

Abstract. We investigate a semi-automated identification of technical problems occurred by armed forces weapon systems during mission of war. The proposed methodology is based on a semantic analysis of textual information in reports from soldiers (war logs). Latent semantic indexing (LSI) with non-negative matrix factorization (NMF) as technique from multivariate analysis and linear algebra is used to extract hidden semantic textual patterns from the reports. NMF factorizes the term-by-war log matrix - that consists of weighted term frequencies – into two non-negative matrices. This enables natural parts-based representation of the report information and it leads to an easy evaluation by human experts because human brain also uses parts-based representation. For an improved research and technology planning, the identified technical problems are a valuable source of information. A case study extracts technical problems from military logs of the Afghanistan war. Results are compared to a manual analysis written by journalists of 'Der Spiegel'.

Keywords: Non-negative matrix factorization, NMF, Text Mining.

1   Introduction

War logs written by soldiers during mission of war are a valuable source of information. They indicate e.g. technical problems occurred by armed forces weapon systems in use. Considering these problems in research and technology (R&T) projects may be necessary for an increase reliability of future weapon systems. Thus, extracting this feedback from war logs is an important task in R&T planning.

We provide a methodology for a semi-automated identification of technical problems in soldiers' war logs. A manual identification of these problems e.g. by human experts is not possible because of the large amount of the logs. Although war logs describe the events of the war, technical problems are just a part of the content e.g. an event is described in detail and besides the malfunction of a weapon system during that event is also mentioned. A frequently occurred malfunction of a specific system in different events can be discovered by identifying the underlying (hidden) semantic textual patterns from the collection of war logs because different soldiers formulize malfunctions by using different words. This excludes the use of text classification

N. Aschenbruck et al. (Eds.): Future Security 2012, CCIS 318, pp. 73–76, 2012.

algorithms based on knowledge structure approaches (e.g. Support Vector Machine, Decision trees) for this identification because they do not consider the aspects of meaning and thus, the identification of hidden semantic textual patterns.

Matrix factorization techniques consider the aspects of meaning [1]. NMF is a matrix factorization technique that can be used for text mining [2]. This algorithm is proposed to identify parts of textual documents [3]. The used parts-based representation is similar to the representation of information in human brain as shown by psychological and physiological studies [4-6]. This makes the results of NMF more comprehensible for a human expert than results of other matrix factorization techniques for text mining e.g. Singular Value Decomposition (SVD) [7]. Based on a term-by-war log matrix of weighted term frequencies, NMF factorizes this m x n matrix $A = [a_{ij}]$ into two non-negative matrices: $U = [u_{ij}]$ and $V = [v_{ij}]$ with m the number of war logs, n the number of different terms, and $r = rank(A) \leq min(m,n)$. U represents the (m x r) matrix that shows the similarity of terms and hidden semantic textual patterns. V is the (n x r) matrix that shows the similarity of hidden semantic textual patterns and war logs. Because of many zero values in the matrixes, the rank r can be reduced to $k < r$ with a compressed approximation $A \approx UV^T$ as calculated by

$$a_i \approx \sum_{j=1}^{k} u_j v_{ij} \tag{1}$$

with u_j be the j-th column vector of U. The vectors a_i of A are approximated by the weighted column vectors of U. Thus, a small number of vectors of U is used to approximate a large number of vectors of A. A good approximation can only be archived if the vectors of U discover structure that is latent in the data [8].

2   Methodology

The provided data are textual information contained in a collection of war logs. This unstructured information is prepared by removing specific characters and tags and by correcting typographical errors [9]. Tokenization is used to separate the different terms and all terms are converted in lower case [10], [11]. The number of terms is reduced by part-of-speech tagging, by stop word filtering, by stemming, and by applying Zipf distribution. For each war log a term vector is created based on vector space model [12]. The vector components consist of weighted term frequencies [13]. All vectors are used to create a term-by-war log matrix A. NMF is used to find two non-negative matrices U and V where the product of U and V provides a good approximation to A and where the rank is reduced from r to k. The selection of k is critical [7]. If k is too large then too many column vectors of U exists that represent many irrelevant or unimportant latent semantic textual information. If k is too small then the product of U and V does not provide a good approximation to A and thus, the column vectors of U are not a parts-based representation of the data. We apply a parameter-selection procedure [14] by constructing several rank-k models [15]. A fivefold cross-validation [16] is used to measure the approximation to A for each rank-k model and the lowest k is selected where the approximation to A is acceptable as defined by a specific threshold [17]. The k column vectors of U represent the latent semantic textual information in form of a parts-based representation. To present the vectors in a comprehensible way to human experts [18], terms are ordered by their corresponding vector components that represent the impact of the terms on a latent semantic textual pattern. As a result, a list of keywords is created for each pattern to support the identification of technical problems in the war logs.

3   Evaluation

In a case study, we use the released US military logs of the Afghanistan war (Kabul War Diary) from January 2008 to December 2009 as published by WikiLeaks.org. The data consists of 42,374 events and for each event a detailed description is given. These descriptions are used in the case study and the methodology is applied as described in Sect. 2. Based on the parameter-selection procedure, k is set to 100 and lists of the 100 latent semantic textual patterns are presented to human experts. To compare the performance of the methodology, we apply a second methodology on the data. The second methodology uses SVD instead of NMF because SVD as matrix factorization technique also can be used for text mining. However, SVD does not use a parts-based representation. Thus, we can measure the effect of parts-based representation on human experts' success for identifying technical problems. To enable comparison, the SVD parameter k is also set to 100 and lists of these 100 latent semantic textual patterns are also presented to human experts.

Human experts identify three patterns from NMF algorithm and two patterns from SVD algorithm where a strong reference to technical problems occurs. Technical problems of ground vehicles, trucks, clinger, convoys etc. as well as hydraulic problems of aircrafts can be identified from patterns of both, NMF and SVD. Further, an NMF pattern shows that in several events, small hand-launched remote-controlled unmanned aerial vehicles have crashed. Many reasons for this can be found in the corresponding list of keywords. Technical reasons are from general system faults via computing errors up to sensor failures. Further reasons are human failures by controlling or the shot down by insurgents. These results are confirmed by 'Der Spiegel' [19] where journalists have analyzed the data manually. They also find out e.g. that very often, unmanned aerial vehicle crash in events by the reasons mentioned above. Further, the human experts say that the NMF results are more comprehensible than SVD results. Thus, the proposed methodology can be used to identify technical problems from war logs semi-automatically, and in this case, the use of NMF outperforms the use of SVD. Further work should focus on a more detailed evaluation.

References

1. Cai, D., He, X., Wu, X., Han, J.: Non-negative Matrix Factorization on Mani-fold. In: 8th IEEE International Conference on Data Mining, pp. 63–72. IEEE Press, New York (2008)
2. Paatero, P., Tapper, U.: Positive matrix factorization: A non-negative factor model with optimal utilization of error estimates of data values. Environmetrics 5(2), 111–126 (1994)
3. Lee, D.D., Seung, H.S.: Learning the parts of objects by non-negative matrix factorization. Nature 401, 788–791 (1999)

4. Logothetis, N.K., Sheinberg, D.L.: Visual object recognition. Annual Review of Neuroscience 19, 577–621 (1996)
5. Palmer, S.E.: Hierarchical structure in perceptual representation. Cognitive Psychology 9, 441–474 (1977)
6. Wachsmuth, E., Oram, M.W., Perrett, D.I.: Recognition of objects and their component parts: Responses of single units in the temporal cortex of the macaque. Cerebral Cortex 4, 509–522 (1994)
7. Thorleuchter, D., Van den Poel, D., Prinzie, A.: Analyzing existing customers' websites to improve the customer acquisition process as well as the profitability prediction in B-to-B marketing. Expert Syst. Appl. 39(3), 2597–2605 (2012)
8. Lee, D.D., Seung, H.S.: Algorithms for nonnegative matrix factorization. In: Advances in Neural Information Processing Systems, pp. 556–562. MIT Press, Cambridge (2001)
9. Thorleuchter, D., Van den Poel, D.: Companies Website Optimising concerning Consumer's searching for new Products. In: International Conference on Uncertainty Reasoning and Knowledge Engineering, pp. 40–43. IEEE Press, New York (2011)
10. Thorleuchter, D., Schulze, J., Van den Poel, D.: Improved Emergency Management by a Loosely Coupled Logistic System. In: Aschenbruck, N., et al. (eds.) Future Security 2012. CCIS, vol. 318, pp. 5–8. Springer, Heidelberg (2012)
11. Thorleuchter, D., Van den Poel, D.: Predicting E-Commerce Company Success by Mining the Text of Its Publicly-Accessible Website. Expert Syst. Appl. (in press, 2012)
12. Thorleuchter, D., Herberz, S., Van den Poel, D.: Mining Social Behavior Ideas of Przewalski Horses. In: Wu, Y. (ed.) Advances in Computer, Communication, Control and Automation. LNEE, vol. 121, pp. 649–656. Springer, Heidelberg (2011)
13. Thorleuchter, D., Van den Poel, D.: Extraction of Ideas from Microsystems Technology. In: Jin, D., Lin, S. (eds.) Advances in CSIE, Vol. 1. AISC, vol. 168, pp. 563–568. Springer, Heidelberg (2012)
14. Thorleuchter, D., Van den Poel, D.: High Granular Multi-Level-Security Model for Improved Usability. In: 2nd International Conference on System science, Engineering design and Manufacturing informatization, pp. 191–194. IEEE Press, New York (2011)
15. Thorleuchter, D., Weck, G., Van den Poel, D.: Usability Based Modeling for Advanced IT-Security – An Electronic Engineering Approach. In: Jin, D., Lin, S. (eds.) Advances in Mechanical and Electronic Engineering. LNEE, vol. 177, pp. 615–619. Springer, Heidelberg (2012)
16. Thorleuchter, D., Weck, G., Van den Poel, D.: Granular Deleting in Multi Level Security Models – An Electronic Engineering Approach. In: Jin, D., Lin, S. (eds.) Advances in Mechanical and Electronic Engineering. LNEE, vol. 177, pp. 609–614. Springer, Heidelberg (2012)
17. Thorleuchter, D., Van den Poel, D.: Using Webcrawling of Publicly-Available Websites to Assess E-Commerce Relationships. In: Annual SRII Global Conference 2012. IEEE Press, New York (in press, 2012)
18. Thorleuchter, D., Van den Poel, D.: Rapid Scenario Generation with Generic Systems. In: International Conference on Management Sciences and Information Technology 2012. Lecture Notes in Information Technology. IERI, Delaware (in press, 2012)
19. Gebauer, M., Goetz, J., Hoyng, H., Koelbl, S., Rosenbach, M., Schmitz, G.P.: Die Afghanistan-Protokolle. Der Spiegel 30, 70–86 (2010)

Safety and Security, Dealing with Risks

Kurt Osterloh and Norma Wrobel

BAM Federal Institute for Materials Research and Testing, Radiological Methods,
Berlin, Germany
{kurt.osterloh,norma.wrobel}@bam.de

Abstract. Reducing risks and confining them to an acceptable level can be regarded as an essential commitment of technical applications for safety purposes and the public security measures.

Rating the efficiency of such measures requires an assessment of the risk that is supposed to be reduced. However, approaching this subject means to face a plethora of existing literature and an ongoing discussion if and how this can be achieved. On one hand, it remains a rather uncertain estimate particularly if it comes to rare interrupting events. On the other hand, making a decision responsibly requires a certain rational base. Several approaches exist for assessing risks, from verbal to quantitative, depending on the individual case. The frequently quoted Delphi technique represents the verbal one, others such as the Bayesian statistics a quantitative one or the consequence/probability matrix in-between.

A problem remains with understanding probability. Even if an event is highly unlikely it may happen right now.

Keywords: Risk definition, risk assessment, Public Safety and Security.

1 Introduction

Safety and security measures are intended to reduce risks by countering threats of various origins. As long as threats are obvious ways could be found to evade and thus to avoid the inevitable consequences. However, this is rarer in reality than expected. As a consequence, something unforeseen may happen any time that might have certain consequences. Since technical safety as well as public security aim to avoid adverse events dealing with risks is a common subject to both areas. The efficiency of measures taken in this direction parallels the estimation if and how far given risks may have been reduced by this way.

2 Understanding Risk

A concise overview on approaches how to understand risk has been presented recently at the 18th World Conference on Nondestructive Testing [1]. The term "risk" has been and is being used in a rather different context such as economics, politics,

N. Aschenbruck et al. (Eds.): Future Security 2012, CCIS 318, pp. 77–80, 2012.
© Springer-Verlag Berlin Heidelberg 2012

natural forces and technology. Though not completely inseparable, different views have been developed within the separate areas. An approach followed by economists was given by KNIGHT [2] who tried to differentiate between risk and uncertainty. However, this one cannot be sustained anymore consequently.

Pertaining to the commitment of safety and security to reduce risks to an acceptable level, it is essential to achieve a common understanding of the term "risk". A commonly acceptable definition of risk taking into account technical considerations can be found in the ISO/IEC Guide 51 of 1999 [3]: "combination of the probability of occurrence of harm and the severity of that harm". This entails both aspects that something unwanted could happen on one side and that this might have considerable consequences. A new definition was introduced by the most recent issue of the ISO Guide 73 of 2009 [4]: "effect of uncertainty on objectives". Surprisingly, the term "uncertainty" that KNIGHT had used distinct from risk now has become part of its definition. Though it is even more concise it should be questioned if it also fits technical requirements. Also the term "objectives" appears to be too common for technical purposes. What really counts are consequences, particularly if they are severe. It might be sufficient for management purposes or in a social context, but it might be too common for technological reasons as proven by still referring to the older ISO/IEC Guide 51 mentioned before.

3   Estimating Risk

All this raises the question whether a risk could be estimated for the purpose of risk management, i.e. to decide responsibly how to efficiently reduce risks [5]. The choice and the implementation of such measures require a rational base to justify the efforts involved. In this context, the lack of predictability has been identified as the main problem when assessing risk. As described in international standards [6], the process of risk assessment is divided into the phases of identifying, analysing and evaluating a risk. The risk analysis may focus on the probability of an event, its consequences and on the level of risk. The evaluation finally forms the base of future decision based on the results and understanding of the previous phases.

Particularly in case of rare events, no assessment has even a glimpse of predictability. A rare event could happen within a decade or even tomorrow. Therefore, the use of oversimplifications such as multiplying a probability of an adverse event by an estimated severity of harm is strongly discouraged since probabilities could shift dramatically while assets etc. could be added up to estimate putative consequences. Within the insurance business where such numerical approaches might be applied, it seems to be quite common to limit the amount of compensation in the case of damage or to decline certain risk from insuring. Some of the numerical approaches that have or may have been tried are sketched in Fig. 1 that includes a formula suggested at the previous Future Security Conference 2011 [7]. Fortunately, methods of risk assessment other than numerical exist.

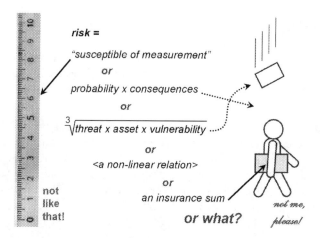

Fig. 1. Attempts to quantify risk: it cannot be measured like a physical entity such as the length nor assigned to a universally applicable formula

A seeming discrepancy becomes apparent that spending resources and efforts for security requires adequate justification on one hand and it seems hard to objectify risk for this purpose on the other hand. Since this inevitably entails a view in the future any assessment cannot exceed the character of an estimate with its inherent uncertainty. This already suggests that several pathways may be chosen even in parallel, at least in the consecutive phases of risk assessment as mentioned above, to achieve an estimate sufficiently convincing for a decision of actions. A comprehensive overview of methods is given in the annex of the IEC/ISO standard 31010 [6]. This list includes verbal, i.e. qualitative approaches such as the Delphi method predestined to identify risk but not applicable for risk evaluation. For the latter purpose, numerical methods such as Bayesian statistics and Bayes Nets may be preferred. An intermediate, semi-quantitative approach, the consequence/probability matrix has become rather popular for risk analysis. As a consequence, it appears not only impracticable but even impossible to combine the results from all the different approaches into a single parameter where the decision may consist of reading a value above or below an "appropriate" threshold. Instead, expressing the results in terms of three bands is suggested by the standard mentioned as a commonly accepted solution:

1. high risk level regarded as totally intolerable so treatment is essential,
2. 'grey' area with opportunities balanced against potential consequences,
3. seemingly unascertainable or acceptably low risk, no action required.

Aspects not considered yet are e.g. a distinction between assessable and perceived risks that also could exert an influence on a decision whether or not to take certain actions. For the sake of completeness it is necessary also to consider the context, i.e. anything related to the particular risk including possible previous events, i.e. experience. However, rare events may happen the first time or the past ones may have a different context.

4   Conclusion

It appears to be rather common sense that measures taken in both, public security and technical safety are intended to reduce risks, whatever that means. Assessing whether this aim is reasonably achievable some sort of risk assessment is required as presented and suggested here.

Acknowledgements. The Authors wish to thank the German Federal Ministry of Education and Research (BMBF) for supporting this work in part (project "FluSs", FKZ: 13N10054 and project "SefLog", FKZ: 13N11225). A forum to continue the discussion on risk pertaining to safety and security can be found at the European Federation for Non-Destructive Testing Working Group 5 "NDT Technologies for Public Security and Safety" (EFNDT WG 5, `http://www.efndt.org/Organisation/WorkingGroups/WorkingGroup5PublicSecurity.aspx`).

References

1. Osterloh, K., Wrobel, N.: Approaching an understanding of risk: a subject for the EFNDT Working Group 5 "NDT Technology for Public Security and Safety". In: 18th World Conference on Nondestructive Testing, Durban, South Africa, April 16-20 (2012), `http://www.ndt.net/events/WCNDT2012/474_wcndtfinal00474.pdf`
2. Knight, F.H.: Risk, Uncertainty, and Profit, 1st edn. Hart, Schaffner & Marx, Houghton Mifflin Company, The Riverside Press, Boston, Cambridge (1921)
3. ISO/IEC Guide 51:1999(E): Safety aspects – Guidelines for their inclusion in standards
4. ISO Guide 73:2009(E/F): Risk management – Vocabulary, Management du risque – Vocabulaire
5. Aven, T., Renn, O.: The Role of Quantitative Risk Assessments for Characterizing Risk and Uncertainty and Delineating Appropriate Risk Management Options, with Special Emphasis on Terrorism Risk. Risk Analysis 29(4), 587–600 (2009), doi:10.1111/j.1539-6924.2008.01175.x
6. IEC/ISO 31010:2009: Risk management – Risk assessment techniques; Gestion des risques – Techniques d'évaluation des risques
7. Nöldgen, M., Nawabi, A., Juszkiewicz, M.: Risk Evaluation for Critical Built Infrastructure, Asset Classification and Evaluation. In: Enders, J., Fiege, J. (eds.) Proceedings of the 6th Future Security, Berlin. Session B.6, pp. 490–497 (2011) ISBN 978-3-8396-0295-9

SECURITY2People – Functionality
of the Final Demonstrator

Wolfgang Raskob[1], Ellen Gers[2], Peter Meyer zu Drewer[3],
Stefan Möllmann[4], Lars Tufte[5], and Frank Ulmer[6]

[1] Karlsruhe Institute of Technology, 76344 Eggenstein-Leopoldshafen, Germany
[2] Federal Office of Civil Protection and Disaster Assistance (BBK), 53127 Bonn, Germany
[3] CAE Elektronik GmbH, 52220 Stolberg, Germany
[4] Karlsruhe Institute of Technology, 76128 Karlsruhe, Germany
[5] PRO DV AG, Hauert 6, 44227 Dortmund, Germany
[6] Dialogik, 70176 Stuttgart, Germany

Abstract. Within the German Security Research initiative, the integrated project SECURITY2People (Secure IT-Based Disaster Management System to Protect and Rescue People) aims at exploring the needs for and the structure of an integrated disaster management system that is applicable for all types of emergencies and at all levels of emergency management from the local to the Federal Government. Having started in mid 2009, the project will end November 2012. Based on modern IT-technology, a web portal with interconnected portlets has been designed. Portlets for functionalities such as Situation Awareness, Message Management, Knowledge Databases, Key Performance Indicators, Multi-criteria Analysis, Strategic Decision Support, Strategic Simulation, Action Force Management, Analysis and a Social Media Component have been designed for the final demonstrator. External components have been integrated via the Interoperability Platform of SECURITY2People. The final version will be demonstrated to potential end users in October/November 2012.

Keywords: Disaster Management, role based, integrated system, interoperability, portlets.

1 Introduction

The project SECURITY2People (Secure IT-Based Disaster Management System to Protect and Rescue People, in short S2P) that is part of the German Security Research initiative, aims at exploring the needs for and the structure of an integrated disaster management system. This system should be applicable for all types of emergencies and at all levels of disaster management from the local to the Federal Government. In addition operators of critical infrastructures and organisations dealing with security issues are also envisaged as future users of that system. The following functionalities are major components of the system:

N. Aschenbruck et al. (Eds.): Future Security 2012, CCIS 318, pp. 81–84, 2012.
© Springer-Verlag Berlin Heidelberg 2012

- Role-based information management;
- Decision support at all levels of management;
- Different types of simulation techniques;
- Applicability in training, exercises, planning and operation.

An important feature of such a system is the appropriate information exchange between different stakeholders and public communications. For this purpose, social and psychological aspects of crisis communication have to be explored. Finally the system has to be designed in such a way that existing specialised management tools can be integrated into SECURITY2People.

The project started in June 2009 and is scheduled for a three years period. In the first stage, the project focused on the analysis of the current status in emergency management and the functional and technological requirements for such an integrated system. Based on the analysis, a concept has been developed describing the functionalities and the simulation models that should be part of the S2P system. As the project has 10 associated partners from police, fire brigade, rescue services, operators of critical infrastructures and public administrations, a cycle of analysis, realisation and validation was established allowing the associated partners to directly provide feedback within workshops scheduled roughly twice per year. In each of the workshops, a demonstrator was presented, reflecting the current state of development (see e.g. Raskob et al. 2010).

2   The Project Security2People – Modules

The S2P-system is under development in terms of a demonstrator with an increasing number of components. The system architecture uses a state of the art data base management system (PostgreSQL) and a modern approach of building web applications (portlets). The user interacts with the system via an open source Web Portal (Liferay). All information for the models is stored in the knowledge data base that also contains information from historic cases to provide a basis for the current one. Also external simulation systems, here the RODOS system (see Raskob 2010a), can be coupled to exchange information; in our example it is the result from a dispersion simulation. An important component is the GESI system that can simulate resources in real-time (see GESI-EM2012).

The basic structure of the S2P demonstrator including its main modules is shown in figure 1. All in all the software comprises the following elements:

- **Interoperability Platform** as a central unit to connect the various modules to each other and to external systems. Uses TSO as a common language for data exchange.
- **Situation Awareness** providing functionalities to display but also manipulate information.
- **Message Management** aiming to inform the user at the various administrative levels.
- **Knowledge Data Base** containing information from historic events and enhanced with case based reasoning (CBR) algorithms allowing the adaptation of the existing scenarios to the current situation.

- **Key Performance Indicators** estimating the time and resources needed for a particular action.
- **Multi-criteria Analysis** supporting the evaluation of different countermeasure strategies.
- **Strategic Decision Support** analysing potential countermeasures with the help of the knowledge data base and CBR functionalities.
- **Strategic Simulation** providing information on critical dependencies.
- **Action Force Management** simulating the deployment and movement of relief units in real-time.
- **Analysis** functions allowing the spatial and temporal display of measures/commands and events in a web browser.
- **Social Media Component** facilitating the efficient gathering of information from Twitter to complete the decision makers' understanding of the situation.

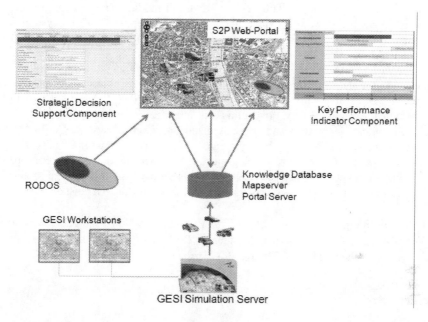

Fig. 1. Demonstrator layout with the various components and the connection to simulations such as GESI and RODOS

3   Summary and Conclusions

The S2P-demonstrator was presented and discussed in several workshops based on a concrete scenario of a large scale emergency. The participating end users from various German government agencies and relief organisations confirmed that the S2P system allows the support of decision making at all levels from the operational (e.g. resource allocation) up to the strategic one (e.g. countermeasure strategy).The possibility to attach existing systems to the interoperability platform was pointed out as a major advantage of S2P. It was made clear that a new system would be much easier accepted when it can complement existing products rather than replace them.

The simulation of resources with the GESI system allows the planning and execution of realistic exercises as decisions taken within the exercise can be directly simulated and thus can be evaluated in terms of performance and expected success. This closes a huge gap in existing approaches utilising predefined scripts that might be far from reality.

The knowledge data bases with the extension of the case based reasoning algorithms are extremely valuable for a first and fast evaluation of the situation. The check of the proposed countermeasure strategy via the Key Performance Indicators provides a first indication if the strategy is applicable. In most cases, in particular when time is short, this can replace the detailed simulation via GESI and might be very useful on the operational level.

The feedback from the potential end users of the S2P system following that demonstration was very positive (Tufte et al. 2011). All modules have been appreciated and recommendations were provided about future developments of the system. The end users stated that S2P is a clear step toward integrating tools for all levels of decision making.

In the last months of the project, the interoperability functionalities will be expanded. Via the interoperability platform of the S2P system, external systems can be integrated and automatically exchange information with the S2P system. This will be demonstrated exemplarily by connecting the chemical simulation system DISMA (TÜV Rheinland, Germany) and the Command and Control system COBRA (ISE GmbH, Germany). In this way, the key requests of the end users will be realised.

Based on the results of the research project, the industry partners of the consortium plan to further develop the demonstrator to an operational system. The final product is envisaged for the usage in emergency centres at the country or federal state level.

Acknowledgment. The project SECURITY2People is funded by the Federal Ministry of Education and Research (BMBF) under its Research Program for Civil Security, which is part of the High-Tech Strategy for Germany.

References

1. GESI-EM (2012), http://www.cae.com/en/military/_pdf/datasheet.GESIsimulation.pdf (visited March 20, 2012)
2. Raskob, W., Hugon, M. (eds.): Enhancing nuclear and radiological emergency management and rehabilitation: Key Results of the EURANOS European Project. Radioprotection 45(suppl. 5) (2010)
3. Raskob, W., Rickers, U., Gers, D.E., Kaschow, D.R., Tufte, D.L., Ulmer, F.: SECURITY 2People. In: 5th Security Research Conference, Berlin, September 7-9 (2010b)
4. Tufte, L., Gers, E., Meyer zu Drewer, P., Möllmann, S., Raskob, W., Stärk, K.: SECURITY2People – Features of and experience with the first demonstrator of an integrated disaster management system. In: 6th Security Research Conference, Berlin, September 5- 7 (2011)

Moving Advanced Safety
to the Cloud: Some Outcomes of SafeCity Project

Roberto Gimenez[1], Diego Fuentes[1], Daniel Oancea[1], Diego Gimenez[2],
Judith Pertejo[2], Tassos Dimitriou[3], Sakis Giannetsos[3],
Sofia Tsekeridou[3], Mario Carabaño[4], and Sofia Virgos[4]

[1] HI-Iberia Ingenieria y Proyectos
{rgimenez,dfuentes,doancea}@hi-iberia.es
[2] ISDEFE
{dgimenez,jpertejo}@isdefe.es
[3] Athens Information Technology – AIT
{tdim,agia,sots}@ait.gr
[4] Everis
{mario.carabano.mari,sofia.virgos.casal}@everis.com

Abstract. Protecting citizens is one of the key factors and also a priority for governments, majors and policy makers in current (and future) smart cities. In this sense, cities and countries' authorities are making a great effort in applying innovative approaches and new technologies in the Public Safety domain in recent years. One of these innovative approaches is to move the advanced safety to the Cloud. This short paper presents an introduction to how cloud hosting can be used by three of the most vital technological fields: Video Analytics, Semantics Data-mining and Communication Security. Part of the results and analysis produced in this paper are the outcome of the work carried out in the FP7 EU project SafeCity, one of the eight Use Cases of the FI Programme.

Keywords: Video Analytics, Data-mining, Security, Safety, Smart Cities, Enablers, Cloud hosting, Future Internet.

1 Introduction

In recent years, cities' authorities have made a great effort in applying innovative approaches and new technologies to drive a fundamental shift from responding to events to anticipating and preventing them, when possible. Expected Future Internet capabilities will drastically increase this innovative Public Safety capabilities adapted to their necessities. Cloud hosting is one of these key technological areas that provides clear flexibility and cost benefits while security and privacy as well as performance and availability are guaranteed.

Recent on-going initiatives, supported by the European Commission through the Future Internet Public-Private Program (FI-PPP), are establishing the technical bases of the *Future Internet* building European-scale technology platforms that provide innovative capabilities suitable for several domains of our society. **SafeCity** (*Future*

N. Aschenbruck et al. (Eds.): Future Security 2012, CCIS 318, pp. 85–88, 2012.

Internet Applied to Public Safety in Smart Cities) [2], an EU-funded project under this FP7 FI-PPP programme, aims at improving the implementation and up-taking of Future Internet services in this safety field by 2015, leveraging the internet infrastructure as the bases of Public Safety centred open innovation schemes. **SafeCity** represents a Use Case domain-area within this program that relies on the Core Platform capabilities, developed within FI-WARE project [1]. The Reference Architecture of the FI-WARE platform is structured along a number of technical chapters, cloud-based enablers, that may clearly enhance public safety capabilities at the same time that security and privacy as well as performance and availability are guaranteed.

2   Video Analytics from the Cloud: New Possibilities, New Approaches, Improved Results

Facilitated by Future Internet capabilities, Intelligent Video Analytics in SafeCity [2] aims to provide advanced capabilities for real-time situational awareness of numerous camera-monitored city areas, for intelligent analysis of many simultaneous video streams from digital surveillance cameras positioned in a city and for high-performance visual detection of a variety of potential life or property threatening situations. It further aims to support efficient decision making and instant alerting of Command and Control (C2) personnel in case of a threatening situation. The architecture of Intelligent Video Analytics during real-time operation and its interaction with other SafeCity C2 components is shown in Fig. 1. To increase the efficiency of the approach and optimize bandwidth usage by minimizing the amount of video feeds forwarded to the C2 centre, Video Analytics is deployed both on the SafeCity gateway (at the cloud edge) and on the SafeCity C2 centre.

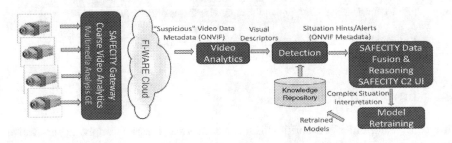

Fig. 1. Video Analytics during real-time operation

3   Cloud-Based Semantics Data-Mining

The raw data generated over time by the SafeCity applications (e.g., vigilance cameras, sensors, etc) might need transformation and is essential for continued functioning. The advance within the SafeCity project is the designing and implementing a Data Fusion framework that will deal with the heterogeneity of data and will overcome these challenges providing a better insight into the aspects which require attention. We believe that Semantic modeling can help with this. Fig. 2 shows the Data Fusion layered architecture, where the basic work flow in Data Fusion application goes as follows: The Data Fusion application receives from different SafeCity collector applications semantics meta-data. Then, through the Interface Layer, any application can make calls to gather information need it. Finally, the Data Fusion application passes any information requests to Service Layer.

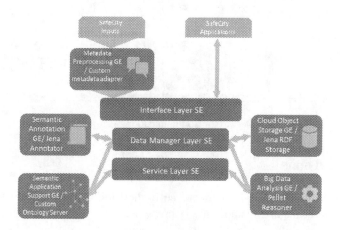

Fig. 2. Data Fusion layered architecture

4   Communication Security in the Context of SafeCity

Our contribution in the context of SafeCity includes the design and development of FI mechanisms and enablers to achieve an appropriate level of security taking into account the wireless nature of sensor networks, the context of the transmitted data and the inherent heterogeneity of the system. We also segregate between important information in order to differentiate among various security levels (e.g., low, high, etc.) for reporting sensitive data in a more appropriate manner. Finally, we provide suitable mechanisms for managing the trade-off between the adopted level of security and the efficient use of resources. The architecture for providing the above described functionalities in the context of Future Internet and FI-WARE revolves around the notion of a *Security Manager*, a Communication Security Specific Enabler (SE) that encapsulates the security aspects of the applications and enforces the desired communication security policies. The end-result is the definition of a cross-layer Security SE, which controls all issues related to secure data transmission and establishment of a device trust relation-ship scheme at different levels of the SafeCity protocol stack.

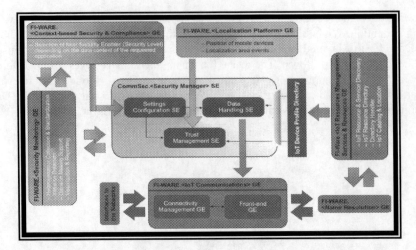

Fig. 3. Architecture of Communication Security Manager

5   Conclusions

Public Safety of tomorrow will be deployed in the Cloud. This innovative approach will bring significant and quantifiable improvements for the citizens' protection as well as service flexibility and costs reduction for the Safety Agencies.

One of the most benefited areas from these breakthroughs will be video analytics, which its main hindrance today is the sheer amount of computing demanded power. Intelligent architectures making profit of local coarse VA and relying on cloud based enablers for most complex tasks, along with properly trained models will shed light on previously uncovered or undetected conditions. Cloud-based semantics data-mining in the context of Public Safety helps to collect data from different processes, systems, and devices and applies intelligence to this mass of data. In addition, cloud-based data mining will help to save time for field personnel and provide costs benefits.   Finally, using appropriate FI mechanisms and enablers, a carefully developed security framework is being developed that specifies appropriate security plans, designs, implementations, and operations with justified benefits.

Acknowledgement. This work was carried out as part of the research project SafeCity, funded by the European Union Seventh Framework Programme (FP7-2011-ICT-FI), under grant agreement n° 285556.

References

1. FI-WARE Project, FI-PPP Programme (2011-2013), http://www.fi-ware.eu/
2. SafeCity Project: FI-PPP (2011-2013), http://www.safecity-project.eu/

Coordination Challenges
for Global Disease Outbreaks Security

Fadl Bdeir[1], Liaquat Hossain[1], Jafar Hamra[1], and John Crawford[2]

[1] Centre for Complex Systems Research, The University of Sydney, Australia
[2] Faculty of Agriculture, Food and Natural Resources, The University of Sydney
Fadl.bdeir@sydney.edu.au

Abstract. We are beginning to observe the management challenges for global security dealing with disease outbreaks. The rapid movement and migration of the world population as well as the transfer of resources across different regions provides immense challenges for developing improved surveillance systems for effectively coordinating our efforts to global security challenges faced by disease outbreaks. There are considerable efforts to collect case data during disease outbreaks (DO) from the spread of infections perspective. However, research for developing reliable framework for the collection of inter-organizational coordination (IOC) response data is lacking to date. Our objective here is to introduce a corpus that can be used in designing and capturing IOC data for facilitating empirical analysis of evolution of networks in a coordinated effort to DO. Since this is new domain, we introduce the main qualitative questions that will discover the characteristics of such coordination and propose a corpus or schema that can be used to classify the quantitative data collection and preparation for further empirical analysis.

Keywords: Pandemic Coordination, Informatics, Disease outbreak data collection.

1 Introduction

Inter-organizational coordination has been the subject of many research quests. What have also received more attention are information collection, sharing and coordination during disasters. This is mainly due to the challenges that such collaboration effort faces [2]. The first step for efficient coordination in disasters is having data characterizing the disasters' intensity, location and related damages as well as the availability of human and physical resources [1]. These data will be usually collected by multiple organizations each with different internal structure, skills, operating procedure and jurisdiction. Such data will ultimately need to be processed and shared with others which can be challenging as it has a tendency to create bottleneck in information gathering, processing, sense and decision making.

This paper will proceed as follow; we will firstly identify types of data that need to be collected. Then we will introduce the qualitative data survey followed by the quantitative data corpus.

N. Aschenbruck et al. (Eds.): Future Security 2012, CCIS 318, pp. 89–92, 2012.

2   Types of Inter-organizational Data to Be Collected

The starting point of data collection is to decide what data need to be collected so to understand the phenomena. Below is what type of data needs to be collected:

1. Organizations: What type of services does the organization provides? This will determine who and why others will outreach to link with it.
2. Organizational Links: The process of accepting or initiating link to another agency. This will form the IOC structure that will be further studied and researched.
3. Link Initiation. Usually the agency that is initiating the link to another one suggests that it in need of the services of the second one hence there is a form of dependency of the first to the second
4. Links Intensity: This is defined by the number of links between two specific organizations over a defined period of time. The intensity will define the dyadic dependency between certain organizations.
5. Links Timeline: A different phases of the outbreak, the need for services / resources will change. Hence some organizations might need to interfere at earlier or later stages of the outbreak timeline.
6. Link Purpose: It will be interesting to investigate the reason that enticed one organization to outreach the other. Was it resource need or information demand or other?

After defining the generally the types of data that need to be collected, we will approach the data collection task from two side, qualitative and quantitative.

3   Introducing the Qualitative Questionnaire

This section introduces the qualitative questionnaire which was primarily motivated by the review of literature related to pandemic coordination. It was decided that the ideas need to be confirmed from the field – that is, the disease outbreak personnel themselves. Hence semi-structured in-depth interviews were conducted. The interview questions were designed and planned carefully so that when executed, a systematic flow to the data collection process was achieved [3]. The interview questions are outlined below.

Table 1. Qualitative Questionnaire

Section:	Example Questions
A. Situational information	• How is outbreak detected? • How is information routed? • What are the outbreak criteria? • What are the containment criteria?
B. Actors	• Identifying the organizations involved. • Identifying organizational characteristics (jurisdiction/domain/location...) • Organizational role: how and when do they get involved in the outbreak? • What is their communication plan and protocols?

Table 1. (*continued*)

C. Processes	• Information production filtering and distribution. • Identifying parties involved in each part of information routing phases. • The inputs feeds and outcome of the decision support system.
D. Determinants	• How to measure coordination gaps? • What are the criteria to determine that coordination is successful? • Can we use epidemiological measures as performance indicators? Historical data? Peer data?

4   Introducing the Quantitative Corpus

In conjunction with qualitative interviews conducted with subject matter experts, the framework is used to further develop and refine a valid and reliable survey instrument. The quantitative method includes a non-traditional "networks" method of data collection and analysis to serve as a fine complement to traditional research methods in behavioral studies. The quantitative research method adds further empirical weight to the disease outbreak coordination model by explaining with quantitative evidence how network properties are associated with coordination.

4.1   Nodes

These represent organizations that have a role in the outbreak management and containment. Table 3 below presents a corpus that links variables to data type. These variables can be used for computational data analysis:

Table 2. Corpus Data variables

Variable	Data	Notes
ORG_NAME	Organization name	
ORG_TYPE	Organization type:	(International/Federal/State/Private)
ORG_ROLE1....n	The role that the organization plays in the pandemic	Leadership and guidance/Information collection and processing/Resource provisioning/Logistical support/Microbiology and epidemiology/Emergency care...

4.2   Relationships

These usually are expressed by exchange of communication or resources. These are called "ties". These ties represent the existence of coordination event between two nodes at a point of time:

Table 3. Relationship Corpus

Variable	Data	Notes
LINK_NUM	number of links between organiza-tions,	
LINK_INI	[ORG_Name]	Agency that initiates the link
LINK_END	[ORG_Name]	The agency which link is directed to.
LINK_TYPE	Reason for link initiation.	Direction of resources or information movement.
LINK_FREQ	Coordination frequency	Daily/Weekly/Monthly
LINK_COMM_METH	Coordination method:	Phone/mobile/Fax/Email/Social media/Web portal

5   Conclusion

This paper seeks to contribute to an improved inter-organizational data collection during pandemics and hence decision for managing global security related to disease outbreaks. To do so, a qualitative questionnaire and a quantitative corpus were developed to capture Inter-organizational coordination data in preparation for further analysis. Beyond data collection, the next step is to arrange, clean and organize the data to prepare it for analysis. It would be useful then to conduct organizational collaboration analysis and statistical analysis to investigate disease outbreak coordination from a social networks perspective.

References

[1] Dantas, A., Dalziell, E.: Opportunities, barriers and challenges for implementing electronic data and information sharing frameworks in organisational response to natural disasters, Citeseer (2005)
[2] Marshall, C.S., Yamada, S., Inada, M.K.: Using Problem-based Learning for Pandemic Preparedness. The Kaohsiung Journal of Medical Sciences 24, S39–S45 (2008)
[3] Miles, M.B., Huberman, A.M.: Qualitative data analysis. Sage Publ. (1999)

Intelligent Multi Sensor Fusion System for Advanced Situation Awareness in Urban Environments

Georg Hummel[1], Martin Russ[1], Peter Stütz[1], John Soldatos[2], Lorenzo Rossi[3],
Thomas Knape[4], Ákos Utasi[5], Levente Kovács[5], Tamás Szirányi[5],
Charalampos Doulaverakis[6], and Ioannis Kompatsiaris[6]

[1] Institute of Flight Systems, Bundeswehr University Munich, Germany
{georg.hummel,martin.russ,peter.stuetz}@unibw.de
[2] Athens Information Technology, 0,8Km Markopoulo Ave, Athens, Greece
jsol@ait.gr
[3] Vitrociset Spa, Via Tiburtina 1020 Roma, Italy
l.rossi@vitrociset.it
[4] Data Fusion International, Dublin, Ireland
thomas.knape@datafusion.ie
[5] Computer and Automation Research Institute, Hungarian Academy of Sciences, Hungary
{utasi,levente.kovacs,sziranyi}@sztaki.hu
[6] Centre for Research and Technology Hellas,
Information Technologies Institute,
Thessaloniki, Greece
{doulaver,ikom}@iti.gr

Abstract. This paper presents a distributed multi sensor data processing and fusion system providing sophisticated surveillance capabilities in the urban environment. The system enables visual/non-visual event detection, situation assessment, and semantic event-based reasoning for force protection and civil surveillance applications. The novelties lie in the high level system view approach, not only concentrating on data fusion methodologies per se, but rather on a holistic view of sensor data fusion that provides both lower (sensor) level and higher level (semantic) fusion. At the same time, we concentrate on easy and quick extensibility with new sensors and processing capabilities. The system also makes provisions for visualizing and processing space-time alerts from sensor detections up to high level alerts based on rule-based semantic reasoning over sensor data and fusion events. The proposed architecture has been validated in a number of different synthetic and live urban scenarios.

Keywords: Sensor Fusion, Common Operational Picture, UAV, JDL.

1 Introduction

During the last fifteen years, the world has witnessed a number of major defense and security incidents in the urban environment. Most prominent examples include the

N. Aschenbruck et al. (Eds.): Future Security 2012, CCIS 318, pp. 93–104, 2012.

events on 09/11/2001, or the bombings in the London and the Madrid subways. These incidents have manifested the vulnerabilities of the urban environment, as well as the magnitude of the social and economic costs that are associated with such incidents. At the same time, there have also been cases where military operations in urban environments were necessary. The complications of the urban environment when compared with open terrain impose particular and very specific challenges at both operational and tactical levels. The urban environment is characterized by the presence of buildings, city infrastructure and other man-made structures in a 3D space, over- and underground, as well as considerable number of civilians.

Facing the complexity of operations in the urban environment, security and defense agencies are increasingly turning to pervasive multi-sensory technologies for enhancing their ability to acquire, analyze and visualize events and situations. Sensor data fusion is among the primary technologies employed towards supporting these goals and such fusion systems can enable the creation of a common operational picture (COP). However, the development of robust data fusion systems is associated with a host of technical challenges. Several of these challenges stem from the need to integrate highly distributed and heterogeneous systems, including multiple sensors (e.g., cameras, microphones, microphone arrays, LIDARs), signal processing algorithms (extracting events from raw multimedia signals) and data fusion algorithms. Furthermore, fusion is likely to take place on multiple levels as specified by the JDL (Joint Director of Laboratories) fusion models [17].

Since the advent of ubiquitous and pervasive computing [1] researchers have been striving to design and develop middleware that could ease the integration of non-trivial multi-sensory context aware systems. As a result, several middleware architectures have emerged, which can generally be classified into three broad categories. The first includes middleware systems for Smart Spaces [2][3][4], characterized by their emphasis on the integration of complex perceptual components such as audio and visual processing algorithms (e.g., real-time processing, extreme heterogeneity in terms of implementation platforms, timing synchronizations, handling of uncertainty due to inaccurate algorithms), and are usually deployed within in-door environments. The second category includes middleware architectures for Wireless Sensor Networks (WSN) [5] and Radio Frequency Identification (RFID) systems [6], which emphasize efficient ways to integrate, link and fuse information from multiple sensor sources [7]. The focus of these systems is mainly on the integration and fusion of sensor data, without emphasis on complex perceptive processing. Finally, the third category refers to semantic middleware systems [8][9][10], which employ ontologies and semantic reasoning to infer context, while also assessing situations.

Systems providing advanced capabilities for urban security and surveillance, as well as situation assessment and common operational picture generation, should advance and integrate all above functionalities in order to handle multiple heterogeneous sensors suitable for the urban war environment (including sensor and data feeds stemming from perceptual processing). At the same time, it needs to support JDL fusion level mandates by deploying various fusion techniques and algorithms.

As a result we introduce the *Multi sEnsor Data fusion grid for Urban Situational Awareness* (MEDUSA) pervasive multi-sensor fusion system, which takes into account the above considerations towards enabling COP generation in urban environments, based on a middleware architecture which extends the state-of-the-art in terms of the properties outlined above. In particular, novelties introduced in the presented system include:

- The facilitation integration of multiple sensors and fusion algorithms, while at the same time supporting fusion at multiple levels (including JDL levels);
- Transparent interfaces for processing modules and data sensors for quick integration of third party components;
- Support for both low-level rule-based and high-level event-based fusion capabilities;
- Providing geo-location and geographic visualization capabilities, which are key prerequisites for COP generation;

Overall, the system acts as a breadboard enabling flexible integration of diverse sensors, processing algorithms, fusion rules, as well as ontologies for semantic-based reasoning and fusion of high-level metadata.

In addition to its novel architecture, the system includes several component level innovations, concerning

- integration of novel visual processing components, and
- integration and utilization of mobile sensor platforms.

In the area of visual signal processing, we have developed and integrated a number of robust real-time context acquisition components. Generic visual detection methods do not possess the necessary capabilities for drop-in application in urban war scenarios, since the environment and circumstances can be versatile and changing. Thus, we developed and adapted a series of novel processing algorithms that can be applied in such situations. These methods have been integrated into the MEDUSA system, used and validated in real-time scenarios.

In the area of mobile sensor platforms the deployment of and interaction with UAVs was specifically addressed. In this respect the conventional paradigm of UAV guidance and control utilizing a dedicated, manned ground control station was replaced by a tighter, immediate coupling to the fusion grid and its mobile sensors.

Overall, the paper is structured as follows: Section 2 presents an overview of the grid architecture emphasizing its novel characteristics, illustrating sensor integration and fusion capabilities. Section 3 describes low-level processing algorithms and fusion capabilities. Section 4 focuses on semantic reasoning capabilities, including integration of ontologies and implementation of reasoning schemes. Section 5 elaborates the integration of geo-location services, also illustrating the COP interface. Section 6 illustrates the integration of mobile nodes (UAVs). Section 7 is devoted to the validation of the system in the scope of synthetic/simulated and live scenarios.

2   Overview of the Multi-Sensor Fusion Grid Architecture

The presented Sensor Fusion Grid (SFG) has been designed as a pervasive middleware system, which combines the merits of state-of-the art middleware for multi-sensor integration of perceptive algorithms and semantic reasoning. In particular, the system supports the following functionalities:

1. Flexible support for heterogeneous sensors and processing algorithms,
2. Implementation of various fusion algorithms and sensor deployment configurations over a single middleware infrastructure,
3. Support for multiple application scenarios,
4. Capability of real-time context-based acquisition and interaction,
5. Information acquisition and integration from mobile nodes and annexed sensors,
6. Provision of high level fusion and reasoning in order to adequately support event generation and decision support.

The sensor fusion grid architecture (see Fig. 1) has been designed as a next generation pervasive grid system [15]. In essence, it is a distributed system comprising multiple nodes, each in charge of collecting and fusing information stemming from sensors, perceptive algorithms or other nodes of the SFG. The core of the system was designed on the basis of the following types of nodes, which can seamlessly communicate and exchange information with each other [16]:

- Low-Level Fusion Nodes (LLF), collecting and combining information from underlying sensors and perceptive processing algorithms. LLF nodes are where sensors and sensor processing algorithms are integrated and executed.
- High Level Fusion (HLF) Node (or Semantic Node), integrating ontologies for situation awareness and high level reasoning.
- Mobile Nodes, including Instrumented Person Nodes (IPN) and Unmanned Aerial Vehicles (UAV).
- Central Control Nodes, which host centralized services such as the COP module and the Environmental Services (ES) module, also providing presentation services.

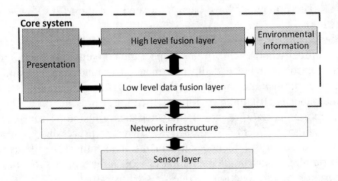

Fig. 1. General system architecture

The MEDUSA system provides support for all the fusion levels specified in JDL model, which is a functionally-oriented. The JDL Fusion Working Group has introduced four different levels for the data-fusion process [17], including: (a) Level 1 (Object Refinement) combining the different information (e.g. location, parametric and identity information, feature extractions) to achieve refined representations of individual objects, (b) Level 2 (Situation Refinement), taking the results of Level 1 to perform situation assessment by fusing spatial and temporal data of entities, to form an abstract representation, (c) Level 3 (Threat Refinement), taking the results of Level

2 to estimate future events by fusing the combined activities and capabilities of entities to infer their intentions and assess the threat that they pose and (d) Level 4 (Process Refinement) providing resource management and feedback for refinement of the previous levels and monitoring the fusion performance. Furthermore, a "pre-processing" level (Level 0) [19] operating at the sensor level and a Human-Machine Interaction Level (Level 5) have been introduced later. The MEDUSA system supports Level 0 and Level 1 fusion through its LLF nodes, and Level 2 and Level 3 fusion through semantic reasoning at HLF. Later paragraphs introduce these nodes, and illustrate HMI capabilities where Level 4 and 5 fusion capabilities are provided.

From an implementation perspective the SFG is based on the following implementation choices: (a) LLF nodes were built based on a customized Global Sensor Networks (GSN) middleware [5][24] which provides support for low-level data access, processing of sensor data sources, timing and sliding windows of the data collection, as well as support for sensor virtualization. (b) Decoupling of the low-level signal processing algorithms from the GSN node, along with the implementation of multiple wrappers for the different algorithms, supporting the integration of third party technologies despite their inherent heterogeneity. (c) Using the Virtuoso platform [19] as a means for ontology integration and associated reasoning mechanisms. The SFG implementation uses the Situation Theory Ontology (STO) [9] as a formal ontology, which is based on situation theory initiated by Barwise and Perry [20] and is developed by Devlin [21]. STO allows inferring new facts about situations from detected events. Note however that MEDUSA is not confined to the use of a single ontology (like STO), since its middleware infrastructure is flexible for the integration of more ontologies. (d) Implementation of standardized distributed interactions (web services), which renders MEDUSA a truly distributed system that can be deployed according to multiple configurations depending on the scenario at hand (i.e. the LLF, HLF, nodes are defined according to the implementation scenario).

3 Low-Level Sensor Processing and Data Fusion

Low level processing is performed on an arbitrary number of LLF Nodes responsible for fusing sensor data, i.e. JDL Level 0 and 1. Low level fusion processes raw sensor data to provide an estimation of physical attributes of specific objects (position, speed, acceleration) along with definition of other entity attributes. The information generated from these elements is fused with geo-location information (fusing data either coming from known sources or calculating position from camera references by Inverse Perspective Mapping [22]). In addition, single data source processing modules were developed and integrated, along with new algorithms for detection of un-usual/abnormal events within large arrays of normal/regular events.

As an example for low level detection, the visual Smoke Detector uses color and image appearance information and background subtraction in order to detect the appearance of smoke. Background subtraction segments moving pixels, based on smoke motion properties. Then, color analysis is performed to produce a threshold that separates smoke colored objects from others in the Region of Interest. Finally, for the remaining moving regions we perform texture analysis to distinguish fast decreases in edge energy, which is generally caused by rigid objects, from slower decreases. We calculate image gradients by a Sobel operator and produce a temporal graph that denotes the declination of edge energies. The combination of these techniques provides fast and robust discrimination among moving objects (e.g. Fig. 2).

Another example, the Unusual Movement Detector is a real-time detector for unusual motions w.r.t. typical motions observed during a training period, based on [14]. It can be used in situations where unusual movement detection can be important, e.g. automatic traffic surveillance, or crowd analysis. The direction of optical flow vectors are first extracted at image pixels; then probability based approaches are used for motion area classification, combined with Mixture of Gaussians modeling and spatial averaging based on Mean-Shift segmentation. A Markovian prior is introduced to get reliable spatio-temporal support. The novelty of the approach is that although outdoor videos are generally of low quality and high complexity, the pixel based approach gives more robust results and spatio-temporal support can be incorporated without object level understanding (which is generally impossible or very computationally expensive for such data) (Fig. 3).

Fig. 2. Examples for smoke detection

Fig. 3. Examples for unusual movement detection. From left to right: Traffic scene. Learned traffic motion direction map. Traffic scene with bicycle going against traffic. Detection mask, where higher intensity means higher probability for unusual movement.

The results of low level processing are used by HLF nodes to further analyze the scene and to provide the C2 operator with better situational awareness of detected threats and support for both risk assessment and decision making. Low level modules of the test system include: (a) multi-view vehicle tracking, (b) detection and tracking of ground objects from UAVs [11], (c) detection and tracking of people and loitering person detection [23], (d) motion detection in regions of interest [12], (e) detection of unusual vehicle or pedestrian movements [13][14], (f) visual smoke detection.

4   Semantic Reasoning Capabilities

The Higher Level Fusion (HLF) layer of the proposed architecture consists of the already introduced STO ontology, which is used as the backbone for performing the reasoning required for situation assessment. We use *Virtuoso*, as underlying Semantic Web technologies integration stack, which provides services like RDF triple storage, SPARQL compilers, and RDF views on relational data. Virtuoso acts as a federation layer for seamless integration of relational and semantic data (Fig. 4.).

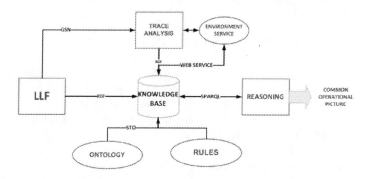

Fig. 4. High level fusion scheme

The chosen STO ontology is the main information gathering point in the proposed architecture. STO supports modeling of artifacts of environment in which the sensor network is deployed. Core modeling is supported with concepts (and sub-concepts) of situation, event and their relations. Alert and detection data originating from processing modules in LLF nodes is stored here, where reasoning is performed to infer new knowledge, which corresponds to events and situation assessment that cannot be performed at the LLF level. STO is written in OWL and models the events/objects and their relationships in a way that can be extended according to the needs of a specific domain in order to support situation assessment [17].

Data coming from local relational databases of the LLF nodes needs to mapped into a semantic notation in order to be exploited by the ontology. This is performed by mapping the relational schema to semantic entities. We adopted a push strategy to process data as soon as they were generated in order to increase system response. A pulling strategy was also an option, however its utilization would have induced delays in the mapping process. The push method forwards relational data from node databases to the ontology as soon as such data are generated. The advantage of this approach is that the transformations are fast and the ontology is always up-to-date.

Additional information are integrated by the HLF layer in order to derive situations. Information from sources like environmental services can be queried, as long as they expose I/O interfaces, and the information can be used for inferencing. Reasoning uses the ontology structure and the stored instances to draw conclusions about the situations. Under this approach, relations between classes like *rdfs:subClassOf*, properties like *owl:sameAs* and relations that are defined by experts in the ontology are used for inference. The knowledge base can be extended further by using rules to describe situations/events too complex to be defined using OWL notation only.

For defining the rules that form the situation assessment inference mechanism, SPARQL CONSTRUCT formulations have been used, since SPARQL is expressive in rule formulation [25]. Another advantage of using SPARQL CONSTRUCTs is their efficiency in terms of speed and memory consumption for evaluation. Using this strategy Virtuoso is treated both as storage and inference layer with high performance both in data volume handing and in query execution times, while also taking advantage of Virtuoso's other features such as query built-ins and geospatial extensions. The reasoning service can also use information from external services in the inference process, e.g. from the Environmental Service which is described in the next Section.

5   Environmental Service and COP

One of the most significant challenges in the development of a multi-sensor data fusion grid is the acquisition and management of the context-based information of the environment in which the sensors are deployed (e.g. restricted areas, critical infrastructures, etc.). Therefore, and due to the needs of the used data fusion algorithms, the system provides a common representation of the environment, the *Environment Service* (ES) [26]. The Environment Service is providing: (a) a common model for representation environment information, (b) an interface to allow uniform access to the environment-related information, (c) specific services allowing users and applications to access geographical and meteorological data for a given location in a specific time and (d) a geometrical algorithm to calculate distances and paths.

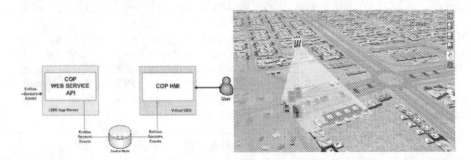

Fig. 5. Architecture and 3D view of the COP

The *Common Operational Picture* (COP) is the presentation layer of the MEDUSA system architecture and uses a graphical interface to provide the user with a common vision of what is happening on the scene from a tactical point of view. It can be subdivided in following main components (Fig. 5): (a) The COP API receives data (e.g. entities, sensors, events, etc.) from LLF and HLF Nodes to store such data in the central control node database. (b) COP Human Machine Interface (HMI) presents information about entities, sensors and events from the database through a graphical interface (2D/3D) to the user.

6   Mobile Nodes

MEDUSA employs various sensors and each sensor is fully integrated by the LLF nodes. The front–end sensor layer includes cameras (visual and infrared), sniper detectors, CBRN detectors, etc. Sensors can be stationary or mobile. Here we illustrate such mobile sensor equipped platforms integrated into the proposed system.

The Instrumented Person Node (IPN) comprises a soldier/person equipped with a wearable device deployed to collect data from the environment. It provides several functionalities, such as GPS localization, video streaming (via a wearable camera), radio communication, and other customizable sensors (e.g. temperature, chemicals).

In addition, the use of airborne sensor platforms such as Unmanned Aerial Vehicles yielding dynamic sensor positioning and particular perspectives (e.g. birds-eye view) for multimodal sensor fusion was considered. One aim was the integration of such a system, bypassing traditional ground control elements. Thus we considered a UAV to be detached from its operating platoon to the network, allowing the network not only to directly receive sensor data but also send control commands to the UAV. We implemented a service-oriented architecture for the deployment of UAVs in order to exploit their capabilities, hiding their complex internals e.g. autopilot and gaze control commands. The UAV platform executes high level tasks using its EO and IR cameras and provides sensor data to the network. The on-board architecture consists of the HW-level SOMA core and the middleware/application oriented SoFiSt layer.

The *SOMA* (Sensor Oriented Missions Avionics Platform) core addresses network monitoring, inter-process communication and sensor virtualization. After an ad-hoc connection is established, the sensor network requests the available capabilities of the UAVs. Each UAV is reporting platform and sensor characteristics: sensor type, resolution, frame rate, stabilization modes, streaming protocols and onboard processing capabilities. The sensor network can send *high-level tasks* such as *Area Search, Sensor Replacement and Road Following*.

A received task is decomposed by sensor and perception management functions using *SoFiSt* (Software Framework for intelligent Sensor Management) into platform, sensor and processing plans, considering resource, context and background knowledge. Sensor data is streamed via RTP, RTSP or UDP. Status information (task ID and type, position, pose, sensor type, field of view) is sent continuously to enable fusion, monitoring and re-tasking of the UAV. During trials, a UAV system, both live and simulated, has been integrated into the proposed architecture, and UAV-derived information has been used in the scope of multi-level multi-layer data fusion.

7   System Evaluation

System components were individually evaluated and their performance was compared with ground truth and state-of-the art algorithms. Due to space constraints, detailed results will not be presented here, but the reader should refer to the related papers in the bibliography [11-14], [16], [23]. The overall MEDUSA system was assessed and validated against challenging scenarios. Specifically, three scenarios have been generated. Two synthetic scenarios, in which an urban war environment is reproduced with deployed simulated sensors, were implemented by means of battlefield simulation software [27]. A third, live scenario, where actors staged the events, was also setup at the UNIBW military campus in Munich in order to showcase the operation of MEDUSA in a real world environment. Here UAVs and IPNs were deployed together with video cameras in order to monitor a specific restricted area. During the test runs in both synthetic and live scenario types, events were reliably detected and processed. Events notifications and threat alarms were displayed on the COP with a maximum delay between 0.5-4s. Table 1 describes one of the storyboards as well as MEDUSA reactions and related Human-Machine Interaction. Here we assume that a vehicle checkpoint (VCP) equipped with MEDUSA technology monitors regular street traffic but also conducts and controls local operations using own patrol vehicles. In the depicted event, a car passes the VCP and starts to closely follow a military patrol, which is considered to be alarming.

Table 1. Storyboard of example event with MEDUSA actions and benefits

Storyboard	MEDUSA actions/interaction
A vehicle approaches a VCP.	Vehicle is tracked automatically and displayed.
The VCP personnel checks vehicle and let it pass.	VCP personnel considers vehicle potentially hazardous and flags it as suspicious.
The vehicle leaves the VCP. This coincides with a patrol setting out for its mission from the VCP.	The vehicle and the patrol are continuously tracked.
The vehicle catches up and to follows the patrol.	High level reasoning within MEDUSA analyzes vehicle status as well as temporal and spatial relations to the patrol and raises an alarm. VCP and patrol are informed about a suspicious vehicle following the patrol.

8   Conclusion

The paper introduced a novel flexible system architecture and prototype for sophisticated multi-sensor data fusion for generation of a common operational picture in urban environments. The system integrates a range of novel algorithms for context acquisition and processing, along with ontologies for semantic reasoning. It is based on a middleware architecture that combines key concepts from state-of-the-art pervasive computing systems, with a focus on successfully responding to heterogeneity-, integration- and intelligence-related challenges. Among the novel points of the introduced system is its ability to leverage a wide range of heterogeneous signal processing components running on various platforms. The system integrates semantic nodes and semantic capabilities, while at the same time it provides support for all JDL fusion levels, based on the distributed collaboration and interaction of the LLF and HLF nodes, but also within the HLF nodes. Furthermore, the system has integrated mobile/roaming nodes such as IPNs and UAVs.

The system has been validated in the scope of urban scenarios handling multiple-sensors and heterogeneous events, while serving the purposes of different applications. Future work includes the implementation of predictive capabilities into the fusion system, with a view to enabling security agencies to anticipate events. This requires the study and integration of advanced reasoning schemes that could predict situations (e.g., based on Bayesian Knowledge Bases and game theory strategies). The MEDUSA system provides a sound basis for the integration of the semantics of such schemes, as well as for experimenting with relevant scenarios.

Acknowledgements. This work has been carried out in the scope of the MEDUSA project (Multi sEnsor Data fusion grid for Urban Situational Awareness), co-funded by the European Defense Agency's Joint Investment Program on Force Protection. The authors acknowledge help and contributions from all partners of the project.

References

1. Weiser, M.: The Computer for the 21st Century. Scientific American 265(3), 66–75 (1991)
2. Yau, S.S., Karim, F., Wang, Y., Wang, B., Gupta, S.K.S.: Reconfigurable Context-Sensitive Middleware for Pervasive Computing. IEEE Pervasive Computing, Joint Special Issue with IEEE Personal Communications on Context-Aware Pervasive Computing 1(3), 33–40 (2002)
3. Soldatos, J., Pandis, I., Stamatis, K., Polymenakos, L., Crowley, J.L.: Agent based middleware infrastructure for autonomous context-aware ubiquitous computing services. Computer Communications (COMCOM) 30(3), 577–591 (2007)
4. Dimakis, N., Soldatos, J., Polymenakos, L., Fleury, P., Curín, J., Kleindienst, J.: Integrated Development of Context-Aware Applications in Smart Spaces. IEEE Pervasive Computing 7(4), 71–79 (2008)
5. Aberer, K., Hauswirth, M., Salehi, A.: Infrastructure for data processing in large-scale interconnected sensor networks. In: MDM 2007, pp. 198–205 (2007)
6. Floerkemeier, C., Roduner, C., Lampe, M.: RFID Application Development with the Accada Middleware Platform. IEEE Systems Journal 1(2), 82–94 (2007)
7. Chatzigiannakis, I., Mylonas, G., Nikoletseas, S.: 50 ways to build your application: A survey of middleware and systems for Wireless Sensor Networks. In: Proc. IEEE Conference on Emerging Technologies and Factory Automation, ETFA (2007)
8. Chen, H., et al.: Semantic Web in the Context Broker Architecture. In: Proc. Second Annual IEEE International Conference on Pervasive Computer and Communications (2004)
9. Kokar, M.M., Matheus, C.J., Baclawski, K.: Ontology-based situation awareness. Information Fusion, Special Issue on High-level Information Fusion and Situation Awareness 10(1), 83–98 (2009)
10. Pfisterer, D., Römer, K., Bimschas, D., Kleine, O., Mietz, R., Truong, C., Hasemann, H., Kröller, A., Pagel, M., Hauswirth, M., Karnstedt, M., Leggieri, M., Passant, A., Richardson, R.: SPITFIRE: toward a semantic web of things. IEEE Communications Magazine 49(11), 40–48 (2011)
11. Kovács, L., Benedek, Cs.: Visual real-time detection, recognition and tracking of ground and airborne targets. In: Proc. of Computational Imaging IX, SPIE-IS&T Electronic Imaging, vol. 7873, pp. 787311-1–12. SPIE (2011)

12. Szlávik, Z., Kovács, L., Havasi, L., Benedek, Cs., Petrás, I., Utasi, Á., Licsár, A., Czúni, L., Szirányi, T.: Behavior and event detection for annotation and surveillance. In: Intl. Workshop on Content-Based Multimedia Indexing (CBMI 2008), pp. 117–124 (2008)
13. Utasi, Á.: Novel Probabilistic Methods for Visual Surveillance Applications. Phd Thesis, University of Pannonia, Veszprém, Hungary (2012)
14. Utasi, Á., Czúni, L.: Anomaly detection with low-level processes in videos. In: Proc. 3rd International Conference on Computer Vision Theory and Applications, pp. 678–681 (2008)
15. Tham, C., Buyya, R.: SensorGrid: Integrating sensor networks and grid computing. CSI Communications 29, 24–29 (2005)
16. Doulaverakis, C., Konstantinou, N., Knape, T., Kompatsiaris, I., Soldatos, J.: An approach to intelligent information fusion in sensor saturated urban environments. In: Proc. IEEE European Intelligence and Security Informatics Conference (EISIC), pp. 108–115 (2011)
17. White, F.E.: Data fusion lexicon. Data Fusion Subpanel of the Joint Directors of Laboratories, Technical Panel for C3 (1991)
18. Steinberg, A.N., Bowman, C.L., White, F.E.: Revisions to the JDL Data Fusion Model. Jrnl. of Sensor Fusion: Architectures, Algorithms, and Applications III (1999)
19. Virtuoso Universal Server, http://virtuoso.openlinksw.com
20. Barwise, J., Perry, J.: Situations and Attitudes. MIT Press (1983)
21. Devlin, K.: Logic and Information. Cambridge U. Press (1991)
22. Mallot, H.A., Bülthoff, H.H., Little, J.J., Bohrer, S.: Inverse perspective mapping simplifies optical flow computation and obstacle detection. Biological Cybernetics 64, 177–185 (1991)
23. Talantzis, F., Pnevmatikakis, A., Constantinides, A.G.: Audio-Visual Person Tracking: A Practical Approach. World Scientific Publication Co., Imperial College Press, London (2011)
24. Salehi, A., Riahi, M., Michel, S., Aberer, K.: GSN, middleware for stream world. In: Proc. 10th International Conference on Mobile Data Management (2009)
25. Konstantinou, N., Spanos, D.E., Stavrou, P., Mitrou, N.: Technically Approaching the Semantic Web Bottleneck. International Journal of Web Engineering and Technology (IJWET) 6(1), 83–111 (2010)
26. Guangyu, L., Kefa, Z., Li, S., Jinlin, W., Qianfeng, W.: Regional Eco-Environmental Information Service System Based on Open Source Projects. Energy Procedia 11, 3892–3898 (2011)
27. Hummel, G., Stütz, P.: Conceptual design of a simulation test bed for ad-hoc sensor networks based on a serious gaming environment. In: Proc. Intl. Training and Education Conference, ITEC (2011)

Collaborative Methodology for Crisis Management Knowledge Integration and Visualization

Ana Laugé, Josune Hernantes, Leire Labaka, and Jose M. Sarriegi

Tecnun - University of Navarra, Paseo Manuel Lardizabal 13, 20018 San Sebastian, Spain
{alauge,jhernantes,llabaka,jmsarriegi}@tecnun.es

Abstract. Crisis management needs intensive cooperation of a significant amount of stakeholders. These stakeholders need to cooperate during the critical peak of crisis, and also during crisis preparation and long term recovery phases. In addition, agents have to learn from each other and from previous events. However, they have different perspectives based on their backgrounds, previous experiences and interests. Collaborative modelling methodologies can help on this knowledge gathering and integration process. This paper presents Group Model Building collaborative methodology and its use on a crisis management research project, where a set of international and multidisciplinary domain experts discussed and contributed to three simulation models development. Through several exercises experts shared and integrated their perspectives, which were initially fragmented. Domain experts also took part in models validation. Resulting models constitute a more holistic, integrated and agreed visualization of crises than the ones each agent had at the beginning of the modelling process.

Keywords: Crisis Management, Collaborative methodology, Knowledge, Learning, Reflection, Simulation model, Group Model Building, System Dynamics.

1   Introduction

Recent crises (whether natural disasters or of human origin) such as the Japanese earthquake with the Fukushima nuclear accident, BP oil spill or hurricane Katrina confirm that the involvement of many multidisciplinary agents is needed for a proper crisis management. Therefore, crisis management, including preparation and response activities, involves many international and multidisciplinary experts' participation such as policemen, fire-fighters, emergency personnel, etc. However, in order to effectively manage a crisis experts' involvement is not enough, a high level of cooperation among them is also necessary.

During crises the existing connections and interdependencies among several sectors spread cascading effects from one to another. Moreover, these cascading effects can transcend international borders affecting more than one country.

Furthermore, the available knowledge about crisis management is fragmented throughout different stakeholders. In order to properly manage a crisis the fragmented

N. Aschenbruck et al. (Eds.): Future Security 2012, CCIS 318, pp. 105–116, 2012.

knowledge of the international and multidisciplinary crisis managers has to be integrated. Crisis managers have partial knowledge based on their experiences and backgrounds. Therefore, a method to integrate the knowledge is necessary. This paper presents a collaborative methodology to integrate this knowledge allowing crisis managers to have a more holistic and complete perspective.

Involving a multidisciplinary team of experts allows gathering information from different mental models. Unifying this information allows obtaining a more holistic and complete knowledge about crisis management. Furthermore, the multidisciplinary team of experts allows not focusing only on technical details but rather on the entire picture of a crisis. In this way, each participant can be enriched with others' perspectives gaining a big insight of the problem.

Modelling is a tool which enables the integration and visualization of knowledge. Through modelling and simulation an overall perspective for a better understanding of complex and dynamic systems, such as crises, can be obtained. Crisis managers use simulation models as a unified visualization of the problem and as a training tool where they can observe how their decisions and policies development affect to crises' evolution. This paper presents a knowledge gathering and simulation models development methodology which improves knowledge integration.

Additionally, this paper presents a case study which illustrates the use of this collaborative methodology in a large crisis caused by an outage. The SEMPOC European project (Simulation Exercise to Manage POwer cut Crises) was funded by EPCIP (the European Programme of Critical Infrastructure Protection). Several multidisciplinary experts took part in the three workshops organized during the SEMPOC project in order to analyze crises triggered by a severe power cut. During these workshops, experts with different background had the opportunity to share experiences and viewpoints, which lead to a better understanding on the matter and to an integration of their initially fragmented knowledge.

The paper is organised as follows. First, it describes the collaborative methodology to gather knowledge from experts. Second, we explain how the knowledge gathered can be analysed and integrated developing and using simulation models. Then, we describe the validation process. Finally, we conclude highlighting the most important issues commented on the paper and giving some recommendations for future research in this field.

2   Method

Crises are complex problems phenomena in which many agents have to cooperate to properly solve them. Crisis management relies on crisis managers, organizations, first responders, etc. but is also dependant on the state of the affected critical infrastructures and on the response of the society. Therefore, it is essential not to analyze each component separately but to consider all the elements together with their corresponding interactions in order to have a more realistic picture of the situation.

Gathering information from different agents and making explicit the initially tacit and fragmented knowledge of domain experts requires a collaborative methodology such as Group Model Building (GMB).

The GMB collaborative methodology is designed to develop consensus and support for organisational interventions [1-3] that has been successfully applied to many different complex and interdisciplinary problems [4], [5]. GMB allows multidisciplinary domain experts to work on one specific problem jointly in order to integrate fragmented knowledge, initially residing in the minds of participants [2], [6], [7].

The main goal of GMB workshops is to learn about one particular messy problem and integrate different perspectives [5]. Furthermore, the knowledge integrating process allows managers to gain a shared understanding of the problem and its potential solutions [8], [9]. Additionally, with the GMB methodology different points of view are presented and discussions are carried out to reach a consensus about the problem under analysis [5].

The GMB methodology is articulated around a number of common components encompassing three stages of activities: pre-meeting activities, activities during the workshop sessions and follow-up activities [10]. Furthermore, to perform GMB workshops several predefined exercises have to be carried out. These exercises have to be developed with the cooperation of domain experts. Firstly, the experts work in small groups and then each group presents their results in plenary to allow discussions and knowledge integration.

GMB methodology defines essential roles to support effective participants' efforts during sessions [3], viz. facilitator, modeller, process coach, recorder and gatekeeper.

The facilitator has the important role to guide the group process. The facilitator's main tasks are eliciting relevant knowledge from the group members and making sure that there is an open communication climate so that in the end consensus and commitment will result. Facilitator's job is to guide workshop participants in model construction, while the experts provided the necessary subject matter knowledge. In SEMPOC the workshops were facilitated by the modelling team.

The process coach's job is to observe the interaction within the group and the group's interaction with the facilitator and advise the facilitator on these issues. The job of the process coach is usually invisible to the workshop participants, but it is important. The process coach should alert the facilitator about potential wrong behaviours of the domain expert's group.

The modellers usually sit at the back of the room with a laptop and their job is to turn group's knowledge into a rough conceptual simulation model. They also should provide feedback to the facilitator about the evolution of the developed models.

The recorder's job is to compile the results of exercises and write down group's thoughts, the most relevant discussions and other potentially relevant observations.

Finally, the role of liaison between the experts and the modelling team is performed by the gatekeeper who validates the process during the GMB exercises not to loose the focus on the problem. This person is the contact between domain experts and the modelling team and has an important role in the decision of which participants to involve in sessions, making decisions to reach a consensus when necessary and supervising the overall process.

3   Results

The SEMPOC project's objective was to assess the European power production and distribution system's ability to deliver service and mitigate damage in face of a major power cut improving prevention, response and recovery issues. This matter required the participation of multidisciplinary experienced stakeholders. Thus, the use of a collaborative approach which could integrate participants' fragmented knowledge enabling them to learn from other experts was a need for this project.

For a complete understanding it is essential to analyze crises using different units of analysis which bear in mind the time scope of the research, the variables that are evaluated and the objectives of the investigation. SEMPOC project has analyzed the crises using three different units of analysis, and the organization of the workshops has been determined accordingly. Therefore, SEMPOC's objective was achieved carrying out three workshops of two days duration. The workshops were arranged in San Sebastian – Spain in order to deep into these three units of analysis (Fig.1).

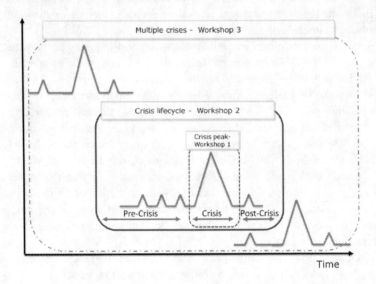

Fig. 1. Structure of SEMPOC workshops

The initial workshop, held in May 2009, concentrated on the first unit of analysis that focuses on the peak of a single crisis. This provides a short term perspective of an energy crisis covering an interval of a few days from the time the event strikes until it is under control. This unit of analysis covers all the details about the main causes of the triggering event and the response phase [11], [12].

During the second workshop (November 2009), the crisis was examined considering its whole lifecycle (the second unit of analysis), covering the pre-crisis, peak of the crisis and post-crisis of a single crisis [13], [14]. This second unit of analysis analyzes the prevention and preparation phases, the immediate response and the recovery process; being its main objective to establish relationships between the activities car-ried out in pre-crisis with the impacts during the peak and post-crisis periods.

The last workshop (April 2010) targeted the learning process from one crisis to another (third unit of analysis), taking into account more than one crisis [6], [15]. During the period in between crises, some crisis indicators can appear and their early detection, comprehension and use provide crisis managers with new insights about the dangers they face allowing them to improve future crisis preparation and response.

In the following subsections the process from gathering to validation of knowledge during the SEMPOC project is explained. Firstly, the experts' knowledge was gathered using the GMB collaborative methodology on the three workshops. Then, the knowledge was analyzed, integrated and translated into simulation models that represent the behaviour of large crises on the energy sector. Finally, the validation of the models was performed through an external validation process in which the experts participated actively.

3.1   GMB Workshops Preparation

As commented previously, preparatory meetings are the first step of the GMB methodology. The preparatory meetings are crucial to accomplish a well-targeted GMB workshop. The first step is identifying the right experts who should take part in the workshops to ensure the best information about the problem under analysis. Logistics is also a critical success factor. The room layout should be comfortable enough to allow participants clustering around in small groups, combining large whiteboards or whole walls covered with cling-sheets for diagramming or showing materials prepared in advance, or the ones obtained from exercises performed during the session.

The GMB roles are assigned for each member of the modelling team and a public agenda for the session is developed. The modelling team also develops the scripts, which are detailed descriptions of each exercise, including its goals and outcomes, the needed materials, detailed timetable and responsibilities for the different roles. In addition to this, potential risks of each exercise are identified and mechanisms to deal with them (plan B) are established.

During the SEMPOC project several materials were prepared during preparatory meetings by the modelling team. For example for the third workshop, knowing that the ability to detect precursors could prevent or lessen the occurrence of a crisis, the modelling team wanted to answer the following questions: what would happen if we do not have the ability to detect crisis precursors in a suitable way? What about if we detect them but we are not able to act accordingly? And, what if we detect them and have the ability to act?

The modelling team prepared the visualization of these three feasible scenarios to work on. These scenarios covered over a 20 year long period. The first scenario was called "No detection" and it represented a situation where many events were taking place but none of them was detected, so that as consequence two crises occurred. The second scenario named "Poor detection & limited resolution" showed that some of the occurred events were detected, so that crisis managers acted upon them consequently and one of the two crises was avoided. In the third scenario, "Detection & resolution", most of the events were detected and managers acted upon them, preventing both crises to occur. This visualization of the three potential scenarios was useful to focus the domain experts' discussion.

3.2   Knowledge Gathering

GMB Workshops' Participants. Fifteen domain international experts from different European countries were invited to provide the work sessions with different cultures, expertise and mental models. The multidisciplinary team of experts allowed not focusing only on technical details but rather on the entire picture of a crisis. Several and diverse institutions such as crisis managers, national agencies, first responders, civil protection, health care, organizations for critical infrastructures protection and agents from the power sector participated in the workshops to obtain the whole picture.

GMB Workshops' Activities. During the GMB workshops several exercises were carried out in order to integrate experts' fragmented knowledge.

As an example, first workshop's exercises are explained here. This workshop's activities started with a one page description of a multi-event scenario. The causes behind the initial scenario were intentionally vague; each expert used their own knowledge to identify what might create or exacerbate the problem. Small groups were formed among the experts to discuss and share their perspectives about the case. Each group reported out their ideas in turn, with the facilitator encouraging the experts to group similar concepts and to clarify each contribution. After that, the experts were asked to identify events that could lead to a crisis. Then, the experts were asked to identify the stakeholders involved in the power cut crisis and to classify them taking into account their influence and interest in the problem. The involved stakeholders were identified and thereafter the experts clustered them in categories. Afterwards, the experts identified the key metrics they would use to evaluate the state of the crisis. The contributors were then asked to create behaviour over time visualizations as an explanation of how they expect a multi-national crisis might unfold. Multiple stories were identified, depicting possible best- and worst-case scenarios that combine the events identified earlier. Finally, experts were asked to think about the policies that should be followed to solve the crisis situation.

To explain the process of team working and consensus reaching in detail, the behaviours over time visualizations exercise will be deeply explained. This exercise deals with the evolution of the variables which best represent the behaviour of the analyzed problem. During the previous exercises, domain experts identified which was the set of variables that according to them more efficiently represents the evolution of a large pan European crisis originated by problems in the electric net.

Then, domain experts were asked to work in small groups in order to draw the behaviour overtime of this set of variables in the best (the crisis is efficiently managed) and worst (the crisis is poorly managed) scenarios based on their experience and intuition. The used scenario related a few days lasting crisis with successive blackouts happened in the first and fourth day caused by overload in the power net and unexplained failures in distribution grid respectively. The combination of these breakdowns and an ineffective coordination between different sectors caused that the crisis was not solved six days after the first failure.

Fig.2 shows the behaviours of two variables (best case in a solid line and worst case in a dashed line), the public disorder caused by the blackout and the number of re-sources that would be deployed to respond to the crisis. After working in small groups, each group presented their results in plenary.

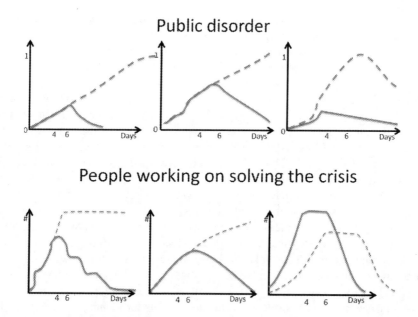

Fig. 2. "Public Anxiety" and "People working on solving the crisis" behaviours over time visualizations developed by each group

After a plenary presentation of these behaviours and their underlying reasons, a discussion was carried out in order to get a consensus about the evolution of each indicator. Consequently, the experts agreed on the final behaviours that could be used as a reference for the best (solid line) and the worst cases (dashed line) (Fig.3). For both variables in the best case they go down to zero earlier whereas in the worst case their effects last for long.

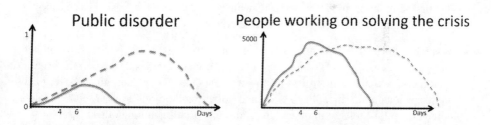

Fig. 3. Behaviours over time visualizations after reaching consensus among experts

3.3   Knowledge Analysis and Integration

During the months in between workshops, the modelling team turned the gathered knowledge into simulation models in order to examine the effects of multi-national power crises in the European Union.

GMB meshes nicely with System Dynamics (SD) computer simulation modelling, as a shared consensus from GMB becomes the problem definition needed to create the SD simulation. When communicated back to the stakeholders, the SD models become the source for proactive review of possible intervention strategies [5].

SD focuses on the behaviour that the combination of several events leads to and not only on isolated events [16-18]. This high aggregation level can capture the broad issues of concern in crisis management across infrastructures and borders. In addition, it allows the analysis of crises as evolutionary processes where the activities carried out on pre and post-crisis stages have significant influence during the whole crisis lifecycle. The scope of these simulation models does not concentrate on the technical details of power system sector, but rather try to embrace the big picture of the crisis including other sectors that may also be affected by the outage. This means inclusion of not only quantitative variables (hard variables), but also aspects that, although they cannot usually be precisely measured (soft variables), which are known to be critical for decision making as they may have significant side effects during a crisis that can even influence the crisis duration [19]. These soft variables are usually related to human behaviour or abstract concepts such as socio-political effects or public anxiety during the blackout, which are indirectly estimated.

Crisis managers can use developed simulation models for training as they enable the integration of knowledge as all involved managers can have a unified representation of the problem. In dynamic complex systems, such as crises, variables change their value over time. Some of these changes are not straightforward to predict, as there are time delays involved between causes and effects and between actions and reactions. The analysis of the generated behaviours allows crisis managers to obtain an overall perspective for a better understanding of crises as they can observe how their decisions affect crises' evolution. The scenarios and policies are degrees of freedom that can be modified in the simulation model to obtain different visualizations and behaviours that enable observing the consequences of each policy in the overall system in addition to understanding the causes of undesirable and unpredicted dynamics.

The first simulation model's structure which is related to the crisis peak is shown in Fig.4. This simulation model has four interconnected sectors:

- Power Network: it represents the system that produces, transports and distributes energy to the customers. The loss in power supply determines the size of the crisis.
- Customers: two different groups of power clients have been distinguished. Regular clients such as non critical businesses and homes, and critical infrastructures which include hospitals, telecommunications and transportation among others.
- Society: this sector includes the variables that reproduce the behaviour of Society during an outage. We have taken into account that Media has also a high influence on public anxiety. Therefore, it is important to satisfy media information needs during a crisis.
- Government: it may help power companies by providing its own resources such as police, civil protection, health emergency and army. The deployment of government's resources is determined by its crisis' perception.

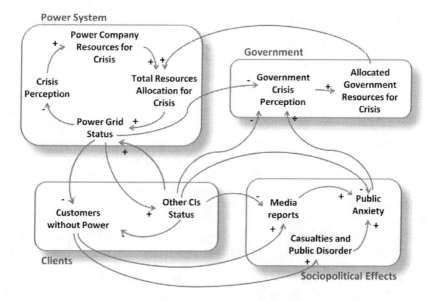

Fig. 4. Workshop 1 model structure

The simulation models developed through the SEMPOC project allow running different scenarios in order to obtain a unified visualization of the problem and to analyze the effect of having different scenarios and developing policies related to crisis management. When designing and implementing those scenarios and policies on the simulation models, different representations of the problem and behaviours are obtained. For example, Fig.5 shows the behaviour of Public Anxiety and Government Deployed Resources variables of the first simulation model when varying the crisis severity. As the Public Anxiety increases, the government also increases the deployed resources in order to solve the crisis as soon as possible. These visualizations are well aligned with the ones developed during the first workshop (Fig.2 andFig.3) as the simulation model has to reproduce the experts' reached consensus during workshops.

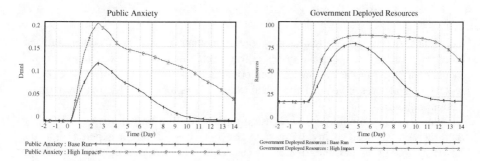

Fig. 5. Simulation model's runs

3.4   Knowledge Validation

Once having developed simulation models, the modelling team performed the validation process through a series of teleconferences with the domain experts who participated on the workshops. The aim of the validation process was to enable experts to analyze the simulation model and the different behaviours obtained when developing several scenarios and to guarantee that they agree on its usability for crisis management improvement Experts clarified some technical questions and verified the simulation model performance providing modelling team with useful information and comments to refine the models. This validation process is also important to build confidence in the developed simulation models engaging experts in the modelling process.

The time elapsed between the workshops and the validation interviews was about four months, time needed by the modelling team to develop each simulation model. In order to engage the experts again in the project and remind them the results gathered with their help, the modelling team developed a document for each developed simulation model explaining model's purpose, the results gathered and the assumptions made during the modelling process.

This document also included some visualizations to show the simulation model's performance under different crisis scenarios and applying diverse policies. This document was sent to experts in advance in order they could review it before scheduling a phone interview. The interviews with experts were helpful to test if the hypotheses and assumptions made in the modelling process were correct. Experts' suggestions also allowed refining the model in order to obtain reliable simulations. This process also triggered interesting discussions that provided simulation models with new insights. For instance, all experts agreed with the assumption that an appropriate level of maintenance and training can reduce the crisis impact and the recovery time after an incident happens, but they had different opinions when asked to quantify their effects. However, the consensus is not always achieved as sometimes the experts have different opinions about an issue based on their different expertise or background. Regarding the level of maintenance just after a crisis, we found two opposite experts' beliefs. Some domain experts who perform crisis management tasks considered that it decreases after a large crisis while experts with a more technical background had the opposite opinion.

4   Discussion

One of the most important drawbacks in the crisis management enhancement process is that relevant knowledge about crises is fragmented in several stakeholders' mental models distributed in various sectors and countries. The integration of these complementary perspectives is a need for the further development of efficient crisis management policies.

Collaborative methodologies such as Group Model Building are especially useful when there is the need of involving several agents from different expertise into the knowledge gathering and integration process. The gathered and integrated knowledge is subsequently represented through System Dynamics models. These models allow the integration of each perspective on the problem holistic simulation models that permit a complete view. These simulation models also make explicit the tacit assumptions about the causal structure of the system which are often misjudged.

SEMPOC project has used GMB to gather initially fragmented knowledge from experts and make it explicit and integrated in simulation models.

However, further research is still required to accurately calibrate these simulation models properly. During the workshops, many qualitative data were gathered but there are not enough quantitative data to establish for instance the influence of a proper training in improving the response during a crisis or the effect of a high level of maintenance in diminishing the crisis impact.

The developed models enable to test a range of policies for alleviating the crisis situation, and to test these against different environmental and structural scenarios, increasing insight in the consequences of some policies which enhances crisis managers perspective on the problem. The simulation model enables crisis managers to analyze and discuss the influence of each policy on the overall crisis impact.

The model facilitates a focused discussion. If domain experts discuss about the influence of a proper training in improving the response during a crisis or the effect of a high level of maintenance in diminishing the crisis impact, they are discussing about some specific parameters of the model and this discussion can remain focused. Although most of the times consensus was achieved in the exercises, in some cases, experts still maintained divergent or complementary perspectives, due to their different backgrounds and past real experiences. These non agreed cases present an excellent opportunity for further research.

Taking part during the model development and validation process also generates a models' ownership feeling. All the model assumptions come from domain experts' explicit comments; which in the one hand makes them co-responsible of models' quality and in the other hand increases their confidence on the potential results.

During the SEMPOC project, a survey was sent to the domain experts to ask about their opinion and usefulness of the workshops. The answers confirmed the value of the collaborative process where multidisciplinary experts worked together. This process led experts better understand how other organizations work, obtaining different perspectives and improving their knowledge for future crises management.

Acknowledgements. The SEMPOC project was supported by the European Commission - Directorate-General Justice, Freedom and Security in the framework of the European CIPS strategic objective, on the "Prevention, Preparedness and Consequence Management of Terrorism and other Security related risks" specific program.

References

1. Vennix, J.A.M., Rouwette, E.A.J.A., Richardson, G.P., Andersen, D.F.: Group model building: Problem structuring, policy simulation and decision support. J. Oper. Res. Soc. 58(5), 691–695 (2007)
2. Andersen, D.F., Richardson, G.P., Vennix, J.A.M.: Group model building: Adding more science to the craft. System Dynamics Review 13(2), 187–201 (1997)
3. Richardson, P., Andersen, D.F.: Teamwork in group model building. System Dynamics Review 11(2), 113–137 (1995)
4. Sterman, J.: Business dynamics. McGraw Hill, New York (2000)

5. Vennix, J.A.M.: Group model building: Facilitating team learning using system dynamics. John Wiley and Sons, Chichester (1996)
6. Rich, E., Gonzalez, J.J., Qian, Y., Sveen, F.O., Radianti, J., Hillen, S.: Emergent vulnerabilities in integrated operations: A proactive simulation study of economic risk. International Journal of Critical Infrastructure Protection 2(3), 110 (2009)
7. Andersen, D.F., Vennix, J.A.M., Richardson, G.P., Rouwette, E.A.J.A.: Group model building: Problem structuring, policy simulation and decision support. Journal of the Operational Research Society 58, 691–695 (2007)
8. Eden, C.: A framework for thinking about group decision support systems (GDSS). Group Decision and Negotiation 1(3), 199–218 (1992)
9. Senge, P.M.: The fifth discipline. Bantam Doubleday Dell Publishing Group, New York (1990)
10. Bérard, C.: Group model building using system dynamics: An analysis of methodological frameworks. The Electronic Journal of Business Research Methods 8(1), 35–45 (2010)
11. American Society of Civil Engineers (ASCE): The new orleans hurricane protection system: What went wrong and why, Reston, Virginia (2007)
12. Union for the Coordination of Transmission of Electricity (UCTE): Final report: System disturbance on November 4, 2006 (2007)
13. Kahan, J.H., Allen, A.C., George, J.K.: An operational framework for resilience. Journal of Homeland Security and Emergency Management 6(1) (2009)
14. Rose, C., Thomsen, S.: The impact of corporate reputation on performance: Some danish evidence. European Management Journal 22(2), 201–210 (2004)
15. Crichton, M.T., Ramsay, C.G., Kelly, T.: Enhancing organizational resilience through emergency planning: Learnings from cross-sectoral lessons. Journal of Contingences and Crisis Management 17(1), 24–37 (2009)
16. Maani, K., Cavana, R.Y.: Systems thinking, system dynamics: Managing change and complexity. Pearson Education, Auckland (2007)
17. Sterman, J.D.: Business dynamics: Systems thinking and modeling for a complex world. Irwin/McGraw-Hill, Boston (2000)
18. Forrester, J.: Industrial dynamics. MIT Press, Cambridge (1961)
19. Lindell, M.K., Prater, C.S.: Assessing community impacts of natural disasters. Natural Hazards Review 4(4), 176–185 (2003)

Prioritisation of Simulation Models for Ensuring Safety and Security in Underground Stations on the Basis of a Detailed Requirements Analysis

Steffen Schneider, Therese Friberg, Tobias Becker, and Rainer Koch

Research Group C.I.K., University of Paderborn, Germany
{st.schneider,friberg,t.becker,r.koch}@cik.upb.de

Abstract. Simulations in the context of public safety and security are an important mean for generating information and enabling a realistic forecast of upcoming events. But since there are numerous different types of simulations by now the selection of the right model gets more and more difficult. This paper presents a method to support decision makers in prioritising the different types based on a detailed requirements analysis. In this paper the requirements are gathered by identifying stakeholders and personas and therewith conducting blue printing based on a specific scenario in an underground station.

Keywords: Scenario-Based Requirements Analysis, Personas, Underground System, Crisis Management, Ishikawa Diagram, Blue Printing, Categorisation and Assessment of Simulation Models.

1   Introduction

Simulation models are too numerous and it is difficult to identify the adequate simulations for a specific context. In this paper we present an approach for gathering requirements for the selection of simulation models with the target to ensure safety and security for the different "users" (cp. section 3.1) of an underground station. Our approach focuses on a scenario-based requirements analysis to identify required useful simulation models.

The value of the scenario-based approach is already stated by several researchers and practitioners (cp. [Carr95], [McHa97]) and Pohl emphasizes the importance of scenarios in the requirements engineering process [Pohl07]. We base on these facts and findings and present our methodology to achieve a prioritisation of simulation models:

1. Initially defining a scenario,
2. identifying the necessary key stakeholders,
3. based on these deducing the relevant personas,
4. gathering the adequate requirements and
5. finally mapping the requirements against the existing simulation models.

N. Aschenbruck et al. (Eds.): Future Security 2012, CCIS 318, pp. 117–128, 2012.

The resulting user requirements of step 4 offer the opportunity to prioritise and choose the most useful simulation models in the context of the specified scenario.

2   Scenario Definition

Scenarios, once they are agreed upon, form the foundation for the requirements [RoRo99]. Scenarios help to reduce the complexity of systems and are applicable to systems of all types, and may be used at any stage of the development life cycle for different purposes [AlMa04]; they are arguably the starting point for all modeling and design [Sutc03]. Normally they include descriptions about the user, the situation, the user's desired goal for the task, procedure and task flow information, a time interval and envisioned features the user will need/use (cp. [CoBa04]). In this work we will primarily focus on the context and environment to constitute the borders. The defined scenario will then build the framework for the following work.

We do not want to describe or refer to a specific city, any parallels to known big cities happened by happenstance. Following a description of the scenario is given:

A manually driven train loaded with 500 passengers arrives in the rush hour in the station which is an interchange node. About 300 people are additionally waiting on the platform to enter the train. At that moment a huge bounce is heard and smoke appears. In underground stations and tunnels there exist significant hazard potential for humans, animals and material in case of operational disturbances and deliberated manipulations. For many passengers a safety hazard like fire, smoke or a toxic substance would build a huge risk in this confined space in the underground station with only few exits and probably crowded. The passengers and all other people have to be protected and saved; furthermore the interchange node has to be considered concerning explosive protection. As the cause is unclear an attack using toxic materials which could be poisonous by inhalation has to be considered. The operators of the station can monitor the interchange node via CCTV and even have access to loudspeakers. In the stations and even in the tunnels sensors for smoke detection are regularly installed.

By defining a specific scenario we formed the framework for the further work. This scenario builds the foundation for all other steps and next the users of the underground system will be identified.

3   Users of an Underground System

In this paper the term user is utilized regarding all people who are affected in the defined scenario in an underground system. As we want to consider these users in detail and identify their requirements towards simulations we firstly conduct a stakeholder analysis and for the key stakeholders we develop personas.

3.1   Stakeholder Identification

Stakeholders include anyone with interest in, an effect on, the outcome of the "product" [RoRo99]. Hence potentially dozens of stakeholders exist for this subject. A valuable way to conduct a detailed stakeholder analysis is to use the so called onion diagram of

Alexander (for more information [Alex03]) which represents a stakeholder map to facilitate a complete detection of the stakeholders. In this paper we will focus on the key stakeholders concerning an underground system: passengers, operators and the organisation. These groups provide input for the scenario and build in a first step the key stakeholders although knowing there exist further stakeholders like the publicity, homeless, architects, etc.

- Passengers: The passengers are travelers and end user of the underground station, they can be in the train or even waiting for or travelling to their next departure.
- Operators: This type of stakeholder is an employee of the operating company and is assigned to support safety and security in the context of urban transportation. For instance this includes surveillance via CCTV or communication with internal and external personnel. This category of stakeholder comprises a broad spectrum of different employees. Due to their common superordinate goal the several groups are combined in this paper.
- Organisation: This stakeholder represents the operating companies providing urban transportation via underground. According to the International Association of Urban Transport (UITP) these organisations are a main player in the context of urban transportation. For a defined scenario normally only one organisation is represented.

3.2   Definition of Persona

By identifying the three key stakeholders we formed the first step concerning the users of the underground system. Sometimes a "generic" user makes it hard to develop a requirements analysis goal-oriented and using personas will assure greater success of hitting the target. A persona is simply a fictional individual created to describe a specific user (cp. [CoBa04]). Personas are useful when real users are not available, too numerous to interview all of them or too time-consuming to introduce the stakeholder into the complexity (cf. section 4 concerning the passengers).

The set of personas should be manageable, three primary personas (for each identified key stakeholder) is a given recommendation by Courage and Baxter. Below exemplary a template to create a persona is given (Fig. 1). Within this template the name, age, disabilities, location, job and goal is required and optional a photo to make the persona more

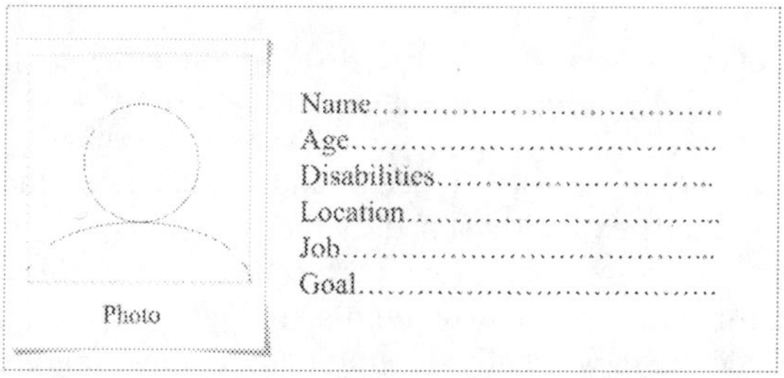

Name...................................
Age.....................................
Disabilities.........................
Location.............................
Job......................................
Goal...................................
Photo

Fig. 1. Persona template

feasible. The characteristics depend on the defined scenario and can vary in each field of application. Following an example for each of the three presented key stakeholder is given.

Passenger:	Operator:
Name: John Doe	**Name:** Jane Miller
Age: 45	**Age:** 55
Disabilities: Heavy baggage and a dog	**Disabilities:** -
Location: At the platform seeing the accident	**Location:** In the control room watching the accident via monitors
Job: Freelancer	**Job/Position:** Senior director, responsible for the department
Goal: Protect himself and his dog, quick information about the ongoing situation, help about rescue	**Goal:** Save the people and the train, inform the organisation, protect herself and her crew

Organisation:
Name: Ben Robertson
Age: 30
Disabilities: -
Location: In the main building located in the city
Job: Contact point to the press
Goal: Forward reliable information, prevent and reduce panic, get information quickly and primary

The personas can be extended if necessary, but often it is useful to generate a new, additionally persona. It is important to cover the needed different characteristics (e.g., at the platform/in the train, with/without disabilities, etc.) and not every possible collocation.

4   Requirements Analysis

In today's literature you will find various publications which deal with different simulation models and point out a series of operating conditions and requirements. Two examples (out of a list of more than 30 specifications) are

1. A simulation should consider the persons' distribution in the architecture [SOL04].
2. A simulation must be very stable and reliable [Fried92].

But the stakeholders have got further needs and expectations that go far beyond. Those requirements can be explicitly stated by the stakeholders or be implied or obligatory [ISO9000]. Interviews can reveal performance requirements but merely an incomplete list of imprecisely stated requirements [MaPf07]. The passengers themselves have got no idea as they usually do not think of simulation models while going by underground. The operators may be unmotivated to support as they either refuse additional tasks or fear for their jobs. The management is mainly interested in economic needs, e.g.:

3. A simulation must be inexpensive in purchase and maintenance.

4. A simulation should require little instruction and training efforts.

However, the implied requirements can be added inductively by using creativity techniques or deductively by reasoning. Improvisation methods like Brainstorming, Brainwriting, 6-3-5 or using cards produce lots of ideas within a very short time. But their quality and completeness is uncertain. A more structured approach is given by mind maps. Nevertheless, discursive methods permit an even more structured and analytic requirements analysis. While Morphological and other analysis are used for creative problem solving and product development the Ishikawa diagram visualises cause and effect relations: Which requirements have to be realised in order to reach a specified goal? In combination with the famous 7 Ms (Men, Material, Machine, Method, Measurement, Milieu and Management) the Ishikawa diagram constitutes a well-structured mind map that allows logic and reproducible requirements engineering. Of course the 7 Ms have to be reinterpreted according to the domain: Men are passengers, employees and other users; material means interior equipment and mobile objects; machines include the trains, ticket machines and shops [Ishi90], [Pfei01]. Fig. 2 shows an extract from the Ishikawa diagram[1] which leads to further requirements, e.g.:

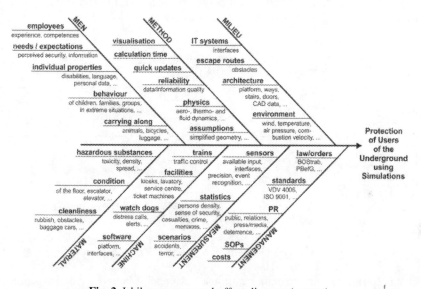

Fig. 2. Ishikawa cause-and-effect diagram (extract)

5. A simulation should consider individual characteristics (blind/wheelchair user, etc.).

6. A simulation should be valid for all realistic scenarios (accident, terror).

7. A simulation must be prepared for updates (altered CAD data, new sensors, etc.)

---

[1] Designed by the authors using multiple creativity techniques in smaller and larger groups.

The term 'valid' in this context refers to the usability of simulation results. It is assumed that the relevant simulation applications associated with a simulation models are based on established theoretical frameworks from various research disciplines like physics, engineering or chemistry.

An example for deductive reasoning is service blue printing, a method for visualisation, analysis, design and control of service processes. All customers' and suppliers' activities that will be carried out during the service delivery are listed chronological. Since the operating company of a critical infrastructure can be seen as a service provider and the safe transport of passengers as a marketable product, the application of methods from service quality management seems reasonable – especially as the end-users' needs have not been sufficiently respected yet [Flie09].

Fig. 3 shows a blue-printed passengers' way through the underground[1]. No passenger will perform all the activities, at least the order will differ from passenger to passenger. But through the detailed analysis of all possible contact points between the customer and the underground system further requirements will be derived, e.g.:

8. A simulation could support the passengers' orientation within the underground system and provide them with additional real-time information.
9. A simulation should monitor/forecast person behaviour at the platform, in order to predict/prevent casualties and to increase other passengers' perception of security.

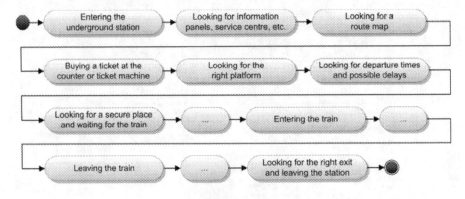

Fig. 3. A blue print of a passenger (extract)

Other blue prints include changing trains, a passenger's behaviour during an emergency and other stakeholder (e.g., shop owners, security staff) and will reveal additional requirements, e.g.:

10. A simulation could render standard operating procedures (SOP) for security staff more adequate through including real-time predictions.

The depicted methods are used to compile a comprehensive requirements document comprising 35 requirements. These are used for the prioritisation of simulation models in section 6.

5   Categorisation of Simulation Models

Hereafter the term simulation represents all aspects concerning simulation models and applications. The term simulation model is used synonymous to simulation types and depicts the distinction of the object to be simulated. As an example most of the main characteristics of pedestrian flow simulators distinguish from the attributes of bushfire spread simulation systems (cp. [XTM09], [JMK05]). Within this paper there are seven different types of simulation models relevant in the context of public safety and security which will be used to make a categorization[2]. These are:

- pedestrian flow (PF),
- traffic flow (TF),
- sensor networks (SN),
- human behaviour (HB),
- stability of constructions (SC),
- spread of hazardous/dangerous substances (includes explosions) (SHS),
- safety & security processes in case of emergency (SSP).

Other types of simulations can be used in the context of public safety and security, but their main purpose cannot be assigned to this domain (like driving simulators to teach driving skills for emergency vehicles).

In the context of this paper PF simulations describe the evacuation of a crowd based on several inputs, like cubage (e.g., the width of paths), expected persons (average person density, velocity, etc.) or - depending on the fidelity of the simulation – effects of their behaviour (e.g., collision due to rival attitude of groups). There are several model approaches for the specification of the simulation, providing different types of analysis and levels of detail [XTM09]. All these will be considered within the prioritisation of simulation types.

"*[TF (author's note)] theory studies the dynamic properties of traffic on road sections.*" [ImLo02, p. 2] In this paper the regarded simulations are assumed to focus on transport routes, traffic volumes and correlations between and within different traffic systems. The movement of pedestrian (cp. [Løvå94]) in a traffic flow is allocated to pedestrian flow simulations.

"*The primary goal of [sensor network (author's note)] simulation is to enable rapid exploration and validation of system designs before deployment, by providing a controlled environment for evaluating design and configuration alternatives [...].*" [TLP05, p. 477] Therefore sensor network simulations are assumed as a virtual execution of scenarios affecting the sensor network.

Human behaviour is a main aspect and has to be considered for modelling pedestrian flow simulations, especially for doing so in a microscopic way. Therefore the distinction between pedestrian flow and human behaviour simulations has to be outlined. In this paper human behaviour simulations are assumed to base on human behaviour models (cp. [SaDe07]) for reproducing behaviour, not the effects on the pedestrian flow.

---

[2] This result is based on simulation relevant tasks in the FP7-Demonstration-Project SECURED (Project Number: 261605, Call identifier: FP7-SEC-2010-1, cp. http://www.secur-ed.eu/).

SC simulations focus on the interaction of weight, movement of load components and consistency of strut components for identifying critical developments causing a maximum load or in the worst case a collapse of the architecture. Especially for underground station in an urban area it is important to consider this aspect [YoKi06].

The exposition of hazardous substances may cause serious damages to the people affected. "*Consequently, determining the possible distribution of the hazardous substances is important for evaluating the suitability of the safety measures to both prevent accidents and mitigate their effects.*" [ATT+10, p. 753] In this context simulations for detecting the spread of these substances are common facilities. In this paper this category includes fire propagation and the spread of explosions.

Here simulations regarding the processes and procedures of public safety and security organizations are assumed to depend on the organizational structure, the work flow process and guidelines. Like in other process management simulations [JEN+10] some of the main results are total process durations, work load statistics and the visualization of work flows.

Depending on the defined scenario the usage of special types of simulation models is more sensible (e.g., the simulation of person flow does not make sense by consideration of a deserted subway station). To address this aspect for the scenario of the paper a prioritisation of these categories according to the derived requirements is described in the next paragraph.

6   Prioritisation of Simulation Models

In this paragraph the simulation types categorised in the previous passage will be evaluated against the requirements derived in section 4. Therefore for every requirement zero, one or two points according to the degree of fulfilment of the respective model were assigned. Zero points imply that the model complies with the requirement in no aspect. One point signifies a low, two points an absolute fulfilment of the considered requirement. This scale was chosen in order to allow an easy and simple method for assessing the models against the requirements. The first of them is related to the consideration of persons' distribution in the relevant architecture. Taking macroscopic simulation (cp. [XTM09]) into consideration this aspect can be regarded in person flow simulations (cp. [Cast05]). Moreover this is one of the results related to the application of these simulations. Traffic flow simulations in the context of underground transportation are able to consider the allocation of individual persons (e.g., persons on the tracks). Because of the categorisation in this paper the distribution of the relevant persons has to be based on a separate pedestrian flow simulation or a definition ex ante. Sensor networks in the depicted context are not able to provide the consideration of the distribution of persons, though sensors for tracking of persons are able to identify pedestrians' positions (cp. [MHEL10]). According to the categorisation this aspect is not regarded within the simulation of the sensor network. The simulation of human behaviour largely depends on the environment of the regarded persons [Osma10]. Therefore the distribution of people has to be considered within this type of simulation, but will be provided by a person flow simulation or a definition ex ante. The stability of constructions is dependent on the weight the relevant elements have to sustain. But a SC simulation in the context of this paper is not able to provide this information. Therefore person positions as inputs from person flow simulations or a definition beforehand are needed. Simulations regarding the spread of hazardous substances do not depend on the allocation of people, though there are projects like the German research project OrGaMIR[3] that consider the spread of dangerous substances within the management of an evacuation of an underground station [PBRK10]. Safety and security processes are referred to the relevant operational units. Therefore they highly depend on the distribution of these and the results of a pedestrian flow simulation as input seems to be sensible in this context. The categorisation in this paper implies that public safety and security simulations do not provide this feature and need to be connected with a person flow simulation or started with an ex ante definition of the person's position.

All these descriptions are summarised in Table 1 in the second row. The person flow simulation is the only category that is able to obtain and provide the dispersion of persons within the architecture. Therefore the field regarding PF simulation and requirement 1 contains the highest amount. Despite of the SN and SHS simulations all other simulation categories seem to be improved by considering person's position. Thus these are able to regard the distribution and are counted with the one point rate. Only the sensor network and the spread of hazardous simulations seem not to be enhanced by incorporating the dispersion and therefore counted with the lowest amount.

As described before the simulation types are hardly evaluable against some kinds of requirements. Concerning the reliability of simulation models there has to be a measure or a method of measurement defined. This can be different even for the same simulation model and therefore reveal diverse results. Due to this fact and the different types of results of the simulation models an assessment and prioritisation of them without these definitions cannot be conducted. But the determination of methods goes beyond the topic of this paper and will therefore not be addressed. The same pertains for the third and fourth requirement. As there are different simulation applications for every simulation model available, the application of one of the models can imply varying amounts of effort. Methods like comparing the average expenses can be an approach for solving this challenge. This requires a detailed analysis of all simulation applications available and will therefore not be addressed within this paper.

The simulation types can be assessed against the fifth requirement 'A simulation should consider individual properties / behaviours'. PF simulation and especially microscopic simulation are already considering this aspect (e.g., group structures due to relationships in [QiHu10]). There are few attempts for addressing this requirement within traffic flow simulations (cp. [PuVa10]). But this can only be done by incorporating human behaviour models into the simulation, which only can be provided by human behaviour simulations. As described before sensor networks are able to track persons and their characteristics, but sensor network simulations do not consider individual properties. Human behaviour simulations highly depend on individual characteristics. Therefore this aspect is addressed in the context of simulations (e.g., Personality representation in [ÖrGh03]). As mentioned above simulations regarding the stability of constructions depend on the weight supporting components have to carry. Therefore the individual

---

[3] The ORGAMIR project is funded by the Federal Ministry of Education and Research in the Research Program for civil security which is part of the hightech strategy of the German government (cp. http://www.orgamir.de/).

characteristics should be considered, but this can only be done by providing these inputs via a person flow simulation or a definition ex ante. SHS simulations do not depend on individual characteristics and a consideration of this aspect cannot improve this type of simulation. SSP simulations are more realistic by considering individual characteristics though these will get more personalised and hence inflexible. In this context the individual behaviour is the relevant parameter. Human behaviour simulations or a definition beforehand can only provide the respective inputs. Moreover the effort for realising this seems to be inappropriate towards the expected results.

The other 25 requirements are assessed in the same way, the respective result is summarised in Table 1. In this paper the requirements are not weighted differently. An adequate quantifier can be found by using a contingency table (cp. in [Lind05]). The assessment according to this weighting results in a use-value analysis.

Table 1. Assessment of the simulation types

Simulation type	PF	TF	SN	HB	SC	SHS	SSP
Requirement 1	2	1	0	1	1	0	1
Requirement 2	-	-	-	-	-	-	-
Requirement 3	-	-	-	-	-	-	-
Requirement 4	-	-	-	-	-	-	-
Requirement 5	2	1	0	2	1	0	0
Requirement 6	1	2	2	1	1	2	1
Requirement 7	-	-	-	-	-	-	-
Requirement 8	2	0	0	1	1	1	1
Requirement 9	2	0	0	2	0	0	0
Requirement 10	1	1	0	1	1	1	2
⋮							
Requirement 35	-	-	-	-	-	-	-
SUM	37	17	8	25	18	19	18

7   Conclusion

This paper once more approved that the scenario-based requirements analysis is a very advantageous approach for gathering needs and expectations from multiple stakeholders. Especially the implied or obligatory requirements can be specified using inductive methods (creativity techniques, e.g., Ishikawa diagram) and deductive methods (reasoning, e.g., service blue printing). For the defined scenario in an underground station we have listed a series of exemplary requirements that have been utilised for the prioritisation of simulation models. Therefore a preferably distinct categorisation for the respective scenario has been made. On this basis the simulation types have been assessed against the requirements. We found out that not all requirements are useful for a comparison of simulation types. Those remaining have enabled an evaluation of their level of compliance. Hence one result of this paper is a categorisation of simulation models in the context of civil safety and security and an assessment of them for a defined scenario. Moreover a method for selecting suitable simulation types was presented.

For further work and validation of the methodology other requirements engineering methods could be used to see potential differences. A deeper and broader gathering of requirements with more stakeholders could be of interest to guarantee the completeness of the requirements. An enhanced evaluation based on the consideration of weightings can be made in order to get more specific prioritisation. With no doubt, the depicted method can be used for other scenarios, too, where the result can be that another simulation type might be more adequate. Though the appropriateness of the techniques used should be reconsidered with respect to the matter of subject.

References

[Alex03]   Alexander, I.: Stakeholders – Who is Your System for? Computing & Control Engineering 14(1), 22–26 (2003)

[AlMa04]   Alexander, I., Maiden, N.: Scenarios, Stories, Use Cases Through the Systems Development Life-Cycle. John Wiley & Sons (2004)

[ATT+10]   Anfossi, D., Tinarelli, G., Trini Castelli, S., Nibart, M., Olry, C., Commanay, J.: A new Lagrangian particle model for the simulation of dense gas dispersion. Atmospheric Environment 44, 753–762 (2010)

[Carr95]   Carroll, J.: Scenario-Based Design. John Wiley (1995)

[Cast05]   Castro, A.: Pedestrian evacuation simulation. J. Comput. Small Coll. 20(5), 141–142 (2005)

[CoBa04]   Courage, C., Baxter, K.: Understanding Your Users: A Practical Guide to User Requirements Methods, Tools, and Techniques. Morgan Kaufmann, San Francisco (2004)

[Flie09]   Fließ, S.: Dienstleistungsmanagement – Kundenintegration gestalten und steuern (Service Management – Modelling and Controlling of Customer Integration). Gabler Verlag, Wiesbaden (2009)

[Fried92]   Friedman, R.: An international survey of computer models for fire and smoke (1992)

[ImLo02]   Immers, L.H., Logghe, S.: Traffic flow theory. Verkehrskunde Basis. Katholieke Universiteit Leuven (2002)

[Ishi90]   Ishikawa, K.: Introduction to quality control. Chapman & Hall, London (1990)

[ISO9000]   DIN EN ISO 9000: Quality management systems – Fundamentals and vocabulary (2005)

[JEN+10]   Jahangirian, M., Eldabi, T., Naseer, A., Stergioulas, L.K., Young, T.: Simulation in Manufacturing and Business: A Review. European Journal of Operations Research 203(1), 1–13 (2010)

[JMK05]   Johnston, P., Milne, G., Klemitz, D.: Overview of bushfire spread simulation systems. School of Computer Science and Software Engineering. University of Western Australia (2005)

[Lind05]   Lindemann, U.: Methodische Entwicklung technischer Produkte – Methoden flexibel und situationsgerecht anwenden (Methodical development of technical products – flexible and appropriate application of methods). Springer, Heidelberg (2005)

[Løvå94]   Løvås, G.G.: Modelling and simulation of pedestrian traffic flow. Transportation Research B 28, 429–443 (1994)

[MaPf07]   Masing, W., Pfeifer, T.: Handbuch Qualitätsmanagement (Handbook Quality Management), 5th edn. Hanser Verlag, München (2007)

[McHa95]   McGraw, K., Harbison, K.: User-Centered Requirements: The Scenario-Based Engineering Process (1997)

[MHEL10]   Mitzel, D., Horbert, E., Ess, A., Leibe, B.: Multi-person Tracking with Sparse Detection and Continuous Segmentation. In: Daniilidis, K., Maragos, P., Paragios, N. (eds.) ECCV 2010, Part I. LNCS, vol. 6311, pp. 397–410. Springer, Heidelberg (2010)

[ÖrGh03]   Ören, T.I., Ghasem-Aghaee, N.: Personality representation processable in fuzzy logic for human behavior simulation. In: Proceedings of the 2003 Summer Computer Simulation Conference, Montreal, pp. 11–18 (2003)

[Osma10]   Osman, M.: Controlling uncertainty: A review of human behavior in complex dynamic environments. Psychological Bulletin 136(1), 65–86 (2010)

[PBRK10]   Pflitsch, A., Brüne, M., Ringeis, J., Killing-Heinze, M.: OrGaMIR – Development of a safety system for reaction to an event with emission of hazardous airborne substances - like a terrorist attack or fire - based on subway climatology. In: 4th International Symposium on Tunnel Safety and Security, Frankfurt, pp. 451–462 (2010)

[Pfei01]   Pfeifer, T.: Qualitätsmanagement (Quality Management), 3rd edn. Hanser Verlag, München (2001)

[Pohl07]   Pohl, K.: Requirements Engineering. Grundlagen, Prinzipien, Techniken (Requirements Engineering. Basics, principles, techniques). Dpunkt Verlag (2007)

[PuVa10]   Pueboobpaphan, R., van Arem, B.: Driver and vehicle characteristics and platoon and traffic flow stability. Journal of Transportation Research Board 2189 (2010)

[QiHu10]   Qiu, F., Hu, X.: Modeling group structures in pedestrian crowd simulation. Simulation Modelling Practice and Theory 18, 190–205 (2010)

[RoRo99]   Robertson, S., Robertson, J.: Mastering the requirements process. ACM Press/Addison-Wesley Publishing Co., New York (1999)

[SaDe07]   Sabeur, E., Denis, G.: Human behavior and social network simulation: Fuzzy sets/logic and agents-based approach. In: Proc. of the 2007 Spring Simulation Multi-Conference, SCS 2007, Norfolk, San Diego, pp. 102–109 (2007)

[SOL04]   Schneider, U., Oswald, M., Lebeda, C.: Evakuierung bei Brandereignissen (Evacuation at Fire Incidents). Brandschutzfachtagung (2004)

[Sutc03]   Sutcliffe, A.: Scenarios, models and the design process in software engineering and interactive systems design. In: Proc. HCII 2003, Crete, Greece (June 2003)

[TLP05]   Titzer, B.L., Lee, D.K., Palsberg, J.: Avrora: Scalable Sensor Network Simulation with Precise Timing. In: Proc. of IPSN (2005)

[XTM09]   Xiaoping, Z., Tingkuan, Z., Mengting, L.: Modeling crowd evacuation of a building based on seven methodological approaches. Building and Environment 44, 437–445 (2009)

[YoKi06]   Yoo, C., Kim, S.-B.: Stability of soft ground tunnelling in urban environment – a numerical investigation. In: International Symposium on Underground Excavation and Tunnelling, Bangkok, Thailand, February 2-4 (2006)

Location and Routing Models
for Emergency Response Plans with Priorities[*]

Ali Oran[1], Kiat Chuan Tan[2], Boon Hooi Ooi[2],
Melvyn Sim[3], and Patrick Jaillet[4]

[1] SMART, Singapore
aoran@smart.mit.edu
[2] DSO National Laboratories, Singapore
{tkiatchu,oboonhoo}@dso.org.sg
[3] NUS Business School, Singapore
melvynsim@nus.edu.sg
[4] EECS & ORC MIT, Cambridge MA, USA
jaillet@mit.edu

Abstract. In emergency planning, consideration of emergency priorities is a necessity. This paper presents new formulations of the facility location problem (FLP) and vehicle routing problem with time windows (VRPTW) with considerations of priority. Our models ensure that higher priority locations are considered before the lower priority ones, for both facility and routing decisions. The FLP is solved using an MIP solver, while a tabu search based metaheuristic is developed for the solution of the VRPTW. Under a set of possible emergency scenarios with limited emergency resources, our models were able to serve higher priority locations better than the much utilized Maximal Coverage Location Problem (MCLP) model. We also present preliminary work and results for an integrated location-routing analysis which improves service results further.

Keywords: Emergency Planning, Facility Siting, MCLP, VRPTW.

1 Introduction

Increasing population growth and high level of urbanization have increased the impacts of disasters, whether natural or man-made. Consequently, there is an increasing need for new methods to better prepare for and manage emergencies. In general, a good emergency response plan (ERP) must yield an efficient and immediate emergency response to locations that will be affected by the actual disasters. As a first stage of an ERP, in the preparation stage, emergency facilities must be sited at optimal locations, and the emergency vehicles (eg. Fire Trucks, First Aid Vehicles etc), that will be bringing relief material to emergency points from these facilities, be allocated to the right facilities. Later, during the actual emergencies, within short decision times, optimal routes for emergency vehicles must be found, and updated dynamically when new information about

---

[*] Research funded in part by NRF (SMART Future Mobility).

N. Aschenbruck et al. (Eds.): Future Security 2012, CCIS 318, pp. 129–140, 2012.

the emergencies becomes available. Both problems have been studied in detail in operations research, under the broader problems of FLPs, and VRPs (see surveys [1], [2]), respectively.

When planning for an ERP, all possible hazards must be considered as part of a thorough risk assessment and prioritized on the basis of impact and likelihood of occurrence. Otherwise, treating all hazards the same in terms of planning resource allocation would ultimately lead to failure [3]. Priority considerations are particularly essential when planning for emergencies with limited resources. In such situations trade off decisions must be made about which emergencies to receive the available resources based on the priority of emergencies. For instance, for fire-related emergencies, it would be prudent to consider serving a petrochemical plant with fire trucks before less fire-sensitive areas because of the possible risks associated with such an emergency in that plant. While essential in emergency planning, priority related problems have not been studied in detail in FLPs except a few studies, e.g. [4].

A major challenge for developing ERPs is the uncertainties involved with emergencies, such as the time and location of their occurrence. In order to account for the uncertainties the 'backup coverage' concept of Hogan and ReVelle [5] could be utilized. It constructs a more reliable or robust facility network, such that in the event of facility failures (or busyness) any remaining facilities can continue to provide a sufficient level of coverage [6]. An ERP with priority considerations can particularly benefit from backup coverage utilization if locations with high risks (high priority) could be covered by more than one facility.

It has been noted that for problems where different customers will be served simultaneously with vehicles from the sited facilities, such as the ERP problem mentioned above, the location and routing decision will be strongly interrelated [7]. This dependency suggests that FLP results might not be indeed optimal when considered without the possible service effectiveness of vehicles dispatched from the sited facilities. For instance, the optimality of an emergency facility location depends on how effectively the vehicles can respond to emergency calls. In general, a combined FLP-VRP analysis could give the planner a more accurate measure of the location decisions for problems that involve the delivery of goods with vehicles dispatched from the facilities. For an ERP, such a combined assessment could improve the reliability of the proposed emergency facility plans.

In this paper we introduce a new methodology for the development of ERPs. Overall, our approach consists of a facility location model, MCLP-PB, built on the MCLP with priority considerations and backup coverage, and a vehicle routing model, VRPTW-P, built on the VRTPTW with priority considerations. VRPTW-P is also used to analyze MCLP-PB results, under different demands characterized by possible emergency scenarios. For the solution of VRPTW-P, we present a fast and accurate metaheuristic that could update vehicle routes dynamically, and which could be utilized in real life emergencies where computation time is critical. Finally, as an extension of our approach, we present an integrated location-routing approach, which finds location and routing decisions in a feedback loop fashion rather than a sequential analysis.

2 Problem Formulation and Model Development

Consider a network $G(V, A)$, with V being the set of locations of interest, and A the set of arcs in the network representing roads in the physical space. In this network, we are given a set of potential sites for emergency facilities $\mathcal{J} \subset V$, and the set of emergency sites (points) $\mathcal{I} \subset V$. To develop a general method, we consider multiple types of emergencies, with each type demanding service by a particular type of emergency vehicle, e.g. fire emergencies demanding fire trucks. The type of an emergency vehicle is represented by an element of the index set $\mathcal{K} \doteq \{1, 2, ...\}$. An emergency point $i \in \mathcal{I}$ is said to be covered by site $j \in \mathcal{J}$ if and only if the shortest distance (or travel time) from j to i is less than a preset coverage standard [1]. We define, $N_i^k \doteq \{j \in \mathcal{J} \mid j$ can cover $i \in \mathcal{I}$ by vehicle type-k, $k \in \mathcal{K}$ under distance (time) standards$\}$. Other parameters and decision variables are defined below.

Parameters:
Q: number of available facilities for operation,
P^k: number of available type-k vehicles for allocation to facilities,
p_i^k: priority (value) of emergency point $i \in \mathcal{I}$ for vehicle type-k,
d_i^k: number of distinct facilities required to cover $i \in \mathcal{I}$ with type-k vehicles,
α_i^k: weight for type-k emergency at $i \in \mathcal{I}$.

Decision Variables:

$$y_j \doteq \begin{cases} 1 & \text{if a facility is sited at } j \in \mathcal{J}, \\ 0 & \text{otherwise.} \end{cases}$$

$$x_j^k \doteq \begin{cases} 1 & \text{if a type-}k \text{ vehicle, } k \in \mathcal{K}, \text{ is allocated to the facility at } j \in \mathcal{J}, \\ 0 & \text{otherwise.} \end{cases}$$

$$w_i^k \doteq \begin{cases} 1 & \text{if } i \in \mathcal{I} \text{ is covered by a type-k emergency vehicle, } k \in \mathcal{K}, \\ 0 & \text{otherwise.} \end{cases}$$

Below, we first reintroduce the basic MCLP model with the notion of priority, which we call MCLP-P, in order to consider it as a benchmark against our model.

$$\max_{y_j, x_j^k, w_i^k} \sum_{k \in \mathcal{K}} \sum_{i \in \mathcal{I}} \alpha_i^k w_i^k \tag{1}$$

$$s.t: \sum_{j \in J} y_j \leq Q, \tag{2}$$

$$\sum_{j \in \mathcal{J}} x_j^k \leq P^k, \qquad \forall k \in \mathcal{K}, \tag{3}$$

$$x_j^k \leq y_j, \qquad \forall k \in \mathcal{K}, \forall j \in \mathcal{J}, \tag{4}$$

$$\sum_{j \in N_i^k} x_j^k \geq w_i^k, \qquad \forall k \in \mathcal{K}, \forall i \in \mathcal{I}. \tag{5}$$

(2) and (3) are the constraints for the available number of facilities, and vehicles, respectively. (4) avoids allocating a vehicle at a point with no facility, (5) ensures that a point $i \in \mathcal{I}$ is covered by a type-k vehicle, only if there is at least one type-k vehicle already sited at a facility that can cover i under the distance (time) standard. The difference between MCLP-P and MCLP comes from the definition of weight α_i^k in (1). In MCLP-P, we define α_i^k by considering the priority of type-k emergency at location $i \in \mathcal{I}$, p_i^k. One particular case is the formulation for absolute priority, where α_i^k should be defined such that the coverage of an emergency point with priority value p is always worth more than the coverage of all points with priorities less than p. In such analysis, the MCLP-P model would yield a solution with as many high priority points covered as possible.

2.1   Location Model, MCLP-PB

As mentioned earlier, our location model is based on introducing extra coverage for emergencies of high priority. We assume that the number of distinct coverage demands, d_i^k, is given for each emergency point $i \in \mathcal{I}$ and emergency type $k \in \mathcal{K}$. To introduce the extra coverage considerations we redefine the objective function as a penalty function as shown (6). The difference term inside the square brackets is the unsatisfied distinct coverage demand of a type-k emergency at location $i \in \mathcal{I}$. The weight α_i^k is again used to reflect the priority of type-k emergency at point i. If the absolute priority case is considered, then minimizing the objective function ensures that higher priority points, together with their backup coverage requirements, are covered first. (7),(8) and (9) are also the first three constraints of the MCLP-P model, and are introduced for the same requirements. The formulation below is transformed into a linear form by introducing the difference term in brackets as a new variable, and adding extra constraints accordingly.

$$\min_{y_j, x_j^k} \sum_{k \in \mathcal{K}} \sum_{i \in \mathcal{I}} \alpha_i^k \left[d_i^k - \sum_{j \in N_i^k} x_j^k \right]^+ , \text{where} \quad [f(.)]^+ \doteq \begin{cases} f(.) & \text{if } f(.) \geq 0, \\ 0 & \text{otherwise.} \end{cases} \tag{6}$$

$$s.t : \sum_{j \in J} y_j \leq Q, \tag{7}$$

$$\sum_{j \in \mathcal{J}} x_j^k \leq P^k, \quad \forall k \in \mathcal{K}, \tag{8}$$

$$x_j^k \leq y_j, \qquad \forall k \in \mathcal{K}, \forall j \in \mathcal{J}. \tag{9}$$

2.2   Routing Model, VRPTW-P

Our routing model is an extension of the VRPTW formulations of Desrosiers et al. [8] with the notion of priority, and the relaxation of the constraint for serving every demand. We assume routing analysis succeeds facility solutions, so that $\mathcal{J}^k \subset \mathcal{J}$, the set of facilities that house type-k vehicles, is already found for all $k \in \mathcal{K}$. New terms consistent with the ones defined earlier are introduced below.

Sets:
$\mathcal{I}^k \subset \mathcal{I}$: the set of emergency points that demand type-k vehicles,
$\mathcal{A}^{j,k} \doteq \{(m,n) \in (\mathcal{I}^k \cup \{j\}) \otimes (\mathcal{I}^k \cup \{j\}) \mid \delta_{mj} \leq C, \delta_{nj} \leq C\}, j \in \mathcal{J}^k, k \in \mathcal{K}$.

Parameters:
β_i^k: weight for serving type-k emergency at $i \in \mathcal{I}^k$,
Δ_i^k: amount of relief material demanded from a type-k vehicle at $i \in \mathcal{I}^k$,
D^k: range (distance) capacity of type-k vehicles,
C^k: emergency relief material capacity of type-k vehicles,
δ_{mn}: minimum distance between $m \in (\mathcal{I} \cup \mathcal{J})$ and $n \in (\mathcal{I} \cup \mathcal{J})$,
$[e_i, l_i]$: the time window at $i \in \mathcal{I}$ within which the emergency must be responded,
t_{mn}^k: travel time for a type-k vehicle on arc $(m,n), m \in (\mathcal{I} \cup \mathcal{J})$ and $n \in (\mathcal{I} \cup \mathcal{J})$,
s_i^k: service time for a type-k vehicle at $i \in \mathcal{I}$, and $s_i^k = 0$, $\forall i \in \mathcal{J}$,
$\bar{t}_{ij}^k \doteq t_{ij}^k + s_i^k$.

Decision Variables:

$$z_{mn}^{jk} \doteq \begin{cases} 1 & \text{if the type-k vehicle housed at } j \in \mathcal{J}^k \text{ travels on arc } (m,n) \in A^{j,k}, \\ 0 & \text{otherwise.} \end{cases}$$

$$T_n^k \doteq \begin{cases} \text{Service start time at } n \text{ if } n \in \mathcal{I}^k, \text{ for type-k vehicle,} \\ \text{Return time to facility } n \text{ if } n \in \mathcal{J}^k, \text{ for type-k vehicle.} \end{cases}$$

We formulate VRPTW-P as:

$$\max_{z_{mn}^{jk}} \sum_{k \in \mathcal{K}} \sum_{j \in \mathcal{J}^k} \sum_{(m,n) \in \mathcal{A}^{j,k}} \beta_n^k z_{mn}^{jk} \tag{10}$$

$$s.t: \sum_{j \in \mathcal{J}^k} \sum_{\{n \mid (m,n) \in A^{j,k}\}} z_{mn}^{j,k} \leq 1, \qquad \forall k \in \mathcal{K}, \forall m \in \mathcal{I}^k, \tag{11}$$

$$\sum_{\{n \mid (m,n) \in A^{j,k}\}} z_{mn}^{jk} = \sum_{\{n \mid (m,n) \in A^{j,k}\}} z_{nm}^{jk}, \; \forall k \in \mathcal{K}, \forall m \in (\mathcal{I}^k \cup \mathcal{J}^k), j \in \mathcal{J}^k \tag{12}$$

$$\sum_{\{n \mid (j,n) \in A^{j,k}\}} z_{jn}^{jk} = 1, \qquad \forall k \in \mathcal{K}, \forall j \in \mathcal{J}^k, \tag{13}$$

$$\sum_{\{m \mid (m,j) \in A^{j,k}\}} z_{mj}^{jk} = 1, \qquad \forall k \in \mathcal{K}, \forall j \in \mathcal{J}^k, \tag{14}$$

$$z_{mn}^{jk} (T_m^k + \bar{t}_{mn}^k - T_n^k) \leq 0, \qquad \forall k \in \mathcal{K}, \forall j \in \mathcal{J}^k, \forall (m,n) \in \mathcal{A}^{j,k}, m \neq j, \tag{15}$$

$$z_{jn}^{jk} (\bar{t}_{jn}^k - T_n^k) \leq 0, \qquad \forall k \in \mathcal{K}, \forall j \in \mathcal{J}^k, \forall (j,n) \in \mathcal{A}^{j,k}, \tag{16}$$

$$e_m \leq T_m^k \leq l_m, \qquad \forall k \in \mathcal{K}, \forall m \in \mathcal{I}^k, \tag{17}$$

$$\sum_{(m,n) \in \mathcal{A}^{j,k}} \delta_{mn} z_{mn}^{jk} \leq D^k, \qquad \forall k \in \mathcal{K}, \forall j \in \mathcal{J}^k, \tag{18}$$

$$\sum_{(m,n) \in \mathcal{A}^{j,k}} \Delta_n^k z_{mn}^{jk} \leq C^k, \qquad \forall k \in \mathcal{K}, \forall j \in \mathcal{J}^k. \tag{19}$$

Set $\mathcal{A}^{j,k}$ is introduced to ensure that the decision variable z_{mn}^{jk} is defined properly for our problem. With that definition, the vehicles can only leave from and return to their own facilities. Also, they can only serve emergency points falling under the coverage area (defined by the distance 'C') of their facilities. The objective function (10) is defined similar to (1) that it considers the priorities of each emergency. Relatedly, constraint (11) is relaxed from an equality to an inequality, in order to let emergency vehicles not serve lower priority emergencies and serve the higher priority ones when the demands are simultaneous. In the absolute priority case, VRPTW-P formulation ensures that emergency vehicles serve the higher priority demands even this might result in not serving lower priority demands independent of the number of lower priority demands. (11) imposes that every emergency point can be assigned to at most one single route according to the type of emergency vehicle demanded at that point. (12), (13), (14) describe the flow for the type-k vehicle from facility j. (15), (16), and (17) ensure that vehicle routes stay feasible with the given emergency time windows at each emergency point. (15) can be transformed into the following linear form:

$$(T_m^k + \bar{t}_{mn}^k - T_n^k) \leq (1 - z_{mn}^{jk}) M, \qquad \forall k \in \mathcal{K}, \forall j \in \mathcal{J}^k, \forall (m,n) \in \mathcal{A}^{j,k}, m \neq j$$

where M is a very large number. The same transformation could be used for (16) as well to keep the VRPTW-P as a linear integer problem. (18) guarantees feasibility for the range capacity, and (19) guarantees feasibility for the emergency relief material capacity of a vehicle.

3   Emergency Response Planning

Now that we have defined our location and routing models, MCLP-PB and VRPTW-P, we are ready to demonstrate how these two models could be utilized in preparation of real life ERPs. As mentioned earlier, for a problem like the ERP, where location and routing decisions will be interrelated, the facility location decisions should be assessed by how effectively the vehicles will respond to actual demands. In order to assess MCLP-PB's performance, we considered various types of emergency scenarios, and analyzed how well the allocated vehicles were able to serve the demands with VRPTW-P. In this assessment, we consider the performance of MCLP-P as a baseline to our model.

For our simulations we consider the 44-node network shown in Figure 1, where red colored nodes represent emergency points (EPs), and the remaining nodes possible locations for the emergency facilities. The network and EP locations are based on a typical metropolitan city, where high priority locations are clustered together in a central region, while low priority locations are sparsely distributed on the city fringes. For a concise argument, we assume that only two types of emergency vehicles, fire trucks and medical vehicles, are demanded at EPs. Each emergency type at each point has its priority, p_i^k, shown next to the EP, with higher values representing more important demands. In the network, there are a total of 14 priority level-1 (L1), 8 priority level-2 (L2), and 2 priority level-3

(L3) emergencies, with L3s having the highest priority. Again, for conciseness we let the number of distinct base coverage demand, d_i^k, equal to p_i^k, consistent with the fact that more important EPs requiring more distinct coverage.

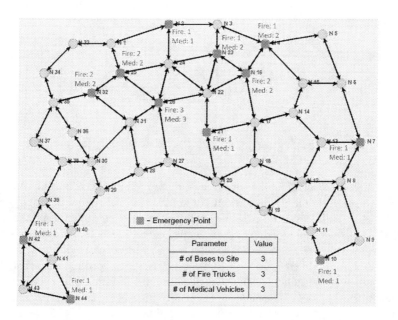

Fig. 1. 44-Node Simulation Network

3.1   Siting of Emergency Facilities and Vehicles

Both MCLP-P and MCLP-PB models are solved to optimality using a binary programming solver, and results are shown in Fig. 2 and Fig. 3, with facilities shown in yellow color. In the MCLP-P facility configuration Fig. 2, the facility sited at node-24, is able to cover all EPs at the upper- center of the network. The facilities sited at node-8 (right-bottom) and node-40 (left-bottom) cover the EPs at the fringes of the network. As a result, the facilities are more spread out, and all the EPs in the network are covered. In the facility configuration of the MCLP-PB model Fig. 3, the facilities are sited closer to the central high priority cluster, due to backup demands. As a result, some of the EPs located at the fringes of the network are not covered. For both configurations, each facility was fully operated, housing one fire truck and one medical vehicle each.

3.2   Vehicle Routing under Various Emergency Scenarios

In this section, we consider various emergency scenarios to test our models. The scenarios vary in the arrival time of emergency demands, $A_i\,(i \in \mathcal{I})$, and the duration of service at EPs, λ, following a disaster. The variation in arrival times

136   A. Oran et al.

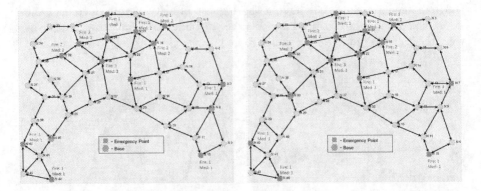

Fig. 2. MCLP-P Facility Configuration   **Fig. 3.** MCLP-PB Facility Configuration

is related to the anticipation factor about an emergency, and is considered to see the performance of our models when some anticipation about an emergency's characteristics could be utilized. The variation in service duration is related to the severity of emergencies (more severe emergencies taking longer time to serve), and is considered to see the performance under emergencies of different severity.

Scenario 1 is modeled after considering a series of coordinated terrorist attacks, where an emergency response system would be suddenly overloaded by simultaneous emergency demands, without any possible earlier warning. Service duration, λ, is kept as a variable, and we assume $A_i = 0, \forall i \in \mathcal{I}$, since there could be no warning (emergency demands would arrive instantaneously).

Scenario 2 is modeled after considering a spreading disaster, such as a flood with an estimated path of spread. In the simulation network, Fig. 1, we assume that the disaster spreads from the right nodes to left, with demands from EPs arriving in phases. The two rightmost EPs, at node-7 and node-10, demand for vehicles at $A_7 = 0$ and $A_{10} = 0$. As the disaster moves from right to left, the next two rightmost EPs, at node-4 and node-16, demand vehicles at $A_4 = \tau$, and $A_{16} = \tau$. Here τ denotes the time interval between phases, and is the variable defining the disaster spread speed. Subsequent demands from the EPs will arrive at $2\tau, 3\tau$, and so on. Based on this scenario, we consider two separate sub-scenarios Scenario 2a and 2b. In Scenario 2a, we assume that the demand arrival times for all EPs are known initially, so we can anticipate the arrival of the disaster at each EP. In Scenario 2b, we assume that the demand times are not known initially, and a demand only occurs when the location has been struck by a disaster. Hence, advance planning is not possible, and we can respond to these demands only when they occur.

In Scenario 3, each demand occurs in a random phase, and each demand will require service only once in the scenario. This scenario is modeled after a normal everyday situation, where demands for service occur independently of each other and the arrival of a demand is random in nature. As in the previous scenario, the time interval, τ, determines the duration between arrival phases. For Scenarios 2a, 2b, and 3, service duration λ is assumed to be zero.

As mentioned in the Introduction section, routing decisions for an ERP should be able to be updated during the actual emergencies with the arrival of new information (such as new emergency demands) in short decision times. For this reason, in this work we present a fast and highly accurate metaheuristic that solves the VRPTW-P. The details of the metaheuristic is given in Appendix 1, and it was was used to find the routes of all vehicles in all scenarios.

MCLP-P and MCLP-PB facility configurations was evaluated by the number of tasks successfully served, ordered by priority, by the vehicles dispatched from the facilities. Results of the simulated scenarios are displayed in Table 1.

Table 1. Comparison of MCLP-P and MCLP-PB

#	Scenario	Parameters	MCLP-P			MCLP-PB			MCLP-PB − MCLP-P		
			L3	L2	L1	L3	L2	L1	L3	L2	L1
1	1	$\lambda = 0.00$h	2	4	7	2	8	5	0	+4	-2
2		$\lambda = 0.17$h	2	3	5	2	7	2	0	+4	-3
3		$\lambda = 0.33$h	2	1	4	2	5	0	0	+4	-4
4		$\lambda = 0.50$h	2	0	2	2	3	0	0	+3	-2
5	2a	$\tau = 0.05$h	2	5	7	2	8	6	0	+3	-1
6		$\tau = 0.10$h	2	5	6	2	8	6	0	+3	0
7		$\tau = 0.15$h	2	4	7	2	8	4	0	+4	-3
8		$\tau = 0.20$h	2	4	3	2	7	4	0	+3	+1
9	2b	$\tau = 0.05$h	2	3	7	2	8	5	0	+5	-2
10		$\tau = 0.10$h	2	5	6	2	5	5	0	0	+1
11		$\tau = 0.15$h	1	3	6	2	4	6	+1	+1	0
12		$\tau = 0.20$h	0	4	6	2	4	4	+2	0	-2
13	3	$\tau = 0.05$h	2	2	8	2	8	6	0	+6	-2
14		$\tau = 0.10$h	2	5	7	2	5	7	0	0	0
15		$\tau = 0.15$h	1	3	7	2	3	7	1	0	0
16		$\tau = 0.20$h	2	2	8	2	3	7	0	+1	-1

For Scenario 1, 2a and 3, the MCLP-P facility configuration results in vehicles serving more L1 EPs, while the MCLP-PB facility configuration results in vehicles serving more L2 EPs. It should be noted that for Scenario 1, even when the service duration λ is 0.5 hours, which is in fact half of the time limit assumed for facility coverage in these simulations, the vehicles in the MCLP-PB facility configuration are still able to serve 3 L2 EPs, whereas none of the vehicles in the MCLP-P facility configuration are able to serve any L2 EP (Table 1, row 4).

In Scenario 2b, it is interesting to observe that when the time interval between phases increases, even the most important L3 EPs are dropped in the MCLP-P facility configuration (Row 11 and 12 of Table 1). On the other hand, with the MCLP-PB facility configuration, all the L3 EPs are always served. When the time interval is large, an emergency vehicle is more likely to be en route to a lower priority EP when a new demand arrives from a higher priority EP. If vehicles are too far away from the higher priority EPs, they will be unable to service those, resulting in dropped demands from the higher priority EPs.

In contrast, with the MCLP-PB facility configuration, the backup facilities (and vehicles housed in them) are able to provide service to the higher priority EPs' demands.

3.3   Integrated Analysis

In the previous section, we compared the effectiveness of emergency vehicles' response to simulated emergencies from the facility configurations found by MCLP-P and MCLP-PB models. Notice that the facility locations did not change after the routing analysis was completed, so the overall planning was in fact carried out in an open loop manner. As mentioned in the Introduction section, this type of independent FLP-VRP solution process could result in an overall sub-optimal solution. For this reason, we designed an extension to this process to include a feedback loop to find better facility configurations. For this analysis, a new method to generate alternate facility configurations based on the solution of the routing algorithm is developed. In this method, we shift the emergency facilities to other possible locations that could improve vehicles' responses to emergencies. This method is described in greater detail Appendix 2.

We conducted additional simulations with Scenario 1 and 2a to observe the effectiveness of the proposed closed-loop planning method. The results of the alternate facility configuration simulations are shown in Table 2.

Table 2. Comparison with Facility Shifting

#	Scenario	Parameters	MCLP-P			MCLP-P shift			MCLP-PB			MCLP-PB shift		
			L3	L2	L1	L3	L2	L1	L3	L2	L1	L3	L2	L1
1	1	$\lambda = 0.00h$	2	4	7	2	4	7	2	8	5	2	8	5
2		$\lambda = 0.17h$	2	3	5	2	3	6	2	7	2	2	8	2
3		$\lambda = 0.33h$	2	1	4	2	1	5	2	5	0	2	6	1
4		$\lambda = 0.50h$	2	0	2	2	0	4	2	3	0	2	4	0
5	2a	$\tau = 0.05h$	2	5	7	2	5	7	2	8	6	2	8	6
6		$\tau = 0.10h$	2	5	6	2	5	6	2	8	6	2	8	6
7		$\tau = 0.15h$	2	4	7	2	4	7	2	8	4	2	8	4
8		$\tau = 0.20h$	2	4	3	2	4	6	2	7	4	2	8	4

As can be noticed from the results, when facility shifting is allowed, there is a small improvement in the number of EPs served by the vehicles for all scenarios and for both base configurations. These results show the potential improvements to emergency plans by utilizing an integrated location-routing analysis particularly for emergencies whose characteristics could be estimated beforehand, such as a flood with an estimated path.

4   Conclusions

In this paper, for emergency response preparation, we have formulated new location, MCLP-PB, and routing, VRPTW-P, models with priority considerations.

MCLP-PB, also utilizes the extra backup coverage concept to introduce robustness to the facility network. A fast and highly accurate metaheuristic, that could be utilized in real life emergencies, is developed for VRPTW-P. We tested our formulations on a 44-node network that is influenced from a metropolitan city. The MCLP-PB model generated facility configurations that are better in achieving the goal of servicing higher priority EPs, as compared to the baseline MCLP-P model. While the MCLP-PB model does neglect the coverage of some lower priority EPs, in crisis management where resources could be scarce and high priority EPs needs to be addressed first, the MCLP-PB model is better able to achieve this goal. We have also proposed an integrated feedback type algorithm involving facility shifting. The algorithm for this integrated model performed better than the algorithms for both the MCLP-P and MCLP-PB models under various scenarios. While this study is developed with the ERP problem in mind, our approach would also be useful for other location problems where priority is a major concern, and the location and routing decisions are interrelated.

References

1. Brotcorne, L., Laporte, G., Semet, F.: Ambulance location and relocation models. European J. of Operational Research 147(3), 451–463 (2003)
2. Eksioglu, B., Vural, A.V., Reisman, A.: The vehicle routing problem: A taxonomic review. Computers & Industrial Engineering 57(4) (2009)
3. Principles of emergency management supplement (September 2008), http://training.fema.gov/EMIWeb/edu/emprinciples.asp
4. Silva, F., Serra, D.: Locating emergency services with different priorities: the priority queuing covering location problem. J. Op. Res. Soc. 59(9) (2008)
5. Hogan, K., ReVelle, C.: Concepts and applications of backup coverage. Management Science 32, 1434–1444 (1986)
6. OHanley, J.R., Church, R.L.: Designing robust coverage networks to hedge against worst-case facility losses. European J. of Op. Res. 209(1) (2011)
7. Klose, A., Drexl, A.: Facility location models for distribution system design. European J. of Operational Research 162(1), 4–29 (2005)
8. Desrosiers, J., Dumas, Y., Solomon, M.M.: Chapter 2 time constrained routing and scheduling. In: Network Routing. Handbooks in Op. Res. & Man. Science, vol. 8, pp. 35–139. Elsevier (1995)
9. Cordeau, J., Laporte, G., Mercier, A.: A unified tabu search heuristic for vehicle routing problems with time windows. J. Op. Res. Soc. 52 (August 2001)
10. Solomon, M.: Algorithms for the vehicle routing and scheduling problems with time window constraints. Operations Research 35(2), 254–265 (1987)

Appendix 1: Vehicle Routing Problem Heuristics

For emergency vehicle routing, we use a tabu search algorithm adapted from the unified tabu search (UTS) algorithm in [9]. In the original UTS algorithm, the solution produced by the initial construction phase is not guaranteed to be feasible. We modified the initial construction phase of the UTS algorithm to use the I1 insertion heuristic from [10], so that the algorithm can return a feasible solution at any time.

In the original UTS algorithm, all EPs have equal priority. We modified the algorithm to consider absolute priorities. During the search, we compare solutions as follows. Suppose the EP priorities from lowest to highest are $1, 2, \cdots, p^*$. The most important criterion is to maximize the number of priority p^* EPs assigned to a solution. The next most important criterion is to maximize the number of priority $(p^* - 1)$ EPs assigned to a solution, and this proceeds until the priority 1 EPs have been considered. Finally, the least important criterion is to minimize the total distance of all the routes in a solution, for a total of $p^* + 1$ criteria. Finally, we adapted the algorithm to be able to perform replanning whenever the situation changes.

Our metaheuristic algorithm performed well on the well-studied Solomon benchmark set of problems [10]. This benchmark set contains over 150 VRPTW instances with differing characteristics in terms of size, location distribution and time window duration, and has mostly been solved optimally, with minimizing total distance as the main criterion. For every instance, our algorithm produces a solution within 10% of optimality, meaning that the total distance of the solution is within 110% of the optimal total distance. For smaller problem instances containing 25 locations, our algorithm takes only a few seconds. For larger problem instance containing 100 locations, our algorithm takes less than 5 minutes. It is important to note that this benchmark set only contains static problems, and does not have locations of different priorities. However, our algorithm's strong performance on this data set together with its ability to perform replanning makes it suitable for our purposes.

Appendix 2: Finding Alternate Facility Configurations

Using the result from the routing algorithm, better alternate facility configurations can be generated. A tabu list of facility configurations is used to widen the exploration of the search space. The facility to relocate is the one covering the dropped highest priority EP. The neighboring nodes to the facility and the nodes on the shortest path between the facility and the dropped EP are put into a list of possible locations to shift to.

In the list, nodes with a facility are dropped from the list. If the facility is relocated to a node that results in a tabu configuration, the node is also removed from the list of possible locations. From the filtered list, the one possible location to consider for relocation is selected by finding the location that can cover the most priority weighted EPs. After obtaining the possible location, we shift the facility if the dropped EP has a priority that is higher or equal to all the EPs that are served by the facility. Otherwise, we will only shift the facility if all the higher level EPs that is served by the facility can still be covered. Once we decide to shift the facility, the current facility configuration is added to the tabu list and the alternate facility configuration is now used as the input into the routing algorithm.

New Building Concepts Protecting
against Aircraft Impact

Alexander Stolz[1], Werner Riedel[1], Markus Noeldgen[2], and Andreas Laubach[2]

[1] Fraunhofer Ernst-Mach-Institut High Speed Dynamics, Freiburg, Germany
{alexander.stolz,werner.riedel}@emi.fraunhofer.de
[2] Schüssler-Plan Ingenieurgesellschaft mbH, Düsseldorf, Germany
{mnoeldgen,alaubach}@schuessler-plan.de

Abstract. Aircraft impact is a decisive load case for critical infrastructure as high-rise buildings in prestigious large-scale urban developments or nuclear power plants. The proposed paper introduces new concepts based on high performance concretes (HPC, UHPC) for the example of the 'Security Scraper' [1,2] and an innovative superstructure for existing power plants [3,4]. Key analysis steps using Two-Degree-of-Freedom (TDOF) and finite element (FEM) methods and their experimental validation [5] are used to predict dynamic response on local and global levels to maintain structural integrity under impact and to keep the fire outside the security zone.

Keywords: Aircraft impact, fire, TDOF, security hull, ballistic limit, high performance concrete.

1   Introduction

Aircraft impact and subsequent kerosene fire has to be considered as realistic threat against critical infrastructure. Typical examples are high-rise buildings in the range of several hundred meters altitude, potentially as part of a large scale urban development, housing several ten thousands of occupants in office and/or residential space. The largest of these buildings worldwide carry symbolic value making them susceptible to attacks. Furthermore, major nuclear facilities have to be considered, especially those designed about 2-3 decades ago without or with low protection requirements against accidental aircraft impact. Especially early designs of boiling water reactor housings with a large control area are principally more vulnerable than pressurized reactors with very localized and often strongly covered reactors.

The paper reviews and compares two recently developed comprehensive and innovative concepts of these building types, based on high and ultra high performance concretes (HPC, UHPC). The 'Security Scraper', designed in [1], [2] and illustrated in Figure 1, is a concept for a high-rise buildings with 500m altitude and more consisting of:

- a UHPC safety and security core shown in blue, providing resistance against the complete aircraft and the most localized penetration loading by the engines

N. Aschenbruck et al. (Eds.): Future Security 2012, CCIS 318, pp. 141–152, 2012.
© Springer-Verlag Berlin Heidelberg 2012

- escape and rescue routes (green) and key installations for fire protection placed inside the security core to remain functional during an impact and the associated fire
- alternate load paths compensating larger scale local failure of columns by outrigger constructions redirecting the static loading forces around the damaged area

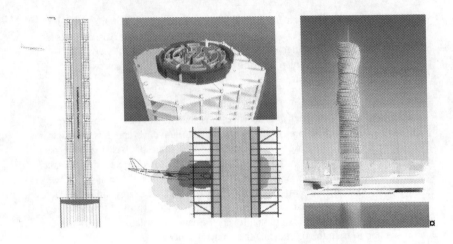

Fig. 1. Security Scraper concept with protective ultra high performance concrete core (blue) housing escape and rescue routes (green); design impression by Dissing + Weitling Architects

The second concept review describes a superstructure for existing boiling reactor type nuclear power (Figure 2) plants with:

- a box girder construction spanning contact free across the plant structure to leave the existing operation license virtually untouched
- a structural design, such that the superstructure can absorb momentum and energy of the global impact forces
- an outer hull as local penetration protection (red in Figure 2) to keep all burning kerosene out of the superstructure and the security zone
- sufficiently low transmission of impact induced vibrations from the superstructure, through the foundations into the existing plant building, to achieve acceptable floor response spectra for critical components

The design of these structures involves the analysis of global integrity, such that the building can absorb the overall momentum and kinetic energy of all impacting aircraft components. In order to protect the security cores from failure caused by kerosene fire, the local penetration resistance must be dimensioned appropriately. The design methods on these two scales are reviewed and applied in the following to quantify the benefit of high performance concretes in innovative concepts.

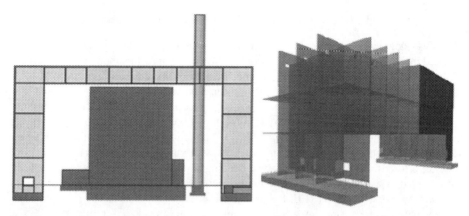

Fig. 2. Power plant superstructure concept: Free-spanning protection of a boiling water reactor type against civilian and military aircraft; right: partly opened 3D view of the HPC security hull (red) onto the bracing structures

2   State of the Art

Buildings in general are designed following the related regulations of the building sector. Impact in general is categorized as an extraordinary loading case for a construction, in which no additional safety factors have to be considered. The actions and influences resulting from an aircraft impact as well as the resistance of the structural elements within the construction against this loading type are covered within the regulations only by simplified analytical formulas basing on empirical correlations, which have been modified to describe effects of an aircraft impact. The most sophisticated method to calculate the local resistance of a reinforced concrete building component for the loading case aircraft crash is with respect to the DIN 25449 the use of a modified, empirical punching strength evidence. For the punching strength the design code differentiates between components with and without stirrup reinforcement. In the virtual evidence loading and calculated resistance are compared neglecting the dynamics. In order to take the dynamics into account static substitute loads have to be derived and dynamic strength increase factors need be calculated. The derivation of the corresponding factors is quite complex and includes a certain amount of uncertainties.

Regarding these uncertainties in the following more enhanced calculation models will be discussed taking dynamics fully into account.

3   Local Penetration Resistance

Before the overall static and dynamic construction in section 3 can be done, the necessary wall dimensions of the security core and hull to avoid penetration have to be derived.

3.1   TDOF and FEM Analysis Methods for Conventional Concrete to UHPC

The Two-Degree-of-Freedom (TDOF) model, illustrated in Figure 3 upper right, and detailed in [3], is a simplified but dynamically coupled engineering approach. It describes global bending with mass M_1 and resistance R_1 and local shear plug formation (M_2, R_2) of plates in dynamic equilibrium with the transient impact forces F(t). Figure 3 upper left, illustrates as example the local shear resistance function of a reinforced concrete plate with failure criteria for concrete in tension (F_c^u), yielding and rupturing of stirrup (F_{stir}^p, F_{stir}^u) and bending reinforcement (F_{ben}^p, F_{ben}^u). The solution of the equation of motion provides the coupled response of impact forces with the concrete member's inertia and resistance forces. Resulting time-resolved bending and shear deformations are shown on the example of two Meppen tests [6]in Figure 3, lower.

Finite element methods (FEM) based on conservation of mass, momentum and energy with explicit time integration schemes are another key for impact analysis. Concrete is modeled in volume elements with strength models describing the dependence on triaxial compression, deformation rates, porous compaction and state of damage. Rebar is explicitly modeled by beam elements with strain and strain rate hardening and thermal softening. Figure 4 shows a sample validation case for conventional concrete [3].

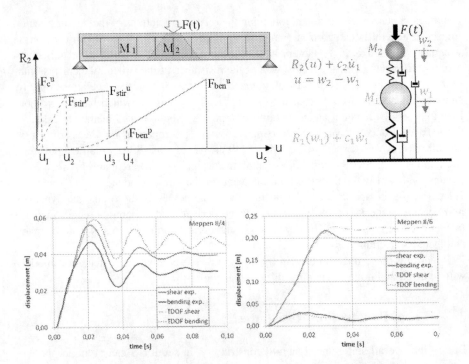

Fig. 3. Comparison of TDOF of local shear (M_2) and bending resistance (M_1) (dashed) to Meppen [6] impact experiments II/4 (solid, left): shearing underestimated, bending very well predicted; and test II/6 (right): shearing and bending very well predicted

Fig. 4. Validation example of explicit FE-Method with discrete rebar and RHT-concrete model for Meppen test II/4 and II/6 on conventional concrete plates

In Figure 5 the same FEM modeling approach is applied together with a UHPC concrete description [1] against a recent own test series [5]. The M1:10 experiments (see also Table 2) are consistent with a large test database of Phantom F4 GE79 engine and representative model impact tests in literature [7]. In both experiments and simulations of Figure 5 can be noted that the ballistic limit velocity increases from about 219 for conventional concrete to remarkable 320 m/s when using UHPC with the same reinforcement degree and 1% fiber content.

Table 1. DIN, TDOF and FEM compared to Meppen experiments [6] on conventional concrete

Analysis method	DIN 25449		TDOF		FEM	
Resistance evaluation	shear	bending	shear	bending	shear	bending
Experiment						
Meppen II/4	~correct*	n.c.	too high	correct	too low	correct
Meppen II/6	~correct#	n.c.	correct	correct	correct	correct

n.c.: not considered; * slightly too high

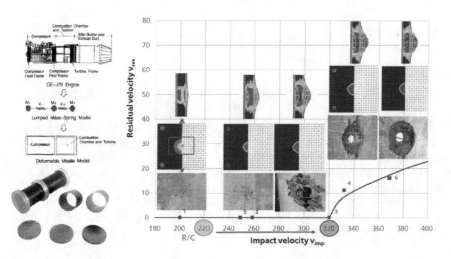

Fig. 5. Engine impact model based on Sugano [8]; increased ballistic limit from 219 m/s for conventional concrete to 320 m/s ±10 m/s in own UHPC tests [5] and FE validation [1]

The conclusions from [1,3] on the validation of TDOF and FEM methods for conventional concrete (Table 1) and UHPC (Figure 5) can be summarized as follows:

- TDOF engineering models and explicit finite element methods show separately often very good agreement, sometimes with slight deviations.
- Combination of both methods, as in Tables 1 and 3, allows well-based predictions of necessary thicknesses and occurring deformation magnitudes.
- TDOF and FEM models are well applicable to high performance concretes with much higher penetration resistance compared to conventional concrete.

3.2   Dimensioning the Protective Core of the Security Scraper

The necessary thickness and steel content in terms of bar and fiber reinforcement is one decisive design and cost parameters for the 500 m high security core. The global bending behaviour is analyzed in section 3.1. The critical load case for local penetration is the engine impact, since this component has most ballistic performance. Engine debris and fuel fire must not enter the escape and rescue routes. Impact of largest civilian airliners with a speed of 250 m/s is considered.

The engine modelling approach by Sugano et al. [7] for the 1,76t Phantom GE-J79 is consistently transferred in [1] to the very large civilian engine type PW4000 with a mass of 6.5t. Key impact parameters are compared in Table 2 on the example of 219 m/s initial velocity.

Table 2. Comparison of the momentum of aircraft engines and the generic jet engine model

		Original	Original	Scaled Model
		GE-J79	PW4000	GE-J79
		1:1	1:1	1:10
Weight	[kg]	1764	6500	1.764
Velocity v_0	[m/s]	219	219	219
Momentum	[Ns]	3.86E+05	1.42E+06	3.86E+02
Area	[m²]	4.54E-01	4.08E+00	4.54E-03
Momentum/ area	[Ns/m²]	8.52E+05	3.48E+05	8.52E+04

Considering as a possibly weakest section a two storey spacing with 8,0m height, the local impact area of the core tube is modeled as shown in Figure 6. Again, concrete and rebar are represented in separate discretisations and material models. 1% of steel fiber reinforcement in the UHPC is used in all cases. Figure 6, left, shows perforation of a 1,0m thick core, with 0,545% (or 54,5 cm²/m) of reinforcement on both sides as insufficient to avoid penetration. Increasing to 1,09% (or 109 cm²/m) will stop the engine, as shown on the right side. 1,3 m thickness with 0,545% or 71 cm²/m rebar are derived as alternative sufficient protection.

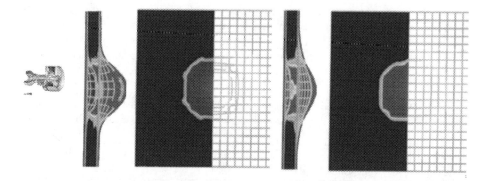

Fig. 6. Impact simulation with the PW4000 engine model (m~6.5 t) at 250m/s on a 1m thick UHPC wall; left: perforation with 0.545 % longitudinal reinforcement on each side; right: no perforation with 1.09 % longitudinal reinforcement; both cases without shear reinforcement and 1% of steel fibers

3.3   Materials and Dimensions of the Power Plant Protection Hull

High performance concretes seems very suitable for the more than 70 m wide spanning power plant superstructure concept considering the substantially improved penetration resistance (Figure 5). In Germany HPC designs can be approved along normed guidelines up to a cylinder compressive strength of 100 MPa with classes up to HPC 80 mostly used in practice. UHPC constructions still require individual concessions which increase the construction costs considerably. The necessary steel fibers and fine and coarse aggregates like microsilica, quarz and bazalt split lead to a further increase.

For this reason, the protection benefit among strength classes is analyzed using Finite-Element-Simulations. With the same rebar content UHPC allows a cross section reduction by 10 cm or about 10% compared to HPC 100 and HPC 80 for the considered load case. Since for the superstructure the additional costs do not justified the benefit, HPC 80 with 1% steel fiber reinforcement is chosen for the concept. Still it should be noted, that the performance and cost benefit strongly depends on the application and load case.

Since the structure is free spanning across more than 70m, zones of considerable pre-loading have to be considered. They occur in Figure 12 in the tensile zone of the box girder span as red elements with high amounts or reinforcement,. A tensile pre-load on the reinforcement of up to 40% of its yield strength is identified in the static calculations. At this amount of preload localized cracking of the concrete cannot be excluded and is considered as a loss of tensile loading capacity of up to 30%. Figure 7 gives a comparison of an impact calculation of the considered civilian airliner, on the left side without and on the right with pre-loading. Both in the finite element simulations (top row) and for the TDOF analysis (lower row) it can be seen, that shear localization of the rebar increases for the preloaded configuration.

Table 3 summarizes the predictions of both analysis methods. For the assumed airliner type and impact speed 110 cm HPC 80 with 1% of fiber content and a reinforcement of 120 cm²/m is suitable to protect the box girder construction and the inner security area of the covered power plant against intrusion of aircraft debris and

148   A. Stolz et al.

burning kerosene. The consistent predictions of two different engineering methods allow high confidence in the calculated result. Additional experimental validation could be achieved by model scale impact tests on HPC consistent with the UHPC campaign shown in Figure 5 and numerous literature values for conventional concrete along [7].

Table 3. TDOF and FEM predictions of HPC 80 limit thickness against the assumed civilian airliner with various pre-loads; 110 cm limit thickness are deduced for the outer hull

wall thickness [cm]	concrete pre-damage [%]	reinforcement pre-load [%]	TDOF	3D-FEM	Con-clusion
100	0	0	√	√	√
100	0	40	√	X	X
100	30	40	√	X	X
110	0	40	(√)	√	√
110	30	40	√	√	√

√ = sufficient resistance;   X = perforation;   ( ) = analogy

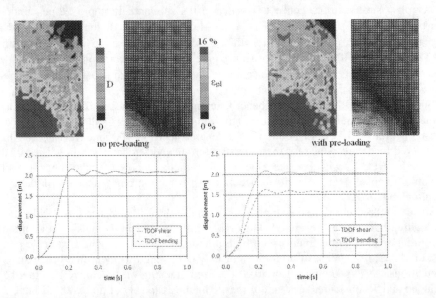

Fig. 7. Upper: larger damage extension and rebar localisation in the case of pre-load (right) than without (left); 40 % preload of rebar yield stress and 30 % tensile pre-damage of HPC 80 assumed; Lower: consistent TDOF results with higher shear localisation under preload (right)

4   Global Building Integrity

With sufficient local penetration resistance ensured, the next step is to design the construction with dead and service loads. The dynamic building response to the full momentum of all impacting aircraft parts has to evaluated and compared to the strength of the construction in the following. For simple shapes, i.e. the slender high-rise building, a single-degree-of-freedom (SDOF) model (see Figure 8, right) with the equation of motion can be used.

4.1   Structural Deflection and Damage Tolerant Construction of the Security Scraper

The SDOF approach is very suitable to analyse the global response of the highrise building. F(t) is the acting load-time function from the aircraft impact, here taken as the impact of a very large airliner at 200 m/s at the top of the building.

Figure 8 shows the solution of the equation of motion at the top of the high-rise building. The static deflection under the design wind case is greater, so that the aircraft impact does not represent the decisive global loading. The maximum deflection is furthermore in the normal design range for high-rise building structures. Further dynamic analysis in [1] with a reduced stiffness by 15% for a worst case of up to 5 destroyed columns on a low story does not affect considerably the result.

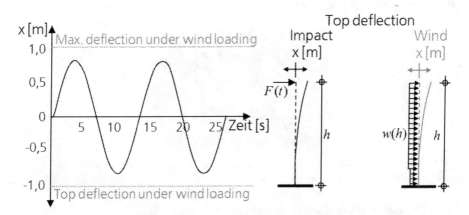

Fig. 8. Top deflection of the building from aircraft impact (calculation without building damping c) in comparison with the maximum top deflection under wind loading

Dynamic finite element methods can subsequently be used on a local level of the storey structures to assess the effect of dynamic failure of statically pre-loaded components. Figure 9 shows a scenario after an impact on a corner resulting in the loss of 5 columns (red). Although the oscillations exceed the loads on the intact level, no overload beyond 100% of the design strength of the adjacent columns is derived. A peak value of 94% of the design strength in column S8 predicts no damage progression on the same level. But on a larger structural scale alternate load paths must be activated and designed such that the forces from the failed structural elements are re-transmitted. A solution to this problem can be an outrigger framework proposed in [1] for every ten storeys. In the outrigger framework the redistributed forces largely exceed 100% of the static design strength (Figure 9). They must be designed thoroughly to various cases of aircraft induced damage to carry loads levels up to 274%.

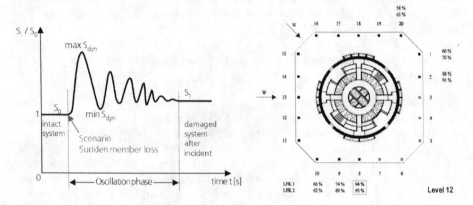

Fig. 9. Left: Dynamic calculation of varying load level during dynamic loss of a number of neighboring columns; right: worst case scenario of losing 5 corner columns (red) and following peak dynamic loading in percent: no progression of collapse

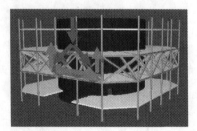

Fig. 10. Left: Security Scraper outrigger framework to provide alternate load pats after loss of columns on the side (left) and the corner (right)

4.2   Dynamics of the Plant Superstructure Using FEM

The complex shape and box girder structure of the nuclear power plant superstructure suggests use of structural finite element codes for static and dynamic analysis. Figure 11 shows the required reinforcement for a representative impact scenario. The resulting 90 cm²/m are lower than the local design reinforcement of 120 cm²/m to avoid local penetration (see section 2.3).

With local and global dynamic resistance approved, impact induced vibrations are the third key aspect for buildings with highly security relevant equipment, such as nuclear containments and their control aggregates. Acceleration response spectra for components characterized by their Eigen frequencies and damping ratios are derived from local displacement-time recordings by exciting SDOF models with varying system parameters. In comparison to earthquake excitation peak spectral accelerations are reached at higher frequencies above 30 Hz. In this last step structural dynamics calculations (2) are combined with SDOF models for equipment (1). It can be shown that the superstructure can be designed such that the impact induced vibrations transferred from the protecting structure through foundations, soil and existing building stay below critical values for the power plant aggregates.

5   Conclusions

The present paper reviews recently developed new structural concepts of a high-hrise building and a power plant superstructure against aircraft impact. They both involve high performance concretes, which showed significantly improved ballistic resistance in recent aircraft engine impact experiments.

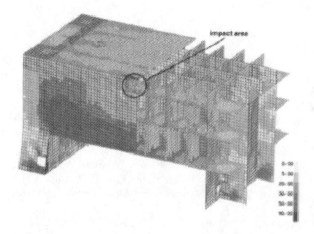

Fig. 11. 90 cm²/m required reinforcement for an impact scenario lower than the needed 120 cm²/m against local perforation; static preloading visible as red areas on the lower edge of the span

Basis for the static and dynamic structural design are in a first step the reliable prediction of necessary thicknesses of the security core and the protection hull. This is mandatory to prevent intrusion of debris and kerosene into the parts of the structure which must remain intact to avoid catastrophic failure. TDOF and FEM tools were shown to provide especially in combination reliable predictive capabilities for the ballistic limit of different concrete qualities. The resulting security scraper core consists of 1 m with 109 cm²/m bar reinforcement of 1% steel fiber reinforced UHPC. 1,1m of HPC 80 with 120 cm²/m where shown to be sufficient for the superstructure hull. HPC showed to be more economic with not too much compromise on higher member thickness compared to UHPC for the power plant application.

After the conventional static design with these basic wall dimensions, the global structural integrity of the building has to be evaluated. The dynamic bending response of the slender highrise building is modeled using an SDOF approach and does not exceed wind loads. The local damage by the aircraft on the storey scale is also uncritical, as long as alternate load paths for lost external columns are provided. Contrary to the adjacent columns, the outrigger structure must provide significantly higher strength of up to 274% of the static limits.

The powerplant superstructure is too complex for a simplified dynamic mechanical model with few degrees of freedom. But it can be well assessed in structural dynamics FEM programs. They show required reinforcement degrees from the global dynamic analysis of 90 cm²/m clearly below the locally required 120 cm²/m. Floor response spectra, derived from the combination of FEM and SDOF calculations, reveal decisive design properties for equipment to withstand the impact induced vibrations.

References

[1] Nöldgen, M.: Modeling of Ultra High Performance Concrete (UHPC) under Impact Loading – Design of a High Rise Building Core against Aircraft Impact. In: Forschungsergebnisse aus der Kurzzeitdynamik, vol. 19, Fraunhofer Verlag, Heft (2011)

[2] Nöldgen, M., Fehling, E., Riedel, W., Thoma, K.: Security Concept for Highrise Buildings – Security Scraper. In: Conference on Highrise Towers and Tall Buildings - HTTB. Technische Universität München (April 2010)

[3] Riedel, W., Stolz, A., Roller, C., Nöldgen, M., Laubach, A., Pattberg, G.: Impact Resistant Superstructure for Power Plants Part I: Box Girders and Concrete Qualities. In: Int. Conf. Structural Mechanics in Reactor Technology, SMIRT, New Delhi, India (2011)

[4] Nöldgen, M., Laubach, A., Lukaschek, F., Riedel, W., Stolz, A., Roller, C., Pattberg, G.: Impact Resistant Superstructure for Power Plants Part II: Structural Concept and Global Response. In: Int. Conf. Structural Mechanics in Reactor Technology - SMIRT, New Dheli, India (2011)

[5] Riedel, W., Nöldgen, M., Straßburger, E., Thoma, K., Fehling, E.: Local Damage to Ultra High Performance Concrete Structures caused by an Impact of Aircraft Engine Missiles. Nuclear Engineering & Design 240, 2633–2642 (2010)

[6] Jonas, W., Rüdiger, E., Gries, M., Riech, H., Rützel, H.: Kinetische Grenztragfähigkeit von Stahlbetonplatten; Bericht RS 165, Hochtief AG, Abt. Kerntechnischer Ingenieurbau, Frankfurt (1982)

[7] Sugano, T., Tsubota, H., Kasai, Y., Koshika, N., Ohnuma, H., von Rise-mann, W.A., Bickel, D.C., Parks, M.B.: Local damage to reinforced concrete structures caused by impact of aircraft engine missiles–Part 1. Test program, method and results. Nuclear Engineering and Design 140, 387–405 (1993)

Safety and Security of Urban Areas through Innovative Architectural and Structural Concepts

Norbert Gebbeken[*], Torsten Döge, and Martin Larcher

Institute of Engineering Mechanics and Structural Mechanics,
University of the Bundeswehr Munich, Germany

Abstract. In the past terrorist attacks were increasingly directed against so-called soft targets. Thus, it is necessary to analyze the threats and to protect "public spaces" in urban areas that are primarily not considered permanent critical infrastructure. Specific threats e.g. explosions, vehicle impact and impact of flying debris, arise from various scenarios. Public spaces are to be protected by structural, architectural and land shaping elements that are not recognized as protective elements by the public. This paper describes architectural attractive, art work, and constructional protective measures as well as intelligent design in landscape architecture for the protection of public spaces in urban areas. Overall, the paper deals with a non-standard development and use of physical protective measures.

Keywords: Lightweight Protective Structure, Explosions, Protective Landscaping, Protective curtains.

1 Introduction and Motivation

Terrorist attacks have been increasingly directed against so-called soft targets rather than against critical infrastructure that, by definition, needs to be protected. Critical infrastructure is comprised of buildings and facilities that are essential for the survivability of a society in case of a catastrophe. Such facilities belong to supply of energy, water and food, transportation, telecommunication, administration, government, financial, command centers, security services, public health, air- and sea ports, military etc. Urban areas or public spaces are considered soft targets if a considerable number of fatalities and casualties must be expected in case of threat. Examples for such a scenario are the Metro attacks of Madrid (2004) and London (2005), the Bali attack (2005) or the horrible attack of Oslo in 2011. These attacks have in common that many people became victims in unsecured urban areas where many people gather because of waiting for a train or bus, shopping at markets, sitting in bars, public viewing, mass events etc. Protection against such asymmetric attacks towards soft targets requires completely new innovative strategies and measures. A video observation in

---

[*] Corresponding author.

N. Aschenbruck et al. (Eds.): Future Security 2012, CCIS 318, pp. 153–164, 2012.

combination with comparative image recognition software is extremely helpful but useless if suicide bombers act. A free, democratic and open society would never accept a surveillance state. Therefore, we need passive safety measures like innovative and architectural attractive building elements, landscape elements, gardening principles or artwork as part of city planning. This is a completely new approach.

From the structural point of view there are in principle four strategies that are combinable:

1. Increase of stand-off distance whenever possible
2. Initial protective design of a structure and its built-in components
3. Hardening of existing structures
4. Application of protective elements apart from a building

Whenever it is possible one should increase the stand-off distance between the source of explosion and the target. If we have to design new buildings, and if the threat is already defined, we have the chance to develop optimal solutions considering safety as well as architectural requirements within a given budget. If existing infrastructure has to be hardened we can use modular systems starting with safety foils to prevent glass breakage and end up with additional structural elements attached to the building or partly rebuilding of the structure. Protective elements apart from the building can be blast walls, bollards, water moat etc. In addition we can use innovative systems that have multiple functions. Especially the USA and Israel have undertaken some research and development efforts towards protection against terrorist threats (Federal Emergency Management Agency (FEMA) e.g. [6], [7]).

2   Potential Hazards

2.1   Explosions

If an explosion happens a huge amount of energy is abruptly released. We have to distinguish between contact explosions, near field explosions, and far field explosions. Contact- and near field explosions generate a localized but intensive damage to the building materials. These effects shall not be discussed here. For detailed information we refer to [8], [11], [12]. In the following we mainly concentrate on the action of far field explosions. A blast wave generated by far field explosions is characterized by its shock front, the peak pressure p_1 and the atmospheric pressure p_0 neglecting the rise time (Fig. 1, left). The difference between the peak pressure p_1 and the atmospheric pressure p_0 is the peak overpressure. Having reached the peak pressure the pressure decreases to the atmospheric pressure. This time period is called overpressure phase. Then the pressure decreases further below the atmospheric pressure resulting in a suction phase. Integration of the overpressure with respect to time yields the impulse of the blast wave.

Once the travelling blast wave front hits an obstacle the overpressure increases due to reflections at a surface. The reflected overpressure can be up to 20 times the initial overpressure [8]. Furthermore there are multiple reflections in built environments or if indoor explosions take place. These multiple reflections cannot be described by analytical or empirical equations. Such situations have to be numerically modeled using computational fluid dynamics (CFD) methods. In addition the materials exhibit an increase of strength and stiffness due to strain rates [10], and a strong compaction under high hydrostatic pressure.

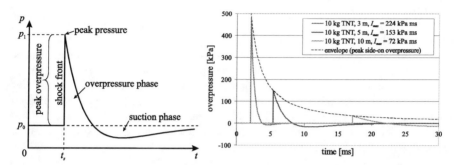

Fig. 1. Far field explosion, ideal pressure-time-distribution (left), Overpressure--histories, explosion of 10 kg TNT, spherical wave propagation, distances of 3 m, 5 m and 10 m (right)

If people are hit by blast waves they might suffer injuries like ear drum failure, lung collapse, or debris impact. Their probability can be estimated using empirical formulae [13].

Figure 1 (right) gives the idealized overpressure-time-histories of three explosion scenarios: 10 kg TNT in stand-off distances of 3 m, 5 m und 10 m and their envelope (dotted line). From Figure 1 (right) we can deduce the simplest and most effective protection rule: distance protects!

2.2   Debris Impact

In an explosion event debris might result from cracking of structural or building elements (concrete fragments, glass splinter etc.) or from missiles. Often IEDs are prepared with metallic bullets, nails or splinters. From the physical protection point of view there are two main strategies to counteract. On the one hand we try to increase the stand-off distance. On the other hand we try to avoid that debris can be originated or that developed debris can fly off. These methods are not discussed here.

2.3   Vehicle Attack, Impact, Violent Access

Vehicles can be loaded with a huge amount of explosives and they have a certain mass that can be accelerated. Therefore a vehicle might break through gates, damage massive walls or drive into groups of people. Such a situation might cause a cascade effect if the vehicle damages a wall or a column heavily such that as a consequence the entire building collapses. An example is the attack against the Murrah Federal Building in Oklahoma City in 1995. Attackers might use vehicles to enforce violent access to buildings, installations or facilities. This is for two main reasons, first to get access, second to bring explosives close to the target. There are several opportunities to reduce such threats. We can create obstacles, like traffic islands, that avoid high speed driving, or install bollards, high curbs, or security gates.

2.4   Landscape Architecture, Terrain Modelling

If the real estate and the infrastructure allow terrain modeling it can be used to reduce the effectiveness of a blast wave or prevent from vehicle entering. Sloping grounds, ditches, hills, sags, or banquettes deflect and reflect blast waves and at the same time they create stand-off distance. Figure 2 shows three cases where each case faces an explosion of 100 kg TNT at a distance of 15 m [9]. The numerical studies show the pressure distribution of the blast wave. On the left the building is not protected. In the middle a blast wall has been chosen as protection. On the right the sloped ground serves as blast wave barrier. In order to assess the real blast load we compare the reflected overpressure and the corresponding impulses at the front of the building (Fig. 3). The unprotected building suffers the highest loading. The blast wall protects better than the sloped ground. But the sloped ground can be optimized or combined with a smaller blast wall. Thus, architectural attractive protection systems can be designed with great creativeness.

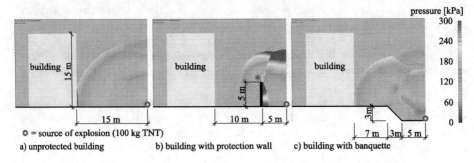

Fig. 2. Building, blast wall, blast wave propagation at sloped ground [9]

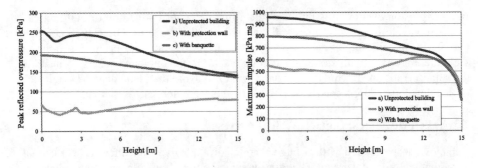

Fig. 3. Landscaping, comparison of the loadings on the buildings (shown over building height)

Numerical studies published in [1], [2] reveal that sloped terrain is more effective than ditches. The decrease of the peak overpressure was roughly linearly with the height of the slope and reached 25% reduction at a height of 3m. The reduction was about 10% using a ditch that was 3 m deep.

Terrain modeling is the three-dimensional design of the terrain using additional structural elements and elements of garden architecture. An example is the "Minneapolis Courthouse Plaza" (Figure 4). The mounds and the tree trunks of the fore court symbolize Minnesota's nature. At the same time they act as safety elements avoiding undesirable access and providing distance. The landscape architectural design of the fore court combines several aspects and functions like attractive architecture, symbolic sculptures, nature, and protection. The non-expert might not recognize that this is a substantial passive element of the safety and security concept of the entire facility.

Fig. 4. Minneapolis courthouse plaza; photo: FEMA [7]

Sloping grounds can also be achieved by creating discontinuous slopes, in other words stairs. One single high stair is a vertical ground offset. Thus we can creatively play around with different options in order to create safety elements.

2.5   Walls, Blast Walls, Wall Elements

Perimeter walls might have several functions like generate distance, blast barrier, view barrier, fragment barrier. The disadvantages of walls are that they are mostly not attractive, and they give the feeling of living behind walls. Therefore, if walls are required it is a challenge to design them such that disadvantages are avoided.

Fig. 2 shows in the middle the numerical blast wave distribution around a blast wall. The shielding of the wall can be seen which is proven quantitatively in building Fig. 3. Noticeably the blast pressure is mainly reduced in the lower area of the building's exterior wall [17]. Protection walls can only exhibit their effectiveness if their distance to the building is not too large. The blast wave streams over the crown of the wall down to the ground and again develops a blast front. Therefore there are three main design parameters: stand-off distance between charge and building, distance between blast wall and building, height of blast wall. A further (limiting) parameter is the resistance of the wall against the blast pressure. The wall cannot have any height or width and the foundation must be possible. Usual blast walls are up to 5 meters tall. This is a compromise between the competing goals of protection requirement and economic solution. In general ordinary walls are not accepted by the open and free society. Therefore we have to find new solutions. One solution might be to arrange wall elements such that the protection requirements are met. In addition the wall elements might look like sculptures. Doing so, the walls might become sculptural elements of city planning artwork. In the following some suggestions are listed (Fig. 5):

- V-, T- or Y-form of wall elements in cross-section and or elevation,
- Staggered walls,
- Modification over height,
- Planting of walls with bushes and or blooms,
- Combination of different materials (e.g. concrete, steel, wood, bulk material cages)
- Combination with water game / fountains.

Just a few of these wall elements have been studied numerically [14], [15]. In order to prevent the blast wave from flowing around the crown of the wall the vertical shape of the wall has to be optimized. At the same time such a wall might prevent from climbing over. There are no limitations for the design of the crown. These walls can be made of arbitrary material. It is not just concrete that can be used. Steel sheets, perforated steel sheets or multi-layered materials can advantageously be applied. The walls shall be elements of architectural city planning. Thus, they might be generally accepted by the society. These walls need not necessarily to be fixed for all times. They can also be mobile installations for temporary use. Protective walls that are known from flood protection are alternatives. They can be made of rubber like material and filled with water (water tanks) or air (pneumatic structures) [3]. Their protection capabilities have to be studied in the future.

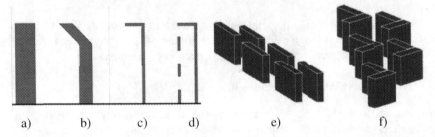

a)   b)   c)   d)   e)   f)

Fig. 5. Protection walls (a) -- d): vertical section, e) and f): perspective drawing), design possibilities for enhancement of reduction of blast wave

Possible protection measures for buildings and installations depend essentially on the property that exist or that shall be purchased. How can we generate stand-off distance, how shall the building be placed on the property, is landscaping possible, is the property surrounded by roads, how is access possible (land, water, air), etc. These are questions that need to be answered. In addition the costs for the property have to be compared with the costs for physical protection. Based on the physics of blast waves a stand-off distance of more than 30 m can be suggested.

In order to characterize stand-off distance a little bit we have to remember how explosives can be transported. There are letter bombs addressed to a specific person or installation. They usually carry explosives of up to 100 g. Parcel bombs might have explosive mass of 10kg or even more. These bombs can be detected if post offices are equipped with detection devices. People walking around with backpacks are not just tourists even managers have realized the comfort of backpacks. Therefore people with backpacks can be seen everywhere. They cannot enter every building but the creation of stand-off distance in the urban environment is practically impossible. So we have to think about how to mitigate the effects of a (dirty) backpack bomb of up to 20 kg explosives in certain defined places (popular bars, public viewing areas, etc.). The access of vehicles (cars, trucks) to buildings, properties and places can be restricted. The applied protection measures depend on the principal question whether force shall be shown (embassies, military installations, ministries, industrial facilities, etc.) or whether force shall be hidden (hotels, banks, shopping centers, theaters, etc.). Besides walls bollards are visible barriers clearly indicating their purpose. Bollard systems are on the market in a huge variety. A simple system is made of concrete elements set into concrete foundations. Bollards of high technology are installations that can slide up and down on demand and they are instrumented with light elements and certain sensors that can operate the bollards. Sensors in the pavement of the access road detect speed and weight of vehicles. These security elements complement the protective bollards. A series of bollards viewed from certain angles gives the impression of a wall (Figure 6, left). Jersey barriers (Figure 6, right) are cheap and easy to bring in place, but they are recognized bothersome.

Fig. 6. Examples of barrier systems, left: bollards, right: Jersey barriers; photo right: FEMA [7]

When we try not to show force or when we have to develop solutions for usual urban areas we have at first the chance to break up the boring series of bollards and combining them with other protection elements like planting buckets, trees or massive elements to sit on (Figure 7, Figure 8). Further elements that can be used are benches, rocks, street lamps, bus stopping areas, or even secured kiosks. Totally inconspicuous are sculptures or artwork as given in Figure 8 with the NOGO-barrier of Rogers Marvel Architects erected in the New York City Financial District. The NOGO-barrier is made of sculptured bronze blocks (Figure 8). These blocks can be mounted to turn tables which allow for open the barrier. These elements have multiple functions like protective elements, sculptures, and playground to be experienced. The ordinary person does not recognize that these elements are there for the purpose of protection, and, therefore, these elements do not affect unfavorably the daily life of the people.

In order to reduce the impact energy of vehicles it is recommended to design access roads such that the driving velocity s reduced to a certain level. Effective elements are pavement sleepers, narrow tracks, traffic islands, indenting bays.

In former time ponds, moats, and moor have been used to protect castles and palaces. Especially moors were insuperable. At the same time these elements might serve as natural habitats thus being recreational places. In winter the water might freeze resulting in loss of protection because ponds and moats become conquerable. But also in summer people might use boats or canoes to cross the water. Therefore, in order to complement the safety and security measures additional installations are necessary like cameras and or smart fences that are able to detect undesirable trespasser.

Fig. 7. Bollards, trees between bollards and different sizes of bollards reduce monotony; photos: FEMA [7]

Fig. 8. NOGO barrier, bronze sculptures as seats; photos: FEMA [7]

Moor and wetlands have been the archetypes of the „TigerTrap-System" (TTS). This not recognizable protection system is comprised of a deformable substrate in a ditch which is covered by a layer (collapsible material) that can carry pedestrians and cyclists but collapses under heavier loads (vehicles). Once a vehicle has broken into the TTS the affected portion need to be repaired.

2.6 Curtains

Architecturally and artistically appealing are curtains that are mitigating the effect of explosions. At the same time curtains can be a collision protection to prevent vehicles from entering. These protective systems can be elements of the building's or city planning architecture, or art elements that can be complemented with illuminations. Curtains can be transparent or non-transparent, translucent or light-proof, permeable to air or air-impermeable, plain or colored. Mostly they are wire meshes. Figure 10 displays a photo of a curtain made of steel ring meshwork which is illuminated at night. Steel ring meshwork is already known form medieval times when knights wore chain armor shirts to protect themselves from being knifed [4].

Fig. 9. Curtains made of steel ring meshwork, illuminated at night (Swarovski, Wattens, Austria); photo: daniel swarovski & co Wattens; alphamesh

Figure 9 gives a good impression of the curtain design. Illumination of buildings, bridges, fountains, and artwork has become very popular. For the curtain a light choreography has been composed which is very impressive. Steel ring meshwork can be designed such that an arbitrary protection goal can be met.

The protection capabilities of steel ring meshwork are hardly studied yet. We are just in the beginning. At the Federal testing center WTD52 first tests have been carried out. These tests showed that we additionally have to consider the fasteners at the boundaries because they have been the weakest elements under blast so far.

The wire mesh is flexible itself but it might be favorable to design additionally flexible fasteners. Thus, the forces that are transferred to the superstructure are smoothed out with time. A main problem that has been observed is the pull out of localized single fasteners. Spring fasteners can be applied that can transform blast energy into elastic deformation energy. The development of such spring-damper-elements is actually under progress [18].

2.7 Natural Protection

The authors have been asked to assess the safety and security of an important facility where it was not advised to show force. When we inspected the property which was nicely planted with bushes and trees (broadleaf trees, conifers) the question came up what their blast protection could be. Plantings, especially trees and plant baskets can ensure stand-off distance being at the same time blast protection. But how can we approach this challenge? Gardeners know that after shredding a huge hill of branches there is almost nothing left than a small crop of biological mass. And, in fact, the biological mass of a usual hedge is just about 7% in volume. In order to have protection all the year the bushes and trees need to be evergreen. Evergreen plants are for example yew tree, thuya, conifers, or hardy laurel cherry. Hedges in urban areas have multiple purposes. They are not just fencing properties, they provide valuable biotope for insects, bugs, and birds, they provide photosynthesis all year round, filtering air, provide protection against wind and noise, and are being screens. This is why usually people feel comfortable in a green environment.

Fig. 10. Hedge plants: coniferous trees (Thuja, left), sketch of the problem (right)

In order to check whether hedges are capable to mitigate the effects of blast waves we have carried out a numerical study. The simulated scenario is given in Figure 10 (right). A 5 kg charge is placed 5 m in front of a rigid wall. Between the charge and the wall a hedge has been planted which is 1m in width and 1m in height. Provided that estimated densities for wood and leaves of 400 to 700 kg/m³ are true we can determine that approximately 1 % to 7 % of hedge volume is organic material. In our numerical study we investigate volume fractions of 1 % and 5 %.

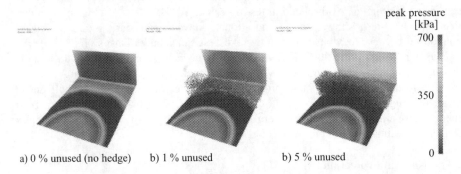

a) 0 % unused (no hedge)   b) 1 % unused   b) 5 % unused

Fig. 11. Hedge, numerical simulation, peak overpressures

The main problem was how to numerically model the hedge. In order to determine a first estimate the hedge was simplified such that the volume was discretized with a numerical Eulerian grid of volume elements from which 1% and 5% respectively were set "unused". Thus, the hedge is numerically modeled a rigid grid (Figure 11). The distribution of the "unused-elements" was randomly. The small hedge elements (unused-elements) are fixed in position and do not move or deform like leaves do. The blast wave will be reflected and scattered at the hedge particles disturbing its free distribution.

The results of the simulation can be seen in Figure 11. In color the overpressure distribution at a certain time is plotted. On the left no hedge is present. In the middle the hedge consists of 1% biological material, on the right 5%. In order to study the effectiveness of the hedge blast protection the maximum reflected peak pressures at the wall are compared (Table 1).

Table 1. Reduction of peak overpressure and of impulse by hedges (simulation)

Model	p_{ro} [kPa]	Reduction	I_{max} [Pa s]	Reduction
No hedge	627	-	537	-
1 %-Hedge	570	9 %	503	6 %
5 %-Hedge	381	39 %	404	2 5%

Table 1 shows the quantitative results in terms of reflected peak overpressure pro and of the related maximum impulse I_{max}. The hedge with 1% mass fraction already reduces the pressure with 9% and the 5% mass hedge reduces the pressure at 39% which is significant. The qualitative result of the study is that hedges reduce the blast loading of the wall. This result needs to be verified and validated in the future.

2.8   Water Games

In various publications (e.g. [5], [16]) investigations concerning the influence of water dust on the distribution of blast waves are reported. A main result is that atomized water can reduce the effect of a blast wave. In [5] a reduction of the peak overpressure of about 45 % is reported. These results might initiate investigations with usual water games that are present permanently. Usual water games are for example waterfalls, water fountains, water curtains or combinations of wire mesh curtains with down running water. The creativeness is not limited. Such water games can be permanently installed or temporarily if certain events need to be protected. The idea of using water games as blast barriers is very innovative. In order to put such systems into practice systematic research and development has to be carried out in the future.

3   Summary

In the past terroristic attacks have been addressed against soft targets. This article provides various protection systems that are especially designed to fit into urban areas where usual protection systems disturb the environment and the desire for freedom. The governing idea is always that distance protects. Most of the systems can help ensuring the standoff distance. Combining all the requirements we were looking for natural solutions using architectural, artwork, gardening, and landscaping measures. This new and innovative field is just in the beginnings.

Acknowledgement. The authors acknowledge the funding that was provided by the department „BauProtect" of the Federal Office of Disaster Management and Civil Protection.

References

1. Barakat, M.A., Hetherington, J.G.: New architectural forms to reduce the effects of blast waves and fragments on structures. Structures Under Shock and Impact V, 53–62 (1998)
2. Barakat, M.A., Hetherington, J.G.: Architectural approach to reducing blast effects on structures. In: Proceedings of the Institution of Civil Engineers: Structures and Buildings, pp. 333–343 (1999)
3. Barnes, I., Thomas, D.B., Diaper, R.L.: The evaluation of a commercial water tank barrier system for mitigation of explosives fragmentation and blast. In: International Symposium on Military Aspects of Blast and Shock (MABS) 18, Bad Reichenhall (2004)
4. Burger, U.: Impactverhalten von hybriden Verbundwerkstoffen mit metallischem Ringgeflecht. Dissertation, Technische Universität Berlin (2009)
5. Chauvin, A., Zerbib, J., Jourdan, G., Daniel, E., Mariani, C., Houas, L., Biamino, L., Tosello, R., Praguine, D.: Investigation of the attenuation of a shock wave passing through a water spray. In: International Symposium on Military Aspects of Blast and Shock (MABS) 21, Jerusalem, (2010)
6. Federal Emergency Management Agency. FEMA 426: Reference Manual to Mitigate Potential Terrorist Attacks Against Buildings. FEMA (2003)
7. Federal Emergency Management Agency. FEMA 430: Site and Urban Design for Security – Guidance Against Potential Terrorist Attacks. FEMA (2007)
8. Gebbeken, N., Döge, T.: Vom Explosionsszenario zur Bemessungslast. Der Prüfingenieur 29, 42–52 (2006)
9. Gebbeken, N., Döge, T.: Explosion Protection – Architectural Design, Urban Planning and Landscape Planning. International Journal of Protective Structures 1(1), 1–22 (2010)
10. Gebbeken, N., Ruppert, M.: A new material model for concrete in high-dynamic hydrocode simulations. Archive of Applied Mechanics 70, 463–478 (2000)
11. Hartmann, T., Pietzsch, A., Gebbeken, N.: A Hydrocode Material Model for Concrete. International Journal of Protective Structures 1(4), 443–468 (2010)
12. Larcher, M., Casadei, F.: Explosions in Complex Geometries - A Comparison of Several Approaches. International Journal of Protective Structures 1(2), 169–196 (2010)
13. Larcher, M., Solomos, G., Casadei, F., Gebbeken, N.: Simulation terroristischer Anschläge in Massenverkehrsmitteln. Bautechnik 88(4), 225–232 (2011)
14. Löhner, R., Baum, J.D.: An assessment of architecturally appealing, semi-open shock mitigation devices. In: International Symposium on Military Aspects of Blast and Shock (MABS) 21, Jerusalem (2010)
15. Löhner, R., Camelli, F., Stück, A.: Adjoint-based design of passive shock mitigation devices. In: International Symposium on Military Aspects of Blast and Shock (MABS) 21, Jerusalem (2010)
16. Mataradze, E., Krauthammer, T., Chikhradze, N., Chagelishvili, E.: Influence of liquid phase concentration on shock wave attenuation in mist. In: International Symposium on Military Aspects of Blast and Shock (MABS) 21, Jerusalem (2010)
17. Smith, P.D.: Blast walls for structural protection against high explosive threads: a review. International Journal of Protective Structures 1, 67–84 (2010)
18. Teich, M., Gebbeken, N., Larcher, M.: Cable net facades subjected to explosion loads. In: International Symposium on the Application of Architectural Glass. Engineering and architectural design of glass, Munich, Germany (2010)

Security for Critical Infrastructure and Urban Areas: A Holistic Approach to Urban Safety, Security and Resilience

William Hynes[*] and Stephen M. Purcell[**]

Abstract. For the first time, more than 50% of the world's population live in urban areas. In 1950, 30% of people were urban dwellers; by 2050 this figure is to rise to 70%. This trend brings with it increased security and safety threats in urban areas. The increased risk of catastrophic events, whether accidental or deliberate, or by way of natural disasters, means there is now more so than ever before, a need to ensure the resilience of our cities. Large scale urban built infrastructure is a critical node within the intertwined networks of urban areas, which include not only physical components, but also integrated hardware and software aspects. To date, a comprehensive and holistic approach to improve the resilience and security of large scale urban developments against attacks and disruptions, has not been developed thoroughly. The background to this paper comes from a forthcoming EUFP7 project, entitled HARMONISE.

Keywords: Resilience, Urban Security, Critical Infrastructure, HARMONISE, Built Environment, State of the Art, SOTA, Holistic Approach, Vulnerability.

1 Introduction: Why Do We Need a Holistic Approach to Urban Security and Resilience?

To date there is no comprehensive, holistic approach to improve resilience and security of large scale urban built infrastructure; this is a situation which is not helped by the lack of a clear definition of what amounts to urban resilience. Vulnerabilities to terrorism and natural disasters of our urban areas, together with the mechanisms to address them, continue to be studied, yet no holistic approach has been formulated to develop a systematic approach to the design and planning of large scale urban built infrastructure with resilience in mind. Cities have been identified, by Bugliarelio,[1] as being 'target rich' environments, within the context of terrorism; however, cities are just as susceptible to natural disasters. In 2010, for the first time since records began, natural catastrophes, such as floods, storms and earthquakes caused more damage (human and economic) than man-made disasters.[2] There is, now more so than ever before, a need for a holistic approach to

---

[*] Director Downey Hynes Partnership, Dublin, Ireland.

[**] Senior Associate Downey Hynes Partnership, Dublin, Ireland.

[1] Bugliarello, G. (2003) "Urban Security in Perspective", *Technology in Society,* Volume 25, Issue 4 : 499-507.

[2] Resilient Cities Forum (2011), Resilient Cities Congress Report, ICLEI.

N. Aschenbruck et al. (Eds.): Future Security 2012, CCIS 318, pp. 165–175, 2012.

urban resilience, with an emphasis on having the tools in place which are capable of dealing with all challenges, whether man-made or natural.

The typical responses taken by authorities when dealing with issues relating to resilience traditionally revolve around physical measures, such as modifications or retrofitting of at-risk buildings, combined with an increase in security personnel. Such measures are typically aimed at tackling issues relating to some form of attack, usually of the more traditional terrorist type, and, as such, are less compatible at dealing with natural disasters and their aftermath. The severity of both terrorism and natural disasters or threatening events over the course of the last decade has prompted a requirement for buildings and related infrastructure to offer not only resistance, but functional capacity (e.g. safe shelter and critical operations) after a destructive incident. In this respect the concept of 'resilience' has become an increasingly utilized metaphor within the policy-making process and in the expanding institutional framework of national security, disaster preparedness and mitigation.[3]

In relation to urban resilience, the objective must be to mitigate the impact and sustain functionality for as far as is practically possible. To achieve this there is a requirement to have the conditions in place so that unforeseen outcomes can nonetheless be accommodated accurately and immediately through collective problem solving with improvisation and innovation.[4]

Resilience therefore in this context refers to a system's capacity "to continue its existence, or to remain more or less stable, in the face of surprise, either a deprivation of resources or a physical threat".[5] Within the built environment literature, resilience of the 'urban form' comprising buildings and related infrastructures has been traditionally construed as being primarily concerned with protection and recovery from natural hazards.[6] Depicting the evolving and increasingly complex nature of modern day security challenges the terminology of resilience – the ability of the urban system to 'bounce-back' - has therefore assumed a dual guise, encompassing the twin threats and challenges of climate change in parallel with the development of modernist counter-terrorism initiatives.

The current State of the Art (SOTA), as shown in Fig. 1 below, depicts the resilience of large scale urban buildings and related infrastructure, as comprising of six interrelated concepts. These concepts support resilience through the promotion of good initial design and construction for new facilities, effective retrofit for existing facilities, and appropriate operational programs to ensure that mitigation plans are in place, and building systems operate as required in response to events of disaster/hazard. The following is an overview of each concept.

---

[3] Coaffee, J., O'Hare, P., and Hawkesworth, M. (2009) "The Visibility of (In) Security: The Aesthetics of Planning Urban Defences Against Terrorism". *Security Dialogue*, 40: 489-511.

[4] Demchak, C. (2010) "Lessons from the Military: Surprise, Resilience, and the Atrium Model", In: Comfort, L., Boin, A. and Demchak, C. (Eds.): *Designing Resilience: Preparing for Extreme Events*, University of Pittsburg Press: Pittsburg.

[5] Longstaff, P. (2005) "Security, resilience and communication in unpredictable environments such as terrorism, natural disasters and complex technology". In: Programme on Information Resources Policy, Centre for Information Policy Research, Harvard University.

[6] Pelling, M. (2003) *The Vulnerability of Cities: Natural Disasters and Social Resilience*, London: Earthscan.

Fig. 1. Overview of the Current State of the Art in resilience of large scale urban buildings

Multi-functionality of Complex Urban Areas – The advent of the 24/7 society incorporating mixed-use/mixed tenure buildings has mitigated many security risks and at the same time enhanced resident perceptions of 'safety' and 'security'. Planning must take place in a way that it accounts for future urban development, the changing climate and the radicalization of modern terrorist threats. It calls for making use of smarter infrastructure, investment and land-use planning, among others. The use of green infrastructure needs to be embedded into urban design and planning for a holistic approach to urban resilience.

Energy Efficiency and Sustainability – There is an inexorable link between resilience and energy use; increasing the energy efficiency of the existing, as well as the future building stock is of crucial importance to this.[7] Energy efficient buildings seek to maximize opportunities for indoor environmental quality and performance; saving money, reducing waste, increasing worker productivity, etc. There is also a need for access to a decentralized power supply system, which maximizes the use of renewable energy; this model of energy provision would boost the security of supply both in the context of an increasing threat of terrorist attack as well as the impending peak oil crisis. In order for this type of energy supply model to be successful, it would require a low energy built environment in order to function effectively. In relation to energy and sustainability the current SOTA focuses predominantly on decision-support systems (DSS) for the integrated management of energy efficiency and emission-reduction requirements as well as developing new methods for automated intelligent energy management that specifically looks to improve building energy efficiency in a cost-effective manner.

Technological Innovation – This has primarily focused on tracking and monitoring of threats over the last decade. The use of CCTV based 'Smart cameras', facial recognition imagery and programmes which monitor crowd behavior patterns have become increasingly important in detecting risks. Technological innovation has not just focused on threat identification; there have also been developments in the use of technology to mitigate the worst effects of events should they happen. It is now possible that buildings could be equipped with information systems which would give up-to-the-minute real

---

[7] ULI (2010) *'Resilient Cities: Surviving in a New World'*. A Urban Land Institute Investment Network Report. November 2010.

time information on escape routes, and in doing so, improve the likelihood of the survival of occupants should some type of attack or natural disaster take place.

Construction Material Resilience – Building materials and designs are constantly developing and evolving. The materials used in particular buildings can be adapted to suit particular threats; similarly, the building design and the arrangement of the core functions within the building can be arranged in such a manner to provide resilience from specific threats.

Smart 'Unconventional' Business Solutions – Use of Smart structures can be seen as a response to the increasing size and, by association, the increasing probability of incidents relating to this size of modern structures. Smart Structures Engineering is a marriage between civil/structural engineering and electronic/IT engineering. Smart Structures are similar to the nervous system of the human body, in that they can detect an unhealthy condition in the building. This then enables the call for a detailed inspection of the structure, the diagnosis of the problem and the provision of a solution and remedial actions.

Integration of Approach – When dealing with urban resilience, the SOTA approach still must encapsulate the need to limit the consequences of failure and accelerate restoration capabilities; this need exists as the risks to buildings and cities are 'managed, never entirely eradicated'.[8] Systems (technological and human) pertaining to the security and resilience of buildings/building complexes/building arrangements are inherently interconnected and are particularly vulnerable to cascading-type failures from a single event.[9] The 'holistic approach' to the development and protection of large scale urban built infrastructure is essential, with an awareness of where failure in one building/building complex can lead to a cascade of failures elsewhere. An 'integrated approach' to the security and resilience of large scale urban built infrastructure is needed to capture the levels of interdependence at the 'operational level'. This will allow enhanced understanding and more effective management of the interactions. It will also facilitate recognition of higher order dependencies which impact upon and emerge from buildings/building complexes.

This paper advocates the view that an 'integrated and holistic strategy' (an integrative philosophy depicting socio-technological innovation) that incorporates technology, people and institutions will achieve fundamentally greater security and resilience pertaining to large scale urban built infrastructure as well as possible ancillary benefits from other hazards.

2   Opportunities for Integration

Under the Seventh Framework Programme (FP7) Research and Technical Development project on urban security and resilience being carried out across Europe; one of

[8] Heng, Y.K. (2006) 'The Transformation of War Debate: Through the Looking Glass of Ulrich Beck's World Risk Society'. *International Relations*, 20:1, 69-91.
[9] Little, R. G. (2002) "Controlling Cascading Failure: Understanding the Vulnerabilities of Interconnected Infrastructures". *Journal of Urban Technology*, 9:1, 109–123.

these projects, scheduled to commence in 2013, is a pan-European program entitled HARMONISE (A Holistic Approach to Resilience and SysteMatic ActiOns to Make Large Scale UrbaN Built Infrastructure SEcure) which will seek to address the shortfall in the integration and standardization of urban resilience systems. The central aim of HARMONISE is to develop a comprehensive, multi-faceted, yet mutually-reinforcing concept for the enhanced security, resilience and sustainability of large scale urban built infrastructure and development.

It seems that in the urban ecosystem, security/resilience solutions are developed by stakeholders based on their own needs and purposes. The most obvious gap in the SOTA is the lack of a comprehensive and strategic approach where large interdependent building complexes/infrastructures are seen holistically, thus paving the way for the design of joint resilience. Such an approach needs to be supported by (web-based) IT-tools, educational multi-media, worked exemplars/case studies and continuing professional development for urban planning professionals. Currently, integration between security, building management systems and energy efficiency systems cannot be achieved effectively, as each level of integration demands considerable specific tailoring between each of the different systems in order to make them compatible with each other.

The security and resilience of large scale urban built infrastructure is a critical subject within the EU. While there is clear direction from the EU in general, the subject area is dealt with in widely different manners across Europe – within individual member states there are often different approaches, different actors, different interests, different results, etc. Greater integration of the theme of security and resilience pertaining to large scale urban built infrastructure can be achieved by the utilization of an integrated framework of the type which is advocated in Fig. 2 below.

Fig. 2. The proposed framework model and how it intends to make advances to the SOTA

The concept of creating linkages between interdependent building complexes draws upon the axioms of several disciplines, including the large scale technical systems field, behavioral studies pertaining to hazardous incidents, the emerging collaboration studies field, organization theory and information systems. This type of approach advances the existing SOTA pertaining to the resilience of large scale urban buildings and their related infrastructures by offering an innovative and integrated approach comprising an interactive semantic intelligence platform, transcending technological systems and multi-stakeholder groupings, and depicting a more integrated and collaborative approach to resilience planning. This cross-disciplinary approach necessitates the bringing together of different professional disciplines, methodologies and occupational cultures to successfully channel their respective expertise and skill sets towards shared goals and outcomes; facilitating organic and emergent processes to stimulate novel and innovative practices.

Existing platforms are developed for individual buildings and do not support large areas with multiple buildings. Moreover the complexity of security and resilience increases radically with multiple buildings. In short, a common view to all systems is missing; there are only separate views to some parts of the systems. Also, a clearly defined interface to exchange information between buildings is currently lacking. One means which could be used to address this inherent shortcoming within the urban resilience framework is by advocating an integrated 'locale' based approach, depicting the urban character, the relationships and technological interface capacities between buildings and related infrastructures within relative proximity, and the occupiers and users of buildings. This type of comprehensive approach, where large interdependent building complexes/infrastructures are seen holistically, would pave the way for the design of joint resilience and would be supported by (web-based) component tools. The development of an interactive semantic intelligence platform would be able to both host and enable a portfolio of search, diagnostic, scenario modeling, management and educational tools.

This kind of interactive platform would be required to host a shared space and knowledge repository in order to adapt to the needs of whatever situation it may be necessary to deal with. Such a workspace setting would facilitate a holistic, multidisciplinary approach which has the capacity to organically transform into an interactive knowledge hub. This type of inter-linked holistic approach would provide a robust and dynamic platform for delivering resilient large scale urban built infrastructure in a way which advances the current SOTA. A platform of this type could be further developed, so that existing applications which are currently used to monitor energy use at the urban area level, could become fully integrated, thus allowing them to be used to promote greater integration and allow for the balancing of sustainability and security as key underlying principles depicting the resilience of the built environment.

The successful use of a combination of integrated systems combined with stakeholder participation across professional institutions will encourage the embedment within building and planning codes or guidance for sustainable construction. In the future a more inclusive and joined-up approach to integrating security and environmental sustainability should be advanced through the greater collaboration between a wide range of stakeholders - architects, engineers, planners, law enforcement, insurers, surveyors, and, importantly, the public.[10]

---

[10] Coaffee, J., O'Hare, P., and Hawkesworth, M. (2009) "The Visibility of (In)Security: The Aesthetics of Planning Urban Defences Against Terrorism". *Security Dialogue*, 40: 489-511.

2.1   Addressing the Challenges: Advancing the SOTA Using the Platform and Toolkit

In conjunction with the development of the above software platform, the introduction of an innovative tool kit, ranging from a best practice guidance document/manual, through to simulation modelling/scenario tools will also enable the assessment and analysis of security and resilience pertaining to large scale urban built infrastructure to establish an evidenced-based body of knowledge. A best practice guidance document/manual will be implemented across Europe and will be generically adopted within urban areas incorporating large scale urban built infrastructures.

The sharing of the information between different systems, and the interfacing of this information in an emergency management, egress strategy and safety application is a challenge, but one which is not insurmountable and can be achieved. Whilst existing platforms are designed for individual buildings and do not extend to support large urban areas with multiple buildings, a platform which can carry out this type of function on larger urban areas would certainly be a significant leap forward in terms of the SOTA. This will allow for the creation of a common platform upon which all systems can be viewed independently and holistically. In addition, and more importantly, a clearly defined interface to exchange information between separate buildings will be developed.

The utilization of information from energy-efficiency systems (monitoring, sensors, building management systems) in combination with security/safety systems will also be used to demonstrate the feasibility of this type of advanced management system. For example, new safety features would enable visualization of the optimal rescue route in case of emergency for the public through the digital signage system of a building. This feature will combine information from several sources, e.g. smoke detectors, temperature sensors, occupancy detectors, from fire alarm system and building automation system, to show optimal routes through the digital signage system.[11]

2.2   The HARMONISE Model

The background to this paper is based upon the forthcoming HARMONISE project, which will be funded under EU Seventh Framework Programme within Topic-2012.2.1-1, Resilience of Large Scale Urban Built Infrastructure – Capability Project. This is aimed at addressing the activity of increasing the security of infrastructures and utilities within the area of design, planning of buildings and urban areas.

HARMONISE will result in significant resilience enhancement methods for large scale urban built infrastructure. This project will be grounded in a holistic view of innovation and will advocate synergies with, and augmentation of, existing FP7 projects such as VITRUV, RIBS and DESURBS among others. The project recognises the necessity to improve the design of urban areas and increase their security against, and resilience to, new threats. The practical objectives of HARMONISE are outlined in Table 1 below.

---

[11] Galea et al., (2006) *BuildingEXODUS V4.06*, User Guide and Technical Manual, Doc Rev 4.05, University of Greenwich, UK.

Table 1. The practical objectives of HARMONISE

HARMONISE Objectives	Practical Objectives
(A) HARMONISE Inter-active Semantic Intelligence Platform (HISIP)	It is intended that the use of the HARMONISE platform will mean that buildings and infrastructure will be planned and constructed with the primary principles of resilience and sustainable development in-built from the first stages of the design process.
(B) Innovative Toolkit	The HARMONISE toolkit will include a series of innovative and purposefully designed applications which will be aimed at improving the safety, security, sustainability and general resilience of large scale built infrastructure.
(C) Dissemination	It is intended that the information which is gathered through the work of HARMONISE will be made widely available, enabling its practical application by the full spectrum of stakeholders actively engaged in the resilience of large scale built infrastructure.
(D) Commercialization	The completed HARMONISE platform and associated toolkit will made available commercially, with ongoing support, continuous updates and adaptations involving a mixture of SMEs, government stakeholders and contractors from both the construction and security industries.

3   Methodology for the Delivery of a Holistic Concept

The development of an integrated approach to urban resilience and the advancement of the SOTA will encompass a five phase methodological framework, as described in Table 2 below.

Each phase will need to be carried out seamlessly, with clear inter-linkages and continual exchange of information permeating through all stages. This type of approach ensures that the results and conclusions of the various phases are incorporated at appropriate stages throughout, enabling the gradual refinement and advancement of the concept.

Through the application of a real life case study module within the methodology, a more thorough examination of the proposed interactive semantic intelligence platform, the associated toolkit, as well as any recommended changes to building or planning codes/rules can be made. Each of the specific case studies would have to be chosen with a focus on large-scale buildings/building complexes/building arrangements such as shopping centres/areas, sports venues or combinations of business centres with underground transportation nodes; in doing so, the selected case studies will be representative of the diversity among the built urban form. This will allow a comprehensive assessment and iterative development process in terms of the tools that will be developed while providing a robust test-bed for the integrated information platform to be developed. The state of the art built infrastructure protection products and planning/engineering tools currently practiced/envisaged at these case study areas will be analyzed to identify existing constraints, shortfalls and capability gaps.

Table 2. Proposed phases and associated actions

Phase	Action Points
Phase 1: Towards an Understanding of Urban Security and Resilience	· Establish a common frame of reference for increased resilience of large urban built infrastructure; · Undertake a thematic review of current SOTA and formulation of gap analysis of approaches, methods, tools; · Commence multi-disciplinary engagement.
Phase 2: Development of a Shared Holistic Concept for Greater Urban Security and Resilience (of Large Scale Urban Development)	· Begin development of a web-based Interactive Semantic Intelligence Platform; · Establish a protocol of access and operational capacity of the platform depending on user type and requirements.
Phase 3: Formulation of Mechanisms/Tools for Delivery of Improved Urban Security and Resilience	· Apply a multi-disciplinary, holistic suite of tools to ensure optimum integration/interactions; · Develop design and planning guidelines.
Phase 4: Case Study Application and Scenario Modelling	· Undertake a case study of Interactive Semantic Intelligence Platform, along with holistic approach and toolkit on five areas within Europe.
Phase 5: Evaluation & Adaptation of Implementation Methods and Integration Process	· Thorough testing and widespread adaptation of Interactive Semantic Intelligence Platform, holistic approach and toolkit.

While the method described is inherently superficial, through the application of the vision outlined above within the methodological approach, a viable and robust framework for a holistic approach to security of large scale built infrastructure can be achieved.

4   Conclusions

In terms of the security and future long term sustainability of the continuously expanding urban areas of the world, addressing issues of urban resilience must be a priority for all involved in the design and planning of our cities. The culmination of threats posed by global terrorism and natural disasters, together with such impending issues as 'peak oil', results in the need to proactively tackle matters concerning urban resilience.

Having identified a means by which the current SOTA can be advanced through the integration and development of existing systems, this paper has sought to highlight the way forward in terms of urban resilience. The primary outcome of an integrated approach, as outlined above, will be to:

— Facilitate a systematic approach (vis-a-vis the proposed HARMONISE Interactive Semantic Intelligence Platform) to develop a security and resilience concept for a combination of complex and dynamic urban systems. This will allow for improved situational awareness across a collection of buildings or building complexes, resulting in the optimization of responses to whatever situation may arise.
— Deliver supporting tools (hosted within the same platform) for the design/planning stage of large scale urban built infrastructure development; these tools will have been tested and enhanced through the evaluation of the quality case studies. This will result in the introduction of a set of new urban design criterion, which encompasses the values of urban resilience. This will ensure that urban designers embrace the need to consider services, security measures and infrastructure into their design, to ensure a properly integrated environment and a viable finished vision of the design from the outset.
— Provide an integrated approach to sharing building infrastructure and security information (building operation systems traditionally work in isolation) including critical flows of materials/energy and sensor technologies etc, while recognizing the important role of security culture and societal acceptance aspects. This will also see the introduction of integrated systems, between complexes of buildings, which are designed to make exiting the wider urban area safer in cases of emergency; this will be possible through the use of systems to adapt to information from sensor technology and to identify the routes which are safe and highlight those which are unsafe.

The results of this study will also be conducive to complementarities with other EU Seventh Framework Projects, specifically those relating to urban resilience and security. The information gathered could be used to feed into other projects at the EU level, not least VITRUV, RIBS and DESURBS. This will also result in the enhancement of the pool of European expertise on matters of urban resilience.

The improvement of the design of urban areas and systems, increasing their security against, and resilience to, new threats, will be the most important outcome of this study.

References

Bosher, L.: Hazards and the Built Environment: Attaining Built-In Resilience. Taylor-Francis, London (2008)

Bugliarello, G.: Urban Security in Perspective. Technology in Society 25(4), 499–507 (2003)

Coaffee, J., O'Hare, P., Hawkesworth, M.: The Visibility of (In)Security: The Aesthetics of Planning Urban Defences Against Terrorism. Security Dialogue 40, 489–511 (2009)

Demchak, C.: Lessons from the Military: Surprise, Resilience, and the Atrium Model. In: Comfort, L., Boin, A., Demchak, C. (eds.) Designing Resilience: Preparing for Extreme Events. University of Pittsburg Press, Pittsburg (2010)

Galea, E., Lawrence, P., Filippidis, L., Blackshields, D., Cooney, D.: Build-ingEXODUS V4.06, User Guide and Technical Manual, Doc Rev 4.05, University of Greenwich, UK (2006)

Heng, Y.K.: The Transformation of War Debate: Through the Looking Glass of Ulrich Beck's World Risk Society. International Relations 20(1), 69–91 (2006)

Little, R.G.: Controlling Cascading Failure: Understanding the Vulnerabili-ties of Interconnected Infrastructures. Journal of Urban Technology 9(1), 109–123 (2002)

Longstaff, P.: Security, resilience and communication in unpredictable environments such as terrorism, natural disasters and complex technology. In: Programme on Information Resources Policy. Centre for Information Policy Research, Harvard University (2005)

Pelling, M.: The Vulnerability of Cities: Natural Disasters and Social Resilience. Earthscan, London (2003)

Resilient Cities Forum, Resilient Cities Congress Report. ICLEI (2011)

ULI Resilient Cities: Surviving in a New World. A Urban Land Institute Investment Network Report (November 2010)

United Nations Department of Economic and Social Affairs/Population Division 1. World Urbanization Prospects: The 2009 Revision, 1–4 (2009)

Vulnerability Identification and Resilience Enhancements of Urban Environments

Kai Fischer[1], Werner Riedel[1], Ivo Häring[1], Albert Nieuwenhuijs[2], Stephen Crabbe[3], Steen S. Trojaborg[4], William Hynes[5], and Ingo Müllers[6]

[1] Fraunhofer Institute for High-Speed Dynamics, Ernst-Mach-Institut
Efringen-Kirchen, Germany
[2] TNO, Defence, Safety and Security, JG The Hague, Netherlands
[3] Crabbe Consulting Ltd, Erfurt, Germany
[4] DISSING+WEITLING Architecture, Copenhagen, Denmark
[5] Downey Hynes Partnership, Dublin, Ireland
[6] Schüssler-Plan Ingenieurgesellschaft mbH, Düsseldorf, Germany

Abstract. Steadily increasing number of the world's population is living in urban centres. The issue of security and citizen safety in densely populated areas is a growing concern. Considering terrorism and large scale accident scenarios, natural disasters and crime, urban planning practice must be complemented with vulnerability identification and resilience enhancements methods.

The VITRUV project, funded by the European Commission under its FP7 Research & Technical Development Programme, is carried out by a consortium of 12 industry partners, public end-users and research institutions drawn from 8 European countries. The aim is the development of software tools for the consideration of extraordinary threats. For the complex process of urban planning the tools supports the planning process through all three planning stages, from concept to plan and detail design, compatible with existing planning formats and software solutions. The qualitative or quantitative hazard and risk analysis of single buildings of infrastructure forms the basis. It consists of the analysis of events, scenarios, hazards, damage, frequency of events, exposure of personnel and risk including options for risk visualization and risk assessment for plan and detail level. Based on an all hazard risk approach, the tools will enable planners.

- to include a security assessment and security knowledge in their planning process, in order to make well-considered systematic qualitative decisions (concept level),
- to analyse the susceptibility of urban spaces with respect to new threats (plan level), and
- to perform vulnerability analysis of urban spaces by computing the likely damage on humans, buildings and traffic infrastructure (detail level).

1 Introduction

Urban planners need support to make decisions concerning the aspects of security and safety planning. This decision support will be made with user friendly software tools in

N. Aschenbruck et al. (Eds.): Future Security 2012, CCIS 318, pp. 176–179, 2012.

the EU-project VITRUV[1]. All three stages (see Fig. 1) will contribute to enable the development of more robust and resilient structures with respect to urban (re)planning, (re)design and/or (re)engineering. Planners who use VITRUV's tools will be able to deliver urban space less prone to and less affected by attacks and disasters, sustainably improving the security of citizens. Fig. 1 gives an overview of the operational stages of urban planning and the connection of each level to the software tools of the VITRUV-project.

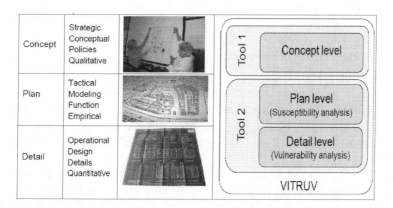

Fig. 1. Operational stages of urban planning (left) and tools overview of the VITRUV project (right)

2   Overview of the Tools

This section gives a brief overview of the three stages of urban planning and the associated tools which will be developed during the VITRUV project.

2.1   Concept Level Tool

The aim of the concept level tool is to provide an easy-to-use, computer assisted support for urban planners in a systematic, qualitative way in order to make decisions with regard to the security of cities concerning specific problems or goals. Although the tools will specifically focus on the issue of security, it recognizes the fact that urban planners work in a holistic environment, i.e. that they have to consider a widely varied range of aspects and interests from a multitude of parties.

This is why the tool will have to place its security information and advice within this context: it will not only widen the knowledge of urban planners in security related issues, but will also place these in relationships with the other aspects of the urban planners' decision space, which will encompass among others, the economic, social, ethical, safety and mobility dimensions.

---

[1] Fraunhofer EMI, Vulnerability Identification Tools for Resilience Enhancements of Urban Environments, 2012, http://www.vitruv-project.eu

The concept tool is composed of two inter-related components: the Knowledge Base (Securipedia) and the Risk Assessment (Securban). These components work closely together in supporting the urban planner: the risk assessment components guides the urban planner via a short questionnaire as quickly as possible to potential security issues.

The tool will output the list of potential security issues in two ways:

- A prioritised (sorted) list of security issues that are deemed relevant for addressing in the project-issues with insufficient relevance will not be displayed.
- A complete (sequential) list of all possible security issues with an indication of its relevance to the project.

The prioritised list will allow the user to quickly get an overview of the issues to be dealt with. The complete list allows the user to quickly compare the results of two risk assessments. This can for example be achieved by presenting all possible security issues in a standard format, with the relevance expressed in a colour or bar indicator behind the issue. By manually overlaying two printed end results, the differences can quickly be found.

In the output of the Securban tool there are direct links to the Securipedia. Here they are explained and more background information can be found about the security issue and possible measures to mitigate the risk. In Securipedia, the security issue and its possible solutions are related to all the various aspects of an urban planning process, such as the impact on economy, mobility, social life, safety or ethics.

2.2   Plan and Detail Level Tool

On the plan level of an urban planning process a susceptibility analysis will be carried out. This includes measures for frequency or probability of events based on specific building types. The susceptibility can be related to different quantities such as the frequency of (all/ selected) attack types for the considered building/ infrastructure types for example.

To get the empirical risk values for items of an urban area the frequency of events must be determined. Currently general crime and terrorist attacks are considered in this project. Further threats, like environmental disasters for example could be considered in future. In this paper examples concerning terrorist attacks will be presented.

To get empirical data of terrorist event the Fraunhofer EMI in-house database TED (Terror Event Database[2]) is used. The information from the TED are used in the project to determine the frequency of terrorist attacks, the tactic (e. g. car bomb), and the number of injuries and fatalities.

The empirical risk in dependency on the target (e.g. embassy or public place) is the result of this analysis. Hence on plan level the new tool can be used to analyse which parts of a city are mostly endangered.

The concept and plan level includes results for the guidance concerning risk assessment and an analysis concerning the susceptibility of targets in an urban area. In a

---

[2] U. Siebold and I. Häring, Terror Event Database and Analysis Software, in Future Security, 4th Security Research Conference, Karlsruhe, 2009.

next step the detail level is used to examine what are the effects of the threats that are identified during the plan level analysis. This examination will be carried out with a vulnerability analysis.

After the empirical risk analysis in the plan level the detail level tool includes algorithms for a quantitative risk assessment. The vulnerability is a measure for consequences risen from possible events. The vulnerability can be related to

- (local) average physical hazard in case of an attack,
- (local) average damage in case of an attack, and
- (local) average risk.

Within the approach the classic definition for risk computation is used. Therefore the quantitative risk is defined as a product of the frequency of an event and a measure for the consequences in the case the event happens.

The frequency is empirical determined during the plan level analysis. The consequences of considered threats can be calculated for persons and buildings. To calculate the structural response of buildings simplified engineering models are used. For this structural damage assessment more detailed information of the components are used, which are only available on detail level. Building costs and personal density are implemented to calculate lethality respectively structural damage and hence the derived risk for persons and buildings. The definition of the risk assessment on plan and detail level is precisely described and defined by Voss[3].

These results are used for risk mapping. In combination with a three-dimensional visualization the user gets a quick overview for the considered urban area. In a next step security measures can be used to minimize the risk. The visualisation of plan and detail level occurs with a user-friendly Graphical User Interface (GUI).

3   Conclusion

In this paper the aims and the contents of the EU-project VITRUV are presented. During this project different risk assessment tools for urban planners are developed. The development of the software allows an identification, detailed analysis and resilience enhancement of "weak points" in urban areas. The tools can be used for planning and (re)design of urban areas to make them less prone for and less affected by terrorist attacks and natural disasters.

Acknowledgements. The research leading to these results has received funding from the European Commission's 7th Framework Programme under grant agreement no. 261741. The contributions of all VITRUV consortium members are gratefully acknowledged.

---

[3] M. Voss, et.al.: „Susceptibility and vulnerability of urban buildings and infrastructure against terroristic threats from qualitative and quantitative risk analyses", in European Safety and Reliability Association, ESREL Conference, Helsinki, 2012.

Determining the Effectiveness of Safety Measures for Self-rescue in the Built Environment

Inge Trijssenaar-Buhre[1], Sandra Wijnant-Timmerman[1],
Remco Witberg[2], and Gerard Veldhuis[3]

[1] TNO, Urban Environment and Safety, Utrecht, The Netherlands
{Inge.Trijssenaar,Sandra.Wijnant}@tno.nl
[2] TNO, Modelling, Simulation & Gaming, The Hague, The Netherlands
[3] TNO, Training & Performance Innovations, Soesterberg, The Netherlands

Abstract. Various types of emergency situations may occur in a city, region or country. In these –safety and security- emergency situations it is important for citizens to know how to handle. Preparation of citizens in the use of appropriate self-rescue measures can save many lives. Examples of self-rescue measures are: (automatic) alert with either limited or extensive evacuation instructions, dynamic signposting or instructions for the best direction of flight. The questions to be answered are: (1) What is the effect of these measures on the self-rescue in various emergencies? And (2) what is the effect of structural measures on buildings such as heat resistant glass or a more solid construction and (3) how do specific safety measures relate to other measures? This paper describes the first developments of a model for determining and comparing the effect of safety measures for self-rescue in various types of emergency situations.

Keywords: self-rescue, safety measures, built environment.

1   Background

During disasters but also in smaller incidents, the government is unable to help all victims at once, despite the high standard of care in prosperous countries such as the Netherlands. Therefore, citizens need to be able or be enabled to rescue themselves.

Possible disasters in a region depend on the sources of risk in that region: for example, the presence of chemical industry, or rivers. If the national or regional government, emergency responders, real estate developers or housing corporations know what measures are most effective in a particular region, they can pay more attention to inform the citizens or take specific precautions in preparation of possible emergencies. In addition, preventive measures can be taken so that the citizens can rescue themselves during a disaster. TNO proposes a model which can be used to determine the effectiveness of self-rescue measures on the overall safety of citizens in a given region.

N. Aschenbruck et al. (Eds.): Future Security 2012, CCIS 318, pp. 180–183, 2012.
© Springer-Verlag Berlin Heidelberg 2012

2   Approach

An inventory is made of possible -safety and security- disaster categories that can happen to a citizen. This inventory uses available methods in the Netherlands for prioritizing disasters such as the "regional risk profile" (regionaal risicoprofiel) [1] and "National Risk Assessment" (Nationale Risicobeoordeling) [2].

Subsequently, a conceptual model is developed in which all possible disasters and measures come together to determine the impact of measures on the safety of citizens. An inventory of available models is made with input of experts on the various disaster categories. In the first version of the model the following disaster categories are evaluated with numerical examples: a fire in a building, flooding and the release of hazardous substances. A software-demonstrator of the model is developed. During the model development, various stakeholders and potential users are involved.

3   Results

3.1   Disaster Categories

The categories of disasters which are selected for inclusion in the model are: flood, fire in a building, accidents with hazardous substances, CBRN terrorism, criminal acts, extreme weather, tunnel accidents, breakdown of utilities, and wild fire. The disaster categories flood, fire in a building and dispersion of hazardous substances and form the basis for the initial elaboration of the model.

3.2   Conceptual Model

The conceptual model is a mathematical model in which the various disaster categories and possible measures and their interactions come together. The safety of citizens is expressed in the risk of injury due to a large range of possible scenarios in a region. The measures for separate disaster categories can reinforce or weaken each other. For example: securely locking the doors of a building has a positive effect on security with respect to burglary, but has a negative effect on safety with respect to evacuation in case of fire. In a database, a large number of safety measures are collected. For each measure is indicated whether the measure has a positive or negative influence on the categories of disaster.

The model inventory showed that complete models exist for calculating self-rescue measures for certain disaster categories, for other disaster categories not even a model exits for calculating the possible amounts of victims. For example, in the field of tunnel safety, models exist for the effect of safety measures such as alerting, emergency exits, etc. If available, existing tools are applied to model the effect of self-rescue measures for these disaster categories. The results of these models can be used as input for the overall model.

182   I. Trijssenaar-Buhre et al.

For disaster categories where no suitable model is available yet, a straightforward model is developed. This model is based on the available time that a person has before he will be injured. The available time is compared to the time the person needs to bring himself into safety. The measures influence the available and / or the time required to get to a safe location. With this we can model the effectiveness of a measure.

3.3   Example

In a specific region three risks are foreseen, as presented in the picture: a toxic cloud, flooding of the region and fire in a building. GIS (Geo Information Systems) can be used to obtain regional data such as population density, characterization of population, location and type of buildings.

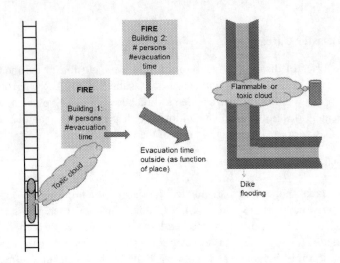

The table shows several safety measures which can be taken to reduce victims and to increase the self-rescue of people for the three disasters. The effect of the measure on the time which is available to flight is given in the table as well. For example in case of fire resistant walls and windows, people are protected from the heat radiation, which gives them more available time before (temperature or radiation) conditions get unbearable. In case of high-rise buildings it takes more time to evacuate the building.

Using the model gives insight in whether measures of different disasters enhance or weaken each other. When avoiding high-rise building, it has a positive effect on evacuation in case of fire. However, this measure has a negative effect on self-rescue in case of a toxic cloud. High obstacles or buildings result in lower concentration in the direction of the wind, behind a building [3]. Therefore avoiding high-rise buildings has a negative effect on self-rescue in case of a toxic cloud. Also in case of flooding, avoiding high-rise buildings has a negative effect on self-rescue: people are unable to escape to a higher point.

Measures	Effect of measure			
Fire measure	Effect on time	Fire	Toxic cloud	Flooding
Fire resistant walls and windows	time available	+	0	0
Avoid high-rise buildings	time required	+	-	-
Toxic cloud measures				
High wall or obstacle between the risk object and the citizen	time available	+	+	-/+
Flooding measures				
Dike or wall around house	time available	+	+	-/+
Avoid obstacles and narrow passages	time required	+	-	+

3.4   Numerical Example

Several numerical examples have been elaborated for the selected disaster categories. For toxic clouds, the effect of alarming citizens on the time required is calculated. A comparison is performed for the following situations 'without an alarm', 'with an alarm but without further information' and 'with an alarm and information'. The number of lethal victims in this specific example are 96, 89, and 63 respectively. For flood the same alarm safety measures have been elaborated for a fast flooding scenario, as well as an average and a slow scenario. No difference in victims is found of the slow and average scenario. For the fast flooding scenario the number of lethal victims is 327, 269 and 191 respectively. To determine the effectiveness of the safety measures for these flooding and toxic cloud scenarios the number of victims needs to be combined with the probability of the scenarios according to [1] and [2].

3.5   Conclusions and Further Developments

A model is proposed for determining and comparing the effect of safety measures for self-rescue in various types of emergency situations. A first conceptual model is developed and a demonstrator is built for three disaster categories: "fire in a building", "a toxic cloud" and "a flood", including several measures. Further developments will include more disaster categories and safety and security measures. Challenges ahead are:

- Integrating various models from various disaster categories in an overall model.
- Creating an accessible model for the user that provides good insight in the effectiveness of the various measures.
- Taking into account the behaviour of people: do people react and how do people react on warnings, alerting and additional evacuation information?

References

1. Regional Risk Profile: Handreiking Regionaal Risicoprofiel, concept 1.10 (2009)
2. National Risk Assessment: Nationale Risicobeoordeling bevindingen rapportage 2010, Ministerie van Veiligheid en Justitie (2010)
3. Wijnant-Timmerman, S.I., Wiersma, T.: Risk reduction by use of a bufferzone. In: Martorell, et al. (eds.) Safety, Reliability and Risk Analysis: Theory, Methods and Applications (2009) ISBN 978-0-415-48513-5

Enhancing Robustness
of Tubbing Tunnels in Case of Extreme Loads[*]

Christoph Niklasch and Peter-Michael Mayer

Ed. Züblin AG, Stuttgart, Germany

Abstract. The effects of extreme loads on tubbing elements have been studied as part of the joint research project "Automated generation of information and protection of critical infrastructures in the event of a disaster (AISIS)".

Novel sensing techniques and protective measures have been developed to monitor and enhance the robustness of tubbing tunnels. Amongst other topics, Ed. Züblin AG developed a new coupling system to increase the resistance of tubbing tunnels in case of explosive loads.

Keywords: Tubbing tunnel, explosion load, robustness.

1 Development of a Coupling System for Dynamic Loads

Public transport tunnels in soft ground are frequently built with tunnel boring machines (TBMs) and lined with segmental linings. In single shell tunnels the segmental lining has to carry the ground loads and the water pressure. Each ring consists of several segments with contact joints in the longitudinal direction. The rings of the segmental lining may or may not be coupled. Lining stiffness can be increased if coupled rings are used. Especially in soft grounds the deformation differences between the rings can be reduced by ring coupling. A common coupling solution is use of cam and plug connectors.

An explosion inside the tunnel generates an air overpressure. Depending on the surrounding ground stiffness a relatively pronounced widening of the tunnel lining with a decompression of the lining is the result.

Depending on the soil state, the bedding reaction will be reduced and the soil tends to fluidize during the event. To reduce upward motions of the tunnel and relative displacements between neighboring rings a permanent coupling of adjacent rings could improve the stability of tunnel linings in soft soil [4] and guarantee the water tightness of the joints.

The developed coupling system comprises of four main components: Two embedded steel parts to distribute the load into the concrete, a steel bolt to transfer the load at the joint, an epoxy mortar for the connection between the steel bolt and the embedded steel parts, and a special reinforcement layout for the load transfer inside the concrete segments. Fig. 2 (a) shows a partial model of the coupling system with the main components.

---

[*] The research work has been supported by the German Federal Ministry of Education and Research in the research program „Forschung für die zivile Sicherheit".

2   Static Tests of Coupling System

To determine the static load capacity and the robustness respectively the ductility of the developed coupling system four tests have been performed at the Institute of Concrete Structures and Building Materials (IMB) of the KIT. Details on the experimental test setup can be found in [1].

All four tests succeeded and showed a ductile behaviour without failure of the coupling system, as can be seen in Fig. 1. After the first test the reinforcement layout in the load application and bearing zones of the specimen has been optimized and strengthened.

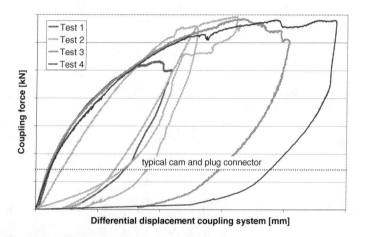

Fig. 1. Static tests – transferred coupling force in relation to the relative displacement between the two connected concrete segments

All three remaining specimen reached their maximum load as indicated by reinforcement yielding and the presence of wide cracks above the support on the passive segment. In the load transfer region close to the coupling system only small cracks without concrete spalling have been observed up to the maximum load, as shown in Fig. 2 (b).

It was possible to increase the relative displacement between the two segments after reaching the maximum load without a large load reduction. The maximum displacements were limited not by the coupling system, but by the bending of the two segments, as they collided in the upper region of the segmental joint.

Compared to a classical cam and plug connector in segmental tunnel linings for tubbings with the same thickness, the maximum connection loads are much higher (cp. Fig. 1) and can help to guarantee the lining integrity after a large event for tunnels in soft soil.

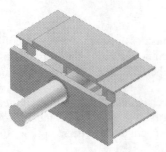 

Fig. 2. (a) Coupling System with embedded steel part, steel bolt and epoxy mortar. (b) Cracks in load introduction zone, but no spalling of concrete cover.

3   Dynamic Coupling Tests

Together with the Fraunhofer Ernst-Mach-Institut (EMI) a 1:4 scaled dynamic test of the coupling system has been performed at the EMI testing site. A scaled medium explosive load was tested [3]. The model tunnel lining consists of four segments, two made of ordinary concrete and two out of a fibre-reinforced ultra-high performance concrete. The four segments are connected with three coupling systems, as shown in Fig. 3. The segments are bedded in sand to simulate the soil around the tunnel.

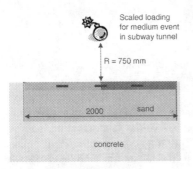 

Fig. 3. (a) Experimental setup for dynamic coupling tests. (b) Specimens with embedded coupling system after dynamic test.

After the tests the specimens are almost undamaged, as shown in Fig. 3 (b).

4   Summary

In the research project AISIS the Ed. Züblin AG developed a new coupling system for segmental tunnel linings subjected to extreme loads.

The initial development goals, ability to withstand high static and dynamic coupling loads, high ductility and robustness have been reached and proven in static and dynamic tests.

References

1. Müller, H.S.: AISIS, Teilvorhaben: Kurzzeitdynamische Baugrund-Bauwerks-Interaktion und Entwicklung brandbeständiger ultrahochfester Betone, Teilbereich: Entwicklung brandbeständiger ultrahochfester Betone für hochdynamische Beanspruchungen: Schlussbericht (2011)
2. Niklasch, C., Mayer, P.-M.: AISIS, Teilvorhaben: Komponentenintegration und baulicher Schutz, Schlussbericht (2011)
3. Millon, O.: AISIS, Abschlussbericht Fraunhofer EMI (2011)
4. Kudella, P., Osinov, V., Huber, G., Chrisopoulos, S., Triantafyllidis, T.: AISIS - Teilvorhaben Kurzzeitdynamische Baugrund-Bauwerks-Interaktion, Schlussbericht (2012)

Security Evaluation of Street Bridges for Fire Exposure

Current Findings of the Project SKRIBT[Plus]

Ulrich Bergerhausen[1] and Sven Priestaff[2]

[1] Federal Highway Research Institute, Bergisch Gladbach, Germany
bergerhausen@bast.de
[2] University of Stuttgart, Stuttgart, Germany
sven.priestaff@ilek.uni-stuttgart.de

Abstract. In a developed society, the achievement of individual and economic goals requires a high degree of mobility. Mobility is the key for an efficient transport infrastructure. This is particularly important for roads and its bridges and tunnels. They play a vital part since the majority of the transport of goods and people of all modes are handled by them. In the joint research project "Protection of critical bridges and tunnels (SKRIBT[Plus]) a method is developed to evaluate the security of bridges and tunnel safety. In particular, this methodology investigated the scenario fire on/under a bridge, which can have serious consequences both technical and economic.

Keywords: criticality, bridges, fire, security evaluation, measures.

1 Introduction

Transport infrastructures, like railway stations, airports, subways and roads, are used by millions of people every day. The dense, highly cross-linked transport systems are the lifelines of our society. However, they can be disrupted by attacks, criminal acts, extreme weather events or major accidents. Hence, it is necessary to tackle these threats in a holistic manner. For the road sector, the research in the joint project "Protection of critical bridges and tunnels (SKRIBT[Plus])" contributes to the security of transport infrastructure and thus significantly increase the security of traffic participants.

In this respect, bridges and tunnels play an important role and can be the vulnerable key points in a road network. Even minor disturbances due to traffic restrictions show that a failure of these structures may lead to adverse effects, which result in high economic costs, as well as negative impacts on the environment.

2 Occurrence of Fire on Bridges

In addition to a variety of other scenarios, a possible security-related scenario is a fire under a bridge. This may be triggered by an accident, a targeted attack or even by an unintentional accident. A recent example is the fire underneath a bridge at Dormagen along the A57 highway on 14/02/2012.

N. Aschenbruck et al. (Eds.): Future Security 2012, CCIS 318, pp. 188–191, 2012.
© Springer-Verlag Berlin Heidelberg 2012

Supply pipes made of plastic material were stored under the bridge and set on fire by employing fire accelerants.

The fire led to an enormous smoke development, which eventually enclosed the structure, causing drivers on the top to break abruptly due to the lack of visibility. The result was a multiple car crash with several injured persons and one fatality. Furthermore, the fire caused immense damage on both bridge-superstructures, which eventually led to the demolishment and replacement of the bridge.

The result was a complete closing of the motorway for two months with considerable congestion on the alternative routes. Additionally, the economic losses are far above the direct costs of demolition and restoration of the bridge.

Fig. 1. Bridge must be teat down after fire (Source: BASt)

With the programme „Research for Civil Security" of the Federal Ministry of Education and Research, innovative research projects regarding the "Protection of traffic infrastructures" should help to understand such incidents, reduce the extent of damage or even prevent the occurrence of the former.

SKRIBT^{Plus} is a project within this programme, which further develops relevant methods and new technologies for the use of new security systems for bridges and tunnels.

3   Fire Damages to Bridges

The fire safety in construction and design of industrial buildings has been well developed and researched for many years. However, the resulting standards cannot be used in bridge design, as they do not consider the variety of possible fire hazards and the differences in design and construction of bridges structures.

On the highways a unknown amount of different fire loads is transported daily. When calculating the fire damage on bridge structures there are numerous factors that need to be considered such as the amount and character of the fire loads, the position of the fire source and the distance relating to the cross section of the bridge deck as well as the construction of the bridge deck itself, the weather conditions and the response time of the fire brigade.

Basically, the damage of the bridge structure can be derived from the temperature distribution in the cross section. This temperature distribution mainly depends on the height and the duration of the fire. Because of the great number of possible fire hazards and the array of variables which have to be considered, the detection of the thermal history of the cross section is even more complex.

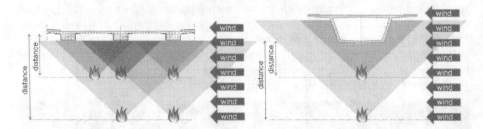

Fig. 2. Influence of variables at different cross sections (Source: ILEK)

When evaluating a number of fire hazard incidents that have occurred on bridges, it becomes evident that steel bridges are more sensitive to fire than reinforced or prestressed concrete structures. This effect is well known and is due to the higher mass of the concrete structures. Especially the different structural components of reinforced or prestressed concrete bridges are more resilient than the commonly used concrete profiles such as floors, walls and binding girders.

Starting at the surface (facing the fire or heated air) the bridge deck begins to rise in temperature. Due to the increasing temperature, the possibility of concrete spallings and changes in the mechanical characteristics of the used materials is evident.Depending on the thermal history and construction of the bridge, the critical temperatures could reach important bearing-type fixtures, for example external tensioning elements inside a box girder or tensioning elements inside a T-beam bridge. Damaging these elements could result in the failure of the bridge structure.

4   Security and Technical Evaluation of Structures

In the context of the project "Protection of critical bridges and tunnels in the course of roads (SKRIPT)" [1] a method for the security and technical evaluation of structures has been developed. In a first step, a threat analysis is performed, in which all relevant threats are identified and described. This is followed by an object analysis, in which the established threats out of step one, are contrasted with the object properties. The parameters which are considered are: structure, user and traffic. In a last step a selection of appropriate protective measures is carried out. These measures have previously been examined with regards to their efficiency and cost-effectiveness under the specific objective properties. The method is universal and hence allows the owner of a structure to evaluate the former in a consistent way. It can be applied equally to tunnels and bridges, and includes all relevant initial events such as fire, explosion, mechanical impact or natural events. The result is an index to describe the criticality of a building, which allows for a relative comparison of the structures. It became evident that structures should be protected by additional safeguards. This method is further developed in SKRIBT[Plus] to assess in particular the change of the criticality caused by applying protection measures.

When applying this method to the previously described case of a fire scenario under bridges there are three sub-areas to determine. These are the structural damage caused by the fire, the number of fatalities and the effects on the traffic. The values can be transferred as part of the identification procedure in assessing classes, so that the three areas can be compared with each other and together lead to a result. The result is an index number which describes the criticality of a structure for the initial event fire. If required, these initial studies can be conducted for other events as well, which allows for a comprehensive assessment of the criticality. If these investigations are also performed for other structures, a ranking of the structures is possible as well.

5   Summary

Bridges and tunnels are special objects on the road network because in the event of a failure they are difficult to replace and the impact inhibits substantial economic costs, as well as negative impacts on the environment. Current events, e.g. the fire at the highway bridge at Dormagen on the A57 motorway, show that the scenarios considered in the project SKRIBT^{Plus} are of importance and the respective analysis, including the development of protective measures, increases the security of structures and their users.

An important scenario is a fire under a bridge where the bridge may be damaged so severely that its demolition and reconstruction is required. In this case, the traffic is redirected on the surrounding routes, which leads to a significantly higher travel time for the users. With the further developed method in SKRIBT^{Plus} a security and technical evaluation of structures can be conducted and the structures can be effectively protected by the developed measures.

Reference

[1] Protection of critical bridges and tunnels in the course of roads (SKRIBT) – Recommended measures used for bridges and tunnels, final report of the joint project for the Federal Ministry of Education and Research (BMBF) (in preparation)

Influence of Orientation Fields
of Fingerprints to Matching Performance

Sebastian Bodó[1] and Thorsten M. Buzug[2]

[1] Westcoast University of Applied Sciences Heide
[2] Institute of Medical Engineering, University of Lübeck

Abstract. Fingerprint recognition and verification make use of the so called minutiae feature of fingerprints. These are points in the fingerprint image where a ridge of the finger is starting, ending, forking or joining. Besides its relative position the relative orientations of the minutiae points are an important information and can be used for matching of two individuals together with the position [1] and sometimes with further features of the image [2]. Classical methods of fingerprint orientation estimation are gradient based [3] or based on filtering/spectral/projection techniques [4]. Orientations are often used to perform directional filtering techniques to improve the image processing [5]. There exist two main techniques to improve the orientation fields. The first technique is to smooth the orientation field values and the second is generally an approximation technique. This second kind of strategy can be found in [6] and [7]. The performance of these two methods will be compared and interpreted. We will show that the accuracy of an orientation field (OF) is an important aspect for the matching procedure and will give hints for the right choice of processing from an independent point of view.

Keywords: fingerprint, identification, matching, approximation.

1 Estimation and Approximation of Orientation Fields

1.1 Estimation

The local orientation values can be used for directional filtering [7] while the global orientation field can be used for for indexing of fingerprints [6], [8]. The importance and benefits of a high quality orientation field estimation can be particularly useful for latent fingerprints [9]. In the later parts of the paper we will describe techniques for estimation and approximation of fingerprint orientation fields in Sec. 1 the testing method in Sec. 2 and show the final results and conclusions in Sec. 3.

Estimating the orientation of the fingerprint image at a certain point is a trade-off between accuracy and robustness. Smoothing will only be desirable to a certain extend to avoid removing critical information. On the other hand the smoothness increases the robustness against noise. The main drawback is that we only judge based on a local information and do not combine it with global information about a fingerprint. The main reason for using approximation

N. Aschenbruck et al. (Eds.): Future Security 2012, CCIS 318, pp. 192–195, 2012.

methods is to improve the robustness against distortions while keeping a high accuracy. We want to compare two popular estimation methods. The first one based on [3] uses the gradient values and the second one based on a discrete Fourier transform (DFT) is explained in [10]. The second strategy is used in [11].

1.2   Approximation

Approximations are used to give a smooth but sound representation of the estimated orientation field values. Each approximation method uses a set of basis functions and a set of parameters $\boldsymbol{p}$ given a liner combination of these basis functions to build a orientation field $\phi(z, \boldsymbol{p})$. This is then set in relation to the estimated orientation field $\Psi(z)$ in an error function

$$E = \int_z \sin(2\phi(z, \mathbf{p}) - 2\Psi(z))^2 dz. \tag{1}$$

The error function (1) $z \in \Omega \subset \mathbb{Z}$ is the coordinate system build under the image domain Ω and it is then the base for an optimization using the analytic derivative of this expression in a Levenberg-Marquardt optimization. The strategy remains the same for any set of basis functions.

2   Evaluation

For the evaluation of different orientation field estimation algorithms in the context of coding and matching of fingerprints we decided to use the NBIS software from http://www.nist.gov/itl/iad/ig/nbis.cfm The software was modified to allow for inserting pre calculated orientation fields. Since the NBIS source provides a simple definable value to adjust the quantization of the orientation values. We used 16 (default) and 32 for each method.

We use the FVC2000 DB3 database fingerprint images to generate the results in this common framework. Extracting the original NIST orientation values and inserting it into the modified code yields the same results as the original code thus we are sure not to have a bug. The following algorithms have been used for calculation of orientation values.

- NBIS internal (NBIS)
- Slightly smoothed Gradient based (GB)
- Strong smoothed gradient based (GB-SMOOTH)
- Not smoothed gradient based (GB-EXACT)
- Legendre Exact (LE) with 240, (LN) with 90 and (LS) with 30 parameters
- FOMFE Exact (FE) with 242, (FN) with 98 and (FS) with 50 parameters

The results are histograms of all scores for matchings of the same person (genuine) and matchings of different persons (impostor). Based on these we calculate the false acceptance rate (FAR) and false rejection rate (FRR) of the resulting systems for the choice of different thresholds applied on the scores. This kind of representation is also called DET curve.

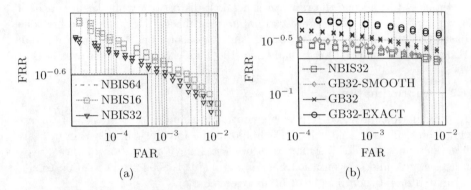

Fig. 1. Results for the NBIS method in Fig. 1a with different quantizations of the orientation values. For the same quantization of 32 steps in both methods the NBIS and GB-SMOOTH method both are comparable Fig. 1b.

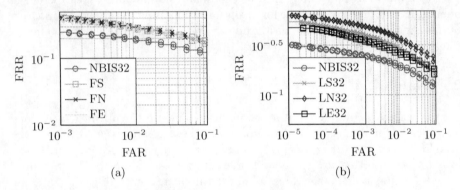

Fig. 2. Compared to the NBIS method the approximation using FOMFE or LP can not reach the same accuracy. The FOMFE method performs a bit better while using the same number of degrees of freedom.

3   Results and Conclusions

In our first experiment we want to evaluate the influence of orientation field quantization. We build the NBIS coding with a total of 16 (NBIS16) up to 64 (NBIS64) quantization steps and found that a quantization of 32 steps yields the optimal trade off between speed and accuracy. Using this quantization we compare the NBIS to the gradient values based method GB. We can see in Fig. 1b that the DFT method delivers slightly higher accuracy. The equal error rate (EER) for the GB method reached a maximum of 10.39% while the NBIS method reached 12.28%. We can conclude from the results in Fig. 2a that the approximation does not result in higher accuracy for any degrees of freedom used. The final EER for the FE method is at 13.73%. We can see in Fig. 2b that the LP approximations can not reach the performance of the NBIS algorithm. The final EER for the LS method is at 15.44%.

The GB method deliver better performance than the approximations although we implemented a very smooth version. The key difference between both methods is that the smoothness of the approximation is given by low order functions. This has the consequence that many local non-linear influences are lost. Thus we can state that the local non-linear information of the orientation image is one key ingredient that makes a person distinguishable from others. An approximation method should be able to maintain this information if we want to keep good matching performances.

Acknowledgement. This project is sponsored by the European Union (EFRE) and the federal state of Schleswig-Holstein, Germany (Zukunftsprogramm Wirtschaft).

References

1. Jiang, X., Yau, W.Y.: Fingerprint minutiae matching based on the local and global structures. In: Proc. 15th Int Pattern Recognition Conf., vol. 2, pp. 1038–1041 (2000)
2. Jain, A.K., Feng, J., Nagar, A., Nandakumar, K.: On matching latent fingerprints. In: Proc. IEEE Computer Society Conf. Computer Vision and Pattern Recognition Workshops CVPRW 2008, pp. 1–8 (2008)
3. Bazen, A., Gerez, S.: Systematic methods for the computation of the directional fields and singular points of fingerprints. IEEE Trans. Pattern Anal. Mach. Intell. 24, 905–919 (2002)
4. Ji, L., Yi, Z.: Fingerprint orientation field estimation using ridge projection. Pattern Recognition 41(5), 1491–1503 (2008)
5. Hong, L., Wan, Y., Jain, A.: Fingerprint image enhancement: algorithm and performance evaluation. IEEE Transactions on Pattern Analysis and Machine Intelligence 20(8), 777–789 (1998)
6. Wang, Y., Hu, J., Phillips, D.: A fingerprint orientation model based on 2d fourier expansion (fomfe) and its application to singular-point detection and fingerprint indexing. IEEE Trans. Pattern Anal. Mach. Intell. 29(4), 573–585 (2007)
7. Sherlock, B.G., Monro, D.M., Millard, K.: Fingerprint enhancement by directional fourier filtering. IEE Proceedings -Vision, Image and Signal Processing 141(2), 87–94 (1994)
8. Henry, E.R.: Classification and uses of finger prints. Routledge, London (1900)
9. Yoon, S., Feng, J., Jain, A.K.: Latent fingerprint enhancement via robust orientation field estimation. In: Proc. Int. Biometrics (IJCB) Joint Conf., pp. 1–8 (2011)
10. Chikkerur, S., Wu, C., Govindaraju, V.: A systematic approach for feature extraction in fingerprint images. Biometric Authentication, 1–23 (2004)
11. National Institute of Standards and Technology: Nist biometric image software

Jamming and Spoofing in GPS/GNSS Based Applications and Services – Threats and Countermeasures

Manuel Cuntz, Andriy Konovaltsev,
Achim Dreher, and Michael Meurer

Institute of Communications and Navigation,
German Aerospace Center (DLR),
Oberpfaffenhofen, Germany
{Manuel.Cuntz,Andriy.Konovaltsev,
Achim.Dreher,Michael.Meurer}@dlr.de

Abstract. GPS positioning and time synchronization have become crucial for a large variety of services and applications. Especially for safety-critical applications and infrastructure networks a reliable and robust service of GPS is essential. However, the availability of cheap jamming devices has recently demonstrated the threat for GPS applications. GPS jamming is no longer only a hypothetical threat, it is already present and will become increasingly dangerous for GPS users. For this reason the German Aerospace Center (DLR) developed strategies to cope with these threats and to retain a valid position solution even in harsh interference environments.

Keywords: Navigation Sensors, GNSS Threats, GPS, Critical Infrastructure, Interference, Spoofing, Jamming, Personal Privacy Devices.

1 Introduction

GPS positioning and time synchronization have become crucial for a large variety of services and applications. Especially for safety-critical applications and infrastructure networks, a reliable and robust service of GPS is essential. As an example, nowadays cell phone networks, as well as banking systems and power grids are time synchronized with GPS. Also safety-of-life applications like landing approaches of airplanes or manoeuvring of ships as well as restricted positioning services for national authorities have to rely on a dependable position service. However, the availability of cheap jamming devices has recently demonstrated the threat to GPS applications. Therefore, corresponding countermeasures have to be taken to ensure a robust and reliable navigation. This paper introduces the jamming and spoofing threats to GPS-based applications and services. Subsequently, selected countermeasures are presented which are able to detect and mitigate jamming and spoofing attacks.

N. Aschenbruck et al. (Eds.): Future Security 2012, CCIS 318, pp. 196–199, 2012.

2   Jamming Threats

The U.S. Federal Aviation Administration reported problems due to jammers at Newark Airport (FAA, 2011). A ground-based augmentation system (GBAS) was installed at the international airport of Newark in 2009, which was meant to allow CAT I automated landing approaches. But several interference events prevented the certification of the system until now. During tests it was found out, that the source of the interfering signals came from a nearby toll road. So-called personal privacy devices, small GPS jammers available at prices down to $25, were used by truck drivers to circumvent the road toll or to disable the GPS-based tracking system of their trucks. Such devices are also known to be used for car thefts.

With respect to maritime navigation, the U.K. General Lighthouse Authorities revealed the threat of jammers during a test campaign at the east coast of Great Britain. It was shown how GPS jamming events can not only prevent a GPS receiver from determing the position, but also how such receivers could be mislead to report a wrong position to the user (Grant, Williams, & Ward, 2010). GPS jamming is no longer only a hypothetical threat, it is already present and will become increasingly a problem for GPS users.

3   Spoofing Threats

Not only jamming is a severe problem for GPS users. Also intended or unintended misleading GPS/GNSS signals can cause a GPS receiver to report a false position. An intended spoofing signal needs a relatively high effort in comparison to GPS jammers, but the impact and consequences to the user as well as the risk of not detecting the false signal are very high. It has to be expected that such spoofing devices will be developed and used in the near future. A simple example of a spoofer is a so called GPS repeater. Such devices consist of a GPS receiver antenna, an amplifier and a GPS transmitter antenna. The received signals of the repeater antenna are just re-emitted with a larger power level than the received signals. A GPS receiver, which locks on these reradiated signals, will always report the position of the repeater antenna and not the true user location. First unintentional incidents of that kind have been already reported to DLR.

4   Countermeasures against Jamming and Spoofing Attacks

Radio frequency interference (RFI) has in general individual characteristics in time, frequency and space domain. Therefore it is necessary to take into account all three domains for an effective and reliable interference detection and suppression.

The German Aerospace Center (DLR) initiated in 2005 the development of a multi-antenna receiver demonstrator to investigate the performance of modern interference detection and mitigation techniques, see Fig. 1.

Fig. 1. DLR Multi-Antenna Receiver Demonstrator

This receiver demonstrator incorporates, besides others, frequency-domain adaptive filtering (FDAF) and antenna-array signal-processing algorithms. FDAF is a well-known and efficient technique to detect and mitigate pulsed and continuous wave signals in frequency and time domain. A detailed description of FDAF can be found in (Denks, Hornbostel, & Chopard, 2009).

With array processing the reception pattern of an antenna array is digitally steered. This allows to point the main beam of the antenna array in the direction of the desired satellite signals and to put a null in the direction of the interference signal. Therefore, this technique is also termed digital beamforming (DBF). This enables the receiver to efficiently suppress jamming signals and enhance the desired satellite signals. For more details on array processing refer to (Konovaltsev, De Lorenzo, Hornbostel, & Enge, 2009).

Beside this jammer suppression functionality, direction-of-arrival (DoA) estimation allows determining the true angles of arrival of tracked GPS/GNSS satellite and interfering signal sources (Konovaltsev, Antreich, & Hornbostel, 2007). This is a very efficient tool to identify jammers and to detect spoofing attacks on the basis of the discrepancy of the expected and the detected directions of arrival.

The DLR demonstrated in several jamming measurement campaigns in 2010 and 2011 the performance gain of such advanced techniques. DBF, DoA estimation and FDAF have been practically tested in the German Galileo Test Environment (GATE) by using GPS and Galileo signals in the presence of interfering signals. The obtained results clearly show the advantages of these technologies, especially with respect to the improved robustness of an antenna-array GPS/GNSS receiver to radio frequency interference. The DLR receiver was able to decode navigation messages and to determine its position in conditions where commercial receivers fail to track a single satellite. The results presented in (Cuntz, et al., 2011) show that the robustness against the radio interference can be improved by up to 30 dB by using DBF alone and up to 45 dB by using the combination of DBF with FDAF compared to the case without mitigation techniques. DoA estimation could be further used for effective spoofing detection. Also in interference-free scenarios array processing was able to improve the navigation quality by benefitting from higher C/N_0 ratios and better signal availability. Due to their interference robustness the GPS/GNSS receivers using a combination of adaptive antenna arrays with other mitigation strategies are a very powerful technology to enable safety-of-life applications in critical signal conditions.

5   Conclusion

GPS jamming already exists today. The threat to the users will become even more severe in the near future (The Royal Academy of Engineering, 2011). This is valid for users requiring reliable position information but also for manifold critical infrastructures like mobile radio systems, power grids, financial networks etc., which rely on GPS/GNSS for synchronization purposes. Also the threat of spoofing is considered as a high risk.

Fortunately, there are methods and techniques to detect and to mitigate jamming and spoofing attacks. Results of several measurement campaigns of the German Aerospace Center (DLR) have demonstrated the performance gain of such methods (Cuntz, et al., 2011). However, today's GPS/GNSS receivers have very limited protection against this type of interference. Therefore, there is an urgent need to push such technologies for integration in GPS/GNSS receivers which are used in (safety) critical applications.

References

Cuntz, M., Konovaltsev, A., Mattheo, S., Hättich, C., Kappen, G., Meurer, M., et al.: Field Test: Jamming the DLR Adaptive Antenna Receiver. In: ION GNSS 2011, Portland, U.S.A. (2011)

Denks, H., Hornbostel, A., Chopard, V.: GNSS Receiver Testing by Use of a Hardware Signal Simulator with Emphasis on Pulsed and CW Interference. In: Cergal 2009, Oberpfaffenhofen, Germany (2009)

Federal Aviation Administration (FAA), GPS Privacy Jammers and RFI at Newark (March 2011), http://laas.tc.faa.gov/CoWorkerFiles/GBAS%20RFI%202011%20 Public%20Version%20Final.pdf (retrieved March 27, 2012)

Grant, A., Williams, P., Ward, N.: The Potential Effects of GPS Jamming on Maritime Navigation. In: Nav. 2010. Church House, London (2010)

Konovaltsev, A., Antreich, F., Hornbostel, A.: Performance Assessment of Antenna Array Algorithms for Multipath and Interference. In: 2nd Workshop on GNSS Signals 2007, Noordwijk, The Netherlands (2007)

Konovaltsev, A., De Lorenzo, D., Hornbostel, A., Enge, P.: Mitigation of Continuous and Pulsed Radio Interference with GNSS Antenna Arrays. In: ION GNSS 2009, Savannah, U.S.A (2009)

The Royal Academy of Engineering, Global Navigation Space Systems: reliance and vulnerabilities (March 2011), http://www.raeng.org.uk/news/publications/list/ reports/RAoE_Global_Navigation_Systems_Report.pdf (retrieved June 13, 2012)

Millimeter-Wave Monolithic Integrated Circuits and Modules for Safety and Security Applications

Michael Schlechtweg[1], Axel Tessmann[1], Axel Hülsmann[1], Ingmar Kallfass[1,2], Arnulf Leuther[1], Rolf Aidam[1], Christian Zech[1], Ulrich J. Lewark[2], Hermann Massler[1], Markus Riessle[1], Martin Zink[1], Josef Rosenzweig[1], and Oliver Ambacher[1]

[1] Fraunhofer Institute for Applied Solid State Physics (IAF), Freiburg, Germany
michael.schlechtweg@iaf.fraunhofer.de
[2] Karlsruhe Institute of Technology (KIT), Karlsruhe, Germany

Abstract. Metamorphic high electron mobility transistor (mHEMT) technologies with 100, 50, and 35 nm gate lengths have been developed at Fraunhofer IAF for operation in the millimeter-wave frequency range up to 600 GHz. Based on these technologies, a variety of multifunctional millimeter-wave and submillimeter-wave monolithic integrated circuits (MMICs and S-MMICs) has been realized. To demonstrate the potential of these technologies, this paper presents some examples of S-MMICs developed for use in next generation systems for safety and security applications: a 460 GHz amplifier and a 300 GHz heterodyne receiver. Furthermore, a complete 94 GHz imaging system for materials testing and concealed object detection is presented.

Keywords: millimeter-wave monolithic integrated circuit (MMIC), metamorphic high electron mobility transistor (mHEMT), amplifier, receiver, active imaging, radar, materials testing, weapon detection, continuous wave radar.

1 Introduction

The millimeter-wave (30 GHz < f < 300 GHz) and submillimeter-wave (f > 300 GHz) frequency range of the electromagnetic spectrum is increasingly addressed by safety and security technologies, due to its fascinating properties. The millimeter waves easily penetrate dust, snow, fog, and fabrics. Operation distances up to a few hundred meters are feasible. The usable frequencies for high-resolution millimeter-wave and submillimeter-wave systems are around 94, 140, 220, 340, 410, 460, and 670 GHz, where the transmission of the atmosphere exhibits local maxima, as shown in Fig. 1 [1]. Examples for millimeter-wave applications are the collision avoidance radar used in the automotive and avionic market, the synthetic aperture radar for reconnaissance and checkpoint screening systems for threat detection. All these systems provide real-time operation and deliver a maximum number of relevant information to enable automatized threat detection. The state of the art of security body scanners is described in some recent publications [2]-[6]. In this paper, we will concentrate on millimeter-wave imagery for detection of hazardous objects concealed in closed containers, such as packages, letters, and luggage. For this application, the higher millimeter-wave

N. Aschenbruck et al. (Eds.): Future Security 2012, CCIS 318, pp. 200–211, 2012.

frequency range features the ability to focus the RF beam effectively without using a large aperture. In addition, the ability to exploit reflection as well as transmission data enhances the information gained about the hidden object.

Analogous to the more familiar optical part of the electromagnetic spectrum the information content increases with increasing bandwidth. Here, higher operational frequencies offer a larger absolute bandwidth, which is an essential reason for the interest of Fraunhofer IAF in the high millimeter-wave and sub-millimeter-wave frequency regime. Additionally, the higher frequencies allow for smaller antenna geometries at unchanged resolution. The demand for real-time capable systems requires architectures with many transmit and receive channels. To lower the costs of such multi-channel approaches it is necessary to develop multifunctional integrated circuits and packaging technologies suitable for mass production. Furthermore, systems for safety and security applications require low error rates in threat detection. High resolution and high image quality are needed for imaging systems.

In this paper, we report on the development of millimeter-wave and submillimeter-wave monolithic integrated circuits (MMICs and S-MMICs) for use in next generation safety and security systems. The circuits are based on an advanced metamorphic high electron mobility transistor (mHEMT) technology of the Fraunhofer IAF. Two circuits are presented: a 460 GHz amplifier and a 300 GHz heterodyne receiver. To demonstrate the capability of millimeter-wave systems for safety and security applications, an active 94 GHz millimeter-wave imaging system for materials testing and concealed object detection is presented.

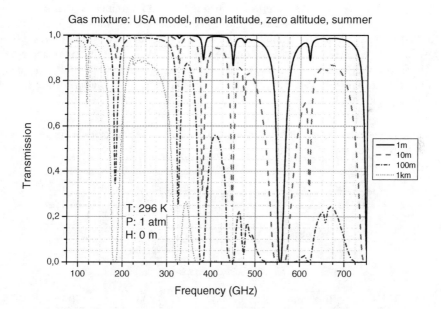

Fig. 1. Transmission spectrum of electromagnetic waves in the atmosphere at zero altitude for different distances

2   Metamorphic HEMT Technologies

The InGaAs-channel-HEMT is one of the most advanced semiconductor device technology for MMICs and S-MMICs. Besides the high transistor gain at millimeter-wave and submillimeter-wave frequencies, the HEMT has the lowest noise figure which is a very important parameter for many system applications.

The high-frequency performance of the HEMT was continuously improved over the recent years by reducing the gate length and increasing the indium content in the channel. The advantages of the higher indium content are the higher electron mobility and the better charge confinement due to larger band offsets. InP, GaAs or Si can be used as substrates for the epitaxial growth of InGaAs/InAlAs heterostructures. In the case of different lattice parameters in the substrate and the active device layers, the devices are called metamorphic HEMTs. Advantages of the metamorphic approach are the larger, cheaper, and less brittle substrates.

For fabrication of MMICs and S-MMICs operating up to 600 GHz, three In-AlAs/InGaAs metamorphic HEMT technologies with gate lengths of 100, 50, and 35 nm have been developed at Fraunhofer IAF as described in [7], [8]. The mHEMT layers were grown on 4" semi-insulating GaAs wafers using molecular beam epitaxy (MBE). For the metamorphic buffer, a linear graded $In_xAl_{0.48}Ga_{0.52-x}As$ (x = 0→0.52) transition was used. For the 100 nm gate technology, an $In_{0.65}Ga_{0.35}As/In_{0.53}Ga_{0.47}As$ composite channel is used to increase the breakdown voltage. For the 50 nm gate mHEMT, the indium content on the upper composite channel layer was increased to 80% to reduce source resistance. In contrast to 50 nm mHEMT with $In_{0.80}Ga_{0.20}As/In_{0.53}Ga_{0.47}As$ composite channel, the 35 nm mHEMT uses a single $In_{0.8}Ga_{0.2}As$ channel. The gate definition of the 100 and 50 nm mHEMTs was performed using e-beam lithography in a three and four layer resist (PMMA) process, respectively, whereas for the 35 nm devices the gate was defined in a two-step e-beam process [8]. Additionally, the transistors are encapsulated in a low-k BCB layer to minimize the parasitic gate capacitance, and passivated with silicon nitride for high reliability and robustness.

Table 1. Electrical DC- and RF-Parameters of the mHEMT Technologies at Fraunhofer IAF

Gate length (nm)	100	50	35
In content (%)	65	80	80
R_c (Ω·mm)	< 0.1	0.05	0.03
R_s (Ω·mm)	< 0.23	0.15	0.1
$I_{d,\,max}$(mA/mm)	900	1200	1600
V_{th} (V)	-0.3	-0.25	-0.3
$BV_{off\text{-}state}$ (V)	4.0	2.2	2.0
$BV_{on\text{-}state}$ (V)	3.0	1.6	1.5
$g_{m,\,max}$ (mS/mm)	1300	1800	2500
f_T (GHz)	220	380	515
f_{max} (GHz)	300	~ 600	~ 900
$MTTF$ (h)	3.0×10^7	2.7×10^6	n.a.

In addition to the active devices, MIM capacitors, thin film resistors, and two inter-connection layers including one plated Au layer in airbridge technology are provided for circuit realization. The RF interconnects at these very high frequencies are of special importance. Because of its good isolation and small dimensions, grounded copla-nar waveguides (GCPW) are used as transmission lines within the MMICs and S-MMICs, enabling successful suppression of unwanted substrate modes. After front side processing, the GaAs substrates were thinned to a final thickness of 50 µm and through-substrate vias were etched.

Some significant electrical DC- and RF-parameters of the metamorphic HEMT technologies at Fraunhofer IAF are summarized in Table 1. The 100 nm gate technol-ogy features an extrinsic transit frequency f_T of 220 GHz as measured for a 2×30 µm common source HEMT. Extrinsic f_T values of 380 and 515 GHz were extrapolated from the on-wafer measured current gain for a 2×10 µm common source device with a gate length of 50 and 35 nm, respectively.

3   460 GHz Amplifier S-MMIC Based on 35 nm mHEMT Technology

To reveal the high-frequency performance of the 35 nm gate length mHEMTs, a four-stage submillimeter-wave amplifier circuit was developed at Fraunhofer IAF, demon-strating reasonable bandwidth and high small-signal gain in the WR-2.2 waveguide band (325 to 500 GHz). The circuit design was described in detail in [7]. The utilized transistors are in common-source configuration and have a gate width of 2×5 µm, each. Special care was taken in the design of the RF shunt capacitance networks to ensure low-frequency stability of the submillimeter-wave monolithic integrated cir-cuits (S-MMICs). Fig. 2 (left) shows a chip photograph of this amplifier S-MMIC. The compact coplanar layout resulted in a die size of only 0.37×0.63 mm^2.

The measurement results were described in detail in [9], [10]. On-wafer S-parameter measurements were performed using an Agilent 8510C VNA system with an 85105A submillimeter controller, two Oleson WR-2.2 T/R frequency exten-sion modules, and two Cascade Infinity 500 RF-probes with a pitch of 60 µm. The measured and simulated S-parameters of the four-stage WR-2.2 amplifier are depicted in Fig. 2 (right). A peak gain of 16.1 dB was achieved at 460 GHz. Between 433 and 465 GHz, a small-signal gain of more than 13 dB was obtained. The amplifier S-MMIC operates in the 500 GHz frequency regime and simultaneously demonstrates an excellent gain-per-stage performance. The input return loss S_{11} is -8 dB and the output return loss S_{22} is -19 dB at 460 GHz. Due to the lack of a suitable noise source, the noise figure of the S-MMIC could not be measured so far, the simulated value is 9.7 dB at 460 GHz.

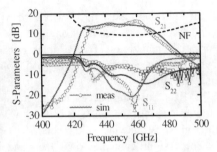

Fig. 2. Left: chip photograph of four-stage 460 GHz mHEMT amplifier S-MMIC, right: on-wafer measured and simulated S-parameters, dotted line: simulated noise figure

4   300 GHz Receiver S-MMIC Based on 50 nm mHEMT Technology

An example of multifunctional S-MMICs developed at Fraunhofer IAF is a subharmonic receiver circuit, described in detail in [11]. Fig. 3 shows the chip photograph of a subharmonic 300 GHz heterodyne receiver circuit, consisting of a frequency multiplier-by-three, a two-stage driver amplifier, a resistive mixer, and a four-stage low-noise amplifier. The corresponding block diagram with the separate components is presented in Fig. 4. Due to high operating frequency, the chip size of the S-MMIC is only 0.5×2.5 mm^2. The S-MMIC was realized in metamorphic high electron mobility transistor (mHEMT) technology with 50 nm gate length. The function of the circuit in high resolution radar systems is the transfer of the high frequency input signal into a lower frequency band for subsequent data processing.

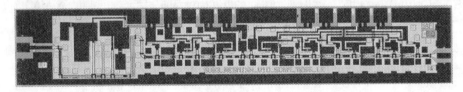

Fig. 3. Chip photograph of the subharmonic 300 GHz heterodyne receiver S-MMIC

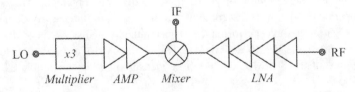

Fig. 4. Schematic diagram of the subharmonic 300 GHz heterodyne receiver S-MMIC

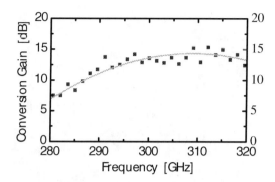

Fig. 5. Conversion gain as a function of frequency of the subharmonic 300 GHz heterodyne receiver S-MMIC, measured at 100 MHz intermediate frequency and 8 dBm input power

The measurement results of the subharmonic 300 GHz heterodyne receiver S-MMIC were described in detail in [11]. The on-wafer measured conversion gain of the heterodyne receiver plotted as a function of frequency is shown in Fig. 5. Because of the integrated four-stage low-noise amplifier a conversion gain of more than 12 dB was achieved in the frequency range from 290 to 320 GHz. The applied input power at the subharmonic LO port was only 8 dBm at 100 GHz. All measurements were performed at an intermediate frequency of 100 MHz.

5   Millimeter-Wave Imaging System for Materials Testing and Concealed Object Detection

Materials testing is a continuously growing application field. Depending on the substance there are different challenges which require new methods. Fraunhofer IAF develops multifunctional MMICs which are needed for non-destructive materials investigation and testing. Millimeter waves penetrate dielectric substances like plastics, paper, and cardboard. On the other hand, they are nearly completely reflected by high-conductive materials (e.g. metals); weakly conductive materials attenuate and absorb millimeter waves. At dielectric interfaces, where different materials get into touch, one part of the incident wave is reflected and the other is transmitted.

Because of low »photonic energy«, millimeter waves are non-ionizing and notably harmless to humans compared to X-rays. The radiation power needed for materials testing amounts to only a few milliwatts and is therefore insignificant.

Fig. 6 shows the photograph of the developed W-band millimeter-wave imaging system. The block diagram of millimeter-wave components used inside this system is shown in Fig. 7, a detailed description is presented in [12].

206   M. Schlechtweg et al.

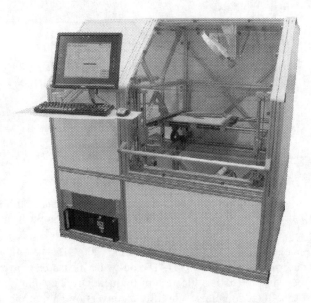

Fig. 6. Photograph of the entire millimeter-wave imaging system developed at Fraunhofer IAF

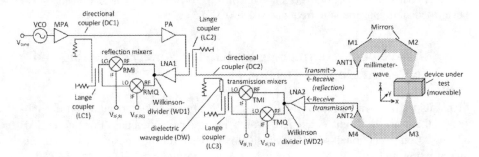

Fig. 7. Block diagram of a material scanner with millimeter-wave components. All RF devices are in-house developments.

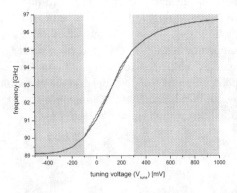

Fig. 8. VCO output frequency as a function of the applied tuning voltage

The scanner was designed to demonstrate the capability of the millimeter-wave technology. The system is build using in-house W-band components. The object is illuminated with low-power millimeter waves in the frequency range between 89 and 96 GHz; mirrors are used to guide and focus the beam. The object is moved through the focus point to scan the object pixel by pixel. Depending on the actual material, some parts of the waves are reflected, the other parts penetrate the object. A single-antenna transmit and receive module is used for illumination and measurement of the material-specific reflected power. A second receiver module is used to measure the transmitted wave. All information is processed for amplitude and phase based images by a computer algorithm.

The system can be used for security applications, such as detecting concealed weapons, explosives or contrabands at airports and other safety areas, but also quality assurance applications, e.g. during production to detect defects. Through a focused beam, materials under test can be precisely moved 300 mm in all three dimensions and can be analyzed by beam transmission as well as reflection. The quasi-optical ray path is shown in Fig. 7 on the right. The setup with four off-set parabolic mirrors is designed to be extremely broadband, which allows using different high-frequency components from 0.1 to 3 THz. Quasi-optical pictures which uncover concealed details can be produced with the aid of this demonstrator.

A voltage-controlled oscillator (VCO) is used for signal generation. Depending on the applied tuning voltage (V_{tune}), a millimeter-wave in the range of 89 to 96 GHz is generated. The frequency response of the VCO is shown in Fig. 8. To generate a linear frequency ramp in the range from 90 to 95 GHz, the tuning voltage is limited to a range from -100 to +300 mV.

The signal is then amplified by a medium power amplifier (MPA). A part of the signal is extracted by a directional coupler (DC1) and split as well as 90 degree phase shifted by a Lange coupler (LC1), to feed the reflection IQ-mixers (RMI, RMQ) as local oscillator (LO). The main signal from the VCO is amplified by a power amplifier (PA) and brought to the antenna (ANT1) by a second Lange coupler (LC2). A 15 dB gain rectangular horn is used as antenna. The radiated millimeter-wave beam is then guided by two offset-parabolic mirrors (M1, M2) and focused into one point at the device under test.

Depending on the material and geometrical surface of the DUT, a part of the wave can be reflected. The reflected wave is directed by the same mirrors (M1 and M2) back into the same antenna (ANT1). The Lange coupler (LC2) separates the transmitted and received signals. Although a circulator would perform better, we used a Lange coupler as a directional coupler, because of the feasibility of MMIC integration. The received reflected signal behind LC2 is amplified by a low-noise amplifier (LNA1) and split in-phase by a Wilkinson-divider (WD1) to support the receive in-phase and quadrature phase mixers (RMI, RMQ). The intermediate frequency reflection signals $V_{IF,RI}$ and $V_{IF,RQ}$ are used for later data evaluation. All above mentioned RF components of the scanner are realized on a single chip MMIC and are included in an enhanced version of an in-house fabricated W-band module which was originally designed as frequency-modulated continuous-wave (FMCW) radar [13].

Millimeter waves, that penetrate the DUT, are directed by two additional mirrors (M3, M4) to a second antenna (ANT2), which is a 25 dB gain rectangular horn. The penetrated signal from the DUT is also amplified (LNA2), split in-phase by a second

Wilkinson divider (WD2) and brought to the transmission in-phase and quadrature mixers (TMI, TMQ). The LO signal for TMI/Q is generated by a discrete 10 dB directional waveguide coupler (DC2) between the FMCW module and the antenna (ANT1). This LO signal is again split and 90 degree phase-shifted (LC3) for the TMI/Q. The transmit IF signals $V_{IF,TI}$ and $V_{IF,TQ}$ are used for later data evaluation as well. For all transmission components (LNA2, WD2, LC3, MTI, MTQ), an in-house single-chip, single-channel IQ-receiver is used.

To demonstrate the possibilities of the developed imaging system for safety and security applications, two examples are presented in the following: imaging of defects in composite materials and detection of concealed weapons inside a package.

Testing of composite materials (e.g. for aerospace) can be advantageously carried out by millimeter waves. At present, testing of the solidity of wind power rotary wings is under discussion, because the number of installed plants constantly increases. Meanwhile, many old wind power plants have already collected huge hours of operation in service with numberless load alternations. Spontaneous wing crashes with incalculable outcomes increase. To ensure safety, new and cost-efficient testing technologies have to be developed, which enable plant vendors and carriers to perform materials testing not only during production but also in the field. Great danger occurs with creeping delamination of composite fiber mattings and consequential spontaneous wing breakdown. This kind of material defect reveals dielectric discontinuities, which can be detected more reliably by millimeter waves than by ultrasound. Fig. 9 shows a photograph of a glass-fiber reinforced plastic wing shaft with a laminated carbon fiber mat and balsa wood and the corresponding millimeter-wave transmission figure at 94 GHz on the right. Destructive interference lines and higher absorption of the carbon fiber can be clearly seen.

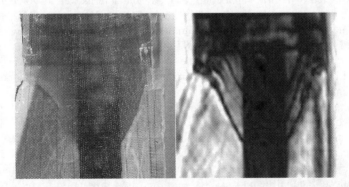

Fig. 9. Wing shaft of a wind power plant made of glass-fiber reinforced plastic with laminated carbon fiber mat and balsa wood next to the corresponding millimeter-wave image at 94 GHz. Interference lines and absorption of the weakly conductive carbon mat can be seen.

Reflections from interfaces can be investigated using radar technology operating at millimeter- or THz-wave ranges. The locations of voids inside the composite material can be distinguished by the echo signal duration time. This new non-destructive radar measurement technology operates at comparatively short distances in strong absorbing and dispersive materials and needs special multifunctional MMICs. Suitable radiation power and ultra-low-noise amplification of weak radar echoes is essential. Additional complex computation is necessary to interpret the signal phase information, which requires the adoption of I/Q mixers. Fig. 10 shows the chip photograph of an MMIC with integrated low-noise amplifier, I/Q mixer, LO amplifier, Wilkinson splitter and Lange coupler for the W-band, as utilized in the developed millimeter-wave material scanner.

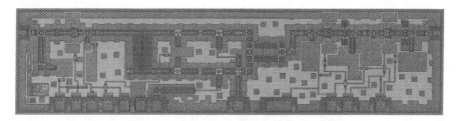

Fig. 10. Chip photograph of a 94 GHz receiver MMIC including LNA and I/Q mixer

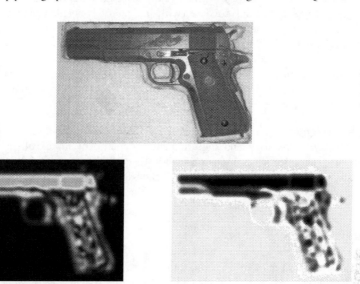

Fig. 11. Top: optical image of a gun taken from the opened package. Bottom: reconstructed millimeter-wave images of the gun concealed inside a closed package (left: reflected amplitude, right: reflected phase). Reflections from the metal can be easily identified. Details of the magazine underneath the molded plastic grip become visible.

Another example of images for security applications is shown in Fig. 11. A handgun is concealed inside a block of extruded polystyrene foam (Styrofoam). While polystyrene is transparent in the millimeter-wave range, the gun becomes visible, although it cannot be seen in the optical range. Furthermore the plastic hand grip also becomes semitransparent, so that even the subjacent magazine and cartridges become visible in the reflection images. The phase image contains information about the surface structure of the gun. In this case a darker area represents a shorter distance from the antenna or respectively a heightening in the object surface. Nevertheless, phase jumps will appear at every $\lambda/2$-change in surface height, meaning that the color will change from black to white.

6   Conclusion

Advanced MMIC technology features two important aspects, namely the ability for multifunctional circuit fabrication and very broadband operation. Particularly, it fosters the development of broadband and multifunctional integrated circuits and modules operating at frequencies up to 600 GHz and above. In this paper, the potential of this technology at very high frequencies was demonstrated by means of two circuits: a 460 GHz amplifier S-MMIC and a 300 GHz heterodyne receiver S-MMIC. These components were realized at Fraunhofer IAF using a well-established metamorphic HEMT technology featuring a grounded CPW process.

A novel millimeter-wave imaging system for concealed object detection and materials testing was presented, together with images of concealed objects. This scanner exploits both amplitude and phase information of the signals which is enabled by multifunctional MMICs as well as a low-loss millimeter-wave packaging. The achieved results reveal the high potential of active millimeter-wave components realized using advanced III/V semiconductor technologies for application in safety and security systems at highest frequencies, which is expected to enable manifold novel applications in the future.

Acknowledgment. The authors would like to thank their colleagues from the Fraunhofer IAF epitaxy, technology and high-frequency department for excellent wafer growth, processing, and characterization. This work was partially funded by the German Federal Ministry of Defense (BMVg) and the Bundeswehr Technical Center for Information Technology and Electronics (WTD81) in the framework of the TERAMOSS program.

References

1. Gas Mixture Spectra, http://hitran.iao.ru/gasmixture/spectr
2. Appleby, R., Wallace, H.B.: Standoff Detection of Weapons and Contraband in the 100 GHz to 1 THz Region. IEEE Trans. Antennas Propag. 55, 2944–2956 (2007)
3. Cooper, K.B., Dengler, R.J., Llombart, N., Thomas, B., Chattopadhyay, G., Siegel, P.H.: THz Imaging Radar for Standoff Personnel Screening. IEEE Trans. Terahertz Sci. Technol. 1, 169–182 (2011)
4. Ahmed, S.S., Schiessl, A., Schmidt, L.-P.: A Novel Fully Electronic Active Real-Time Imager Based on a Planar Multistatic Sparse Array. IEEE Trans. Microw. Theory Tech. 59, 3567–3576 (2011)
5. Friedrich, F., von Spiegel, W., Bauer, M., Meng, F., Thomson, M.D., Boppel, S., Lisauskas, A., Hils, B., Krozer, V., Keil, A., Löffler, T., Henneberger, R., Huhn, A.K., Spickermann, G., Bolivar, P.H., Roskos, H.G.: THz Active Imaging Systems With Real-Time Capabilities. IEEE Trans. Terahertz Sci. Technol. 1, 183–200 (2011)
6. Hantscher, S., Schlenther, B., Hägelen, M., Lang, S.A., Essen, H., Tessmann, A., Hülsmann, A., Leuther, A., Schlechtweg, M.: Security Pre-screening of Moving Persons Using a Rotating Multichannel W-Band Radar. IEEE Trans. Microw. Theory Tech. 60, 870–880 (2012)

7. Leuther, A., Tessmann, A., Kallfass, I., Lösch, R., Seelmann-Eggebert, M., Wadefalk, N., Schäfer, F., Gallego Puyol, J.D., Schlechtweg, M., Mikulla, M., Ambacher, O.: Metamorphic HEMT Technology for Low-Noise Applications. In: Proc 21st Int. Conf. Indium Phospide Related Mater., pp. 188–191 (2009)
8. Leuther, A., Tessmann, A., Kallfass, I., Massler, H., Loesch, R., Schlechtweg, M., Mikulla, M., Ambacher, A.: Metamorphic HEMT Technology for Submillimeter-Wave MMIC Applications. In: Proc. 22nd Int. Conf. Indium Phospide Related Mater., pp. 425-430 (2010)
9. Tessmann, A., Leuther, A., Hurm, V., Kallfass, I., Massler, H., Kuri, M., Riessle, M., Zink, M., Lösch, R., Seelmann-Eggebert, M., Schlechtweg, M., Ambacher, O.: Metamorphic HEMT MMICs and Modules Operating Between 300 and 500 GHz. IEEE J. Solid-State Circuits 46, 2193–2202 (2011)
10. Tessmann, A., Leuther, A., Loesch, R., Seelmann-Eggebert, M., Massler, H.: A Metamorphic HEMT S-MMIC Amplifier With 16.1 dB Gain at 460 GHz. In: IEEE Compound Semicond. IC Symp. Dig., pp. 245–248 (2010)
11. Tessmann, A., Massler, H., Lewark, U.J., Wagner, S., Kallfass, I., Leuther, A.: Fully integrated 300 GHz Receiver S-MMICs in 50 nm Metamorphic HEMT Technology. In: IEEE Compound Semicond. IC Symp. Dig., pp. 219–222 (2011)
12. Zech, C., Hülsmann, A., Kallfass, I., Tessmann, A., Zink, M., Schlechtweg, M., Leuther, A., Ambacher, O.: Active Millimeter-Wave Imaging System for Material Analysis and Object Detection. In: Krapels, K.A., et al. (eds.) Proc. SPIE Millimetre Wave and Terahertz Sensors and Technology IV, Bellingham, WA, vol. 8188, pp. 81880D-1–81880D-9 (2011)
13. Tessmann, A., Kudszus, S., Feltgen, T., Riessle, M., Sklarczyk, C., Haydl, W.J.: Compact Single-Chip W-Band FMCW Radar Modules for Commercial High-Resolution Sensor Applications. IEEE Trans. Microw. Theory Tech. 50, 2995–3001 (2002)

Data Simulation and Testing of Visual Algorithms in Synthetic Environments for Security Sensor Networks

Georg Hummel[1], Levente Kovács[2], Peter Stütz[1], and Tamás Szirányi[2]

[1] Institute of Flight Systems, Universität der Bundeswehr München, Neubiberg, Germany
http://www.unibw.de/lrt13
[2] Computer and Automation Research Institute, Hungarian Academy of Sciences, Hungary
http://web.eee.sztaki.hu

Abstract. Current development of security sensor networks and their processing algorithms use pre-recorded or abstract data streams for testing, often missing important ground truth for validation. This paper proposes a simulation-based test bed, presenting an approach to use commercial off the shelf virtual reality environments to create adaptive simulations of sensors, data streams and scenarios for training and testing perceptive algorithms. An example using airborne visual multi object tracking is discussed and validated.

Keywords: virtual reality, simulation, security networks, computer vision.

1 Introduction

Security sensor networks are designed to analyze the current situation to detect possible threats in urban environments. To achieve this, information processing modules on different inference layers are commonly chained together (e.g. signal processing, fusion and reasoning) [1-2]. To develop and test such systems, coherent datasets for different sensors are needed to stimulate reasoning algorithms [3]. Taking into account today's highly complex scenarios, the traditional way to stage and record live data often turns out to be problematic because of limited financial, time and human resources. Therefore, simulations and virtual reality have been reviewed as suitable substitutes [4]. This paper presents a first validation for using a virtual environment to stimulate perceptive algorithms, evaluated with a multi object tracking algorithm. Using the presented test approach, our vision is to be able to test perceptive modules in early development stages without the final system, which can mean large cost savings, since the effort to generate real test data for large scale scenarios, multiple synchronized sensors or complex mobile sensor platforms can be reduced.

2 Integrated Test Bed for Experimentation on Mission Sensors

The *Integrated Test bed for Experimentation on Mission sensors* (ITEM) [5] consists of a virtual environment and a virtual sensor layer. Our platform of choice for the simulation of scenarios, sensors, objects and events in a virtual environment was

N. Aschenbruck et al. (Eds.): Future Security 2012, CCIS 318, pp. 212–215, 2012.

VBS2 [9], which can provide multiple synchronized visual sensor streams through a shared scenario. Main components of the virtual environment are the mission scenario, the scenario environment and the simulation engine. Entity behavior and their interaction with the world are described in the Mission Scenario. Environmental conditions such as weather, time and terrain are declared in the Scenario Environment. The simulation engine renders the situation based on the above modules.

The virtual sensor layer modifies image and semantic data received from the virtual environment to model sensor characteristics compliant with their real counterparts. Sensor Models define the nature of simulated sensors, which can be EO or IR cameras, light barriers, sniper detectors, NBC sniffers, etc. Since the simulated world and simulated sensor parameters can be "perfect" from different aspects (e.g. location, quality, accuracy, availability), custom signal perturbation filters can be added to create a more realistic sensor output (e.g. resize, signal/transmission noise, optical distortions). Sensor output is accessible for testing clients through common distribution methods like MPEG-TS, RTP and Spread [10]. Ground truth data for validation can also be generated, logically separated from sensor data. Sensor models can be configured from outside the test bed to allow hardware-in-the-loop simulation of automated mechanisms or systems (e.g. self managing networks, unmanned aerial vehicles). Thus, ITEM is able to simulate a mission scenario in a virtual world with virtual sensors, to provide sensor data for processing applications including security networks, surveillance systems, or visual processing algorithms.

3   Reference Application and Test Results

The following proof-of-concept setup has been built (Fig. 1): ITEM interfaces with the GSN middleware [11], which handles registration and control of processing modules. Modules can be plugged into GSN either as direct implementations (e.g. C++ through JNI wrapping) or as external applications (e.g. native Linux applications), connecting through Web services or local XML data sources.

For performance comparisons of real and synthetic test data, a real video stream was reverse engineered for the synthetic environment (Fig. 2). The real stream shows a busy road in Budapest from a camera mounted to a hovering flying platform. Camera settings (Field of View, Aperture and Focus) and Platform movement (X-, Y-direction and Angles) have been modeled after the real footage using a simplified dynamic model (see Table 1). The reference test application shall monitor the moving entities on the street, which can be valuable for security applications.

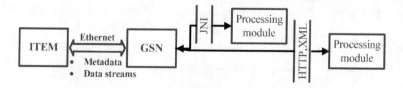

Fig. 1. Proof-of-concept architecture

Table 1. Ranges of the airborne camera motion model

variable ranges	Position	Heading	Pitch	Bank	Height
length/angle	x±2m	0±0°	-90±10°	0 ±10°	50±0m
linear/angular speed	x±1m/s	0±0°/s	0±2,5°/s	0±2,5°/s	0±0m

The purpose of the airborne object tracker is to provide real-time ground target detection and tracking. The goal was to use fast solutions running on cheap commodity hardware, providing passive visual detection, tracking and traffic analysis capabilities for area surveillance and protection. The method is a novel approach based on [6,7], developed considering real-time applicability, built on the following steps: (a) Feature point extraction (Harris corners [8] for performance). (b) Frame stabilization and warping of consecutive frames based on motion information and extracted feature points. Corresponding points from consecutive frames are searched by Lucas-Kanade optical flow, and since camera motion is not restricted to translation or rotation, a more general perspective transformation is used. (c) Background-foreground separation: the background is modeled and updated in the common coordinate system, calculating the pixel-based running average and variance of consecutive frames. Generic Mixture of Gaussians cannot be used because of the free camera motions. (d) Object detection: object candidates are the blobs from the foreground obtained in the previous step. (e) Object tracking using motion information, object features and Kalman filtering, with the Hungarian method [7] for object-track assignment.

3.1   Test Results

Table 2 contains evaluation data on real and simulated video footage, in order to compare the performance of the UAV object tracker given different inputs. Three numerical evaluations have been performed: (a) PDR (presence detection ratio): the ratio of detections vs. all possible locations during the ground truth presence of an object (i.e. if object A is present on N number of frames and detected for M times: $PDR=M/N$). (b) P (precision): the ratio of good detections vs. all detections. (c) R (recall): the ratio of good detections vs. all possible detections.

The results show that numerical performance values are usually fairly similar, but values are better when the algorithm runs on simulated data. The reason for this is that: i). Simulated footage is usually lacking real life noise (optical, environmental, network, etc.) and ii). Objects in the simulated feed are easier to detect and track (sharp edges, constant speed, constant size, repeating textures and objects, etc.). However, preliminary results confirm the usability of simulated data from virtual environments for the purposes of developing and testing visual processing modules.

Table 2. Evaluation for real and simulated data (Presence Detection Ratio, Precision, Recall)

Test data type	PDR	P	R
Real footage	84%	77%	84%
Simulated footage	90%	93%	85%

Fig. 2. Ground object detections from real (left) and simulated (right) UAV camera feeds

4   Conclusion and Future Work

The presented test approach demonstrated the viability of using simulated data for testing and development of perceptive modules (especially visual algorithms), and shows general usability for detection and tracking. The lack of optical and signal errors can simplify processing in synthetic feeds, and these issues will be addressed in future work. The benefits of such an approach are the availability of ground truth data for automatic evaluation, closed loop simulations and prompt repeatability. Also, testing the performance of classification and identification methods in such simulated environments is of high interest, due to the limited variety in textures and entities. For supplementary information please visit http://web.eee.sztaki.hu/fs.

References

1. Medusa Consortium: Multi Sensor Data Fusion Grid for Urban Situational Awareness, http://medusa-project.eu
2. Collins, R., Lipton, A., Fujiyoshi, H., Kanade, T.: Algorithms for cooperative multisensor surveillance. Proc. of the IEEE 89(10), 1456–1477 (2001)
3. Doulaverakis, C., Konstantinou, N., Knape, T., Kompatsiaris, I., Soldatos, J.: An approach to intelligent information fusion in sensor saturated urban environments. In: Proc. of IEEE European Intelligence and Security Informatics Conference (EISIC), pp. 108–115 (2011)
4. Burger, W., Barth, M.J.: Virtual Reality for enhanced computer vision. In: Proc. IFIP 5.10 Workshop on Virtual Environments (1994)
5. Hummel, G., Stütz, P.: Conceptual design of a simulation test bed for ad-hoc sensor networks based on a serious gaming environment. In: Proc. Intl. Training and Education Conference, ITEC (2011)
6. Kovács, L.: Benedek, C.: Visual real-time detection, recognition and tracking of ground and airborne targets. In: Proc. Computational Imaging IX, SPIE-IS&T Electronic Imaging, vol. 7873, pp. 787311-1–787311-12. SPIE (2011)
7. Máttyus, G., Benedek, C., Szirányi, T.: Multi target tracking on aerial videos. In: Proc. of ISPRS Workshop on Modeling of Optical Airborne and Space Borne Sensors (2010)
8. Taixe, L.L., Heydt, M., Rosenhahn, A., Rosenhahn, B.: Automatic tracking of swimming microorganisms in 4D digital in-line holography data. In: Proc. of WMVC, pp. 1–9 (2009)
9. Virtual Battlespace 2, Bohemia Interactive Simulations, http://armory.bisimulations.com/products/vbs2/overview
10. Amir, Y., Nita-Rotaru, C., Stanton, J., Tsudik, G.: Secure Spread: An Integrated Architecture for Secure Group Communication. IEEE Trans. on DSC 2(3), 248–266 (2005)
11. Salehi, A., Riahi, M., Michel, S., Aberer, K.: GSN, middleware for Stream World. In: Proc. of 10th Intl. Conf. on Mobile Data Management, MDM (2009)

Unmanned Inspection of Large Industrial Environments

Insights into the Research Project RoboGas[Inspector]

Thomas Barz[1], Gero Bonow[2], Jens Hegenberg[3], Karim Habib[4], Liubov Cramar[3], Jochen Welle[1], Dirk Schulz[1], Andreas Kroll[2], and Ludger Schmidt[3]

[1] Fraunhofer Institute for Communication, Information Processing and Ergonomics FKIE,
Research Group Unmanned Systems, Neuenahrer Straße 20, 53343 Wachtberg, Germany
{thomas.barz,jochen.welle,dirk.schulz}@fkie.fraunhofer.de
[2] University of Kassel,
Faculty of Mechanical Engineering, Measurement and Control Department,
Mönchebergstraße 7, 34125 Kassel, Germany
{gero.bonow,andreas.kroll}@mrt.uni-kassel.de
[3] University of Kassel, Faculty of Mechanical Engineering,
Human-Machine-Systems Engineering Department,
Mönchebergstraße 7, 34125 Kassel, Germany
{j.hegenberg,l.cramar,l.schmidt}@uni-kassel.de
[4] BAM Federal Institute of Materials Research and Testing,
Departement 2 "Chemical Safety Engineering",
Unter den Eichen 87, 12205 Berlin, Germany
karim.habib@bam.de

Abstract. Industrial plants are a vital and common asset of modern society in a various number of ways. Safety of large industrial complexes that handle hazardous chemical materials is of utter importance to prevent harm to employees, general population, our natural environment and valuable infrastructure. Therefore, besides the plant owner's own financial interest to guarantee faultless and safe operation, legal regulations have to be adhered as well. An important measure to ensure safety is the implementation of regular inspection tours by maintenance personnel, who examine the often widely-stretched process infrastructure on foot and locally search for signs of beginning leakage. The research project RoboGas[Inspector] was started to develop new means of aiding with the fulfillment of this essential task. This article gives an overview of this ongoing research project, where autonomous mobile robotics is combined with laser-based remote gas detection technology in order to create a proof-of-concept inspection system prototype, which can relieve humans of this monotonous and highly repetitive work.

Keywords: unmanned system, industrial inspection, mobile robot, plant safety, gas detection, leak localization, remote sensor technology, human-machine interface.

1 Introduction and Motivation

Using an autonomously acting robot system equipped with all the measuring equipment needed for leakage inspections, instead of a human worker, seems a promising

N. Aschenbruck et al. (Eds.): Future Security 2012, CCIS 318, pp. 216–219, 2012.
© Springer-Verlag Berlin Heidelberg 2012

approach with a lot of benefits. The robot system would guarantee a constant quality level of the inspections and their documentation, which could be used to satisfy the legal safety authorities. Remote sensor technology enables the system to inspect locations that may be difficult to access otherwise and can yield a better coverage of inspected objects. Plant personnel could be relieved of a great deal of monotonous and highly repetitive inspection work, so that they could focus on more appropriate tasks, where their professional expertise, experience and human judgment are needed.

Fig. 1. Infrastructure of industrial project partners and possible application domain for a robotic inspection system: petroleum refinery (left) and gas compressor station (right)

2   System RoboGas^{Inspector}

The RoboGas^{Inspector} is composed of three main software and hardware components. Together they provide a complete system to perform inspection duties in different industrial facilities like shown in Fig. 1.

2.1   Robot System

The measurement robot prototype itself essentially consists of three major components: a robust chain-driven chassis, which also houses the system's main batteries; an autonomy compartment module, that contains technical devices needed for autonomous operation, while also serving as central infrastructure hub and baseplate for necessary superstructures; and a top-mounted inspection module that features remote sensing technology and intelligence for leak detection (see Fig. 2). A more technical description of hardware and software can be found at [3].

Localization and Navigation: A fundamental prerequisite for navigation, and hence autonomous mobility, is to determine and continuously monitor the current location of the robot. For that purpose the system design follows a two-fold approach which combines GPS measurements with well-known SLAM approaches. Provided with adequate means of localization, a navigation system was implemented that is able to maneuver the robot to a specified target position.

Obstacle Detection: Two planar-mounted laser range scanners at the compartment module serve as main devices for obstacle detection and SLAM purposes. While the robot is moving, the obstacle detection system additionally takes control of the tiltable laser scanner of the inspection module and monitors the ground in front of the robot to detect smaller obstacles that are below the scanning plane.

2.2   Remote Gas Detection and Leak Localization

Many technical gases (e.g. methane) absorb radiation at different wavelengths in the infrared spectrum. The absorption behavior of every gas is unique, thus it can serve as means of identification. This absorption effect is used by the inspection module's remote gas measuring devices (see number 3 and 6 in the left part of Fig 2). If the wavelength dependent absorption behavior of the gas is known, the integral gas within the optical path can be determined by using the Lambert-Beer Law [4].

Measuring Gas Concentrations: The detection of gas clouds in industrial environments occurs in two steps. In the first step an area measurement is carried out by scanning interesting inspection frustums that were defined by the system operator before. If a significant integral gas concentration is ascertained, the direction of the maximum gas concentration will be iteratively searched by using the raster based searching strategy DRS, which is described in [2].

Leak Localization: The results from the DRS method will be forwarded to a localization routine in order to find the leak position. For this task, the uncertainties of the measured pose of the robot, uncertainties in sensor readings and the dynamic of gas clouds have to be considered. Two different methods have been tested: the maximum method which iteratively moves the robot towards the maximum, and the triangulation method which uses measurements from different angles for leak triangulation. The maximum method has turned out to be more robust while the triangulation method requires less execution time (approx. four times less than the maximum method).

2.3   Human-Robot Interaction

The presented system is designed as a human-robot system, which synergistically combines the capabilities of human beings and autonomous robots. [5]

Supervisory Control: The implemented human-robot interaction is based on the concept of supervisory control [1]. Humans are involved by fulfilling the supervisory functions of planning inspections, monitoring their conduction, interpreting their results and teleoperating the robot.

User Interface: The user interface supports three phases common to all considered inspection processes: planning, conducting and documentation. Beside the current video image of the robot a satellite image is shown in the GUI. It can be overlaid with multiple information layers showing the current robot pose, sensor readings, measured distances to obstacles and risk zones based on gas detections.

Teleoperation Interface: The teleoperation interface is specifically designed for complex teleoperation tasks which need enhanced perception and control facilities. It allows immersive and stereoscopic visualization to support telepresence and the perception of depth. A head-mounted display shows the gathered 3D video images.

Fig. 2. Inspection module (left), fully assembled robot (middle), teleoperation interface (right)

3   Summary and Outlook

In this paper we gave a quick overview of the motivation and different aspects of the research project RoboGas^Inspector. Although the project phase of comprehensive outdoor tests and final evaluation is just about to come, a positive conclusion from the gathered experience can already be drawn. The general concept of a robotic system for unmanned inspection of large industrial environments seems to be feasible.

Acknowledgements. The project RoboGas^Inspector is funded by the German Federal Ministry of Economics and Technology due to a resolution of the German Bundestag. The authors would like to thank the project partners for their valuable support and collaboration.

References

1. Sheridan, T.B.: Humans and Automation: System Design and Research Issues. Wiley series in systems engineering and management 3. Wiley, New York (2002)
2. Baetz, W., Kroll, A., Bonow, G.: Mobile Robots with Active IR-Optical Sensing for Remote Gas Detection and Source Localization. In: Kazuhiro Kosuge, K.I. (ed.) IEEE International Conference on Robotics and Automation (ICRA 2009), Kobe, pp. 2773–2778 (2009); IEEE Catalog Number: CFP09RAA-DVD
3. Soldan, S., et al.: Towards Autonomous Robotic Systems for Remote Gas Leak Detection and Localization in Industrial Environments. In: International Conference on Field and Service Robotics (2012)
4. Frish, M.B., et al.: The next generation of TDLAS analyzers. In: Society of Photo-Optical Instrumentation Engineers Optics East, vol. 6765, pp. 76506–76517 (2009)
5. Hegenberg, J., Cramar, L., Schmidt, L.: Task- and user-centered design of a human-robot system for gas leak detection: From requirements analysis to prototypical realization. In: 10th International IFAC Symposium on Robot Control (2012)

The LabDisk – A Fully Automated Centrifugal Lab-on-a-Chip System for the Detection of Biological Threats

Thomas van Oordt[1], Oliver Strohmeier[1], Daniel Mark[1], Roland Zengerle[1,2,3],
Michael Eberhard[4], Josef Drexler[4], Pranav Patel[5], Manfred Weidmann[6],
Andrea Zgaga-Griesz[7], Wolfgang G. Bessler[7], and Felix von Stetten[1,2]

[1] HSG-IMIT - Institut für Mikro- und Informationstechnik, Villingen-Schwenningen, Germany
[2] Laboratory for MEMS Applications, Department of Microsystems Engineering - IMTEK,
University of Freiburg, Freiburg, Germany
[3] BIOSS-Centre for Biological Signalling Studies, Universiy of Freiburg, Freiburg, Germany
[4] QIAGEN Lake Constance GmbH, Stockach, Germany
[5] Robert Koch Institut, Berlin Germany
[6] Department of Virology, University Medical Center Göttingen, Göttingen, Germany
[7] Institute for Molecular Medicine and Cell Research, University Medical Center Freiburg,
Freiburg, Germany

Abstract. The world's growing mobility, mass tourism and the threat of terrorism increase the risk of a fast spread of infectious microorganisms and toxins. Therefore, there is a growing demand for small, mobile, easy to use diagnostic systems for automated detection of those agents directly at the point of need. However, the state of the art for pathogen detection requires complex stationary devices and trained personal limiting the capability for a rapid and effective response. We present an alternative solution to this demand: the LabDisk platform, a portable fully automated Lab-on-a-Chip system which performs complex biochemical analyses at the point of need. We applied the LabDisk platform to an automated nucleic acid analysis for the detection of *Bacillus anthracis* and *Francisella tularensis* and to an immunoassay for the detection of ricin.

Keywords: Lab-on-a-chip, immunoassay, nucleic acid assay, portable point-of-care devce, LabDisk.

1   The LabDisk Platform

The platform consists of a disposable centrifugal-microfluidic cartridge, the "LabDisk", in which completely integrated biochemical protocols for nucleic acid or protein analyses can be performed. For cartridge processing, a portable device, the "LabDisk Player" was developed. This device automatically controls fluid processing, heating and signal acquisition via fluorescence or luminescence. Due to the size and weight of the processing device (178 x 283 x 150 mm^3; 2 kg), the system is suitable for use at the point-of-need.

N. Aschenbruck et al. (Eds.): Future Security 2012, CCIS 318, pp. 220–223, 2012.
© Springer-Verlag Berlin Heidelberg 2012

1.1   LabDisk Player

The LabDisk Player is able to run a fully automated and defined rotation- and temperature protocol to control the complete analysis. The processing device incorporates a heater for isothermal incubation or nucleic acid amplification at up to 60 °C and two detection units for either fluorescence or chemiluminescence readout (Figure 1).

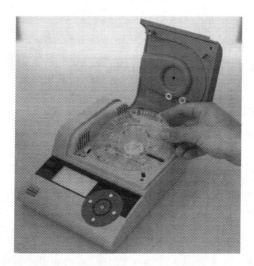

Fig. 1. The portable LabDisk Player. Integrated magnets can be used for the automated control and manipulation of magnetic beads e.g. for nucleic acid purification or bead based immunoassays

1.2   LabDisk

Disposable micro-thermoformed polymer films, the LabDisks [1] were used to implement a nucleic acid analysis and an immunoassay. For both assays, the complete microfluidic structures have been integrated into the foil-based cartridges and all the microfluidic unit operations required to perform the assays have been verified.

Nucleic Acid Analysis
The LabDisk for nucleic acid analysis includes blood plasma sample preparation featuring initial pathogen lysis and subsequent DNA extraction according to a standard bench top bind-wash-elute protocol (Figure 2, left). As a solid phase, silica coated magnetic particles are applied that can be manipulated by the magnets that are integrated into the processing device [2]. After DNA extraction the sample solution is aliquoted in up to 11 cavities with 10 μL volume each. In each cavity, a set of pathogen specific primers and probes is prestored and enables specific amplification and detection via isothermal real time recombinase polymerase amplification (RPA). The systems functionality was demonstrated by automated detection of *Bacillus anthracis* and *Francisella tularensis* from blood plasma samples in less than 45 minutes (Figure 2, right).

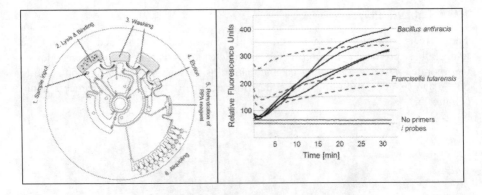

Fig. 2. The nucleic acid analysis. Left: Fluidic design of the disposable LabDisk. Right: On-disk detection of *Bacillus anthracis* and *Francisella tularensis*.

Immunoassay

The immunoassay is based on a sandwich ELISA where one anti-ricin antibody is covalently linked to magnetic beads as solid phase. It will allow the detection of ricin from blood plasma samples. Figure 3 shows a LabDisk with the microfluidic design for the immunoassay with integrated aluminum pouches for reagent pre-storage. Primary tests show the successful detection of 10 ng/ml ricin from a citrated blood plasma sample in 45 minutes of which 30 minutes are needed for incubation. For the primary tests reagents were stored in cavities on the cartridge without the aluminum pouches. In the current stage, the readout is performed by absorption measurements. For that, the LabDisk is taken out of the processing device and readout in an external photometer. Completely automated testing and chemiluminescence detection in the LabDisk player is currently under validation.

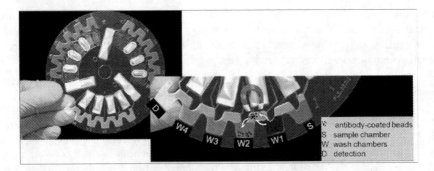

Fig. 3. Disposable LabDisk for immunoassay: reagents are stored in aluminium pouches

2   Conclusion and Outlook

A fully integrated system that provides rapid detection of pathogens is being developed. The LabDisk platform is able to perform a wide range of analyses such as immunoassays and nucleic acid detection. Fabrication of the microstructured disposable LabDisks and the detection of different pathogens have been successfully demonstrated. Currently the performance of the assays is under validation. The fabrication of a pilot series of cartridges in a prototyping line will enable us to perform field tests with the LabDisk platform.

Acknowledgement. We acknowledge funding by German Federal Ministry of Education and Research (BMBF), grant number 13N10116.

References

1. Focke, M., Kosse, D., Al-Bamerni, D., Lutz, S., Müller, C., Reinecke, H., Zengerle, R., von Stetten, F.: J. Micromech. Microeng. 21(115002), 11 (2011)
2. Strohmeier, O., Emperle, A., Focke, M., Roth, G., Mark, D., Zengerle, R., von Stetten, F.: The 14th Int. Conference on Miniaturized Systems for Chemistry and Life Sciences (MicroTAS), Groningen, The Netherlands, October 3-10, pp. 402–404 (2010)

Susceptibility of Two Deployable C4I Systems to HPM – Improvement by Hardening

Christian Adami, Christian Braun, Peter Clemens, Michael Jöster,
Michael Suhrke, and Hans-Joachim Taenzer

Fraunhofer INT, P.O. Box 1491, 53864 Euskirchen, Germany
{christian.adami,christian.braun,
peter.clemens,michael.joester,michael.suhrke,
hans-joachim.taenzer}@int.fraunhofer.de

Abstract. This report deals with high power microwave (HPM) vulnerability tests on two generations of configurable military IT network communication systems. The tests have been conducted within joint actions in two NATO RTO Task Groups. The systems based on state-of-the-art Commercial Off The Shelf (COTS) components have been adapted to the military environment with boxes, connectors, data cables and power supplies hardened in various ways. The investigation of susceptibility thresholds at Fraunhofer INT has been done in its TEM waveguide which allows the generation of field strengths up to some kV/m, depending on location of test objects. We find that besides the use of shielded data cables the application of state-of-the-art electrical equipment protection implemented in the second generation communication network system allows avoiding severe system failures due to HPM irradiation.

Keywords: C4I, hardening, HPM, high power microwave, IT network components.

1 Introduction

Several successive NATO RTO Task Groups have investigated the influence of tactically interesting high-power microwave sources on various electronic equipment for military use. In the most recent working phase a current C4I system (Command, Control, Communications, Computers, and Intelligence) has been chosen as test object for a joint effort involving different test facilities available in the group. The new C4I system replaces a first generation installation tested in a previous Task Group and consists of various rack-mounted EMC-compliant commercial IT network equipment interconnected by both fiber optic (FO) and electric data cables (various forms of twisted pairs). It connects users that are spread over several kilometers or more to a common IT network and common communication systems. Fig.1 shows an exemplary structure of an army field camp. A single high power microwave attack or exposure cannot be effective over such an area. Consequently, the Task Group selected certain test geometries that reflect likely individual exposures.

N. Aschenbruck et al. (Eds.): Future Security 2012, CCIS 318, pp. 224–232, 2012.
© Springer-Verlag Berlin Heidelberg 2012

The agreed test setups were retained unchanged during the test campaign to achieve comparable results from laboratories of the different participating nations. Likewise, the parameters of the irradiating fields were kept the same as during the test series with the first generation system to be able to compare the measured vulnerability thresholds of the different generations.

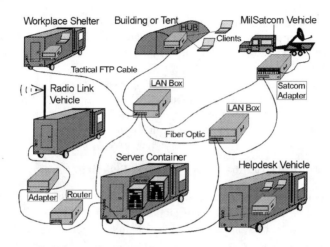

Fig. 1. Exemplary IT infrastructure of an army field camp

The tests were focused on the vulnerability of the critical IT network components of the two systems but not on connected PCs and other peripherals as monitors or keyboards. To this end, several subsystems were set up and network traffic was generated involving the relevant network components. In order to detect malfunctions due to microwave illumination data traffic was monitored with network diagnostics software.

2   Military Network Communication Systems

The main components of the systems consist of different boxes (HUB, LAN Access and Backbone) containing IT network components (switches, routers, media converters) and uninterruptible power supply units. For the new system particular attention was focused on electrical equipment protection in contrary to the 1st generation. The most important improvements concerning the boxes are EMI (Electromagnetic Interference) filters at the power input, conductive cases with gaskets and screened patch cables inside. Furthermore EMC RJ45 connectors for harsh environment are used at the entry panel. At the older system also bad screened boxes and plastic shells were in use. The data transmission between the network boxes over long distances took place via fiber-optic and for shorter distances via shielded or unshielded TP (twisted pair) Ethernet cables.

3   Testing and Diagnostics for Susceptibility Measurements

The aim of the test campaigns conducted in 2005/2006 and 2009/2010 was to find susceptibility thresholds of the system components irradiated by HPM fields for different relevant setups with possible modifications of wired shielded (SFTP) or unshielded (UTP) cables as well as fiber optic cabling.

To compare the results of the different laboratories from Czech Republic, France, US, and Germany taking part in the recent test campaign a well-defined arrangement of boxes and cables was agreed for the new system and similar field parameters were used if possible.

Based on the experiences in developing the necessary configurations for the network devices of the older system Fraunhofer INT was responsible for system setup and configuration prior to the actual tests. As mentioned before the tests were intended to be more uniform than in previous campaigns.

3.1   Test Facility at Fraunhofer INT and Test Planning

The test facility of Fraunhofer INT consists of a waveguide built as an open pyramidal asymmetric three plate TEM transmission line housed in a shielded hall (Fig.2). Susceptibility tests can be done with a pulse modulated generator in the frequency range from 150 to 3425 MHz for different pulse widths and repetition rates. The pulse generator allows pulse widths from 0.25 – 15 µs with pulse repetition rates from 1 Hz – 10 kHz, whereas the majority of the measurements was done with 1 µs pulses at a repetition frequency of 1 kHz. It permits electric field strengths of up to some kV/m at the test object depending on its size and position. In the tests the field strength was increased linearly within 30 seconds from some minimum value to the threshold for disruption or upset or to the maximum achievable value.

Fig. 2. Fraunhofer INT TEM waveguide with pulse generator and typical test object

The test plan includes the following items:

- Definition of test setups with fixed layout of boxes and cabling
- Use of tactical FO and SFTP between diagnostic PC (DPC) and system boxes
- Specified illumination area
- Irradiation of front side of boxes
- Generation of data traffic between selected hardware
- Monitoring of data traffic with diagnostic software
- Placing peripheral equipment and diagnostic PC outside of illumination area
- Use of corresponding field parameters if possible.

For examination of effects of field coupling into TP cables, one cable within the waveguide was formed to a rectangular loop (1 x b = 1.5 x 0.5 m^2) in some tests in order to simulate the worst case cabling of a simple PC network with cables parallel to the electric field vector. Usually the panel of a box is screwed up with locking screws. To simulate an unintentional gap at the panel or dirt/corrosion at the gaskets in some experiments the hatch was left ajar ("hatch open"). An important goal of the tests was to find weak points of the system.

In principal three different setups are used for each system as shown in Fig.3. In each case a diagnostic PC (DPC) is inserted to monitor the data traffic. It is connected to the boxes alternately via tactical fiber optic or TP cables. In setup 1 the data traffic proceeds between notebook NB2 and notebook NB1 via the HUB Box and Access Box AC2 respectively, whereas it takes place via LAN1 and LAN2 Box (1st) and Access and Backbone Box BB2 (2nd) in setup 2. In the old system the HUB and LAN2 Boxes are made of plastic (indicated as dashed lines in fig.3).

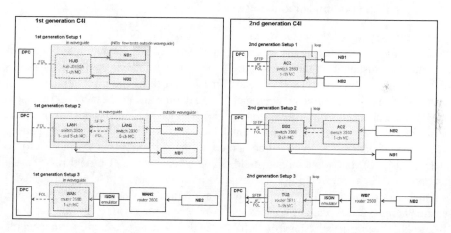

Fig. 3. Principal measurement configurations of the two systems

In setup 3 the data are transferred from NB2 to the diagnostic PC via an inserted router and ISDN emulator realizing a telephone network. The shaded areas in the figure represent the disturbing field of the irradiation area within the waveguide. As demanded for the new system, the notebooks, diagnostic PC, router and ISDN emulator are always outside the field. In each case we used a well-defined arrangement of the loop and the cabling. In the measurements with the predecessor system this strict condition was not always fulfilled, as can be seen in the figure above. A further difference is the restriction to the FO link between box and diagnostic PC for the old system. Obviously, the use of boxes with plastic shells would be a weak point regarding immunity.

In Fig.4 an example is shown for a typical test arrangement of the network boxes and the Ethernet cable loop. The equipment to be investigated is positioned near the end of the TEM waveguide, whereas notebooks and diagnostic PC are outside of the illumination area in the laboratory.

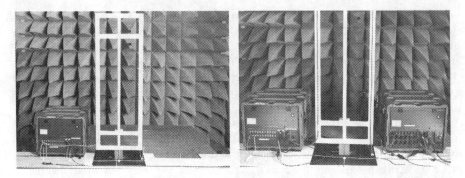

Fig. 4. Typical arrangement of network boxes with cable loop (attached on wooden frame) for setup 1 and setup 2

3.2   Diagnostic Equipment and Software

The proper working of the network components was monitored using network diagnostics software included in the tool collection SolarWinds Engineers Edition. SolarWinds was installed on the diagnostic PC and on the notebooks. The SolarWinds tools used in the tests were SNMP Real-Time Graph to monitor network traffic at particular ports of the network equipment in real time using the network protocol SNMP and Enhanced Ping to ping to multiple IP addresses for round-trip time and packet loss rate. Furthermore, the program TimeServer was installed on the diagnostic PC for time synchronization of the computers in the network. This was necessary to relate occurrence time of failures to field strength for our use of a field ramp in the susceptibility tests. For Windows XP installed on the computers the network activity was also monitored locally with Windows Task Manager. Data traffic between the selected hardware was realized by sending a 500 MB sample with FTP from notebook NB2 to NB1 (setup 1 and 2) or from NB2 to the diagnostic PC (setup 3). An example for the diagnostic analysis is shown in Fig.5. In this configuration the network traffic between NB2 and NB1 via the LAN Access Box is monitored by Enhanced Ping at each involved network component.

As an example typical screenshots from the monitors of the diagnostic PC and notebook 2 regarding the diagnostic software running on the computers are shown in Fig.6. Both SNMP Real-Time Graph and Task manager show the quality of the file transfer. Some seconds after the disturbing field ramp has been started the transfer broke down.

By switching off the illumination after 30 s the traffic started again until all data are transferred. Enhanced Ping shows the packet loss observed at the different PCs. The different kinds of effects occurring during the illumination are summarized in Table1.

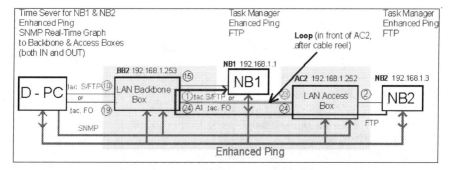

Fig. 5. Network traffic and diagnostics for setup 1

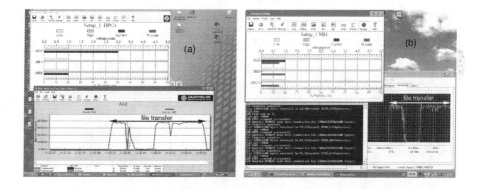

Fig. 6. Typical screenshots of the diagnostic software at (a): DPC (Enhanced Ping, SNMP Real-Time Graph) and (b): NB2 (Enhanced Ping, Task manager) for setup 1

Table 1. Classification of the effects

Level	Effect	Description	Failures observed during tests
0	Unknown	Unable to determine due to effects on another component	
1	No Effect		
2	Interference	Effect is only present during illumination	- Loss of packets - Interruption of ftp traffic
3	Disturbance	Effect is present during illumination and self corrects over a short period of time once illumination is removed.	Interruption of ftp traffic until some seconds after illumination is off
4	Upset	Effect that occurs during illumination and requires human intervention to correct (e. g. restart of computer).	Interruption of ftp traffic remains, data transfer has to be restarted
5	Damage	Effect that damages hardware to the point it must be replaced or software to the point it must be reloaded.	

4   Comparison of the Measured Susceptibilities of the Old and New System

As previously mentioned particular attention was focused on electrical equipment protection at the new system in contrary to the preceding one. The most important improvements of the boxes are EMI filters at the power input, conductive cases with gaskets and screened patch cables inside. Furthermore EMC RJ45 connectors for harsh environment are used at the entry panel. This upgrade should lead to more immunity against disturbing fields in any case.

The main similarities and differences between the setups are summarized in Table 2. At the old system only the tactical FO connection to the diagnostic PC was examined and in the most tests the notebooks were within the waveguide or outside close beside the waveguide in the shielded hall. However, no tests with enhanced coupling with UTP loops were done. A weak point regarding immunity was the use of boxes with plastic shells in setup 1 and setup 2. But basically the setups of the two communication systems are very similar and comparable regarding the corresponding features.

Table 2. Similarities (shaded) and differences between setups of 1st and 2nd generations

Configurations	1st Generation	2nd Generation
Connection DPC - Box	FOL	FOL, SFTP
Diagnostic PC	laboratory	laboratory
Notebooks	within waveguide, in shielded hall and in laboratory	laboratory
Connections to notebooks	UTP, (SFTP)	loop: UTP, SFTP
Setup-1:	hub	switch
Box	plastic shell	excellent shielded, filter
Notebooks	within waveguide, (few outside)	laboratory
Connections to notebooks (illuminated)	3 m UTP; NB2 cable 0.8 m parallel E.field	loop: UTP, SFTP
Media converter	1-port (metal case)	1-port
Setup-2:	Switch, switch	Switch, switch
Boxes	LAN1: metal shell LAN2: plastic shell	excellent shielded, filter
Connection between boxes	FOL, SFTP	FOL, SFTP
Notebooks	Outside waveguide, (laboratory)	laboratory
Connections to notebooks (illuminated)	3 m UTP	UTP, SFTP
Media converter	LAN1: integr. 6-port, 1-port LAN2: 6-port (metal case)	AC2: 1-port BB2: 8-port
Setup-3:	Router, ISDN, router	Router, ISDN, router
Box	metal shell	excellent shielded, filter
Notebook	laboratory	laboratory
ISDN emulator, router	laboratory	laboratory
Connection to ISDN device (illuminated)	SFTP	loop: UTP
Media converter	1-port	1-port

An example for the reduction of the susceptibility of the new system is shown for setup 3, where the layout of the two systems coincide sufficiently. As can be seen in Fig.3 and Fig.7 the data transfer is from the notebook to the diagnostic PC via the illuminated router. The shaded area in the figure represents the disturbing field within the wave guide.

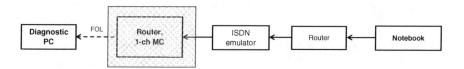

Fig. 7. General measurement configuration for setup 3

Fig.8 shows the interruption of the data traffic between the network components at the 1st generation system. Obviously, nearly at all selected test frequencies the communication was disturbed, with the effects ranging from interferences to disturbances, to upsets (see Table 1).

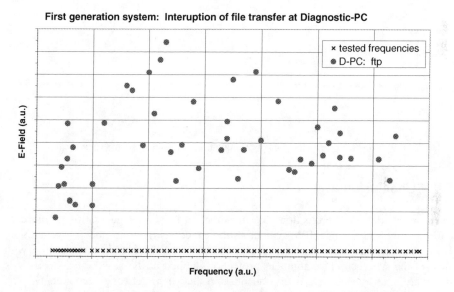

Fig. 8. Influence on file transfer by illumination of router in setup 3 (old system)

Fig.9 shows the influence on the data transfer for the upgraded system with the box lid fully closed. Although the configuration was illuminated with susceptible UTP cables the system showed only packet losses at the low frequencies but no interruption of the data transfer. With the router box slightly open at the higher frequencies additional losses occurred. This condition of the box can roughly be compared with the conventionally shielded enclosure of the predecessor box.

Regarding the results of setup 1 the disturbed frequency ranges due to UTP cable coupling and field penetration through openings were similar for the two systems, but at the old one effects ranging from interferences to upsets could be observed, whereas at the new system only interferences occurred and the number of these effects was remarkably decreased in the considered frequency range. In setup 2 interferences, disturbances and upsets appeared at each system, but at the new system there were fewer failures and the impact on the data transfer was smaller.

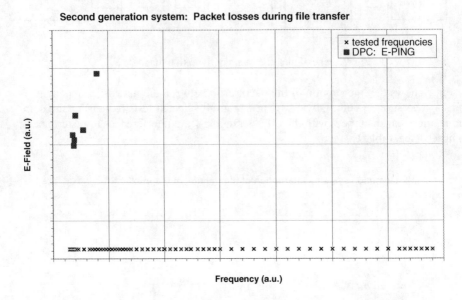

Fig. 9. Influence on file transfer by illumination of router in setup3 (new system)

5   Conclusion

In summary, the EMC protection measures applied for the 2nd generation C4I system considerably reduce its HPM vulnerability in comparison to the 1st generation. However, only the exclusive use of well-shielded SFTP cables in combination with state-of-the-art electrical equipment protection applied at the new system leads to a relatively interference-free data transmission between network components. The usage of unshielded UTP cables induces severe effects like interference and distur-bance in the low frequency range. In the case of not fully closed or conventionally shielded boxes and for application of fiber optic connections, additionally interrup-tions can occur in the medium and higher frequency range due to field coupling to the media converter as a result of bad case shielding. Consequently, the reliable operation of these links which are necessary for longer distances requires the utilization of EMC hardened media converters. For application in the services only shielded cables should be used and the boxes have to be really fully closed.

Detector Array with Gas Chromatograph for On-Site Analyses

Hendrik Fischer[1], Jörn Frank[1], Bert Ungethüm[2], Matthias Drobig[3],
Andreas Walte[2], and Gerhard Matz[1]

[1] Hamburg University of Technology, Institute of Measurement Technology,
Hamburg, Germany
{hendrik.fischer,joern.frank,matz}@tuhh.de
[2] Airsense Analytics GmbH, Schwerin, Germany
{ungethuem,walte}@airsense.com
[3] Federal Office of Civil Protection and Disaster Assistance, Bonn, Germany
matthias.drobig@bbk.bund.de

Abstract. Toxic and environmentally threatening gaseous substances can be released on purpose or by accident e.g. during transportation or handling. In this cases fast, reliable detection, identification and quantification is needed to face the threat effectively. Therefore the handheld measurement device DACHS was developed. It combines different sensor technologies to an array to provide a quick on-site analysis for the most important industrial substances. The most sensitive sensor in the developed instrument is an ion mobility spectrometer (IMS), but the IMS cannot detect all toxic gases. Therefore additional sensors are needed. To obtain reliable identification during the presence of mixtures of different chemicals a short column gas chromatograph with enrichment unit is included. The device and the results of its evaluation are presented.

Keywords: on-site analysis, ion mobility spectrometer, multi capillary gas chromatograph, handheld device.

1   Introduction

The production of chemical substances has heavily increased in the recent years. This leads to the need of powerful measurement devices to detect and identify these often gaseous substances in the case of a spontaneous release.

A very accurate and reliable analysis is provided by many laboratory devices. But these devices are mostly not applicable in the field because of size, weight, speed and complexness. As on-site detectors often broadband gas sensors such as photoionization detectors or semiconductor gas sensors are used. These single detectors show a fast response to their target gases, but are not able to distinguish between different compounds in a mixture. By the combination of different broadband detectors to an array with pattern matching, an identification and for most substances even a quantification is possible. This principle in combination with a gas chromatograph is used in the presented device DACHS. The gas chromatographic separation leads to additional information especially when it is used for substances that are in a mixture.

N. Aschenbruck et al. (Eds.): Future Security 2012, CCIS 318, pp. 233–236, 2012.

The measurement device is developed to detect chemical agents listed in the ETW ("Einsatztoleranzwerte" – concentration limits for exposure (DE)[1]) and the ERPG (Emergency Response Planning Guidelines(US)[2]).

2   Detector Array

The array combines four different sensor principles. It consists of a photoionization detector (PID), three metal oxide semiconductor gas sensors (MOS), two electro-chemical cells (EC) and an ion mobility spectrometer (IMS).

Within the PID gas is exposed to an UV-lamp with an ionization potential of 10.6 eV. This makes the PID mainly detect volatile organic compounds (VOCs) with a limit of detection in the low ppm range. Quantification over some orders of magnitude is possible due to its linear behaviour..

Metal oxide semiconductor gas sensors consist of a heatable semiconductive substrate. Substances are oxidized or reduced on its hot surface which leads to a change of its resistance. With the three MOS a broad range of substances like hydrocarbons, nitrous gases and hydrogen sulphide can be detected.

The two electrochemical sensors are based on the principle of a galvanic cell. Their electrolytes, electrodes and filter materials are matched to their target gas.

The IMS is the most sensitive detector of the array. Molecules are ionized and their drift time through a drift tube is measured, to obtain time of flight spectra. These spectra and the related reduced mobility (K_0) are specific for each substance. To measure positive and negative charged molecules simultaneously the IMS contains two drift tubes.

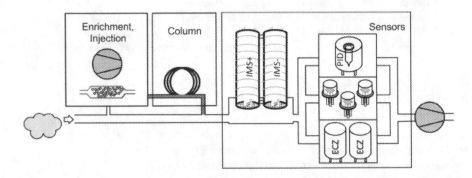

Fig. 1. Fluidics of the sensor array

The principle of the fluidics is shown in Fig. 1. The sample gas is sucked in front of the inlet membrane of the IMS. Parts of the gas are diffusing through the membrane into the reaction region of the IMS while the remaining gas is directed to the other sensors. The gas flow is divided into three parts and led to the different detector types separately, to avoid interferences between the sensors. The gas flow is established by a rotary pump sucking at the outlet of the sensor block.

3   Measurement Modes

The DACHS can be used in different measurement modes. In the on-line mode the sample gas is led directly to the sensor array. Because of the short path from inlet to the sensors also low volatile compounds are traceable. To increase the dynamic range of the instrument the sucked in gas can be diluted with clean air to avoid a saturation of the sensors even at high concentrations.

In the second mode the GC is used to separate the substances before their detection. Therefore the gas is collected on an adsorbent. The used adsorbent is Tenax. After sampling gas on the adsorbent the compounds are released through thermal desorption and are injected into the GC column. Air from the outside of the instrument, cleaned by a charcoal filter, is used as carrier gas. The eluted substances are sucked by the sample pump to the array of sensors.

Pre-tests showed that the column AT624 provides a good separation of the substances of interest despite its length of only 34 cm. 38 capillaries are used in parallel in order to provide adequate gas flow rates for all sensors. The capillaries are united with both ends in a fitting. The bundle is fixed in a U-shaped mounting, which contains a controlled heater.

The next figure 2 shows a picture of the prototype instrument.

Fig. 2. The developed instrument DACHS

4   Evaluation

The evaluation of the developed instrument was done in laboratory conditions. Substances listed in the ETW were tested as single compounds and in mixtures. In Fig. 3 the sensor signals of a gas chromatographic separation of the substances acetone, 2-pentanone and xylene is shown.

The bottommost graph shows the signal of the PID, the three MOS and the two EC over time. A separation of the two substances can be observed clearly in the signals of the PID and the MOSs. The two EC are not sensitive to the applied substances. On top of this graph the signals of the IMS are plotted. It shows IMS drift time over measurement time of the positive spectrum. The negative spectrum is not shown. White areas show a high detector signal, black areas a low signal. All three substances can be found well separated.

The displayed measurement shows the need of a gas chromatographic separation within the presence of mixtures. The PID and the MOSs themselves are not able to discriminate the tested substances at all. The single IMS leads to no reliable information for mixtures as well. In its spectrum the signatures of the substances are interfering each other or leading to suppression of substances because of different proton affinities.

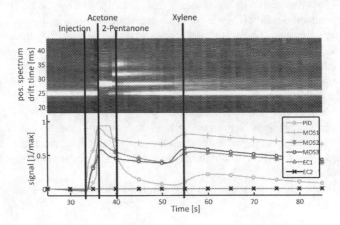

Fig. 3. GC separation of Acetone, 2-Pentanone and Xylene

Other sensor arrays achieve comparable results with single substances. But they are not able to discriminate substances in a mixture.

5   Conclusion

A novel handheld gas measurement system was developed, which combines several detection principles to a heterogeneous sensor array. The included gas chromatograph with its enrichment unit and multi capillary is adapted for the use in a handheld device. The system has been evaluated with substances regarding current references and is now applicable in field test.

Acknowledgements. The authors acknowledge the founding for the project by the German Federal Ministry of Education and Research.

References

1. vfdb-Richtlinie 10/01, Bewertung von Schadstoffkonzentrationen im Feuerwehreinsatz (2005)
2. Emergeny Response Planing Guidlines, American Industrial Hygiene Association (2008)

User-Centric Protection and Privacy in Smart Surveillance Systems

Hauke Vagts[1,2], Erik Krempel[2], and Jürgen Beyerer[1,2]

[1] Vision and Fusion Laboratory, Karlsruhe Institute of Technology,
Karlsruhe, Germany
[2] Fraunhofer Institute of Optronics, System Technologies and Image Exploitation
IOSB, Karlsruhe, Germany
{hauke.vagts,erik.krempel,juergen.beyerer}@iosb.fraunhofer.de

Abstract. During the last decades surveillance systems developed from
analog one camera one monitor systems to highly complex distributed
systems with heterogeneous sensors that can handle surveillance tasks
autonomously. With raising power and complexity, ensuring privacy became a key challenge. An event-driven SOA architecture that follows the
privacy by design principle is a promising approach to realize a smart
surveillance system and is described in this work.

Enforcement of privacy is not only complex for engineers and system
designers; rather it is not understandable for the average user, who cannot even assess potentials and limitations of smart surveillance systems.
This work presents an approach for privacy that is focused on the user,
i.e., the observed subject. By using a mobile device the user can interact
with the surveillance system and is not passive anymore, as in conventional surveillance deployments. This restores the balance between the
observed and the observers, enhances transparency and will raise the
acceptance of surveillance technology.

In the highlighted approach the user can control his individual-related
data and privacy preferences and can use services that are beneficial for
him.

1   Introduction

The overall number of surveillance systems is still increasing. In the UK, more
than 4,000,000 cameras have been deployed. Modern surveillance systems are
enhanced with acoustic sensors or can read RFID tags. Simultaneously, new algorithms for identification, risk detection and automated data processing appear.
Observed people got scared by powerful and complex systems. In [1] Hempel et
al. point out that 40% of the European Society thinks that CCTV invades privacy. Even if acceptance highly differs between countries, surveillance must be
more transparent to achieve trust of the users and to restore the balance between
data controllers and data subjects.

Smart surveillance services can also provide a benefit for the observed objects,
e.g., people might want to book a surveillance service when walking home in the

N. Aschenbruck et al. (Eds.): Future Security 2012, CCIS 318, pp. 237–248, 2012.

dark or special observation for their car in public parking. Also non-security related services as inhouse navigation are possible. They all require active communication between the user and the surveillance system.

This work is structured as follows. Section two gives an overview about privacy protection technologies in conventional surveillance systems, smart surveillance systems and adjacent areas. Section three specifies an architecture for a smart surveillance system that is based on the privacy by design principle. Section four integrates a new system for user interaction, evaluated in detail in section five. The last section gives a short overview of the achievements and shows potential fields for further research.

2   Recent Work

With the recent increase of video surveillance systems, privacy protection in surveillance has become an active field of study. More information about intelligent video surveillance can be found in, e.g., [2][3]. Most research work considers conventional video surveillance systems with CCTV cameras and improves privacy by disguising regions of interest (ROI). The work from Dufaux and Ebrahimi [4] uses private key encryption to scramble ROIs. Privileged users, e.g., law-enforcement authorities possess the needed private key to unscramble the video, while unauthorized users can only view the distorted version of the content. Another approach from Schiffer et al. [5] proposes a practical real-time system that blurs the faces of people wearing special markers. This enables selective privacy protection, e.g., for employees, while the camera observation stays usable for its surveillance task.

More extensive privacy approaches for video completely prevent the visualization of video streams. In [6] Fleck and Straßer use smart cameras, which are capable of processing data, to detect events in an observed area, such as a falling person. Only these events, secured by encryption, are transmitted to a central server for visualization. The operator is completely decoupled from the live video stream and can only see the resulting movements and events within a map. Similar work was done by Senior et al. [7]. Their system processes video streams and constructs an abstract model of the observed environment. Access to this model is regulated by privacy rules, enabling, e.g., anonymous access to statistical data and law-enforcements authorities to receive the original stream with additional annotations.

All these systems try to increase privacy by blocking access to certain data, mask the identity of the user and secure the communication channels. The integration of the user was forgotten and the user had only a "take it or leave it" choice when he was confronted with a surveillance systems. This results in activist projects, like i-SEE[1] of the Institute for Applied Autonomy. Their system generates a route between two points in Manhattan with the least amount of passed surveillance systems possible.

---

[1] http://www.appliedautonomy.com/isee.html; 2012-04-12.

New approaches have to focus on the surveillance subject and its fears and demands on a surveillance system.

To gather new approaches for transparency and acceptance, research in the areas of pervasive and ubiquitous computing must be considered. These systems have many similarities with modern surveillance systems, i.e., a big amount of personal data is collected and different services access the data to perform certain tasks. As these systems were designed to serve individual users and not to secure areas, privacy concerns are more in focus of development.

In [8] Langheinrich proposes a system, called PAWS, to process data with a high level of transparency for the users. Whenever a user enters a new area, a privacy beacon informs him about services in place and what personal data they process. The user can set his own trust in the services and decides, which services are allowed to process his personal data, so that he can use their functionality. The shortcoming of this system is that it completely relies on social and legal norms to prevent the misuse of private data, since there is no system wide control over the distributed data. Bagués et al. [9] extend the work and suggest a complete architecture for privacy protection in pervasive computing environments. They consider three stages of data lifetime: collection, access and secondary use and use different techniques to prevent misuse.

Contrary to pervasive environments, main object of surveillance system is to ensure security. Hence, transparent and accepted surveillance systems must still process certain data without permission of the user, while still giving the users the maximum right for privacy. This makes the design of privacy aware surveillance systems even more complex.

3   An Architecture for Privacy in Smart Surveillance Systems

To cope with the requirements for smart surveillance systems and to ensure privacy of observed subjects, a new architecture for smart surveillance was developed. More details can be found in [10]. Four main components realize a privacy preserving smart surveillance system. The *task-oriented approach* ensures that data is only captured and processed when needed. A surveillance task can be broken down in multiple steps and is executed through an *event-driven SOA architecture*. The captured data, from heterogeneous sensors, is stored in an abstract representation inside the *Object-Oriented World Model*, where it can be accessed for further processing. The *Privacy Manager* ensures, that data is accessed in a way that agrees with the desired privacy level.

3.1   Task-Oriented Approach for Surveillance

Most existing surveillance systems operate in a *sensor-oriented* way, i.e., many sensors are deployed in the monitored area and all available data is collected and stored. After the transmission to a central storage, intelligent algorithms process the data to extract as much relevant information as possible. A big number of

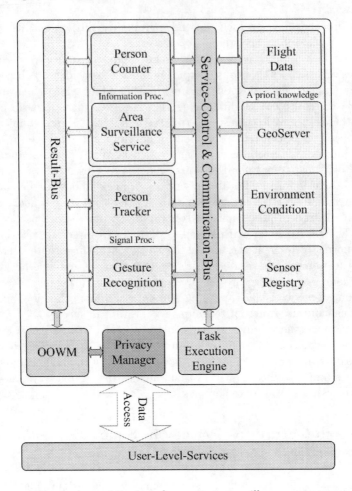

Fig. 1. An architecture for a smart surveillance system

sensors directly results in a big amount of data and ineffective systems, as most of the data is not required. In addition, this has a huge impact on privacy. In contrary, task-oriented systems avoid the collection of data whenever possible. Data is only gathered and processed for a specific purpose/task. This has to two benefits. Fewer resources, e.g., bandwidth are required and less sensitive data is gathered and processed. An example for a task is the observation of a single person from its current position to a specified destination. Only one person is tracked, instead of all persons in the area.

3.2 An Event-Driven SOA Architecture for Surveillance

A system following the task-oriented approach must be capable of executing small pieces of functionality (services) and combing them to complex workflows. A smart system also runs multiple surveillance tasks in parallel for different users. To extend the functionality of smart surveillance systems, it should be easy to integrate new sensors and services. An event-driven SOA controls the collaboration of the services. Services can either be signal-oriented, if they encapsulate sensors and gain information about the environment, or can process information. The architecture is shown Figure 1. Services generate events, e.g., person identified, fight detected etc., which are received by the task execution engine that coordinates all involved components. Triggered by such events other services are started. Depending on the scenario an operator can integrate different kinds of prior knowledge. In the evaluation scenario, the system has multiple prior knowledge sources such as the current weather conditions to recalibrate its sensors and a geo data repository with information about the building and prohibited areas, etc.

Different kinds of *Signal Processing Services* (SPS) are used to interpret data captured by sensors. Services exist to, e.g., track persons over multiple cameras or to identify a person with biometric data or other means. The Sensor Registry provides information about existing SPS and connected sensors, e.g., field of view of used cameras. The preprocessed data is delivered to the Object-Oriented Word Model (OOWM) that acts as central data storage for further processing in the surveillance system.

Information Processing Services (IPS) process the data stored in the OOWM. Typical examples are the "Person Counter Service", which checks that not too many people are in a certain area or the "Area Protection Service" which sends an alarm when people enter a restricted area.

User Level Services (ULS) provide additional services to the surveillance subjects. They even can be integrated by third parties and are therefore not completely trustworthy. To cobe with law requirement, ULS are detached from the core processing system. Typically ULS are activated by users themself and elaborate privacy related check of the used data are performed. In Chapter 4 ULS are looked at in detail.

3.3   Object-Oriented World Model

The Object-Oriented World is the central data store in the system. It transforms all observations from SPS into a consistent object representation and acts as high-level information source for IPS and ULS. The OOWM performs the following tasks:

- Information Representation: The OOWM offers an application-independent representation of real world objects. It distinguishes different types of objects, e.g., persons, luggage, animals and stores them for later access.
- Data Association: For each new object observation the OOWM decides, whether it corresponds to a new object, or if an existing object must be updated.
- Data Fusion and Tracking: Updated information from new observations is fused with previously assessed information.

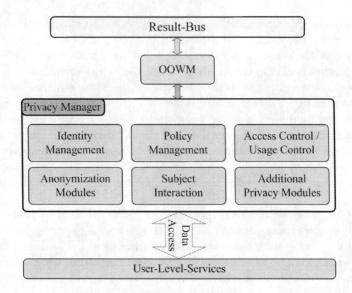

Fig. 2. Privacy Manager

– Data Access: Different types of services need an easy way to access the stored data. Therefore every object is represented by a unique ID and can be polled as a list of attributes with their corresponding values.

More details about the technical implementation of the OOWM can be found in [11].

3.4 Privacy Manager

The task-oriented approach reduced the capture of privacy concerning data and allows controlled processing. But it is not addressing all legal issues and not capable to offer the required level of transparency. The *Privacy Manager* (PM) is designed to enforce privacy respecting access to the OOWM and enable transparency for the users. ULS can only access data from inside the surveillance system via the PM. All access from ULS to the OOWM, or similar data representation in other smart surveillance system, is managed by the PM. It groups different Privacy Enhancing Technologies (PET) in a single place. Thereby the system is very flexible and new methods can be easily integrated. The current implementation realizes the following components and is sketched in Figure 2:

– Identity Management (IdM): In a privacy preserving surveillance system, every component should only get access to required data. To prevent services to exchange data several security methods exist. One is the use of pseudo IDs for all objects. When two or more services access data of the same object, they know the object with different IDs, preventing the services from merging attributes. More Details can be found in [12].

- Policy Management: Multiple modules use policies for specifying configurations, e.g., XACML access control policies, IdM policies or policies for anonymization. The Policy Management controls the access to these policies for users. It also merges user specific policies with system policies. More details can be found in [13].
- Access and Usage Control: To enforce privacy requirements Access Control is integrated in the PM. Due to expressiveness and extendibility for privacy needs, the PM utilizes XACML. By deploying, changing or revoking policies, the access rights of a service can be altered at runtime. More details can be found in [13]. Current research aims at integrating Usage Control, to ensure that access to data can be controlled, even when it has left the system.
- Anonymization Modules: Besides simple permit or deny decisions, XACML is capable of obligation handling. It is possible to write policies that only grant access to attributes after they have been anonimized. The PM uses different kinds of anonymization modules. A typical job would be to anonymize position data to reach certain k-Anonymity or l-Diversity values [14].
- Subject Interaction: The Subject Interaction module handles the interaction between an observed subject, the users, and the surveillance system. Different options for interaction with a surveillance system exist. Section 5 explains user interaction based on a mobile device in detail.
- Additional Privacy Modules: The PM also performs additional tasks, like key-distribution and management, which are implemented in additional modules.

4   Data Access for User Level Services

User Level Services are a new approach for surveillance systems and are not yet fully explored. Especially, the opportunity to allow third parties the development of their own ULS leads to a high complexity. So far three different types of ULS can be distinguished:

- *Security ULS accessing user data*: Users can request additional security related services. These services offer a higher level of security than the core system, but are only activated on request of the user.
- *Convenience ULS accessing user data*: Each user can start ULS processing his data for additional services, e.g., in-house navigation.
- *ULS accessing anonymized data*: Some ULS operate on anonymized data to provide statistical information, e.g., a service generating a heat map of a shopping area for shop operators. When processing proper anonymized data, no risk for privacy exists, but especially with multiple possible data sources, it is hard to decide whether a sufficient level of anonymization is reached or not.

This work only addresses services accessing user data. Further research is required for ULS accessing anonymized data for statistical reasons.

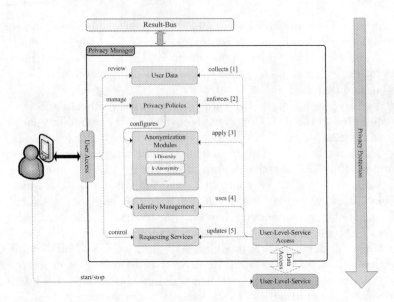

Fig. 3. Data Access for ULS

4.1 User Level Service Communication

Figure 3 shows the user-centric approach for data management. When a user wishes to use a ULS, he needs a way to interact with the surveillance system at first. this work proposes (smart) mobile phones. They provide enough resources for complex computations and with the increasing sales, it can be assumed that most people will own one in future. The smart phone allows to interact with the system in many different way, e.g., to review, which ULS are running, to manage personal privacy policies or to start and stop ULS. When a user started an ULS, a generic communication takes place:

1. The ULS registers at the Privacy Manager (PM) and sends a data request. The PM then collects all requested data from the OOWM.
2. XACML based privacy policies are applied to the collected information. Either a default policy or personal policies managed by the concerned users. Afterwards, every attribute that the ULS is not allowed to access is removed[13].
3. If the privacy policies include obligations for further anonymization of the data the Privacy Manager applies its corresponding anonymization module[14].
4. The Identity Management replaces the identifiers from the OOWM with new unique identifiers only used for this ULS [12].
5. In the last step, the Privacy Manager updates its intern database with service names and used data. This database is used to show to the users, which services access their data.

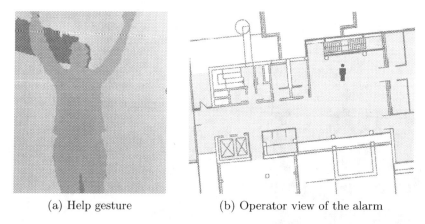

(a) Help gesture   (b) Operator view of the alarm

Fig. 4. Gesture Recognition

Only after performing all steps the Privacy Manager provides the requested data to the ULS. The user can review the stored data corresponding to him. His privacy policies also let him stay in charge of his personal data.

5   Evaluation

The proposed privacy preserving techniques and the new user-centric approach are evaluated in the Network Enabled Surveillance and Tracking (NEST) [10] demonstrator system. Multiple cameras are deployed throughout the entire site of Fraunhofer IOSB. The operator has access to a screen that shows pixelated video streams. These streams allow him to detect crime or accidents, but are not fine-grained enough to identify the employees. Additionally, the operator can access a terminal showing alarm events. In a demonstration setup, three exemplary technologies show the potential of the new user-centric surveillance and privacy technologies. At first, users can send an alarm to the operator by performing a certain gesture. Then a security related ULS is shown to increase the surveillance level in a certain area. The last scenario shows a convenience related ULS for indoor navigation.

5.1   Gesture Recognition

The first example task is a gesture recognition system. This technology is part of the core system and data access is not regulated by the PM, due to the the high security value and the little privacy impact. An information processing service analyses the video streams and tries to detect a special gesture. If one is detected the operator receives an alarm event and access to the non-pixelated steam of the camera that detected the gesture. This allows users easy contact to security when feeling in danger or seeing others in danger.

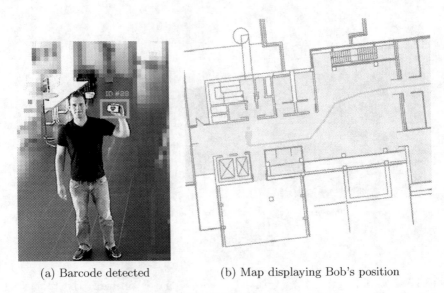

(a) Barcode detected   (b) Map displaying Bob's position

Fig. 5. WatchMe Application

5.2   WatchMe Smartphone App

The second realized example is a security related ULS. The general idea of the application is that sometimes people want a higher level of surveillance, e.g., at an empty subway station at night. Bob might feel threatened and wants extra attention of the surveillance system and its operator. Therefore he starts the "WatchMe" application and demands a higher surveillance level by pressing a button. After that, the system sends a special bar code to his device. Bob has to present this barcode to the next camera (see Figure 5a) to start his surveillance task. As soon as the system has detected the barcode the mobile device vibrates to notify the user about the successful log in. At the same time the operator sees a marker for Bob's position and his movement trace in the area (see Figure 5b). The operator can now pay extra attention to Bob.

As soon as Bob wants the extra surveillance to stop he can use his smart phone to cancel the surveillance task. The system deletes all collected information of the WatchMe task. The same happens when Bob leaves the observed area.

5.3   Indoor Navigation

The last example shows a pure convenience ULS in action. Navigation in an unknown buildings can be hard. Therefore the system offers an indoor navigation support. At first, the user has to pick his desired destination. Afterwards the system sends a special bar code to his device, which needs to be presented to the next camera. The app loads a privacy policy in the system that allows the usage of the user's position for the navigation purpose. Therefore the ULS can calculate the shortest path to the user's destination. This path gets plotted inside a map of the building and is transmitted to user.

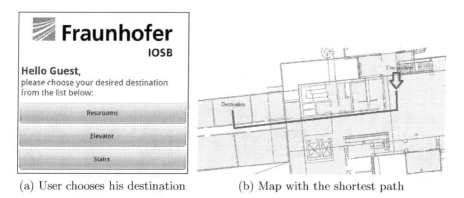

(a) User chooses his destination   (b) Map with the shortest path

Fig. 6. Inhouse navigation

When the user reaches his destination or wishes to cancel the tracking, the system deletes all collected data and the default privacy policies are reactivated.

6   Conclusion and Future Work

Complex surveillance systems can be realized by an event-driven SOA, following the task-based approach. To realize privacy by design, multiple PETs are integrated in the Privacy Manager. Even if the PETs are very promising from a technological perspective, users do not really understand them and cannot distinguish between them, which lead to a user-centric approach for privacy enforcement that realizes a communication channel between the user and the system. He is now in charge of his privacy preferences and can also use additional services offered by the system. Transparency is enhanced and it is easy for the users to control the system and his privacy setting. Further user studies are necessary to see, if the user-centric approach is really enhancing the acceptance of surveillance technology and if it is understood by the user. The results from the evaluation in the demonstrator system are very promising and have shown that the new system is capable to protect user data inside a surveillance system. It must still be investigated, if it can be used in practice. Therefore image processing and video analysis must improve first.

Still, a lot of research needs to be done in the field of privacy preserving smart surveillance. More PETs must be evaluated, especially for non-video data, e.g., audio information. The current demonstration system is going to extend with more PETs and further demonstration scenario are realized.

References

1. Hempel, L., Töpfer, E.: CCTV in Europe. Final Report, Urbaneye Working Paper No. 15 (August 2004)
2. Regazzoni, C.S., Fabri, G., Vernazza, G.: Advanced video-based surveillance systems, vol. 488. Springer (1999)
3. Remagnino, P.: Video-based surveillance systems: computer vision and distributed processing. Springer, Netherlands (2002)
4. Dufaux, F., Ebrahimi, T.: Scrambling for video surveillance with privacy. In: Computer Vision and Pattern Recognition Workshop (CVPRW 2006), p. 160. IEEE (2006)
5. Schiff, J., Meingast, M., Mulligan, D.K., Sastry, S., Goldberg, K.: Respectful cameras: Detecting visual markers in real-time to address privacy concerns. In: Senior, A. (ed.) Protecting Privacy in Video Surveillance, pp. 65–89. Springer (2009)
6. Fleck, S., Straßer, W.: Smart camera based monitoring system and its application to assisted living. Proceedings of the IEEE 96, 1698–1714 (2008)
7. Senior, A., Pankanti, S., Hampapur, A., Brown, L., Tian, Y.L., Ekin, A., Connell, J., Shu, C.F., Lu, M.: Enabling video privacy through computer vision. IEEE Security & Privacy 3, 50–57 (2005)
8. Langheinrich, M.: A Privacy Awareness System for Ubiquitous Computing Environments. In: Borriello, G., Holmquist, L.E. (eds.) UbiComp 2002. LNCS, vol. 2498, pp. 237–320. Springer, Heidelberg (2002)
9. Bagüés, S., Zeidler, A., Klein, C., Valdivielso, C., Matias, I.: Enabling personal privacy for pervasive computing environments. Journal of Universal Computer Science 16(3), 341–371 (2010)
10. Moßgraber, J., Reinert, F., Vagts, H.: An architecture for a task-oriented surveillance system – a service and event based approach. In: Fifth International Conference on Systems ICONS (April 2010)
11. Bauer, A., Emter, T., Vagts, H., Beyerer, J.: Object oriented world model for surveillance systems. In: Elsner, P. (ed.) Future Security: 4th Security Research Conference, pp. 339–345. Fraunhofer Verlag (October 2009)
12. Vagts, H., Krempel, E., Beyerer, J.: Privacy enforcement by identity management in smart surveillance systems. In: Proceedings of the International Conference on Distributed Multimedia Systems. Knowledge Systems Institute Graduate School, vol. 16, pp. 64–69 (October 2010)
13. Vagts, H., Krempel, E., Fischer, Y.: Access controls for privacy protection in pervasive environments. In: The 3rd Workshop on Privacy and Security in Pervasive Environments PSPAE (2011)
14. Vagts, H., Bier, C., Beyerer, J.: Anonymization in intelligent surveillance systems. In: 2011 4th IFIP International Conference on New Technologies, Mobility and Security (NTMS), pp. 1–4. IEEE (2011)

Methodology for Analysing Unstructured Usability Evaluation Data

Therese Friberg, Christina Schäfer, and Rainer Koch

Research Group C.I.K., University of Paderborn, Germany
{friberg,c.schaefer,r.koch}@cik.upb.de

Abstract. This paper presents a methodology to analyse unstructured end user feedback gathered from usability evaluations. Usability can mean the difference between success or failure of a product. There exist a significant number of methodologies for measuring usability. However just a very few general, structured approaches for analysing unstructured usability evaluation data gathered in interviews is published. This paper regards on the deficit and presents the methodology Sum-SARSEP. After the preparation phase with the clustering of the user requirements, generation of hypotheses, definition of user-oriented scenarios and designing of the interviews the analysis phase follows. The seven steps provide a result about the fulfillment of the user requirements and additionally a prioritisation list to implement the findings drawn from the end user feedback.

Keywords: Usability Evaluation, User Requirements, Evaluation Data Analysis, Fire Department, Thinking-Aloud Technique, Interviews, Scenario-Based Evaluation.

1 Introduction

Every project arrives at some stage in its lifecycle at an evaluation phase as it is cost effective and useful across various methods and domains [BiMa05]. When you arrive at this point, you can find a lot of advices how to evaluate your product; in this paper we will from now on focus on an IT-product, a kind of software which will be described more detailed later. Even if you bear all the guidelines and principles in mind, you will get problems concerning the representing of your results. The one side just wants to hear a formal description of "succeeded" and the other side just sees the evaluation phase as a "necessary evil". As the evaluator you will present your results and derive an added value out of it. During the evaluation phase of the research project AirShield[1] we developed a methodology focusing on the analysis of the gathered data. Our motivation was one the one hand to achieve a result concerning the fulfillment of the user requirements and on the other hand a priorisation list for the further development.

---

[1] Airborne Remote Sensing for Hazard Inspection by Network Enabled Lightweight Drones - funded by BMBF "Research for civil security" HighTech-Strategy.

N. Aschenbruck et al. (Eds.): Future Security 2012, CCIS 318, pp. 249–260, 2012.

Before describing the methodology an introduction of the project AirShield is given: The project acts in the domain of civil security and focuses on IT-based information management and decision support for fire fighters. More concrete, by using the AirShield-system fire fighters have in case of a CBRN[2]-operation no longer the need to measure the concentration of dangerous substances under risk conditions. Therefore autonomous, wireless networked drones with corresponding, mobile sensors have to be researched. The obtained data are used to receive a spatial visualisation of the current situation and to achieve a context-sensitive decision support for the fire fighters in the disaster. The Fig. 1 shows the graphical user interface of the AirShield-system at the time of the conducted evaluation.

Fig. 1. Screenshot of AirShield-system (Client mainly developed by Gis Consult GmbH)

While validation concentrates on the proof of correctness of an actual system or design, during an evaluation process the discharge of criteria like before gathered requirements are tested. Hence, from our point of view evaluation can be seen very close to the term verification. The aim of this paper is to illustrate the used evaluation process in AirShield and to describe the analysis and interpretation of evaluation data in general. Furthermore a used methodology how to fill the gap between end user, developers and evaluators is shown, who all should be different from each other to assure an objective assessment [Niel93]. The usability of assigned software is important [Niel93], especially in the described context where goal-oriented, rapid and flexible decisions are requested. "Usability within a certain context of use characterizes the quality of product use" [DATe06]. Hence this is one aspect of the AirShield evaluation. The planning and conducting of usability evaluation is a huge challenge, e.g., you have to choose the method, to design the procedure, to prepare the probands and to plan the conduction. In this work we chose the "thinking aloud" technique and refer

---

[2] Chemical, biological, radiological, and nuclear.

to work in [DuRe99] and [NoHo06]. But these steps are not enough, you need to analyse and interpret your data and communicate your findings to developers and other stakeholders. Furthermore the acting on the findings presents a difficult task [FLH10]. In this paper we will exactly focus on this analysis of the observations, usability problems, and recommendations.

2   Target Group

Structure and human resource planning of fire departments during an operation follows a strict hierarchy with a predefined command level. This paper references to the structure of German fire departments. Every role has its own range of duty and for that reason requires different information or opportunities from an IT-system. In case of a CBRN-incident the task of the officer-in-charge is to control and lead the whole operation. Related to the dimension of the incident the officer-in-charge is able to establish specific sections concerning "measurement" to retrieve information about the potential contaminated area. Under a section leader several fire fighters who are skilled in CBRN-operations explore the situation ([FWDV100], [FWDV500]). Such a disaster is affected by dynamic conditions. For that reason fire fighters assume multiple roles or change it during the incident and an applied IT-system has to react on it [TCVX04].

Designers are not user, so knowing the user is crucial for designing a reasonable system [Niel93]. It makes a difference if novice or experts in a special domain are the expected end user, hence the system design should refer to the certain qualifications of the users. The AirShield-project wants to support every described (officer-in-charge, section leader "measurement", CBRN-fire fighters) role and implemented various system-views with a deviating range of functions. Therefore concerning the usability evaluation participants who are familiar with the working conditions of the specified role and have deep knowledge in that context are required for the evaluation. They have to be experts in their domain; they have technical, process- and conjectural knowledge which are related to a specific field of work. An expert is not alone characterized by a high professional knowledge; he has furthermore an established practical notice about his operating range [BLM09].

In practice twelve probands were interviewed who all take an active part full-time or voluntary in a fire department. Four participants conducted the scenario for the CBRN-fire fighters; three took part in the test for the section leader and five for the officer-in-charge. To demonstrate the high professional experience the participants are involved in the fire department for a long time, in average about 16,7 years.

3   Related Work

There exist a lot of different methodologies in the literature to evaluate an IT-system and to measure usability (e.g., heuristic or guideline evaluation [Niel93], [ShPl10], cognitive walkthrough [MSK10], competitive usability testing [ShPl10]). An overall approach for structuring and designing a usability-test and moreover how to analyze the gathered data is given in [TuAl08]. It is described as a simple technique intended to capture what the participants are thinking while working: confusion, frustration and also delights. Furthermore it is described as especially effective for conducting exploratory research because it exposes the participant's expectations and impressions about how the system works. The "thinking aloud" technique should be complemented through specific requesting to continuously gather feedback from the users (cf. [MaMu02]), a fact we made use of by designing the interviews.

The International Standards Organisation (ISO 9241-11) defines usability as "the extent to which a product can be used by specified user to achieved specified goals with effectiveness, efficiency, and satisfaction in a specified context of use". Thereby [TuAl08] mentioned that "Usability can sometimes mean the difference between life and death" and even more when the corresponding system is used by a fire department. Once more a confirmation of the subject we focus on concerning the evaluation of the IT-system.

As already mentioned the performing of usability evaluation is challenging but a lot of support can be found in literature. Concerning the procedure to analyse the collected data and additionally derive recommendations of interviews is very little to find (cf. also [FLH10]). Suggestions about the protocols and data analysis are briefly given (e.g., [RuCh08]), but primarily for structured data like 'Task Accuracy', comments and open feedback is rarely regarded. The study of Følstad, Law and Hornbæk [FLH10] investigates how usability professionals conduct analysis and reveals a lack of structure in the analysis process.

4   Approach

The following section describes the approach of the AirShield-project for the evaluation. Initially the preparation phase is shown, then the design and the conducting of interviews. Finally the methodology to analyse the gathered unstructured data is described in detail.

4.1   Preparation

During the phase of requirements engineering on the one hand specific, technical requirements which are related to the system or underlying subsystem are gathered and on the other requirements which deals with the indeed needs of the user are analysed. In the context of the AirShield-project end users were early integrated in the design specification to consider their specific requirements. For our further work we define that a user requirement can only or at least optimally be evaluated by the end user.

In case of the project the inquiry was done by using the syntax of [Rupp07] to follow a standardized approach and all collected requirements used the same template. Overall 178 requirements were summarized in a catalogue whereof 16 fulfilled the characterisation of a user requirement. Due to the importance of the user requirements a separate evaluation process was initiated to direct the intention on the user's needs. Therefore the involvement of end users was necessary to evaluate the realised system.

To prepare the evaluation phase in a first step the user requirements have to be clustered to get an outline about the topics to evaluate and to generate open issues (in the form of hypotheses). In the context of AirShield accrued the following aggregation in Fig. 2.

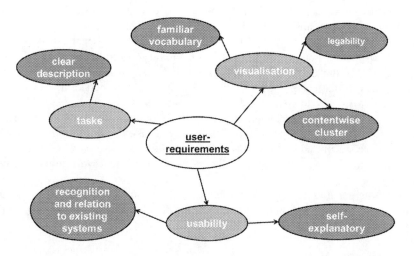

Fig. 2. User requirement cluster

There exists of course dependencies between the generated clusters (e.g., usability contains legibility), but an adequate assignment is necessary to continue goal-oriented in the evaluation and does not have to be bijective. Out of these assignments the hypotheses can be derived. The list is extensible; we want to show exemplary how to proceed.

- The AirShield-system integrates aspects concerning visualization like legibility and familiar vocabulary. (H1)
- In the AirShield-system the tasks to be performed have a clear description. (H2)
- The AirShield-system considers issues concerning the usability like the recognition and relation to existing similar systems. (H3)

In a next step deducted from the user requirements role-based test-scenarios have to be specified referring to existing evaluation-methods like expert-reviews and contextual analysis [Rich10]. Scenarios are important for the following usability-test in which participants have to solve typical, expected tasks with the respective product. In relation to the usability-method "exploratory study" the probands have no detailed knowledge of the system, so that the precognition conducts their completed actions

[RuCh08]. Therefore three scenarios for each considered role (officer-in-charge, section leader "measurement", CBRN-fire fighters) based on the described approach was developed to provide user-oriented tasks with the system.

Therefore test tasks "should be chosen to be as representative as possible of the users to which the system will eventually be put in the fields" [Niel93]. Additional in the preparation phase in AirShield three severity levels of tasks emerged. General tasks constitute the first level. Here the focus lays on small, completed tasks which are in circumstances are similar to other systems like login or zoom if the system provides a map-view like in AirShield. The next level contains specific tasks which represent the corresponding system. In case of AirShield the planning of a route for drone flight is an example of this task-group. As a last type aggregated tasks can be mentioned. In this particular instance the tasks combine several subsystems. In AirShield the use of the decision support system and then plan a resulting route for drones belongs to that category. Every type of task should be part of a scenario and moreover the tasks have to cover the defined hypotheses.

The clusters of user requirements and hence the hypotheses are the basis for creating tasks, so that a relation between requirement and task can be established during the analysis phase. But additionally the task has to be a realistic part of the working field. Furthermore the sequence of tasks has to fit into the actual workflow of the end user.

After having generated a scenario for the usability evaluation with regard to the user requirements the preparation phase ends and the detailed design and planning of the interviews proceeds.

4.2   Design of Interviews

A good and comprehensible documentation is essential for a sufficient analysis of the gathered data. Consequently the use of different recording media is recommended (i.e. audio, video, manual notes, digital pen). During the conduction of the scenario-based tasks several minute taker should be on-site and recording should be installed. In AirShield the proband[3] (indistinguishable) and the IT-system is filmed to have an objective view from the evaluation. Furthermore it is recommendable to arrange a projector in the field of view of all involved people to facilitate the documentation and common comprehension. The recommended test-setup is shown in Fig. 3.

The tests in AirShield took place under laboratory conditions. Consequently the simulated environment and the course of the scenario are substantial to give probands the feeling to work with the system as realistic as possible. In that context a second system worked in the background to simulate the drone flight and the progress of the spreading of dangerous substances.

During the interviews the probands have to be supported by a moderator with deep knowledge of the functionalities and handling of the presented system. The probands have to be introduced into method of thinking-aloud to gather impressions and comments concerning each step of the interview. Each iteration of an interview lasts about two hours and should contain the following steps:

---

[3] The agreement of the participants has to be sought beforehand.

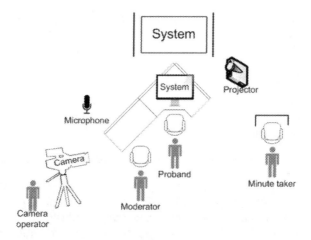

Fig. 3. Test setup

(a) Introduction

In the beginning the organization team has to be introduced to the test person. A short description of the context, the underlying project and research questions should be given and thereby the intention and intended goal of the evaluations are explained.

(b) Introducing the IT-System

In the next step the evaluated object and its functionalities are explained. It is important to "emphasize that it is the system that is being tested, not the user" [Niel93] themselves and the interviewees have the possibility to try out the system to allow a feeling of confidence.

(c) Performing the Pre-Defined, Role-Based Scenario

This step builds the main part of an iteration of an interview. A detailed description of the scenario is given in section 4.1. After performing the simulated incident the GUI of the IT-system contained several new generated information and objects.

(d) Collecting General Feedback

After finishing the scenario every test person was asked about the added value of the IT-system, if they would use and work with such a system to improve the processes during an incident.

4.3   Analysis of Collected Data

After the interview the observations have to be collated and brought synchronous together to analyze the data. An important fact is that the used evaluation method does not influence the analysis. We describe in this paper the interviews with structured scenarios, but every kind of gathering unstructured data from end users can be adapted in the described method below. Necessary are the clustered user requirements and the derived hypotheses in the beginning to get the relation afterwards.

The procedure for the detailed analysis is described in the following and depicted in Fig. 4. In every step the main activity is marked in bold and furthermore represents the acronym of the method SumSARSEP.

1. **Summarization (Sum)** of all protocols of each minute taker

All recordings have to be captured in an understandable way within its context. The goal is to have one protocol for each interview partner. Multiple recordings have to be identified and just collected once in the final protocol.

2. **Sorting (S)** of the statement into the clusters of the collected user requirements

Positive and negative statements of the probands have to be sorted into the defined hypotheses (the more fine-grained the hypotheses are defined the more detailed will the integration of the statements be). Furthermore a section with identified errors and one for general feedback are needed. All protocols of step 1 are sorted into the hypotheses. The result will be one document for each hypothesis with statements of all probands.

3. **Aggregation (A)** of statements in every protocol

Statements made by more than one person have to be weighted stronger. Similar statements have to be grouped and afterwards aggregated by stating the frequency. As we are evaluating results from research projects and hence innovative ideas and systems are presented, often suggestions for modifications or extensions were mentioned. These ideas present an important input for the further development and should not get lost through low mentioning. So it is important to emphasize frequently named comments but on the other hand rarely statements contain important feedback. Based on this fact comments stated by at least half of the test persons get weighted with number 1 and all the others get zero. Hence, the frequency will intendedly thereby get a low impact on the result, but it could be adapted in another context, i.e. the market introduction of an e-shop where the frequency may play a decisive role.

4. Identification of **recommendations (R)** for adjustments

Based on the feedback of the experts recommendations for modifications are derived to improve the system. Criteria for the identification are feasibility and meaningfulness. Recommendations are just identified for negative comments and errors as these need improvement. Costs and practicability for implementing the recommendations are not taken into account, only the fulfilling of the feedback.

5. Identification of the **severity (S)** from users' perspective

In this step the severity of the statement for performing the work process is assessed independent from the effort to implement the recommendation. The value 7 represents a high relevance for the user and 1 a low relevance for the processes performed by the experts. Zero represents non-compliance from the view of the usability-experts, i.e. like a suggestion about a feature which already is implemented but was not used during the interview.

6. Identification of the **effort (E)** to implement the recommendations

In this phase the effort to implement the identified recommendations for adjustment in step 4 is determined. In this step the developer team plays the most important role. They have to define the effort to implement the recommendations, independent from the importance for the end users. The value 1 means a very high effort, 7 accordingly a low effort.

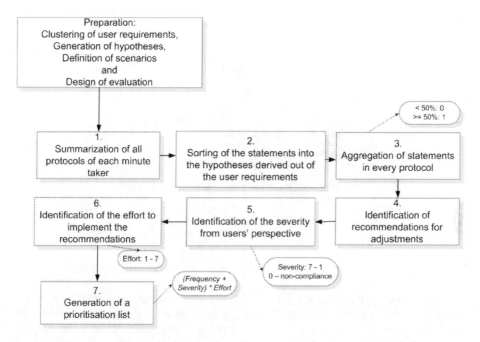

Fig. 4. Methodology SumSARSEP for analysing unstructured evaluation data

7. Generation of a **prioritisation (P)** list

In this last step a list with prioritisations based on the derived indexes is generated. The indicator concerning the frequency (0 or 1) of step 3 is added to the severity for the user (step 5). This sum is multiplied with the effort for implementing the recommendation (step 6). The possible maximum and hence 'best' result could be 56 (cf.: (1+7)*7 = 56). The higher the result is the higher is the position in the prioritisation list. These results should be considered at first for improvement: Often stated things, with high severity and low effort for implementing.

5   Results

By using the SumSARSEP method to analyse the collected data we could achieve a valuable result in the project AirShield to satisfy the different stakeholders by presenting useful results with connection to the user requirements and a list of recommendations based on the gathered feedback.

One of the predefined results was the measuring of the degree of fulfillment of the hypotheses and hence the user requirements collected in the beginning of the project. The Fig. 5 represents the result of the evaluation and its analysis in the AirShield-project. Nearly 80% requirements listed in the catalogue of requirements were satisfied (up to 80% fulfilling) and further 10% of the initial requirements were rejected from the end users during the project. The rejection was based on new findings and insights and also a stronger focusing on other components than suggested in the beginning. Hence, in AirShield only about 10% of the user requirements were not fulfilled or just with restrictions.

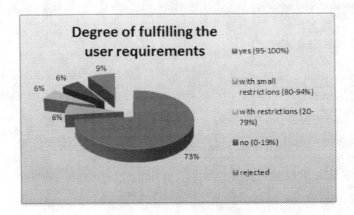

Fig. 5. Fulfilling of user requirements

Furthermore by using the SumSARSEP-method we were able to present a prioritisation list which built the foundation for the next development phase. We maintained the collected feedback in the initially defined hypotheses (out of the user requirements) to achieve the list more structured. To every hypothesis   were in the end (out of twelve interviews) 5 to 20 different feedbacks integrated (e.g., statements like "font size is too small", "the button to start the drones is difficult/not to find" and "a versioning of the measured data should be integrated"). Whereby the first example had a quite high prioritisation as many end users mentioned it, the level of severity is medium and the effort to change it is very low. The prioritisation of the second example is very high as some assumed it, the severity level is very high and the effort for changing is low again. The third example showed a low prioritisation as only a few end users mentioned it, the severity level is low and the effort is high. By using excel files for the documentation we offered the possibility to sort the list according to the prioritisation independent from the originally topics.

The three scenarios for each role (officer-in-charge, section leader "measurement", CBRN-fire fighters) were adopted quickly and easily by the experts and offered a beneficial foundation to gather useful feedback. The recordings during the interviews in Air-Shield were in the beginning done manual and by video, later additionally with digital pens. By using these methods we experienced the advantages and disadvantages.

6   Conclusion and Recommendation

After the evaluation process besides an overview about the fulfilling of the user requirements a prioritisation list of the feedback can be given. Furthermore by using the methodology SumSARSEP a team consisting of end users, usability professionals and developers grow together. The consequent use of the described methods SumSARSEP is very time-consuming but offers you the possibility to get useful and recyclable results out of end user feedback which often not is used.

Additionally to the results about the fulfilling of the requirements and generation of a prioritisation list interesting insights concerning the analysis procedure were made:

- The designing of the scenario may not be underestimated because there the clustered user requirements and hence defined hypotheses have to be integrated. If requirements are missing at that point, it will be hard to integrate them afterwards and hence to draw a conclusion about the fulfilling. Especially if different system views or roles exist, it will take time to define, discuss, prepare and train the scenarios with the organisation team.
- Another fundamental point is the recording of data. One essential task is to master the great quantity of accrued evaluation data. So several, different possibilities should be taken under account. Manual recordings are easy made, but the analysis strongly interdepends from the minute taker. Also the storage space is negligible but especially video needs a lot of storage space and a high-end equipment is needed. Every type of recording should be tested beforehand.
- One important fact is the timeliness of the analysis of the interviews. As Courage and Baxter [CoBa04] already mentioned the collected data should be analysed shortly after conducting each interview, otherwise it will be really hard to remember and classify your notes and minutes.

As mentioned the evaluation method to collect the unstructured end user feedback can be changed or modified. To start the analysis with the methodology SumSARSEP it is important to have the clustered user requirements or at least core themes the findings should be about to define the hypotheses. Then our described definition of scenarios and conducting of interviews can be used or any other kind of method.

The method has to be tested and applied more detailed, at or institute already two further projects are in use of it. An interesting point would be to adapt it in other domains, not just the civil security to see the differences.

References

[XTM09]   Xiaoping, Z., Tingkuan, Z., Mengting, L.: Modeling crowd evacuation of a building based on seven methodological approaches. Building and Environment 44, 437–445 (2009)

[BiMa05]   Bias, R., Mayhew, D.: Cost-Justifying Usability: An Update for the Internet Age. Morgan Kaufmann, San Francisco (2005)

[BLM09]   Bogner, A., Littig, B., Menz, W.: Interviewing experts. Palgrave Macmillan (2009)

[CoBa04]   Courage, C., Baxter, K.: Understanding Your Users: A Practical Guide to User Requirements Methods, Tools, and Techniques. Morgan Kaufmann Publishers Inc., San Francisco (2004)

[DuRe99]   Dumas, J., Redish, J.: A Practical Guide to Usability Testing, Intellect Ltd. (1999)

[DATe06]   Akkreditierungsstelle DATech: DATech-Prüfhandbuch Gebrauchstauglichkeit (DATech Test Handbook Usability), Akkreditierungsstelle DATech, Frankfurt a.M (2006)

[FWDV100]   Feuerwehr-Dienstvorschrift 100 - Führung und Leitung im Einsatz (fire department manual 100 – leadership and conductorship in operation). Deutscher Gemeindeverlag, Stuttgart (2003)

[FWDV500]   Feuerwehr-Dienstvorschrift 500- Einheiten im ABC-Einsatz (fire department manual 500 – units in CBRN-operation). Deutscher Gemeindeverlag, Stuttgart (2004)

[FLH10]   Følstad, A., Law, E., Hornbæk, K.: Analysis in usability evaluations: an exploratory study. In: Proceedings of the 6th Nordic Conference on Human-Computer Interaction: Extending Boundaries (NordiCHI 2010), pp. 647–650. ACM, New York (2010)

[Lewi82]   Lewis, C.: Using the 'thinking-aloud' method in cognitive interface design. Research Report RC9265. IBM T.J. Watson Research Center, Yorktown Heights, NY (1982)

[MaMu02]   Manhartsberger, M., Musil, S.: Web Usability - Das Prinzip des Vertrauens (Web Usability - the principle of trust). Galileo Press (2002)

[MSK10]   Mahatody, T., Sagar, M., Kolski, C.: State of the art on the cognitive walkthrough method, its variants and evolution. International Journal of Human-Computer Interaction (2010)

[Niel93]   Nielsen, J.: Usability Engineering. Morgan Kaufmann (1993)

[NoHo06]   Norgaard, M., Hornbaek, K.: What Do Usability Evaluators Do in Practice? An Explorative Study of Think-Aloud Testing. In: Proc. DIS 2006. ACM Press (2006)

[Rich10]   Richter, M.: Effiziente Implementierung von UCD-Methoden in Unternehmen (2010)

[RuCh08]   Rubin, J., Chrisnell, D.: Handbook of Usability Testing. Wiley Publishing (2008)

[Rupp07]   Rupp, C.: Requirements-Engineering und -Management. Professionelle, iterative Anforderungsanalyse für die Praxis (Requirements-Engineering and Management. Professional, iterative analysis for practice). vol. 4. Aufl., Hanser Fachbuchverlag, München (2007)

[ShPl10]   Shneiderman, B., Plaisant, C.: Designing the user interface. Pearson (2010)

[TCVX04]   Turoff, M., Chumer, M., van der Walle, B., Yao, X.: The Design of a Dynamic Emergency Response Management Information System (DERMIS). The Journal of Information Technology Theo7ry and Application (JITTA) 5(4), S.1–S.35 (2004)

[TuAl08]   Tullis, T., Albert, B.: Measuring the User Experience. Morgan Kaufman (2008)

Creating and Testing Holistic Crisis Management Strategies: The Crisis Management Balanced Scorecard and Systems Modelling

Jose M. Sarriegi, Eliot Rich, Ana Laugé, Leire Labaka, and Josune Hernantes

Tecnun - University of Navarra, Paseo Manuel Lardizabal 13, 20018 San Sebastian, Spain
{jmsarriegi,erich,alauge,llabaka,jhernantes}@tecnun.es

Abstract. A priori evaluation and monitoring of crisis management strategy effectiveness should lead to more effective use of scarce and expensive resources. We propose a two part process: First, a Crisis Management Balanced Scorecard (CMBSC), based on Kaplan and Norton's Balanced Scorecard, guides the monitoring and implementation of a crisis management strategy. In support of the CMBSC we propose a systems-based structuring of the tangible and intangible concerns that are the basis of crisis management.

Keywords: Crisis Management, Balanced Scorecard.

1   The Need for a Crisis Management Strategic Framework

We live in an interconnected world, where industrial accidents, volcano eruptions, terrorist attacks and pandemics have consequences extending past their geographic borders. The recent Japanese tsunami created unanticipated damages and concern well beyond the initial cataclysm [1, 2]. The consequences of crisis cascade and enlarge over time, and local efforts to mitigate them might not be effective or even desirable from a holistic point of view.

Planning and evaluating crisis management strategies should therefore be developed through an inclusive, coordinated and multidisciplinary approach. Operation of critical infrastructures upon which Society depends requires sophisticated knowledge, particularly when pressed in unanticipated ways. The number of agents involved in crisis preparation and response has increased, and with them the complexity and opacity of the problem. These agents may speak different languages, may have different cultures, and may come from different technical training, expertise and mental models. Without tools that bridge these differences, emergency response will suffer from poor coordination and low integration. Thus, crises will be inefficiently managed.

The successful avoidance and mitigation of crises often go unnoticed and unappreciated [3]. When a critical event occurs, information travels world-wide almost immediately, triggering a rush of resources and intangible reactions that affect the evolution of subsequent actions. Before the event, however, information does not travel as far or as fast. It is hard to estimate the adequacy or robustness of crisis preparation. When the

N. Aschenbruck et al. (Eds.): Future Security 2012, CCIS 318, pp. 261–264, 2012.

triggering event occurs, its impact tends to surprise: the real preparation level was not the expected one. Therefore we also argue for tools that treat crises as a confluence of temporal events and emergent vulnerabilities [4], and support experimentation and testing, particularly in the absence of hard data. Otherwise we can only judge the adequacy of our preparation after the fact.

2   Creating a Scorecard for Crisis Management

The importance of indirect factors and intangible assets in the development of strategy was recognized by business management community two decades ago. Companies adopted process and quality measures as timely proxies for delayed financial measures. This led to the adoption of various innovations, including Balanced Scorecard (BSC) [5], Quality Management [6] and Six Sigma [7], to name a few. Each of these techniques had advocates and success stories [8], and they remain influential in industry [9]. Notably, they share at least one common thread: To obtain excellent results, the firm must perform excellently.

The BSC is particularly useful for consideration of crisis management, as it is particularly integrative and outward-focused. It is deployed through the identification of objectives and indicators grouped into four linked perspectives: Organizations exist to achieve some key results. While these are often financial, non-profits, government franchises, and non-governmental organizations often have service concerns as their strategic focus. To achieve its results, the firm relies on developing a set of satisfied and loyal customers. Monitoring customers' behavior identifies performance data and anticipates potential problems. The relative attractiveness of a company depends on the company's process quality. Having well-designed, implemented, and managed processes results in satisfactory products and services for the customers.

The forward-looking firm expects that the future behavior of customers will depend on the excellence of its current processes. To this end, processes need to be up-dated, improved and replaced to avoid obsolescence. A reflective perspective, accepting the role of learning and growth within the firm, brings all these elements together as the basis for the long-term direction of the firm. The combination of these four perspectives creates a methodology to design and deploy a strategy within a company with an integrated set of objectives and indicators that capture the current status of the company and information that anticipates its future behavior and environment.

3   Adaptation of the BSC to Crisis Management

We propose an adaptation of the traditional BSC to match the characteristics of crisis management. The four perspectives listed above are matched to ones closer to our present concern. Starting at the bottom of the figure, key results become crisis "impacts," as the focal result of the crisis management activity. The size and frequency of impacts are conditioned by system's "resilience," its ability to perform during anticipated and unanticipated conditions. Thus, estimating system's resilience anticipates crisis impacts. Analogously, systems resilience is a consequence of "mitigation policies," the actions implemented in order to increase system's resilience level. Finally, we match learning and growth with "awareness," the ability to identify and adapt to the changes in resilience, crisis context, risk, performance, resources, and other concerns that affect the implemented mitigation policies' intensity and presumptive results.

4   The Challenge of Strategy Identification and Evaluation

While the value of the BSC is recognized widely, complex strategic problems re-quire additional and continuing effort to achieve significant results. The identification and evaluation of potential strategies must be accomplished before selecting the best ones for implementation. Metric monitoring must be linked with learning and adaptation for internal process improvement. BSC measures may not capture the differences between short-term and long-term measures of success, or even why this distinction is important to the success of the firm.

These concerns have been addressed through a variety of approaches. Strategy maps, proposed by Kaplan and Norton [10] as a supplement to their scorecard, articulate the rationale and vision of the strategic effort. They improve on how the story of the strategy is told and made clear to those charged with its implementation. Others have made causal mapping the central element when developing strategic options, with the goal of capturing the mental models underlying the choices being proposed. These approaches range from detailed capture of ideation and linkages [11] to more macro-level causal structures [12]. The articulation of perceptions and multiple perspectives provides a linkage to the strategic choices that become part of the BSC.

The evaluation of strategic choices requires more than causal mapping. Systems-oriented analysis that do not include simulation provide value through their articulation of critical actors and concerns [viz., 13], but they provide limited value when considering complex problems [14]. Extending the process to include formal modeling to simulate the effects of organizational policy, resource allocation, and information delays provides insight into the hidden or delayed side-effects that reduce or neutralize effectiveness [15-17]. A simulation-based policy "sandbox" provides a low-cost and low-risk opportunity to experiment with policy changes and consider conflicting assumptions. Experience with a simulation tool can be used to reduce the stress and uncertainty faced during real crises.

The broad organizational and contextual scope of crises complicates the development of comprehensive strategy. Crisis management among multiple independent actors conflicts with the hierarchical leadership and control structures found in corporations. Decisions that produce satisfactory outcomes for one organization generate or amplify problems for other stakeholders. Stakeholders may have different timetables for involvement, response, and withdrawal of their resources, depending on their own definition of crisis.

5   Systems Based Crisis Management

This combination of Balanced Scorecard and systems modeling creates a robust tool set for examining and implementing a comprehensive crisis management strategy. We will apply our framework to strategy examination of a hypothetical large scale power failure in the European Union. While the case is necessarily abstracted, it is based on a series of workshops run with the assistance of multidisciplinary experts in power, critical infrastructure, healthcare, and public safety from several EU countries.

References

1. Broad, W.J.: Scientists project path of radiation plume. New York Times, New York (2011)
2. Dempsey, J., LaFraniere, S.: In Europe and China, Japan's Crisis Renews Fears About Nuclear Power. New York Times, New York (2011)
3. Repenning, N., Sterman, J.: Nobody Ever Gets Credit for Fixing Defects that Didn't Happen: Creating and Sustaining Process Improvement. California Management Review 43, 64–88 (2001)
4. Roux-Dufort, C.: Is Crisis Management (Only) a Management of Exceptions? Journal of Contingencies and Crisis Management 15, 105–114 (2007)
5. Kaplan, R.S., Norton, D.P.: The Balanced Scorecard. Harvard Business School Press, Boston (1996)
6. Juran, J.M.: Made in U.S.A.: A renaissance in quality. Harvard Business Review 71, 42–50 (1993)
7. Hammer, M.: Process Management and the Future of Six Sigma. MIT Sloan Management Review 43, 26–32 (2002)
8. Rigby, D., Bilodeau, B.: Selecting Management Tools Wisely. Harvard Business Review 85, 20–22 (2007)
9. Lubin, D.A., Esty, D.C.: The Sustainabililty Imperative. Harvard Business Review 88, 42–50 (2010)
10. Kaplan, R.S., Norton, D.P.: Strategy Maps: Converting intangible assets into tangible outcomes. Harvard Business School Press, Boston (2004)
11. Bryson, J.M., Ackermann, F., Eden, C., Finn, C.B.: Visible thinking: Unlocking causal mapping for practical business results. Wiley, New York (2004)
12. Checkland, P., Scholes, J.: Soft Systems Methodology in Action: A 30-Year Retrospective. Wiley & Sons, Chichester (1999)
13. Abrahamsson, M., Hassel, H., Tehler, H.: Towards a System-Oriented Framework for Analysing and Evaluating Emergency Response. Journal of Contingencies and Crisis Management 18, 14–25 (2010)
14. Richardson, G.: Probems with causal-loop diagrams. System Dynamics Review 2, 158–170 (1986)
15. Morecroft, J.: Strategic Modelling and Business Dynamics. Wiley, West Sussex (2007)
16. Warren, K.: Competitive Strategy Dynamics. John Wiley West Sussex, UK (2002)
17. Akkermans, H.A., van Oorschot, K.E.: Relevance assumed: a case study of balanced scorecard development using system dynamics. Journal of the Operational Research Society 56, 931–941 (2005)

How Is Positive-Sum Privacy Feasible?

Christoph Bier[1], Pascal Birnstill[1], Erik Krempel[1],
Hauke Vagts[1,2], and Jürgen Beyerer[1,2]

[1] Fraunhofer Institute of Optronics, System Technologies and Image Exploitation
IOSB, Karlsruhe, Germany
[2] Vision and Fusion Laboratory, Karlsruhe Institute of Technology, Germany
{christoph.bier,pascal.birnstill,erik.krempel,hauke.vagts,
juergen.beyerer}@iosb.fraunhofer.de

Abstract. This work discusses Ann Cavoukian's fourth *Privacy by Design (PbD)* principle, which is known as *Full Functionality – Positive-
Sum, not Zero-Sum*. The authors argue that this principle regulating
trade-offs between privacy and functionality is questionable from a the-
oretic as well as from an operational point of view. A more consistent
and pragmatic definition of *positive-sum privacy* is proposed and demonstrated using an example scenario in the context of video surveillance.

1 Introduction

Ann Cavoukian's seven principles of *Privacy by Design (PbD)* are as well recognized as appreciated in the privacy community. Nevertheless, according to their
rather abstract nature, they are often hard to apply in practice. In particular
the fourth PbD principle of *Full Functionality – Positive-Sum, not Zero-Sum*
seems overly dogmatic. Hence, Section 2 illuminates this principle and its consequences in detail. Given these insights, Section 3 proposes a revised definition of
Positive-Sum Privacy. Section 4 applies this new notion of *Positive-Sum Privacy*
to a video surveillance example, before concluding in Section 5.

Related Work

Besides the discussed PbD Principles by Ann Cavoukian [1], who introduced the
term in the early 1990s, Langheinrich [2] was one of the first researchers who
focussed on the application of a PbD framework. His principles for system design
are based on the Fair Information Practices Principles (FIP) by the OECD [3].
Guerses et al. [4] criticise the missing distinctiveness of the PbD principles. They
propose to start from data avoidance as the best and first step towards PbD.

2 Discussion

Ann Cavoukian's fourth PbD principle *Full Functionality – Positive-Sum, not
Zero-Sum* [1] addresses the compatibility of privacy and functionality.

N. Aschenbruck et al. (Eds.): Future Security 2012, CCIS 318, pp. 265–268, 2012.

"Privacy by Design seeks to accommodate all legitimate interests and objectives in a positive-sum 'win-win' manner, not through a dated, zero-sum approach, where unnecessary trade-offs are made. Privacy by Design avoids the pretence of false dichotomies, such as privacy vs. security, demonstrating that it is possible, and far more desirable, to have both."

Figure 1 illustrates the three different concepts from game theory needed for understanding Cavoukian's definition as well as the revised version in Section 3. Depending on a starting point (dots in Figure 1), functionality F and privacy P can evolve. Changes are denoted with ΔP and ΔF respectively.

- zero-sum: A concept in the field of game theory in which the sum of the outcomes is equal to zero (cf. Figure 1a), i.e., a positive ΔP results in a negative ΔF with the same quantity and vice versa.
- positive-sum: A concept in the field of game theory in which the sum of the outcomes is greater zero (cf. Figure 1b), i.e., either ΔP or ΔF can be negative, but the sum is positive.
- win-win: A special case of a positive-sum game where it is necessary that every participant has a outcome greater zero, i.e., privacy and functionality increases (cf. Figure 1c).

In other words, fulfilling this principle of PbD requires that a given system's functionality must only be extended if at the same time the systems privacy-awareness is improved. This requirement inhibits any kind of pragmatic trade-offs, i.e. neither tolerating a minor cut of functionality for significantly improved privacy nor sacrificing a bit of privacy for undoubtedly beneficial functionality is possible.

The principle is also inconsistent from a theoretical point of view. Starting with a situation of full privacy and zero functionality, adding functionality that requires personal information necessarily reduces privacy. Generally speaking, there have to be trade-offs between functionality and privacy in some cases.

In order to assess whether a new design results in a win-win, positive-sum or zero-sum situation, the degrees of privacy and functionality have to be measured. For this, privacy as well as functionality requirements have to be prioritized and weighed against each other. After determining to which fraction the requirements are actually fulfilled by a given design, the weighted sums over the fractions of privacy and functionality fulfillment can be calculated. From an operational point of view, however, weighting of requirements is a controversial issue and developing a method for objectively resolving conflicting requirements is an open research question.

3   Positive-Sum Privacy

As discussed in 2, a more pragmatic regulation for trade-offs between functionality and privacy during a concrete design process requires a new definition of *Positive-Sum Privacy*. A design process does not necessarily start from scratch,

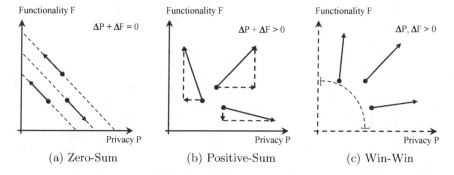

Fig. 1. Comparing zero-sum, positive-sum and win-win

i.e., privacy invasive features are often created by adding new functionality to an existing system. Thus, the new definition also has to be applicable as a guideline for the evolution of a system.

Definition 1 (Positive-Sum Privacy). *Positive-Sum Privacy consists of a starting point (cf. Figure 1), an evolutionary step and an assessment of the method:*

- *Starting point of a comparative evaluation is an outdated predecessor with less than full functionality and less than full privacy, both greater than zero.*
- *In an evolutionary step, a trade-off between privacy and functionality is acceptable if and only if it results in a positive-sum of functionality and privacy.*
- *The positive-sum has to be clear and not based on biased evaluation methods. If there is reasonable doubt, Positive-Sum Privacy is not fulfilled.*

It must be stressed that PbD cannot assure that a system is not privacy invasive. When adhering to all seven principles of PbD, however, one can come up with a design that is as little privacy invasive as possible given the purpose of the system. As a consequence, particularly for a system whose purpose is intirinsically privacy invasive, it makes perfect sense to establish a PbD compliant design process. This insight will be illustrated in the subsequent section.

4   Positive-Sum Privacy in Intelligent Video Surveillance

As starting point for this example assume an airport being monitored using a conventional video surveillance system, which is supposed to be replaced for efficiency reasons. The purpose of the video surveillance system is to observe critical infrastructures of the airport, i.e., regions of the airport that must not be accessed by unauthorized persons. The system is also used for manual tracking of intruders, thus its cameras do already cover the airport to a great extent. The security personnel is faced by a large number of live video screens.

Video surveillance is often criticized as an unselective measure putting people under general suspicion, i.e., a very high privacy impact is inherent to video surveillance. Nevertheless, modernizing video surveillance due to efficiency needs is an opportunity for carrying out a PbD compliant redesign.

The new system shall enable security personnel to observe critical regions more efficiently, i.e., intrusions have to be detected autonomously, so that an operator can concentrate on handling incidents. In the default setting the system performs rather noninvasive intrusion detection. Person detector algorithms are only running on specific cameras that cover critical regions and the cameras' video streams are not shown to the operator. Thus, *no* personal data is stored. If and only if an intruder is detected, the system is put into *alert mode*, which enables logging of the operator's interactions and tracking of the intruder.

By this means, system functionality is separated into a less privacy-invasive default operational mode, i.e., intrusion detection for critical regions, and a highly invasive alert mode, i.e., tracking or locating of intruders. This design is compliant to *Positive-Sum Privacy* as in total the system is less privacy invasive and only in highly selective situations trades privacy for valuable functionality.

5   Conclusion

The new definition of *Positive-Sum Privacy* allows for pragmatic trade-offs between privacy and functionality as often required in practice. The field of intelligent video surveillance illustrates the benefit of such trade-offs. An entirely rephrased and complemented definition of PbD as a set of explicit requirements of a design meta-process is ongoing work.

Acknowledgment. This work was partially funded by Fraunhofer Gesellschaft Internal Programs, Attract 692166, the KASTEL project by the Federal Ministry of Education and Research, BMBF 01BY1172 and the SURVEILLE project in the 7th Framework Programme by the European Commision (Project reference: 284725). The views expressed are those of the authors alone and not intended to reflect those of the Commision.

References

1. Cavoukian, A.: Privacy by Design - The 7 Foundational Principles (2011)
2. Langheinrich, M.: Privacy by Design - Principles of Privacy-Aware Ubiquitous Systems. In: Abowd, G.D., Brumitt, B., Shafer, S. (eds.) UbiComp 2001. LNCS, vol. 2201, pp. 273–291. Springer, Heidelberg (2001), http://www.springerlink.com/index/y9reah898fcuc2n8.pdf
3. OECD: Guidelines on the Protection of Privacy and Transborder Flows of Personal Data. Organisation for Economic Cooperation and Development (1980)
4. Gürses, S., Troncoso, C., Diaz, C.: Engineering Privacy by Design. In: Proceedings of the 4th International Conference on Computers, Privacy & Data Protection, Brüssel (August 2011)

Concept for Scenario-Development for Foresight Security Scenarios: Mapping Research to a Comprehensive Approach to Exogenous EU Roles

Thomas Benesch, Johannes Göllner, Johann Höchtl,
Andreas Peer, and Walter Seböck

Danube University Krems, Dr.-Karl-Dorrek-Straße 30, 3500 Krems, Austria
{thomas.benesch,johannes.goellner,johann.hoechtl,
andreas.peer,walter.seboeck}@donau-uni.ac.at

Abstract. Europe still has to find its way to become a truly united state, overcoming diverse legal and political frameworks and moral understandings and ethical values. The FOCUS project, EU funded under the FP7 research program, has the goal to identify future EU roles in security research. One important aspect is an agreed and comprehensive set of security themes. This paper presents possible major security scenarios, their methodological finding and identified obstacles on the way to a more coordinated EU security strategy.

Keywords: European security research, comprehensive approach, scenario identification, security taxonomy, transversal security aspects.

1   Scope of Security Research

Each EU Member State is an open system, influenced by internal and external threats and hazards. In the context of a comprehensive approach, the concept of internal security cannot exist without an external dimension, since internal security increasingly depends on external security.

Challenges in the coming decades will continue to be fraught with uncertainty, involving state and non-state actors combining conventional and asymmetric methods. They will go beyond traditional domains to encompass space and cyberspace, and strongly influence the conceptual and operational ingredients of the comprehensive approach. Problems related to the proliferation of weapons of mass destruction will persist. Cyber threats will also proliferate, with possible capabilities to organize a high-consequence attack against European critical infrastructures [1,2].

2   FOCUS Methodology Development

The FOCUS project (Foresight Security Scenarios – Mapping Research to a Comprehensive Approach to Exogenous EU Roles, http://www.focusproject.eu) is co-funded under the Security Research theme of the EU's 7th EU Framework Programme, for the period of April 2011 to March 2013. FOCUS aims a wide coverage of research

N. Aschenbruck et al. (Eds.): Future Security 2012, CCIS 318, pp. 269–272, 2012.

topics, with a high level of practical utility in mind: to define the most plausible threat scenarios that affect the "borderline" between the EU's external and internal dimensions to security; to derive guidance for possible future EU security roles and related security research – building on and reaching beyond conclusions from expert bodies and other projects [3]. The main contribution of the FOCUS project is the development of effective long-term prediction and assessment tool. Moreover, it will deliver tangible products (as an IT platform) and contents (as a roadmap) for planning of research and deciding on priorities. To realize this contribution, FOCUS will design and apply an "embedded scenario" method to develop scenarios for security research (methodologically speaking: alternative futures) [4].

2.1   Scenario Perspective

Based on extensive literature review of European Member States security frameworks and grounded work within the security research community [5,6], the FOCUS consortium developed the following vertical perspective of a security scenario taxonomy [4]: Global scenarios, Local scenarios, Drive/trend scenarios, Defence related scenarios (incl. situational scenarios), Threat scenarios. This taxonomy served as a building block for the scenario discovery process of the following project iteration.

2.2   Scenario Finding Process

Scenario development was based on context scenarios of FOCUS deliverable 3.2 [7] and critical assessment. The weighing was done according to relevance from a dual perspective: (a) nation/member state vs. EU-level/international approach to civil security and security research; (b) position of the scenario on the continuum of internal/external security. The scenarios for alternative futures of security research in support of the "comprehensive approach 2035" represent the major outcome of deliverable 3.3 [8].

1. Generalised security research system: a common securitisation model and national security research programmes on the European level.
2. Nationalisation of security research: Member States consult each other on a regular basis and establish common security research initiatives.
3. Research system for European critical infrastructure protection (EUCIP): support of European critical infrastructure protection [8,9].
4. Security incident management research: includes research for monitoring instruments.
5. Security economics research system: to improve the protection of the European Union from within or outside the EU.
6. Public health research system: includes all health care systems of the respective Member States.

2.3   Guidance for Possible Future EU Security Roles

The FOCUS project consortium identified a list of cross-cutting, or "transversal" aspects that generally all of the six scenarios for "security research 2035" have in common. Those transversal aspects relate to future fields of action and needed expertise in most of the six future scenarios [8]. The following research lines appear of particular future interest: Tools for policies and national views integration and Standards for national organisation for a comprehensive approach to security. Socio-demographic developments across the European Union have an impact on the development, as well as the capacity to act and on the effectiveness of the used instruments [10]. Government bodies hold an enormous amount of data which carries the potential to raise security, welfare, trust and create new economic opportunities[11]. Social media plays an increasingly important role in crisis communication. This has implications for the practical work of emergency services and media organisations, as well as for further scholarly research. Future security research will have to provide results for uptake also on the level of dedicated training material in the context of online education, or advanced distributed learning.

3   Transversal Aspects of Scenarios in Relation to Alternative Futures

Future EU security research should contribute to prepare rules for the processing and implementation of a suitable concept, leading to security of both the Member State and the Union as a whole. To overcome present and future weaknesses, as anticipated by FOCUS scenario foresight, any concept for a "comprehensive approach 2035" should address the following aspects: terms, human system /- assets are understood in different ways, safety and crisis management, EU basic legislation, security training for EU citizens. To overcome these problems, it would be necessary to elaborate the concept of sustainable development, a long-term plan of implementation of sustainable development concept into practice and the plan of enforcement of sustainable development principles into practice. Possible concrete measures include education and training of citizens, specific technical education and training, technical, medical, environmental, cyber and other standards, executive units to defeat emergency and critical situations, adapted security, emergency and crisis planning.

4   Conclusion and Outlook

For all thematic embedded scenarios an appropriate standardized terminology work as the root for the processing of every scenario has to be developed. A general thesaurus catalogue for scenario research will act as the basis and prerequisite for more fine grained thesauri which will follow. In order to meet the these requirements, an efficient and strategic as well as operative documentation, information and knowledge management (system) has to be formulated with a view to a strategic Foresight-Risk Assessment. Further transversal aspects have to be identified. Multiple scenarios based on IT-supported foresight in the form of alternative futures for support of security research for exogenous EU security missions, will have to be developed. The increased complexity of security research will amplify the importance of identified transversal security aspects, rendering security research an even more interdisciplinary field of research.

FOCUS is co-funded by the European Commission under the 7th Framework Program, theme "security", call FP7-SEC-2010-1, work program topic 6.3-2 "Fore sighting the contribution of security research to meet the future EU roles"

References

1. Focus Consortium: Problem space report: Critical infrastructure & supply chain protection, Deliverable 5.1, p. 20 (January 2012)
2. Maguire, R.: Safety Cases and Safety Reports: Meaning, Motivation and Management. Ashgate Publishing, Ltd. (2006)
3. Focus Consortium: Summary of problem space descriptions, p. 2, http://www.focusproject.eu/documents/14976/15033/Summary+of+FOCUS+problem+space+descriptions?version=1.0 (retrieved March 29, 2012)
4. Focus Consortium: Report describing and defining the methodology (Deliverable 2.1) (September 2011)
5. Merlingen, M., Mireanu, M., Stavrevska, E.B.: Europäische Sicherheit. Wo stehen wir heute? In: Jahrbuch 2008, Center for OSCE research (CORE). Center for OSCE Research (CORE) am Institut für Friedensforschung und Sicherheitspolitik (IFSH) an der Universität Hamburg (2008), http://www.core-hamburg.de/documents/jahrbuch/08/pdf-gesamt.pdf
6. Fry, M.J., Jan, H.: European Union and Strategy: An Emerging Actor. Routledge Chapman & Hall (2007)
7. Focus Consortium: Report on alternative future models of comprehensiveness, Deliverable 3.2 (December 2011), http://www.focusproject.eu/web/focus/downloads/-/document_library_display/1QpQ/view/15032
8. Focus Consortium: Foresight Security Scenarios: Mapping Research to a Comprehensive Approach to Exogenous EU Roles: Deliverable 3.3 (March 2012)
9. Lopez, J., Setola, R., Wolthusen, S.D. (eds.): Critical Infrastructure Protection. LNCS, vol. 7130. Springer, Heidelberg (2012)
10. Dostal, E., Cloete, A., Járos, G.: Biomatrix: A Systems Approach to Organisational and Societal Change. BiomatrixWeb (2005)
11. Höchtl, J., Reichstädter, P.: Linked Open Data - A Means for Public Sector Information Management. In: Andersen, K.N., Francesconi, E., Grönlund, Å., van Engers, T.M. (eds.) EGOVIS 2011. LNCS, vol. 6866, pp. 330–343. Springer, Heidelberg (2011)

Establishment of the European Reference Network for Critical Infrastructure Protection (ERNCIP)

Naouma Kourti, Ferenc Borsos, and Peter Gattinesi

European Commission Joint Research Centre, Ispra, Italy
{naouma.kourti,ferenc.borsos,peter.gattinesi}@jrc.ec.europa.eu

Abstract. The lack of EU-wide conformity assessment for security-related equipment, systems, and services is a barrier to the development of security-related products. The ERNCIP project provides a framework for CIP-related experimental facilities and laboratories to share knowledge and expertise, and to harmonize test protocols throughout Europe, aiming at improved protection of critical infrastructure in the EU against all types of threats and hazards. Following a preliminary phase, the project was endorsed by the Member States and was launched in 2011. This paper presents the preliminary results from ERNCIP from its first year, describing in detail the foundation of the first Thematic Areas and the development of the Inventory.

Keywords: Critical Infrastructure, network, experimental facility, laboratory, test protocol, harmonisation, ERNCIP, Inventory, security.

1   Introduction

Security solutions in Europe need to be conformity tested and certified in each of the 27 Member States. This leads the industry to invest unnecessary resources to conduct such tests and obtain related certifications within a virtually absent Single Market for Security. This hampers the transition to the market and hinders market acceptance, jeopardising the ability of the EU to protect its critical infrastructure against emerging threats and hazards.

EU Member States and the European Commission (EC) believe this situation can improve by increased availability and networking of existing experimental facilities. The ERNCIP project has been formulated to provide the platform to satisfy this rationale. Its mission statement is: *To foster the emergence of innovative, qualified, efficient and competitive security solutions, through the networking of European experimental capabilities.*

ERNCIP has been established under the umbrella of the European Programme for Critical Infrastructure Protection[1], and operates within the organisational framework of Institute for the Protection and Security of the Citizen (IPSC) of the EC's Joint Research Centre.

---

[1] http://ec.europa.eu/home-affairs/policies/terrorism/
terrorism_infrastructure_en.htm

N. Aschenbruck et al. (Eds.): Future Security 2012, CCIS 318, pp. 273–276, 2012.

IPSC works in close collaboration with research centres, universities, private companies and international organisations in a concerted effort to develop research-based solutions for the security and protection of citizens.

Following preparatory work in 2009-10 by the EC's Joint Research Centre, Member States agreed that ERNCIP should be a long-term, sustainable network of experts from research and technology organisations within the EU, with capabilities relevant to critical infrastructure protection. A four-year project is under way to fully establish this network. The priorities of the first year were the inception of the priority thematic areas to be addressed, and the development of an on-line inventory of relevant experimental facilities in the EU.

2   Governance of ERNCIP

During the first year of operation the ERNCIP Office has been set-up and a fully functional organisation put into place. The main duties of the ERNCIP Office are:

- Manage, coordinate and administer the ERNCIP project;

- Identify and prioritise the thematic areas (through the sponsors) and subsequently supervise and promote them

- Address the legal-regulatory issues, as well as the relevant ERNCIP management policies and security

- Develop and operate the ERNCIP Inventory, including the tasks of data population and marketing

The organisation of ERNCIP follows a lean management approach, effected through the key support functions of ERNCIP project i.e. the Expert Group, the Key User Group for the Inventory, the Legal Issues Group, and Thematic Area Coordinators. These four groups have the following roles:

Table 1.

Supporting body	Roles
Expert Group (EG)	represent the interests of the stakeholders and sponsors especially on issues concerning the ERNCIP deliverables
Key User Group (KUG)	represent the different types of users to support the development, data population and marketing of the Inventory
Legal Issues Group (LG)	represent the legal interests of the stakeholders in order to support the development of a legal framework to run ERNCIP in a trusted and regulated manner
Thematic Area Coordinators (Coos)	coordinate the work within their respective thematic area, report the findings (interim or final) of their work and liaise with the ERNCIP Office.

3   Thematic Areas

The ERNCIP work programme addresses several thematic areas ('TA), as prioritised by our sponsors. The work within each thematic area is planned and undertaken by a dedicated working group of experts in that area, led by the TA coordinator.

ERNCIP provides the structure, governance and support funding for these thematic groups, which have been set the high-level objectives of:

*   Harmonisation of test protocols, promotion of standard test methods;
*   Proposing methodologies for measurement, quality assurance, calibration and metrology;
*   Proposing recommendations for EU-wide evaluation / certification / labelling procedures;
*   Proposing recommendations for research and investments.

The first year of ERNCIP has seen seven priority TAs identified, and their coordinators appointed. Another three TAs are to be launched in the project's second phase. These are listed in Table 2.

Table 2.

ERNCIP Thematic Area	Coordinator
Aviation Security Detection Equipment	JRC, Geel, Belgium
Explosives Detection Equipment (non-Aviation)	CEA, France
ICS and Smart grids	CPNI, Netherlands
Structural Resistance against Seismic Risks	JRC, Ispra, Italy
Resistance of Structures against Explosion effects	Fraunhofer-EMI, Germany
Chemical & Biological Risks in the Water Sector	Austrian Environmental Agency
Space Security	CNES, France
Biometrics	*To be decided*
Video surveillance and analysis	*To be decided*
Nuclear & Radiological Threats	*To be decided*

Work in six of these thematic areas has now started. Kick-off meetings of the thematic groups have been organised by their coordinators, by assembling experts in experimental facilities for their thematic area from across the EU. The number of experts for each thematic group varies, according to the specialisation of that thematic area, and ranges from nine experts to 33 experts.

Each thematic group has discussed the key areas of concern to the assembled experts, with the aim of identifying the programme of activities that the thematic group will address over the next three years.

4   Inventory of Experimental Facilities

The ERNCIP Inventory is a free-to-use on-line search tool for open-source information on European security experimental and testing facilities. The profiles in the Inventory contain basic information about the facility, including scientific contact points for potential customers; description of competencies; offered services; accreditations and certifications hold; and available experimental or testing equipment.

The objective of the Inventory is to help all types of critical infrastructure stakeholders (e.g. government authorities, infrastructure operators, and research institutions) to identify and make contact with CIP-related experimental expertise located in the EU, when they have a need for:

- Specific knowledge or expertise on CIP security-related problems;
- Certified solutions to CIP security-related problems; or
- Research partners to conduct CIP-related experiments, or to form partnerships to bid for EU funded projects.

The use of Inventory's search features are limited to organisations working in the field of CIP, thus the access requires a registration. When an organisation has successfully registered as a Search User, any employee of that organisation will be able to access the Inventory. The members of the Inventory are EU-based facilities and laboratories that have been granted the privilege by the ERNCIP Office to record their profile.

A beta version of the Inventory was successfully demonstrated to the ERNCIP Expert Group in February 2012. The Inventory is due to be launched in May 2012.

5   Way Forward

In the next phases of the project, the ERNCIP Office will continue to support the existing Thematic Areas; and will also discover and start new areas that are in the interest of our stakeholders.

The ERNCIP Office would like to launch new services that encourage sharing best practises and dissemination of knowledge within the Thematic Areas. Based on the results of the Thematic Areas' work, we will assess the possibility of creating EU-wide certifications and an ERNCIP labelling system that would create the premise for a stronger EU security market, and thus would foster the emergence of innovative, qualified, efficient and competitive security solutions.

Reference

1. European Commission Home Affairs, Protection of Critical Infrastructures,
   http://ec.europa.eu/home-affairs/policies/terrorism/
   terrorism_infrastructure_en.htm

Designing a Cyber Attack Information System for National Situational Awareness

Florian Skopik, Zhendong Ma, Paul Smith, and Thomas Bleier

AIT Austrian Institute of Technology
Safety and Security Department
2444 Seibersdorf, Austria
firstname.lastname@ait.ac.at
http://www.ait.ac.at/it-security

Abstract. Information and communication technology (ICT) systems underpin many of today's societal functions and economic development. Consequently, protecting a nation's ICT infrastructure from deliberate cyber attacks and unintentional disruptions is of paramount importance. Collaboration among all parties across all domains of cyberspace is the key to effective and coordinated effort to cope with cyber threats. This is particularly the case as cyber threats become increasingly sophisticated and distributed. In this paper, we introduce the foundational building blocks to realize an efficient incident response cycle on a national level, and propose the design of a conceptual framework – the Cyber Attack Information System (CAIS) – for establishing national cyber situational awareness.

Keywords: cyber attack information system, situational awareness, national incident response, collaborative detection and response.

1 Introduction

Information and communication technology (ICT) is of fundamental importance for our society and economy. For example, in Europe the most important factor for growth in productivity is the application of modern ICT [8]. ICT offers unique opportunities, but introduces a significant new vulnerability to a society that increasingly relies on electronic services. A deliberate or unintentional disruption as a result of technical or human failure, or due to natural causes could lead to social destabilization. As a consequence, IT security measures are rapidly being adopted in almost all areas utilizing ICT. However, the complexity and interconnectedness of modern ICT facilities and the rise of mobile data traffic and cloud computing pose further challenges to securing today's infrastructures.

A number of recent high-profile incidents have shown the vulnerability of critical infrastructures, which depend on ICT, to sophisticated cyber attacks. For example, the Stuxnet virus [9], explicitly designed to attack industrial process automation facilities, impressively demonstrated the vulnerability of critical infrastructures. Thorough analysis revealed that due to its complexity it must have

N. Aschenbruck et al. (Eds.): Future Security 2012, CCIS 318, pp. 277–288, 2012.

been developed or at least financed by a state; created to be used against another state. Furthermore, highly distributed botnets can cause major problems for national organizations and private enterprises, in many cases via denial of essential services. Distributed Denial of Service (DDoS) attacks were the main tactic used in the cyberattacks on Estonia in 2007 [15] and Georgia in 2008 [19] to paralyze a nation's ICT infrastructure.

In order to cope with such threats, we argue that tight cooperation between all parties in the digital society is necessary. In some domains, such as the banking sector, strategic alliances and public information sharing are already commonplace (e.g., to deal with phishing attacks [3]). Furthermore, there exist ad-hoc relationships between organizations, such as national Computer Emergency Response Teams (CERTs), to support collaborative incident response activities. However, these tend to be informally arranged between individual groups and are largely focused on securing infrastructures in the same operational domain. Whilst these activities have proven useful, a more comprehensive and formal approach to ensuring the security of national critical infrastructures, which spans numerous operational domains, will become necessary with the increasing use of ICT in interdependent critical infrastructure provisioning, e.g., as with Smart Grids.

In this paper, we discuss a number of foundational building blocks that can be used to realize an effective cyber incident response cycle on a national level, and propose the design of a conceptual framework – the Cyber Attack Information System (CAIS). The ultimate goal of this framework is to strengthen the resilience of today's interdependent networked services, and increase their overall availability and trustworthiness. The rationale for our framework is as follows:

- *Linking and Coordinating Existing Initiatives*: important work performed by CERTs and other agencies need to be coordinated on a national level to tackle current and future sophisticated highly-distributed cyber threats.
- *Establishing Situational Awareness on a National Level*: developing situational awareness is important for determining effective responses to cyber attacks, this needs to be done on a national level to fully understand any risks to our society's interdependent infrastructure.
- *Facilitating Public-Private Partnerships*: interconnected national infrastructures, which are operated using numerous public-private partnerships, require a suitable intermediary in order to facilitate a national cyber incident response strategy.
- *Maintaining Organizational Responsibility*: it is essential that participants in a national cyber incident response initiative clearly understand their role, including obligations, and the interfaces with other organizations; these are outlined in our framework.
- *Activating Inter-organizational Collaboration*: essential to improving national resilience to cyber attacks is inter-organizational collaboration – our framework aims to facilitate this. A further benefit of such collaboration is a decreased dependency on a national coordination point, which may be necessary or desirable in some cases.

The remainder of the paper is organized as follows. Section 2 introduces the notion of situational awareness and essential methods for its establishment. As mentioned earlier, developing situational awareness is critical in order to define well-informed and effective national cyber incident response strategies. Furthermore, Sect. 2 introduces an extended incident response cycle, which underlies our CAIS framework and supports the development of situational awareness. Section 3 highlights the basic stakeholders in the framework and their associated responsibilities. Subsequently, Sect. 4 outlines the high-level CAIS architecture and a mapping to organizational roles in order to implement the framework. The purpose of the architecture is to inform potential participants in a future national CAIS of the activities they need to undertake, the interfaces they must support, and the kinds of data they need to maintain. Furthermore, the architecture can be used to understand the human resources necessary to support the CAIS framework. Related work and international initiatives are presented in Sect. 5. Section 6 concludes the paper.

2   Situational Awareness for Incident Response

Central to taking an informed and coordinated approach to cyber security incidents is determining Situational Awareness (SA). A number of models of SA exist [6][10][16], but arguably the most pervasive is that proposed by Endsley [6], which describes three increasing levels of awareness: *perception, comprehension,* and *projection.* As one advances through these levels, decision making capabilities are improved.

Previous work from the EU-funded ResumeNet project proposed a mapping of information sources and mechanisms to the first two levels of SA [17] for identifying *challenges*, e.g., attacks, to computer networks. It is proposed there are two key sources of information for situational perception: *(1) multilevel network measurement information* and *(2) context information,* which is external to the network under scrutiny, such as news items about an ongoing situation. These two forms of information – network and context – are used as inputs to various techniques that are used to build situational comprehension. There are three proposed main approaches to comprehension: *(1)* detection of the presence of a challenge, e.g., provided by anomaly and intrusion detection systems; *(2)* identification of the characteristics of the challenge, e.g., provided by classification [14] and data fusion [18] techniques; and *(3)* the impact an attack is having on the network and associated services. Situational projection, which was not addressed by the ResumeNet project, estimates possible future situations, such as the continued behaviour and impact of a cyber attack. A way to approach determining situational projection is via the continued simulation of an ongoing cyber security incident, using output (data and events) from perception and comprehension mechanisms to drive the simulation. To support this process, we propose the use of an extended incident response cycle.

In short, we distinguish a preventive (green) and reactive (red) phase in our extended incident response cycle, as depicted in Fig. 1. While the preventive phase focuses on identifying and characterising potential attacks and the deployment of sustainable defence mechanisms, the reactive phase deals with short-term counter measures to tackle those that are ongoing.

Fig. 1. Incident response cycle incorporating modeling and simulation phases

The cycle starts with the creation of an infrastructure model and simulation of potential threats and future attacks ((1)). The infrastructure model is created with information collected from organizations that are participating in the proposed national CAIS framework – such information is typically maintained in asset management systems. The threats to be simulated are identified in a number of ways, such as from databases managed by CERTs and by using threat and vulnerability analysis techniques. The outcome of these simulations is an understanding of the potential impact of attacks and how they may manifest. Based on the simulation findings, which can form an input to a suitable risk assessment process, the deployment of mechanisms for an in-depth protection is performed in the next step ((2)). In particular, this should include mechanisms for enabling situational perception and comprehension, as discussed earlier. A key addition, in order to participate in the national CAIS, are interfaces to enable exporting of monitoring data and alarms generated by the various mechanisms used for situational comprehension. Once an anomaly, such as an attack, is detected ((3)), its potential impact on the whole infrastructure is evaluated using models and the simulation from the first step ((4)). The aim of these simulations is to *project* how an anomaly may continue to manifest across the institutions participating in the CAIS, and determine its potential impact. Studying potential effects allows for informed and targeted counter measures in order to mitigate negative effects ((5)). After a current attack has been successfully repelled, the basic security plans and measures must be updated ((6)) to ensure preparedness for future threats. This phase closes the cycle. Based on this extended incident response cycle, we can derive a number of responsibilities for the organizations that participate in the CAIS.

3   CAIS Stakeholder Responsibilities

The basic principle to establishing situational awareness on a national level, and consequently deriving a national cyber incident response strategy, relies on collecting information from single organizations that are involved in running critical infrastructures. Stakeholders, being *single organizations* or a *national cyber defence centre*, have numerous responsibilities, as discussed here.

3.1   Responsibilities of Single Organizations

A single organization in the CAIS framework can include entities such as banks, utility providers, telecommunication network providers, and so on. Collectively, they provide the ICT-coupled critical infrastructures our society depends on, and have a number of responsibilities in the CAIS:

1. *Asset Management*, i.e., knowing what hardware and software is deployed and the design of their own infrastructure, is essential since this is the basis for determining vulnerabilities of certain organizations.
2. *Infrastructure Monitoring* is about the thorough observation and logging of own network traffic reflected by e.g., firewall logs, proxy logs, DNS queries. This is the basis for discovering and tracking anomalies which can be potentially caused by ongoing attacks.
3. *Organization-Wide Anomaly Detection* through aggregation, correlation, and analysis of distributed network logs from various devices, services, and components is required to respond on a local level to identified exploits.
4. *Local Incident Response* deals with the deployment of immediate counter measures once an attack has been detected in order to mitigate the effects as fast as possible.
5. *Reporting to the National Cyber Defence Centre* enables the establishment of situational awareness on a larger scale. Besides actually identified attacks and threats, also relevant asset configurations need to be reported so that the Cyber Defence Centre can estimate an organizations's vulnerability to identified attack vectors.

Complementary to organizations that provide critical national infrastructures are those that provide security-related tools and information, such as CERTs and security enterprises (antivirus software companies, for example). Their role within the CAIS is typically to fulfil responsibilities two to five in the list above. Furthermore, they can support critical infrastructure providers with their participation in the CAIS.

3.2   Responsibilities of the National Cyber Defence Centre

We propose that a national cyber defence centre should collate information from single organizations, develop country-wide situational awareness, and provide guidance on how to respond to incidents. The national cyber defence centre is intended to act as a trusted third-party and coordinate activities between public-private organisations, for example. Correspondingly, the national cyber defence centre has a number of responsibilities:

1. *Collective Asset Management* aggregates asset information from all involved organizations. This is a vital aspect, e.g., for the estimation of the effects of spreading malware or for goal-oriented planning of counter measures.
2. *Centralized Report Collection and Evaluation* enables the cyber defence centre to be informed about the ICT states of single organizations and with what anomalies they have to deal with.
3. *Complex Attack Simulations* are used to evaluate the causes and effects of certain attacks. These simulations use infrastructure models created from asset management data and further account for the organizational states according to their most recent reports. This way, the impact of ongoing attacks can be identified on a national level (this is particularly important for dealing with coordinated attacks) as well as various scenarios for counter measures tested before they are even deployed.
4. *Establishing Situational Awareness* by combining (i) data sent from single organizations, (ii) intelligence data gathered from simulations, and (iii) co-ordination with international cyber centres (similar as CERTs do today)
5. *Planning Coordinated Counter Measures* deals with finding an effective way to mitigate the impact of ongoing attacks; and finally helps to re-establish a normal state of operation.
6. *Policy-based Advice and Recommendation* are the means to inform attacked organizations (and also potential future targets) how to reconfigure, update, or reshape their network and components in order to close open vulnerabilities, and thus, harden their infrastructure.

4   A Cyber Attack Information System Architecture

Building on the extended incident response cycle presented in Sect. 2 (which faciltitates the development of Endsley's three levels of SA), and the stakeholders and their roles that are identified in Sect. 3, we have developed a high-level architecture for a national cyber attack information system. The CAIS architecture, shown in Fig. 2, describes the flow of information and activities that are undertaken to implement two incident response cycles within a single organization and nationally within the cyber defence centre. Furthermore, the architecture identifies the necessary data repositories that are required to support the activities and information flow, along with the interfaces between the various stakeholders in the CAIS. Next, we briefly summarise the operation of the organizational and national aspects of the architecture, then we identify the necessary human resource roles, including the competencies and tasks, that must be filled to realise the architecture.

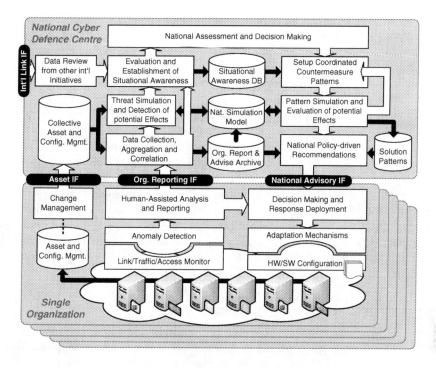

Fig. 2. High-level architecture for a national CAIS

4.1   CAIS Architecture – Organizational Level

Every organization essentially runs its own infrastructure to support their business processes. Monitoring links, traffic and service accesses is state-of-the-art of IT administration. In case of (mostly automatically) detected anomalies (e.g., a triggered alarm of an intrusion detection system), a human-assisted analysis is performed to, first, find out if an attack is going on at all, and second, which services are concerned. Based on these investigations, a decision for solving these issues is reached by a security manager and counter measures deployed by security administration staff. Here, hardware or software is adapted or reconfigured.

While such an incident response cycle in one form or another is usually applied today in every professional IT environment, we foresee an extension to integrate with our CAIS approach. Here the results of the human-assisted analysis need to be reported to the defence centre, where reports from participants all over the nation are collected. Additionally, to help address locally identified anomalies, feedback and advice from the defence centre is considered in the decision phase.

4.2   CAIS Architecture – National Level

The national cyber defence centre applies a higher-level version of the cycle introduced in Fig. 1 – in addition to the single-organization cycles. It collects reports about detected anomalies and identified attacks from single organizations (via the `Org. Reporting IF`). Using this intelligence data, a nation-wide threat simulation (on an abstract level) is used to assess potential effects of ongoing attacks – not only for a single enterprise but spanning numerous interconnected organization and domains. An approach to realising the national simulation is to use an agent-based simulator [13], which can model autonomous, interacting agents, such as the organizations in our CAIS. The simulation model captures the rough organizational assets and their interdependencies (using the `Asset IF`) in order to enable the identification of cascading effects and estimation of rolling breakdowns. This is important input for the evaluation of situational awareness and ultimately, for national decision making. Decisions include, for instance, to extend/fund backup systems of a frequently attacked organization providing a critical service. Decision are evaluated by applying changes to the simulation model and running simulations from previous attacks. Therefore, the improved resilience of the whole infrastructure can be evaluated and finally, the strategy with the best value for money is propagated to concerned organizations (using the `National Advice IF`).

Table 1. Organizational and national roles in the framework

Role	Competencies and tasks
Network Op. Centre (NoC)	Running the technical infrastructure; monitoring the operational state; anomaly detection; deploying counter measures on advise
Security Team	Human-assisted threat analysis; incident reporting to the Chief Security Officer and the Organizational Report PoC (see below)
Chief Security Officer	Decision making; keeping an overview of the operational status of the organization
Head of IT	Decision making together with Chief Security Officer; processing recommendations from the Advisory PoC from the National Defence Centre
Organizational Report PoC	Collecting reports from single organizations, maintaining a public-private partnership; optionally stay in touch with international initiatives
Data Analyst	Reviewing, aggregating and correlating reports; maintain an up-to-date data base of organizations' identified attacks
Simulation Task Force	Large-scale infrastructure simulation; making forecasts and predictions; feed the situational awareness model; evaluation of counter measures (solution patterns)
National Security Council	National decision making about the strategic evolution of the IT infrastructure on a higher level
Advisory Point of Contact	Advise heads of IT in single organizations in order to realize the evaluated counter strategy to an identified threat
National Asset Management	Requesting asset information from single organizations; keeping an overview about critical assets

4.3   Roles, Interactions and Information Exchange

In order to implement the CAIS framework, we need to map tasks and responsibilities onto dedicated roles. For that purpose, Table 1 describes mandatory roles (i) to realize fast incident response within an organization, (ii) to enable long-term strategic evolution of the IT infrastructure from a national perspective, (iii) to manage national assets, which is an essential input for simulation and risk assessment.

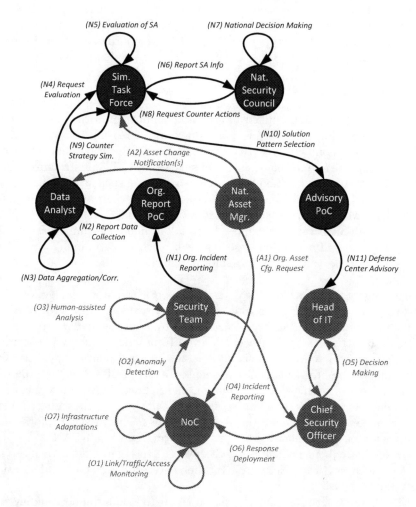

Fig. 3. Sequential steps for incident response: *(O)*rganizational level, *(N)*ational level, and *(A)*sset management

Furthermore, Fig. 3 depicts the relationships between these roles and how a detected incident within an organization is propagated. The starting point is at the Network Operation Centre which monitors infrastructure links, traffic, and service accesses (*O1*). All blue elements represent actions within an organization (*O1* to *O7*), including monitoring, anomaly detection, incident reporting, decision making, response deployment and optional infrastructure adaptations. The black elements reflect roles and interactions in the cyber defence centre (*N1* to *N11*), such as the collection of reports from all single organizations, aggregation and correlation of data, evaluation of situational awareness, informing of decision makers and decision making itself, requesting counter actions, counter strategy simulation, solution pattern selection, and defense centre advisory provisioning. The National Asset Management (in red) is part of the defence centre, however it provides the Data Analyst and Simulation Task Force (*A1* to *A2*) with essential data about infrastructure assets (e.g., deployed hardware and software in the single organizations).

5   Related Work

As ICT systems are being applied in a greater number of critical areas, cyber attacks are becoming more frequent and have an increasing impact (see [12] for a list of reports on cyber security and cyber attacks). Situational awareness plays an important role in the defence and survival of ICT infrastructures amid a cyber attack. Attack detection relies on cyber sensors, such as intrusion detection systems (IDS), log file sensors, anti-virus systems, malware detectors, and firewalls [11]. Many of the sensor techniques used today are based on sophisticated anomaly detection techniques, i.e., finding non-conforming patterns in data [5]. The results from various research fields, such as data mining, statistical analysis, machine learning, as well as information theory are applied to anomaly detection.

Since many of the attack detection tasks are performed at a local level, within a single organization, such as an Internet Service Providers (ISP), cross-domain security information sharing is a crucial step to correctly understanding the situation for national cyber defence. However, in practice, security information sharing is usually accomplished via ad-hoc and informal relationships [20]. Often, national Computer Emergency Response Teams (CERTs) assume the role of national contact points for coordinating and aggregating security incidence reports via communication channels such as email, instant messaging, file exchange/storage, VoIP, IRC and the Web [7]. Other means exist for information sharing. Internet forums such as the Internet Storm Center from SANS [2] collect and provide data about malicious activities on the Internet. Commercial service providers, such as Arbor Networks [1], offer network-wide threat information updates and analysis services.

Although many of the existing efforts contribute to a better understanding and response in light of cyber attacks, many technical and organizational challenges remain for establishing a national situational awareness infrastructure. As situational awareness is multi-faceted and multi-disciplinary, a holistic framework is needed to ensure systematic development and cooperation. The architecture proposed in this paper provides such an overview on the building blocks which contribute to reaching this goal.

6   Conclusion and Future Work

Because of the increasingly sophisticated and distributed nature of cyber attacks, e.g., that use botnets as a platform, and our dependence on ICT-coupled critical infrastructures, a coordinated multi-domain approach to cyber incident response is required. This paper has introduced the building blocks in the form of a framework to realize an incident response cycle and a design of a cyber attack information system (CAIS) for establishing situational awareness to strengthen the resilience and trustworthiness of today's national ICT infrastructure. Our design aims at linking existing initiatives, maintaining organizational responsibility, and activating inter-organizational collaboration on a national level.

The cyber attack information system introduced in this paper is the first step towards establishing national cyber situational awareness. In order to reach this goal, the following major open research challenges need to be addressed: (i) secure and privacy-preserving data sharing across organizational boundaries (for example, building on secure multi-party computation (MPC) approaches [4]); (ii) methodologies and techniques for efficient and scalable data synthesis and processing, and information reasoning to generate full situational awareness; (iii) evaluation of proven techniques on hypothesis and reasoning for projection and decision making under high uncertainty.

Acknowledgments. This work was partly funded by the Austrian security-research programme KIRAS and by the Austrian Ministry for Transport, Innovation and Technology.

References

1. Arbor networks, http://www.arbornetworks.com/
2. Internet storm center, http://isc.sans.org/
3. Phishtank, http://www.phishtank.com/
4. Burkhart, M., Strasser, M., Many, D., Dimitropoulos, X.: SEPIA: Privacy-Preserving Aggregation of Multi-Domain Network Events and Statistics. In: USENIX Security Symposium, Washington, DC, USA (August 2010)
5. Chandola, V., Banerjee, A., Kumar, V.: Anomaly detection: A survey. ACM Comput. Surv. 41(3) (2009)
6. Endsley, M.: Toward a theory of situation awareness in dynamic systems. Human Factors 37(1), 32–64 (1995)
7. ENISA: Practical guide/roadmap for a suitable channel for secure communication: secure communicatio with the CERTs & other statkeholders (December 2011)
8. EU Press Release IP/07/453: ICT drives 50% of eu growth, says commission's annual report on the digital economy (2007)
9. Falliere, N., Murchu, L.O., Chien, E.: W32.Stuxnet Dossier. Tech. rep., Symantic Security Response (October 2010)
10. Fracker, M.: Measures of situation awareness: Review and future directions. Tech. Rep. AL-TR-1991-0128, Wright-Patterson Air Force Base, OH: Armstrong Laboratories (1991)

11. Jajodia, S., Liu, P., Swarup, V., Wang, C.: Cyber Situational Awareness: Issues and Research, 1st edn. Springer Publishing Company, Incorporated (2009)
12. Lewis, J.A.: Selected bibliography for cyber security,
    http://csis.org/publication/selected-bibliography-cyber-security
13. Macal, C.M., North, M.J.: Tutorial on agent-based modelling and simulation. Journal of Simulation 4, 151–162 (2010)
14. Nguyen, T.T.T., Armitage, G.J.: A survey of techniques for internet traffic classification using machine learning. IEEE Communications Surveys and Tutorials 10(1–4), 56–76 (2008)
15. Ottis, R.: Analysis of the 2007 cyber attacks against estonia from the information warfare perspective. In: Proceedings of the 7th European Conference on Information Warfare, p. 163. Academic Conferences Limited (April 2008)
16. Sarter, N., Woods, D.: Situation awareness: A critical but ill-defined phenomenon. International Journal of Aviation Psychology 1, 45–57 (1991)
17. Smith, P., Hutchison, D., Sterbenz, J.P.G., Schöller, M., Fessi, A., Doerr, C., Lac, C.: D1.5c: Final strategy document for resilient networking. ResumeNet Project Deliverable (August 2011), http://www.resumenet.eu
18. Tadda, G., Salerno, J.J., Boulware, D., Hinman, M., Gorton, S.: Realizing situation awareness within a cyber environment. In: Multisensor, Multisource Information Fusion: Architectures, Algorithms, and Applications, Orlando, FL, USA (April 2006)
19. Tikk, E., Kaska, K., Rünnimeri, K., Kert, M., Talihärm, A.M., Vihul, L.: Cyber attacks against georgia: Legal lessons identified (Novermber 2008),
    http://www.carlisle.army.mil/dime/getDoc.cfm?fileID=167
20. U.S. Homeland Security Cyber Security R&D Center: A roadmap for cybersecurity research (November 2009)

Towards Sound Forensic Acquisition of Volatile Data

Sebastian Eschweiler and Elmar Gerhards-Padilla

Fraunhofer FKIE, Germany
{sebastian.eschweiler,elmar.gerhards-padilla}@fkie.fraunhofer.de

Abstract. This work discusses shortcomings of current forensic acquisition tools aimed at securing volatile data. Recent developments in the area of anti-forensics have effectively disabled current forensic methods. The development of new methods towards sound forensic acquisition of volatile data is necessary as to keep up with the arms race. After an overview over current hardware-based and software-based acquisition methods, attacks and evasion techniques will be presented. Concluding, novel techniques are discussed to cope with anti-forensics.

Keywords: Forensics, Malware, Anti-Forensics, Volatile Data.

1 Introduction

Today, many users protect their privacy by relying on modern hard disk drive encryption tools. These tools encrypt parts of the drive or the complete drive and only decrypt portions of data on demand, once the user entered the correct password. However, for usability reasons, the secret key has to persist somewhere in the computer. Law enforcement agencies often are unable to decrypt devices, once the computer is shut down. After a recent U.S. Federal Court ruling [3], the defendant does not need to incriminate himself, hence he can deny revealing the decryption password.

Modern malware, especially highly sophisticated targeted malware,lo leaves virtually no traces on the hard disk drive. Payloads to enumerate local folders or passwords are injected into the compromised computer on demand and at will of the usurpers. For example, Kaspersky discovered a malware distributed on news sites that is never written to hard disk [8]. Hence, mere forensic acquisition of non-volatile data is insufficient. Techniques capable of acquiring volatile data have been developed in the last years, but the arms race does not stop here.

Recent developments against the forensic acquisition of volatile data, especially against the acquisition of main memory, lead to a series of problems that current forensic methods are not equipped for. Examples include altering the underlying operating system to return arbitrary data upon a read request on main memory or instructing certain chips on modern mainboards to become unresponsive upon reading main memory.

N. Aschenbruck et al. (Eds.): Future Security 2012, CCIS 318, pp. 289–298, 2012.
© Springer-Verlag Berlin Heidelberg 2012

In the first part of this work current methods for forensic acquisition of volatile data are enumerated and their shortcomings in modern computer environments are derived. Following the discussion, techniques are presented that are targeted against today's forensic acquisition methods. Here, attacks against software-based and hardware-based acquisition methods are presented, followed by a different technique, namely the avoidance of main memory. Concluding, these techniques are discussed. The urgent need for new tools able to cope with the presented techniques is deduced. Finally, novel techniques are presented and discussed.

2   Forensic Acquisition of Volatile Data

The main memory of a computer offers a vast source of information about the user. It contains passwords from visited web sites and even secret keys that enable foreign parties to decrypt the computer's hard drive, providing it is encrypted. Extracting the secret keys from memory is fairly easy, for example the software Passware Kit Forensic is able to derive the secret key from a memory dump within minutes [11]. Consequently, integrity of acquired data is extremely important.

Currently, there exist two methods for replication of main memory. The first method is software-based, the second method exploits design weaknesses in hardware to read live memory. In the following, both approaches are presented and discussed with respect to their strengths and weaknesses.

2.1   Software-Based Acquisition Methods

Forensic acquisition of memory with software programs requires elevated privileges on the examined computer. Once these permissions are granted, the software has low-level access to the complete memory. Thus, it is able to extract its content and to store it on a forensic hard disk drive. To mention just some examples for software-based tools for Windows are the Windows Memory Toolkit by Moonsols [12], FastDump by HBGary [10] and EnCase by Guidance Software [19]. For the Linux operating system the software dd [7] and Second Look by PikeWerks [15] are most notable and for MacOS there exists Mac Memory Reader by Cyber Marshal [4].

To successfully examine a computer with aforementioned software, the computer must not be locked and permissions have to be gained to access the whole memory. On the upside, software-based acquisition has the advantage of not needing a second computer or special hardware. Hence, the computer itself can be used to examine it for malware.

On the downside, it is necessary that software has to be executed on the examined computer. Hence, the memory will inevitably be tainted and memory integrity on the examined computer cannot be guaranteed, and even worse, potentially crucial parts of the memory are overwritten.

2.2 Hardware-Based Acquisition Methods

Modern computers are capable of outsourcing I/O-intensive transactions in order to save CPU time. The so-called direct memory access (DMA) allows hardware to access main memory bypassing the CPU. Hardware-based memory acquisition methods exploit a weakness in the current computer architecture. By registering as DMA-capable device they are able to bypass restrictive access set by the CPU and gain direct control over the complete memory. While it is basically possible to access the whole memory through each DMA-capable device, hitherto only few notable approaches have been made.

Carrier and Grand present Tribble [2], a hardware device for the PCI bus that is capable of acquiring the complete memory range without CPU interception. However, it has to be installed in the computer while it is powered off, hence limiting the usefulness in a common forensic scenario. Their scenario suggests a large company where Tribble cards are installed into the servers as forensic capture devices in case of a server compromise.

The most widely used technique, however, for hardware-based forensic acquisition is the IEEE-1394 interface (Fire Wire). In order to achieve high transfer rates, the Fire Wire bus delegates read and write commands to the interface hardware. Hence, the Fire Wire bus is capable of DMA mode. This allows special hardware and even a second computer direct access to the examined computer's memory. The USB protocol, in contrast, relies on the CPU and thus is not susceptible to this kind of attack. For detailed information on this technique, we refer to [6].

Laptops often have extension card slots, e.g. PCMCIA or Cardbus, that is susceptible to the mentioned acquisition method as well. The forensic investigator inserts an appropriate card into the notebook and can read arbitrary memory.

A drawback of hardware-based acquisition methods is their need of special hardware. Hence, not all computers that are subject to a forensic investigation can be scrutinized based on this method.

The most notable advantage of hardware-based techniques is that memory on the computer to be scrutinized is left unaltered, as no process has to be started on the target computer. Until recently, no techniques were known to attack hardware-based methods. This changed with a publication from Rutkowska [17], as shown in chapter 3.1 (see below).

3 Techniques against Forensic Acquisition of Volatile Data

Basically, we identified two different techniques against forensic acquisition of main memory. First to name are attacks specifically directed against forensic acquisition of memory. The second technique is evasion of the acquired memory in order to be invisible to the analyst. In the following, both techniques are presented and discussed.

3.1   Attacks against Forensic Acquisition

In the following section, attacks targeted against forensic acquisition of volatile data are presented. All methods commonly rely on the fact that acquisition of memory happens on the same computer that has been compromised beforehand. Hence, the attacker can erect very specific defenses on the computer. The methods have in common that they are implemented in software. Hence, they can be executed remotely as no physical access to the computer is necessary. In the following, we fist present attacks directed against software-based acquisition methods are presented. Second, attacks against hardware-based methods are shown and discussed.

Attacks against Software-Based Acquisition Methods

Attacks against software-based acquisition methods rely on the fact that the main memory has to be accessed through the operating system. On a compromised system and on driver level, it is possible to arbitrarily alter memory read requests. For example, the Shadow Walker rootkit [18] conceals its presence by patching the Windows kernel, such that instead of displaying the actual rootkit code, completely different data content is returned. The rootkit accomplishes this by setting up a new page fault handler that distinguishes between read and execute access on its code. If the memory region where the rootkit resides is executed, the altered handler returns the actual machine code. But if a read request reaches the handler, the rootkit assumes an effort of detection, hence the data returned is altered.

Hence, by this technique forensic software can be effectively deceived.

Attacks against Hardware-Based Acquisition Methods

Until recently, there was no way for software intercept and alter hardware-based memory extraction. In [17], Rutkowska presents a novel technique based on memory-mapped input/output (MMIO) remapping against hardware-based forensic acquisition methods.

Newer north bridge chips offer the feature of MMIO mapping. MMIO is a communication method between CPU and other devices that are attached to a common bus, such as the PCI bus. Here, the I/O registers of the devices connected to the bus are mapped into the address space of the main memory. Hence, from the CPU point-of-view, direct access to the device memory is possible. The MMIO mapping feature allows to instruct the north bridge chip a remapping of arbitrary memory regions onto device memory.

Deducing from that, there exist several scenarios: if the device that is mapped to a memory range does not exist, the north bridge sends a query to the bus that is never answered. Hence, an infinite waiting cycle is created and the computer stops responding. Hence, hardware-based forensic acquisition is effectively thwarted.

A different behavior can be provoked if the mapped device exists, but the memory range on the device does not exist. The device will then output garbage data, usually being 0xFF, says Rutkowska. Furthermore, she discusses the possibility of concealing parts of existing memory by swapping it to unused regions. For instance, parts of the video card memory could be used to overlay the real values in memory in order to send arbitrary data to hardware-based forensic acquisition methods.

Concluding, she notes the inability of hardware-based techniques to undo MMIO mapping. The only way would be running special software on the system, bearing all the consequences, as discussed in section2. Hence, hardware-based acquisition methods can be deceived with similar results to software-based methods, ranging from system compromise to arbitrary alteration of data.

3.2   Avoiding Main Memory

In modern computers, main memory is not the only place where data can be stored. These alternative memory locations can serve as retreat for malware or data. Modern volatile forensic acquisition methods concentrate on main memory. Hence, if code or data can escape from main memory, it is safe from further detection.

Alternative memory has to meet some preconditions: it has to be reliable in terms of read/write access. Additionally, in the case of binary code, there has to be a way of executing it. This can be on the CPU, but other processors in a computer may be exploited as well, for example the graphic cards processor (GPU) or the network card processor. By means of the following examples one will see that increasingly alternatives to main memory are found in today's computers.

Graphic Card. Modern video cards offer rich potential regarding their computing power and memory. Current software increasingly employs the computing power as it often surpasses the computing power of the CPU by orders of magnitude.

In an unpublished work the video card is shown to be a secure storage for secret keys. Standard encryption algorithms are implemented for the GPU, hence the video card can be seen as black box, encrypting and decrypting data at will. Only the initial key setup remains a potential security risk. The researchers state that even algorithms specially crafted for the CPU run faster on the GPU because of its high computing speed. Cryptographic algorithms specifically suited for the GPU might well exceed current throughput by multiples.

Additionally, malware is exploiting the computing powers of the video card. BitCoin is an anonymous electronic cash system based on cryptography. It is designed such that there exists a maximum amount of around 21 million BitCoins, which have to be found or mined. The process of mining BitCoins is computationally expensive and thus costly by means of power consumption. In August 2011, Symantec identified a malware specimen that generates the electronic currency BitCoin on the GPU of infected computers [20,16]. Through the massively parallel and distributed nature of the botnet, the malware authors attempt to gain large amounts of BitCoins.

As none of today's forensic frameworks is capable of acquiring the video memory, there is no possibility of obtaining the secret key once it is stored on the video card.

CPU. Also the CPU can be used to store data that is inaccessible to common forensic methods. The CPU cache is a very fast piece of memory directly embedded into the CPU. In his FrozenCache presentation [14] Pabel shows on the basis of the cryptographic algorithm AES the possibility to store the secret key completely in the CPU cache. After copying the secret key into CPU registers the key is deleted in memory and the CPU cache is "frozen". Hence, traditional acquisition methods are unable to access the key. However, as system performance drastically breaks in, he recommends only moving the secret key into the CPU cache when the computer is locked.

Another storage place on the CPU are rarely used registers. Mï¿œller et al. present a similar method in [13], using the debug registers as permanent storage for secret keys. The central benefit is the drastic performance gain compared to the FrozenCache technique. In performance evaluations, Mï¿œller et al. see virtually no difference between classic AES implementations and theirs. The software is available as kernel patch for Linux.

The aforementioned methods of evading main memory all have their discontinuity in common. Upon reboot, they have to be saved into the specific memory location again. In contrast to that, the next two examples are embedded into memory locations persistently.

The BIOS (basic input/output system) is executed first upon the start-up of a computer. It is stored on a firmware flash chip and serves as bootstrap loader for the actual operating system. Currently, a rootkit named Mebromi is spreading that infects the BIOS of a compromised computer [1]. If Mebromi finds an AwardBIOS on the compromised computer, it infects the BIOS. Once the computer is rebooted, the BIOS part of Mebromi starts successive stages of the malware.

Almost all other hardware parts also have firmware chips that can be exploited to evade main memory. Similar to infecting the BIOS chip Delugrï¿œ presents a rootkit completely residing on a network interface card [5]. If an attacker has administrative privileges on a compromised computer, he is able to re-program the firmware of the network interface card and embed a rootkit that is completely outside conventional memory. Through DMA access it is still possible to read from and write to main memory, undetected by the CPU. Hence, a remote attacker gains full control over the complete computer, a transparent bridge head is established on the system, not detectable by current forensic software.

4   Discussion

In this work, we presented a detailed overview about current anti-forensic techniques directed against volatile data and resulting shortcomings of current forensic methods. It shows that current forensic acquisition methods of volatile data are insufficient, taking developments in the area of anti-forensics into consideration. The following discussion is divided into two parts. First, attacks against the acquisition process are considered. Second, strategies avoiding main memory are presented and discussed.

Attacks against Acquisition

As shown in chapter 3.1, there exist several techniques to attack the acquisition process of main memory. While altering the page fault handler in order to return arbitrary data relies on changes in the operating system and hence is able to deceive software-based acquisition methods, Rutkowska's method of remapping the MMIO has to meet special hardware requirements in order to succeed. It is able to attack hardware-based acquisition. Be it software- or hardware-based acquisition methods, both suffer of their susceptibility to deception. The returned data can be altered arbitrarily and thus integrity and completeness of data cannot be guaranteed.

In most cases, primary goals of forensic acquisition of volatile data are

- identification of malicious processes
- identification of network transactions
- extraction of secret keys aiming at deciphering encrypted persistent data storage.

All information can be active, hence still be actively managed by the underlying operating system or inactive, meaning that the information still resides as artifact in memory. While active information is not likely overwritten by changes in the system state, inactive information is sensitive to overwriting. As the amount of data subject to forensic acquisition is considered very low, the probability of overwriting inactive data during the start of a process is low. However, the probability of overwriting inactive data has not been subject to research and thus remains an open question and is left for future research.

Looking at techniques directed against forensic acquisition, there is a clear distinction between concealment of data, thus tampering with the integrity of data and the technique of denial of service, resulting in abortion of the forensic process.

As both results are undesirable, developing a software that prepares a computer for actual forensic acquisition should be considered.

Assuming the impact of starting a new process on an examined computer has a low probability of destroying inactive memory, the consequences are considerably lower than above mentioned results of a successful concealment or denial of service. Goals of the pre-forensic software are identification of measures against forensic acquisition and disabling them. In the further forensic process traditional tools can be applied.

Halderman et al. describe in their so-called Cold-Boot attack publication [9] the possibility to circumvent many anti-forensic methods and to properly acquire large portions of the main memory. In order to achieve that goal, they cool down the main memory of the examined computer after cutting off its power supply. The memory is then transferred to a different computer where it is forensically acquired. However, this method is not forensically sound, as the acquisition computer has to be started with a minimal operating system that is inevitably overwriting main memory and thus possibly destroying valuable evidence.

Extending this idea, a special read-only device for main memory modules would be certainly helpful towards sound acquisition of volatile data. After opening the examined computer case and cooling down the main memory, it is cut off from power and the main memory is removed and transferred to the device. Here, the memory can be obtained without aforementioned obstacles, as the memory chip can be regarded as just holding data for the purposes of forensic acquisition. However, the runtime state of the system has to be recovered, e.g. all running processes have to be retrieved. The software Volatility offers recovering the runtime state of the system in an easy way [21].

However, possible mitigation of aforementioned techniques against forensic investigation inevitably go along with restrictions in data integrity.

Avoiding Main Memory

In chapter 3.2 several ways of effectively evading main memory have been discussed. While some methods are persistent and detectable by extracting the firmware on the appropriate hardware, others are volatile and highly sensitive to shutting down the system. Hence, forensic software specially dealing with new types of memory has to be developed. While it is relatively easy to access special registers of the CPU of an examined computer, there is no method known to access the memory of the graphic card. As its GPU and memory is increasingly becoming an alternative to traditional main memory and computing power it is important to devise new methods to acquire the video memory.

Accessing persistent data on other hardware cards, e.g. the firmware of the network interface card is not as easy and requires special equipment. This is outside the scope of this work and will not be discussed further.

5   Summary and Future Work

Introducing, the de-facto standard of forensic acquisition techniques of volatile data were presented. The techniques can be distinguished into software-based and hardware-based acquisition methods. While software-based methods are more generic, as they can run on almost any standard computer, inevitably they alter the main memory and need extensive permissions on the examined computer.

Hardware-based acquisition methods do not alter main memory but have to meet special hardware requirements.

Next, we enumerated approaches against the presented acquisition methods. At the example of the Shadow Walker rootkit, techniques against software-based acquisition were shown. Rutkowska presented a novel technique to counter hardware-based acquisition methods. Following, strategies aimed at avoiding main memory have been shown at several examples. Outsourcing data from main memory to the GPU was discussed, as well as outsourcing it to the CPU cache or special registers of the CPU. Furthermore, code evading main memory was presented by means of a rootkit completely residing on a network interface card and BIOS rootkits.

In order to accomplish comprehensive and forensically sound acquisition of volatile data, new methods have to be devised that are able to cope with state-of-the-art anti-forensic techniques. New pre-forensic software that identifies and disables anti-forensic methods has become necessary. Additionally, acquisition methods for other memory types have to be developed.

References

1. Qihoo 360. Description of the Mebromi Rootkit,
   http://bbs.360.cn/4005462/251096134.html (last access September 2011)
2. Carrier, B.D., Grand, J.: A hardware-based memory acquisition procedure for digital investigations. Digital Investigation 1(1), 50–60 (2004)
3. U.S. Federal Court. Forcing Defendant to decrypt Hard Drive is unconstitutional, appeals Court Rules, http://www.ca11.uscourts.gov/opinions/ops/201112268.pdf (last access March 2012)
4. Cybermarshal. Mac Memory Reader, http://www.cybermarshal.com/index.php/cyber-marshal-utilities/mac-memory-reader (last access March 2012)
5. Guillaume Delugröe Closer to metal: Reverse engineering the Broadcom NetExtreme's Firmware. In: Hack.lu (2010)
6. Maximilan Dornseif. Owned by an iPod. In: PacSec (2004)
7. GNU. dd, http://www.gnu.org/software/coreutils/manual/html_node/dd-invocation.html (last access March 2012)
8. Golovanov, S.: A unique 'fileless' bot attacks news site visitors, http://www.securelist.com/en/blog/687/A_unique_fileless_bot_attacks_news_site_visitors (last access March 2012)
9. Alex Halderman, J., Schoen, S.D., Heninger, N., William, et al.: Lest We Remember: Cold-boot Attacks on Encryption Keys. Commun. ACM 52, 91–98 (2009)
10. HBGary. FastDump PRO, http://www.hbgary.com/fastdump-pro (last access March 2012)
11. Passware Inc. Passware Kit Forensic,
    http://www.lostpassword.com/kit-forensic.htm (last access March 2012)
12. Moonsols. Windows Memory Toolkit,
    http://www.moonsols.com/windows-memory-toolkit (last access March 2012)
13. Müller, T., Freiling, F.C., Dewald, A.: TRESOR runs encryption securely outside RAM. In: Proceedings of the 20th USENIX Conference on Security, SEC 2011, p. 17. USENIX Association, Berkeley (2011)

14. Pabel, J.: FrozenCache – Mitigating cold-boot Attacks for Full-Disk-Encryption Software. In: 27C3 (2010)
15. Pikewerks. Second Look, http://pikewerks.com/sl/ (last access March 2012)
16. Plohmann, D., Gerhards-Padilla, E.: Case Study of the Miner Botnet. In: Proceedings of the 4th International Conference on Cyber Conflict (to appear, 2012)
17. Rutkowska, J.: Beyond The CPU: Defeating Hardware Based RAM Acquisition. In: Black Hat DC 2007 (2007)
18. Butler, J., Sparks, S.: Shadow Walker – Raising The Bar For Windows Rootkit Detection. Phrack 11(59) (2005)
19. Guidance Software. Encase Forensic, http://www.guidancesoftware.com/forensic.htm (last access March 2012)
20. Symantec. Description of Trojan.Badminer (2011), http://www.symantec.com/business/security_response/writeup.jsp?docid=2011-081115-5847-99&tabid=2 (last access September 2011)
21. Volatile Systems. Volatility, https://www.volatilesystems.com (last access September 2011)

The New Counter-Espionage Concept at Deutsche Telekom[*]

Thomas Königshofen

Group Security Commissioner, Deutsche Telekom AG

1 Threat and Challenge

With the globalization of the markets has come the development of information as a raw material into an increasingly important commodity for international competition. Unsurprising, then, that tip-offs regarding espionage between companies, as well as intelligence activities against individual companies, are on the up (see figure 1 below).

The challenge: protecting the "CROWN JEWELS" from Espionage attacks

As a consequence, companies that feel exposed to this growing risk are forced to step up measures to protect their business secrets in order to maintain their existing level of security. Astonishingly, according to a recent survey carried out by Ernst&Young in April 2011[1], two-thirds of the companies surveyed recognized the growing threat posed by industrial espionage, but 83 percent of these companies considered themselves to be sufficiently protected, and at 66 percent of companies the IT department was responsible for defense against industrial espionage.

---

[*] Based on a contribution to the event in Cologne "5. Sicherheitstagung des BfV und ASW", dated June 2011.

[1] Ernst&Young "Datenklau" data theft study, April 2011.

N. Aschenbruck et al. (Eds.): Future Security 2012, CCIS 318, pp. 299–302, 2012.
© Springer-Verlag Berlin Heidelberg 2012

It became clear, however, at the very latest with the discovery of Stuxnet malware and its mode of operation, that conventional IT protection mechanisms are no longer sufficient to protect against these kinds of virus attacks, which means corporate IT departments alone are no longer able to stay on top of the situation (see figure 2 below):

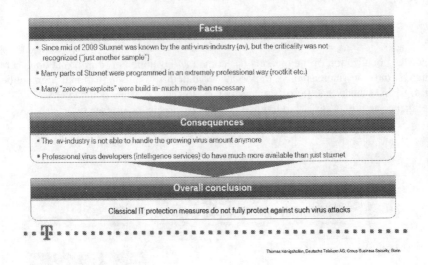

Example Stuxnet: what to learn...

Facts

* Since mid of 2009 Stuxnet was known by the anti-virus-industry (av), but the criticality was not recognized ("just another sample")
* Many parts of Stuxnet were programmed in an extremely professional way (rootkit etc.)
* Many "zero-day-exploits" were build in- much more than necessary

Consequences

* The av-industry is not able to handle the growing virus amount anymore
* Professional virus developers (intelligence services) do have much more available than just stuxnet

Overall conclusion

Classical IT protection measures do not fully protect against such virus attacks

Thomas Königshofen, Deutsche Telekom AG, Group Business Security, Bonn

2   Solution

In 2009, Security Management at the Deutsche Telekom Group took these basic assumptions and started work on a project aimed at developing new, binding security requirements for the international Group to protect top business secrets (TBS). Internal security experts joined the project from Group subsidiaries in Europe, Asia and the United States, with the Pinkerton Group (USA), a subsidiary of the SECURITAS group, brought in as external consultant. The German security authorities were represented by the Federal Criminal Police Office (BKA), the Federal Office for the Protection of the Constitution (BfV), and the North Rhine-Westphalia State Office for the Protection of the Constitution (Verfassungsschutz NRW).

The basic goal of the joint project force was to protect the TBS with a special set of technical and non-technical protection measures, such as encrypted cell phones and presentation documents for security awareness training (e.g. social engineering), out of the so called toolbox. The toolbox elements are provided out of a pool which is hold available by the Security Management department (see figure 3 below).

The solution: Building comprehensive counter measures around "Top Business Secrets" (TBS), the CROWN JEWELS of Deutsche Telekom

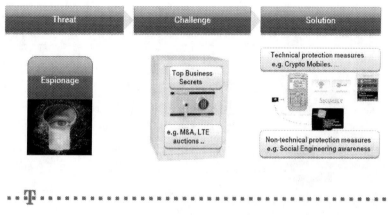

Thomas Königshofen, Deutsche Telekom AG, Group Business Security, Bonn

3   General Process and Role Model

The counter-espionage concept is based on the existing comprehensive measures across the Group to protect information and data. These serve as the foundation for specific supplementary protection measures.

A risk assessment has been integrated to enable the identification of top business secrets that – based on the impact of their disclosure – classifies TBSs as belonging to the Group's highest information category "strictly confidential," but which takes account of the special risk posed by attacks using intelligence-gathering techniques.

To help identify and determine protection measures, a role-based model has also been developed on the premise that top-level management as a rule is aware or gains knowledge of top business secrets. This group, known as the TBS owners, is thus given training with a particular focus on the new security requirements.

From the group of TBS owners, the respective TBS identifier is appointed who has primary responsibility for protecting a specific business secret (e.g., the head of Mergers & Acquisitions in the event of a planned acquisition/sale of a company unit).

As soon as the identifier learns of or expects a TBS (e.g., the target acquisition and the maximum offer for a company purchase), he/she can get in touch with the counter-espionage officer, CE officer). They then jointly perform a special, project-oriented risk analysis and agree on specific technical and non-technical protection measures out of the so called toolbox (see figure 4 below). CE officers are appointed by the management of each independent Group company and authorized by the respective company's Chief Security Officer (CSO).

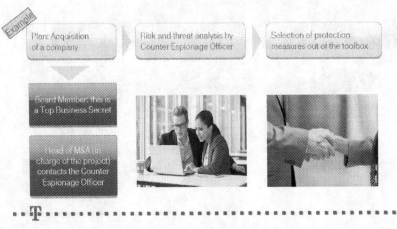

The whole process: Based on the new security requirement "Protection of Top Business Secrets from espionage"

Thomas Königshofen, Deutsche Telekom AG, Group Business Security, Bonn

4   Implementation across the Group

Based on the principle of making life harder for agents of industrial espionage, the new concept is being rolled out across the Group on a step-by-step basis, to insure that Top Business Secrets are protected group wide by the same standards. In the last years training sessions for counter-espionage officers in the Group's subsidiaries were held in Bellevue (USA), Kuala Lumpur (Malaysia), Madrid (Spain), Vienna (Austria), Athens (Greece) and Warsaw (Poland).

5   Next Steps

The concept was very successful within Deutsche Telekom, proven by various successfully secured TBS projects. We are convinced that our new counter espionage concept can be adapted also by external companies, efficiently. Therefore it is planned as a next step to market this concept externally at medium-sized businesses and big enterprises as pilots.

An Approach for Independent Intrusion Detection Management Systems

A Standardized Intrusion Detection Parameterization Format

Björn-C. Bösch

Carl-von-Ossietzky-University Oldenburg
Faculty II - Department of Computing Science
System Software and Distributed Systems Group
Oldenburg, Germany

Abstract. Efficiency of Intrusion Detection Systems depends on their configuration and coverage of services. The coverage depends on used Intrusion Detection Systems with currently vendor-specific configurations. In case of usage of multiple systems the operations could become complex. This work provides an approach for a multi-vendor IDS implementation under one central administration and notification entity based on standardized communication between analyzer and manager.

1 Introduction

Intrusion Detection Systems (IDS) protect critical infrastructures and services against malicious actions. Detailed knowledge of application and communication are necessary to protect services adequate. IDS are scoped on a single application (special kind of Host based IDS), a single operating system (Host based IDS) or communication protocols (Network IDS). To detect intrusions in an IT composite, different IDS are required to protect and monitor computer systems at all levels, top to bottom.

Application-based IDS become more and more specialized and focusing to one single application. So, vendors provide own specialized IDS for their products. Current multi-vendor IDS architectures do not interact with each other. Additional IDS requires a full independent coexisting IDS solution. A full functional integration in an existing IDS is currently not possible. Based on the Intrusion Detection Message Exchange Format (IDMEF) [1] it is possible to integrate an additional general monitoring system as notification umbrella. This research is focused to separate the manager from the rest of an IDS, so that the manager is an independent entity to IDS analyzers and sensors.

The remaining paper is organized as follows: Section 2 describes the architectural solution approach and the methodology of parameterization. Subsequent the integrations in three different free open source IDS are briefly described. Section 3 concludes this work.

N. Aschenbruck et al. (Eds.): Future Security 2012, CCIS 318, pp. 303–306, 2012.
© Springer-Verlag Berlin Heidelberg 2012

304   B.-C. Bösch

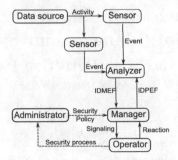

Fig. 1. IDS model with standardized communication to and from the manager

2 Approach

This section describes current IDS architectures and the architectural approach
to separate the IDS manager. Subsequent the parameterization methodology was
pointed out on a high level. This section is closed with a brief illustration of the
IDPEF integrations.

2.1 Current IDS Architectures

The entities analyzer and sensor are vendor-specific entities. The manager is the
only entity that could be shared with other IDS. The communication between a
general manager and vendor-specific analyzers has to be standardized to manage
a multi-vendor IDS architecture with one manager.

Today, IDMEF standardizes notifications to a monitoring application. As
transport protocol the Intrusion Detection eXchange Protocol (IDXP) [2] is already created on top of the Blocks Extensible Exchange Protocol (BEEP) [3].
The BEEP framework provides confidentiality, integrity and authentication for
the communication. IDXP provides a streamtype option and the value "alert"
is already used by IDMEF. This work uses IDXP with the streamtype value
"config" as communication framework.

The manager was separated from the rest of the IDS with a standardized
communication between analyzer and manager. The communication between
sensor and analyzer is continuously vendor-specific. The communication in the
IETF IDS model [4] was modified. As visualized in fig. 1, the security policy will
be applied to the manager and distributed to the analyzers and forwarded to the
sensors instead of directly from the administrator to all IDS entities. Operators
and administrators use the manager as single point of human interface to operate
the entire IDS.

2.2 Parameterization Methodology

IDS have their individual structure, syntax and semantic for management and
operations. Today, sharing of configuration files or references between IDS is not

possible and an interaction is not in place. On the other hand, all IDS compares activity against a reference database. References consist of a baseline part and a customizing part. The baseline part describes the event itself (intrusion activity, vulnerability or baseline). Baseline parts are customized for the individual implementation. For example, a SYN flood contains in the baseline part the attack description. In this case the TCP/IP protocol with a set SYN flag. The customizing part defines threshold and a time interval for the individual implementation of the event. As result the SYN request (attack description) has to occur more than 200 times (threshold) within 1 second (time interval) to cause a SYN flood signalization.

The baseline part of a rule is vendor-specific and out of scope for parameterization. The customizing part of a rule will be mapped into the standardized parameterization format. Analog to IDMEF the standardized parameterization format is named "Intrusion Detection Parameterization Exchange Format" (IDPEF).

2.3   IDPEF Integration

IDPEF was initially defined [6] as theoretical green field approach. Subsequent the attributes of IDPEF are mapped to the open source IDS Snort [7], Samhain [8], OSSec [9] and Bro [10]. Improving adjustments of IDPEF were carried out within this phase. Based on these theoretical mappings the software implementations were carried out.

This theoretical approach was implemented first in three open source IDS, the network IDS Snort [7] and the host based IDS Samhain [8] and OSSec [9], to test the common applicability of this format. The implementations do not modify IDS executables. Only existing configuration files are processed and modified. The implementation in Bro [10] will be following.

As human interface an IDPEF web front-end was created that enables IDXP based communication to a selected analyzer. Attribute values are modified over the front-end and send back as IDPEF update to the analyzer. Additional software updates including upload of update files and new signatures are scheduled within the front-end and send to the analyzer.

On site of the analyzer individual IDXP / IDPEF communication modules are created. These modules modify configuration files of operating system and IDS software and schedules updates and their execution. Each attribute of individual IDS configuration files was assigned as baseline parameter or customizing parameter. Baseline parameters are not transferred into or modified by IDPEF. Customizing parameters are bi-unique mapped to an IDPEF attribute.

3   Conclusion

The configurations of three different IDS were mapped into one common parameterization format covered by one consistently administration front-end. These three IDS were operated under one common independent IDS manager. As result, the IDS manager was separated from the rest of different IDS and integrates analyzers of different vendors and analyzing levels. Further IDS integrations have to substantiate this conclusion. Customizing of IDS could be due to a small amount of parameters and values. Baseline configuration and references depend on the internal processing and are not able to standardize by external modifications.

The implementations demonstrate that one central independent manager is able to operate IDS of different vendors and analyzing levels. With this single central administration entity it is necessary to operate, manage, maintain and administer a heterogeneous IDS composite based on a small format. All connections are initialized from the central manager to the distributed analyzer entities. All updates (parameter and software) could be controlled, downloaded and distributed to each single IDS entity from one central management entity. The communication is easier to control, because there is only one communication port from the manager to all IDS entities necessary and the content could be inspected by security devices. Connections from an IDS analyzer entity to a system outside the administrative IDS LAN are not necessary. The manager entity defines the boarder of autonomous acted IDS. The concerting entity of the IDS is continuously the manager, but this entity is no longer vendor-specific.

On the whole, the manager is an independent system of IDS and could be separated from the rest of the IDS. It is possible to operate different IDS with one consistently administration front-end. This findings enable new and independent evolution streams for IDS analyzer as well as manager. As a consequence this enables new business cases for IDS manufacturers to provide enriched IDS management systems.

References

1. Debar, H., Curry, D., Feinstein, B.: The Intrusion Detection Message Exchange Format (IDMEF), RfC 4765 (2007), http://www.ietf.org/rfc/rfc4765.txt (last visit September 01, 2007)
2. Feinstein, B., Matthews, G.: The Intrusion Detection Exchange Protocol (IDXP), RfC 4767 (2007), http://www.ietf.org/rfc/rfc4767.txt (last visit September 01, 2007)
3. Rose, M.: The Blocks Extensible Exchange Protocol Core, RfC 3080 (March 2001), http://www.ietf.org/rfc/rfc3080.txt (last visit September 01, 2007)
4. Wood, M., Erlinger, M.: Intrusion Detection Message Exchange Requirements, RfC 4766 (March 2007), http://www.ietf.org/rfc/rfc4766.txt (last visit September 01, 2007)
5. Bösch, B.-C.: Standardized Parameterization of Intrusion Detection Systems. International Journal of Advanced Research in Computer Engineering & Technology (IJARCET), 1–5 (May 2012)
6. Bösch, B.-C.: Intrusion Detection Parameterization Exchange Format, work in progress (2012)
7. SNORT, http://www.sort.org (last visit: December 03, 2011)
8. Samhain: http://www.la-samhna.de/ (last visit: December 03, 2011)
9. OSSec: http://www.ossec.net (last visit: December 03, 2011)
10. Bro: http://www.bro-ids.org (last visit: December 03, 2011)

Modularizing Cyber Defense Situational Awareness – Technical Integration before Human Understanding

Gabriel Klein, Heiko Günther, and Susan Träber

Fraunhofer FKIE, Wachtberg, Germany
`firstname.lastname@fkie.fraunhofer.de`

Abstract. Human cyber situational awareness can only be achieved through appropriate visualization. Observation, understanding and projecting the status of cyber resources need to be supported by novel display and interaction techniques. These displays can only be realized if the cyber security-related data is sufficiently structured. We propose a two-stage creation of human cyber situational awareness: the first stage consists of technically integrating all security-related knowledge about the defended systems into a comprehensive model. In the second stage, this semantically enriched data can be visualized in a way that intuitively supports the operators' understanding of the current security situation as well as analysis techniques that go beyond the current state of the art.

Keywords: Cyber defense, situational awareness, security visualization.

1 Introduction

The concept of situational awareness (SA) is well-known in the cognitive sciences [1]. When applied to the context of cyber defense, the three SA stages are retained but their respective semantics differ. The observation phase is typically equated with security monitoring of vital resources, e. g. system components, services or users. Understanding their interdependencies involves modeling the effects these different resources have on each other and integrating data delivered by employed security tools. The semantics of the projection phase are similar to that of the physical world. The behavior of resources in the near future is predicted.

Translating the technical representation of the situation into a human awareness regarding the cyber situation is a challenge that requires appropriate interface design and visualization strategies. Existing security analysis environments, so-called security information event management (SIEM) systems, offer data aggregation mechanisms and rudimentary visualization approaches. While well-suited for in-depth analyses, these displays lack intuitive situation perception and the lack of projection capabilities.

2 Model-Based Technical Cyber Defense Situational Awareness

The integration of all available cyber security-related knowledge about defended systems is crucial for creating a meaningful cyber situation picture. The model constituting

N. Aschenbruck et al. (Eds.): Future Security 2012, CCIS 318, pp. 307–310, 2012.

the cyber situation representation (CSR) is described in more detail in [2]. It is initialized once at system start and continuously updated with real-time security information. Due to the large volume of information from security sensors, an online mapping of external data to the different resources in the system model is performed.

2.1   Automatic Network Modeling

Consistency between the CSR and the real network is essential for the quality of situational awareness. An imprecise CSR can lead to misinterpretation of the situation and inaccurate predictions about the impact of security-relevant events or counter-measures against attacks. Therefore, both the initial creation and the frequent update of the CSR need to be performed as effectively and efficiently as possible. Manually creating a complete network model is very time consuming and error-prone. There-fore, we use a best-effort approach that uses automatic modeling and limits the manual contribution to the verification of the identified model and minor adjustments.

For the identification of components and dependencies, we focus on passive network monitoring techniques. They are supported by active techniques where this is possible and useful. It has been shown in [3] and [4] that passive and active network discovery cover different views on the network and should therefore be used in parallel. For example, it is possible to identify hosts and applications by inspecting network traffic, but it is not possible to identify open ports which are not addressed during the passive inspection.

Many dependencies can be identified by inspecting the network communication streams. Dependencies between applications on the same host cannot be seen in the network traffic. However, it is possible to use local agents on the host system or make use of existing network analysis techniques that can be extended to suit our needs.

We implemented this approach and successfully tested it in an experimental test environment. If the network traffic is monitored continuously, the CSR can dynamically adapt to changes in the network infrastructure. Frequently performed active scans can additionally unveil changes in the structure that cannot be detected by passive scanning techniques.

We believe that this approach for both the initial modeling and for continuous updates helps to maintain an accurate model of the network and significantly lower the administrative overhead for the CSR.

2.2   Mapping External Information to System Model Entities

A wide variety of tools deployed in networked systems are capable of delivering security-relevant information about important resources; e. g. system/application logs, intrusion detection or network management systems. This information needs to be structured in a fashion that is compatible with the system model. Because the association of security-relevant data to model entities is not generally known, data from external sources needs to be mapped to model entities so that meaningful analysis and display can take place. Advantages of this mapping include the ability to meaningfully infer a resource's state, clustering of huge data repositories, and insight into structural aspects of security-relevant information.

The mapping process consists of two stages. During the first, data items are mapped to resources. The second stage seeks to determine the effects that data items matched to a resource in the first phase have on that resource's status indicators. This is theoretically possible both in a qualitative and also in a quantitative manner, although the practicability of the latter case has not yet been proven in the general case.

Standards such as the Common Platform Enumeration [5] and Common Configuration Enumeration [6] provide guidelines for characterizing model entities so that they can be more easily matched with features extracted from external data items. A first implementation uses regular expressions to detect known patterns, but more mature approaches such as artificial intelligence and machine learning are being investigated.

3   Human Cyber Defense Situational Awareness

The visualization of IT infrastructures becomes increasingly difficult with the increasing scale and complexity of the underlying networks. These factors require an appropriate visualization that enables a comprehensible overview and provides detailed technical information. For security monitoring, SIEM systems are used to collect all relevant messages, but their graphical capabilities are limited to data aggregation, statistical overviews and presentation of text messages.

We pursue a different approach by developing a visualization that represents the security-relevant information in the context of our system model. Our first goal is to represent large-scale networks in a clearly arranged manner that is based on the principles of different viewpoints and hierarchical layers. The second goal is to represent the occurrence of security-relevant events in a way that allows an intuitive understanding of their impact on different parts of the network.

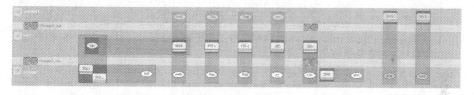

Fig. 1. Overview of network tasks and services

A GUI prototype provides a general overview of the security situation of the monitored network and allows drill-down analysis where further information is required. The interface design concept is based on ecological interface design (EID, [7]). EID relies on the development of a work domain model [8] which allows the user to explore monitored systems in breadth and depth in a structured manner. Thus, users are able to enhance their system understanding and therefore – combined with the presentation of security-relevant events – improve their information security/cyber defense situational awareness.

Fig. 1 shows an overview of the monitored system. It displays the fundamental task of the networked system by showing the client/server applications and their dependencies. In case of a security-relevant event such as an attack, the corresponding areas in the visualization are highlighted for instant perception by administrative personnel.

Further information is available by performing a drill-down analysis. The monitored computers are represented by horizontal bars and icons within these bars symbolize the chronological sequence of status indicator values (e. g. availability) for the respective applications. For more information about the attributes of a single machine, a sliding panel can be opened to the left. Another panel can be opened to the right to display detailed information about the lower-level network connectivity.

4   Outlook

We believe that human cyber defense situational awareness can only be attained through appropriate visual mechanisms which in turn require extensive model-based integration of all available security-relevant data.

In the future, we plan to intensify our efforts in the areas of automated network modeling and the mapping of security-relevant data to model entities. Both will be implemented prototypically in realistic reference scenarios. To further support the proactive aspects of our graphical user interface design, we will investigate the appropriateness of visual analytics as a means to promote a deeper system understanding.

References

1. Endsley, M.: Theoretical Underpinnings of Situational awareness: A Critical Review. In: Endsley, M.R., Garland, D.J. (eds.) Situational Awareness Analysis and Measurement, Mahwah, NJ, USA (2000)
2. Klein, G., Hunke, S., Günther, H., Jahnke, M.: Model-based Cyber Defense Situational Awareness. To be Published in Praxis der Informationsverarbeitung und Kommunikation (PIK). K. G. Saur Verlag, München (2012)
3. Webster, S., Lippmann, R., Zissman, M.: Experience Using Active and Passive Mapping for Network Situational Awareness. In: Fifth IEEE International Symposium on Network Computing and Applications (2006)
4. Bartlett, G., Heidemann, J., Papadopoulos, C.: Understanding Passive and Active Service Discovery. In: Internet Measurement Conference, San Diego, California, USA (2007)
5. MITRE Corporation. Common Platform Enumeration, http://cpe.mitre.org/ (accessed March 2012)
6. MITRE Corporation. Common Configuration Enumeration, http://cce.mitre.org/ (accessed March 2012)
7. Vicente, K., Rasmussen, J.: Ecological interface design: Theoretical foundations. IEEE Transactions on Systems, Man, and Cybernetics 22, 589–606 (1992)
8. Vicente, K.J.: Cognitive Work Analysis: Towards Safe, Productive, and Healthy Computer-based Work. Lawrence Erlbaum Associates, Mahwah (1999)

Underwater Inspection Using the AUV SeaCat

Joerg Kalwa

ATLAS ELEKTRONIK GmbH, Bremen Germany
joerg.kalwa@atlas-elektronik.com

Abstract. Supported by the R&D-Project CView Atlas Elektronik together with further partners has recently developed an autonomous underwater vehicle (AUV) named SeaCat which is able to carry a multitude of payloads for various inspection tasks. A specific pan/tilt-inspection head has been created by the Bremen based institute DFKI Robotics Innovation Center, comprising a multibeam sonar and a camera/laser imaging system. Among possible tasks are inspections of the bottom, walls and underwater structures of harbors and waterways. This configuration marks a starting point for further development leading to a unique underwater inspection system. In the near future this will support closing the safety gap which exists today.

Keywords: AUV, SeaCat, harbor security, pipeline inspection, CView.

1   Introduction

In spite of today's expanding road- and air traffic, harbors and waterways are the backbone of international freight business. More than 90% of the world exports and imports are moved by sea transport. In Europe more than 1200 Seaports are in operation to wind up nearly the complete foreign trade of the Union. The uninterrupted functionality of the dedicated infrastructure is of greatest economical importance. Today, many harbors are built on foundations which are older than 100 years. In order to secure their continuous use it is necessary to avoid damages and risks which can be seen in unattended wear and degradation of underwater structures (safety) but also in possible criminal affairs or even terrorism (security).

Until today inspections of these structures are done by human divers which are faced with a multitude of difficulties or even dangers mainly due to low visibility and limited diving time. Thus, manual inspections can be performed at pre-known neuralgic spots only.

The same problem affects inland water supply which utilises drinking water pipelines. Partially these ducts are tunnelling mountains for several kilometres. Often these pipes cannot be emptied so that there is no possibility for inspection at all!

Autonomous underwater vehicles which are sufficiently small to be highly manoeuvrable but still big enough to carry substantial payload sensors and energy storage may contribute to bridge this gap. This paper shows the current state of the art using the ATLAS SeaCat as a typical example.

N. Aschenbruck et al. (Eds.): Future Security 2012, CCIS 318, pp. 311–314, 2012.
© Springer-Verlag Berlin Heidelberg 2012

2   Lessons Learned from the SeaWolf

In 2006 the German MOD awarded a study to ATLAS to demonstrate the potential benefit of operating AUVs for harbor security. To save development time and costs the body of a former SeaWolf mine disposal vehicle prototype was reactivated from storage and upgraded by many components which stemmed from a parallel product development aiming at a long range AUV, today known as SeaOtter MK II. The result of the project, the SeaWolf HPT, was a bit short-winded as maximum operating time was about 3 hours but it gave interesting insights in the pros and cons of harbor operations using AUVs.

The payload sensor was an Edgetech 2200 dual frequency Sidescan Sonar operating at 250 kHz and 850 kHz; the selection of which was very suitable for the detection of smaller objects on the sea bottom. The basic idea was to establish a sonar map of the bottom and then run missions in regular intervals to detect changes.

The areas of interest inside a harbor are typically terminals as those in ferry ports. It was found that there is a significant change of the seabed due to the operation of powerful propellers and bow thrusters. This makes change detection much more difficult than anticipated.

Furthermore, the principle of the sensor does not allow resolving any vertical structure for all sound energy is reflected at once. Thus, harbor structures and ship hulls could be inspected using a video camera only. But without the possibility of image mosaicing video inspection is limited to few spots of interest only.

3   The CView Project

In order to fill this gap with emphasis on harbor safety, ATLAS together with four further partners started a R&D project called "CView" in 2009, supported by the German Ministry of Economy. The project, which ended recently, aimed on the creation of an underwater inspection system for vertical harbor structures like piers and ship hulls. The basic idea was to allow a 3D perception of structures in a parallel approach.

On one hand there should be a high resolution multibeam echosounder, provided by the Fraunhofer Institute IBMT, which measures a line of points on a wall. Moving forward, the point lines add to a full 3D image of the illuminated structure. On the other hand a similar procedure should be conduced by optical imaging. A laser should project a pattern onto the structure. By taking a photo of the pattern the 3D structure can be constructed. Later it had been decided that a single line laser is sufficient for this task. This system had been developed by the DFKI Robotics Innovation Center who also built the multifunctional head. The Institute WSS of the University of Applied Sciences in Bremen was in charge of analyzing the sonar images and the Fraunhofer Institute AST of Ilmenau provided control methods for an automatic inspection so that the missions need not to be planned in detail.

ATLAS modified the SeaWolf HPT in order to be able to carry the multifunctional head. At the same time the performance of the SeaWolf could be increased by magnitude. The changes were that radical that it gave rise to re-name the vehicle "SeaCat". The SeaCat AUV (Fig. 1) is a torpedo-shaped underwater vehicle about 2.6

m in length and about 30 cm in diameter. Driven by a single propeller, steering is achieved by four fins which also allow control of the roll motion. A unique feature roots in the fact that SeaCat is a so called hybrid vehicle. It can be operated either remotely controlled, using a 2 mm thin fibre-optic Ethernet cable, or fully autonomously with an endurance of up to 8 hours and a range of up to 30 km.

The CView system has been tested at various places with special emphasis on video data recording. It was found that the laser line recording was quite sensitive to ambient light. Together with certain requirements for good visibility this leads to the fact that the distance between vehicle and objects needs to be rather close. Conditions as found in Baltic Sea ports require a maximum distance of 1.5 m in daylight. The situation improves if the head can be operated at night.

For accurate distance control a sector scanning sonar (Tritech Micron) was used to determine the shape and distance of the adjacent wall. The information was processed in a specific module which takes advantage of a backseat driver mechanism. It allows implementing reactive control strategies which are based on in-situ processing of sensors.

Fig. 1. CView pan tilt unit mounted on SeaCat (Photo by DFKI). The small insert shows a 3D structure as result of the scanning process.

4   Internal Pipe Inspection

The usability of the SeaCat for challenging inspection tasks had been proven in March of this year. In a mission lasting almost seven hours, the AUV was able to dive through a water supply tunnel of 24 km length in the vicinity of Stuttgart, successfully investigating the tube for damage. Although the concrete duct had been checked regularly in the course of it's over 40-year life-time through measurements of the hydraulic friction losses and through the leakage rate, a visual inspection of its condition over the entire length had not been technically possible until now. Based on the technical progress in UUV technology the idea was born to inspect the water tunnel by means of an autonomous diving robot.

Fig. 2. SeaCat ready to start. Note the Laser beam in the small photo used for distance control.

The SeaCat Team of ATLAS designed a specific inspection head which allows recording high resolution video data over the total length of the tunnel, while moving continuously through the tube at a speed of about 2 knots and remaining centered with the aid of optical distance sensors.

The exit point of the trip was a surge chamber at Talheim, a concrete structure comprising a shaft 38 m deep and about 8 m in diameter. A diver's lamp was positioned at the bottom of this well which was switched on, when the vehicles entered the basin. This visual signal was detected by the vehicle's camera, causing the autonomous guidance system to stop the vehicle and let it rise to the surface.

This pioneering accomplishment was made possible by the outstanding teamwork between the staff of BWV and of Atlas Elektronik. While the mission demonstrated the technical reliability of the SeaCat, initial evaluation of the data showed that the water tunnel was still in good condition after 40 years of continuous use.

Probing the Seafloor in Order to Find Dumped Ammunition and Other Hazardous Materials

Wolfgang Jans[1], Matthias Reuter[2], Stefan Behringer[1], and Sabine Bohlmann[2]

[1] Bw Technical Center for Ships and Naval Weapons,
Naval Technology and Research (WTD71),
Research Department for Underwater Acoustics and Marine Geophysics (FWG),
Klausdorfer Weg 2-24, 24148 Kiel, Germany
WolfgangJans@bwb.org
[2] Clausthal University of Technology,
Institute for Computer Science /
CUTEC Institute GmbH, Julius-Albert-Str. 4, 38678 Clausthal-Zellerfeld, Germany
matthias.reuter@tu-clausthal.de

Keywords: Probing the Seafloor, Sediment Sonar, Neuronal Networks, Dumped Ammunition.

1   Introduction

On one hand North and Baltic Sea are contaminated with ammunition. On the other hand these areas are of particular economic interest - as a direct consequence of the so called energy-turn – mainly due to the planning and construction of off-shore- energy parks for 21st century. Therefore it will be one of the largest challenges in the early future to detect, to map out and finally to recover all kinds of dangerous legacies of the past.

Ammunition may be accidently lost during military conflicts or is disposed during and after these conflicts. This is especially true for Europe, where a large amount of ammunition was dumped in the North and Baltic Sea after World War I and II. Fig. 1 shows potentially contaminated sites with dumped ammunition of the coast of Germany[1]. The marked sites indicate a reasonable suspicion that these sites are contaminated with dumped ammunition based on the sometimes contradictory and often incomplete known information. In total, the amount of dumped ammunition just for German waters after WW II is estimated to be in the order of 1,800,000 t. Considerable quantities of this ammunition was recovered and destroyed during the early postwar years. But, it is assumed that up to 1,600,000 t of conventional ammunition is still in the North and Baltic Sea[1]. In addition, up to estimated 230,000 t of chemical ammunition are also present[1].

Dumped ammunition is not just a German problem. This method was adopted by many nations after World War II in Europe for disposing ammunition and other surplus materials. As a consequence, dumping sites are scattered all over the coast of Germany, France, Italy, Great Britain, Ireland and parts of the coast of Spain, Denmark, and Norway. In UK for example, after World War II some 1.200.000 t of army ammunition and 500,000 t of air force ammunition in the stocks were believed to be no longer necessary. This ammunition was dumped since sea dumping was

N. Aschenbruck et al. (Eds.): Future Security 2012, CCIS 318, pp. 315–326, 2012.

considered to be the safest and most efficient method for disposal at this time. In particular, the British Ministry of Defense has dumped more than a million tons of munitions in the Irish Sea, including 14,600 t of phosgene-filled artillery rockets since the 1920s[2]. This kind of disposal method continued until 1972 when international agreements were reached to control the dumping of material at sea. Today dumping at sea is regulated by international treaties and national law.

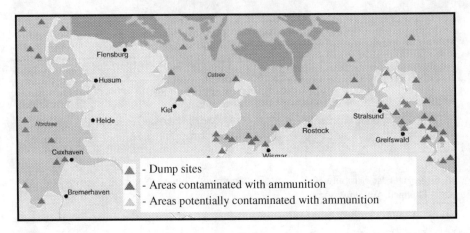

Fig. 1. Simplified map with potentially contaminated sites with dumped ammunition in the Baltic and North-Sea of the coast of Germany[1]

On the other hand the interest in the economic use of coastal waters is constantly growing. This starts with technical installations like offshore wind parks and ends with cables and pipelines connecting neighboring countries. This is supported by the European Commission in order to secure energy supply of the European Union and to establish a European electricity market. Recently the wind parks EnBW Baltic 1 (2011) about 16 km north of Fischland-Darss-Zingst in the Baltic Sea and Alpha Ventus (2010) about 45 km north-west of Borkum in the North Sea have been brought on line. And, a lot more parks are under construction or planned. Also 2011, the first line of the North Stream natural gas pipeline through the Baltic Sea from Vyborg in Russia to Greifswald in Germany was inaugurated. Additionally, offshore electricity cables are more and more installed on the seafloor. An example is the planned NorGer Cable, which will connect the electricity market in Germany and Norway. This direct current cable trough the North Sea with a transmission capacity of 1.400 MW will start in Tonstad in Norway and will end in Moorriem in Lower Saxony, Germany. Initial operation is planned for 2018 or later. A similar cable (NorNel) connecting Norway and the Netherlands is in operation since 2008.

A first evaluation of a chemical ammunition dump sites in the Baltic Sea was carried out in the framework of the EC-FP6 project "MERCW" (Modeling of Environmental Risks related to sea dumped Chemical Weapons) from 2005 to 2009[3]. Within this project two surveys[4] were undertaken at the known chemical ammunition dump site in the Bornholm Basin. East of the island of Bornholm approximately 32.000 t of chemical ammunition were dumped 1947 in some 80 m of water depths on the order of the Soviet military administration in Germany. Although, this site is marked in maps as "anchoring and fishing not recommended", the area has always remained a popular fishing area. Corrosion of this ammunition has been steadily advancing over the period of approximately 50 years. While most of the collected ammunition was only partly corroded during the first decades, today nearly all collected ammunition is either empty or is very heavily corroded. However, one should keep in mind that the ammunition had been located largely proud or open on the seafloor. Ammunition buried in the sediments seem to be much more intact[5].

Especially during the second survey within the MERCW project geophysical data were collected with parametric echo sounder sonar and simultaneously with a deep-towed magnetic array in two roughly 0.5 x 2 km large areas within the dumping site. The high resolution of the collected acoustic data enabled the authors[4] to detect several hundreds of buried objects per survey area. Only four larger proud objects, exposed on the seafloor in the vicinity of ship wrecks, were found. 80 % of the buried objects were covered by less than 70 cm of soft muddy sediments in the Bornholm Basin. All buried objects were detected within the first 1.5 – 2 m thick layer of sediment. 60 % of the detected objects had a size less than 2 m - the rest was larger. The number of detected objects in the acoustic data set was significantly larger compared to the number of detected magnetic anomalies. Correlating the echo sounder data with the magnetic data did also not always result in a good match for the considered two areas due to navigation uncertainties and lateral deviations[4].

These sited results from the Bornholm Basin indicate some of the issues related to the detection of dumped ammunition. Some are mentioned here:

- Dumped ammunition is often buried.
- The complex underwater environment causes a very high number of false alarms for buried objects, which needs to be reduced.
- The detection performance depends on the different seafloor sediment types within a dumping site, which may vary from mud to sand and rock. In addition, the water – sediment interface is often rough, occasionally smooth and shows sometimes periodical structures (ripple). Fishing activities and bioturbation may also constantly modify this interface.
- Dumped ammunition has a very broad size distribution ranging from single projectiles over 10.5 cm shells to 1000 Kg mines / bombs. Detecting this entire size spectrum puts a challenge on all available detection systems and basically requires an optimized use of these systems.

These issues will be addressed by a new research project SOAM which will start this year in order to detect dumped ammunition within the seafloor prior to construction projects. Our research project will focus on three main goals:

- the selection and improvement of suitable detectors for the detection of buried ammunition,
- a performance modeling approach in order to optimize the detection performance for all sediment types under all sorts of environmental conditions,
- an autonomous, neuronal based detection and classification process for false alarm suppression, and
- the development of an autonomous prototype vehicle for area search.

2   Sensors for Detecting Buried Ammunition at Sea

While proud objects (e.g. dumped ammunition) lying on the sea floor can be detected and classified rather well with high-frequency sonar systems[6], the detection and classification of buried objects is a much more difficult task. In principle, acoustic and magnetic sensors as well as the chemical analysis of collected sediment samples have been used for this task[4]. All of these sensors together with a visual (stereo) camera will be used during the SOAM project.

2.1   Low Frequency Sonar

Sediment sonars seem to be standard tools in the field of marine technology, however, their development, mainly in regards to resolving power, area search rate and inter- pretability are far from complete, especially for the task of detecting buried ammuni- tion. Resolving power, for example, is an important system feature in this context, since dumped ammunition has a broad object size distribution ranging from single rifle bullets over 10.5 cm shells to 500 – 1,000 Kg sea mines and torpedo or doodle- bug warheads. This demand for a high resolution is on the other hand in some way a conflicting requirement to a appropriate search rate in order to be able to survey a construction site within a reasonable time.

Today most sonars for surveying the sub-bottom base on the conventional or para- metric echo sounder principle. Short pulses are transmitted by these systems. The corresponding echoes are recorded in the interval between two adjacent transmissions, and the depth is calculated by converting the travel time between pulse transmission and echo reception using the speed of sound. By traveling along a track a depth sec- tion of the sub-bottom develops over time, which permits identification of sub-seafloor features.

Due to high absorption losses in the sediment, only low frequencies penetrate rea- sonable well into seafloor sediments. Parametric echo sounders generate this low frequency by transmitting two high frequency primary signals with high power. The bottom penetrating secondary frequency, which is the difference between the two primary frequencies, is produced by the non-linearity of water. Parametric echo sounders have the advantages of broad bandwidth and narrow beam since these characteristics are determined by the primary signals. When fully developed, the secondary frequency shows no side lobes. Major disadvantages are the very low efficiency for the secondary frequency and the very low area search rate. A single parametric antenna allows to measure one depth profile per ping at a small, single spot and a sub-bottom image develops over time by slowly moving along a track line. Fig. 2 shows an example for a bottom section image including a detected object.

In order to detect small buried objects a full 3D scan is needed. This results for parametric sonars in a search pattern with very low track line spacing. To increase this track line spacing and consequently the area search rate several parametric antennas can be combined in principle. This is certainly one issue which needs to be addressed during the research project SOAM. Another issue is the high number of buried objects detected by the sonar or a magnetic sensor. An example can be found in [4], which shows on average 5 – 10 likely or certain buried objects per 100 x 100 m.

In order to increase the area search rate the principle of multi-beam or swath echosounding can be used for systems with conventional antennas. This technique is common for high frequency systems, and produces some 90 beams across a 90° 135° broad swath for mapping the seafloor. In contrast, low frequency bottom penetrating multi-beam echosounder are not state of the art. Only a few experimental systems exist – one is the SEDISON System of WTD 71[8]. SEDISON was developed by ATLAS Elektronik as demonstrator system and bases partly on the results of an earlier experimental system[9,10]. It has significantly other system parameters compared with the parametric sediment sonar SES-2000.

Both systems have been deployed for investigating the problem of buried mine detection by repeatedly conducting experiments in the Baltic Sea. A great variety of test targets were buried for this at different depths in fine sand or soft, muddy sediments.

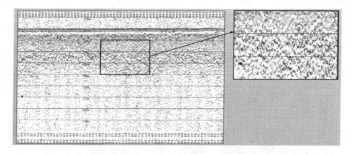

Fig. 2. Parametric echo sounder profiles produced with the INNORMAR SES-2000 system showing the water-sediment interface and about 2.5 m beneath this a small object[7]

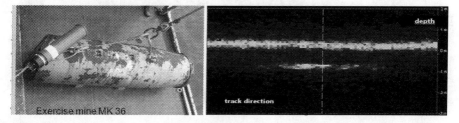

Fig. 3. Exercise Mine MK 36 (left) and sonar image of this mine covert by 80 cm of sediment (right)

Multi-beam echosounder which penetrate into the sediment have a low angle resolution due to the required low frequency and the fact that the conventional antenna needs to stay within a manageable size. Along the track the lateral resolution can be significantly enhanced by Synthetic Aperture Sonar processing (SAS). This fact together with a high number of detected buried objects results in a high false alarm rate, which needs to be reduced for the detection of buried ammunition by means of intelligent data analysis. Fig. 3 shows an example for a buried mine detected with the SEDISON system in the Baltic Sea.

The echo of naturally buried objects can be masked by bottom reverberation. This is for example the case, if the echo of an object and bottom reverberation contributes to the same 3D resolution cell – a problem for lower grazing angles or sloping seaf-loors (see Fig.4). Of cause, this effect depends amongst others on the ratio between the object-size-and-shape-dependent target strength, which is also aspect angle or track direction dependent, and the bottom reverberation level, which depends on seaf-loor type and roughness and may also show angle dependence.

If objects are flush buried or only slightly covered by sediment, the echo from the object will always be masked more or less by the bottom reverberation due to the just mentioned reasons[10]. If objects are buried very deeply, echoes will very often fade out by transmission loss. Therefore, the detection performance of sediment sonars depends on the depth of object burial.

These are just two factors which determine the performance of sediment sonars. Other environmental or system related factors like the background noise level, which is wind speed and carrier dependent influence this performance as well. Therefore, proper performance modeling is necessary in order to collect the best possible date[11,12]. In this context the entire processing chain: expected buried ammunition - environment – signal processing – intelligent data analysis – sensor carrier needs to be analyzed for each and every measurement.

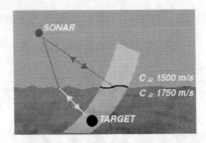

Fig. 4. Physical principle for a sediment sonar: Sound penetration is limited to approx. ±60° (Brewster Angle), high absorption losses in the bottom reduce an echo return significantly and an object echo competes with bottom reverberation

3   Methods for Classifying Buried Landmines

Any sediment sonar or metal detector system detects apart from buried ammunition natural structures like e.g. sediment layering, boulders and other embeddings, sediment changes caused by marine life or traces caused by fishing activities. These natural structures cause a significant number of false alarms which needs to be reduced significantly by an autonomous detection and classification system.

For this task a neuronal-based detection and classification method will be improved and used, which was designed for the detection of land mines. Typical sensors for land mine search are bottom penetrating radar and metal detectors, which are used in a similar configuration compared to the considered sensors for detecting dumped ammunition. The performance of these land based systems is also significantly limited by high false alarm rates[13,14,15,17]. Thus, the University Clausthal developed and tested neural-based automatic detection and classification software, which improves the detection and classification probability significantly[16, 18].

3.1   Metal Detectors and Neural Nets

The operator sequence to classify and detect predetermined objects consists of four sequential working modules. The first one is responsible for smoothing only the relevant part of the raw signal, which is that part of the raw signal belonging to the default integration window in the receiving phase. This first module works as a preprocessing stage to obtain optimal input vectors for the neural classificators, as described below.

That part of the information of the received data, which allows to discriminate different objects (as far as possible), can be found on the one hand in the time-dependent decay of the induced pulse, but on the other hand definitely also in the spatial shape of the signals when moving the search head over the object. For this reason our neural classifier consists of two sequential feed-forward nets. The fact, that objects to be detected are known a priori, implies the application of a supervised learning scheme, wherefore we used back propagation working with the Generalized Delta Rule.

After a successful training phase of such networks the classification results obtained by propagating a smoothed decay curve v_s are given by

$$BPP^{(1)}(v_s(n_1,p),v_s(n_1+1,p),...,v_s(n_2,p)) \mapsto \left(\psi_1^{(1)}(p),\psi_2^{(1)}(p),...,\psi_{o^{(1)}}^{(1)}(p)\right)$$
$$=: \vec{\psi}^{(1)}(p) \in (0,1)^{o^{(1)}} \qquad , (1)$$

with $BPP^{(1)}$ the classification mapping evaluated by the neural net via the training process. $o^{(1)}$ denotes the number of output neurons and equals the number of training vectors (decay curves). We considered that the combination of three different sample signals denoting no, low and high metal content is sufficient to categorize different (position independent) response signals, so just three output neurons are enclosed in this first stage of the neural classificator: $o^{(1)}:=3$.

The output activities of the first back propagation net are accumulated to a new spatial input vector while moving the sensor head over the examined slice of ground. These spatial vectors work as inputs for the system's third stage, which is another feed-forward net in order to classify the spatial trend of the induced voltage signals. Assuming a fixed number of the to be discriminated objects[1] N, a fixed maximum number of sample curves w(N) defined by the maximum elongation of the N objects and a uniform motion[2] of the sensor head from positions p1 to pw(N) defining the vector of movement $\vec{p}$, the second backpropagation net performs the transformation

$$BPP^{(2)}\left(\vec{\psi}^{(1)}(p_1),\vec{\psi}^{(1)}(p_2),...,\vec{\psi}^{(1)}(p_{w(N)})\right) \mapsto \left(\psi_1^{(2)}(\vec{p}),\psi_2^{(2)}(\vec{p}),...,\psi_N^{(2)}(\vec{p})\right)$$
$$=: \vec{\psi}^{(2)}(\vec{p}) \in (0,1)^N \qquad , (2)$$

---

[1] If an object should be detected in different depth stages, each stage has to be defined as a single object.

[2] A uniform motion is possible only if using a robot. The use of the detector by a human deminer requires an exact position acquisition and an algorithm to transform the data into a suitable format.

whereas the desired output activity $\vec{\psi}_{des}^{(2)}$ for each object $k \in \{1,2,\ldots,N\}$ is given by

$$\vec{\psi}_{des}^{(2)}\left(\vec{p}^{(k)}\right) := \left(0,\ldots,0, \underset{k-th\ component}{1}, 0,\ldots,0\right). \tag{3}$$

The last module of the supporting system acts as a postprocessor and consists of different smoothing and visualizing routines, e.g. a 3D-imaging system (Fig. 5), spatial smoothing routines both in x- and y-direction, scale- and zoom-operators, etc., that can be manually switched on or off by the deminer to deal with different soils and environmental conditions.

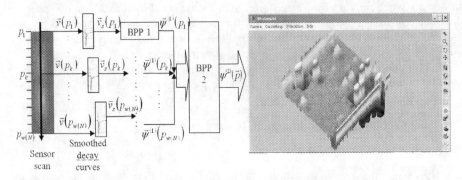

Fig. 5. Screenshot of the user-interface of the post-processing and 3D-imaging system (left); Schematic overview of the processing mode of the supporting system (right)

Fig. 6 shows the results after successful training with six objects (mine surrogate of type "M3B" buried in depths 0cm, 5cm, 10cm and 15cm, high metal content reference object on the surface and one pure soil measurement).

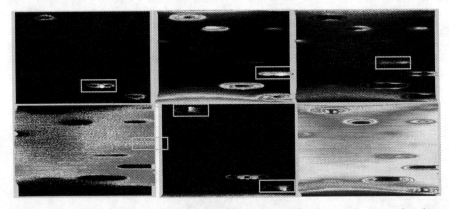

Fig. 6. Color-coded activities of the six output neurons of a trained network when using data of the JRC test site, Ispra, field 4C. Displayed are the activities at each position of the analyzed area (size: 6m×2m) of the output neuron trained with signals of (from upper left to lower right) mine on surface, in 5cm depth, in 10cm depth, in 15cm depth, high metal content reference object, sample ground signal [16,18].

3.2   Analyzing Ground Penetrating RADAR by Neural Nets

Based on the task to detect, classify and identify objects with high accuracy (centimeter range) in the soil, we adapted the neural based system described above [16] in that way that signals of ground penetrating radars and electromagnetic probes are analyzed in a way that a virtual glassy ground of the area down to a depth of 4 meters was created. The reference of the objects is based on a differentiated GPS and – as special in urban areas GPS technology is working not adequate – on odometric or tachometric technology.

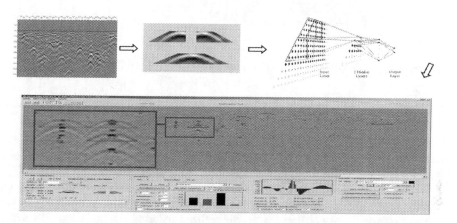

Fig. 7. Data processing to define adequate learning pattern for detecting hyperbolas out of radar-grams by feed-forward neural networks

The detection system records radar-grams from six 200 MHz and 600 MHz antennas at the same time. These data are pre-processed again by using a low-pass filter for reducing the high-frequency noise, followed by a background removal based on moving average subtraction and an energy decay gain to amplify the data depth-dependently. Furthermore, an entropy based algorithm evaluates parameters to allow assumptions about the geological and hydrological parameters of the underground.

The cleaned radar-grams are fed to the more or less similar neural net structure as described above, whereby we use in modification two-dimensional image sections as a kind of focus of attention. The dimension of these sections depends on the properties of the measurements, e.g. scans per meter; means they have to be adapted accordantly by a special algorithm.

As shown in Fig. 7 right hand side on top the neurons of the first hidden layer are not fully connected to the input layer, as the get just a small area of the presented image section. Adjacent neurons thereby are responsible for adjacent. Furthermore the neurons input scheme is freely configurable and may overlap arbitrarily. The idea of this method: neurons in the first layer merely identify small parts of the object, which will be composed to higher, more complex concepts in the subsequent layers similar to the biological image processing. Furthermore by this way the network has the capability to detect faint and disturbed hyperbolas. After finding the space points of a hyperbola, it can be fitted and their different parameters calculated. Out of these parameters the form and the line-parameters themselves can be evaluated, means the line can be identified, as shown in Fig. 8.

Fig. 8. Quasi 3 dimensional cadastral map including the detected lines (engeneering version)

4   Summary and Discussion

In addition to sediment sonars and metal detectors including neural net based data analysis a camera system shall be used for navigation purposes and for detecting ammunition lying upon the ground. The algorithm of them are widely used and tested.

The entire detection process is shown in Fig. 9. This detection process including the required sensors will be tested in a lake and in the Baltic Sea. Finally, a prototype of an autonomous vehicle will be designed; partly realized and used within the test sites. Difficulties in this context are that the vehicle imposes limitations to the detection sensors in terms of weight, size and available energy. Interferences between sensors belonging to the guidance system of the vehicle and the sensors for detection are also an important issue. One research issue in this context is the navigation uncertainty of the vehicle, which needs to be very small for relocation of detected and classified ammunition.

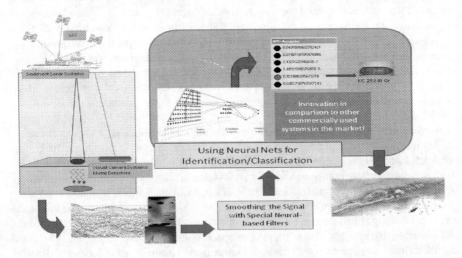

Fig. 9. Principle scheme of the detection, identification/classification of dumped ammunition

The performance of the sediment sonars will be determined using adequate sound propagation and sonar modeling in order to adjust the sonars for the obtained environmental conditions including observed seafloor conditions and the type of dumped ammunition looked for. In addition, modeling will permit to evaluate different sonar systems for the same task, identify room for improvement and optimize the integration of such sonars in a platform. If feasible, this modeling will also be extended to other sensors. Furthermore, the investigations will be complemented by first attempts to use Raman Spectroscopy in a chemical sensor for detecting dumped ammunition in the field.

Acknowledgements. The Project SOAM – Sounding of Ammunition –is coordinated by Clausthaler Umwelttechnik-Institut GmbH (CUTEC), Clausthal. Further project partners are the Research Department for Underwater Acoustic and Marine Geophysics (FWG), Kiel, of the Bw Technical Center for Ships and Naval Weapons, Maritime Technology and Research (WTD 71), ATLAS Elektronik, Bremen, Heinrich Hirdes EOD Services GmbH (HH EOD) in cooperation with Challenger Technologies Dr.-Ing. Klaus Köhler (CTK), Muster.

References

1. Böttcher, C., Knobloch, T., Rühl, N.-P., Sternheim, J., Wichert, U., Wöhler, J.: Munitions-belastung der deutschen Meeresgewässer - Bestandsaufnahme und Empfehlungen, Sekretariat Bund/Länder-Messprogramm für die Meeresumwelt von Nord- und Ostsee (BLMP) im Bundesamt für Seeschifffahrt und Hydrographie (BSH), Bernhard-Nocht-Straße 78, 20359 Hamburg, Germany (2011)
2. Peterkin, T.: MoD dumped munition in the Irish Sea, The Telegraph, April 22, 2005 and The British MoD, Disposal of Munitions at Sea (May 15, 2009),
   http://www.mod.uk/DefenceInternet/AboutDefence/CorporatePubl ications/HealthandSafetyPublications/DSEA/DisposalOfMunition sAtSea.htm (last update May 18, 2012)
3. http://mercw.org/, http://cg.cs.uni-bonn.de/en/projects/mercw/
4. Missiaen, T., Söderström, M., Popescu, I., Vanninen, P.: Evaluation of a chemical munition dumpsite in the Baltic Sea based on geophysical and chemical investigations. Science of the Total Environment 408(17, 1), 3536–3553 (2010)
5. Sanderson, H., Fauser, P.: Historical and qualitative analysis of the state and impact of dumped chemical warfare agents in the Bornholm Basin from 1948–2008. Internal Report DMU-75-00061B. National Environmental Research Institute, p. 25 (2008)
6. Jans, W., Schmaljohann, H., Langner, F., Knauer, C., Middelmann, W.: Scanning for Hazardous Objects on the Seafloor – State of the Art Technologies. In: Proc. Future Security 2011, Berlin, Germany, September 5-7 (2011) ISBN 978-3-8396-0295-9
7. Wever, T.: WTD 71, NEST 2006, Sea Trial (2006)
8. Peine, H.: Sedison High-resolution Towed Sediment Sonar System. 2007 Annual Research and Technology Report, BMVg, Rü IV, Fontainengraben 150, 53123 Bonn (2007)
9. Peine, H., Brecht, D., Fedders, B.: Detection of Objects Buried in the Seafloor. Acta Acoustica United with Acustica 92(1), 150–152 (2006)
10. Peine, H., Brecht, D.: Detection of objects buried in the Seafloor. In: Proc. Oceans 2005 Europe, Brest, France, June 20-23 (2005)

11. Homm, A., Jans, W., Numerische Berechnungen zum Zielmaß von Objekten in Wasser und im Sediment: Teil 1, Kugel und Zylinder, TB 2003 - 9, FWG – Kiel, 2003 (VS – NfD) (2003)
12. Ehrlich, J., Fiedler, C., Peine, H.: Scattering from proud and buried sherical targets in the time domain. In: Proc. Seventh European Conference on Underwater Acoustics, ECUA 2004, July 5-8, Delft University of Technology, The Netherlands (2004)
13. Lewis, A.M., et al.: Multisensor Mine Signatures. Final Report of ITEP Project 2.5.1.2 (2004), http://demining.jrc.it/msms/MsmsFinalReport.pdf
14. Mcgrath, R.: Landmines and Unexploded Ordnance – A Resource Book. Pluto Press (2000) ISBN 0-7453-1259-4
15. Nelson, C.V., et al.: Wide Bandwidth Time-Domain Electromagnetic Sensor for Metal Target Classification. IEEE Trans. on Geoscience and Remote Sensing 39(6), 1129–1138 (2001)
16. Reuter, M., Tadjine, H.H., Harneit, S.: Localisation and Detection of Buried Objects like Mines in Diverse Soils with Soft-Computing Methods. In: 9th European Conference on Non-Destructive Testing, ECNDT, Berlin, Germany (2006)
17. Kaczkowski, P.J.: Pulsed Electromagnetic Induction (PEMI) for UXO discriminaton in JPG Phase IV- Preliminary Results. In: Proc. UXO Forum (1998)
18. Reuter, M., Harneit, S., Tadjine, H.H.: Multi-Stage Neural Supporting Systems for Time Domain Metal Detectors. In: World Automation Congress (WAC 2006), 6th International Symposium on Soft Computing for Industry (ISSCI), Budapest, Hungary (2006)

An Experiment for Detection of Underwater Intruders with Different Kinds of Sensors

Dietmar Stiller[1], Stephan Benen[2], and Paula Berkel[2]

[1] Wehrtechnische Dienststelle für Schiffe und Marinewaffen, Maritime Technologie und Forschung, Eckernförde, Germany
[2] Atlas Elektronik GmbH, Bremen, Germany

Abstract. Ships and infrastructure in harbours can be threatened by underwater intruders. Possible intruders are e.g. divers. A common characteristic of these threats is their low velocity and target strength, which makes them very difficult to detect. Further problems are the challenging environmental conditions in harbours and in the roads. Due to the usual extremely shallow water conditions, there are a high number of false alarms. Furthermore, ambient noise is very high because of ship traffic and harbour infrastructure. In the EDA project HaPS (Harbour and Base Protection Systems), which is a cooperation of Sweden, Italy, Norway and Germany, the detection of and reaction to possible threats in harbours are investigated theoretically and in sea trials.

1   Introduction

Ships and infrastructure in harbours can be threatened by underwater intruders. Possible intruders include divers - with or without scooter -, AUVs (Autonomous Underwater Vehicles) or mini-submarines. A common characteristic of these threats is their low velocity and target strength, especially in the case of divers equipped with closed circuit breathing systems, which makes them very difficult to detect. Further problems are the challenging environmental conditions in harbours and in the roads. Due to the usually extremely shallow water conditions, there are a high number of false alarms. Furthermore, ambient noise is very high because of the ship traffic and harbour infrastructure [2]. As the threat in harbours and on anchorages exists permanently, continuous surveillance is necessary. To avoid overloading the operator, the detection, classification and alarm generation should be automated as far as possible. Therefore the surveillance system has to meet the requirements of an extremely low false alarm rate and a high probability of detection. In the EDA project HaPS (Harbour and Base Protection Systems), which is a cooperation of Sweden, Italy, Norway and Germany, the detection of and reaction to possible threats in harbours are investigated theoretically and in sea trials [1]. Active acoustic sensors in horizontal and vertical orientation and passive acoustic, electric and magnetic sensors were used for detection. Additionally it is investigated how the different information from various sensors can be combined in order to fulfil the requirements described above. In Section 2 the layout of the experiment is shown and

N. Aschenbruck et al. (Eds.): Future Security 2012, CCIS 318, pp. 327–333, 2012.

the used sensors and effectors are described shortly and some preliminary results are shown. A first approach for data fusion is described in section 2.2.

2 HaPS Sea Trial in Eckernförde

In the HaPS project different sensors and countermeasures were investigated theoretically and in sea trials. The first sea trial was conducted in Eckernförde in 2011. The goal was to test sensors and effectors, which are described shortly in sections 2.1 and 2.3. The sensors were two active sonars and several trip-wires with passive acoustic, active acoustic, magnetic and electric sensors. A loudspeaker and an airgun were used as effectors. During the experiment the effectiveness of the single systems and also their mutual influence was investigated. The detections of the sensors were recorded for later data fusion.

Different scenarios with divers equipped with open and closed circuit system gears were conducted. In order to use sensors and effectors at the same time in accordance with safety regulations, an air-filled sphere of glass was also used as a target. The glass sphere was towed by a rubber dinghy and had a sonar target strength similar to that of a diver.

The scenarios which were used in this project are set up to cover both operational requirements and the requirements of this research and technology project itself. The expertise of the naval forces of the participating nations and of the NATO Centre of Excellence for Confined and Shallow Waters (COE CSW)was included in the layout of the scenarios. The location of the experiments, the "Kranzfelder Hafen" is shown in figure 1.

Fig. 1. The location of the Sea Trial in Eckernförde. Depicted are sensor and effector positions and containers on the pier. Also two types of scenarios are depicted.

2.1   Sensors

In this sea trial different types of sensors were used. For one thing tripwires were laid out at the bottom to detect crossing objects in the water column, for another thing active sonars were installed. They serve as sensor of higher detection range and they generate tracks of moving objects. In figure 2 the tripwires that were used are shown.

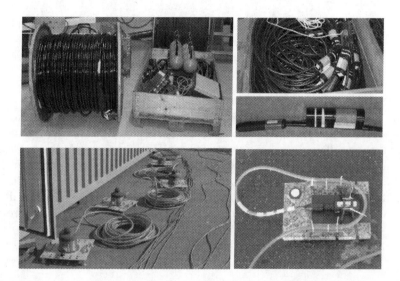

Fig. 2. Tripwires used for detection. Passive Acoustic Tripwire (PAT) from FOI (upper left). Passive Electric Tripwire (PET) from FOI (upper right). Vertical active Sonar (ACTAC) from WASS (lower left). Magnetic Tripwire (MAG) from WASS (lower right).

The four tripwires that were used in the HaPS project detect passing objects based on measurements of physically different properties. The PAT system analyses the sound which is emitted by the divers crossing the system. The PET system detects changes in the electric field. In the ACTAC system sound is transmitted from the bottom to the surface. By analysing the echoes a detection of a crossing object is realized. The MAG system analyses changes in the magnetic field caused by the presence of a diver.

One of the active sonars is a 120 kHz Sonar from Saab (DDS - Diver Detection Sonar) with a surveillance sector of 120 degrees, the other sonar which was used is the Cerberus diver detection sonar from Atlas Elektronik UK. It has a centre frequency at 100 kHz and an adjustable surveillance sector up to 360 degrees. Both sonars were installed in the classic horizontal orientation to insonify the harbour entrance and the area in front of the harbour. The echoes were used for contact- respectively track-generation. The Saab-DDS-system works with a Track-Before-Detect algorithm. A modified version for Cerberus developed by Atlas and WTD 71 builds tracks from the contacts with a MHT-algorithm, as described in [3]. Both sonars are shown in figure 3.

Fig. 3. Active sonars DDS from Saab with 120 kHz (left) and Cerberus from Atlas UK with 100 kHz (right)

During the experiments the detections of the tripwires and the tracks of the active sonars were depicted in an online common picture display. An enlarged part of the surveillance area with tracks of Saab DDS (green) and Cerberus sonar (blue), the tripwire position (yellow) and the tripwire detections (red) of WASS ACTAC is shown in figure 4. In white and grey colour the GPS-tracks of the divers and the safety boats are also depicted. The GPS-receivers of the divers were mounted on a buoy connected to the divers with a rope. Hence there is a difference between the GPS-position and the true position of the diver.

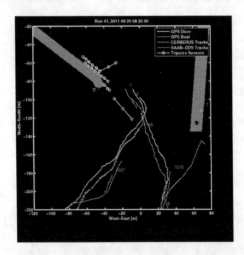

Fig. 4. Example of the sensor detections with active sonar tracks (Saab-DDS: green, Cerberus: blue), GPS tracks (divers: white, boats: grey), position of the tripwires (yellow) and tripwire detections (red)

2.2   Data Fusion

During the experiments the tracks of the active sonars and the detections of the tripwires were recorded in order to investigate various fusion methods after the trial. Different sensor combinations and fusion concepts are considered and investigated and the gain of the data fusion is evaluated. The goal of the data fusion is to combine the available data from the different sensors in order to extract comprehensive information about the presence and type of potential threats.

The data fusion is still in progress, so only preliminary results can be shown. The data fusion will be realised with a multiple hypothesis approach [3], [4], [5], in which several different possible data associations are considered in parallel. As only the tracks of the active sonars are available, a decentralised data fusion concept [6] has to be applied. In case of the tripwires the detections are used directly in the fusion process.

A preliminary result of the fusion is shown in figure 5, which corresponds to the sensor data shown in figure 4. In comparison to the original data the probability of detection was increased and the false alarm rate was reduced. Furthermore the track fragmentation was reduced as detection losses of single sensors can be compensated by the other ones.

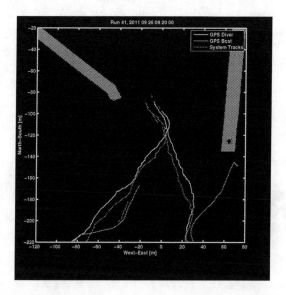

Fig. 5. Example of fused result with fused tracks (red) and GPS tracks (divers: white, boats: grey)

2.3   Non-lethal Countermeasures

In the experiments the effectiveness of non-lethal countermeasures (NLC) was
also investigated. Therefore two different kinds of effectors were used. One was
an underwater loudspeaker and the other was an airgun. Both devices are shown
in figure 6.

Fig. 6. Non-lethal countermeasures loudspeaker from Saab (left) and airgun from KDA
(right)

The loudspeaker was transported to a predefined position in the harbour and
lowered onto the bottom. The airgun was brought to the predefined position with
a rubber dinghy and operated from there. Sound pressure level of both devices
were measured and a possible influence on the detection rates of the acoustic
sensors was investigated.

Therefore different types of signals were transmitted with an underwater loudspeaker as well as the emissions of shots from the airgun at half water depth
were measured. In figure 7 two results are shown.

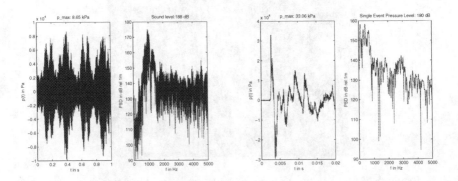

Fig. 7. Sound pressure and PSD of an alarm tone of the loudspeaker (left half) and
sound pressure and PSD of a shot of the airgun (right half) back calculated to 1 m
distance. For the short signal of the airgun the single event sound pressure level is
calculated.

For the alarm tone of the loudspeaker the continuous time equivalent sound level is calculated. For the short signal of the airgun the single event sound level is calculated. In both cases the measurement distance was 30 m and for back calculation spherical spreading was assumed.

3   Summary and Outlook

If naval forces are called into a foreign harbour, a cooperative operation of all available sensors in the underwater domain should be achieved. In the EDA project HaPS this cooperative operation is investigated. The data of the sensors are fused and the impact of the non-lethal countermeasures on divers and on the sensors are considered. In the next experiment an additional active sonar and an USV as carrier of additional effectors will be used. The information of all sensors is then combined for classification and alarm-generation.

References

1. Harbour and Base Protection Systems, Project Arrangement (B-0387-ESM1-GC), EDA, Brussels (2010)
2. Urick, J.: Principles of Underwater Sound, 3rd edn. McGraw-Hill, New York (1983)
3. Blackman, S., Popoli, R.: Design and Analysis of Modern Tracking Systems. Artech House, Boston (1999)
4. Blackman, S.: Multiple hypothesis tracking for multiple target tracking. IEEE AES 19(1), 5–18 (2004)
5. Seget, K., Schulz, A., Heute, U.: Multi-Hypothesis Tracking and Fusion Techniques for Multistatic Active Sonar Systems. In: Proceedings of the 13th International Conference on Information Fusion, Edinburgh, UK (July 2010)
6. Chong, C.-Y., Mori, S., Barker, W.H., Chang, K.-C.: Architectures and Algorithms for Track Association and Fusion. IEEE AES Systems Magazine (January 2000)

Electro-optical Surveillance in Maritime Environments

Joerg Kushauer, Nicolai Kuenzner, Stefan Katzenbeisser, and Klaus Wingender

Diehl Defence GmbH & Co. KG
88662 Überlingen, Germany
Nicolai.Kuenzner@diehl-bgt-defence.de

Abstract. Asymmetric attacks against maritime platforms often emerge suddenly, non-predictably and from civil environments. Adequate reaction to intercept possible threats requires a quick and overall perception of the emerging situation. For this purpose close-in range surveillance systems capable of day- and night imaging can provide powerful support with respect of enhancing operator's situational awareness and therefore platform security. We report here on a staring wide area surveillance sensor. The system is suited for integration to military and civil maritime platforms.

Keywords: Electro-optic imaging system, surveillance systems, asymmetric threats.

1   Introduction

Transport on safe sea routes provides the backbone of the global economy. The increasing incidence of piracy and asymmetric attacks on ships in waters remote from coastal areas has prompted the need for enhanced onboard protection measures for both civil ships and warships. A key element to effectively countering an attack is its early detection. Over the past several years Diehl Defence has been developing a system for the automatic surveillance of a ship's surrounding at day and nighttime. Our system enables the early detection of approaching objects. Using video imagery of the surrounding, a single crew member can essentially monitor the whole ship and raise the alarm to initiate adapted counteractive measures if needed. Focusing on the detection of asymmetric threats it follows that detection range is not the only relevant measure. Rather the reaction time remaining after threat detection by the surveillance system and perception of the situation is crucial for decision takers.

2   System Layout

Sensor modules for wide angular coverage are distributed over the platform and equipped with an individual number of infrared cameras sensitive in the spectral range 7-14 μm. An example configuration for a warship of about 150 m length consists of four sensor modules containing a single imaging infrared sensor head and two sensor modules containing five imaging infrared sensor heads, respectively.

N. Aschenbruck et al. (Eds.): Future Security 2012, CCIS 318, pp. 334–336, 2012.
© Springer-Verlag Berlin Heidelberg 2012

The integration of the sensor module containing multiple sensor heads is per-formed starboard and portside into the ship's hull. Four sensor modules containing a single sensor head cover the astern and ahead domain, respectively. Together, the 14 infrared sensor heads provide coverage around the ship as depicted in Figure 1.

Fig. 1. Full coverage around ship platform obtained using six sensor modules

Image data are transmitted from the infrared sensors to the Processing Cabinet con-sisting of 19''-standard-server PC's based on multi-core architecture via an IEEE 802.3 network. Results of the image processing, namely threat data and alarm events, can be provided to men on guard and operators. The full video panoramic images of the platform surrounding together with object data are visualized on a human machine interface (HMI).

3   Signal Processing

The real-time processing of the image data obtained from electro-optical sensors in-volves the application of a variety of digital filters for object extraction. In the second step the kinematic behavior of conspicuous objects is determined, e.g. their relative motion to the own ship. Tracks of objects representing a high threat potential trigger an alarm event to be displayed on a stand-alone HMI or forwarded to the CDS. An electronic horizon-stabilization of the panoramic image is performed as well as an image enhancement.

Human operators require the contrast of the imagery to be improved because of the human eye is limited in terms of the range of contrast distinguishable. To improve the contrast, we use a range of algorithms to process the imagery. Figure 2 shows the result of employing these algorithms to enhance the human operators' ability to cap-ture the full visual content of the image. The top-left image is the raw data; simple adjustments to brightness and contrast highlight details of the area marked by the red

336   J. Kushauer et al.

rectangle whereas information outside this area is lost. Image enhancement algorithms automatically perform a local adjustment of brightness and contrast based on the image content; the result is the detailed image on the bottom right.

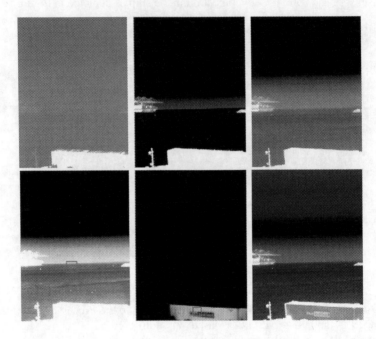

Fig. 2. Image enhancement supporting perception of detailed image content

The application of imaging sensors with an update rate of 20 Hz provides a huge advantage for decision takers over classical radar type sensors. The object type can be determined instantaneously by the operator and the estimation of the objects behaviour, eventually taking into account the behaviour of persons on board, provides a substantial contribution to situational awareness.

Acknowledgment. Authors acknowledge the support from BWB, WTD71 and Deutsche Marine.

References

[1] Künzner, N., Kushauer, J., Katzenbeißer, S.: SIMONE – Ship Infrared Monitoring, Observation and Navigation Equipment. Strategie und Technik, 52–55 (November 2008)
[2] Stockfisch, D.: Fregatte Klasse 125. Strategie und Technik, 54–59 (September 2008)
[3] Künzner, N., Kushauer, J., Katzenbeißer, S., Wingender, K.: Modern electro-optical imaging system for maritime surveillance applications. In: 2010 International Waterside Security Conference, WSS (2010)
[4] Künzner, N., Kushauer, J., Katzenbeißer, S.: An electro-optical sensor system for maritime surveillance. To be published in SPIE Newsroom

PITAS: Pirate and Terrorist Aversion System

Boris Culik[1], Thomas Lehmann[2], and Christoph Zebermann[2]

[1] F³: Forschung . Fakten . Fantasie, Heikendorf, Germany
bculik@fh3.de
[2] Raytheon Anschütz, Kiel, Germany
Thomas_Lehmann@raykiel.com

Abstract. The Pirate and Terrorist Aversion System PITAS is a joint R&D project led by Raytheon Anschütz, Kiel. It aims at improving the safety on merchant and leisure vessels as well as on offshore facilities. PITAS connects to existing infrastructure and consists of a variety of modules. The system is flexible and can be installed permanently, or temporarily from a mobile container. Key elements are:

- knowledge data base tapping various communication networks
- data analysis providing threat scenarios and routing options
- systems design integrating sensors and effectors, alarms and reactions
- novel optical sensors and repellents
- novel sonar sensor array for diver detection
- novel close-range RADAR
- track management based on radar and sonar data
- situation-specific reactions, alarms and communications
- automated pan and tilt platform for effectors
- safety and security concepts
- integrated and ergonomic human machine interface.

1   Introduction

Piracy is one of the biggest threats to international merchant shipping – and is particularly acute in tropical seas: off West and East Africa, in Southeast Asia and on the Northeast and Northwest coast of South America [1].

The International Maritime Bureau (IMB) reports ongoing high numbers of pirate attacks: in 2011 a total of 439 ships were attacked, 45 of them highjacked and 802 seafarers taken hostage by pirates. One of the nations most affected by piracy was Germany (14,5 % or 64 incidents; [1]). The Association of German Shipowners (Verband Deutscher Reeder VDR) estimates total costs associated with piracy in 2011: ransom US$ 160 m, insurance policies US$ 635 m, additional equipment US$ 500 m and costs for re-routing and high speed steaming US$ 3,3 bn [3]. Costs for vessel protection teams range from US$ 1.500 to 5.000 per day. In 2012, global numbers remain at high levels: between Jan 1 and June 7, 157 attacks were reported, 12 ships were highjacked and 188 hostages taken [2].

In addition to the hijacking of ships, holding the crew hostage, and the theft of cargo, other targets of the attackers include cash in the ship's safe, crew possessions and any portable ship's equipment. And there is no end in sight: in a recent study [4] both piracy,

N. Aschenbruck et al. (Eds.): Future Security 2012, CCIS 318, pp. 337–346, 2012.
© Springer-Verlag Berlin Heidelberg 2012

focused on economic interests, and terrorism with its underlying political interests, were seen as ongoing threats for at least another 20 years.

2   System Requirements

In a recent analysis, Engerer and Gössler [5,6] outlined the technical requirements sought by German shipping companies with respect to a system such as PITAS:

- Continuous real-time evaluation of piracy relevant websites (e.g. ICC, US Naval Intelligence, MSCHOA, others)
- Continuously updated situation analysis with the potential of route adjustment to avoid high risk areas
- improved RADAR (detection and tracking of small targets)
- improved night vision and CCTV to cover dead angles, for early detection and documentation of attack.

In addition to these requirements, which are aimed at the merchant fleet, offshore facilities (such as e.g. oil and gas, wind power) would benefit from additional sonar protection from underwater threats [5,6]. These requirements match closely the goals set by the PITAS developer team.

3   PITAS System Components

The PITAS project aims at developing an anti-piracy and counterterrorism system on merchant and leisure vessels based on a variety of modules. These can be permanently installed on board or integrated into a mobile container. The project was initiated in 2010 and will extend into 2013. It has an overall budget of Euro 5 m, 60% of which are funded by the German Federal Ministry of Economics and Technology (BMWi).

PITAS project partners are the Kiel-based companies and institutions: Raytheon-Anschütz (project management), L-3 Communications ELAC Nautik, Thales Defence and Security Systems, the Dept. of Computer Science and the Technical Faculty of Kiel University, and the Maritime Cluster Northern Germany. Further partners are the Bundeswehr Technical Center for Ships and Naval Weapons (WTD 71 and FWG) in Eckernförde and Kiel as well as WISKA CCTV in Kaltenkirchen.

3.1   Knowledge Database and Threat Evaluation System

The knowledge database and threat evaluation system are at the core of PITAS. They are based on a series of threat scenarios determined by the project's expert group, covering attacks on merchant vessels while underway, moored in a harbour or anchoring in the roads. Attack patterns are specified by several variables, including type of attack (piracy or terrorism), approach behavior, as well as the type and quantity of the deployed equipment (e.g. vessels and weapons).

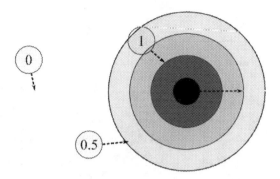

Fig. 1. Periphery of merchant vessel in a heavy traffic situation: the threat analysis yields "0" for harmless traffic, "0.5" for unidentified or approaching vessels and "1" for unidentified, approaching vessels within the first self-defense perimeter.

Both PITAS components, the knowledge database and the threat evaluation system, interact as a deductive system. Attack patterns are transformed into a computable model, where each scenario is represented by a set of if-then-rules. A wide range of potential sensors, their effectiveness and the required data analysis were thoroughly analyzed. Each trajectory, incrementally reported by the track management (sec. 3.4), is evaluated in terms of the rule base (Fig. 1). Based on the results of this evaluation, probable threat scenarios are determined and appropriate and specific reactions suggested by the system.

The proposed approach is similar to others [e.g. 7], the main difference being that PITAS must react in real-time. For that purpose, data structures and algorithms for the analysis of moving objects are adapted from the fields of moving object databases [8] and computational movement analysis [9]. Furthermore, to ensure consistency of the database as well as extensibility of the attack scenario descriptions, innovative techniques for crawling, mining and fusing textual data from the web have been developed and implemented [10].

Currently, data recorded during field tests in the Baltic Sea are used to check the performance of the system. Next steps involve the integration of real-time track management (sec 3.4) and the development of a prototype user interface. The effectiveness of the system will be investigated using a series of sophisticated test scenarios.

3.2   Integrated System Design

PITAS is open for the integration of a wide range of sensors, communication-, fire fighting-, entertainment- and information systems as well as effectors (Fig.2). One of the pre-requisites for this is the development of an appropriate and flexible interface.

Primary sensors include IMO required X- and S-Band RADAR, ARPA and AIS. Additional sensors include SONAR for diver detection, close-range radar and opto-electronical devices such as low-light, color and infra-red imaging. Identification of personnel in various sectors of the vessel, at doors and bulkheads can be implemented for access control.

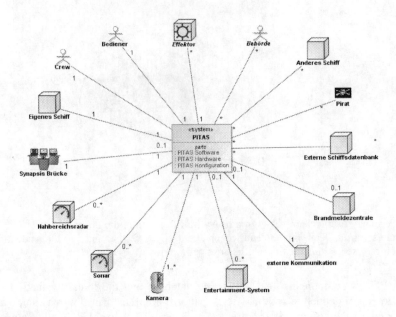

Fig. 2. Integration of sensors, effectors, users and crew into the PITAS system

Potential effectors range from acoustic alarms to electrical fence activation, high intensity light (see 3.5), acoustic and thermal sources, to water monitors or automated access denial. While these can be included into PITAS, the project focuses on developing automated target tracking as well as multi-purpose pan and tilt units for a variety of close- to medium-range, non-lethal effectors.

3.3   Track Management

The main aim of this sub-project is to improve the analysis of raw IMO-RADAR data in a way as to be able to reduce the false alarm rate and to detect small, fast moving boats and skiffs in a complex situation. We conducted sea trials in Eckernförde Bight, Baltic Sea, with two 6 m long rigid hull inflatable boats (RHIBs), while RADAR and optical equipment were installed on the jetty of the German navy testing facilities (WTD 71). Fig. 3 shows the dense traffic conditions during these trials. Added to this, there was RADAR clutter due to a passing shower (not shown). The task consisted in detecting the two RHIBs travelling at 25 - 30 kn away from and back to the detection equipment (red dotted line).

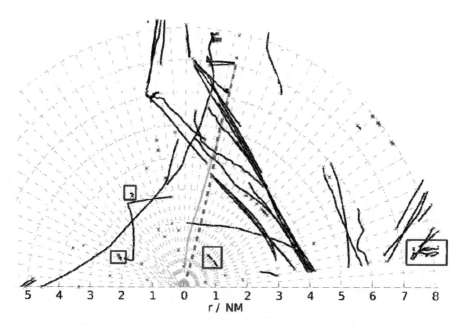

Fig. 3. RADAR tracks recorded in Eckernförde Bight in November 2011 using the newly developed small target tracker. Two RHIBS were detected 6.7 nm out (grey and red-dotted diagonal lines from 0 to about 1o'clock).

Two major algorithms, namely constant-false-alarm-rate (CFAR; [11]) and multi-hypothesis tracking (MHT; [12]) were implemented for the task. As an alternative, we tested the global nearest neighbor (GNN) approach to reduce computational effort [13] but obtained a poorer performance in a cluttered environment. MHT was modified using adaptive clutter density [14] to improve false track elimination and a two-stage gating procedure was implemented to enhance computation time [15]. As a result, maximum detection distance of the RHIBs was successfully increased to 6.7 nm.

In the next step, a reduction of the time required for data analysis and improvement of false track elimination will be pursued. The goal is to achieve real-time data acquisition and filtering. Further information on the detection and tracking algorithms used in PITAS can be found in this volume [15].

3.4   Alarm and Reaction System

Acquisition of a wide range of data by the knowledge data base yields a continuously updated situation analysis. This entails the requirement for a graded and situation specific alarm scheme based on the evaluation of the threat level (Fig. 4). The alarm doctrine, the specification and classification of alarms, their representation on the human machine interface (see 3.9), the devices employed in alarming crew and other personnel are key elements of this work package.

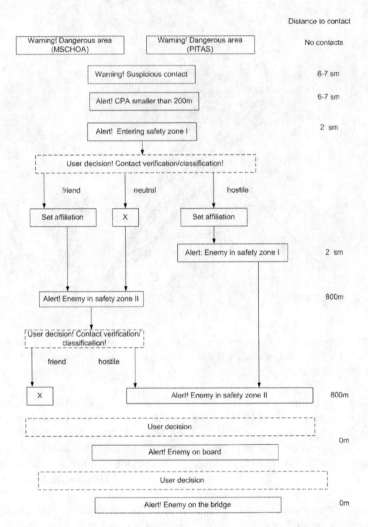

Fig. 4. Graded alarm scheme depending on the proximity of a detected threat and on a continuously updated situation analysis

3.5   Detection and Reaction System

Detection of piracy threats by merchant vessels is to date based on the ships RADAR as well as on human lookouts. PITAS aims at improving this by integrating a newly developed daylight and infrared camera with automated image analysis. One of the functions of this system will be the automated focus and lock-on on a pre-determined element. This can be a pirate skiff or a man at sea, which adds an interesting feature for the improvement of safety on board.

The fully marinized cameras include a heater and windshield wiper system. They are mounted on a pan and tilt head stabilized mechanically and electronically and remote-controlled via the human-machine interface. The full system will be tested on board a ferry line operating in the Baltic Sea.

The aim of the newly developed optical **reaction** system is to temporarily blind potential attackers from a distance of up to 200 m and to induce temporary illness by pulsed light [e.g. 16]. The powerful floodlight consists of a 1000W Xenon-Lamp, with a light density of approx. 60.000 Candela /cm² (the sun at full noon reaches 100-150.000 Candela/cm²). It is installed on the same pan and tilt head as the above described cameras and commanded by the PITAS system or the operator on the bridge.

Besides carrying the optical system, the pan and tilt head may carry other effectors. To be truly modular and to enable a wide series of applications, a real-time software was developed for the determination and implementation of contact and elevation angles based on the ships reference point, as well as for roll, pitch and yaw compensation of the carrying vessel. These are pre-requisites for the automated deployment of e.g. water canons. A functional pan and tilt subsystem was tested successfully in conjunction with the Raytheon-Anschütz navigation bridge by simulating a variety of realistic on-board situations.

3.6   Safety and Security Concept

A safety and security concept is of paramount importance, since PITAS includes elements aimed at effectively repelling attackers at close range: any unwanted incidents harming crew or passengers must be excluded at the early planning stage.

The analysis includes the determination of threat levels of the various system modules according to the 4 safety integrity levels (SIL). Based on this, we develop strategies and methods for the reduction of potential hazards to acceptable levels. For example according to IEC 61508 [17], it is acceptable if in 10% of all vehicles the airbags do not activate after a crash (SIL 1). However, the same norm only tolerates the unmotivated activation of airbags in 7^{-10} airbags per hour in the entire vehicle fleet (SIL 3), to prevent unwanted accident hazards.

3.7   Sonar Sensor Array

The requirement to detect small underwater threats such as divers led to the development of novel detector arrays. In this sub-project we have selected and characterized appropriate emitters and receivers, developed a new concept for a sonar array including element position and coupling and focused on further developing the van-Atta antenna array (Fig.5).

The antenna array invented by L. C. Van Atta in 1959 [18] is known in the fields of satellite communication [19] and bullet detection [20]. Its main principle is the ability to automatically focus the transmission energy on a target. We have developed a numerical simulation on the basis of Matlab and Bellhop, conducted first simulations with new signal forms and reduced feedback.

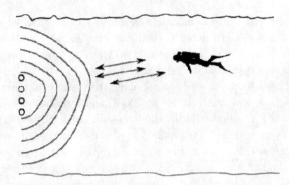

Fig. 5. Diver detection by self-focusing sonar array based on the van-Atta priciple

First results of the simulation indicate a high capability of detecting small moving targets and led to the submission of two patents. At current we are developing new transmission signals, testing a laboratory prototype and preparing for performance tests during sea trials. These are required for the comparison and optimization of various detection algorithms.

3.8   Close-Range RADAR

RADAR systems currently operated on board of merchant vessels are unable to detect small targets at very close range. At the same time, the ships crew is limited and in scenarios with multiple skiffs attacking simultaneously, it is of paramount importance to keep track and to prioritize the different potential aggressors.

For this purpose, we designed and built a new type of close range 34 GHz RADAR sensor with 420 Msps sampling rate in 7 channels and a corresponding signal analysis system. In the next step, we aim at reducing clutter in the near field (20-25 dB) and improving the detection algorithm of the close-range RADAR.

3.9   Human Machine Interface (HMI)

The interface between PITAS and the safety personnel on board is the human machine Interface (HMI) which can be integrated into the ships bridge (Fig. 6) or only temporarily made available together with other PITAS modules using a transportable container. The HMI depicts maps, tracks and target information, warnings and alarms, thus combining   and fusing all the elements of PITAS.

The HMI communicates between sensors and effectors, permits the manual input of data and commands, suggests appropriate reactions, initiates automated (and low level) processes, alarms and communications and requests confirmation for proposed higher level reactions. The HMI is currently being designed by Raytheon-Anschütz on the basis of its standard merchant vessel bridge and mobile surveillance systems and will successively integrate all PITAS modules as these become available.

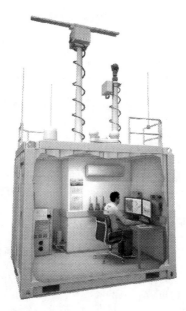

Fig. 6. The mobile, containerized human machine interface integrates all elements of PITAS and is the interface to the safety officer. It depicts maps, AIS and visual information, integrates remote controls and response systems.

References

1. Bundespolizei See: Piraterieberieht der Bundespolizei See 4. Quartal 2011 / Jahresbericht 2011. Bundespolizei See, Sachbereich 12, Polizeiliche Auswertung und Analyse (PAA), Wieksbergstr. 54/0, 23730 Neustadt in Holstein (2012)
2. ICC 2012: International Chamber of Commerce, Piracy news and figures (2012), http://www.icc-ccs.org/piracy-reporting-centre/piracynewsafigures
3. Wallrabenstein, T.: Rechtliche Rahmenbedingungen für die Pirateriebekämpfung. Verband Deutscher Reeder. Kolloquium Seefahrt heute- zwischen Freiheit und Geiselhaft FH Flensburg (March 22, 2012)
4. Jopp, H.-D., Kaestner, R.: Eine globale Übersichtsanalyse von möglicher politisch oder ökonomisch motivierter maritimer Gewalt in den nächsten 20 Jahren. PiraT Arbeitspapier zur Maritimen Sicherheit Nr. 15, Hamburg (2012)
5. Engerer, H., Gössler, M.: Maritimer Terrorismus und Piraterie aus Sicht der deutschen Versicherungswirtschaft – Ergebnisse einer Befragung deutscher Transportversicherer. PiraT Arbeitspapier zur Maritimen Sicherheit Nr. 12, Hamburg (2011)
6. Engerer, H., Gössler, M.: Piraterie und maritimer Terrorismus aus Sicht deutscher Reeder – Ergebnisse einer Befragung. PiraT Arbeitspapier zur Maritimen Sicherheit Nr. 11, Hamburg (2011)
7. Van Hage, W.R., Malaisé, V., de Vries, G., Schreiber, G., van Someren, M.: Combining ship trajectories and semantics with the simple event model (SEM). In: Proceedings of the 1st ACM International Workshop on Events in Multimedia, pp. 73–80. ACM (2009)

8. Güting, R.H., Schneider, M.: Moving Object Databases. Morgan Kaufmann, San Francisco (2005)
9. Laube, P., van Kreveld, M., Imfeld, S.: Finding REMO - detecting relative motion patterns in geospatial lifelines. In: Fisher, P.F. (ed.) Proceedings of the 11th International Symposium on Spatial Data Handling Developments in Spatial Data Handling, pp. 201–214. Springer, Heidelberg (2004)
10. Böhm, M.: Integration von Informationen zu Piratenangriffen aus heterogenen Internetquellen mit einer Text-Mining-Komponente. Bachelor Thesis, Christian-Albrechts-University, Kiel (2011)
11. Skolnik, M.: Radar Handbook. McGraw Hill, Inc. (1990)
12. Daun, M., Ehlers, F.: Tracking Algorithms for Multistatic Sonar Systems. EURASIP Journal on Advances in Signal Processing 35, 1–28 (2010)
13. Konstantinova, P., Udvarev, A., Semerdjiev, T.: A Study of a Target Tracking Algorithm Using Global Nearest Neighbor Approach. In: Proceedings of the 4th International Conference on Computer Systems and Technologies: e-Learning, CompSysTech 2003, New York, USA, pp. 290–295 (2003)
14. Wilkens, K., Nguyen, V.D., Heute, U.: Adaptive Clutter Density in Multi-Hypothesis Tracking. In: Proc. IEEE ISIF GI Workshop Sensor Data Fusion, Berlin, Germany (2011)
15. Nguyen, V.D.: Small-Target Radar Detection and Tracking Within the PITAS Hard- and Software Environment. In: Aschenbruck, N., et al. (eds.) Future Security 2012. CCIS, vol. 318, pp. 335–346. Springer, Heidelberg (2012)
16. Harding, G., Harding, P., Wilkins, A.: Wind turbines, flicker, and photosensitive epilepsy: Characterizing the flashing that precipitate seizures and optimizing guidelines to prevent them. Epilepsia 49(6), 1095–1098 (2008)
17. DIN EN 61508-0: Funktionale Sicherheit sicherheitsbezogener elektrischer/elektronischer/programmierbarer elektronischer Systeme; Teil 0: Funktionale Sicherheit und die IEC 61508
18. Van Atta, L.C.: Electromagnetic Reflector, U.S Patent No. 2,908,002 (October 6, 1959)
19. Belfi, C., Rothenberg, C., Schwartzman, L., Tilley, R.E., Willis, A.: A satellite data transmission antenna. Transactions on IEEE Antennas and Propagation 2, 200–206 (1964)
20. Gupta, S.: Retro-directive noise correlation radar with extremely low acquisition time. In: IEEE Microwave Symposium, vol. 1, pp. 599–602 (2003)

Small-Target Radar Detection and Tracking within the PITAS Hard- and Software Environment

Viet Duc Nguyen

Christian-Albrechts-Universität zu Kiel, Kiel, Germany
vng@tf.uni-kiel.de
http://www.dss.tf.uni-kiel.de

Abstract. The number of piracy attacks on cargo ships has increased significantly over the past years. Countermeasures often rely on early threat detection.
Hence it must be possible to track small targets such as pirates' skiffs. Navigation
radar systems for cargo ships are not designed to do so. Advanced radar tracking
systems may be capable of small-target tracking but may lack in affordability for
ship owners. Thus, a software-based extension is more cost efficient.

In this paper an overview of algorithms for detection and automatic tracking of
small targets using a navigation radar is presented, and all sufficient steps to process raw radar video up to final tracks are given. Detection and tracking is carried
out by Constant-False-Alarm-Rate and Multi-Hypothesis Tracking approaches,
respectively. The way of implementing these methods given here ensures long-
range tracking of small objects. Tracking results are obtained by applying the
methods to a real radar dataset.

Keywords: Small-Target Tracking, Constant-False-Alarm-Rate, Multi-Hypothesis
Tracking, Piracy.

1 Introduction

Piracy attacks, as they occur for example off the coast of Somalia, are an increasing
problem for merchant shipping. Every year hundreds of ships are attacked and seafarers'
lives endangerd. The resulting costs are not only caused by ransom payments but also
by insurance, re-routing of ships or protective steps taken by ship companies and they
are estimated to go up to billions of dollars.

Possible countermeasures such as anti-piracy maneuvers, sending a distress call or
approaching a citadel rely on early threat detection. The project PITAS (Ger.: *PIraterie-
und TerrorAbwehr auf Seeschiffen*, Engl.: Pirate and Terrorist Aversion System) is a
joint project of the university of Kiel and German companies[1] and addresses the problem of piracy. Besides implementing defense technology, such as sonic weapons or
water cannons, PITAS also seeks for methods of threat detection. A major task within
threat detection is the automatic tracking of possible attackers. Here, the focus is on

---

[1] Thales Deutschland GmbH, Raytheon Anschütz GmbH, L-3 Communications ELAC Nautik
GmbH, Wiska GmbH.

N. Aschenbruck et al. (Eds.): Future Security 2012, CCIS 318, pp. 347–358, 2012.
© Springer-Verlag Berlin Heidelberg 2012

the tracking of small targets such as the fast skiffs used by pirates. The problem is that radars of freighters, oil tankers or fishing vessels are rather made for navigation and detection of other large objects for collision avoidance than for small-target tracking. Replacing the existing navigation radar system of a ship by a more powerful and advanced radar system is a costly solution and employing additional personnel to monitor the radar display is even more expensive. To solve this specific problem, PITAS develops a software extension to enhance the navigation radar's detection and automatic tracking capability. This extension, i.e. the tracker, should have long-range capabilities and avoid false tracks as much as possible. In addition, it must not be too complex, since it is supposed to be easily adaptable to other radar systems.

In this paper a first approach of such a tracker is described and all procedures to process a raw radar video up to final tracks are given. A Multi-Hypothesis tracking (MHT) algorithm is used for tracking [1]. Modifications, namely two-step-gating and distance-dependent probability of detection, are implemented to improve tracking results or accelerate the system. Tracking results are obtained by applying the algorithm to a radar dataset recorded at a sea trial and assessed by means of tracking-performance metrics [2]. The structure of the paper is as follows:

Sec. 2 provides information about the radar system and the sea trial. Sec. 3 describes the process of generating contacts out of raw radar images using Constant-False-Alarm-Rate methods (CFAR). The next section presents the MHT algorithm and its modifications. The results of the tracking simulations are shown in Sec. 5. A conclusion and an outlook are given in Sec. 6.

2   Radar System and Test Environment

The sea trial took place in the Eckernförde Bight[2] in the Baltic Sea in northern Germany. In the considered scenario two rigid-hulled inflatable boats (RHIB) ($2 - 3$ m wide, 6 m long) were approaching the position of the radar at a speed of about 30 kn, starting at a buoy 7.2 NM away. This scenario simulates an attack by skiffs on open sea. The objective is to track the boats as early as possible.

Besides the two boats many non-trial-related objects such as freighters, sailing boats or buoys were in the surveillance area of the radar. On the day of the trial, the sea state was 2 and it was partly cloudy. During the mentioned scenario rain showers occured.

The used X-band navigation radar was positioned about 15 m above waterline. Its pulse width is 250 ns, the beamwidth is $1°$ and it has 25 kW peak power. After return echoes from targets are received by the antenna and processed by the signal processing unit of the radar, the resulting data stream delivers normalized values of the echo power for each of the 8192×4096 cells (#range bins $\times$ #azimut bins), i.e. the radar image (s. Fig. 1). Each range bin's size is of 1.875 m and each azimut bin covers $360/4096$ degree. This image, usually the input data for plan-position indicators, serves as a base for further detection and tracking procedures. As the rotation speed of the radar is 24 rpm, the image refreshes every 2.5 s.

---

[2] http://maps.google.com/?ll=54.5,10&z=12

Fig. 1. Example of an raw radar image on the day of the sea trial. The coastline of the Eckernförde Bight[2] is clearly visible. Red areas indicate strong radar echoes and black areas (background) indicate weak echoes. Extended blue areas indicate clouds.

3   Detection

Before MHT (s. Sec. 4) can be applied, contact data has to be derived from the radar image data, i.e. potential targets have to be detected on the base of the radar image. As such a decision has to be made whether a cell's value refers to a target echo or not (clutter or noise). A well-known method which is used in this work is the Cell-Average Constant-False-Alarm-Rate (CA-CFAR, short: CFAR) approach [3]. Before applying CFAR, the image cells' values are compared to a threshold and only cells whose values exceed the threshold are considered for CFAR-processing. There is always a trade-off between a high threshold D_T which results in a small number of false detections but also small number of true detections, and a low threshold which causes more false detections but also gains a higher probability of target detection. Here, $D_T(r)$ is chosen range-dependent and decreases stepwise as the range r increases.

Despite thresholding there are still 'active' (still in the calculation process) not-target-related cells, caused by areas with a return echo which is stronger than the threshold D_T, e.g., cloudy areas or areas with much seaclutter. Compared to return echos of ships, echos from these areas are also usually widely visible over the radar image due to their large spatial dimension. CA-CFAR takes advantage of this fact by comparing a cell's value with the average signal power of its surrounding area. Only if a cell's value $\theta(r_\ell, \varphi_m)$ exceeds the average $\overline{\theta}_s(r_\ell, \varphi_m)$ by a factor α it is considered to be a detection (s. Fig. 2):

$$\theta(r_\ell, \varphi_m) > \alpha \overline{\theta}_s(r_\ell, \varphi_m). \tag{1}$$

$\overline{\theta}_s$ is given by

$$\overline{\theta}_s(r_\ell, \varphi_m) = \begin{cases} \frac{\psi_1 + \psi_2}{L} & , \text{for } s = 0 \\ \frac{max(\psi_1, \psi_2)}{L/2} & , \text{for } s = 1 \\ \frac{min(\psi_1, \psi_2)}{L/2} & , \text{for } s = 2 \end{cases} \tag{2}$$

with L being the number of reference cells and ψ_s being the sum of the reference cells (s. Fig. 2). The determination of α depends on the desired purpose of the CFAR implementation. The higher α is, the less false contacts occur, but also the probability of missing target contacts increases. The choice of s depends on the detection environment. E.g., if high sensitivity is required, s should be 2. Adjacent cells of the cell which is tested by CFAR are called guard cells. They must not be included as reference cells as in case of a target, they may include echo power of the target as well. The number of guard cells or their corresponding spatial length, respectively, should cover at least the radar pulse length.

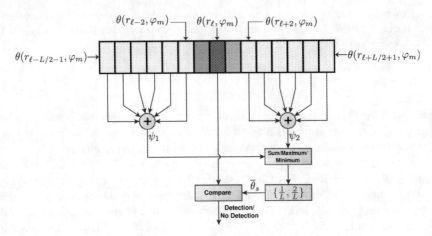

Fig. 2. Principle of CA-CFAR [4]. Adjacent cells (guard cells) of the tested cell are not taken into account as reference cells. The figure shows one guard cell on each side. In general, the number of guard cells depends on the pulse length and the resolution of the radar image. The block $\{1/L, 2/L\}$ indicates the different cell-average calculations depending on s.

4 Multi-Hypothesis Tracking

MHT is a widely known approach for tracking in cluttered environments. There is actually not one specific MHT-algorithm but there are different variants of the MHT approach [5]. The one used here is precisely described in [1].

The basic principle of MHT is to create differently weighted hypotheses about the state of a target track. Hypotheses are generated by associating contacts to existing hypotheses without knowing *a priori* whether the contact is target-originated or a false contact (clutter). The decision, which of the hypotheses is the true trajectory is postponed until sufficient information is available. Despite high clutter densities and missing detections MHT can generate tracks of target-originated contacts. In addition, MHT includes an estimation step to compensate noisy measurements and to incorporate kinematic models of the objects which are to be tracked. Estimation is realized by the Unscented Kalman filter (UKF) [6], a nonlinear variant of the Kalman Filter. This is neccessary due to the nonlinear relation between the radar measurements and the target state. As the number of contacts within one scan may be high, the number of hypotheses increases quickly with time. Hence different methods such as gating, pruning and merging are necessary to limit the number of hypotheses.

4.1   Kalman Filter

Kinetic Model and Measurement. A state-space representation is used to model the system. The *Nearly Constant Velocity* (NCV) model is chosen to be the kinematic model for the target motion. As the state estimation is done in a 2-dimensional Cartesian plane, the state vector at time step t_k is defined by

$$\boldsymbol{x}_k = [p_x, v_x, p_y, v_y]^\top \tag{3}$$

and the system dynamic is linear:

$$\boldsymbol{x}_k = \boldsymbol{A}\boldsymbol{x}_{k-1} + \boldsymbol{w}_{k-1}. \tag{4}$$

p_x and p_y are the coordinates of position and v_x and v_y are the corresponding velocities. $\boldsymbol{A}$ is the system matrix, and the process noise, representing deviations from the assumed kinematic model, is represented by the white Gaussian noise $\boldsymbol{w}$.

As detections are given in polar coordinates, the measurement vector $\boldsymbol{y}_k$ consists of the bearing φ and the distance r between receiver and target:

$$\boldsymbol{y}_k = [r, \varphi]^\top. \tag{5}$$

The nonlinear functional relation between the state vector $\boldsymbol{x}_k$ and the measurement vector $\boldsymbol{y}_k$ is given by the function h and added with white Gaussian noise $\boldsymbol{v}$ to model measurement errors:

$$\boldsymbol{y}_k = h(\boldsymbol{x}_k) + \boldsymbol{v}_k. \tag{6}$$

$\boldsymbol{A}$ and h are chosen according to [7] and [8].

Filtering. In order to incorporate the process noise $\boldsymbol{w}$ and the measurement noise $\boldsymbol{v}$ into the estimation, the Kalman filter is used. Hence estimation is carried out in two steps: time update and measurement update.

The time update step calculates an *a priori* estimation $\hat{\boldsymbol{x}}_{k|k-1}$ of the target state $\boldsymbol{x}_k$ by considering the kinematic model. As indicated by the subscript $k|k-1$, this step takes all measurements up to time step t_{k-1} into account. The *a posteriori* estimation $\hat{x}_{k|k}$ is calculated within the measurement update step which considers all measurements up to time step t_k. In this paper the Unscented Kalman filter [6] is used since the relation between x_k and y_k is not linear.

4.2 Data Association and Hypotheses Weighting

Since it is not known *a priori* whether a contact is target-originated or clutter, in principle all contacts are considered in the process of hypotheses forming [9]. Given a set $X_{k-1} = \{\hat{x}^1_{k-1|k-1}, \hat{x}^2_{k-1|k-1}, ..., \hat{x}^{\hat{n}_{k-1}}_{k-1|k-1}\}$ of $\hat{n}_{k-1}$ hypotheses states at time step t_{k-1}, subsequent hypothesis states X_k are obtained by associating each hypothesis of X_{k-1} with each of the n_k contacts at t_k of the set $Y_k = \{y^1_k, y^2_k, ..., y^{n_k}_k\}$.

Each hypothesis state i is weighted according to its probability of being the actual target state. In doing so one has to calculate the preliminary weights $\hat{\omega}$ first [10]:

$$\hat{\omega}^{ij}_k = \begin{cases} \omega^i_{k-1} \frac{P_d}{f_c} \mathcal{N}(y^j_k; h_{UT}(\hat{x}^i_{k|k-1}), S^{ij}_k), & 1 \le j \le n_k, \\ \omega^i_{k-1}(1 - P_d), & j = 0, \end{cases} \quad 1 \le i \le \hat{n}_{k-1}. \quad (7)$$

$j = 0$ considers the hypothesis of no contacts belonging to the target. $h_{UT}(\hat{x}^i_{k|k-1})$ is the result of the Unscented Transformation of the prediction $\hat{x}^i_{k|k-1}$ of the Kalman filter. Furthermore, S is the innovation covariance which is calculated by the Kalman filter during the measurement update. P_d and f_c denote the assumed probability of detection of the targets and clutter density, respectively. Their parameterization is described in Sec. 4.4.

By normalizing the preliminary weights, the final weights are obtained:

$$\omega^{ij}_k = \frac{\hat{\omega}^{ij}_k}{\sum_{i=1}^{\hat{n}_{k-1}} \sum_{j=0}^{n_k} \hat{\omega}^{ij}_k}. \quad (8)$$

As indicated by (7) the number of hypotheses increases by the factor $n_k + 1$ at each time step. This exponential growth would lead to an incomputability of the algorithm. Hence different techniques of hypothesis management such as gating, pruning, and merging are used [1] and further described in Sec. 4.3. In addition, confirmation and deletion of tracks as part of the track management of MHT is carried out by means of Sequential Track Extraction [11].

4.3 Hypothesis Management

The task of hypotheses management is to reduce the number of hypotheses to a computable extent. One measure is pruning by which either the number of hypotheses within a track is limited to a fixed number of the most weighted hypotheses [12] or all hypotheses with weight smaller than a suitable threshold are terminated [10]. In merging procedures, similar hypotheses (state vector and covariance) are either merged together or the less weighted one is simply removed as it is done in this work.

Furthermore, unlikely associations of contacts and hypotheses can be avoided by gating [5]. Here, a statistical gate is formed around the predicted measurement $\hat{\boldsymbol{y}}_k = h_{UT}(\hat{\boldsymbol{x}}_{k|k-1})$. A contact j is only considered for association with hypotheses i if it meets the condition

$$\left[\boldsymbol{y}_k^j - \hat{\boldsymbol{y}}_k\right]^\top \left(\boldsymbol{S}_k^{ij}\right)^{-1} \left[\boldsymbol{y}_k^j - \hat{\boldsymbol{y}}_k\right] \leq G \qquad (9)$$

with G indicating the gate size and the left side of the inequation being the Mahalanobis distance. Although gating is a powerful tool for hypotheses reduction, it is very time consuming on its own due to the inversion of the matrix $\boldsymbol{S}$ which has to be done for every potential contact-hypothesis association. Hence in this paper a two-step-gating (2SG) is used to accelerate the gating procedure. In the first step contact j and hypothesis i must meet the requirement

$$|\hat{p}_{x,k}^i - \tilde{p}_{x,k}^j| < l_x \quad \wedge \quad |\hat{p}_{y,k}^i - \tilde{p}_{y,k}^j| < l_y \qquad (10)$$

with $\hat{p}_{x,k}^i, \hat{p}_{y,k}^i$ being the position of the predicted state vector $\hat{\boldsymbol{x}}_{k|k-1}^i$ and $\tilde{p}_{x,k}^j, \tilde{p}_{y,k}^j$ being the Cartesian coordinates of corresponding contact j. Only if this condition is fulfilled the pair ij of hypothesis and contact goes on to the statistical gating given in (9). Hence the number of Mahalanobis distance calculations and also matrix inversions can be reduced. Furthermore, in this work the first gating step is efficiently implemented by using Quicksort. To assure that the first step does not influence the gating result but only accelerate the gating procedure the limits l_x and l_y must be set sufficiently large [8].

4.4 Parameterization

The choice of the parameters f_c and P_d in (7) effects the hypothesis weights and therefore the hypotheses and the track management, i.e., track confirmation and deletion. Thus, their setting influences the tracking result significantly. In order to adapt the parameters to the tracking environment, they are determined as follows:

The clutter density f_c is the spatial density of false contacts. It can be low at certain spots and high at other spots and it is also time variant. To take this fact into account, f_c is calculated adaptively following the idea of density contributions [9].

Usually, navigation radars of cargo ships are made to detect other cargo ships or in general large targets to avoid collisions. Due to the objects large radar cross sections they are almost always detectable and the corresponding probability of detection can be considered to be very high and constant over time and range. This does not apply to small targets. Due to their small radar cross section their detectability decreases as the distance increases. This effect is even enhanced when pitching occurs as it changes the radar cross section. Hence a range-dependent probability of detection $P_d(r)$ is used to take this issue into account.

5   Results Analysis and Discussion

5.1   Tracking Result

The final tracking result is shown in Fig. 3 with the track of the two boats being marked in red. The assessment of the result is based on existing tracking-performance metrics [2]. Since the dataset was recorded at a sea trial and not synthesized, the track probability of detection TPD can only be obtained for the "skiffs" and not for any other targets. Furthermore, the number of false tracks can not be quantified precisely as it is not known for sure, which track is a false track and which one originates from a real target (e.g., ships, buoys). Nevertheless, the number of false tracks is most likely very low as almost all tracks shown in Fig. 3 are not zig-zag shaped and last for a long duration. Clutter-originated tracks are rather short tracks. The TPD_p, the ratio of the time the boats are tracked to the time they were present, is about 93%. Considering the time between the occurence of the first and the last contact of the boats, the TPD_c is 96%. Regarding the tracking range, the tracking of the boats starts at 7 NM distance and track confirmation is achieved at 6.75 NM or at the 14th scan after the appearance of the first target contact, respectively. The corresponding latency L is 32.5 s. No track loss occures and hence the track fragmentation is 0.

Although two boats were used in the trial, only one track exists. The reasons are the high radar-pulse width and wide beam angle (s. Sec. 2) and, especially, the fact that the boats were driving very close to each other.

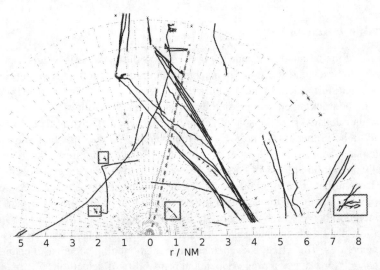

Fig. 3. Tracking result using the contacts shown in Fig. 6. The track of the "skiffs" is marked in red (dashed line). Potential false tracks are marked by blue rectangles. Land areas are already cut out but can be seen in Fig. 5. One track is marked in grey to ensure visibility of the skiffs' track.

5.2   Influence of Distance-Dependent Detection Thresholds

Figs. 4, 5, and 6 show contacts obtained by using the detecion methods described in Sec. 3. Each of the figures use different detection thresholds. In Fig. 4, D_T is very high which results in fewer contacts compared to the other two figures. Not only false contacts but also likely target-originated contacts are missing. Especially, the contacts of the RHIBs are missing (red ellipse). In Fig. 5, a low threshold D_T is chosen and hence the target contacts of the boats are visible even in far distance (narrow red ellipse). As a drawback, the number of false contacts increases (big blue ellipses) significantly. Fig. 6 shows the detection result using range-dependent thresholds $D_T(r)$ with values which are high in close range and decrease as the distance increases. Hence the number of false contacts is small in close range but increases with distance (big blue ellipses). However, the advantage is that the RHIB-contacts are visible up to the 7 NM range (narrow red ellipse). As this contact data has a suitable balance between the number of false contacts and target-originated contacts, it is chosen to be the input data for obtaining the tracking results given in Sec. 5.1.

It is likely that the benefits of range-dependent thresholds can also be achieved by choosing an overall low detection threshold but a higher CFAR-factor α. This option is not investigated since CFAR-calculations have a higher computational load than a matching of a cell's value with pre-determined thresholds. Hence it is more time efficient to eliminate cells by setting range-dependent thresholds first and then applying CFAR.

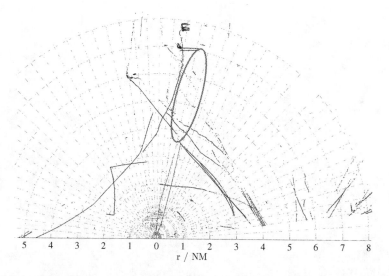

Fig. 4. All contacts of the scenario using a high detection threshold and CFAR. Very few false contacts occur compared to Fig. 5 and 6 but the desired target contacts of the RHIBs are missing (red ellipse).

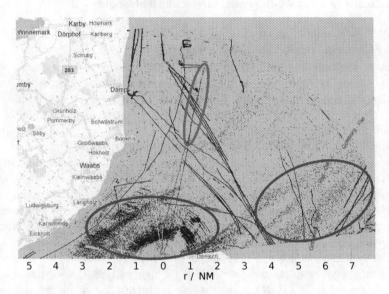

Fig. 5. All contacts of the scenario using a low detection threshold and CFAR. The number of false contacts is extremely high (big blue ellipses). Target contacts are clearly visible (narrow red ellipse).

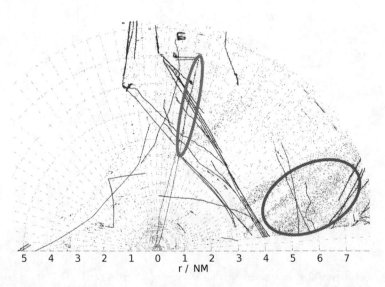

Fig. 6. All contacts of the scenario using range-dependent detection thresholds and CFAR. False contacts occur only in far distance (big blue ellipse). Target contacts are clearly visible (narrow red ellipse).

5.3   Speedup of the Two-Step-Gating

A significant acceleration of the tracking system is achieved by applying the 2SG proce-dure described in Sec. 4.3. By using 2SG, the number of the calculations of Mahalono-bis distances is cut down by 98.8%. Although additional time is needed for the first gating step, the total time saving comes to 92%, i.e., it is about 12 times faster. The time for the total tracking procedure was reduced by 49.5%. A crucial and necessary part of implementing the first gating step efficiently is the usage of sorting algorithms such as Quicksort.

5.4   Discussion on Performance Metrics

Using the performance metrics given in [2], trackings results are assessed either by analysing the quality of target-tracks or by counting the number of false tracks. As long as the tracking of controlled objects such as the RHIBs is analyzed, in general, the analysis of the target-track quality is possible. In Sec. 5.1 the target-track-quality perfor-mance metrics are the track probability of detection TPD, the latency L, and the track fragmentation rate TFR, and they can be obtained without problems. As mentioned above, the number of false tracks cannot be counted and hence the tracker's ability to avoid false-tracks can only be estimated. This performance metric is only suitable if reference data is given. So, although the given performance metrics are well known and widely used for different tracking algorithms (e.g. in [12–16]), one must consider that a complete analysis of the tracking results would only be possible if the scenario was fully controlled or simulated.

6   Conclusion

In this paper all steps for processing a raw radar video up to final tracks are given. It is shown that it is possible to enhance a navigation radar's ability for small-target track-ing with long-range capability without actually replacing the hardware but only by a software extension. The detection and tracking extension uses range-dependent detec-tion thresholds, CFAR methods, and an MHT algorithm. The range-dependent detec-tion thresholds improve the quality of contact data significantly and the implementation can be easily adapted to other radars. Furthermore, the implemented two-step-gating method is proven to be a lot faster compared to the usage of statistical gating only. The complete system is applied to a radar dataset recorded at a sea trial. In the scenario of the trial in which two RHIBs approached the radar position, the two boats can be tracked in a distance of 6.75 NM (12.5 km). Despite false contacts the occurance of false tracks is extremely rare.

So far, the tracking system is applied to recorded data. In the next step the system will be modified to be able to take the image data directly from the radar system. Tests have to be done in order to further validate the tracking system's ability of small-target tracking and false-tracks termination as well as to ensure real time capability. As only one track is calculated although two boats are in the scenario, additional investigations are necessary in order to separate them as far as possible. The final step within PITAS is the incorporation of additional sensors such as sonar, other radars (e.g. S-band), and camera into the tracking and thus developing an efficient sensor-fusion system.

Acknowledgements. This work was made possible by Thomas Lehmann and Carsten Reiter from Raytheon Anschütz who organized the sea trial. The author would like to thank Kathrin Wilkens for helpful discussions and support.

This work was supported by the Federal Ministry of Economics and Technology (Germany).

References

1. Daun, M., Ehlers, F.: Tracking Algorithms for Multistatic Sonar Systems. EURASIP Journal on Advances in Signal Processing, 35:1–35:28 (February 2010)
2. Coraluppi, S., Grimmett, D., de Theije, P.: Benchmark Evaluation of Multistatic Trackers. In: Proceedings of the 9th International Conference on Information Fusion, Florence, Italy, pp. 1–7 (July 2006)
3. Skolnik, M.: Radar Handbook. McGraw Hill, Inc. (1990)
4. Ludloff, A.: Praxiswissen Radar und Radarsignalverarbeitung. Viewegs Fachbücher der Technik. Vieweg (1998)
5. Bar-Shalom, Y., Tian, X., Willet, P.K.: Tracking and Data Fusion: A Handbook of Algorithms. YBS Publishing (2011)
6. Julier, S., Uhlmann, J.K.: Unscented Filtering and Nonlinear Estimation. Proceedings of the IEEE 92, 401–422 (2004)
7. Bar-Shalom, Y., Li, X.R.: Estimation and Tracking: Principles, Techniques, and Software. Artech House, Inc., Norwood (1993)
8. Blackman, S., Popoli, R.: Design and Analysis of Modern Tracking Systems. Artech House radar library. Artech House (1999)
9. Wilkens, K., Nguyen, V.D., Heute, U.: Adaptive Clutter Density in Multi-Hypothesis Tracking. In: Proc. IEEE ISIF GI Workshop Sensor Data Fusion 2011, Berlin, Germany (2011)
10. Koch, W., Koller, J., Ulmke, M.: Ground target tracking and road map extraction. ISPRS Journal of Photogrammetry & Remote Sensing 61(3–4), 197–208 (2006)
11. van Keuk, G.: Sequential Track Extraction. IEEE Transactions on Aerospace and Electronic Systems 34(4), 1135–1148 (1998)
12. Seget, K., Schulz, A., Heute, U.: Multi-Hypothesis Tracking and Fusion Techniques for Multistatic Active Sonar Systems. In: Proceedings of the 13th International Conference on Information Fusion, Edinburgh, Scotland, pp. 1–8 (July 2010)
13. Coraluppi, S., Carthel, C.: Distributed Tracking in Multistatic Sonar. IEEE Transactions on Aerospace and Electronic Systems, 41(3), 1138–1147 (2005)
14. Seget, K., Schulz, A., Heute, U.: Maneuver-Adaptive Multi-Hypothesis Tracking for Active Sonar Systems. In: Proc. IEEE ISIF GI Workshop Sensor Data Fusion 2010, pp. 818–823 (2010)
15. Georgescu, R., Schoenecker, S., Willet, P.: GM-CPHD and MLPDA Applied to the SEABAR07 and TNO-Blind Multi-static Sonar Data. In: 12th International Conference on Information Fusion, FUSION 2009, pp. 1851–1858 (July 2009)
16. Grimmett, D., Coraluppi, S., La Cour, B., Hempel, C., Lang, T., de Theije, P., Willett, P.: MSTWG Multistatic Tracker Evaluation Using Simulated Scenario Data Sets. In: 11th International Conference on Information Fusion, pp. 1–8 (2008)

Open and Interoperable Maritime Surveillance Framework Set to Improve Sea-Borders Control

Cengiz Erbas[1], Fulya Tuncer Cetin[1], Burcu Yilmaz[1], Erdem Akagunduz[1], Yildiray Kabak[2], and Aykut Bulca[2]

[1] ASELSAN Elektronik Sanayi ve Ticaret A.Ş. PK.30 Etlik, Ankara, 06011, Turkey
{cerbas,ftuncer,buyilmaz,eakagunduz}@aselsan.com.tr
[2] Software Research, Development and Consultancy Ltd., Silikon Building, No: 14, METU Technopolis 06531, Çankaya/Ankara Turkey
{yildiray,bulca}@aselsan.com.tr

Abstract. This study presents an open and interoperable maritime surveillance framework with multimodal sensor networks and an automated decision-making. The intention is to improve sea-border control, plugging the gaps in the maritime security with interoperability solutions and have wide-area situational awareness, thus particular reducing the number of illegal immigrants crossing sea borders in small boats, with a cost-effective approach. In this paper initial results are presented. This research is a part of a European project supported by ITEA2, Eureka Cluster Programme (RECONSURVE Project, no: ITEA2 09036).

Keywords: maritime surveillance, interoperability, situational awareness, threat analysis, vessel classification.

1 Introduction

In the context of EU enlargement, Europe's maritime borders have expanded with Europe's coastline containing 85 per cent of the EU's international borders [1]. To sustain security over expanded maritime borders there is a need to tackle problems such as intrusion of protected areas, and other illicit activities such as drugs smuggling, and illegal immigration without impeding the flow of commerce and travelers. In order to address these problems it is recognized that there is a need of advanced and innovative surveillance and information-sharing technologies in the maritime border surveillance field [2]. Currently available systems widely use of complex sensor networks, integrated information techniques, effective decision aids, and robust command and control systems in order to provide an effective support for several border security authorities. However, the development of advanced and innovative surveillance and information-sharing technologies in the maritime surveillance field is still a challenging issue and it needs deeper studies in order to address the interoperability of maritime surveillance systems and situational awareness concepts as well as identifying and evaluating threat situations.

N. Aschenbruck et al. (Eds.): Future Security 2012, CCIS 318, pp. 359–362, 2012.
© Springer-Verlag Berlin Heidelberg 2012

This paper reports an ongoing study aiming at developing and evaluating an open interoperable maritime surveillance platform, which will enable easy access to a wide range of situational awareness and tactical communication data.

The organization of paper is as follows: Second section describes the architecture of reconfigurable smart surveillance system, while the third section details each RECONSURVE component separately and presents initial results and design choices. Finally, the last section describes future work and concludes the paper.

2   A Reconfigurable Smart Surveillance System Architecture

The proposed reconfigurable surveillance system architecture offers a complete interoperable maritime surveillance system which is capable of utilizing data from several platforms with a variety of sensor types to provide higher situational awareness The system is designed based on standards to the extent possible. The high level picture of the reconfigurable surveillance system architecture can be seen in Fig 1. The research team focused its efforts on the development of service-oriented architecture.

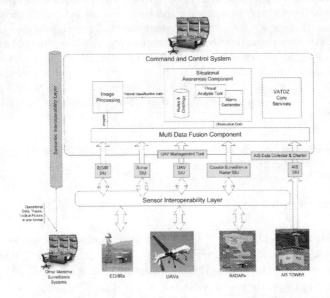

Fig. 1. High Level Architecture of the proposed system

The details of these components will be given in Section 3.

3   Methodology and Technology Description

The maritime surveillance system is designed based on VATOZ® product. VATOZ® is a Naval Command and Control (C2) System Software Product line developed by ASELSAN Inc. It is a real-time distributed and data-driven and can be deployed to Ship Combat Management Systems and/or Harbor Control Locations.

This section briefly presents the technical progress that was achieved so far.

3.1   Situational Awareness Component

The surveillance system is capable of performing behavior analysis of the vessels, which might result in labeling them as suspicious. The system evaluates the sensors data considering available domain knowledge in order to decide whether there is a suspicious situation or not.

When we consider the complexity of continuous maritime monitoring of a large region, there are a huge number of objects and relations that can be defined for situation knowledge. Up to now, about 60 rules (e.g. Check whether the ship has an illegal activity record, Is the speed of the track is above normal?) already identified and stored in knowledge base, which are editable for accommodating future arising rules.

Suspicious label to be exchanged among C2IS systems is compatible in OASIS Common Alerting Protocol (CAP) v1.2 format, which defines an upper format for alarm messages. This issue is presented in details in [3].

3.2   Semantic Interoperability Layer

RECONSURVE project aims to create an interoperability platform in order to enable the exchange of situational awareness and tactical data between maritime surveillance systems. Initial design of the system architecture is based on results of research initiative of NATO RTO IST-075 R&D group, which includes methodologies and guidelines for the conceptual construction of the Semantic Interoperability Logical Framework (SILF) [7]. The details of this layer is presented at [8].

Situational Awareness Ontology [6] is developed as a semantic domain information model, which is the common ground of the SILF architecture in this implementation. The ontology is the harmonization of semantic models of some well-accepted standards such as   Joint Consultation, Command and Control Information Exchange Data Model (JC3IEDM) [5], Open Geospatial Consortium's Sensor Web Enablement (OGC-SWE), Automatic Identification System (AIS), OASIS CAP.

3.3   Multi Data Fusion Component

In RECONSURVE project, information required to construct the common picture is gathered from a diverse set of sensors such as radar, AIS, EO/IR, and UAV. Data fusion creates a real-time, unified situation picture by encompassing all detected entities and activities in the monitored area. Fused data is passed to Situational Awareness Component to conduct in-depth geospatial data mining and behavioral analysis for threat and pattern detection, including classification of vessel activity and intent.

3.4   Sensor Interoperability Layer

Currently most of the surveillance systems lack of dynamically employing available sensors in the environment and requires performing a manual customization or integration effort. Sensor Interoperability layer addresses this problem and provide abstraction by adoption of OGC-SWE standard during observation gathering and querying [8]. Furthermore, the same mechanism also enables publishing the sensor data to other platforms. The project will also utilize the OpenGIS® Sensor Planning Service Interface Standard (SPS) to task the sensors remotely in a standardized way.

3.5   Image Processing Component

Image processing mainly concentrates on small vessel classification problem as mostly illicit activities linked to organized crime are realized by these types of vessels.

First an image database is constructed with virtual thermal images from 475 different angles and/or ranges by working on various 3D civilian vessel models in simulation environment as having a comprehensive image database increases the classification success at the end. Then a vessel classification algorithm has been designed to process the thermal image taken by IR camera on UAV platform. In the future the algorithms will be adapted to day light images as well. Since the thermal images do not have many features but an easily segmentable silhouette, a novel silhouette-based recognition algorithm is developed in the project to classify the object with a scale (resolution) and rotation invariant representation of them.

4   Future Work and Conclusion

This study presents an initial result of this study and details on-going work on development of RECONSURVE project developing an open and interoperability maritime surveillance framework. .

As a future work, we aim to proceed according to the project plan and have a maritime surveillance framework complying with the goals set at the beginning of the project in order warrantee improved border security at EU level. Currently, the development activities are on-going and needs to be finalized at the end of year 2014. The final product will be deployed in Turkey and France to be demonstrated.

References

1. Ex-post Evaluation of PASR Activities in the field of Security and Interim. Evaluation of FP7 Security Research. CBRN Case Study, P O Box 159 (January 2011)
2. European Commission, Communication on examining the creation of a European Border Surveillance System, COM (2008) 68 final, Brussels (February 13, 2008b)
3. Dogac, A., Kabak, Y., Bulca, A., Namli, T., Erbas, C., Yilmaz, B., Tuncer Cetin, F.: RECONSURVE: JC3IEDM and EDXL based Emergency Management Service Oriented Architecture for Maritime Surveillance. To be appear on eChallenges, Proceedings (2012)
4. JC3IEDM, Joint Consultation, Command and Control Information Exchange Data Model, MIP. 'True' JC3IEDM ratified as NATO STANAG 5255. MIP
5. Situational Awareness Ontology, http://www.srdc.com.tr/projects/reconsurve/documents/SAO/SituationalAwarenessOntology.owl
6. Bacchelli, F., Boury-Brisset, A., Isenor, A., Kuehne, S., Martinez, R.B., Miles, J., Mojta-hedzadeh, V., Poell, R., Rasmussen, R., Uzunali, A., Wunder, M.: Final Report of Task Group IST-075 Semantic Interoperability (July 2010)
7. Tuncer, F., Kabak, Y., Yilmaz, B., Dogac, A., Erbas, C.: Semantic Interoperable C4I systems for maritime surveillance: The RECONSURVE Approach. In: NATO Information Systems Technology Panel Symposium (IST-101 / RSY-024)
8. OGC Sensor Web Enablement, http://www.opengeospatial.org/projects/groups/sensorwebdwg

Threat and Potential of High Power Electromagnetics Technology (HPEM)

Robert H. Stark, Franke Sonnemann, Jürgen Urban, and Dieter Weixelbaum

Diehl BGT Defence GmbH, Fischbachstraße 16, 90552 Roethenbach/Peg. - Germany
Robert.Stark@diehl-bgt-defence.de

Abstract. Modern electronic systems are susceptible to intense electromagnetic fields. Due to the small feature size and the low supply voltage of the electronics, the currents and voltages induced in signal and power lines cause malfunction of electronic circuits and components. During decades high power electromagnetic sources have been developed providing electromagnetic fields in the order of several hundreds of Mega Watts up to the Giga Watts level. For electronic components and smaller electronic systems, protection against the powerful electromagnetic radiation may be realized on a component or on a sub-system level. However, for larger electronic systems or electronic based infrastructures like communication centres, control centres or power plants, provision of a protected "hotel room atmosphere" and therefore shielding of the room or building itself may be mandatory.

A new time domain measurement technique has been developed, which allows to measure shielding efficiencies already during the construction phase of a building in order to ensure proper shield installation.

High power electromagnetic pulses may also being used to defeat against modern electronic weapon systems and other electronic threats. Various HPEM sources have been developed emitting high power electromagnetic radiation in a single pulse or a burst of pulses targeting the control and computer electronics of modern electronic systems and infra structures. Those sources are able to disrupt the control units of engines and may be used to stop cars, to control admission to sensible or high value areas or to stop speed boats or jet-skis in order to control access to harbours and moored ships from sea side.

Keywords: BoatStop, CarStop, DIEHL, EMC, Electromagnetic Compatibility, eT-Wall, HPEM, High Power Electromagnetics, HPM, High Power Microwave.

1 Susceptibility of Electronics and Protection

Electronic systems are sensitive to damage or upset from external electromagnetic (EM) transients such as lightning, radar, electrostatic discharge (ESD), switching spikes, nuclear high altitude electromagnetic pulse (HEMP) and high-power electromagnetics (HPEM) in general. Because lightning is a frequently happened natural phenomenon, in many buildings the electrical installations are equipped with lightning protection systems. Similar, static electric discharges can be avoided by proper choice of floor materials and ESD protective clothing, which is especially useful for

N. Aschenbruck et al. (Eds.): Future Security 2012, CCIS 318, pp. 363–365, 2012.
© Springer-Verlag Berlin Heidelberg 2012

workers in sensible areas (e.g. electronic manufacturing or server rooms). An electromagnetic protection against radar, EMP and HPEM pulses in general is at most provided for military systems but typically not for civilian infrastructure. However, the loss of electrical power and circuitry for high-value buildings and facilities may lead to fatal environmental conditions.

Therefore, as an act of precaution and risk minimisation, it might be useful to establish a complete electromagnetic shield for high-value buildings. This does not necessarily mean that the building itself or its content is of high value rather than the amount of loss and the consequences on civil infrastructure in the event of damage can be fatal.

A novel time domain measurement technique has been developed, which allows to verify the required shielding quality at time of shield installation for every wall segment separately. The measurement technique utilizes sub-ns UWB HPEM pulses. The basic idea of the proposed method is that the propagation time of a very short UWB pulse of several 100 ps duration through a potential leakage is much shorter than the propagation time of the scattered signal around the shield. Due to the different time delays both signals can be separated from each other by a time-gating technique. Using FFT-method the shielding effectiveness of a certain wall area under test can be determined. The measurement system consists of a transmitter and receiver unit which are placed at the opposite side of the wall on top of the area under test. The method can be applied even if the shielding of the building is not fully accomplished.

A forecast for the development of the susceptibility of target electronics may be given by the roadmap of the leading semiconductor companies[1]. Development of semiconductor devices with further reduced structure size, layer thickness and lower supply voltage will further increase susceptibility of electronic systems. In future, on-chip protection concepts may be replaced by concepts which will offer a "hotel room atmosphere" to electronic components and circuits with moderate temperature and humidity and electromagnetic field free environment in order to ensure proper system operation. However, the sensible point will be the interfaces to the environment, which are necessary to communicate and transfer signals and data.

2   Applications of HPEM Technology

HPEM pulses induce currents and voltages in signal and power lines causing disruption or even destruction of electronic circuits and components. HPEM technology is a non-lethal technology. It enhances the capabilities and allows reacting more flexible in critical situations. In the following some examples for applications of HPEM technology will be given.

(a) Admission Control with HPEM CarStop

Studies of the susceptibility of engine control electronics against HPEM pulses have shown that vehicle and engine electronics is very susceptible to HPEM. Currents and voltages induced in power and signal lines forces the engine to stop operation. This effect can be used in various scenarios.

[1] http://www.itrs.net/Links/2011ITRS/Home2011.htm

(i) HPEM Mobile CarStop System

The HPEM Mobile CarStop System allows stopping target cars trying to pass by on the highway. The system consists of high voltage DC power supply, Marx bank and DS resonator antennas mounted on the back of a carrier vehicle. Due to the high power electromagnetic pulses, the engine electronic and as a consequence the engine of the vehicle will fail. The HPEM CarStop Mobile System is adapted to a HPEM qualified carrier vehicle.

(ii) HPEM eT-Wall Stationary Vehicle Stopper

The HPEM eT-Wall Stationary Vehicle Stopper may be used in a typical check-point scenario on the road or at the entrance to a high valued facility or building (power plants, airports, harbours, military installations etc.). If the driver of a car does not stop at the check-point and does speed up instead in order get away, the HPEM et-Wall Stationary Vehicle Stopper may be activated automatically or manually in order to stop the vehicle.

(b) Admission Control with HPEM BoatStop

HPEM technology may also be used to control access to harbours or moored ships from sea side. In this case HPEM technology may be integrated into floating buoys or on top of a speed boat or ship. The HPEM radiation emitted by the source couples to signal and power lines inducing voltages and currents causing malfunction of engine operation. The HPEM BoatStop system may run in stand-by mode and can be activated automatically or even manually by the user, depending on scenario requirements. A selection of representative watercrafts like outboard engines and jet boats has been tested successfully.

3   Conclusion

High power electromagnetic (HPEM) radiation targets modern electronic systems. The electromagnetic pulses induce currents and voltages in signal and power lines which are able to disrupt or even destroy electronic systems. For large buildings and high value facilities and infrastructures which include a manifold of sensible and critical electronic devices, it is important to provide a protected "hotel room atmosphere" for the susceptible electronics. A novel time domain measurement technique has been developed in order to measure the installed shielding efficiency already during the construction phase of a building. HPEM technology can also being used in order to defeat modern electronic based threats. HPEM technology is a non-lethal technology and targets the electronic system only. It offers new capabilities in order to deescalate situations and to react more flexible. HPEM technology has been successfully tested to stop car and speedboat engines in checkpoint scenarios or in order to protect ships in harbour.

Reference

1. http://www.itrs.net/Links/2011ITRS/Home2011.htm

Designer Drugs and Trace Explosives Detection with the Help of Very Recent Advancements in Proton-Transfer-Reaction Mass Spectrometry (PTR-MS)

Philipp Sulzer[1,*], Simone Jürschik[1], Bishu Agarwal[2], Thomas Kassebacher[1,2],
Eugen Hartungen[1], Achim Edtbauer[1], Fredrik Petersson[1], Johannes Warmer[3],
Gerhard Holl[3], Dave Perry[4], Christopher A. Mayhew[4], and Tilmann D. Märk[1,2]

[1] IONICON Analytik GmbH., Eduard-Bodem-Gasse 3, 6020 Innsbruck, Austria
{philipp.sulzer,simone.juerschik,eugen.hartungen,
achim.edtbauer,fredrik.petersson,tilmann.maerk}@ionicon.com
[2] Institut für Ionenphysik und Angewandte Physik, Leopold-Franzens Universität Innsbruck,
Technikerstr. 25, 6020 Innsbruck, Austria
{bishu.agarwal,tilmann.maerk}@uibk.ac.at,
thomas.kassebacher@student.uibk.ac.at
[3] Institut für Detektionstechnologien, Hochschule Bonn-Rhein-Sieg, von-Liebig-Strasse 20,
53359 Rheinbach, Germany
{johannes.warmer,gerhard.holl}@h-brs.de
[4] Molecular Physics Group, School of Physics and Astronomy, University of Birmingham,
Edgbaston, Birmingham, B15 4TT, UK
{d.b.perry,c.mayhew}@bham.ac.uk

Abstract. At the "Future Security 2011" we presented an overview of our studies on the "Detection and Identification of Illicit and Hazardous Substances with Proton-Transfer-Reaction Mass Spectrometry (PTR-MS)" including first results on explosives, chemical warfare agents and illicit and prescribed drugs detection. Since then we have considerably extended these preliminary studies to the detection of defined traces of some of the most common explosives, namely TNT, PETN, TATP, and DATP deposited into aluminum foam bodies, and to the detection of a number of novel and widely unknown designer drugs: ethylphenidate, 4-fluoroamphetamine and dimethocaine. Moreover, we have dramatically improved our time-of-flight based PTR-MS instruments by substantially increasing their sensitivity and hence lowering the detection limit, making them even more suitable and applicable to threat agents with extremely low vapour pressures. Data from measurements on certified gas standards are presented in order to underline these statements. The data demonstrate that, in comparison to the first generation instruments, a gain of one order of magnitude in terms of sensitivity and detection limit has been obtained.

Keywords: Proton-Transfer-Reaction Mass Spectrometry, PTR-MS, drug detection, designer drugs, explosives detection, TOF, low detection limits.

---

[*] Corresponding author.

N. Aschenbruck et al. (Eds.): Future Security 2012, CCIS 318, pp. 366–375, 2012.
© Springer-Verlag Berlin Heidelberg 2012

1   Introduction

Proton-Transfer-Reaction Mass Spectrometry (PTR-MS) is a well established analytical technology in many fields of application. Environmental research [1], food and flavor science [2], biological research [3] and medicine [4] are just a few examples. This has resulted from the high selectivity, high sensitivity, low detection limits and simple real-time sampling procedure capabilities of PTR-MS. Although these advantages make PTR-MS ideal for use as a versatile detector for illicit and/or dangerous substances, it is only recently that PTR-MS is being applied to the area of homeland security, as is indicated by several publications of military research organizations using PTR-MS instruments, e.g. the "Wehrwissenschaftliches Institut für Schutztechnologien" in Germany [5] and the Dstl in the UK [6]. In addition to these "end user" publications, we performed various proof-of-principle and fundamental studies on the detection capabilities of PTR-MS explosives from small amounts of bulk samples [7, 8], explosives dissolved in water [9], chemical warfare agents (CWAs) [10] and illicit and controlled prescription drugs [11].

Here we present unpublished data on the detection of defined trace amounts of explosives deposited into aluminum foam bodies and novel designer drugs (so called "research chemicals", which are readily available to a broad community of consumers via the internet). We will cover not only details on these applications, but also describe recent instrumental developments of our Proton-Transfer-Reaction Time-of-Flight Mass Spectrometry (PTR-TOFMS) instrumentation. We demonstrate that the new generation of PTR-TOFMS considerably exceeds the selectivity and meets the sensitivity of quadrupole mass filter based systems [12]. In particular the resolution is now sufficiently high to permit the separation of many isobaric compounds. Until recently the sensitivity of PTR-TOFMS instruments was somewhat limited in comparison to quadrupole based models, because for TOF mass spectrometers ions have to be pulsed into the flight path. Through major development work, we have been able to make significant improvements to the PTR-TOFMS, with the result that we have achieved an increase in the overall sensitivity by approximately one order of magnitude, and thereby reaching sensitivities which until now have only been possible with our high sensitivity PTR-QMS devices [13]. These improvements will considerably support the use of PTR-MS towards being a commonly-used and reliable technology in the detection of threat agents.

2   Instrumental Setup

Many publications already describe the operational principles of PTR-MS, which e.g. have been extensively reviewed by Blake et al [14], and therefore no details are presented here. However, we highlight in this work that our instruments are equipped with the switchable reagent ions (SRI) feature [13], so that either water vapor from a container holding distilled water (for H_3O^+ mode), charcoal filtered air (for NO^+ mode) or oxygen from an O_2 cylinder (for O_2^+ mode) is introduced into the ion source. Owing to the sophisticated design of our ion source, a high level of purity in the production of the reagent ions results, which makes the need for an inlet (and hence signal diminishing) mass filter, as required for Selected Ion Flow Tube-MS instruments, obsolete. In the drift tube the chemical ionization takes place.

Finally, a transfer lens system guides the ions either into a TOF mass spectrometer, where they are analyzed by their mass and detected on a microchannel plate detector or into a quadrupole mass filter with an attached secondary electron multiplier.

The most important operational parameter in the drift tube of a PTR-MS instrument is the reduced electric field strength E/N (in Td), which results from the pressure, temperature and voltage applied to the PTR drift tube. By varying the E/N value (usually this is done by only varying the voltage) fragmentation can either be enhanced (high E/N) or suppressed (low E/N). This can be utilized as an experimental parameter to obtain further information for the identification of a substance in a complex chemical environment. This will be discussed in more detail in the results section.

2.1   PTR-TOFMS Improvements

Between 2009 and 2010 we introduced two different types of TOF based PTR-MS instruments, namely the PTR-TOF 8000, with a mass resolution of up to 8000 m/Δm and sensitivity of about 25 cps/ppbv, and the PTR-TOF 2000, with a somewhat lower mass resolution of about 2000 m/Δm but with an increased sensitivity of approximately 250 cps/ppbv [12, 7]. These were already benchmark values for TOF based PTR-MS instruments. However, for the detection of hazardous substances with low vapour pressures, the sensitivity cannot be high enough. Therefore, we undertook an extensive R&D programme to improve these sensitivity values even further. As a direct result of this we are now obtaining sensitivities of approximately 280 cps/ppbv for the PTR-TOF 8000 and up to 740 cps/ppbv for the PTR-TOF 2000, while lowering the detection limits (3σ method, 1 min integration time) down to 800 ppqv (previously around 10 pptv) and to 640 ppqv (previously around 5 pptv), respectively. The detailed results of the sensitivity measurements on a certified gas standard (Restek, US) are presented in Fig. 1.

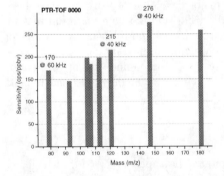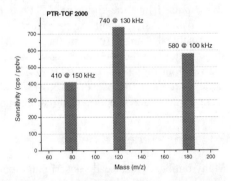

Fig. 1. Measured sensitivities in cps/ppbv for two different TOF based PTR-MS instruments, obtained from measurements on a certified gas standard (TO-14A; Restek, US) with appropriate extraction frequencies (stated in kHz)

With these improvements, we have achieved about a one order of magnitude increase in the sensitivity of a PTR-TOF 8000 instrument. This now makes the sensitivity of PTR-TOFMS comparable to that currently achievable using our high sensitivity

PTR-QMS instruments (ppqv detection limit; several hundred cps/ppbv sensitivity [13]), but with the advantage of high mass resolution and thus high selectivity. Fig. 2 provides an example of the separation power of a PTR-TOF 8000. Although for TOF instruments the mass resolution is increasing with increasing mass with a steep slope up to about 100 m/z, it can be seen that already at around 57 m/z a resolution of nearly 7000 m/Δm is reached and two isobaric compounds, methylketene and butene, can be easily separated. It has to be noted that the intensity of these two compounds differs by about one order of magnitude, i.e. mass separation at 50% peak height would only lead to the formation of an indefinable, non-quantifiable shoulder.

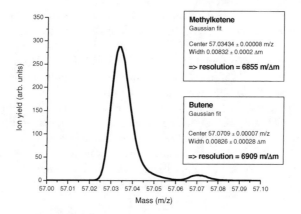

Fig. 2. Example for the separation of two low mass isobaric compounds at different intensities and calculated mass resolutions utilizing a PTR-TOF 8000

3   Results and Discussion

In this section we present novel and previously unpublished data on designer drugs and trace explosives measurements. The combination of these two compound classes in one study might seem arbitrary at a first glance. However, as most commonly utilized real-time detection technologies (e.g. ion-mobility spectrometry (IMS) in positive or negative ion mode, chemical test strips, etc.) are limited or at least optimized for one of the two substance classes, it is a remarkable fact that with PTR-MS both substance classes (and any other compound which has either a proton affinity greater than H_2O (for H_3O^+ reagent ions) or an ionization potential less than the recombination energies of O_2^+ and NO^+) can be detected and analyzed, in contrast to GC-MS in real-time, without any instrumental modifications.

3.1   Designer Drugs

Collecting scientific information about legal designer drugs is a very difficult task owing to their short-lived nature (i.e. they are released to the market, get banned after some time and new substances follow nearly instantly), and hence hardly any reliable publications exist. Therefore, the main sources of information about which substances are currently on the market are various "consumer" internet forums which we carefully consulted.

According to these, one very recent substance in common use since the beginning of 2012 is ethylphenidate ($C_{15}H_{21}NO_2$), an analogue of methylphenidate, which is better known to the public under its brand name of "Ritalin". Ethylphenidate is legal in most countries and should produce effects such as raised alertness, mild euphoria, increased productivity, etc. We obtained an off-the-shelf sample from a vendor in the UK and analyzed the white crystalline powder with a PTR-TOF 8000.

Fig. 3 shows the result of this analysis. Surprisingly, although the origin of this chemical is not from a state-of-the-art chemical lab, the ethylphenidate from this vendor seems to be exceptionally pure. It has to be mentioned that with PTR-MS one usually analyzes the headspace above a (solid) substance, i.e. highly volatile solvents will be much more pronounced in the obtained mass spectra than the less volatile substance itself. However, in Fig. 3 the dominating ion is at 248.165 m/z, which is the exact mass for protonated ethylphenidate. One "high mass" impurity (or a fragment from PTR reactions) is found at 156.081 m/z (probably $C_{11}H_{10}N^+$). In the lower mass range (i.e. 84, 75, 61, 58 m/z in Fig. 3) we expect mainly impurities originating from solvents during the production process and preliminarily identify them via their exact mass as (protonated) $H_9C_5N^+$, $H_6C_3O_2^+$, $H_4C_2O_2^+$, $H_7C_3N^+$. In summary we conclude that we cannot only easily detect the novel designer drug ethylphenidate with PTR-MS but we have also found out that the ethylphenidate sample, bought as a so-called "research chemical" from a rather obscure source, is surprisingly pure, especially when compared to street bought illegal drugs like cocaine or heroin, which are reported to often contain less than 30% of the active ingredient.

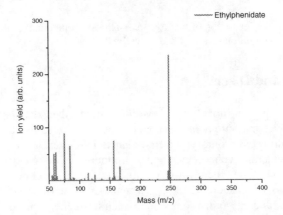

Fig. 3. Mass spectrum of the designer drug ethylphenidate obtained with a PTR-TOF 8000

Two further designer drugs reported here are dimethocaine (DC, $C_{16}H_{26}N_2O_2$) and 4-fluoroamphetamine (4-FA, $C_9H_{12}FN$). Both substances are considerably strong stimulants with DC having very similar properties to cocaine and 4-FA being more on the entactogenic side. DC is still legal in most countries, while 4-FA is getting banned in an increasing number of countries. However, at the time of the experiments 4-FA (and DC) was legally available from an internet vendor in the Netherlands where we bought it.

Again, the substances were found to be surprisingly pure. In Fig. 4 we present branching ratios of DC (upper graph) and 4-FA (lower graph). It can be seen that the two molecules behave completely different upon protonation. Whereas DC is rather stable at all E/N values, with some fragmentation only occurring at very high E/N, 4-FA is a nice example of a "fragile" molecule where the protonated parent ion is the most abundant ion only at very low E/N values. This information could be used to provide an unambiguous confirmation of its detection, i.e. if an ion at 154.10 m/z is detected at low E/N and the ion yield virtually vanishes when the E/N value is increased, this is a strong indicator that the substance detected is really 4-FA.

In addition to the three designer drugs presented here, we measured and analyzed a large number of research chemicals and related and/or precursor compounds. All of them were easily detectable with PTR-MS at room temperature.

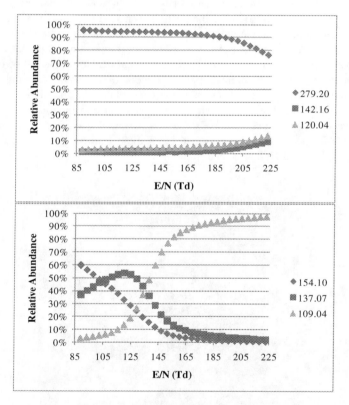

Fig. 4. Branching ratios of the "stable molecule" dimethocaine (upper panel; 279.20 = protonated parent, 142.16 = loss of $C_7NO_2H_7$ from protonated parent, 120.04 = loss of C_9NOH_{21} from protonated parent) and the "fragile" molecule 4-fluoroamphetamine (lower panel; 154.10 = protonated parent, 137.07 = loss of NH_3 from protonated parent, 109.04 = loss of C_2NH_7 from protonated parent)

3.2   Trace Explosives

For our investigations of explosive traces we utilized aluminum foam bodies containing less than 1 mg of the respective explosive substances (ExploTech, Germany). A picture of one of these test bodies is displayed in Fig. 5. These standards had been developed to validate trace detectors, especially explosive detector dogs. The test bodies (made entirely of inorganic compounds) are mechanically impregnated with a small amount of the respective explosive. No solvents are used for this process. Many different types of explosives (solid, paste-like or liquid) can be incorporated. In spite of the energetic material, they are not considered to be explosives or objects with explosives by law. From the data determined by static thermogravimetry (μ-TG) the strength of the source can be calculated for various temperatures. For example the rate of sublimation for TNT at 293 K can be estimated to be in the range of 15 ng/h.

The test bodies were put into glass vials and charcoal filtered air was drawn through these vials and introduced into a high sensitivity PTR-QMS for analysis. From previous studies we already knew that the explosive trinitrotoluene (TNT, $C_7H_5N_3O_6$) shows a very unusual E/N behavior, i.e. the protonated parent ion shows the highest abundance at elevated E/N. This is unusual because it cannot be explained by fragmentation (high E/N should support fragmentation) and because this behavior has only been observed for the TNT analogue trinitrobenzene and no other molecule investigated with PTR-MS so far. However, this bizarre behavior can be used to provide a very strong indicator that a signal at a nominal mass of 228 m/z is indeed protonated TNT and not an isobaric substance, which is not be distinguishable utilizing a quadrupole based PTR-MS instrument.

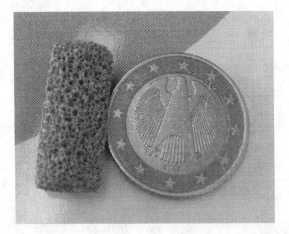

Fig. 5. Picture of an aluminum foam test body containing explosive traces (ExploTech, Germany) used in the present study

In Fig. 6 this E/N dependence for TNT detection sensitivity is nicely illustrated. On the left the ion yield on mass 228 m/z is plotted as a function of time. As expected, the observed ion yield increases after the introduction of the test body into the vial, as the test body is evaporating TNT molecules into the dynamic headspace in the vial until an equilibrium TNT concentration is reached. However, as soon as the E/N value is reduced from 150 Td to 125 Td the signal intensity drops by nearly 50% and at 100 Td by nearly one order of magnitude. In total contrast to this observation is the analysis of pentaerythritol tetranitrate (PETN, $C_5H_8N_4O_{12}$) which is shown on the right side of Fig. 6. Again, as soon as the test body is introduced into the vial, the signal intensity for the protonated PETN ion increases. The E/N value is set to 75 Td at the beginning of this measurement and it can be clearly seen that as soon as the E/N value is increased by 25 Td the ion yield drops significantly and disappears at 150 Td.

In summary, with the information about the E/N dependence of a substance we get an additional dimension for identification. With this data dimension even a low resolution quadrupole based PTR-MS instrument could be used for TNT detection with very low false positives.

Acetone peroxide (DATP, $C_6H_{12}O_4$ (dimer); TATP, $C_9H_{18}O_6$ (trimer)) is a commonly used explosive by terrorists for so-called "improvised explosive device". It is relatively easy to synthesize TATP from common household chemicals without the need of a fully equipped chemistry laboratory. TATP and its explosive dimer DATP contain no nitrogen, thus many established explosive detectors cannot detect these two substances. Fig. 7 shows that PTR-MS has no problem with the detection of TATP and DATP. Again, the x-axis represents the time and the y-axis the ion yield. At the beginning, a test body containing TATP is introduced into the vial. Due to the very high vapor pressure of TATP the substance quickly reaches an equilibrium in the dynamic headspace, as is illustrated by the nearly constant intensity of 223 m/z as a function of cycle (time). At an arbitrary cycle time, the TATP test body is removed and exchanged for a DATP test body, which leads to an immediate increase in the ion yield of the protonated DATP parent.

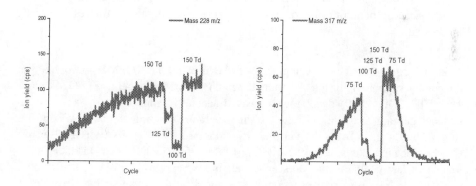

Fig. 6. Measurements on two aluminum test bodies (left: TNT; right: PETN) placed in vials

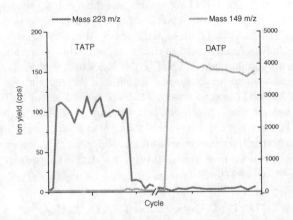

Fig. 7. Measurement of a test body containing TATP and subsequently a second test body containing DATP

4   Conclusions

In conclusion, in this present study we have demonstrated that PTR-MS is indeed capable of detecting two completely different classes of threat agents; designer drugs and explosives. In combination with our previous publications dealing with illegal and controlled prescription drugs [11] and chemical warfare agents [10] this confirms our claim that PTR-MS is a versatile, sensitive and selective analytical detector for virtually all kinds of illicit and/or dangerous substances. Moreover, due to either the high mass resolution of a PTR-TOFMS or the additional information about E/N dependence, or both information combined, the risk of false positives is greatly suppressed.

Acknowledgement. The development of the initial PTR-TOFMS prototype was financially supported by the Austrian Research Promotion Agency (FFG, Vienna). The PTR-TOF 2000 development was financially supported by the Tiroler Landesregierung (Austria) via the FuEuI program. We want to acknowledge the support by the EC (Brussels) via the FP7-IAPP project "PTR-TOF" (GA 218065). CAM wishes to acknowledge the EPSRC (EP/E027571/1). DBP's PhD studentship is funded under the Innovative Research Call in Explosives and Weapons Detection (2010), a cross-government programme sponsored by a number of UK government departments and agencies under the CONTEST strategy.

References

1. Biasioli, F., Yeretzian, C., Märk, T.D., Dewulf, J., Van Langenhove, H.: Direct-injection mass spectrometry adds the time dimension to (B)VOC analysis. Trends in Analytical Chemistry 30(7) (2011)
2. Biasioli, F., Yeretzian, C., Gasperi, F., Märk, T.D.: PTR-MS monitoring of VOCs and BVOCs in food science and technology. Trends in Analytical Chemistry 30(7) (2011)
3. Brilli, F., Ruuskanen, T.M., Schnitzhofer, R., Müller, M., Breitenlechner, M., Bittner, V., Wohlfahrt, G., Loreto, F., Hansel, A.: Detection of Plant Volatiles after Leaf Wounding and Darkening by Proton Transfer Reaction "Time-of-Flight" Mass Spectrometry (PTR-TOF). PLoS One 6(5), e20419 (2011)
4. Herbig, J., Müller, M., Schallhart, S., Titzmann, T., Graus, M., Hansel, A.: On-line breath analysis with PTR-TOF. J. Breath Res. 3, 027004 (2009)
5. Ringer, J.: Detection of Chemical Warfare Agents using Proton Transfer Reaction Mass Spectrometry. In: 5th International Conference on Proton Transfer Reaction Mass Spectrometry and its Applications, pp. 156–157. Innsbruck University Press, Innsbruck (2011)
6. Hickey, P.J., Cairns, S., Kilgour, D.P.A.: Towards using artificial intelligence to detect anomalies in atmospheric mass spectrometry or other spectroscopic data. In: 5th International Conference on Proton Transfer Reaction Mass Spectrometry and its Applications, p. 151. Innsbruck University Press, Innsbruck (2011)
7. Mayhew, C.A., Sulzer, P., Petersson, F., Haidacher, S., Jordan, A., Märk, L., Watts, P., Märk, T.D.: Applications of proton transfer reaction time-of-flight mass spectrometry for the sensitive and rapid real-time detection of solid high explosives. International Journal of Mass Spectrometry 289, 58–63 (2010)
8. Sulzer, P., Petersson, F., Agarwal, B., Becker, K., Jürschik, S., Märk, T.D., Perry, D., Watts, P., Mayhew, C.A.: Proton Transfer Reaction Mass Spectrometry and the unambiguous real-time detection of 2,4,6 TNT. Analytical Chemistry 84, 4161–4166 (2012)
9. Jürschik, S., Sulzer, P., Petersson, F., Mayhew, C.A., Jordan, A., Agarwal, B., Haidacher, S., Seehauser, H., Becker, K., Märk, T.D.: Proton transfer reaction mass spectrometry for the sensitive and rapid real-time detection of solid high explosives in air and water. Anal. Bioanal. Chem. 398, 2813–2820 (2010)
10. Petersson, F., Sulzer, P., Mayhew, C.A., Watts, P., Jordan, A., Märk, L., Märk, T.D.: Real-time trace detection and identification of chemical warfare agent simulants using recent advances in proton transfer reaction time-of-flight mass spectrometry. Rapid Commun. Mass Spectrom. 23, 3875–3880 (2009)
11. Agarwal, B., Petersson, F., Jürschik, S., Sulzer, P., Jordan, A., Märk, T.D., Watts, P., Mayhew, C.A.: Use of proton transfer reaction time-of-flight mass spectrometry for the analytical detection of illicit and controlled prescription drugs at room temperature via direct headspace sampling. Anal. Bioanal. Chem. 400, 2631–2639 (2011)
12. Jordan, A., Haidacher, S., Hanel, G., Hartungen, E., Märk, L., Seehauser, H., Schottkowsky, R., Sulzer, P., Märk, T.D.: A high resolution and high sensitivity time-of-flight proton-transfer-reaction mass spectrometer (PTR-TOF-MS). International Journal of Mass Spectrometry 286, 122–128 (2009)
13. Jordan, A., Haidacher, S., Hanel, G., Hartungen, E., Herbig, J., Märk, L., Schottkowsky, R., Seehauser, H., Sulzer, P., Märk, T.D.: An online ultra-high sensitivity proton-transfer-reaction mass-spectrometer combined with switchable reagent ion capability (PTR+SRI-MS). International Journal of Mass Spectrometry 286, 32–38 (2009)
14. Blake, R.S., Monks, P.S., Ellis, A.M.: Proton-Transfer Reaction Mass Spectrometry. Chem. Rev. 109(3), 861–896 (2009)

On the Detection and Localization
of Radioactive Sources in Public Facilities

Monika Wieneke[1], Wolfgang Koch[1], Hermann Friedrich[2], and Sebastian Chmel[2]

[1] Fraunhofer FKIE
{monika.wieneke,wolfgang.koch}@fkie.fraunhofer.de
[2] Fraunhofer INT
{hermann.friedrich,sebastian.chmel}@int.fraunhofer.de

Abstract. The localization and tracking of radioactive sources in public facilities like airports or stations is a problem of highest security relevance. The accumulation and the severity of terrorist attacks during the past decade give reason to the assumption that future attacks could also involve radioactive material packaged with conventional explosives. The only way to avoid such kind of attacks is to localize and arrest the person carrying the material to its destination. But since radiation is not perceivable by human beings, the security guards are largely dependent on technical decision support to perform this task. We consider a security assistance system comprising three gamma scintillation detectors that are distributed along a corridor wall to check passing people for radioactive material. Furthermore, the system consists of a set of tracking sensors simultaneously providing the positions of all persons during their walk through the corridor. In this paper we propose techniques to estimate the assignment of radioactive detections to person tracks. These techniques provide a measure for each person that reflects the probability that the person is a radioactive source carrier. The problem of source localization is thus reduced to a matching problem between person tracks and sequences of count rates.

Keywords: Radiation Detection, Source Localization, Person Tracking, Data Association, Estimation.

1   Introduction

In the context of intelligent surveillance of public places, the observation and analysis of persons by distributed sensor systems increasingly gains in importance. The detection of hazardous material in busy areas as well as its assignment to a person is a challenging task that cannot be performed without technical decision support. However, the application of conventional technologies and the corresponding courses of action lead to long waiting times and pressure of work for the security personnel. This situation can be extremely relieved by security assistance systems with the ability to continuously observe an area by distributed sensor systems. Ideally, these systems call the security guards only in case of detection and finally give a hint to those persons who can be assumed to carry the detected source. These persons can then be separated for further investigation.

N. Aschenbruck et al. (Eds.): Future Security 2012, CCIS 318, pp. 376–387, 2012.
© Springer-Verlag Berlin Heidelberg 2012

In this work we concern ourselves with the localization of radioactive source carriers in person streams. The discussions about potential substances used for terrorist attacks are not only coined by the already applied improvised *explosive* devices (IED) but also by the fear of improvised *nuclear* devices, or radiological dispersion devices (RDD) like dirty bombs [3]. An RDD consists of a conventional explosive wrapped up with radioactive material. The conventional explosive conduces to disperse the radioactive material in the environment. Although this type of threat has not been put into practice so far, of growing concern are numerous incidents involving a loss or theft of radioactive sources that could be possibly used for an RDD. Hence, there is an increasing need for security assistance systems that are able to localize the material while it is transported.

In this work we consider the transportation of radioactive material by a person walking through a public facility. In such a scenario a security assistance system for source carrier localization is ideally equipped with multiple sensors of complementary type. We propose a combination of scintillation counters for radiation detection with tracking sensors for determining the positions of the persons. While the strength of radiation detectors lies in their detection capability, their substantial weakness is given by a limited spatio-temporal resolution capability. Hence, a single detector is not able to reliably localize the source and to assign it to a person. Tracking sensors in contrast enable a precise localization of all persons but have no detection abilities. A combination of these complementary types of sensors reduces the search space to a countable set of potential source positions. The problem of source localization thus becomes a matching problem between the person tracks and the sequences of count rates. A security assistance system combining sensors for chemical substances with tracking data has first been proposed by Wieneke and Koch [1]. Within this sensor system localization means the calculation of assignment probabilities between a series concentration measurements and each person track. The decision whether a person is a source carrier or not can thus be interpreted as a task of classifying the persons. This paper is dedicated to the localization of radioactive source carriers. We propose two techniques to estimate the assignment between a series of radiation counts and person tracks. The techniques are evaluated on the basis of real and simulated data.

2   Measurement Process and Sensor Model

The radiation strength of a radioactive source is called the activity [2]. The activity A of a source is defined as the expected number of radioactive decays per second. The SI unit[1] of activity is Becquerel (Bq). One Bq corresponds to one decay per second. From a statistical point of view the activity is the expected value of the number of decays per second. The actual number of decays randomly deviates from the expected value. The frequency of the numbers follows a Poisson distribution. Let a_k be the number of decays during the time interval k. The Poisson distribution is a discrete probability distribution that assigns probabilities to numbers $a_k \in \mathbb{N}_0$ according to

$$\mathcal{P}_A(X = a_k) = \frac{\exp(-A)A^{a_k}}{a_k!}. \tag{1}$$

---

[1] SI - International System of Units.

Gamma radiation is electromagnetic radiation of high frequency. A gamma scintillation detector counts the number of emitted gamma rays that hit the detector surface.
The expected number of gamma rays per decay, denoted G, is given by the decay
scheme of the radiator. For example, the decay of Co-60 causes two gamma rays with
a probability of 99.88% and one gamma ray with probability 0.12%. In the following,
the expected number of gamma rays per second is called the *gamma intensity*. It is
designated by α, with $\alpha = G \cdot A$. The unit of α is counts per second (CPS). The
number of gamma rays registered at detector r is inversely proportional to the square
of the distance d_r from the detector to the source (inverse square law). In other
words, the emitted rays are equally distributed on the surface of a sphere with radius
d_r. The area D_r of the absorbing part of the detector marks a section of this surface.
Further influences due to the intrinsic detector efficiency are comprised by factor E_r.
Besides the source rays, the detector registers gamma rays of the background radiation with count rate β^r in CPS.

For a stationary source the relation between the measured counts c^r at detector r
and the gamma intensity is hence given by Eq. (2), where $\theta = [x, y, \alpha]^\mathsf{T}$ is the source
parameter vector with position $[x, y]^\mathsf{T}$ and gamma intensity α. Of course, in case of a
moving source the distance d_r and the count rate c^r are time dependent.

$$\mathcal{P}_{\lambda(\theta)}(X = c^r) \quad \text{with} \quad \lambda(\theta) = \beta^r + \alpha \cdot \frac{E_r D_r}{4\pi d_r^2} \tag{2}$$

Recall that both the actual gamma ray emission and the actual background radiation
result from a Poisson distributed process. The decision whether a measured count rate
is greater than the background rate β^r, i.e. whether a real source is present or not, is a
problem of statistical testing. A decision threshold with a type I error of 0.05 for a
measuring time τ_0 is given by Eq. (3).

$$q^r = \frac{1}{2\tau_0}\kappa^2 \left(1 + \sqrt{1 + \frac{4\beta^r \tau_0}{\kappa^2}\left(1 + \frac{\tau_0}{\tau_\beta^r}\right)} \right) \quad \text{with } \kappa = 1.645 \,, \tag{3}$$

where κ is the quantile of the normal distribution for type I error. The background rate
β^r is determined in advance by a long-term measurement with measuring time τ_β^r.

3   Accumulation of Counts

The first proposed approach to the problem of radioactive source carrier localization
is the accumulation of counts. This is referred to as the Accum-C approach in the
following. Let C_r^m be the count accumulation variable of person m with respect to
detector r. This variable is gradually increased as follows:

1. The procedure starts when person m enters the detection area of detector r. The
   personal count accumulation variable is initialized: $C_r^m := 0$.

2. As long as person m is inside the detection area, all measured counts c_k^r are accumulated: $C_r^m = C_r^m + c_k^r$. When person m leaves the detection area r, then the accumulated counts are divided by the amount of time the person has spent in this area: $C_r^m = C_r^m / T_r^m$. This leads to a personal count rate, which has to be compared with the decision threshold q^r in Eq. (3). If $C_r^m - \beta^r > q^r$, we accept the hypothesis that a source is present and assign the source-related count rate to the accumulation variable: $C_r^m = C_r^m - q^r - \beta^r$. If $C_r^m - \beta^r \leq q^r$ we accept the hypothesis that the source is not present, set $C_r^m := 0$ and continue.
3. Step 1 up to step 3 are repeated for all persons and all passed detectors.

In the Accum-C approach each person m collects a personal count rate C_r^m for each detector $r \in [1 : R]$. When person m leaves the surveillance area, the personal accumulation variables C_r^m with respect to all detectors are summed up to the total personal count rate according to Eq. (4).

$$C^m = \sum_{r=1}^{R} C_r^m \qquad (4)$$

The greater C^m the more suspicious is the person. After normalization with respect of the persons, the variable C^m can be interpreted as a source carrier probability. It is worth mentioning that in the Accum-C approach the detector counts are either fully taken into account with respect to a person (if person is inside the detection area) or completely ignored (if person is outside). It can thus be expected that the ability to discriminate between carrier and non-carrier persons decreases significantly if the persons walk closely and spend most of the time together inside the detection areas. This expectation is verified in the experimental section.

4   Gamma Intensity as Additional State Estimate

The second approach proposed in this paper is able to also discriminate between the persons if they move rather closely to each other. For example, two persons are walking in line at a distance of merely 1 m. A core component of the proposed algorithm is the estimation of a *personal* gamma intensity α^m for each person. In other words, each person is assumed to be the carrier and based upon the measured count rates and the estimated track, the gamma intensity of the fictitiously carried source is derived. To perform the task of intensity estimation, an appropriate filter is required. Therefore, this section is dedicated to the derivation of a Poisson filter for simultaneous tracking and gamma intensity estimation of a moving radioactive source. This is a preparation of Section 5, where the Poisson filter is exploited within the PMHT-C framework for classification of persons into carriers and non-carriers.

Let $\mathcal{Z}^k$ be the series of all measurements recorded up to scan k, including the position measurements of the tracking sensors. Here, we assume that person m is inside detection area r and we want to calculate the joint density $p(\mathbf{x}_k^m, \alpha^m | \mathcal{Z}^k) = p(\alpha^m | \mathbf{x}_k^m, \mathcal{Z}^k) p(\mathbf{x}_k^m | \mathcal{Z}^k)$ for person m. The second factor is calculated by the tracker. Since the conjugate prior of the Poisson distribution is the Gamma distribution, the first factor can be transformed to Eq. (5) (m is omitted in the following).

$$p(\alpha|\mathbf{x}_k, \mathcal{Z}^k) = p(\alpha|\mathbf{x}_k, c_k^r, \mathcal{Z}^{k-1}) \propto \underbrace{\mathcal{P}(c_k^r|\mathbf{x}_k, \alpha)}_{\text{Poisson}} \times \underbrace{\mathcal{G}(\alpha; \mu_{t|t-1}, \nu_{t|t-1})}_{\text{Gamma}}$$

$$\propto \frac{\alpha n_k \exp(-\alpha)}{n_k!} \times \frac{\nu_{t|t-1}^{\mu_{t|t-1}}}{\Gamma(\mu_{t|t-1})} \alpha^{\mu_{t|t-1}-1} \exp(-\nu_{t|t-1}\alpha)$$

$$\propto \alpha^{\mu_{t|t-1}-1+n_k} \exp(-(\nu_{t|t-1}+1)\alpha),\tag{5}$$

where n_k is the number of gamma emissions that is required at the person's position to cause the count measurement c_k^r at the detector. Note that the source is moving and that a person may move a lot during the detector interval of 1 second. Gamma scintillation counters typically work at rate of 1 Hz. Therefore, an integration is required to get the number n_k. For a source moving in parallel to the x-axis, this can be carried out analytically. The relation between the measured count c_k^r and the emitted number of gamma rays n_k is then given by Eq. (6), where p_x^r is the x-position of detector r, $v_{k\Delta}$ is the person's velocity at time $k\Delta$, and h_r designates the shortest distance between person and detector. $\Delta = 1$ sec is the detector interval. b_k^r is the number of background counts during Δ.

$$c_k^r = b_k^r + \int_{(k-1)\Delta}^{k\Delta} \frac{n_k E_r D_r}{4\pi d_{rt}^2}\, dt = b_k^r + \int_{(k-1)\Delta}^{k\Delta} \frac{n_k E_r D_r}{4\pi(h_r^2 + (x_t - p_x^r)^2)}\, dt$$

$$= b_k^r + \int_0^\Delta \frac{n_k E_r D_r}{4\pi(h_r^2 + (x_{(k-1)\Delta} + v_{(k-1)\Delta}t - p_x^r)^2)}\, dt$$

$$= b_k^r + \frac{n_k E_r D_r}{4\pi v_{k\Delta} h_r}\left[\tan^{-1}\frac{x_{k\Delta} - p_x^r}{h_r}\right] - \frac{n_k E_r D_r}{4\pi v_{(k-1)\Delta} h_r}\left[\tan^{-1}\frac{x_{(k-1)\Delta} - p_x^r}{h_r}\right]\tag{6}$$

Clearly, the integration formula in Eq. (6) is applicable for arbitrary path segments as well, after the segment has been brought into the described parallel position via rotation. Solving Eq. (6) for n_k yields the required number of gamma emissions during a path segment. Note that tracking sensors typically work at much higher rates than gamma scintillation counters. For example, if a tracking sensor works at a rate of 5 Hz, then five path segments per detector interval are provided by the tracker. In this case, the n_k-values of the segments are simply added up.

Since we now have the formula to calculate n_k, the focus is again on the filtering problem in Eq. (5). Obviously, Eq. (5) is a Gamma density with the parameters $\mu_{k|k-1} + n_k$ and $\nu_{k|k-1} + 1$. The expected value of this Gamma distribution is $(\mu_{k|k-1} + n_k)/(\nu_{k|k-1} + 1)$, which leads to the following update formulae:

$$\mu_{k|k} = \mu_{k|k-1} + n_k$$
$$\nu_{k|k} = \nu_{k|k-1} + 1\tag{7}$$

The estimated intensity is thus the mean over all numbers of person-related gamma emissions n_k. Note that only the true source carrier is able to produce a sequence of intensity estimates that converges quickly to its expected value. Only the movement profile of the true source carrier "matches" the sequences of count rates measured at the detectors. Therefore, the average deviation of n_k from the expected value is inversely proportional to the probability of being the source carrier. The greater the deviation the less suspicious is the person. This is shown in a simulated example.

In this example, a fictitious surveillance corridor of length 20 m was simulated with three gamma scintillation counters, equally distributed at distances of 5 m on one side of the corridor. Two persons traversed the corridor from the left to the right, walking one after the other at a constant distance of 0.8 m between the persons. The movement corresponded to a straight horizontal line. The distance from the movement line to the detector wall was 0.8 m as well. The persons walked at a velocity of 1 m/s. One of them carried a gamma source of intensity 250 kilo-CPS. The detection radius of each scintillation counter was assumed 2 m. The detectors worked synchronously at a rate of 1 Hz. The background radiations β^r were set to 10 counts per second. The count rate data of each detector was simulated according to the inverse-square law in combination with Eq. (6). Tracking data was not simulated. The true positions and velocities were used within the Poisson filter. Fig. 1 visualizes the output of the filter in case the source was carried by the leading person (left plot) and by the following person (right plot). The circles represent the current n_k-values. The solid line is the final estimated gamma intensity. Obviously, the n_k-values of the non-carrier have a large deviation from the intensity estimate. This is because the movement of the non-carrier does not obey the radioactive dispersion model.

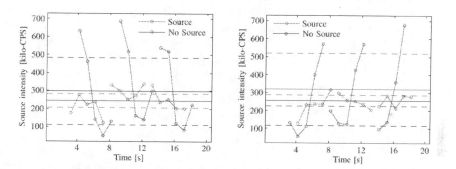

Fig. 1. Deviations from estimated intensity as carrier criterion (example). The red lines correspond to the source carrier. The solid lines mark the final estimated intensity. The dashed lines are the average deviation. The carrier was in the front (left plot) and in the back (right plot).

5   PMHT with Classification Measurements

The original motivation for the development of the PMHT with classification measurements (PMHT-C) [4] was to exploit available classification data for improved tracking and data association.

Basically, the algorithm processes *pairs* of position measurements and classification data and derives estimates for both the kinematical state and the class of each target. This enables to exploit the "attached" classification data as an additional assignment measure, besides the usual position likelihood. The class estimation consists in successively refining a confusion matrix $C \in \mathbb{R}^{J \times M}$, where J is the number of classes and M is the number of targets. The PMHT-C belongs to a class of approaches called classification-aided tracking. However, the motivation in the source localization problem is different: Since sensors for hazardous substances typically have a rather limited spatio-temporal resolution, a simultaneous tracking component enables to reduce the search space to a countable number of possible source positions. In this sense, the source localization problem requires something like a tracking-aided classification approach. Wieneke and Koch showed how the source localization scenario has to be interpreted to make the PMHT-C applicable in this way [1].

With regard to radiation detection, the basic idea is to interpret each pair of detector location and quantized count rate measurement as a pair of position and classification measurement (as mentioned above). With this interpretation, the standard processing of PMHT-C works as follows: In the *assignment phase* the algorithm calculates assignment probabilities between each detector and each person at each scan. In the standard version, these probabilities are governed by the position likelihood evaluating the distance between detector and person. In the PMHT-C version proposed in this paper, the assignment probabilities are additionally controlled by a velocity likelihood and an intensity likelihood. The velocity likelihood compares the slope of the count rate sequence (increasing or decreasing) with the detector-related velocity of the person (approaching or moving apart). The intensity likelihood evaluates the deviations of the person-related counts from the current gamma intensity estimate as described in the previous section. In the following optimization phase, the entries of the confusion matrix are refined by using the probabilities of the assignment phase. Note that each assignment probability reflects how *relevant* the corresponding class measurement (i.e. the quantized count rate) is for the classification of the person. Let w_t^{rm} be the assignment probability of detector r and person m at scan t. Then each entry in the confusion matrix C is updated by

$$
C(j, m) = \frac{\sum\limits_{t=1}^{T} \sum\limits_{r=1}^{R} \delta(z_t^r - j) w_t^{rm}}{\sum\limits_{t=1}^{T} \sum\limits_{r=1}^{R} w_t^{rm}} \quad \text{with } z_t^r := \left\lfloor \frac{c_t^r - \beta^r}{\hbar} \right\rfloor, \tag{8}
$$

where δ is the Kronecker delta symbol and z_t^r is the classification measurement, i.e. the quantized count rate output, which can also be interpreted as an alert level. Actually, PMHT-C works iteratively. However, in the following evaluation only a single iteration is carried out on a growing data window.

6   Experimental Results

The Accum-C approach and the PMHT-C approach are now compared on the basis of real and simulated data. The measure of performance is the ability of each approach to discriminate the carrier person from the non-carrier person. The greater the difference between the carrier probability of the true carrier and the carrier probabilities of the non-carriers, the better is the discrimination ability and thus the performance of the considered approach. The carrier probabilities are normalized w.r.t. the persons.

6.1   Experiments with Real Data

The experiments with real radioactive sources of Cobalt 60 (0.22 MBq) and Caesium 137 (0.25 MBq) were carried out in the experimental environment of the Fraunhofer INT institute. Fig. 2 (bottom) shows a screen shot of the evaluation software. The environment consists of a corridor of length 18 m and width 1.5 m. The person tracking component was realized by a standard PMHT on the basis of laser measurements. The measurements were produced by two laser range scanners at a rate of 5 Hz and with an angular resolution of 0.5°. One of the scanners is shown in Fig. 2 (top, middle). The positions of the scanners are marked by black crosses underlayed with a gray rectangle. Three gamma scintillation counters were distributed along the right corridor wall. The distance between two neighbored detectors is 5 m. An example of the devices is shown in Fig. 2 (top, right). In Fig. 2 (bottom), the positions of the detectors are marked by black crosses underlayed with a yellow rectangle. The screen shot shows intermediate tracking and classification results of a scenario with three persons. The middle person is the source carrier, which is correctly determined by the PMHT-C already during the walk through the second detection area. The detection areas are rectangular and visualized by the light yellow areas in the screen shot. Systematic experiments were carried out with two persons. They walk from left to right. The source was carried on the right, except for the last experiment.

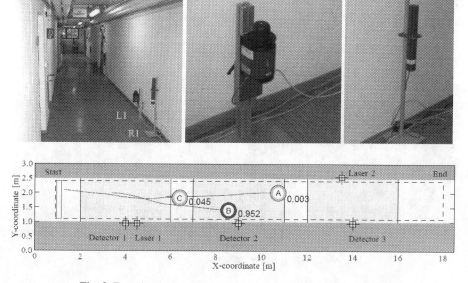

Fig. 2. Experimental environment at the Fraunhofer INT institute

Tab. 1 comprises the final carrier probability of the true carrier calculated by each of the two approaches. The experiments can be divided into four groups. The first group consists of distance experiments with two persons walking in line, having a distance of 3.0 m, 2.0 m and 1.0 m between each other. The source was Cobalt 60

(Co-60). The second group consists of overtaking experiments, in which the carrier is overtaken by the non-carrier and vice-versa. The third group comprises distance experiments with the Caesium 137 (Cs-137) source.

Table 1. Results of the Accum-C and the PMHT-C approach

Scenario	Accum-C	PMHT-C
2 persons, distance 3.0 m, Co-60 in the front	0.995	0.985
2 persons, distance 3.0 m, Co-60 in the back	0.989	0.985
2 persons, distance 2.0 m, Co-60 in the front	0.770	0.978
2 persons, distance 2.0 m, Co-60 in the back	0.824	0.997
2 persons, distance 1.0 m, Co-60 in the front	0.526	0.937
2 persons, distance 1.0 m, Co-60 in the back	0.570	0.894
2 persons, Co-60 is overtaken on the left	0.618	0.989
2 persons, Co-60 is overtaking on the left	0.680	0.646
2 persons, Co-60 is overtaking on the right	0.668	0.767
2 persons, Co-60 is overtaken on the right	0.540	0.732
2 persons, distance 3.0 m, Cs-137 in the front	0.936	0.854
2 persons, distance 3.0 m, Cs-137 in the back	0.998	0.991
2 persons, distance 1.0 m, Cs-137 in the front	0.608	0.976
2 persons, distance 1.0 m, Cs-137 in the back	0.582	0.863
2 persons in parallel, Co-60 on the right	0.502	0.986
2 persons in parallel, Co-60 on the left	0.500	0.929
Average	0.707	0.907

Fig. 3. Real scenarios for radioactive source localization

And finally, in the fourth group of experiments two persons passed the detector array in parallel. In this case the second detector was placed on the left wall of the corridor at position [9.0, 2.5] m. The photos in Fig. 3 show examples of a distance experiment and an experiment with an overtaking source. For each experiment, the better performance result is highlighted by a yellow cell color in the table. The results confirm, what was already expected in Section 3: The closer the persons walk, the worse is the discrimination ability of the Accum-C approach. For the 1.0 m distance experiments the carrier probability is rather close to 50%, which means almost no discrimination. The PMHT-C in contrast results in a source carrier probability of about 90% in these cases and has thus a much better performance than the Accum-C.

Fig 4 provides the classification results of the PMHT-C approach over time. The red and blue bars mark the time range, during which a person was inside the respective detection area. Analogous plots are presented in Fig. 5 for the Accum-C approach. The performance difference is clearly visible.

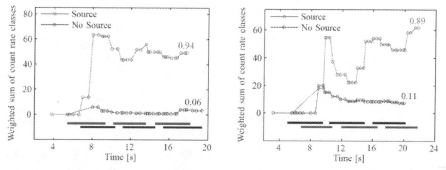

Fig. 4. Results of the PMHT-C approach over time. Two persons walk in line at a distance of 1.0 m. In Fig. 4 (left) the source is in the front. In Fig. 4 (right) the source is in the back.

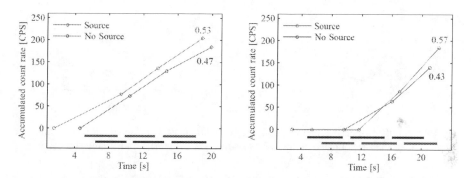

Fig. 5. Results of the Accum-C approach over time. Two persons walk in line at a distance of 1.0 m. In Fig. 4(left) the source is in the front, in Fig. 4(right) it is in the back.

Fig. 6 shows the gamma intensities of the persons estimated by the Poisson filter of PMHT-C. Here, the results are shown for the 1.0 m distance experiment with the Co-60 source in the front. The estimates of the source carrier form an almost horizontal line. However, the essential feature for the discrimination is given by the *deviations* of the person-related numbers of counts (the n_k-values) from the estimated intensity. The n_k-values are plotted as black circles connected by lines. The values of the non-carrier show large deviations from the estimated gamma intensity, while the values of the carrier are constantly close to the mean. Fig. 7 refers to the same experiment and show the distribution of the class probabilities in the confusion matrix, which is estimated by the PMHT-C. Considering the probability distribution of the true carrier, most of the count rate classes referring to the presence of a source have a peak in the plot. Computing the weighted sum of classes thus leads to the large values in Fig. 4. The non-carrier person, in contrast, has a high peak for the zero class indicating that there is no detection caused by this person.

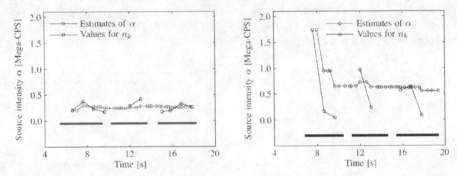

Fig. 6. Gamma intensity estimates for two persons at a distance of 1.0 m and a source of Co-60. The source was carried by the front person.

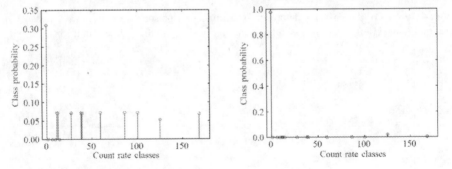

Fig. 7. Distribution of class probabilities in the confusion matrix. Two persons walk in line at a distance of 1.0 m. The source is in the front. Red refers to the carrier, blue to the non-carrier.

Looking at Tab. 1, some more conclusions can be drawn. In the second group of experiments, a decreasing performance of the PMHT-C can be observed. These are experiments with overtaking which are naturally influenced by shielding. However, shielding is out of the scope of this paper. Finally, in the group of parallel person movements, the PMHT-C fully proves its superiority. In these cases, the Accum-C approach is not able to distinguish between the persons anymore, since both persons enter and leave the detection areas at the same time. However, the detector placement has to be adjusted, so that during the walk the property of being closest to the detector changes from one person to the other. The table shows the results after the persons have passed the first two detectors. Computing the average over all experiments, leads to the result that the PMHT-C is significantly better than the Accum-C.

6.2   Simulation Study

A simulation study for scenarios with two persons walking in line was done. The assumed surveillance area and the detector placement were identical to Fig. 2. The background rate β^r was set to 230 CPS for each detector, which corresponds approximately to the values in the experiments. The gamma intensity of the source was 220 kilo-CPS. In this analysis, it is assumed that the positions of the persons inside the surveillance area are exactly known. Persons are considered as point objects. 200 runs for each distance between the persons were simulated. Fig. 8 shows the average carrier probability of the true carrier for each distance. The two plots verify what could be expected by considering Tab. 1. The performance of the Accum-C decreases significantly, when the distance between the two persons gets smaller. The PMHT-C approach in contrast, is able to discriminate fairly well.

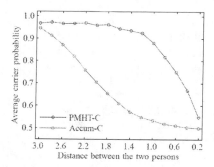 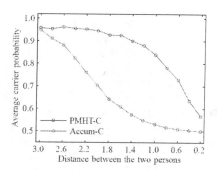

Fig. 8. Results of a simulation study. Two persons walking in line were simulated. The distance between the persons varied from 3.0 m down to 0.2 m. For each distance 200 runs were done.

7   Conclusion

In this work we presented two approaches to the problem of source carrier localization in person streams. The PMHT-C with additional gamma intensity estimates could be proven to be the best in terms of source carrier discrimination. The intensity estimation is realized by a recursive Bayesian filter using Gamma densities. The methodical future activities will consider persons as extended objects and shielding.

References

1. Wieneke, M., Koch, W.: Combined Person Tracking and Classification in a Network of Chemical Sensors. Elsevier Journal of Critical Infrastructure Protection 2(1–2) (2009)
2. Knoll, G.F.: Radiation Detection and Measurement, 3rd edn. John Wiley & Sons (January 2000)
3. Proceedings of the International Conference on Security of Radioactive Sources, Vienna, Austria (2003), http://www-pub.iaea.org/MTCD/publications/PDF/Pub1165_web.pdf (last checked March 30, 2012)
4. Davey, S.J., Gray, D.A., Streit, R.L.: Tracking, association and classification - a combined PMHT approach. Elsevier on Digital Signal Processing 12(2–3), 372–382 (2002)

Imaging Standoff Detection of Explosives
by Diffuse Reflectance IR Laser Spectroscopy

Frank Fuchs, Jan Phillip Jarvis, Stefan Hugger, Michel Kinzer, Quankui Yang,
Wolfgang Bronner, Rachid Driad, and Rolf Aidam

Fraunhofer Institute for Applied Solid State Physics (IAF),
Tullastrasse 72, 79108 Freiburg, Germany
Frank.fuchs@iaf.fraunhofer.de

Abstract. In this work we demonstrate standoff detection of traces of explosives using mid-infrared laser spectroscopy. We apply active laser illumination and use an infrared camera for collection of the diffusely backscattered laser radiation. The key component of the system is an external cavity quantum cascade. Different numerical hyperspectral image analysis methods are evaluated with respect to target detection performance and false alarm rate using both synthetic and real spectroscopic data. Traces of TNT, PETN and RDX could be identified and discriminated against non-hazardous materials by scanning the illumination wavelength over several characteristic absorption features of the explosives.

1   Introduction

During the last years various techniques for detection of explosive materials have been proposed and demonstrated. These can be coarsely divided into two main classes, using the boundary conditions of the scenario in which they can be applied as a classification criterion. So-called cooperative situations provide the possibility of sampling close to the object to be investigated, e.g. by accumulation of air, preparation of swipe samples, and setting up well-defined measurement conditions. Under these conditions, very high sensitivity can be achieved with state-of-the-art techniques such as ion-mobility spectrometry and related methods [1-4].

However, there also exists a strong demand for techniques that allow standoff detection and identification of hazardous substances without any sample preparation, ideally from safe distances. In case of improvised explosive devices, these distances can range from several tens to hundreds of meters e.g. for car bombs.

Up to now, no established techniques were able to accomplish all of these demands though there have been numerous reports on possible approaches. For the detection of larger amounts of hidden explosive material (> 100g) microwave based techniques show potential for short distances (< 5m). For standoff detection of small traces, only laser based techniques have the potential to provide sufficient sensitivity [5-9]. Impressive results were obtained using stand-off Raman spectroscopy [9] with excitation

N. Aschenbruck et al. (Eds.): Future Security 2012, CCIS 318, pp. 388–399, 2012.

in the near UV spectral range. However, questions arise regarding eye-safety when using laser radiation. This issue will be addressed below in more detail.

In this paper we describe a technique using mid-infrared-laser spectroscopy. Optical detection techniques based on this approach have already delivered promising results [5-7], [10]. There are a number of reasons why the mid-IR spectral range is an attractive choice for chemical stand-off detection. Among these perhaps the most important one is that most organic compounds exhibit characteristic absorbance patterns in this spectral range, which, for this reason, is often referred to as molecular fingerprint region.

The transparency of the atmosphere constitutes a critical prerequisite for detection over distances of at least a few meters. In figure 1 we present absorption spectra of several relevant explosives together with the air transmission over a distance of 8 m. The spectra were obtained using attenuated total reflectance (ATR). It becomes clear that the 7 µm - 10 µm region comprises many characteristic absorption features while providing a sufficiently high atmospheric transmission.

Laser sources: Over the last years tremendous progress has been made in the field of mid-IR quantum cascade laser development, regarding output power, wall-plug efficiency and tuning range. This type of semiconductor laser represents an ideal illumination source for the application at hand. Not only does it provide both the necessary bandwidth and output power, the technology also allows the realization of compact, rugged laser modules as building blocks for mobile measurement systems for field applications.

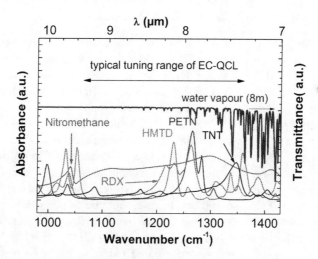

Fig. 1. Absorption spectra of some explosives from 7 µm -10 µm. Several strong, characteristic absorption bands suitable for identification of the compounds lie in this spectral range. For wavenumbers 1300 < cm⁻¹, the atmosphere is sufficiently transparent for stand-off detection using laser light at these frequencies.

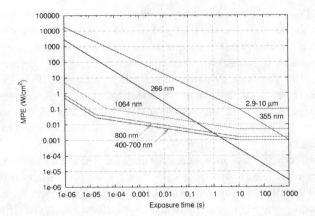

Fig. 2. Maximum permissible exposure (MPE) as power density versus exposure time for various wavelengths (according to IEC 60825, [11])

Detectors: The detection side is another key issue of mid-IR standoff spectroscopy, especially if imaging capabilities are required. High performance is obtained by cooled MCT cameras, however, availability and high prices are an issue. A more cost effective variant are uncooled micro-bolometer arrays, with the drawbacks of a lower sensitivity (the noise-equivalent temperature difference, NETD, is typically three times higher) and lower frame rate compared to their high-end MCT counterparts. Nevertheless, recent developments of bolometric detectors show promising results towards a reduction of the sensitivity gap to MCT-based detectors.

Eye-Safety: An advantage of the mid-IR spectral range is that much higher power levels are allowed than in the near-IR to UV-regions. In figure 2 the maximum permissible exposure (MPE) is shown for different wavelengths from the UV to the IR spectral region according to IEC 60825 (from [11]). Here the maximum permissible power density is plotted as a function of exposure time. Beyond wavelengths of 3 μm, laser intensities up to 100 mW / cm^2 can be tolerated for long exposure times. This is mainly due to the fact, that the human eye is not transparent for radiation in the infra-red spectral range. Even higher power levels can be accepted if lower duty cycles are employed. For stand-off Raman techniques visible and near-UV lasers are predomi-nantly used, resulting in lower tolerated intensity levels, with one exception for wave-lengths between 320 nm and 400 nm. Even though the human eye is transparent for the radiation in that spectral band, the light cannot be efficiently focused on the retina any more, and thus eye-safety is re-accomplished [12],[13]. Finally, the aspect of unconcealed scanning using invisible infrared radiation might be considered as an advantage in certain situations.

2   External Cavity Quantum Cascade Laser

Quantum Cascade Lasers establish a new class of unipolar infrared laser sources which can operate in the infrared spectral range between 3.3 μm to 12 μm wavelengths [14]. Applying band structure engineering, the gain spectrum of such a QC laser can be designed according to the specific needs of the application. Our QC lasers are based on $Ga_{0.47}In_{0.53}As$ quantum wells and $Al_{0.48}In_{0.52}As$ barriers which are grown by molecular beam epitaxy (MBE) lattice matched on InP substrates. To ensure a broad gain spectrum, we rely on a bound-to-continuum design (B-to-C, [15]). A further increase of the spectral range covered by a single chip is obtained by growing an active region comprising two different B-to-C active regions with central emission wavelengths of ~7.8 μm and ~8.8 μm, respectively (a so-called heterocascading design, [16]). The QC laser chips were placed in an external cavity (EC) setup in standard Littrow-configuration using a diffraction grating as a wavelength-selective cavity mirror. The radiation is coupled out through the back facet which acts as the second cavity mirror with a residual reflectivity of ~30%. The lasers were operated in pulsed mode (100 ns pulses) at room temperature. For our B-to-C laser chips, the emission can be tuned over ~190 cm^{-1}, corresponding to 14 % of the central emission wavelength of ~7.5 μm. The heterocascading chip allows tuning over 300 cm^{-1}, thus matching the tuning range needed for explosive detection (see figure 1).

3   Experimental Setup

For our experiments we used samples that were prepared by deposition of artificial fingerprints of the explosives on various substrates, using a synthetic replicate of a human thumb. It is clear that this approach does not yield well-defined surface coverages on the substrate (total amounts vary roughly from about 100μg to > 1mg). However, the morphology of actual residues left by a person handling explosives is more realistically represented, than common laboratory methods of sample deposition (e.g. deposition by a nano-plotter, solvent evaporation). As substrates we used pieces of factory-painted sheets from the autobody of common cars as well as polyamide (PA) and different types of tissue.

The object under investigation is illuminated by the tunable laser, and the backscattered radiation is collected by a detector, synchronized with the tuning of the laser wavelength. Under realistic circumstances, it can be considered a rare case that the sample is oriented such that the light originating from the specular reflection is collected. Therefore, we measured only the much weaker diffusive scattering at directions far away from the specular reflection.

Using a camera, rather than a single element detector on the collection side allows spatially resolved spectroscopy, i.e. hyperspectral imaging. In our system, the backscattered light is recorded by a MCT focal plane array camera. Due to the integration mode of the camera (frame rate: 400 Hz, integration time: 100 μs), the EC-QC laser was driven in a pulse-burst mode (100 ns pulses, up to 1.7 MHz repetition rate) during the integration period of the camera. The resulting average duty cycle of lower than 1% for this mode of operation allows uncooled operation of the laser. With an average laser power during the pulse burst of ~50 mW at the center wavelength, the total time-averaged output power remains below 2 mW, and thus well below power levels at which eye-safety becomes an issue. An enhancement of the current operation distance of a few meters, or alternatively the illuminated area, is therefore possible by using a more powerful laser or multiple illumination sources without violating the conditions for eye-safety. To eliminate the thermal background we subtract two consecutively recorded frames, one frame with active illumination by the EC-QC laser and one frame with the laser turned off. We found that taking a reference every second image instead of a single one for the whole measurement is advantageous especially in non-laboratory situations where the thermal background can change significantly during the recording time of a full spectrum, which can range from a few up to tens of seconds, depending on the desired signal to noise ratio. Reasons for changes in thermal background can include air circulation or the strong thermal signature of moving persons who enter the field of view of the camera either directly or by generating reflections on surfaces. Note that in the thermal infrared spectral region flat surfaces in most cases are mirror-like with significant reflectance.

4   Hyperspectral Image Processing

In the remote sensing community there are several analysis methods available for spectral un-mixing and target detection in hyperspectral image data. In a first step we investigated four detection algorithms with respect to their detection sensitivity and false alarm rate for the task of explosives detection and identification: The Normalized Cross-Correlation (NCC), Constrained Energy Minimization (CEM), Orthogonal Subspace Projection (OSP), and Adaptive Matched Subspace Detection (AMSD).

4.1   Target Detection Algorithms

The first two algorithms NCC and CEM are direct target detection methods that do not require a data model. In contrast the OSP and AMS target detection methods employ a linear mixing model of background and target spectra and therefore require an estimate of the endmembers (substance characteristics) comprising the image background. The NCC target detector uses the normalized cross-correlation coefficient as a similarity measure between target spectrum and each pixel vector in the image to detect pixels containing the target. This approach requires bulk pixel coverage by the target substance, and therefore cannot perform detection on a sub-pixel level. The same holds for the CEM target detector described in [17], which is an approach based on linear finite impulse response filtering. The algorithm calculates the coefficients of a linear finite impulse response filter, for which the average output energy across all pixel vectors is minimized subject to the constraint, that the filter output energy is one, if applied to the target vector.

The OSP target detector was proposed by Harsanyi and Chang in [18]. It is an approach using the linear mixing model, thus enabling target detection on a sub pixel level. The linear mixing model for an arbitrary pixel vector $\vec{r}$ is given by

$$\vec{r} = \vec{t}\,\alpha_t + S\,\vec{\alpha}_s + \vec{n} \tag{1}$$

where $\vec{t}$ denotes the target spectrum with the abundance fraction α_t, and S denotes a matrix of spectra comprising the image background with the vector of abundance fractions $\vec{\alpha}_s$. Image noise is modeled by the additive noise vector $\vec{n}$ which is usually assumed to be uncorrelated Gaussian white. The OSP target detector makes use of the orthogonal complement projector $P_S^\perp = I - S\,(S^T S)^{-1}S^T$ that maps data onto a subspace orthogonal to the space spanned by the signatures in the background matrix S. An estimate of the target abundance fraction α_t for an arbitrary pixel vector $\vec{x}$ is then used for target detection and is computed using the OSP detector

$$T_{OSP}(\vec{x}) = \left(\vec{d}^T P_S^\perp \vec{d}\right)^{-1}\vec{d}^T P_S^\perp \vec{x} \tag{2}$$

under the Gaussian white noise assumption (see [18] for further detail).

The AMS detector also adopts the linear mixing model for target detection and is described in more detail in [19]. A slight modification of equation 1 allows the usage of multiple target spectra that are collected in the target matrix S_t. In this case, the model takes the form

$$\vec{r} = S_t \vec{\alpha}_t + S_b \vec{\alpha}_b + \vec{n}. \tag{3}$$

Here the target fraction scalar in the previous model (equation 1) is now substituted by the fraction vector $\vec{\alpha}_t$. The AMS detector performs hypotheses testing, using the likelihood ratio of the two hypotheses:

- $H_0 : \vec{r} = S_b \vec{\alpha}_b + \vec{n}$ (target absent, i.e. reduced model considering the background spectra only is sufficient)
- $H_1 : \vec{r} = S_t \vec{\alpha}_t + S_b \vec{\alpha}_b + \vec{n} = S\vec{\alpha} + \vec{n}$ (target present, i.e. full model required).

Utilizing the maximum likelihood estimates for noise variance and abundance fraction vector the following target detector can be derived (see [19] for further detail):

$$T_{AMSD}(\vec{x}) = (\vec{x}^T P_b^\perp \vec{x})^{-1}\,\vec{x}^T (P_S^\perp - P_b^\perp)\,\vec{x} \tag{4}$$

Here $P_S^\perp$ and $P_b^\perp$ denote the orthogonal complement projectors for the full and reduced model spectra matrix, respectively.

The OSP and AMS detector have in common, that an estimate of the endmembers comprising the background matrix S_b is essentially required. As in general these endmembers are not available, they have to be estimated from the image data. For this purpose a variety of methods have been proposed some of which are compared in [20]. We propose the usage of the Adaptive Target Generation Process (ATGP) [21]. This algorithm is also based on the linear mixing model and is related to the orthogonal subspace projection target detector. The first step requires a known image endmember $\vec{t}_0$ and calculates the vector norm of all image pixel vectors in the orthogonal subspace received using the orthogonal complement projector $P_{\vec{t}_0}^\perp$. The pixel vector with the largest vector norm in this subspace is then added to the endmember matrix U. Until a pre-selected cutoff criterion is met, the algorithm iteratively adds pixel vectors $\vec{t}_i$ to this matrix, by choosing

$$\vec{t}_i = \arg\{\max_{\vec{r}}[(P^\perp_{[\vec{t}_0 U_{i-1}]}\vec{r})^T (P^\perp_{[\vec{t}_0 U_{i-1}]}\vec{r})]\}, \tag{5}$$

that is: the pixel vector having the largest vector norm in the subspace orthogonal to the space spanned by the current endmember matrix $[\vec{t}_0 U_{i-1}]$. Ren and Chang suggest the cutoff criterion $\mu_i = \vec{t}_0^T P^\perp_{U_i}\vec{t}_0 < \epsilon$ [21]. However, as this yielded highly unstable results in our setup, we chose to use a fixed number of endmembers. This is justified by the fact, that the laser illuminates a comparatively small scene containing only a limited number of materials and therewith a limited amount of endmembers.

Common to all mentioned detection methods is that the output of the target detectors are scalars in varying ranges, which have to be binarized employing a fixed threshold to gain a classification system. In the following section we will evaluate and compare the classifier performances in terms of true positive and false alarm rates employing the target detection methods mentioned. In many image processing applications including that at hand, a common problem is to obtain the ground truth necessary for such an analysis, as true positions and target amounts are not known. Thus, we propose to use synthetic data where all target and background abundances are specified. Our data model for synthetic data is based on the linear mixture model and includes factors for beam profile and laser intensity functions. Given a spatial laser beam function $I_L(x,y)$ and a wavelength dependent laser intensity distribution $I_L(\lambda)$ the intensity value at a given pixel $p_{kl}(x,y,\lambda)$ is given by:

$$p_{kl}(x,y,\lambda) = I_L(x,y)\,I_L(\lambda)\,[\,\sum_{i=1}^k t_i(x,y)T_i(\lambda) + \sum_{i=1}^l b_i(x,y)B_i(\lambda)\,] + w(x,y,\lambda)$$

Here, the l background and k target spectra are denoted $B_i(\lambda)$ and $T_i(\lambda)$ while the corresponding spatial distribution functions $b_i(x,y)$ and $t_i(x,y)$ constitute the abundance fractions. The additive noise term $w(x,y,\lambda)$ is usually chosen Gaussian white.

4.2 Analysis of Target Detection Performance

From the ROC plots in figure 3 we follow, that for the NCC detector it is not possible to choose a threshold value that yields reasonable TPR values while avoiding false alarms. The NCC classifier proves to be especially sensitive to false alarms of RDX; a further analysis revealed that the background spectrum (polyamide) was often mistaken for RDX. The CEM detector outperforms the NCC detector in these characteristics, having a superior ROC. In figure 4 we present the classification results of the model based target detection methods OSP and AMSD, which consider the background spectra. It can be seen, that the ROC of the OSP detector is well comparable to that of the CEM detector.

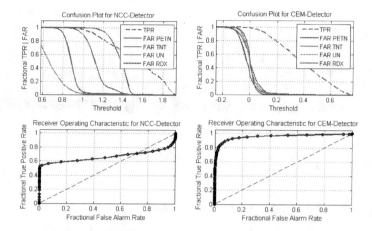

Fig. 3. Confusion plots and Receiver Operating Characteristic for NCC (left) and CEM target detection (right) of PETN on a Polyamid substrate

However, while the OSP detector suffers of being sensitive to both PETN and TNT it is preferable to the CEM detector for explosives detection, as the latter proved to be very sensitive to slight deviations from target to reference spectrum. The confusion and ROC plots for the AMS detector suggest that this method is strongly favored for the task at hand among the detection methods described. The false alarm rates are exceptionally low while true positive rates of 80% can be achieved. In conclusion, we propose the combination of the AMS target detector using the ATGP endmember generation process to estimate the endmembers comprising the background.

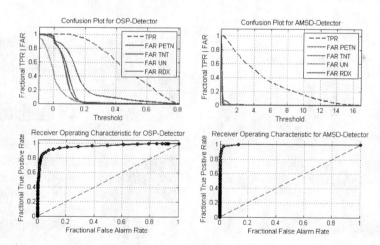

Fig. 4. Confusion plots and Receiver Operating Characteristic for OSP (left) and AMSD detection (right) of PETN on a Polyamid substrate

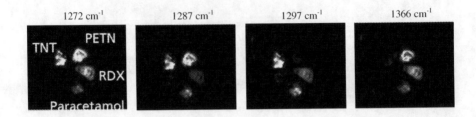

Fig. 5. Wavelength selective illumination of artificial TNT, PETN, RDX and Paracetamol finger prints on car paint

4.3   Results on Real Hyperspectral Image Data

In figure 5, we illustrate the effect of wavelength-selective illumination on both explosive and non-hazardous materials on a factory-painted autobody sheet. Artificial finger prints of TNT, PETN, RDX, Paracetamol and skin powder were illuminated at different, characteristic wavenumbers. At 1272 cm^{-1}, all four compounds show a clear backscattering signal. At 1287 cm^{-1}, the signal from RDX weakens, at 1297 cm^{-1}, PETN is hardly visible and at 1366 cm^{-1} the signal from TNT becomes very low.

Figure 6 shows a polyamide (PA) substrate on which 8 consecutive fingerprints have been deposited. The green area indicates the illuminated part of the sample, i.e. the 7th fingerprint. The amount of deposited material was ~20 µg, the measurement distance was about 1.5 m. In contrast to the autobody sheets shown above, the PA surface acts as a source of diffusive scattering, therefore the measured signal contains significant contributions from the substrate.

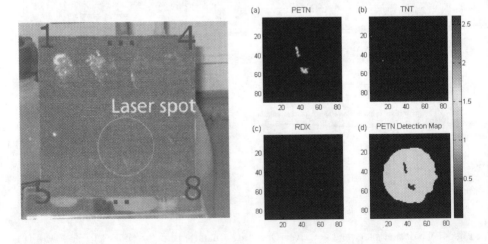

Fig. 6. Left: Photograph of the sample. Right: (a)-(c): detection results for PETN, TNT and RDX traces, (d): detection map with applied threshold for detection of PETN (green: background detected, red: target detected).

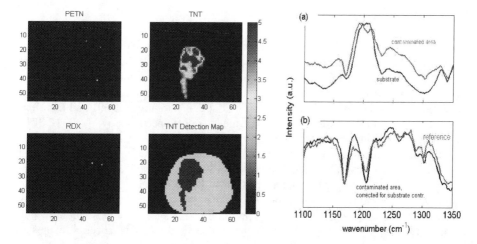

Fig. 7. Left: Detection results of the AMS detector applied to a TNT fingerprint on cloth from a jacket. TNT is identified; no false alarms for PETN or RDX are obtained. Right (a): Normalized spectra from bare substrate (blue) and TNT contaminated area (red). (b) After subtracting the substrate spectrum from the blue curve in (a), a trace closely resembling the TNT reference spectrum is obtained.

Using the reference spectra obtained as discussed in section 3, we applied the suggested AMS target detector in combination with the ATGP background endmember extractor to the collected hyperspectral image and present the results in figure 6. It can be seen, that with this fully generic approach, our algorithm successfully detected the PETN residues, while no false alarms for TNT and RDX were obtained. An example for strong background contribution is shown in figure 7. Here, we investigated a TNT fingerprint on a strongly scattering substrate (cloth from a jacket). Again, the AMS detector was applied to the hyperspectral image. The TNT contaminated region was identified, while searching for the PETN and RDX produced no false alarms. In figure 7 we also present the spectral information averaged over the detected area as well as over the illuminated part of the substrate where no TNT was detected. The signal from the contaminated area still contains strong substrate contributions. Therefore, a detection algorithm seeking for pure reference spectra will most likely fail in this case. The reference spectrum for TNT is recovered by correcting this trace by the spectrum of the uncovered substrate. Treating the spectrum on a single pixel as a sum of different contributions, as assumed in the linear mixing model, is justified by the fact that the coverage of the explosives on the substrate is strongly inhomogeneous on a length scale not resolved by the camera. Therefore, the signal on one pixel effectively averages over regions hardly covered by the explosive and such where the coverage is the dominant source of scattering.

F. Fuchs et al.

5 Conclusions

In this work we present imaging stand-off detection of explosive traces on surfaces using backscattering laser spectroscopy in the spectral range of the thermal infrared at wavelengths between 7 μm and 9 μm. The laser source is an external cavity quantum cascade laser with a maximum tuning range of about 300 cm^{-1}. The technique uses harmless laser radiation in the thermal infrared at eye-safe power levels and therefore enables concealed observation. As an example, standoff spectroscopy of PETN, TNT and RDX fingerprints on different real world materials has been demonstrated. Regarding image processing we investigated the receiver operating characteristics and false alarm rate of several detection algorithms such as normalized cross correlation, orthogonal subspace projection and adaptive matched subspace detection on synthetic image data. Preliminary investigations show, that the latter algorithm provides very promising results regarding efficient suppression of background contributions which corresponds to low false alarm rates in both synthetic and real hyperspectral images.

Acknowledgments. Helpful discussions with J. Wagner (Fraunhofer IAF) and J. Beyerer (Fraunhofer IOSB) are gratefully acknowledged. Part of the results have been obtained within the collaborative project IRLDEX, funded by the German Federal Ministry of Education and Research (contract number FKZ 13N4543). Samples and targets have been prepared during the IRLDEX project by F. Schnürer and co-workers at Fraunhofer ICT.

References

1. Cornish, T.J., Antoine, M.D., Ecelberger, S.A., Demirev, P.A.: Arrayed Time-of-Flight Mass Spectrometry for Time-Critical Detection of Hazardous Agents. Anal. Chem. 77(13), 3954–3959 (2005)
2. Bauer, C., Sharma, A.K., Willer, U., Burgmeier, J., Braunschweig, B., Schade, W., Blaser, S., Hvozdara, L., Müller, A., Holl, G.: Potentials and limits of mid-infrared laser spectroscopy for the detection of explosives. Appl. Phys. B 92(3), 327–333 (2008)
3. Orghici, R., Willer, U., Gierszewska, M., Waldvogel, S.R., Schade, W.: Fiber optic evanescent field sensor for detection of explosives and CO$_2$ dissolved in water. Appl. Phys. B 90(2), 355–360 (2008)
4. Dunayevskiy, I., Tsekoun, A., Prasanna, M., Go, R., Patel, C.K.N.: High-sensitivity detection of triacetonetriperoxide (TATP) and its precursor acetone. Appl. Opt. 46(25), 6397–6404 (2007)
5. van Neste, C.W., Senesac, L.R., Thundat, T.: Standoff photoacoustic spectroscopy. Appl. Phys. Lett. 92(23), 234102 (2008)
6. Furstenberg, R., Kendziora, C.A., Stepnowski, J., Stepnowski, S.V., Rake, M., Papantonakis, M.R., Nguyen, V., Hubler, G.K., McGill, R.A.: Stand-off detection of trace explosives via resonant infrared photothermal imaging. Appl. Phys. Lett 93, 224103-1–224103-3 (2008)
7. Pushkarsky, M.B., Dunayevskiy, I.G., Prasanna, M., Tsekoun, A.G., Go, R., Patel, C.K.N.: High sensitivity detection of TNT. Proc. of the National Academy of Sciences of the United States of America 103(52), 19630–19634 (2006)

8. Hummel, R.E., Fuller, A.M., Schollhorn, C., Holloway, P.H.: Detection of explosive materials by differential reflection spectroscopy. Appl. Phys. Lett. 88(23), 231903 (2006)
9. Wallin, S., Petterson, A., Östmark, H., Hobro, A.: Laser-based standoff detection of explosives: a critical review. Analyt. and Bioanalyt. Chem. 395(2), 259–274 (2009)
10. Fuchs, F., Hugger, S., Kinzer, M., Aidam, R., Bronner, W., Lösch, R., Yang, Q.K., Degreif, K., Schnürer, F.: Imaging standoff detection of explosives using widely tunable midinfrared quantum cascade lasers. Opt. Eng. 49(11), 111–127 (2010)
11. British and European Standard BS EN 60825-1 2007, International Standard IEC 60825-1 (2007)
12. Barker, F.M., Brainard, G.C.: The direct spectral transmittance of the excised human lens as a function of age. FDA 785345 0090 RA, US Foodand Drug Administration: Washington DC (1991)
13. Laube, T., Apel, H., Koch, H.-R.: Ultraviolet Radiation Absorption of Intraocular Lenses. Ophthalmology 111, 880–885 (2004)
14. Bismuto, A., Beck, M., Faist, J.: High power Sb-free quantum cascade laser emitting at 3.3 μm above 350 K. Appl. Phys. Lett. 98, 191104 (2011)
15. Faist, J., Beck, M., Aellen, T.: Quantum-cascade lasers based on bound-to-continuum transition. Appl. Phys. Lett. 78, 147–149 (2001)
16. Maulini, R., Mohan, A., Giovannini, M., Faist, J., Gini, E.: External cavity quantum-cascade laser tunable from 8.2 μm to 10.4 μm using a gain element with a heterogeneous cascade. Appl. Phys. Lett. 88, 201113 (2006)
17. Du, Q., Ren, H., Chang, C.: A comparative study for orthogonal subspace projection and constrained energy minimization. IEEE Transactions on Geoscience and Remote Sensing 41, 1525–1529 (2003)
18. Harsanyiand, J., Chang, C.: Hyperspectral image classification and dimensionality reduction: An orthogonal subspace projection approach. IEEE Transactions on Geoscience and Remote Sensing 32, 779–785 (1994)
19. Manolakis, D., Siracusa, C., Shaw, G.: Hyperspectral subpixel target detection using the linear mixing model. IEEE Transactions on Geoscience and Remote Sensing 39, 1392–1409 (2001)
20. Plaza, A., Martinez, P., Perez, R., Plaza, J.: A quantitative and comparative analysis of endmember extraction algorithms from hyperspectral data. IEEE Transactions onGeoscience and Remote Sensing 42, 650–663 (2004)
21. Ren, H., Chang, C.: Automatic spectral target recognition in hyperspectral imagery. Transactions on Aerospace and Electronic System 39, 1232–1249 (2003)

Development of an Experimental Multi-robot CBRNE Reconnaissance Demonstrator
System Description and Technical Validation

Frank E. Schneider, Dennis Wildermuth, Markus Ducke, and Bernd Brüggemann

Research Group Unmanned Systems
Fraunhofer Institute for Communication,
Information Processing and Ergonomics FKIE
Wachtberg, Germany
frank.schneider@fkie.fraunhofer.de

Abstract. This paper presents a prototype of a multi-robot reconnaissance system for detection of chemical, biological, radiological, nuclear and explosive (CBRNE) threats. Our system consists of different robot platforms which are able to carry highly modularized payload platforms: either a multi-purpose CBRNE sensor suite or a mobile manipulator for semi-autonomous sample collection. A variety of sensors is available for detection and identification of chemical and radiological hazards as well as for collecting potentially dangerous airborne biological particles. A manipulator can be used to gather chemical and biological samples directly from surfaces in the environment. A detailed description illustrates the robot platforms, the CBRNE sensor suite and relevant parts of the user interface. For a technical validation preliminary real world experiments are presented.

Keywords: multi-robot, CBRNE, hazard detection, emergency response.

1 Introduction

Chemical, biological, radiological, nuclear and explosive (CBRNE) incident response becomes increasingly important in our days. On one hand, threats by terrorist groups can cause great damage with relatively small effort. On the other hand, disasters in industrial areas may release dangerous and not easily detectable chemicals. If such an emergency occurs, information about what has happened and how the situation develops is crucial for an effective response. However, it is difficult to explore these scenarios without mortal danger for the involved action force, be it fire fighters, army or police. Unmanned systems help reducing the number of human beings which are required within the danger zone. Robots can support response planning and situational awareness. They can help removing responders from dangerous situations or even allow for immediate site feedback prior to human entry. A robot can be sent ahead, assess the situation at hand and return information and sensor data back to the controller. In [1] Humphrey and Adams classified eight fields of robotic applications in the domain of CBRNE emergency response. Using Cognitive Task Analysis (CTA) and

N. Aschenbruck et al. (Eds.): Future Security 2012, CCIS 318, pp. 400–411, 2012.
© Springer-Verlag Berlin Heidelberg 2012

Fig. 1. Pictures of the two tracked CBRNE vehicles, the QinetiQ Longcross with the CBRNE sensor platfrom and the tEODor carrying the manipulator platform (*left*). Both platforms can be easily dismounted and exchanged (*right*).

Information Flow Analysis (IFA) they proved the feasibility of these tasks and also stated requirements for the acceptance of robots in the human-centric field of CBRNE response activities.

A mobile manipulator greatly enhances the vehicle's utility beyond pure sensor capabilities. On the one hand, its mobility could be increased because the manipulator and the attached gripper can be used to open doors and gates or to push obstacles away. On the other hand, a manipulator-equipped vehicle has the capability to gather images and video from a wider variety of perspectives or to open packages of interest. In addition, the manipulator can be used to collect samples of the hazardous material or from potentially contaminated surfaces for later analysis. So far, for biological and some chemical threats there exists no classification equipment suitable for mobile employment. Thus, samples have to be taken to be analysed in adequate laboratories.

Moreover, the use of more than a single vehicle offers further advantages. When a large area has to be inspected and monitored more robots can simply divide the work spatially. If the area of interest is too far away for reliable communication, robots can act as relay points for data transmission. Or there could be direct cooperation between differently equipped robots. Since general purpose robots usually result in very heavy and complex systems, often a variety of smaller and specialized systems is preferred. Thus, for example, a robot with a manipulator could be used to take a specific sensor from another vehicle carrying a variety of sensor devices. With the help of a mobile arm the operator could then try to have a closer look at the hazardous material and, afterwards, re-attach the sensor to the reconnaissance robot.

Important disaster response requirements, which have to be met by any robot system in this domain, include the ability to

- operate in areas with high radiation or danger of explosives,
- take samples and manipulate,
- do long-time surveying in contaminated areas,
- probe in problematic environments and conditions,
- monitor the movements of a threat, and
- provide real-time data from multiple mobile sensor sources.

Several reasons lead to the additional requirement that commercial off-the-shelf (COTS) and in-use CBRNE sensor components should be used. Firstly, these systems are usually easier to purchase and less expensive than prototypes or custom solutions. Secondly, it is not necessary to develop new training methods for equipment that is already in use.

In this paper, we describe the development of a CBRNE multi-robot system for the German Armed Forces. One important design goal for the system was the fast and easy introduction into service. Therefore and because of the above stated prerequisite, we rely on sensor equipment which is already in use in the German forces or at least commercially available. In principle, all deployed sensors can be used independently from the robot base, turning the vehicle into a mobile toolbox.

The remainder of this paper is structured as follows: After a short review of related work we describe the robot platforms in detail in section 3. Afterwards, we cover the sensor platform and the different types of sensor devices. Section 5 presents the actual user interface for the whole system. The demonstration of the current system state is described in section 6.

2   Related Work

Besides Humphrey's study [1] mentioned in the introduction other work can be found in literature which explores the feasibility of robotic applications in the field of CBRNE incidents as well as in the related domains of Explosive Ordnance Disposal (EOD), fire fighting or emergency response in general. Casper et al., for instance, look at demands and constraints regarding urban search and rescue (USAR) [2]. Lundberg et al. analyse whether the same type of robot could be deployed for CBRNE contamination control, military operations in urban terrain (MOUT), military and civil EOD, and fire fighting [3]. They conclude that, in principle, two types of robots can be used for all these tasks: a small man-portable and rugged vehicle for difficult terrain and a heavy-duty one to carry more payload. Some authors look at concrete incidents like a huge mudslide in California in 2005 [4] or the 2001 attack on the World Trade Center towers [5]. They derive demands and recommendations from the experiences of the rescue personnel with their robot systems. Among the statements frequently found in all this work one can find: easy handling and improved human factors design, high reliability and ruggedness, or adjustable autonomy.

There exists a variety of research projects related to robotic CBRNE response activities, some of which are already in a mature state or even in use. The Canadian Forces, for example, employ a tele-operated all-terrain vehicle with an integrated CBRN sensor suite [6]. The vehicle is used in combination with a ground station which belongs to a remote mobile command post. As one major result, the importance of proper training for the prospective users is mentioned. Similar to our system, this problem is partially mitigated by employing sensors that are already in use. Recently a commercially available hydraulic robotic arm was integrated into the system. In [7] the authors examine a variety of scenarios, like retrieving objects for inspection, opening a building or vehicle inspection. Although the operators turned out to be able to cope with these tasks after a few days of training, remote operation of the arm remained mentally taxing. Neilsen et al. [8] improve a purely tele-operated system by introducing semi-autonomous features, which can help to reduce the amount of training that the operator needs. Jasiobedzki et al. [9] describe a system to increase the situation awareness of the operator, which is called CBRN Crime Scene Modeller (C2SM). Its main purpose is the construction of a three-dimensional model that contains points of interests (e.g. chemical, biological and radiological agents).

A considerable amount of research is related to the automated source localization of chemical agents. Many of the applied methods emulate the biological olfactory systems of lobsters, ants and moths [10]. The chemotaxis approach means following the local concentration gradient, which works best if the chemical agent is spread mostly by diffusion. The anemotaxis approach means following the upwind direction, which works best if the chemical agent is mainly spread by convection without turbulences. A second class of techniques estimates the spread by numerical simulation of the assumed environmental conditions [11, 12, 13].

The major drawback of these approaches is that their assumptions about the environment are easily violated in actual deployments. Searching for the source of a pollution based on these models, therefore, is no actual development goal in our system. Nevertheless, the automated discovery of pollution sources remains a long-term goal of the project.

3   Robot Platforms

The first project stage tackled the development of the CBRNE sensor platform. As only one robot was necessary at this stage, we decided to use a wheeled version of the QinetiQ Longcross, with an additional diesel power generator, as vehicle. Details of this robot platform can be found in [14].

With the concept of a manipulator platform, in a second step the need for multiple vehicles arose. We switched to a QinetiQ Longcross with tracks and an additional tEODor, a tracked robot by Telerob, originally used for Explosive Ordnance Disposal (EOD). Using two vehicles with tracks leads to comparable driving characteristics and, hence, similar kinds of surmountable obstacles. The left part of figure 1 shows both robots: the left one is the Longcross equipped with the sensor platform, the right one is the tEODor with the manipulator arm. It is important to mention that – due to the use of standardized connectors – the two platforms can be simply dismounted and exchanged between the different robots as one can see in the right part of figure 1.

The QinetiQ Longcross is a quite large and heavy platform with a weight of about 380 kg and a possible payload of another 150 kg. It can reach a top speed of 4 m/s and has battery capacity for about 30 minutes. The operational range is around 3000 to 5000 m. The robot can cope with very difficult terrain and is able to turn around on the spot, although this draws a substantial amount of motor current and significantly reduces the operation time. Telerob's tEODor has a weight of only 280 kg and a slightly lower payload capacity. But its major drawback is the very low speed of only 1 m/s which results in a limited operational range.

In order to provide sufficient situation awareness, the robot is equipped with a number of non-CBRNE-related sensors. As one can see in figure 1 these include standard laser scanners and pan-tilt cameras. The Topcon Legacy-E$^+$ GPS receiver, for example, is able to receive both GPS and GLONASS satellite data and to use a variety of differential augmentation services. In the best case, a positioning accuracy in the centimetre range can be reached. The pan-tilt cameras provide visual feedback for the operator and are, therefore, the main sensors for tele-operation.

In addition to simple remote controlled operation, the robots are capable of GPS-based autonomous waypoint navigation. Since our vehicles are designed as tele-operated EOD platforms, they lack a velocity controller, a feature which is essential for classic local navigation and collisions avoidance algorithms. To make motion planning still possible, we introduced a novel template-based local navigation algorithm, which is called Adaptable Motion Patterns. Regrettably, a full description of this approach is beyond the scope of this paper. An overview with respect to this CBRNE project is given in [14]; all details can be found in [15].

4   CBRNE Sensors

Depending on the mission parameters, different sets of sensors can be required. Therefore, the sensor platform of the CBRNE robot is equipped with a variety of devices for all possible aspects of chemical, biological, radiological, nuclear and explosive threats. Figure 2 shows a top view of the platform with all sensors attached. Due to the modular platform design the sensor suite as a whole can be mounted on different robots. Additionally, the sensor configuration itself can be changed. Any device can be freely removed at any time and used in a stand-alone mode, for example when the exact location of a radiation source must be figured out. On the one hand, a specially trained CBRNE operator could take off the sensor and use it manually. On the other hand, the second vehicle with the manipulator arm could be employed, using the sensor platform as a mobile toolbox. Currently, the arm and its gripper have to be tele-operated. As a part of this experimental demonstrator an implementation of semi-autonomous manipulation functions is under development. Refer to section 6 for first results.

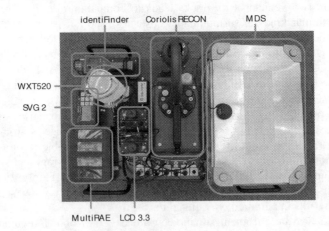

Fig. 2. The complete CBRNE sensor suite, dismounted from the robot platform

In figure 2 the sensor devices are labelled for better differentiation. The LCD 3.3 and MultiRAE devices are sensors for detection of chemical hazards in the air as well as – in case of the MultiRAE – explosive gases. MDS, SVG 2 and identiFinder are used to find different kinds of radiological and nuclear threats. The Coriolis RECON collects airborne biological particles into liquid samples. And, finally, the WXT520 is a sophisticated sensor for a wide range of environmental conditions. Wind speed and direction, for example, are important to predict the dispersion of gases and airborne threats. The sensor suite will be described in detail in the following sections.

4.1   Lightweight Chemical Detector

The Lightweight Chemical Detector (LCD) 3.3 is a chemical sensor. It samples the air continuously, searching for different Chemical Warfare Agents (CWA) or Toxic Industrial Chemicals (TIC).

The LCD 3.3 uses a kind of Ion Mobility Spectrometry, as described in [16] for example. Ambient air is continuously taken into an ionisation chamber. This chamber produces ions from the air as well as possible sample ions of chemicals in that air. A cluster of these ions is passed on to a drift area with two different drift regions, one with negative ions and another with positive ones. By detecting the speed and amount of ions, the different substances can be identified. An alarm is triggered if a certain concentration of an identified agent threshold is exceeded. For the analysis a predefined dataset is used. The LCD 3.3 limits the number of concurrently monitored chemical agents to six. Thus, one should know in advance which chemical agents might be encountered in the target area. To increase the number of detectable substances we employ two LCD 3.3 devices simultaneously, one for TICs and one for CWAs.

4.2   MultiRAE Plus

The MultiRAE Plus is a multi-gas sensor designed to monitor CO_2, combustible and toxic gases, oxygen and so-called Volatile Organic Compounds (VOC). For this purpose, different internal sensors are employed, among them a Photo-Ionisation Detector (PID), which illuminates the gas with a special UV lamp. The high-energy photons ionize the gas. Depending on the substance, different amounts of the UV light are absorbed, leading to different levels of ionization.

The MultiRAE Plus simultaneously measures up to five different gas concentrations. An infrared light sensor detects CO_2. The oxygen level is determined all the time. The described PID identifies a broad range of organic vapours. By changing the electrochemical toxic sensor, several different inorganic toxic gases can be detected. As for the LCD, up to four devices can be mounted in parallel to increase the total number of detectable gases.

4.3   Mobile Detection System

The Mobile Detection System (MDS) is a gamma ray sensor, which can be easily mounted on nearly any type of moving vehicle. The gamma radiation is measured by a large-volume synthetic scintillator. It uses a special Natural Background Rejection (NBR) technology to find even small amounts of radiation. Using this NBR technique, the MDS is able to distinguish between natural (background) and artificial radiation. Even an artificial radiation level below the natural radiation background level can be detected. As the natural radiation is fluctuating depending on the location, the MDS is designed to find artificial sources of radiation in a large area. The synthetic scintillator is supersensitive with a measurement range of 1 nSv/h up to 20 µSv/h. Additionally, two large neutron detector tubes are included in the sensor.

4.4   SVG 2 Radiacmeter

The SVG 2 Radiacmeter is a NATO approved ruggedized ratemeter for gamma and neutron radiation measurement. Both the current gamma dose rate and the integrated gamma and neutron dose can be measured. The internal semiconductor detection device with hardened microprocessor technology is supposed to provide the specified sensibility even in very hostile environments. The SVG 2 has a large measurement range, but it is not as supersensitive as the MDS. The current dose equivalent is measured from 1 µSv/h up to the very high value of 20 Sv/h; the range for the integrated dose is from 1 µSv to 20 Sv with an energy interval from 70 keV up to 3 MeV. Hence, SVG 2 and MDS together cover the full range of conceivable radiation rates.

4.5   ICX identiFinder

The ICX identiFinder detects gamma radiation. But in contrast to the MDS it is not able to distinguish between natural and artificial radiation. Instead, the type of the radioactive nuclide can be identified. For this task, the identiFinder uses a NaI(Tl) (sodium iodide/thallium) detector as gamma spectrum analyser. It has a measurement range up to 500 µSv/h. Above this limit, the identiFinder uses a Geiger-Müller tube. Using a database of nuclide gamma spectra, the identiFinder is able to identify the nuclide. Whenever a gamma source is detected, the identiFinder records a spectrum of the radiation energy. This spectrum is compared to a database of radioactive decay probabilities and the corresponding spectrum of energy. As a result, the identiFinder automatically provides the most likely classification of the gamma source. Naturally, this identification can be only as good as the underlying nuclide database.

4.6   Coriolis RECON

The Coriolis RECON is a ruggedized bio-aerosol sampler developed by Bertin Technologies, France. As already mentioned, up to now there are no biological sensors available which can identify biological threats directly on a mobile platform. Instead, the Coriolis device collects and concentrates airborne biological particles into a liquid sample for examination in a suitably equipped laboratory. Using a special wet cyclone technology, large amounts of biological particles from 0.5 up to 10 µm are concentrated in the sample.

Looking at figure 3 one can see the functional principle of the Coriolis. Air is first aspirated into a liquid-filled cone in a whirling motion to form a vortex. Particles are pulled against the wall due to centrifugal force, separated from air and concentrated in the liquid. This process lasts for 5, 10 or 15 minutes depending on the user's choice. Afterwards, the glass cone can be detached and is ready for later analysis.

Fig. 3. Functional principle of the Coriolis RECON. Air is aspirated into a liquid-filled cone in a whirling motion. Particles are pulled against the wall and concentrated in the liquid. *(Illustration by courtesy of Bertin Technologies, France).*

4.7   Vaisala WXT520

The Vaisala WXT520 weather transmitter measures barometric pressure, humidity, precipitation, temperature, and wind speed and direction – maintenance-free and in real time. The measurement principle of the pressure, temperature and humidity sensors is based on an RC oscillator and two reference capacitors, against which the capacitance of the sensors is continuously measured. According to the manufacturer, air temperature can be measured with an accuracy of ±0.4 °C, barometric pressure with ±0.5 hPa and relative humidity with ±3%. To determine wind speed and direction special ultrasound sensors are used. The resulting accuracy is supposed to be ±5% for speed and ±3° for wind direction. The WXT520 precipitation measurement is based on an acoustic sensor which detects the impact of individual rain drops. The signals exerting from the impacts are proportional to the volume of the drops and can be directly converted into rain intensity and accumulated rainfall.

5   User Interface

Since one of the design goals was to keep the sensors independent from the underlying robot platform, the connection to the robot platform as well as the communication with the control station had to be standardized. Perle IOLAN serial-over-LAN converters are used to forward serial ports directly over a radio link to a dedicated control station. The CBRNE sensors are attached via standard plug-and-socket connectors and can be easily exchanged. The Perle converter translates the various serial data streams into standard TCP/IP network traffic, which is directly processed by the UI software. An advantage of this approach is that, besides to the dedicated control station, the data can be forwarded to other users simultaneously.

Although there is no technical limitation regarding the actual setup of the control station, it was decided to install all required equipment into the trunk compartment of a Ford Transit transporter. The storage space is large enough to host a control station, that can be manned by two operators, as well as the necessary radio transmitters and at least one of the robots. In order to achieve better performance and efficiency, two operators share the workload of running the CBRNE system. One operator is responsible for the navigation of the robot platforms, while the other concentrates on the analysis and evaluation of the incoming sensor data. Both operators have two large displays which provide a detailed overview of the actual workflow. The operator who is responsible for steering and navigating the robot can see a map-based representation of the robots' environment and the available camera views. In addition, he has access to detailed low-level system information. Apart from pure tele-operation, target points can be set for GPS-based autonomous navigation.

The user interface for controlling the CBRNE sensors integrates all sensor devices into one application. The software was developed in Matlab and, afterwards, compiled into a standalone application to be deployable independently from Matlab licensing issues. The user interface consists of two windows, each of them presented on a large display (see the screenshot in figure 4).

Fig. 4. The MATLAB-based user interface for controling the CBRNE sensor suite. The upper window displays the readings of the currently mounted sensors. In the lower window the positions of the involved robots are visible. Any necessary adjustments also can be done in this display.

The upper window visualizes the measurement data. In the upper left corner one can see the data of the ICX identiFinder with its cumulative spectrum of energy and, right of this, dose rate and nuclide count plotted over time. Additionally, the actual measurements are given. Below this, the data of the MDS and SVG 2 devices are printed numerically and plotted in a time diagram. On the right hand side, one can see the separate sensor measurements of the multiple MultiRAE devices as a series of line graphs over time. The bottom left area belongs to the LCD data for CWAs and TICs. When detected, the chemical agents' names are presented together with their intensity. Generally, the corresponding 2D positive and negative spectra are drawn in a waterfall diagram with time in the z-direction.

The bottom window offers different options to control the sensors and also gives a map-based overview. The operator can choose between various kinds of maps. Additionally, specific options for the sensor devices can be triggered: inclusion or exclusion of a sensor's visualization, a colour-coded status display, or start and stop of the measurement. GPS information and weather data are shown near the map in the upper right section. To get a feedback about the system state, informational messages are posted in a text window in the bottom right.

All data are collected and stored in a standard Matlab data format. An extended module of the GUI can be used to display the sensor data history in conjunction with the corresponding vehicle's positions for a specific mission. Of course, also any Matlab analysis or visualization tool can be applied to the recorded, time-stamped and GPS-referenced data.

6   Demonstration

After an initial prototyping phase of about 10 months the first version of the CBRNE capability concept demonstrator was ready to be tested. One of the key strengths of this Concept Development & Experimentation (CD&E) research approach is the close involvement of the future customer. For further tests and demonstrations we used an iterative evolutionary design process to ensure a fast response time to requirements of the involved nuclear, biological and chemical (NBC) disposal experts. This procedure highly improves the acceptance by the prospective end-user.

To ensure a maximum of reconcilement, the NBC Defence School in Sonthofen, Germany, and the Research Institute for Protective Technologies and NBC Protection in Munster, Germany, contributed with their expertise. In detail, the following parts of the system have been tested:

- The sensors were tested regarding their detection, identification and localization capabilities as well as the ability to record and transmit the measured data. The mechanical requirement of dismounting the equipment without tools was fulfilled.
- The vehicle was especially checked for deployment range, mobility and manoeuvrability. Unfortunately, the mechanical implementation of the design showed some weaknesses, which have to be eliminated in the production phase.
- Tests with the manipulator included handling and probing of typical objects and material from the application domain. Preliminary tests on the autonomous sampling function have been carried out.
- The communication system is still in the phase of research and development. Since the customer is looking for high bandwidth in all operational environments and under all weather conditions, radio based communication channels show their limit very fast.

The software for the demonstrator is in a quite mature state. It has been successfully tested on the last European Land Robot Trial (ELROB 2011) where, in particular, the Longcross platform managed to travel nearly 2 km autonomously through dense forest [17]. As for all robotic projects supported by the German Armed Forces, the software architecture has to be based on the Robot Operation System (ROS) [18]. Additional modules for assistance functions, situation awareness and sensor data analysis are included.

7   Conclusion

In this paper the authors described the development of an experimental CBRNE system for the German Military Forces. The system consists of different robot platforms, which are able to carry highly modularized payload platforms: either a multi-purpose CBRNE sensor suite or a mobile manipulator for semi-autonomous sample collection. The vehicles are operated through a mobile control station. All sensor readings and robot status information are forwarded to the operators, displayed in near real time and recorded in a database. A detailed description illustrated the robot platforms, the CBRNE sensor suite and relevant parts of the user interface.

Important future work includes improvements in the mechanical implementation of the robots as well as further tests on the robustness of the employed communication channels. New sensor equipment will be added, including additional MultiRAE devices, an advanced version of the identiFinder and the Proengin AP4C-V chemical detector. The usage of the manipulator arm has to be improved and integrated into the user interface. Additional assistance functions for the various components as well as for the system as a whole are under development.

References

1. Humphrey, C.M., Adams, J.A.: Robotic Tasks for CBRNE Incident Response. Advanced Robotics 23(9), 1217–1232 (2009)
2. Casper, J., Micire, M., Murphy, R.R.: Issues in Intelligent Robots for Search and Rescue. In: Unmanned Ground Vehicle Technology II - Proceedings of SPIE, vol. 4024, pp. 292–302 (2000)
3. Lundberg, C., Reinhold, R., Christensen, H.I.: Evaluation of robot deployment in live missions with the military, police, and fire brigade. In: Carapezza, E.M. (ed.) Sensors, and Command, Control, Communications, and Intelligence (C3I) Technologies for Homeland Security and Homeland Defense VI – Proceedings of SPIE, vol. 6538 (2007)
4. Murphy, R.R., Stover, S.: Rescue Robots for Mudslides: A Descriptive Study of the 2005 La Conchita Mudslide Response. Journal of Field Robotics 25(1), 3–16 (2008)
5. Casper, J., Murphy, R.R.: Human-Robot Interactions During the Robot-Assisted Urban Search and Rescue Response at the World Trade Center. IEEE Transactions on Systems, Man, and Cybernetics - Part B: Cybernetics 33(3), 367–385 (2003)
6. Penzes, S.G.: Multi Agent Tactical Sentry (MATS) Project Review. In: Gerhart, G.R., et al. (eds.) Unmanned Systems Technology VIII - Proceedings of SPIE, vol. 6230 (2006)

7. Giesbrecht, J., Fairbrother, B., Collier, J., Beckman, B.: Integration of a High Degree of Freedom Robotic Manipulator on a Large Unmanned Ground Vehicle. In: Gerhart, G.R., et al. (eds.) Unmanned Systems Technology XII – Proceedings of SPIE, vol. 7692 (2010)

8. Neilsen, C.W., Gertman, D.I., Bruemmer, D.J., Hartley, R.S., Walton, M.C.: Evaluating Robot Technologies as Tools to Explore Radiological and Other Hazardous Environments. In: Proceedings of the American Nuclear Society Emergency Planning and Response, and Robotics and Security Systems Joint Topical Meeting, Albuquerque (2008)

9. Jasiobedzki, P., Ng, H.-K., Bondy, M., McDiarmid, C.H.: C2SM: a mobile system for detecting and 3D mapping of Chemical, Radiological, and Nuclear contamination. In: Proceedings of Sensors, and Command, Control, Communications, and Intelligence, Technologies for Homeland Security and Homeland Defense VIII (2009)

10. Zarzhitsky, D., Spears, D., Spears, W., Thayer, D.: A Fluid Dynamics Approach to Multi-Robot Chemical Plume Tracing. In: Proceedings of the International Joint Conference on Autonomous Agents and Multiagent Systems, vol. 3, pp. 1476–1477 (2004)

11. Kathirgamanthan, P., McKibbin, R., McLachlan, R.: Source Term Estimation of Pollution from an Instantaneous Point Source. Research Letters in the Information and Mathematical Sciences 3, 59–67 (2002)

12. Christopoulos, V., Roumeliotis, S.: Multi Robot Trajectory Generation for Single Source Explosion Parameter Estimation. In: Proceedings of the IEEE International Conference on Robotics and Automation (ICRA), Barcelona, pp. 2803–2809 (2005)

13. Christopoulos, V., Roumeliotis, S.: Adaptive Sensing for Instantaneous Gas Release Parameter Estimation. In: Proceedings of the IEEE International Conference on Robotics and Automation (ICRA), Barcelona, pp. 4450–4456 (2005)

14. Schneider, F.E., Wildermuth, D.: An Autonomous Unmanned Vehicle for CBRNE Reconnaissance. In: Proceedings of the 12th International Carpathian Control Conference (ICCC 2011), Velke Karlovice, pp. 351–356 (2011)

15. Hoeller, F., Roehling, T., Schulz, D.: Offroad Navigation Using Adaptable Motion Patterns. In: Proceedings of the International Conference on Informatics in Control, Automation and Robotics (ICINCO), Milan (2009)

16. St. Louis, R.H., Hill Jr., H.H., Eiceman, G.A.: Ion Mobility Spectrometry in Analytical Chemistry. Critical Reviews in Analytical Chemistry 21(5), 321–355 (1990)

17. Schneider, F.E., Wildermuth, D.: Results of the European Land Robot Trial and Their Usability for Benchmarking Outdoor Robot Systems. In: Groß, R., Alboul, L., Melhuish, C., Witkowski, M., Prescott, T.J., Penders, J. (eds.) TAROS 2011. LNCS, vol. 6856, pp. 408–409. Springer, Heidelberg (2011)

18. Robot Operating System (ROS) documentation, http://www.ros.org/wiki

Research for the Detection of Explosives at CEA: Towards Operational Use

Didier Poullain[1], Pierre Montmeat[1], Lionel Hairault[1], Thierry Maillou[1], Rodrigue Rousier[2], Anthony Larue[3], Aurélie Martin[3], Guillaume Lebrun[3], François Simoens[2], Jérôme Meilhan[2], Claude Fermon[4], Myriam Pannetier-Lecoeur[4], Joachim Tabary[2], Caroline Paulus[2], Anne-Sophie Lallemand[5], Gilles Ferrand[5], Guillaume Sannie[3], Bertrand Perot[6], and Cédric Carasco[6]

Commissariat à l'Energie Atomique et aux Energies Alternatives,
[1] CEA/DAM, Le Ripault, BP 16, 37260, Monts, France
[2] CEA/DRT/LETI, 38054, Grenoble Cedex 9, France
[3] CEA/DRT/LIST, 91191, Gif/Yvette Cedex, France
[4] CEA/DSM/IRAMIS, 91191, Gif/Yvette Cedex, France
[5] CEA/DAM Bruyères-le-Châtel, 91297, Arpajon Cedex, France
[6] CEA/DEN Cadarache, 13108 St Paul Lez Durance, France
didier.poullain@cea.fr

Abstract. CEA, a prominent player in research, development and innovation has developed extensive expertise in a number of topics which are now central within the global security research issues. As an example, CEA is developing research of new technologies for the detection of explosives. This article gives an overview of the main activities regarding to the detection and identification of bulk or traces explosives. The document focus on high TRL projects aiming to develop demonstrators for testing in real configurations.

Keywords: detection, identification, explosives, demonstrator, THz, NQR, chemical sensors, X Ray backscattering, neutron.

1 Introduction

Among missions of CEA, Global Security took an increasing place in the last years, CEA is involved in this field through national (ANR, national authorities), European (FP6, FP7, ISEC,...) and international (NATO) projects. In particular, CEA is coordinating the French global Research and Development program dealing with Chemical, Nuclear, Radiological, Biological and Explosive threats. Among these ones, explosive is the main vector used by terrorists. Based on its important knowledge in the fields of materials, spectroscopy, microelectronic, metrology, software technologies, CEA has engaged studies for the development of explosives detection devices. The approach is based on a closed collaboration with end users and national authorities for usable equipments. In particular, concept of operations are taken into account and applications like aviation security (passengers screening, cabins baggage), unattended luggage, maritime containers are targeted.

N. Aschenbruck et al. (Eds.): Future Security 2012, CCIS 318, pp. 412–427, 2012.

Detection of explosives at CEA goals traces or bulk forms. This article describes the most significant studies in this field aiming to detect and identify the explosives. In particular, we focus on high TRL projects aiming to develop demonstrators for tests in real configurations.

5 technologies will be discussed:

- Chemical sensors for explosives traces detection,
- THz imaging and spectroscopy for the detection of bulk explosive hidden on the body (under clothes),
- Nuclear Quadrupolar Resonance for the detection of bulk explosives in luggage;
- X Ray Backscatter system for imaging and identifying explosives in an abandoned baggage;
- Fast neutron interrogation for the identification of explosives in maritime containers.

2   Chemical Sensors

Explosives traces are present as particles or vapours. Particles detection is well covered by commercially available technologies like IMS (Ion Mass Spectroscopy) or colorimetric tests kits. However, these technologies need physical contact for sampling. Few devices for vapours detection are commercialized. CEA develops an approach based on a physicochemical interaction between explosives vapour and a sensitive material selected for its affinity with the target.

The figure 1 represents the detection principle.

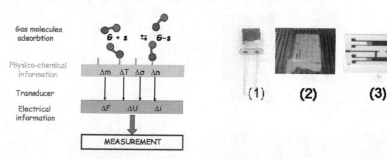

Fig. 1. The gas is adsorbed onto the surface of the sensitive material involving a physicochemical modification of it. Trough a transducer, this signal is transformed into an electrical information.

Fig. 2. QCM (1), Fluorescence (2) and SAW (3) sensors

To achieve our goals, e.g. operational demonstrators for testing in real conditions, several competences are developed:

- Modelling of the interaction between sensitive materials and explosives vapours;

- Design and synthesis of sensitive materials;
- Thin layer deposit on different substrates depending of the detection technology;
- Generation of calibrated vapours concentrations for testing the performances of the detectors;
- Prototyping of the laboratory's equipment for field use.

3 technologies are studied at CEA in this goal (figure 2):

- Quartz Crystal Microbalance (QCM)
- Fluorescence
- Surface Acoustic Waves (SAW)

The targets are explosives, precursors and taggants with vapour pressure up to ppb. For very low vapour pressure compounds, other sampling methods are studied in order to be coupled with vapours detectors. They are not discussed in this article.

Based on the development of the single technologies which have exhibited a high level of performance [1,2,3,4], we designed a new multisensors system combining Quartz Crystal Microbalance, Fluorescence and Surface Acoustic Waves. The response is based on an early fusion of the signals provided by each technology. This approach allows a positive synergy between the 3 technologies (response time, sensitivity, selectivity). The device intends to detect the presence of a threat in a few seconds and to identify in 2 minutes the nature of the detected explosive.

The concept was demonstrated through a first prototype associating a single measurement chamber and the 3 devices.

The fluidic simulation of the chamber was done with a 3D CFD software "Solidworks flow" an add-on of Solidworks. The fluidic simulation allowed to optimize the flow on the sensors, and to identify and reduce dead zone. This simulation was necessary to adjust accurately the flow for each sensor accordingly theirs features. Thanks to optimization, the fluidic volume was reduced to only 9 ml. This volume was calculated from the inlet connector to outlet connector. Figure 4 shows the simulation in the case of fluorescence sensors. The flow is laminar for saw sensors and fluorescence sensors.

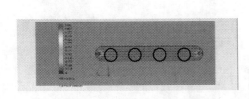

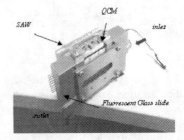

Fig. 3. This figure shows the simulation of the gas flow associating velocity for the fluorescent sensor channel. The flow is laminar for the 4 fluorescent sensors (black circles)

Fig. 4. Single measurement chamber QCM, SAW and fluorescence sensors

The chamber (figure 4) was validated experimentally with a gas test bench delivering 4-nitrotoluene vapour (figure 5).

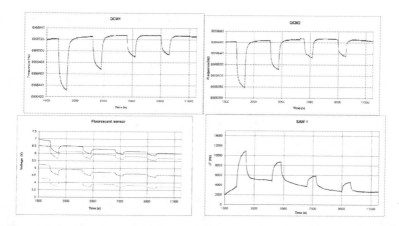

Fig. 5. Example of results obtained with a multi-sensors chamber, only the response of one saw is represented here, but the chamber has 8 saw sensors. The analyte was 4NT and 1 g was set inside the bubbler. The flow rate in the chamber was 330 sccm. Several dilutions were tested 50%, 25%, 12.5% and 10% (proportion of flow rate passing in the bubbler). Each sensor response is synchronized due to the design of chamber.

This validation was the starting point of the new integrated portable demonstrator.

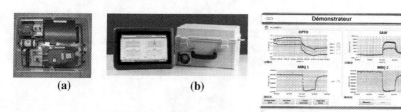

(a)   **(b)**

Fig. 6. Based on the first demonstrator ($60*40*30cm^3$) (a), a portable demonstrator (b) ($30*20*18cm^3$)) was designed and built integrating the measurement chamber, pump, electronic,…In this V1, data processing is monitored through an external laptop

Fig. 7. Responses of QCM/Fluorescence/SAW sensors to EGDN

The device integrates 14 sensors (4 Fluorescence, 2 QCM, 8 SAW).

An extended database on the detection of explosives vapours and potential interferents (solvents) at various concentrations led to a refinement of the data processing [5]. The identification is done in 2 steps:

– Analysis of the signal's form to confirm the presence of one target;
– Analysis of the absorption kinetic to identify the compound.

The identification is confirmed when the probability of presence of the compound is higher than a fixed threshold and higher than the sum of the probabilities of presence of all the other compounds.

The demonstrator has already been validated for the identification in less than 1 minute of 2 explosives (TNT and EGDN) and 3 solvents (Ethanol, Methylethylketone, Dichloromethane) at concentrations closed to vapour pressure (figure 7).

These very encouraging results clearly demonstrate the potential of this new device for the identification without contact of explosives traces. In addition, this system does not include radioactive source.

The next step is the increasing of targets number. The 14 sensors provide large possibilities for sensitive materials choice and will contribute to this goal. In addition, the coupling of particles samplers will be developed in order to detect very low vapour pressure explosives.

3   Terahertz Imaging and Spectroscopy

Most of solid explosives present specific spectral signatures in the Terahertz (THz) electromagnetic range (0.3 –10THz). In addition, THz radiation penetrates a wide range of materials such as plastics or tissues which are opaque to visible and near infrared light or produce only low-contrast x-ray images. A THz system coupling spectroscopic information to active imagery of a stand-off scene is likely to provide at the same time information on the location of potential hidden objects under clothes and on its chemical composition.

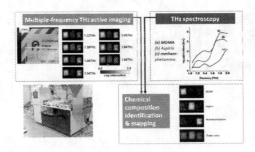

Fig. 8. Riken demonstration of THz spectro-imaging applied to mail scanning

Such frequency-sensitive THz imaging requires the combination of a multicolor illumination source with a broadband detector. The Riken institute (Japan) has successfully applied this technique for the detection and identification of illicit drugs concealed in envelopes. Its system (figure 8) relied on a frequency-tunable THz wave parametric oscillator (TPO) as source and a single pixel pyroelectric detector. The use of single pixel detector implied mechanical scanning to image $20\times38mm^2$ samples (3040 pixels), resulting in approximately 10 minutes acquisition time to be multiplied by the number of frequencies [6].

Practical systems require reduced acquisition time that can be achieved by the use of focal-plane array cameras, such as uncooled resistive microbolometer sensors, that can directly detect THz signals with sufficient speed. On the base of its more than two decades experience in such technology applied to thermal infrared (IR) imaging [7], CEA-Leti started a few years ago the development of fully THz customized amorphous silicon based thermistors [8].

Very innovative (patented) pixel architecture has been defined where, unlike for standard IR bolometers, optical collection and thermometer functions are ensured by separate elements, respectively antennas associated to a resonant cavity and a microbridge bolometer (figure 9).

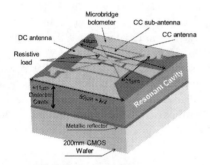

Fig. 9. CEA-Leti uncooled THz antenna-coupled microbolometer pixel structure

Fig. 10. 320x240 pixels FPA

Unlike NEC [9] and INO [10] THz bolometers that do not integrate antennas, the Leti pixel can be tuned without sensitivity decay to sense any frequency range, provided that the dimensions of the antennas and cavity are adequately dimensioned.

320x240 bolometer arrays (figure 10) have been designed and collectively fabricated above CMOS Application-Specific Integrated Circuits (ASIC) in the Leti 200mm silicon facilities. Thanks to state-of-the-art Si microelectronic processes and robust bolometer technology know-how, a very high yield has been achieved with 56 functional arrays out of 63 chips available per 200 mm wafer.

The detector sensitivity has been accurately characterized [11]; at 2.5 THz, the measured threshold detection is close to 30 pW, placing this uncooled THz array better than the international state-of-art (Published values of 70pW at INO and <100pW for NEC).

The pixel design has been optimized for 1.5-3.5 THz spectral absorption range where most of the explosives exhibit specific fingerprints (figure 13).

Fig. 11. CEA THz spectro-imaging demonstrator

To demonstrate the capabilities of spectro-imaging using its bolometer array, Leti in collaboration with other CEA divisions and French universities develops a complete system that mobilizes multi-disciplinary skills. The multiple-frequency source consists in associated high-power (typ. 10 mW CW) THz Quantum Cascade Lasers (QCL) of the French Paris 7 University [12] integrated in a CEA designed cryogenic pulse tube cooler.

A specific illumination optical setup guides the THz beams towards the scene. Then the reflected and backscattered radiation from the scene is collected and focused by a Newton telescope onto the 16x12 mm^2 sensitive surface of the bolometer array. The FPA images in real-time a 40x60 mm^2 illuminated surface (the following figure illustrates the better than 0.5cm resolution achieved by the demonstrator (figure 12).

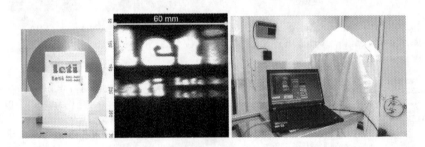

Fig. 12. Real time reflected image of 40*60mm^2 target hidden by cotton white coat

Up to now the Labview® driven system control limits the frame rate to 1 Hz, but higher acquisition speed is expected with forthcoming driving by FPGA electronic cards.

On-going works address the demonstration of spectroscopic identification of chemical samples extracted from reflection images.

In parallel of these system developments, tests are run with explosives samples. Reflectivities extracted from 2D active images exhibit clear variations and contrasts with respect to the chemical compositions and frequencies (figure 13).

In addition a databank of spectral fingerprints of materials -including explosives- is being built in collaboration with the University of Savoie. Special efforts are carried out to acquire reliable reflectivity spectra on a wide range (example of figure 14). In a complementary way, a CEA group develops specific multispectral detection algorithms that analyse stand-off images in combination to spectral signatures.

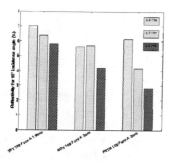

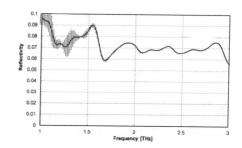

Fig. 13. Measurement of explosives reflectivities at .5 / 2.7 / 2.9 THz

Fig. 14. Example of the reflectivity spectral:2 signature of a sugar pellet sample

As a conclusion, present achievements show encouraging results for applying bolometer arrays to both stand-off imaging and identification of the composition of concealed objects. It opens the way to industrial transfer for several applications like passenger screening or pharmaceutical tests.

4   Nuclear Quadrupolar Resonance

Nuclear Quadrupolar Resonance (NQR) is a solid state spectroscopic technique that applies to nuclei of spin $I \geq 1$ in a non cubic environment. Nuclei with an electric quadrupolar moment, such as ^{14}N, ^{35}Cl and ^{63}Cu, have their energies split by an electric field gradient, created by the electronic bonds in the local environment. The resonance frequencies are compound specific and allow detection of various kinds of objects (bombs, drugs, oil...) on the basis of their chemical composition, which is an important advantage over other methods that detect extrinsic properties such as metallic mine detectors. The resonance frequencies lie in the 500 kHz-5 MHz range, where conventional resonant coils have a limited sensitivity (figure 15).

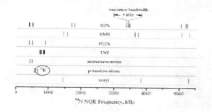

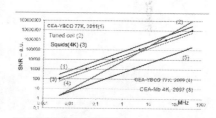

Fig. 15. Resonance frequencies of common solid explosives

Fig. 16. SNR response compared to frequency for new GMR-hybrid sensors, squids and tuned coils sensors

It is therefore interesting to improve the performance of this detection by means of other type of detectors, more sensitive on the low frequency range. Alternative solutions for detection of explosives by NQR have been offered for few years by Superconducting Quantum Interference Devices (SQUIDs) [13-14] and more recently by Giant Magnetoresistive (GMR) sensor, associated to a superconducting pick-up loop to enhance the sensitivity [15]. These sensors are both wideband and exhibit a flat response as function of frequency allowing operation in an untuned configuration, the same device being able to detect various products. Contrary to SQUIDs, GMR-hybrid sensors developed by CEA are robust and can experience directly the RF pulse required for the NQR experiment, with a very short recovery time. We can therefore detect NQR signals using complex sequences, such as Spin-Lock Spin-Echo, in order to increase the signal, especially in the case of long relaxation time products [16].

Figure 16 compares the SNR/frequency for successive CEA's GMR-hybrid sensors generations and classical technologies. New GMRs exhibit a higher sensitivity than squids. Furthermore, they don't need liquid helium temperature and the coils are not tuned. In addition, the sensors are fabricated above classical CMOS wafers (figure 17).

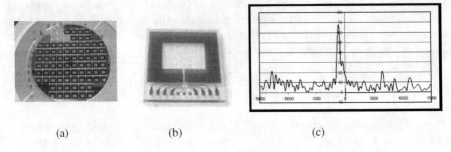

(a)   (b)   (c)

Fig. 17. Wafer (a), GMR hybrid sensor (b) and response to PETN at 890kHz (c)

Based on this innovative sensor, a program aiming to develop a prototype for the identification of nitrogenous explosives in cabin's baggage was launched 2 years ago (figure 18).

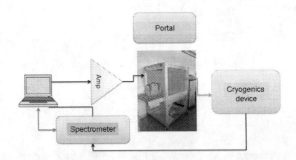

Fig. 18. Elements of the global system for the identification of solid nitrogenous explosives by NQR

All elements were designed by CEA and manufactured in collaboration with industry.

Portal: designed for baggage's screening with an armour plate for protection against environment's interferences. This portal can be equipped with a metal detector.

Spectrometer: 3 frequencies areas for the simultaneous measurement of the whole spectrum of targeted explosives;

Detection System: GMR hybrid sensors and cryogenics device (77K).

Software-User Interface: monitoring of RF sequences and data processing for the identification.

The demonstrator was recently tested with real explosives (figure 19).

Goal is the detection in less than 15s of explosives quantities which could lead to dramatic damages in an airplane.

The system is highly selective. Several interferents as metal can, mobile phone, keys, soap or path tooth didn't modify the signal of the target.

Different nitrogenous explosives and related commercial compositions have been tested. The presence of binders did not affect the resonance wavelength of pure compound.

First results demonstrate the efficiency of the identification of Ammonium nitrate, pentrite, RDX and their associated compositions (figure 19).

Product	Hexomax	Formex	Ammonium nitrate-fioul	Dynamite
Frequency	3.41MHz	890kHz	423kHz	423kHz
Identification time (s)	1 s	14s	1 s	12

Fig. 19. Demonstrator and response time for the detection of several nitrogenous explosives compositions

Detected quantities are relevant compared to the objective. The detection of dynamite is longer due to its low concentration in ammonium nitrate inside. Formex needs more time to be identified due to the long relaxation time of pentrite. It's interesting to note that humidity doesn't modify the detection of PETN.

Next steps will aim to increase the performances by increasing the SNR and validating the detection limit.

Based on this innovative sensor, research is also on progress at CEA/DSM on very low field NMR and MRI. Preliminary results showed the possibility of identifying liquids which could be used in the formulation of explosives. The mT range field is acceptable for electronic devices and produces negligible stray field on people. The final objective is to couple NQR and MRI in the same device for a simultaneous detection of solid and liquid explosives.

5   X-ray Backscattering Demonstrators

Currently, the abandoned luggages are inspected by portable and ergonomic systems, based on static X-ray radiography, searching for presence of an explosive threat. But this technique has limitations, especially in case of large or dense objects or if they are placed close to a wall not allowing access to the rear side for radiography. Portable systems using backscattered X-rays can be an alternative solution to analyze a suspicious object from one side, without any contact, but no commercially available one exists.

In this article, a portable dual X-ray backscatter system is described, in terms of technical specifications, methods and performances. It couples the two following functionalities:

- firstly, to image the object components in order to reveal and localize the presence of a suspicious content hidden inside the luggage;
- secondly, to discriminate between its explosive or inert nature by targeted spectral backscatter measurements.

Two corresponding laboratory demonstrators have been developed on the basis of a manufactured portable X-ray tube for both functionalities [17]. The imager utilizes a flat panel detector; a good energy-resolved spectrometric CdZnTe probe is employed for discrimination. Such equipments have been chosen in order to be operationally deployed in the future by end users (Explosive Ordinance Disposal EOD teams, policies, customs…). Experimental campaigns on both inert and explosive materials have been performed and have led to system characterization. Main results are presented in the following paragraphs.

5.1   X-ray Backscatter Imaging

A portable continuous X-ray tube, about 10 minutes battery powered, is one of the basis of the system. For the further described experiments, the constant potential is set to 120 kV and the current to 1 mA. The portable detector is a high resolution digital X-ray flat panel offering a small pixel size, better than 150 micrometer and a 15 cm ×·15 cm useful area.

To achieve simultaneously a high spatial resolution, a high sensitivity and a large magnification, a multi aperture disposal has been developed. A specific process is then applied on the raw data by a dedicated software, related to the imaging apparatus placed in front of the detector. The final result is a digital image of the "emissive object". The imager and the tube are typically placed, with an approximately 30° angle, 40 to 100 cm far from object under investigation. "Long" distances are not convenient for this laboratory demonstrator because the backscattered signal becomes too weak to perform an image.

Preliminary tests were performed in laboratory with inert materials. Referring to intensity level obtained experimentally in backscattered images, this laboratory demonstrator imager reveals less than 100 g explosive-like material, depending of the nature of the luggage.

The results were confirmed by tests with real explosives, as shown in figure 20 in the case of PETN explosives.

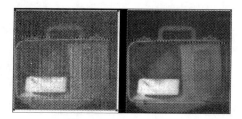

Fig. 20. Backscattered images of pseudo IED luggage containing a ~500 g explosive, PETN based. Left image corresponds to 2 minutes X-ray emission; right image corresponds to 8 minutes X-ray emission.

5.2   X-ray Backscatter Discrimination Technique

The discrimination system aims at focusing at second level a suspicious content identified in the image resulted from the backscatter imaging system, and at determining whether the material is inert or explosive. In this context, a methodology has been developed and tested thanks to a first laboratory test bench.

Many Compton backscatter system have been developed for densitometry purpose in medical [18,19] or non destructive testing applications [18,20]. As in all of those systems, our proposed system uses a double collimation on both irradiation and detection in order to target a small volume of the examined part. More precisely, the method is based on the scanning in depth of the inspected part with a highly collimated spectrometric CdZnTe sensor in order to fully process the backscattered spectral signature of materials. To be easily brought close to the abandoned object, the system is also supposed to use the same portable X-ray tube than the imaging system.

The idea was then to measure the attenuation function and to exploit it to recognize the crossed material. For that, X-ray backscattered spectra are measured at several depths of the suspicious object.

From this consideration, an original identification process has been developed to estimate, from the "mean scattered" attenuation function, the density and the effective atomic number. This processing method, based on a model constructed with calibration measurements on reference materials, is precisely described in [21]. It intrinsically takes into account multiple scatter, which can be significant and depends both on the material and on the depth of investigation. The estimation of both density and effective atomic number is a relevant key to identify the inspected material as an explosive.

A first laboratory discrimination demonstrator has been designed and tested under portable configuration. The probe consists in one 5mm thick CdZnTe pixel detector with a specific capacitive Frish grid providing a good resolution detected spectra (resolution of about 3% at 122 keV). Thus, to rapidly increase statistics in order to estimate correctly the performances of our system, experimental tests have been performed with a more powerful industrial X-ray tube but in the same conditions as a portable X-ray tube, i.e. with a current of 10 mA and a time acquisition of 30 seconds per depth. The working voltage is still 120 kV.

Experiments were done with different bulk (based on TATB, Hexogen, Pentrite) and flakes (TNT) explosives.

424   D. Poullain et al.

A major result is that the three bulk explosives are well localised in the bulk explosives area shown on figure 21. On the other hand, only the effective atomic number value of TNT flakes is in the critical range, for the estimated density corresponding logically to the apparent one. Another interesting result for liquid explosive detection is the discrimination of pure water from hydrogen peroxide (H_2O_2) at 30%.

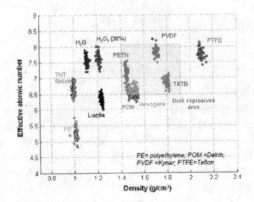

Fig. 21. Experimental results of the X-Ray backscatter discrimination laboratory demonstrator on different inert and explosive materials. Each point corresponds to a set of 6 acquisitions performed at different depths.

Based on commercially available products, we have developed two portable laboratory demonstrators, based on X-ray backscattering using multi aperture imaging and multi energy processing methods in order to reveal, localize and characterize explosive materials. An industrial prototype of an integrated system is envisaged in the future to optimize portability and flexibility of the whole system and operating time by the use of a multi-pixels spectrometric detectors.

6   Fast Neutron Interrogation

In recent years, hazardous material detection in cargo containers has become a key problem due to terrorism activities. Controls are usually performed by the X- or gamma-ray scanners already used for contraband or illicit drugs detection. This approach is satisfactory for determining the shape and density of the inspected content but fails to analyze chemical elements present inside the container.

Controls can be greatly improved by the use of fast neutrons, which provide information about the elemental composition of the irradiated goods.

The EURITRACK project [22] was leaded by CEA and aimed to develop a non intrusive system for the identification of potential explosives in maritime containers. An innovation of this project is the association of X-Ray imaging for the localisation of a threat and fast neutron interrogation for the identification of the organic explosive or illicit drugs, with the associated particle technique to focus neutron interrogation in

3D on the threat area. Finally, EURITRACK led to the first prototype in the world for this purpose. It was tested in real conditions in the port of Rijeka (Croatia).

Explosives and illicit drugs are discriminated from common goods by their specific oxygen-to-carbon (O/C) and nitrogen-to-carbon (N/C) chemical ratios.

Reactions induced by fast neutrons produce gamma rays, which are detected in coincidence with the associated alpha particle to determine the neutron direction. In addition, the neutron path length is obtained from a time-of-flight measurement, thus allowing the origin of the gamma rays inside the container to be determined. Information concerning the chemical composition of the target material is obtained from the analysis of the energy spectrum.

To obtain the chemical O/C and N/C ratios from the gamma ray energy spectra, data processing was based on a method mixing Monte Carlo simulation with an analytical formulation [23]. In addition, special attention was given to HMI for an easy use by operators.

The prototype included the following elements:

- Associated particles 14Mev neutrons generation;
- 22 Gamma detectors shielded with iron and lead;
- Neutron detector: liquid organic scintillator;
- Electronic and data processing;
- Remote control system for monitoring and data acquisition

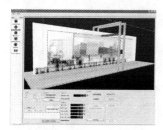

Fig. 22. Portal management   **Fig. 23.** EURITRACK Prototype

First validation was done in laboratory through the identification of a metallic can containing 75kg of ammonium acetate as a TNT surrogate. The can was placed among metal boxes filled with ferrous materials (density=0.2). Ammonium acetate was identified without ambiguity and the measured ratio C/O versus C/N was in accordance with theory.

Full scale experiments [24,25] were done in the port of Rijeka (Croatia) with real containers. Around 150 containers were scanned and compared to the official content statement. Containers containing inorganic materials (metal, ceramic, glass) are favourable to the discrimination of an explosive due to the different chemical composition. In case of organic freight, the identification of the product is more difficult, particularly because of neutron scattering on hydrogen nuclei. However, the identification given by the device was effective for several compounds (paper, wood, polyester, cotton). The accuracy of the result was confirmed by the comparison with the official content declaration.

EURITRACK project validated the feasibility of the concept. The tests in Rijeka gave precious information for the specifications of a future operational device. Future work will target the miniaturisation of the system (neutron generator, electronic devices) for portable on intervention systems, and the accuracy of data analysis [26].

7   Conclusion

Thanks to its fundamental research in material science [27] for the development of innovative technologies, CEA built several demonstrators for the detection of bulk and traces explosives. Diverse conops are proposed (maritime container, unattended luggage, passenger screening, cabins baggage) for first or second level controls. The first experimental results are promising and testing campaigns in real conditions will be processed soon. Furthermore, axes for improving the performances of these first generation's devices are already identified.

In a future global security organisation where no single solution will exist, the performances of these detectors give new alternatives to enhance the security by the identification of several explosives families. These devices are ready for a technological transfer to industry.

Acknowledgements. The authors thank SGDSN and CEA/DSNP for their support.

References

1. Nimal, A.T.: Sensors and Actuators B: Chemical 135(2), 399–410 (2009)
2. Clavaguera, S.: Talanta 82(4), 1397–1402 (2010)
3. Caron, T.: Talanta 81(1-2), 543–548 (2010)
4. Parret, F., Montméat, P., Prené, P.: Detection of explosives vapors with a portable detector based on Quartz-Crystal microbalance. IEEE Sensors, 248–251 (2007), doi:10.1109/ICSENS 2007.4388383
5. Patent, F.: YD 12078 (February 2011)
6. Kawaze: Terahertz parametric sources and imaging applications. Semicond. Sci. Technol. 20, S258–S265 (2005)
7. Yon, J.J., et al.: First demonstration of 25μm pitch uncooled amorphous silicon microbolometer IRFPA at LETI-LIR. In: Proc. SPIE, vol. 5783, pp. 432–440 (2005)
8. Peytavit, E., et al.: Room Temperature Terahertz Microbolometers. In: Proc. IRMMW-THz, pp. 257–258 (2005)
9. Oda, N.: Uncooled bolometer-type Terahertz focal plane array and camera for real-time imaging. C. R. Physique 11, 496–509 (2010)
10. Bolduc, et al.: Noise-equivalent power characterization of an uncooled microbolometer-based THz imaging camera. In: Proc. SPIE, vol. 8023, 80230C (2011)
11. Meilhan, J., et al.: Active THz imaging and explosive detection with uncooled antenna-coupled microbolometer arrays. In: Proc. SPIE, vol. 8023, pp. 80230E–80230E-13 (2011)
12. Barbieri, S., et al.: 2.9THz quantum cascade lasers operating up to 70K in continuous wave. Appl. Phys. Lett. 85, 1674 (2004)
13. Tonthat, D.M., Clarke, J.: Rev. Sci. Instrum. 67, 2890–2893 (1996)
14. He, D.F., Tachiki, M., Itozaki, H.: Superconductor Science and Technology 21 (2008)
15. Pannetier, M., et al.: Science 304, 1648–1650 (2004)

16. Pannetier-Lecoeur, M., Fermon, C., Dyvorne, H., Cannies, G., Le Goff, G.: Explosives Detection using Magnetic and Nuclear resonance Techniques. NATO Science for Peace and Security Series – B: Physics and biophysics. Springer (2009)
17. Lalleman, A.S., Ferrand, G., Rossé, B., Thfoin, I., Wrobel, R., Tabary, J., Billon Pierron, N., Mougel, F., Paulus, C., Verger, L.: A dual X ray backscatter system for detecting explosives: image and discrimination of a suspicious content. In: IEEE Nuclear Science Symposium Conference Record, NP1.M-93, pp. 299–304 (2011)
18. Harding, G.: Inelastic photon scattering: effects and applications in biomedical science and industry. Radiat. Phys. Chem. 50(1), 91–111 (1997)
19. Speller, R.D., Horrocks, J.A.: Photon scattering – a new source of information in medecine and biology. Phys. Med. Biol. 36(1) (1991)
20. Zhu, P., Peix, G., Babot, D., Muller, J.: In-line density measurement system using x-ray Compton scattering. NDT&E International 28(1), 3–7 (1995)
21. Paulus, C., Tabary, J., Mougel, F., Billon Pierron, N., Mathy, F., Rinkel, J., Verger, L.: Explosive detection with an x-ray backscattering system based on CdZnTe spectrometric detector. In: IEEE RTSD, R13-3 Oral Presentation (2011)
22. Szabo, J.-L., Pérot, B., Sannié, G.: EURITRACK: inspection neutronique pour la lutte contre le trafic illicite, Techniques de l'Ingénieur, Editions T.I. IN 82 – 1 (2008)
23. Carasco, C., Pérot, B., et al.: Photon attenuation and neutron moderation correction factors for the inspection of cargo containers with tagged neutrons. Nuclear Instruments and Methods in Physics Research A 582, 638–643 (2007)
24. Pérot, B., Carasco, C., et al.: Measurement of 14MeV neutron-induced prompt gamma-ray spectra from 15 elements found in cargo containers. Applied Radiation and Isotopes 66, 421–434 (2008)
25. Carasco, C., Pérot, B., et al.: In-field tests of the EURITRACK tagged neutron inspection system. Nuclear Instruments and Methods in Physics Research A 588, 397–405 (2008)
26. El Kanawati, W., Perot, B., Carasco, C., Eléon, C., Valkovic, V., Sudac, D., Obhodas, J.: Conversion Factors from Counts to Chemical Ratios for the EURITRACK Tagged Neutron Inspection System. Nuclear Instruments and Methods in Physics Research A 654, 621–629 (2011)
27. Olmedo, L., Bossuet, C., Simonet, F., Gallou, C., Bergonzo, P., Gmar, M., Carrel, F., Mayne, M., Fermon, C., Gillet, D., Volland, H., Delapierre, G., Simoens, F., Amans, J.L., Poullain, D.: Research against CBRN-E terrorism: a real opportunity for materials Science. In: Proceeding Future Security Conference, Berlin (2011)

A Biophotonic Sensor for the Specific Detection of DMMP Vapors at the ppb Level

Karine Bonnot[1], Benny Siegert[1], Nelly Piazzon[1], Denis Spitzer[1], Jose Sansano[2], Manuel Rodrigo[2], Francisco Cuesta-Soto[2], Antonio Varriale[3], Sabato d'Auria[3], Nuria Sanchez[4], Francisco Lopez-Royo[4], and Jorge J. Sanchez[2]

[1] Nanomatériaux pour les Systèmes Sous Sollicitations Extrêmes (NS3E),
UMR 3208 CNRS/ISL, Saint Louis, France
karine.bonnot@isl.eu
[2] DAS Photonics, Valencia, Spain
[3] Istituto di Biochimica delle Proteine (IBP), CNR, Napoli, Italy
[4] Nanophotonics Technology Center (NTC), Universidad Politécnica de Valencia, Spain

Abstract. In defense and security, there is a need to develop more sensitive and selective sensors to allow the detection of toxic and illicit compounds at trace levels. Photonic Integrated Circuits combined with specific protein bio-recognition allowed us to detect DMMP vapors down to 20 ppb in the gas phase. This strong increase in sensitivity results from the specific binding of DMMP molecules in the protein cavity. A high coverage ratio of the ring resonator with proteins permits the enhancement of the wave propagation signal resulting from the adsorption of one DMMP molecule on each biosensing protein, resulting in an amplified optical signal.

Keywords: photonic, detection, sensors, bio-recognition, odorant binding proteins, DMMP, chemical warfare.

1 Introduction

Due to their versatility, optical biochemical sensors are powerful detection and analysis tools with many applications: environmental and industrial monitoring, defense and border security and for the surveillance of large areas such as airports and stadiums [1]. In the framework of the NANOCAP project, we are developing bio-photonic sensors based on photonic integrated circuits (PIC) [2]. Here we present such a sensor for the sensitive detection of dimethyl methylphosphonate (DMMP), a precursor of Sarin (GB) nerve gas and a simulant for many toxic organophosphorus compounds. The sensing element is a ring resonator (Fig. 1) which is functionalized with a modified bovine odorant binding protein (b-OBP) that selectively binds the analyte, modifying the refractive index of the resonator. The use of targeted proteins ensures a high sensitivity and selectivity [3]. Another advantage of this method is that it is not necessary to tag the proteins with fluorescent labels [4].

Biosensors based on ring resonators have been proposed by other groups [5,6]; however, to our knowledge, this is the first time that bio-recognition combined with photonic measurements is used to detect chemical warfare agents or simulants like DMMP, although the technique has already been used with success for the detection of explosive compounds like TNT [7].

N. Aschenbruck et al. (Eds.): Future Security 2012, CCIS 318, pp. 428–431, 2012.
© Springer-Verlag Berlin Heidelberg 2012

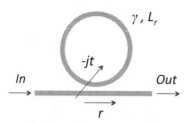
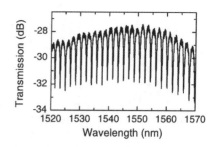

Fig. 1. Schematic of a ring resonator on a PIC (left); optical transmission spectrum of the functionalized ring resonator used for DMMP detection (right)

Due to its low stability in air, DMMP detectors often work in aqueous media [8]. DMMP vapor detection has mainly been done using acoustic wave techniques with detection levels as low as 1ppm [9,10]. Using Raman spectroscopy as an optical technique, Wang et al. achieved a limit of detection of 50 ppb for sensing DMMP vapor on chemiresistive sensors coated with carbon nanotubes [11]. We show the detection of even lower concentrations in the range of 20 ppb.

2 Experimental Investigations

The chips with photonic structures were produced in silicon nitride. The photonic structures consist of a set of twelve ring resonators coupled to waveguides. The total surface of Si_3N_4 resonator is 628 μm^2. A change in the refractive index of the ring resonator leads to a shift in resonance wavelengths, which are seen as dips in the transmission spectrum (Fig. 1). The transmission spectrum is measured using a tunable laser source ($\lambda \approx 1.5\ \mu m$), optical fibers placed at the edge of the chip and a component tester. Most of the chip and photonic structures are covered by a silicon oxide layer to protect the structures. An open window above the resonators allows their functionalization.

The ring resonator was functionalized with bovine odorant binding proteins (b-OBP) whose amino acid sequence was modified to selectively bind DMMP. The chips were first treated with 5% HF solution to remove the oxide layer from the Si_3N_4. Then they were exposed to UV illumination (280 nm) for 30 minutes under a nitrogen atmosphere before deposition of droplets of a protein solution on the surface. A second UV exposure of the surface for 120 min allowed the fixing of the protein. The excess was removed by washing the chip several times with pure water.

To test the sensor, functionalized and non-functionalized chips were introduced in a gas cell for contact with DMMP vapor. The ends of the waveguides and optical fibers were not in contact with the gas flow. Gas tightness of the measurement area was provided by a rubber seal. DMMP vapor was generated using a permeation tube (Owlstone Ltd, UK) enclosed in a glass reactor connected to a gas entry and to the measurement cell at its exit. The permeation tube was maintained at a controlled temperature of 24°C during the experiment. The nitrogen flow was fixed at 200 mL/min. These experimental conditions ensured a delivery of a 20 ppb concentration of DMMP during the experiment. Before injecting DMMP, the system was stabilized for few minutes under

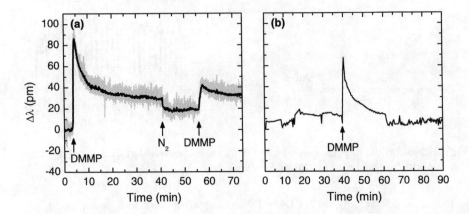

Fig. 2. Mean resonance wavelength shift $\Delta\lambda$ induced by the injection of DMMP vapor (20 ppbv concentration) on a b-OBP functionalized (a) and non-functionalized PIC (b). The light gray area indicates the noise level in a single measurement. The total flow rate of DMMP + nitrogen is 200 mL/min.

nitrogen flow. Pulse injections of DMMP were then performed for 40 minutes on functionalized chips before switching back to nitrogen. In the case of blank chips, no switch back to nitrogen occurred.

3 Results and Discussion

AFM characterization of the chip surfaces (not shown) shows that the protein film on the ring resonators is dense and homogeneous, with a mean coverage ratio of 96%. Taking into account the size of a protein (a sphere with a diameter of 4 nm), the number of active binding sites is estimated as $7 \cdot 10^8$.

Pulse injections of a 20 ppb DMMP vapor were applied to both a functionalized (Fig. 2a) and a blank chip (Fig. 2b). There are about 20–30 resonances in the observed wavelength domain (typically 1520–1570 nm).

The optical sensing system instantaneously reacts to the concentration changes, resulting in a peak wavelength shift of 60 and 90 pm respectively for the blank and functionalized chips. When no proteins are present on the resonator surface, the signal then returns to its initial value (Fig. 2b). However, for the functionalized resonator, the value stabilizes at a shift of +40 pm for a stable DMMP concentration of 20 ppb. The presence of DMMP molecules specifically bound to the surface proteins results in a change in the chemical and optical properties of the protein layer, which explains the change in refractive index and the resulting shift in resonance wavelength. This is consistent with specific adsorption of DMMP on proteins.

Changing the flow to pure nitrogen ("N$_2$" mark on Fig. 2a) led to a decrease of 10 pm of the signal, which could be attributed to desorption of less strongly adsorbed DMMP molecules. A second DMMP pulse was performed around 100 minutes leading to a response similar to the previously attained base value. Comparing the signal obtained on the two chips, we assume that non-specific adsorption or even condensation of DMMP molecules on the naked silicon nitride surface leads to the observed 60 pm peak (Fig. 2b). The rapid return of the signal to its zero value means that the analyte molecules do not bind to this surface. The comparison of these two results shows that the DMMP-sensitive proteins immobilized on the resonator surface allow the accurate detection of a concentration of 20 ppb of DMMP in nitrogen due to a change in the refractive index of the functionalized resonator by specifically binding DMMP molecules on active protein sites.

4 Conclusion

We built a highly sensitive photonic sensor based on the targeted bio-recognition of an analyte in the gas phase. Based on the optical detection of a change in refractive index when a molecule specifically binds a protein, it allows the detection of a concentration of 20 ppb of DMMP vapor in nitrogen. As a first attempt in the development of bio-photonic sensors to achieve highly sensitive detection, this result shows promising features for the development of a portable and low cost device based on photonic bio-recognition for trace detection of toxic and illicit compounds in the gas phase.

Acknowledgements. This work was supported by the NANOCAP project A-1084-RT-GC that is coordinated by the European Defense Agency (EDA) and funded by 11 contributing Members (Cyprus, France, Germany, Greece, Hungary, Italy, Norway, Poland, Slovakia, Slovenia and Spain) in the framework of the Joint Investment Program on Innovative Concepts and Emerging Technologies (JIP-ICET).

References

1. Narayanaswamy, R., Wolfbeis, O.: Optical sensors. Springer, New York (2004)
2. Jokerst, N., Royal, M., Palit, S., Luan, L., Dhar, S., Tyler, T.J.: Biophoton 2, 212–226 (2009)
3. Bañuls, M.J., González-Pedro, V., Barrios, C.A., Puchades, R., Maquieira, A.: Biosens. Bioelectron 25, 1460–1466 (2010)
4. Moerner, W.: Proc. Nat. Acad. Sci. U.S.A. 104, 12596–12602 (2007)
5. Claes, T., Bogaerts, W., Bientsman, P.: Optics Express 18, 22747–22761 (2010)
6. Barrios, C., Gylfason, K., Sanchez, B., Griol, A., Sohlström, H., Holgado, M., Casquel, R.: Opt. Lett. 32, 3080–3082 (2007)
7. Orghici, R., Lützow, P., Burgmeier, J., Koch, J., Heidrich, H., Schade, W., Welschoff, N., Waldvogel, S.: Sensors 10, 6788–6795 (2010)
8. Hou, C., Yang, L., Huo, D.: Spectrophotometric detection of dimethyl methyl-phosphonate using plant-esterase. In: The 2nd International Conference on Bioinformatics and Biomedical Engineering, ICBBE 2008, pp. 1640–1643. IEEE (2008)
9. Grate, J., Rose-Pehrsson, S., Venezky, D., Klusty, M., Wohltjen, H.: Anal. Chem. 65, 1868–1881 (1993)
10. Zimmermann, C., Mazein, P., Rebiere, D., Dejous, C., Pistre, J., Planade, R.: IEEE Sensors Journal 4, 479–488 (2004)
11. Wang, F., Gu, H., Swager, T.J.: Am. Chem. Soc. 130, 5392–5393 (2008)

Light-Weight Optical Sensor for Standoff Detection of Fluorescent Biosensors

Martin Wehner[1,*], Ulrich Thombansen[1], Nicole Raven[2],
Christoph Kühn[2], and Stefan Schillberg[2]

[1] Fraunhofer ILT, Aachen, Germany
{martin.wehner,ulrich.thombansen}@ilt.fraunhofer.de
[2] Fraunhofer IME, Aachen, Germany
{nicole.raven,christoph.kuehn,
stefan.schillberg}@ime.fraunhofer.de

Abstract. Cell-based biosensors can be modified to express fluorescent proteins when in contact with trace substances like TNT. Stand-off detection of activated fluorescent biosensors becomes feasible by optical sensors which shine excitation light on the biosensor and collects the fluorescence light. We propose a low cost, light-weight sensor solution which consists of a LED illuminator, a large aperture light collector and a solid state detector. The irradiance level and the detection efficiency are expected to be sufficient for short range detection.

Keywords: cell-based biosensor, fluorescent marker protein, LED illuminator, optical sensing, large aperture detector.

1 Introduction

In human demining there are two main issues: First, large areas have to be cleared to assure save land use, and second, the reliability of the clearing process has to be very high. Usually mine action starts in a suspect region with a non-technical survey to define the confirmed hazard zone [1]. A technical survey with close visual inspection or partial mine detection in probe lanes follows. In those identified high hazard zones animals like mine dogs and manual deminers come into action for close-in detection of buried mines. Unfortunately, anti-personnel mines contain virtually no metal parts and therefore cannot be detected by electromagnetic sensors. In practice that means that area reduction and demining action can be very time consuming. Adequate tools for scanning of a large suspect area are not available yet. Detectors for fast technical survey would be very helpful to concentrate on high hazard zones and to speed up the clearing process.

To meet that need we propose the use of biosensors which are spread over a suspect area and transform the close range chemical signal into a long range optical signal. A whole-cell bacterial biosensor is modified to react to trace amounts of TNT or DNT as a byproduct by the expression of fluorescent proteins. In principle, the biosensor

---

* Corresponding author.

could be as sensitive as a dog's nose, but without the need to step on the terrain. The replacement of a dog's nose which is the most sensitive and – under certain conditions – most reliable sensor by an artificial biosensor for large area scanning is considered.

A bacterial biosensor containing a TNT-sensitive promoter for detection of TNT has been described in 1999 by Burlage [2]. Bacteria were modified to express a green fluorescent protein which can be excited by UV-light. But after demonstration of the principle there was no further information that this idea led to a practical solution. A different approach was pursued by Danish company ARESA Biodetection [ARESA] who developed a thale cress variety whose leaves turn from green to red in the presence of nitrogen oxide within a growth period of a few weeks.

Own work concentrated on modification of soil bacterium *Pseudomonas putida* to express the red fluorescent protein *td Tomato* [FutSec2010] which can be efficiently excited by the radiation of frequency-doubled Nd:YAG laser at 532 nm wavelength. In our first approach a laser scanner was used to irradiate the biosensor and to detect the fluorescence signal. These experiments showed the capability to detect 2 – 4 activated biosensor beads at 10 m distance under daylight conditions or even at 300 m distance at night [CBRN 2010]. The principle has been demonstrated but increasing sensitivity, reduction of cross reactivity and improvement of environmental stability are still under investigation.

Airborne laser scanners in combination with sophisticated signal processing are high performance tools for construction of digital height models and detection of forest canopy [Anderson]. But airborne scanners are expensive and do need costly infrastructures like air services. Due to the complex signal processing a commercial laser scanner cannot be modified easily by the user to adapt to the special requirements of fluorescence detection. Even though detection of fluorescent biosensors has been performed using our laboratory-type laser scanner we now propose a simpler technical solution.

2   Experimental Approach

2.1   Construction of Bacterial Biosensor

Our sensor is constructed from genetically modified *Pseudomonas putida* bacteria to produce the red fluorescent protein td-Tomato upon uptake of TNT-signatures from liquids or soil [FutSec2011]. The specific response is achieved by a genetic switch that is activated by direct binding of TNT or its derivatives inducing the production of fluorescent proteins (see figure 1). The bacterium *P. putida* is a ubiquitous soil bacterium and is expected to show good compatibility with environmental conditions in different soil habitats. The excitation and emission peaks of td-Tomato do not overlap with the emission spectra of chlorophyll, a chromophore that is abundantly present in green plant tissue. Since the vitality of the biosensors is crucial for their functionality, we intend to build biosensors that in vital stage constantly produce blue fluorescent proteins independently from the production of the red fluorescent proteins.

434   M. Wehner et al.

For practical reasons sensor beads are prepared from bacterial cells in alginate solution by adding Calcium ions to form gel beads. These beads serve as containments
for water to prevent from drying and seeping into earth. It also helps to place a
sufficient number of cells at one spot to get a high signal strength compared to the
surrounding. The bacterial biosensor is provided either ready-to-use as alginate formulated beads that can be stored at 4°C for up to one week. Alternatively, the bacterial can be lyophilized for long-term storage at ambient temperature. The lyophilisate
then serves as a starting material for the production of alginate beads at the site of
application requiring minimal technical equipment.

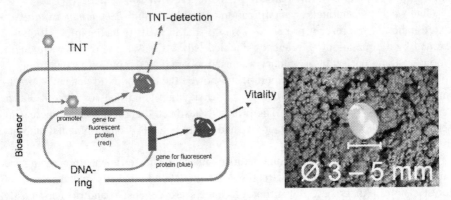

Fig. 1. Principle of bacterial whole-cell biosensor for detection of TNT and its derivates (left);
example of a biosensor bead on soil (right)

2.2   Design of the Optical Sensor Head

The new concept for the optical sensor consists of a LED illuminator and a large aperture Fresnel lens for light collection. For excitation of td-Tomato the green LED from
Cree Inc. (see fig. 2) may be appropriate, for excitation of tagBFP an UV power LED
for photo curing of resins will be used at a wavelength of 400 nm. The maximum
power density in short range application is calculated to about 10 mW/cm² and exceed
the accessible emission limits (AELs) of a laser scanner under eye-safe conditions. As
extended incoherent light sources like LEDs can't be focused to a small spot as a laser
beam, the allowable power density can be higher, but the illuminator has to be tested
before to assure eye safety.

The beam paths for excitation and detection do interfere at a distance of approximately 5 meters with long overlapping zone. A controller alternatively switches the
blue and green excitation LED on and reads out synchronously the signals of both
channels to perform a subtraction of background signals.

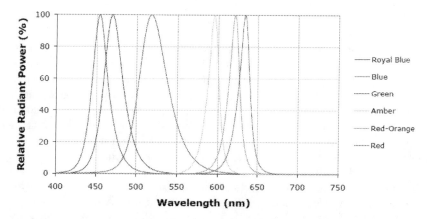

Fig. 2. LED emission spectra for excitation of fluorescent proteins by visible light power LEDs, copyright © 2008-2010 Cree, Inc.

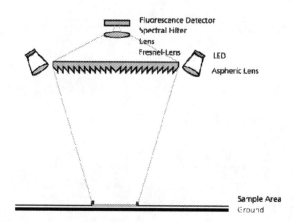

Fig. 3. Sketch of optical design of the detector device (not to scale)

2.3   Conditions of Use

Preliminary work [BioSens] with the laser scanner revealed a detection limit of 3 – 4 sensor beads under daylight conditions. If a similar sensitivity can be obtained in short range detection with the new optical sensor a number of 5 sensor beads inside an illumination spot of 10 cm dia. is required. This corresponds to a mass distribution of about 50 g/m².

Biosensor beads can be spread by a small land vehicle or a sowing device. For instance, a sower may be mounted on an articulated arm on a street vehicle to cover lanes besides the road. Later after incubation the same device carries the optical sensor head. The mass of the optical sensor will be limited to a pay load of less than 1 kg such that a small unmanned vehicle like quadrotor drone would be able to sweep the sensor over the suspect area. The optical sensor can be used simply as a handheld light designator for indication of buried mines or in combination with a carrier system collecting reference data from GPS and tilt angle information.

3 First Results

For the field application of the biosensor alginate encapsulation of the bacteria is advantageous, because it allows the concentration of the fluorescence signal and enables the supplementation of the bacteria with nutrients. Alginate is a natural polysaccharide that is isolated from brown algae. It is cheap, readily available and biodegradeable. Consequently, the alginate encapsulation of the biosensor is economically reasonable and does not impose any threat/risk to the environment. It was successfully demonstrated that alginate encapsulation of the bacteria did not interfere with the production of the fluorescence marker protein. Experiments indicate an optimal read-out time of 48 h after deposition.

Measurements of the fluorescence signal from excitation by green LED revealed the emission peak in the expected spectral region (see fig. 4). Also the wavelength of 525 nm from the LED was below the excitation peak of 554 nm of td-Tomato a strong signal has been measured.

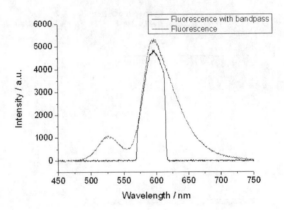

Fig. 4. Fluorescence spectra of td-Tomato from excitation by green LED; red curve: Fluorescence spectrum with excitation peak centered at 525 nm; black curve: fluorescent light with band pass filtering 573-613 nm

4 Outlook

The first calculations for a LED-illuminator seem worthy to construct and test a light weight optical sensor which can be easily adapted to any carrier system.

The genetic modification of the biosensor, namely the integration of a novel amplification loop is intended, because we expect an increase of the signal intensity as well as a reduction of the response time compared to the current biosensor. Moreover, all genetic elements could be integrated into the bacterial chromosome to optimize the acceptability of the biosensor in respect to biosafety issues. Finally, in-depth investigations for the determination of realistic application scenarios by studying simulated and real environmental conditions can be conducted.

Acknowledgement. We gratefully acknowledge the funding by the Ministry for Economic Affairs, Energy, Building, Housing and Transport of the State of North Rhine-Westphalia.

References

1. A Guide to Land Release, A Guide to Mine Action, http://www.gichd.org
2. Burlage, et al.: United States Patent 5,972,638 (October 26, 1999)
3. Aresa Biodetection APS, patent application 2003, WO 2003/100068 A1 (2003)
4. Wehner, M., Wirtz, T., Poprawe, R., Schillberg, S., Kühn, C., Raven, N., Hund-Rinke, K., Meurer, H.: Biosensors for Stand-Off Detection of Mines and Explosives by Laser Induced Fluorescence. In: 5th Security Research Conference, Berlin, September 7-9 (2010)
5. Wehner, M., Poprawe, R., Schillberg, S., Kühn, C., Raven, N., Hund-Rinke, K.: Biosensors for Stand-Off Detection of explosives and CBRN threats: options and challenges. In: 1st International Symposium on Development of CBRN Defence Capabilities, Berlin, November 30- December 1 (2010)
6. Wehner, M., Raven, N., Schillberg, S., Hund-Rinke, K., Kühn, C., Poprawe, R.: Fluorescent Biosensors for Stand-Off Detection of Gamma Raiation. In: 6th Security Research Conference, Berlin, September 5-7 (2011)
7. Andersen, H.-E., McGaughey, R.J., Reutebuch, S.E.: Estimating forest canopy fuel parameters using LIDAR data. Remote Sensing of Environment 94, 441–449 (2005)

Detecting and Quantifying Toxic Industrial Compounds (TICs) with Proton-Transfer-Reaction Mass Spectrometry (PTR-MS)

Thomas Kassebacher[1,2], Philipp Sulzer[1,*], Simone Jürschik[1], Bishu Agarwal[2], Fredrik Petersson[1], Eugen Hartungen[1], Hans Seehauser[1], and Tilmann D. Märk[1,2]

[1] IONICON Analytik GmbH., Eduard-Bodem-Gasse 3, 6020 Innsbruck, Austria
{philipp.sulzer,simone.juerschik,eugen.hartungen,hans.seehauser,
fredrik.petersson,tilmann.maerk}@ionicon.com
[2] Institut für Ionenphysik und Angewandte Physik, Leopold-Franzens Universität Innsbruck, Technikerstr. 25, 6020 Innsbruck, Austria
thomas.kassebacher@student.uibk.ac.at, bishu.agarwal@uibk.ac.at,

Abstract. In the course of the FP7-SEC project "SPIRIT" (Safety and Protection of built Infrastructure to Resist Integral Threats) we focused our research with Proton-Transfer-Reaction Mass Spectrometry (PTR-MS) on C-agents, specifically Toxic Industrial Compounds (TICs). Most TICs are readily available and represent a considerable threat when used in terroristic attacks. We show the principal procedure of PTR-MS detection measurements on two chemicals, namely phosgene and chloroacetone. With studies of the former we want to point out principle differences between measurements on a quadrupole mass filter based and a Time-of-Flight-based PTR-MS instrument and point out the respective benefits and drawbacks. For the latter we present the results of a diluted headspace measurement and illustrate the connection with security standards in buildings.

Keywords: Toxic Industrial Compounds, TICs, Proton-Transfer-Reaction Mass Spectrometry, PTR-MS, PTR-TOFMS, threat detection.

1   Introduction

Proton-Transfer-Reaction Mass Spectrometry (PTR-MS) is well known in analytic research and a commonly used technique in many fields of application, e.g. in food and flavor science [1], environmental research [2], biological research [3] or medicine [4]. These wide-spread possibilities of application mainly originate from the high selectivity, high sensitivity, low detection limit and an easy way of real-time sampling of PTR-MS instruments. For the present studies these factors are highly important for a quick and secure monitoring of public places, where the response time is the one of the most crucial factors.

---

[*] Corresponding author.

N. Aschenbruck et al. (Eds.): Future Security 2012, CCIS 318, pp. 438–447, 2012.

The detection of TICs (Toxic Industrial Compounds), which can be misused as weapons in terrorist attacks, is getting more and more important for maintaining public security, as they are on the one hand readily available due to their importance for industrial products and on the other hand cheap because of mass production. Nevertheless, TICs often have a severe toxicity and high vapor pressure, which not only means that they are a threat to human health, but also that they can spread quickly in buildings via the air conditioning system. Therefore the main object is to detect small concentrations as fast as possible in order to begin with countermeasures as soon as possible. Here lies one of the biggest advantages of PTR-MS. The detection limit is extremely low (depending on the model used down to the ppqv region) and the response time is around 100 ms. Therefore PTR-MS seems to be ideal for contamination detection and triggering presumably life-saving alarms.

As there exists a countless amount of toxic chemicals used in industrial production, for our present research we picked out some representatives (an extensive list of TICs can be found in [5]) that on the one hand possess high toxicity but are on the other hand still rather safe for handling in a laboratory environment (e.g. chemicals in liquid or solid state or bound to other substances instead of pure gas phase TICs). Another reason for choosing these compounds is the collection of "Acute Exposure Guideline Levels (AEGLs)" by the National Advisory Committee for the Development of Acute Exposure Guideline Levels for Hazardous Substances (AEGL Committee [6]), which provides us official detection limits that have to be reached when constructing a TIC monitoring instrument. With these limits in mind (AEGL-1 (experience of notable discomfort, irritation or nonsensory effects), AEGL-2 (suffer from adverse health effects), AEGL-3 (suffer from life threatening health effects)), one can decide which PTR-MS model is best suited for detection purposes, i.e. which are the requirements on sensitivity, mass resolution in comparison to the instrumental costs, size and portability, etc. . Instruments like e.g. the quadrupole mass filter based PTR-QMS 300, which we used in the present study, are not only less expensive but also much smaller and lighter as high resolution time-of-flight (TOF) based models. Therefore they can be installed much easier in places of limited space, e.g. somewhere in an HVAC (heating ventilating and air-conditioning) system for on-line monitoring.

In Table 1, we list some of our studied chemicals, three of them, namely chloropicrin, DMMP and sulfur mustard, have already been studied in a previous paper [7], but only on a time-of-flight based instrument, while the others were chosen, apart from the above mentioned criteria, because of their simple availability at common chemical suppliers and their proton affinity, which has to be higher than that of water for the analysis with a PTR-MS instrument. Out of this still long list, we picked the most hazardous, i.e. the most toxic ones. Studies on those chemicals with a lower proton affinity than water could be performed utilizing alternative reagent ions, such as O_2^+ or NO^+ [8].

Table 1. List of some studied chemicals

Name	Composition
Acrolein	C_3H_4O
Chloroacetone	C_3H_5ClO
Chloroacetophenone, Phenacyl chloride	C_8H_7ClO
Chloropicrin	CCl_3NO_2
Diphosgene	$C_2Cl_4O_2$
Dimethyl methylphosphonate (DMMP)	$C_3H_9O_3P$
Phosgene	CCl_2O
Sulfur Mustard	$C_4H_8Cl_2S$

However, in the present work we mainly focus on two chemicals, phosgene and chloroacetone, not only because of the scientifically interesting results we obtained from them but also because of their known AEGL-2 (see Table 2) and AEGL-3(see Table 3) limits (only for the AEGL-1 there is insufficient data).

Table 2. AEGL of phosgene in ppm

	10 min	30 min	60 min	4 h	8 h
AEGL-2	0.60	0.60	0.30	0.080	0.040
AEGL-3	3.6	1.5	0.75	0.20	0.090

Table 3. AEGL of chloroacetone in ppm

	10 min	30 min	60 min	4 h	8 h
AEGL-2	8.0	5.5	4.4	1.1	0.53
AEGL-3	24	17	13	3.3	1.6

2   Instrumental Setup

The operational principles of PTR-MS were already discussed in numerous publications (e.g. in an extensive PTR-MS review by Blake et al. [9]), therefore we do not present any details here. We utilized two different types of PTR-MS instruments, one quadrupole based PTR-QMS 300 and one PTR-TOF 8000. The former provides compact and mobile dimensions (less than 80 kg) with a detection limit of about 300 pptv, but with a unit mass resolution, whereas the latter features high resolution, high sensitivity (150 cps/ppbv) and a low detection limit (5 pptv), with the disadvantages of being more cost intensive and less mobile. As with PTR-MS only gas phase samples can be analyzed, we had to sample the headspace above the liquid's surfaces.

For the following quantification of TICs, we used the following relations to estimate the concentration in this headspace:

After Dalton's Law for a mixture of two ideal gases, the pressure p holds

$$p = p_1 + p_2 = X_1^g p + X_2^g p , \tag{1}$$

where p_1, p_2 are the partial pressures and X_1^g, X_2^g are the relative mol-fractions in the air, and Raoult's Law

$$p_1 = X_1^f p_1^{sat}, p_2 = X_2^f p_2^{sat} , \tag{2}$$

with p_1^{sat}, p_2^{sat} as the vapor pressures and X_1^f, X_2^f as the relative fractions in the liquid, one gets for $p_1^{sat} \ll p_2^{sat}$,

$$X_1^g \approx \frac{p_1^{sat}}{p} . \tag{3}$$

This means that for vapor pressures much smaller than the ambient pressure of about 1000 hPa, we can easily estimate the fraction (and therefore the concentration) in air by this simple calculation. For chemicals with vapor pressures of about the ambient pressure or higher, we estimate the fraction in the saturated gas between 0.1 and 1, which is sufficient precise in this case (see below).

To reach equilibrium, we waited about half an hour at room temperature till the gas in the recipient was sufficiently saturated. As we wanted to detect concentrations below the AEGL-2, which is in the ppb-range, while the typical concentrations in the headspace were in the high ppb-range and above, we had to dilute the saturated headspace. Therefore we used a syringe to take some of the headspace-gas out of the sample vials and subsequently injected it into a 5 L PTFE bag (Tedlar, CEL Scientific Corp) containing 5 L of pure nitrogen (N_2). Depending on the vapor pressure and the final concentration we wanted to achieve, we chose different injection amounts (between 0.1 mL and 5 mL). The resulting average dilution was about $1:10^3$ to $1:10^6$ (for 10^6 we diluted twice). In this way, we obtained for a dilution of e.g. $1:10^6$ a final concentration between 0.1 ppmv and 1 ppmv for liquids with a high vapor pressure (about 100 hPa and higher). E.g. for acrolein, with a vapor pressure of about 350 hPa at room temperature (calculated by the Antoine Equation Parameters in [10]) - the 8 h AEGL-2 of acrolein is of 100ppb - we checked, if we could still detect it at a dilution of more than $1:10^7$ (concentration between 10 ppbv and 100 ppbv), which is below the required detection limit.

In most applications it is not only necessary to detect a compound but also to discriminate it from overlapping substances. Probably the most sophisticated, but also rather cost intensive method to achieve this is the utilization of a high resolution PTR-TOFMS (e.g. the PTR-TOF 8000 with a resolution of up to 8000 $\frac{m}{\Delta m}$) [11] , i.e. it is possible to resolve most common isobaric molecules. In our case, we used this instrument to rectify the two other used techniques applied to a quadrupole based PTR-MS instrument.

Another method is to look at the isotope pattern of the compound. For common organic molecules (i.e. containing only C,O,N,H), they are quite similar but in case of TICs we have got the advantage, that a large number contains at least one chloride atom, which has isotopes at 35 amu and 37 amu with relative abundances of 75.77% and 24.23%, respectively. Therefore mass spectrometric patterns of molecules containing chloride can be easily identified.

For various substances (e.g. DMMP) valuable information can be derived from the fragmentation patterns. Those patterns mainly depend on the reduced electric field strength (E/N ratio) in the PTR-MS drift tube, i.e. they show the abundance of fragment ions compared to the parent ion in dependence of the applied voltage, the temperature and pressure in the drift tube. However, it is necessary to check the fragmentation pattern first with a high resolution instrument, in order to determine the chemical composition of the different fragment ions.

3   Results and Discussion

In this presentation, we select two representative examples for TICs, namely phosgene and chloroacetone.

3.1   Phosgene (CCl_2O)

Phosgene was used as a chemical warfare agent (CWA) in the First World War, nevertheless even nowadays it is of high relevance for industrial use, e.g. in the production of isocyanates [12]. Since Phosgene is gaseous at room temperature we used a mixture of phosgene dissolved in toluene (Sigma Aldrich), so that it could be handled rather safely. For the detailed study of phosgene we used a PTR-TOFMS.

We observe three main ions in the mass spectrum of Phosgene: CCl_2OH^+ at m/z =98.94 Th, m/z=99.95 Th, m/z=100.94 Th and $CClO_2HH^+$ at m/z=80.97 Th, m/z=81.98 Th, m/z=82.97 Th, and $CClO^+$ at m/z=62.96 Th, m/z=63.97 Th, m/z=64.96 Th, whereas the signal intensity for $CClO^+$ is the most abundant one. This results due to a loss of chlorine during the chemical ionization in the drift tube.

In the case of $CClO_2HH^+$ we observed an interesting reaction for low E/N values in the drift tube: $CClO_2H$ reacts with H_3O^+ in the drift tube in a way, that $CClO_3H_4^+$ at m/z=98.98 Th is formed, which has got almost the same m/z-value as CCl_2OH^+ itself. Utilizing a quadrupole based PTR-MS instrument one could not distinguish the cluster, but as one can see in Figure 1, with a PTR-TOF 8000 the two isobaric compounds can be easily discriminated. Additionally the isotopes at m/z=99.45 Th resp. m/z=99.99 Th or m/z=100.95 Th resp. m/z=100.98 Th can be seen and appear in the right isotopic ratio. Therefore we can be rather unambiguously sure that we really observed those compounds not only because of identification via their exact mass, but also because of the distinctive isotopic distribution.

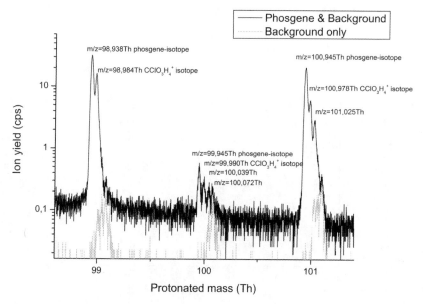

Fig. 1. Protonated phosgene-isotopes (CCl_2OH^+) and isotopes of a fragment ion ($CClO_3H_4^+$) measured on a PTR-TOFMS at E/N=69 Td

However, one can still avoid this clustering reaction by using higher E/N values, which results in a much lower clustering probability. It should be mentioned that as far as concentration measurements are concerned, this does not change the result, because for calculation of concentration one has to count up all the significant fragments, including water-clusters.

Equipped with this knowledge about fragmentation patterns, when using a PTR-QMS 300, one can still easily discriminate phosgene from other substances due to its characteristic chlorine-influenced pattern. This means, the signal intensity of the isotope of CCl_2OH^+ at 101 Th is still 64% of the signal at 99 Th, while the isotope at 100 Th has only got a relative abundance of 1.1 %, a similar situation can be found for the fragment ions. When doing a study for different values of E/N this ratio must always stay the same, unless an isobaric component that appears at the same mass becomes more dominant. In our case, one can see that for 69 Td, the above mentioned $CClO_3H_4^+$ slightly distorts this ratio, since its isotope at 101 Th is only of about 32% of the ion yield at 99 Th. Therefore a precedent analysis with a PTR-TOFMS is always necessary when dealing for the first time with a new chemical in order to understand the reactions in the drift tube, while for use as a threat agent monitor on public places a PTR-QMS would be still sufficient in this case.

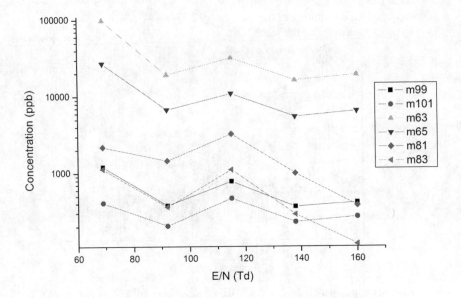

Fig. 2. E/N study of a diluted phosgene headspace. Although the signal is seriously varying, the isotope-ratio remains constant (m99 (=99 m/z) to m101, m63 to m65, m81 to m83). Only at very low E/N one can see that the signal is a bit distorted due to the reaction of $CClO_2H$ mentioned in the text.

3.2   Chloroacetone (C_3H_5ClO)

Like phosgene, also chloroacetone (CA) was used as a CWA in WWI (as a tear gas). Nowadays CA is used mainly for industrial purposes, e.g. for the production of furans [13]. As its vapor pressure at room temperature is of about 20 hPa [14], which is far below 1000 hPa ambient air pressure, we can use the above mentioned formula and get a headspace concentration of about 2% inside the vial filled with almost pure CA (Sigma Aldrich). Keeping this concentration in mind, we calculated, together with the dilution parameters, the final concentrations in the PTFE bags.

In the preliminary analysis utilizing a PTR-TOFMS we not only saw a signal for $C_3H_5ClOH^+$ at m/z=93.01 Th and its isotopes, but also at m/z=126.98 Th, which probably originates from an impurity of dichloroacetone ($C_3H_4Cl_2O$), rectified by the exact mass value of the protonated ion $C_3H_4Cl_2OH^+$ and the fitting isotope fractions at m/z=128.97 Th resp. m/z=130.07 Th of 63.9% resp. 10.2% of the $C_3H_4Cl_2OH^+$ abundance. However, as one can see in Figure 3, there is a rather high background signal at m/z=95.05 Th, originating from the PTFE bag, which we can nicely discriminate with the PTR-TOF 8000 in order to check the right isotope fractions of protonated CA. We also notice two mass peaks identified as $C_2H_3ClH^+$ at m/z=63.00 Th and m/z=64.00 Th, but their relative abundance compared to the parent ion of protonated CA is only about 0.3%. This means that for a concentration of

100 ppbv CA, only a signal intensity corresponding to about 0.3 ppbv can be detected, which is at the lower end of the detection limit of a PTR-QMS 300. That is why one has to concentrate on looking at the isotope-pattern for the discrimination of CA compared to other molecules of the same mass when working with a PTR-QMS.

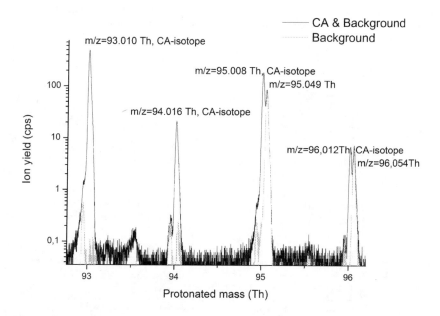

Fig. 3. Protonated chloroacetone isotopes measured on a PTR-TOFMS. One can distinguish very well the background and the CA mass peaks at 95 Th and 96 Th due to the high mass resolution.

To test the applicability of the PTR-QMS 300 for measuring given concentrations, we took five different dilutions $(1:5 \cdot 10^4; 1:2 \cdot 10^4; 1:10^4; 1:5 \cdot 10^3; 1:2,5 \cdot 10^3)$ of the saturated headspace which results in calculated concentrations of about 0.4 ppmv, 1 ppmv, 2 ppmv, 5 ppmv and 8 ppmv, respectively. Compared to the AEGLs it would fit perfectly for the AEGL-3 (min 1.6 ppmv) and also for the AEGL-2 up to 8 hours (min 0.53 ppm).

In the experimental setup we measure these concentrations on a PTR-QMS 300 by coupling its inlet directly to the fitting of the PTFE bag. For the calculation of the cumulative concentration of CA, we only sum up the most abundant isotopes at 93 Th and 95 Th and no other fragments because other compounds at lower masses, e.g. $C_3H_6OH^+$, protonated acetone at m/z = 59 Th, are to abundant in ambient air. As this loss of concentration causes a change in signal intensity of less than ten percent, the disregard of fragment ions is within the technical limitations of the instrument, but it should be kept in mind that this always leads to a light underestimation of the concentration. Therefore we observe a lower measured concentration for higher E/N values due to harder collisions in the drift tube and thus stronger fragmentation of the parent ion. Nevertheless, detection is no problem and the agreement between the calculated and the measured concentration is quite good as the dwell-time for each measurement was only of about two seconds. Only for the highest dilution, the measured concentration is about one magnitude lower than the expected value, mainly because of the systematic error in our dilution. Anyhow, AC is even at this concentration below the AEGL-2 detectable and furthermore identifiable by isotopic comparison. If it was necessary to detect traces of AC even below that limit, a more sensitive PTR-MS model would provide higher accuracy.

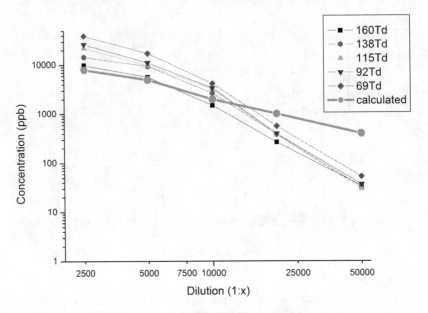

Fig. 4. Results of the concentration measurement of a diluted chloroacetone-headspace for different dilutions with different values of E/N compared to the calculated estimated values of the concentration for the corresponding dilution

Acknowledgement. This work was partly supported via the FP7-SEC project "SPIRIT" (GA 242319; European Commission, Brussels).

References

1. Biasioli, F., Yeretzian, C., Gasperi, F., Märk, T.D.: PTR-MS monitoring of VOCs and BVOCs in food science and technology. Trends in Analytical Chemistry 30(7) (2011)
2. Biasioli, F., Yeretzian, C., Märk, T.D., Dewulf, J., Van Langenhove, H.: Direct-injection mass spectrometry adds the time dimension to (B)VOC analysis. Trends in Analytical Chemistry 30(7) (2011)
3. Brilli, F., Ruuskanen, T.M., Schnitzhofer, R., Müller, M., Breitenlechner, M., Bittner, V., Wohlfahrt, G., Loreto, F., Hansel, A.: Detection of Plant Volatiles after Leaf Wounding and Darkening by Proton Transfer Reaction "Time-of-Flight" Mass Spectrometry (PTR-TOF). PLoS One 6(5), e20419 (2011)

4. Herbig, J., Müller, M., Schallhart, S., Titzmann, T., Graus, M., Hansel, A.: On-line breath analysis with PTR-TOF. J. Breath Res. 3, 027004 (2009)
5. Fatah, A.A., Barrett, J.A., Arcilesi, R.D., Ewing, K.J., Lattin, C.H., Helinski, M.S., Baig, I.A.: Guide for the Selection of Chemical and Biological Decontamination Equipment for Emergency First Responders, NIJ Guide 103-00, National Institue of Justice, vol. I (October 2001)
6. United States Environmental Protection Agency Webpage (March 21, 2012), http://www.epa.gov/oppt/aegl/index.htm
7. Petersson, F., Sulzer, P., Mayhew, C.A., Watts, P., Jordan, A., Märk, L., Märk, T.D.: Real-time trace detection and identification of chemical warfare agent simulants using recent advances in proton transfer reaction time-of-flight mass spectrometry. Rapid Commun. Mass Spectrom. 23, 3875–3880 (2009)
8. Jordan, A., Haidacher, S., Hanel, G., Hartungen, E., Herbig, J., Märk, L., Schottkowsky, R., Seehauser, H., Sulzer, P., Märk, T.D.: An online ultra-high sensitivity proton-transfer-reaction mass-spectrometer combined with switchable reagent ion capability (PTR+SRI-MS). International Journal of Mass Spectrometry 286, 32–38 (2009)
9. Blake, R.S., Monks, P.S., Ellis, A.M.: Proton-Transfer Reaction Mass Spectrometry. Chem. Rev. 109(3), 861–896 (2009)
10. National Institute of Standard and Technology Webpage for Acrolein (March 21, 2012), http://webbook.nist.gov/cgi/cbook.cgi?Name=Acrolein&Units=SI
11. Jordan, A., Haidacher, S., Hanel, G., Hartungen, E., Märk, L., Seehauser, H., Schottkowsky, R., Sulzer, P., Märk, T.D.: A high resolution and high sensitivity time-of-flight proton-transfer-reaction mass spectrometer (PTR-TOF-MS). International Journal of Mass Spectrometry 286, 122–128 (2009)
12. Organic Syntheses Database (March 21, 2012), http://www.orgsyn.org/orgsyn/orgsyn/prepContent.asp?prep=CV2 P0453
13. Smith, J.O., Mandal, B.K., Filler, R., Beery, J.W.: Reaction of ethyl 4,4,4-trifluoroacetoacetate enolate with 3-bromo- 1, 1,l -trifluoroacetone: synthesis of 2,4-bis (trifluoromethyl) furan. Journal of Flourine Chemistry 81, 123–128 (1997)
14. National Institute of Standard and Technology Webpage for Chloroacetone (March 21, 2012), http://webbook.nist.gov/cgi/cbook.cgi?Name=chloroacetone&Units=SI

Vulnerability Assessment
in the Food Chain – A Way to Do It

Anja Buschulte, Britta Müller-Wahl, Annemarie Käsbohrer, and Bernd Appel

Federal Institute for Risk Assessment, Dep. Biological Safety, Germany
anja.buschulte@bfr.bund.de

Abstract. The food chain is regarded as a possible target for bioterrorism at-tacks and the intentional contamination of food may pose a serious public health threat. Whereas Hazard Analysis and Critical Control Points (HACCP) principles and good hygiene practice is well established by the food business operators, a system which assesses the risk of malicious contamination of food within the food chain is not available in Germany yet. The main objective of our work is the development of a vulnerability assessment tool which helps to identify the most vulnerable points in a process chain and gives recommenda-tions to reduce them. In order to do this we evaluated the existing CARVER-system. During the translation process the content was adapted to German requirements. Particular attention has been laid to German legal and practical conditions. Legally inadmissible contents have been removed or adapted to German conditions.

After adaption of the CARVER-system to the national needs the system was applied in selected meat processing companies. The gained experiences were used to evaluate the system, check its practicability and to improve the usability for the potential user. The CARVER-system serves already as a useful software tool to assess vulnerable points in the food supply chain. It enables the compa-nies to identify their most vulnerable points for bioterrorist attacks and to focus on protecting these. Nevertheless the system still needs substantial adaptations to German needs. Then it may become a quite relevant vulnerability assessment tool.

Keywords: Vulnerability assessment, microbiological risks, meat production chain.

1   Introduction

The food chain is regarded as a possible target for bioterrorism attacks and malicious contamination of food for terrorist purposes is a possibility that responsible govern-ments and private companies cannot ignore [1]. In Europe the primary responsibility for food safety rests with the food business operator. According to the European law food business operators who produce, process or place food on the market have to ensure the safety of food [2]. The corresponding legislation applies to all stages of production, processing and distribution of food. In order to fulfil his responsibility the

N. Aschenbruck et al. (Eds.): Future Security 2012, CCIS 318, pp. 448–453, 2012.

food business operator is reinforced by general implementation of procedures based on the Hazard Analysis and Critical Control Points (HACCP) principles, together with the application of good hygiene practice. HACCP is a systematic preventive approach to food safety that identifies possible hazards in production processes that can cause the finished product be unsafe, and designs measurements to reduce these risks to an acceptable level. Factors which may influence food safety are biological, chemical or physical agents in food with the potential to cause an adverse health effect. The instruments to identify, cover and manage these naturally occurring or production-related hazards are well known and established for years. They therefore guarantee a high level of "biosafety". In contrast to this however a system which assesses the risk of malicious contamination of food within the food chain is not available in Germany yet.

2   Aims

The main objective of our work is the development of a vulnerability assessment tool which on one hand helps to identify the most vulnerable points for malicious contamination in a process chain and on the other hand gives recommendations to reduce vulnerability.

The Food and Drug Administration (FDA) has developed a prioritization tool for the US market that can be used to assess the vulnerabilities within a system or infrastructure in the food industry. This system is called „CARVER + Shock" (Center for Food Safety & Applied Nutrition, 2007) [3]. CARVER has been used by Federal US Agencies to evaluate the potential vulnerabilities of farm-to-table supply chains of various food commodities but it can also be used to assess the potential vulnerabilities of individual facilities or processes. CARVER is a software tool that can be downloaded free of charge. It enables food companies to perform a vulnerability assessment of their facilities and processes in a confidential manner. The purpose of this work was to evaluate whether CARVER could be the basis for a German or European vulnerability assessment tool.

3   Material and Methods

Structure, content and functioning of the CARVER system was analyzed. In order to do this the underlying relational database was translated and adapted to German requirements. This adaption of the system was followed by a practical application in food companies. For this purpose selected food companies from the meat chain were requested to perform a vulnerability assessment in their facilities. The practical experiences were used to evaluate the system, to check its practicability and to improve the usability for the potential user.

4   Results

CARVER uses the following attributes to evaluate the vulnerability of the process chain:

— Criticality - measure of public health and economic impacts of an attack
— Accessibility - ability to physically access and egress from target
— Recuperability - ability of system to recover from an attack
— Vulnerability - ease of accomplishing attack
— Effect - amount of direct loss from an attack as measured by loss in production
— Recognizability - ease of identifying target
— Shock - combined health, economic and psychological impacts of an attack within the food industry.

The assessment-process consists of 3 steps (see Fig. 1):

1. Process flow chart: building a flow diagram for the specific process chain or operation; each processing step, material, ingredient is represented in different kind of "nodes". These nodes are represented as icons. Each icon belongs to a specific item category and usually sub-category (the icon "meat, raw" for example belongs to the category "materials" and the sub-category "unprocessed ingredients")
2. Interview: answering a questionnaire for each process flow diagram node
3. Ranking: Based on the answers given, the software calculates a score; conditions that are associated with lower vulnerability are assigned lower values (e.g. 1 or 2), whereas, conditions associated with higher vulnerability are assigned higher values (e.g. 9 or 10)

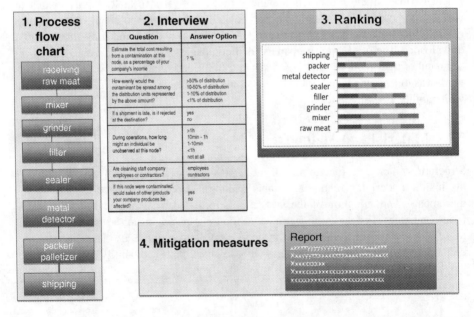

Fig. 1. Consecutive steps of the assessment process

The Ranking step is followed by a fourth step: Mitigation Measures. These measures provide suggestions for improving security for each node based upon the answers to the interview questions.

The programme interface accesses an underlying relational database. The database schema (see Fig. 2) shows the structure of the database and refers to the organization of data. It defines the tables, fields, relationships, views, indexes, procedures, functions and other elements.

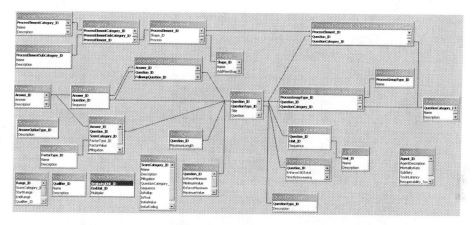

Fig. 2. Database schema of the underlying database for vulnerability assessment

During the translation process the content was adapted to German requirements. Particular attention has been laid to German legal and practical conditions. Legally inadmissible contents have been removed or adapted to German conditions.

This adaption was followed by a practical application in selected food companies from the meat chain. Using the CARVER-system a vulnerability assessment of a company specific process chain was accomplished on-site. The analyzed process chains included raw products like minced meat as well as processed products like cooked ham. To get a better picture concerning the usability companies of different sizes and types have participated. The gained experiences were used to evaluate the system, check its practicability and to improve the usability for the potential user. In addition the knowledge acquired served as a source of ideas for further enhancement. Based on the practical application the advantages and disadvantages are compared in Table 1.

Table 1. Experiences from practical application of the vulnerability assessment system in German meat processing facilities

Advantages	Disadvantages
General: - system is helpful to adopt the perspective towards bio-terroristic risks - large companies are well interested in such an assessment tool	General: - application time-consuming and too complex - low usability for small companies
Technical: - almost no previous technical experience necessary	Technical: - further technical features needed (e.g. export of the icon properties; printing options)
Application: - user friendly interface - self-explanatory - structured approach is appreciated	Application: - pre-constructed generic process-flow diagrams of products ("templates") as well as software supplied icons for the creation of flow diagram process nodes are insufficient - ambiguous questions (intention unclear) - questions and answers far too detailed - existing process flow charts (e.g. from HACCP) cannot be used (too extensive)
Results: - identifies mitigations to reduce vulnerability	Results: - mitigations measures are mostly very unspecific

5   Conclusions

The CARVER system serves already as a useful software tool to assess vulnerable points in the food supply chain. From the microeconomic view CARVER enables the food industry companies to identify their most susceptible points for bioterrorist attacks and could be used to focus resources on protecting these points. From the macroeconomic view potential vulnerabilities of the food supply chains can be evaluated.

Nevertheless summing up our experiences based on the practical usage and application of the system in German food companies one can say that CARVER still needs substantial adaptations to be useful for German requirements. Then it may become a basis for a German or European vulnerability assessment tool.

Acknowledgements. This work has been funded by BMBF (13N11202) and BMELV (BLE No. 07HS019) research grants.

References

1. World Health Organization 2008. Terrorist threats to food: guidance for establishing and strengthening prevention and response systems (2008),
   http://www.who.int/foodsafety/publications/general/en/terrorist.pdf (revision May 2008)
2. Regulation (EC) No 178/2002 of the European Parliament and of the Council of 28 January 2002 laying down the general principles and requirements of food law, establishing the European Food Safety Authority and laying down procedures in matters of food safety. OJ L 31, pp. 1–24 (February 1, 2002)
3. http://www.fda.gov/Food/FoodDefense/ToolsResources/ucm295900.htm

Improving the Security of Food Chains against Natural, Accidental and Deliberate Contaminations

Bernd Appel, Anneluise Mader, Juliane Braeunig,
Heidi Wichmann-Schauer, and Annemarie Käsbohrer

Federal Institute for Risk Assessment, Germany
Bernd.Appel@bfr.bund.de

Abstract. Ensuring an effective and rapid handling of natural, accidental and deliberate contaminations, which can result in food borne outbreaks, countries requires alert, preparedness and response systems to prevent public health threats from actual or threatened intentional contamination of the food supply. Timely and scientific correct risk assessments are essential for a comprehensive crises management. Both should be seen as multidisciplinary approaches with the participation of stakeholders from all sectors of the "farm-to-fork" continuum including the public health sector. Further capabilities to prevent and simulate the spread of diseases as well as defined criteria for use and interpretation of data in a crisis context are crucial. This paper summaries progresses made in the field of food chain security that can support risk assessment tasks in food borne outbreak events.

Keywords: Food, Contamination, Risk Assessment, Risk Ranking, Predictive Microbiology, Vulnerability, Tracing and Tracking, Supply chain, Epidemiology.

1 Introduction

Over the last years international organizations, such as World Health Organization (WHO), Food and Agricultural Organization (FAO) and the World Organization for Animal Health (OIE) have repeatedly expressed concerns that accidental and deliberate contaminations in the food chain can harm the civilian population and cause tremendous economic losses. They therefore joined their efforts to evaluate the risks and define strategies to encounter the threat of food contamination together with various international and national institutions and organizations. The increased awareness that the food supply is vulnerable to (deliberate) contaminations have resulted in several guidelines on how to respond to these threats, including "Report of the CBRN Task Force" (EC, 2009), "Terrorist Threat to Food" (WHO, 2008), "Green Paper on Bio-preparedness" (EC, 2007), "Communication on Strengthening Coordination on Generic Preparedness Planning for Public Health Emergencies at EU Level (EC,2005), "Communication on Cooperation in the European Union on Preparedness and Response to Biological and Chemical Agent Attacks" (EC, 2003) and " White Paper on Food Safety" (EC, 2000). The research needs addressed therein are related to prevention, monitoring and surveillance, detection, biotraceability and clinical treatment. The four main challenges with respect to biopreparedness are: threats to humans; threats to animals, and food and feed for the animals;

N. Aschenbruck et al. (Eds.): Future Security 2012, CCIS 318, pp. 454–461, 2012.

threats to crops, food and feed; as well as biological detection (EC, 2009). Nevertheless the European Community concluded: "There is no need to establish new systems, but rather to adjust the current mechanisms in order to improve their functioning, taking into account the threat of bioterrorism" (EC, 2003).

Food safety and food security are still major concerns worldwide due to repeated food borne outbreaks and contamination problems. Securing the food chains from primary production to ready-to-eat food against contaminations is closely connected with the safety of food products, especially as the complexity of food supply chains continuously increases. Therefore, available resources, that help to protect the food supply chain, such as (food safety) systems, have to be further evaluated, optimized and developed. The Federal Institute for Risk Assessment is developing an infrastructure that is mainly based on current mechanisms aiming to improve prevention of, detection of, response to and recover from possible natural, accidental as well as deliberate contamination events, especially in the field of risk assessment and crisis management.

2   Material and Methods

2.1   Establishment of a General Framework Related to the Assessment of Natural, Accidental and Deliberate Contaminations

The main challenge is to develop structures that ensure the systematic collection, analysis and interpretation of data and communication to all public and private stakeholders involved. Based on literature from international, European and national organizations general basic theses for the development of solutions that will improve efficient science based risk assessments were defined.

2.2   Possibilities to Improve Prevention, Detection, Response and Recovery

Surveillance and damage mitigation can be optimized by various factors such as an improved assessment of threat potential, implementation of specific methods for early detection, analysis of supply chain vulnerability, education of private and public stakeholders and the public in general, gathering of scientific knowledge on agents, knowledge regarding intra- and interplant supply chains, optimal intervention points, decontamination and disposal strategies, development of matrix-optimized detection methods for relevant agents, cost-benefit analysis, timely and scientific correct risk assessment of crisis situations and recommendations to private and public stakeholders. These issues, the list is not intended to be exhaustive, were addressed in various international and national projects coordinated or contributed to by the Federal Institute for Risk Assessment. Further information related to a project including some of the issues mentioned above is presented within the Future Security Conference 2012 by Mader et al. "SiLeBAT – Securing the Feed and Food Supply Chain in the Event of Biological and Agroterrorism (BAT) Incidents".

In case of a food borne outbreak timely and scientifically correct risk assessments are of highest relevance for all stakeholders. Risk assessments serve as guidance for governmental and private sector crisis management and can affect international trade relationships. Therefore, it is necessary to continuously explore data sources and data analysis technologies which support the risk assessment process.

In frame of this paper results and progress on key issues with the main focus on the risk assessment of biological agents will be discussed.

3   Results and Discussion

3.1 Establishment of a General Framework Related to the Assessment of Natural, Accidental and Deliberate Contaminations

A set of basic theses was established by the Department of Biological Safety at the Federal Institute of Risk Assessment that represents a general framework of aspects that should be considered when one deals with the topic of securing food chains against natural, accidental and deliberate contaminations. These are given in table 1.

Table 1. Basic theses related to the development of systems dealing with the threat of natural, accidental and deliberate contamination

1	Deliberate, accidental or natural contaminations can occur at any point in the food chain.
2	Attacks on the food supply chain for political, financial and other purposes are possible and can have a tremendous impact on global public health.
3	Reducing critical failures within the food supply chain and improving the system requires understanding the relationships between production systems, ingredients, people, utensils, equipment, machinery, intra- and inter-corporate food chains.
4	Strengthening of food safety infrastructures including prevention, detection, response and recovery systems will improve handling the burden of food borne outbreaks.
5	It is impossible to completely avoid contamination of food and therefore effective and rapid systems for alert, preparedness and response are crucial.
6	Cooperation between public and private stakeholders of international, European and national organizations, institutions and companies has to be an integral part of strengthening any kind of crisis management. This implies that no stakeholder alone will be able to provide comprehensive solutions for these specific scenarios on his own.
7	Governments should support the food industry that holds the best position to rapidly address threats through the food supply system "from farm to fork" in strengthening existing food safety management systems.
8	By increasing the security for people (maintenance and inspection workers), premises (access to critical areas in production, processing, transport and storage) and (raw) materials the opportunities for contaminations can be minimized.
9	New solutions to improve the security of food chains against contaminations should be mainly based on current mechanisms and the existing regulatory framework.
10	Mechanisms that improve security of the food chain against deliberate contaminations are applicable for natural and accidental contaminations.
11	The misuse of developed solutions must be avoided.

3.2   Possibilities to Improve Prevention, Detection, Response and Recovery

Development of a Generic System for Comparative Ranking of High Pathogenic Agents

To ensure that prevention, detection, response and recovery methods are developed for hazards that can have the most adverse impact on food safety and food security, the development of ranking schemes to prioritize possible agents is necessary. A criteria set for the scoring of biological agents that naturally occur and/or could be used for malicious purposes is needed for the optimization of the recognition and categorization of biological agents in the terms of threats. Such a criteria set can serve to improve security and surveillance measures, especially in order to prevent bioterroristic incidents.

For the development of the ranking system assessing the risk of biological agents, the term "risk" was defined as the product of probability and impact. The knowledgebase, generated while validating the ranking scheme in combination with a set of relevant criteria, will support decision-makers in the worst case of an attack. In contrast to other ranking systems, which are mainly based on expert opinions, the generated set of criteria allows to categorize relevant biological agents based on an objective and scientific approach. By a generic ranking scheme, the risk for different target populations (farm animals (especially zoonoses), humans) can be assessed and it is adjustable to the requirements of specific member states (e.g. differences in agent dissemination or the existing surveillance systems) (Figure 1).

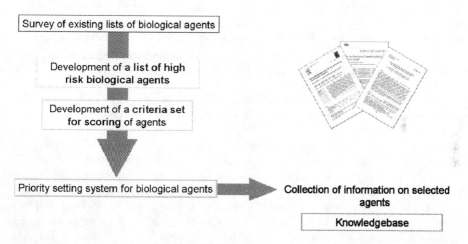

Fig. 1. Approach in the development of a risk ranking scheme for high pathogenic biological agents

Predictive Microbiology and Quantitative Risk Assessment

Once a contamination in a food product is detected, it has to be clarified if it poses a health risk to the public. Therefore, it is necessary to predict the growth, survival or inactivation of microorganisms in different food matrices and processing conditions. Such a quantitative microbiological risk assessment (QMRA) can be achieved by various mathematical models, collectively subsumed under the heading "predictive microbial models" (PMM). Unfortunately, the currently publicly available PMM are characterized by a great heterogeneity with respect to applicability, quality, validity, documentation, application limits and software requirements.

The Federal Institute for Risk Assessment is developing a community resource that facilitates the calculation of predictive microbiological models and their model parameters (e.g. D-, Z- values, lag-times, maximum growth rates etc.). The creation, collection, sharing and application of PMM can extend existing community resources like the ComBase database. Such a community software infrastructure could pave the way for collaborative efforts to improve food safety globally. Further information related to this topic is presented within the Future Security Conference 2012 by Weiser et al. "An open-source community resource for creating, collecting, sharing and applying predictive microbial models (PMM-lab)".

An epidemiological tool for the assessment of microbiological risks, which may originate from intentional contamination of the feed chain, was developed by the Federal Institute for Risk Assessment. It covers several elements such as the feed processing chain, the microorganism and the modeling approach. Different scenarios were defined and evaluated as well as a sensitivity analysis was performed. Further information related to this topic is presented within the Future Security Conference 2012 by Käsbohrer et al. "Model for the Assessment of Microbiological Risks Originating from Intentional Contaminations in Feed Chains".

Detection of Vulnerable Points in Food Processing Facilities
The assessment of the vulnerabilities within a system or infrastructure in the food industry can help to identify areas that may be vulnerable to natural, accidental and deliberate contaminations. Therefore, data including details on facilities and process steps and parameters, as well as information on raw material and suppliers are needed to conduct a vulnerability assessment of a food production facility or process for evaluating the most susceptible points in the system.

CARVER+ Shock, provided by the U.S. Food and Companies, was the first available Vulnerability Assessment Software Tool and supports to evaluate the attractiveness of a target for an attack.

Currently a system is being developed to assess the vulnerability of company facilities and processes handling food materials in Germany. It will meet and include legal framework conditions and allow process mapping by constructing a flow chart, process analysis by conducting of interviews, process review by ranking the obtained information and providing recommendations on mitigation measures. Further information related to a project including the key issues mentioned above is presented within the Future Security Conference 2012 by Buschulte et al. "Vulnerability Assessment in the Food Chain - A Way to Do It".

Commodity Flows, Tracing, Recording and Reporting
Once a contaminated in food (ingredient) occur, all products containing this contaminated material must be identified. In order to define all products at risk the knowledge about the commodity chains is important and therefore forward and backward tracing is necessary. According to Regulation (EC) No 178/2002, business operators shall have systems available to ensure the ability of identifying sources and targets of materials and products to serve tracing investigations. However, at present there is no specification or

standard available on how these systems should be structured and how fast the data have to be made available to the respective governmental institution and/or quality management system.

In case of an outbreak an efficient set of tools for product related information management and backtracing are crucial to enable quick and reliable identification of the source and/or vehicles of the outbreak. Interviewing infected people to define probable vehicles and tracing them back through the specific supply chains were for example the methods of choice within the EHEC outbreak 2011 in Germany. Data on all steps of the respective food supply chains were gathered using spreadsheets (MS Excel) and a relational database was developed at the Federal Institute for Risk Assessment to import and collate these data for further analysis. Additionally, several criteria for consistency checking were implemented, i.e. checking the lot numbers, seed names, quantities and delivery timelines through the supply chain. A graphical representation of relationships between suppliers, distributors and producers were integrated as well and could substantially contribute to the successful identification of common sources and communication processes. (BfR, 2011).

The applied method prooved to be quick and effective and was implemented within a very short time frame. Available information was automatically double-checked and analyzed immediately. Therefore, connections between suppliers have been promptly visualized. In the near future, the implementation of a data management system for all involved parties ensuring electronic provision of trade data in time while ensuring confidentiality of data is needed.

Product Supply Chains

Tracing and tracking of product supply chains can contribute to risk assessment tasks. Commercial data from retail tracking services can be used to explore spatial and temporal properties of products, generate hypotheses on contamination sources, as well as forecast product distribution. Especially during a food borne outbreak it is necessary to have an overview of food product distribution to include this knowledge in the risk assessment and in the recommendations for stakeholders and consumers.

B2B (business-to-business) data from retail tracking services - usually used for marketing or market share analyses - might significantly support the work of risk assessors in food chain crisis investigations. To allow a seamless integration with epidemiological modelling tasks - which are crucial to understand the spreading of diseases itself - it is planned to integrate core functionalities of these workflows into the open-source spatiotemporal epidemiological modeler (STEM) software (www.eclipse.org/stem). Further information related to this topic was presented within the Future Security Conference 2012 by Filter et al. "Exploitation of Commercial B2B Data for Risk Assessment Tasks in Foodborne Crisis Events".

Epidemiological Modeling of Food Contaminations

The ability to predict the spread and effects of pathogens in the population by simulating the transmission of a pathogen-induced disease from the food chain to the human population can improve the possibilities of risk assessment within a food borne outbreak tremendously. However, a software for computer-based simulations on the fate of biological hazard contaminations within the food processing and trade networks is currently not available elsewhere.

The Spatiotemporal Epidemiological Modeler (STEM, available at http://www.eclipse.org) is being used in this context to model the spread of diseases along the supply chain. The synthesis of models that describe the dynamics of a disease on a population level (e.g. with stochastic or deterministic SIR/SEIR models) with those that calculate microbiological behavior of pathogens in the production process is a new approach. This epidemiological community resource can be used by governmental and scientific bodies for the simulation of user-defined intervention scenarios in crisis situations and is thus a useful tool to advice and support decision-making. As a proof-of-concept, the distribution of Salmonella from animals to humans via consumption of contaminated meat has been modelled. Further information related to this topic was presented within the Future Security Conference 2012 by Falenski et al. "An Open-Source Community Resource for Epidemiological Modeling in Bioterroristic or Agroterroristic Crisis Situations".

Differentiation between Natural and Deliberate Contamination
In case of a deliberate contamination without a claim of responsibility it is reasonable to assume that the intentional cause of an outbreak will not be revealed precociously. However, the criminal background of a contamination is an important fact strongly influencing the investigations for the source of an outbreak, the crises management responsibilities and the countermeasures to be taken. Thus, guidelines are needed which assist producers and administrators in differentiating between natural and deliberate food borne disease incidents.

Currently guidelines are being developed at the Federal Institute for Risk Assessment and it is expected that the revelation of the intentional or unintentional nature of the contamination supports the investigators in the detection of the outbreak source and could aid to prevent further attacks. The differentiation is inevitable for the decision to involve the police as well as further distinct authorities as their responsibilities may vary depending on the outbreak's origin.

4   Conclusion

The Federal Institute for Risk Assessment plays an important role in improving consumer protection and food safety. It coordinates and contributes in various national and international projects to further evaluate and optimize available (food safety) systems aiming to improve the security of the food supply chain against deliberate and accidental contaminations with the overall target to enhance food safety and food security, which are still major concerns worldwide due to repeated food borne outbreaks and contamination problems.

Integral part of the concept is the development of a knowledge base on food matrices, food production processes, process parameters, microbial agents and predictive models. The database structure integrates a citation management resource (e.g. for scientific literature) and an information quality scoring feature. This lays the foundation to a comprehensive documentation on model quality considering the data used for model generation and the results from sensitivity analyses of the models. Depending on the available and integrated (experimental) data the developed software and data infrastructure can become an integral part of a strategy to safeguard the food supply chain in case of food borne outbreaks.

References

1. BfR, Methodisches Vorgehen zur Rück- und Vorwärtsverfolgung. In: Appel, B., Böl, G.-F., Greiner, M., Lahrssen-Wiederholt, M., Hensel, A. (eds.) EHEC-Ausbruch 2011 - Aufklärung des Ausbruchs entlang der Lebensmittelkette. Federal Institute for Risk Assessment, Berlin (2011)
2. EC 2000 White Paper on Food Safety Com (1999) 719 final, Commission of the European Communities, Brussels (2000)
3. EC 2003 Communication from the Commission, June 2, to the Council and the European Parliament on cooperation in the European Union on preparedness and response to biological and chemical agent attacks (Health security) (COM (2003) 320 final – not published in the Official Journal), Commission of the European Communities, Brussels (2003), http://eur-lex.europa.eu/LexUriServ/LexUriServ.do?uri=COM:2003:0320:FIN:EN:PDF (accessed April 12, 2012)
4. EC 2005 Communication From the Commission to the Council, The European Parliament, The European Economic and Social Committee and the Committee of the Regions on strengthening coordination on generic preparedness planning for public health emergencies at EU level COM (2005) 605 final, Commission of the European Communities, Brussels (2005)
5. EC 2007 Green Paper on Bio-Preparedness. Commission of the European Communities, Brussels (2007)
6. EC 2009 Report of the CBRN Task Force. Freedom and Security (ed.), Directorate General Justice, Commission of the European Communities, Brussels (2009)
7. WHO 2008 Terrorist Threats to Food — Guidance for Establishing and Strengthening Prevention and Response Systems. Revised version. Z.a.F.D. (ed.), Department of Food safety, World Health Organization, Geneva (2002)

An Open-Source Community Resource
for Creating, Collecting, Sharing
and Applying Predictive Microbial Models (PMM-Lab)

Armin A. Weiser, Matthias Filter, Alexander Falenski, Jörgen Brandt,
Annemarie Käsbohrer, and Bernd Appel

Federal Institute for Risk Assessment, Dep. Biological Safety, Germany
armin.weiser@bfr.bund.de

1   Introduction

Quantitative microbiological risk assessments (QMRA) in the farm-to-fork continuum heavily rely on mathematical models for growth, survival and inactivation of micro-organisms in different food matrices and processing conditions, collectively sub-sumed under the heading "predictive microbial models" (PMM). Unfortunately, the currently publicly available PMM are characterized by a great heterogeneity with respect to applicability, quality, validity, documentation, application limits and software requirements.

2   Aims

The objective of this research is to develop a community resource that facilitates the creation, collection, sharing and application of PMM extending existing community resources like the Combase database on experimental microbial data.

Such a community software infrastructure could pave the way for collaborative efforts to improve food safety globally.

3   Results

On the basis of the open source software framework Konstanz Information Miner (KNIME) [1], R [2] and a HSQL database engine [3] the open-source community resource "PMM-lab" was developed.

The PMM-lab plugin extends the KNIME software framework such that QMRA-specific modeling tasks can easily be accomplished. Due to the available R-software integration no restrictions with respect to applicable model types exist. The implementation of the PMM-lab plug-in allows the integration of data in any format. It already includes several models and some example data, and it is open-ended regarding data, models and other modelling implementations.

N. Aschenbruck et al. (Eds.): Future Security 2012, CCIS 318, pp. 462–465, 2012.

The integrated database is structured as a knowledge base on food matrices, food production processes, process parameters, microbial agents and predictive models. The database structure integrates a citation management resource (e.g. for scientific literature). This forms the basis for a comprehensive documentation on model quality considering the data used for model generation and the results from sensitivity analyses of the models.

The PMM-lab plug-in allows all information necessary for documentation and quality assessment to be accessed immediately and in a standardized fashion.

ID	Name	Manually	Score	RSquare	RSS	Comments
1	Linear model	false	0	0.137	0.279	
2	Geeraerd	false	0	0.255	0.243	
3	Baranyi without Nmax	false	0	0.365	0.0735	
4	Buchanan without Nmax	false	0	0.355	0.0743	
5	Buchanan without lag	false	0	0.0826	0.106	
6	Linear model	false	0	0.355	0.0744	
7	Bilinear without Nres	false	0	0.355	0.0743	
8	Bilinear without Sl	false	0	0.0826	0.106	
9	Baranyi without Nmax	false	0	0.438	0.179	
10	Buchanan without Nmax	false	0	0.171	0.263	

Fig. 1. Model Editor for viewing estimated models and for manually adding new models into the database

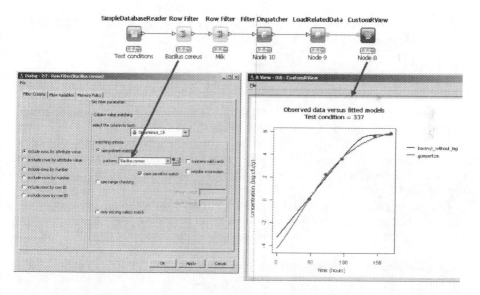

Fig. 2. Example workflow in KNIME for configuration and estimation of primary models. Visualization and reporting are integral parts of KNIME and the plug-in.

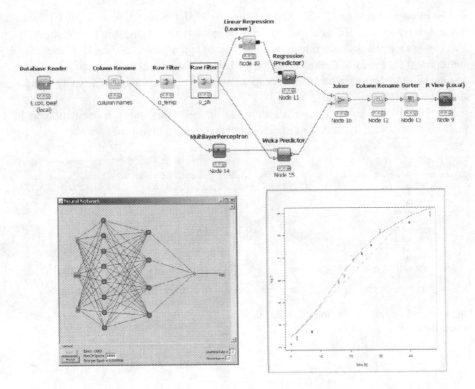

Fig. 3. Implementation of neural networks using the WEKA [4] plugin in KNIME as alternative method for modelling

4   Conclusions

The PMM-lab KNIME-Plug-in is the first full featured community resource in the field of microbial modelling. This infrastructure will open the path for a high quality community PMM model repository. The developed solution has the potential to empower lab scientists to create and document PMM in a standardized fashion which in the end will be beneficial with respect to scientific transparency and model validation opportunities.

Depending on the available and integrated (experimental) data the developed software and data infrastructure can become an integral part of a strategy to safeguard the food supply chain in case of bio-terroristic attacks.

Acknowledgements. This work has been funded by BMBF (13N11202) and BMELV (BLE No. 07HS019) research grants.

References

1. Michael, R.B., Nicolas, C., Fabian, D., Giuseppe, D.F., Thomas, R.G., Florian, G., Thorsten, M., Peter, O., Christoph, S., Bernd, W.: Knime: The Konstanz Information Miner (2006), http://www.knime.org
2. R Development Core Team. R: A language and environment for statistical computing (2008), http://www.r-project.org
3. HyperSQL, http://hsqldb.org
4. WEKA, http://www.cs.waikato.ac.nz/ml/weka

Model for the Assessment of Microbiological Risks Originating from Intentional Contaminations in Feed Chains

Annemarie Käsbohrer, Matthias Filter, Angela Körner, Anneluise Mader, Jürgen Zentek, and Bernd Appel

Federal Institute for Risk Assessment, Department for Biological Safety, Berlin, Germany
Annemarie.kaesbohrer@bfr.bund.de

Abstract. A model for the assessment of microbiological risks, which may originate from intentional contamination of the feed chain, was developed by the Federal Institute for Risk Assessment. It covers different feed processing chains and different microorganisms. Numerous scenarios were defined and evaluated as well as a sensitivity analysis performed. The application of the model allowed the identification of process parameter combinations which would be inefficient in worst case scenarios, e.g. where a highly heat resistant strain was selected for the intentional contamination. Equally important, this analysis can help to target specific control efforts. Based on the outcome of these simulations, recommendations can easily be given in crisis situations to which temperature-time combination processes should be adjusted to ensure the production of safe compound feeding stuff. This research will help to better understand and predict the consequences of bioterrorist attacks in the feed processing chain.

Keywords: Bacillus species, risk assessment, intentional contamination, feed chain, deterministic model.

1   Introduction

Mathematical modeling is considered a useful approach to understand or even predict the survival and spread of microbial agents in a certain environment. Based on knowledge / hypotheses generated by modeling approaches different mitigation strategies can be developed or evaluated. Although the principles of predictive microbiological modeling are well-known among microbiologists, up to now only few approaches have tried to use this knowledge in the context of intentional spread of microorganisms especially in the feed production chain.

   The objective of one module of the project 'Pathosafe', which was financially supported by the German Ministry of Education and Research (BMBF), was to develop epidemiological tools for the assessment of microbiological risks, which may originate from intentional contamination of the feed chain. Based on the outcome of the modeling exercise, recommendations for the appropriate application of analytical test methods available or developed within another module of the project Pathosafe as well as strategies for measures to mitigate these risks were developed.

N. Aschenbruck et al. (Eds.): Future Security 2012, CCIS 318, pp. 466–470, 2012.

2   Material and Methods

In a stepwise approach models covering the feed processing chain and potential bioterrorist agents were developed. Then different scenarios were defined, evaluated and a sensitivity analysis was performed.

2.1   Feed Processing Chain

In a first step, the major processing steps of commercial feed processing chains were described. Based on this a simplified feed chain model for compound feed was build. Figure 1 depicts the major steps of the chain. As the major characterizing parameters, temperature during the process, duration of the process, pH-value and a_w-value of the ingredients were identified. Pressure was identified as another relevant parameter, but due to a lack of data it was not included into the simplified model. For the three major processing steps, namely mixing, conditioning and forming (with three variations: pelleting, expanding or extruding) the range of processing conditions was collecting from literature and in expert consultations.

2.2   Characteristics of the Microorganism

For spore forming bacteria of the genus Bacilli, especially for the species Bacillus anthracis and the surrogate organism, Bacillus cereus, parameters like D-values and z-values were identified as most relevant to predict growth or survival of the spores. The D-value reflects the time needed to inactivate 90% of the cells. The z-value describes the change in an environmental parameter (e.g. temperature) needed to reduce the D-value by 90%. For modeling purposes D- and z-values were collected from literature and entered into a specific spreadsheet.

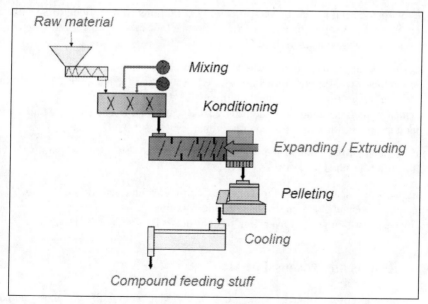

Fig. 1. Schematic representation of the simplified feed processing chain

2.3   Modeling

A deterministic model based on the Bigelow formula was developed. Additional the model for Bacillus cereus (Leguerinel et al. 2004) on the survival of bacterial spores was re-implemented. The formula used was:

$$N = N_0 \times 10^{\frac{-t}{D_T}} \qquad log(N) = log(N_0 - \frac{t}{D_T})$$

or as

(1)

where N = bacterial count at the end of the processing step; N0: = bacterial count at the beginning of the processing step; T = temperature at the processing step; t = duration (time period) of the processing step; DT = D-value for the temperature at the processing step.

To be able to consider also changes in characteristics of the matrix considered, namely the pH-value and the aw-value adjusted D-values (2) were calculated on the basis of the reference D-value and included in the main model (1) using the formula:

$$\log D_T = \log D_{ref} - (\frac{T - T_{ref}}{z_T}) - \left| \frac{pH - pH_{ref}}{z_{pH}} \right| - \left| \frac{a_w - 1}{z_{a_w}} \right|$$

(2)

where z_T, z_{pH} and z_{aw} describe the relative resistance of the bacteria under given conditions for T = temperature, pH-value or aw-value of the matrix. The model formulas were implemented in Excel.

2.4   Scenarios Considered

Different processing scenarios and processing conditions were defined to account for different technical solutions used the field. For each of these scenarios three processing conditions were considered:

— Normal situation: most frequently described processing conditions
— Favorable situation: conditions considered destructive for bacteria, e.g. high temperature; upper limit of reported conditions
— Critical situation: conditions considered not harmful for bacteria, e.g. high temperature; lower limit of reported conditions

Heterogeneity of bacterial strains was taken into account by selecting parameter values for different 'model agents':

— highly heat resistant germ: upper limit of confidence interval for the D-value
— medium resistant germ: mean value for the D-value
— low heat resistant germ: lower limit of confidence interval for the D-value

3   Results and Discussion

The application of the model for the identified 'model agents' allowed the systematic evaluation of different parameter combinations, e.g. of temperature and duration of the process, or the combination of temperature and pH-value. Figure 2 depicts the effect of temperature and pH-value on the D-value. For example, for a matrix with pH 7, temperatures above 98°C might be necessary to achieve a D-value below 10 minutes. Thus, even without any knowledge of actual processing conditions, the tool allows for calculation the data of these complex interactions. Display of results helps to get an overall view on the outcome.

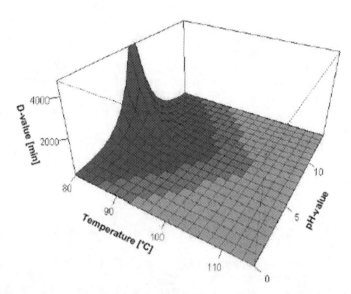

Fig. 2. Example for the effect of temperature and pH-value on the D-value

For each of the individual processing steps and also for the scenarios defined, the model showed that combinations exist which diminish the bacterial load considerably. Lowering the pH-value showed an additional beneficial effect. Figure 3 gives an insight into the effect of two scenarios with quite a difference in the survival rate of the spores. Whereas in scenario I, only a small reduction of log10 (CFU) could be achieved, in scenario II most of the spores could be inactivated.

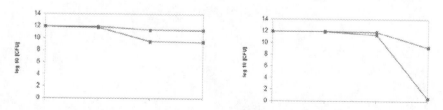

Fig. 3. Example for the modeling outcome for two processing scenarios (mixing, conditioning, processing) considered with different temperature-time-processing conditions. The green and red lines show results for two different pH-values of the matrix.

The application of the model allowed the identification of those processing combinations and the consideration of worst case scenarios, e.g. by assuming that a highly heat resistant strain was selected for the intentional contamination, to target specific control efforts. Furthermore, based on the outcome of the simulation, recommendations can be easily given in a crisis situation to which temperature-time combinations the processes should be adjusted to ensure the production of safe compound feeding stuff.

Validation of the model on the basis of published data for Bacillus cereus toyoi spores (Simon, 2005) was successful. In a next step, the results of this modeling approach should be evaluated by application of the new diagnostic techniques, developed in a separate module of the project.

The results help to better understand and predict the consequences of bioterrorist attacks in the feed processing chain. On the basis of the outcome of the model, possible risks for animal populations feed and in consequence for human health can be calculated based on the mean infective dose for the agent taken from the literature.

Acknowledgements. This work has been funded by the BMBF (13N550) research grant.

References

1. Simon, O.: Micro-Organisms as Feed Additives - Probiotics. Advances in Pork Production 16, 161–167 (2005)
2. Leguerinel, I., Spegagne, I., Couvert, O., Gaillard, S., Mafart, P.: Validation of an overall model describing the effect of three environmental factors on the apparent D-value of Bacillus cereus spores. International Journal of Food Microbiology 100, 223–229 (2004)

Exploitation of Commercial B2B Data
for Risk Assessment Tasks in Foodborne Crisis Events

Matthias Filter, C. Thoens, Annemarie Käsbohrer, and Bernd Appel

Federal Institute for Risk Assessment, Dep. Biological Safety, Germany
{Matthias.Filter,Christian.Thoens,
Annemarie.Kaesbohrer,Bernd.Appel}@bfr.bund.de

Abstract. In foodborne crisis events timely and scientifically sound risk assessments are of utmost relevance for all stakeholders. Risk assessments serve as guidance for governmental and private sector crisis management and affect international trade relationships as well. Therefore it is necessary to continuously explore data sources and data analysis technologies which support the risk assessment process.

This research analyses whether B2B data in combination with an open-source data analysis platform can contribute to risk assessment tasks. Specifically it is shown that commercial data from retail tracking services can be used to explore spatial and temporal distribution properties of products and generate hypotheses on possible contamination sources. Equally important, the developed data analytics workflows can help to decide which food product (group) is unlikely to be the source of the crisis. To make these resources available internationally it is planed to integrate these functionalities into the Spatiotemporal Epidemiological Modeler (STEM) project (www.eclipse.org/stem).

Keywords: foodborne disease, disease distribution, food distribution, risk assessment, KNIME.

1 Introduction

Over the last decades globalization has dramatically influenced all areas of society including food industry [1]. As a result, the health and economic risks associated with an intentional or natural food contamination event have increased significantly [2]. Foodborne disease outbreaks like the EHEC O104:H4 outbreak in Germany 2011 [3] show also the high public pressure originating from these crisis situations.

As the trend towards globalization will continue governmental institutions like the Federal Institute for Risk Assessment have to be prepared for increasingly complex and challenging foodborne crisis situations. Thus risk assessors have to explore new data sources and data analytics tools to be equipped for increasingly challenging tasks. This research analyzed whether commercially available business-to-business (B2B) data from retail tracking services - usually used for marketing or market share analyses - can support risk assessment tasks in foodborne outbreak events.

N. Aschenbruck et al. (Eds.): Future Security 2012, CCIS 318, pp. 471–474, 2012.

2   Material and Methods

2.1   Data

B2B retail sales data from German food retailing companies covering years 2008-2010 were purchased from SymphonyIRI Group. Data covered e.g. commodity groups fresh milk, soft cheese and self-service sausages. Each commodity data set contained information on the amount (weight) of each product (down to EAN code) sold per week in each German postal code 2 region. Weekly product sales amounts from discounter companies Aldi, Norma and Lidl could only be delivered as estimates based on GfK consumer survey data with a spatial resolution of 16 federal states.

2.2   Data Analytics

All data processing steps were performed within the open-source data-mining software Konstanz Information Miner KNIME [4]. Using the "KNIME R Statistics Integration" plugin R scripts [5] were employed for data visualization (libraries: maptools, RColorBrewer and classInt) and statistical analyses (libraries: ecespa, forecast).

3   Results and Findings

Within the KNIME framework several workflows were developed for analysis of B2B data from retail tracking services. Each workflow addresses one of the following specific topics: spatial distribution of products, temporal distribution of products including prognosis feature, comparison of spatial distribution patterns, general commodity and market information.

As a result risk assessors can now explore the spatial (Fig 1) and / or temporal (Fig 2) distribution of products that are under suspicion. Moreover they can test, which product specific spatial distribution pattern is significantly different from a given reference distribution, which e.g. may represent the distribution and number of diseased people (Fig. 3).

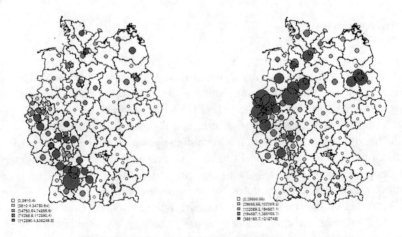

Fig. 1. Spatial Distribution of Two Fresh Milk Products

To compensate for the four week time gap inherent in the commercial data sets the temporal analyses workflow contains a prognosis model which gives product sales (amount) estimates for time points "in the future".

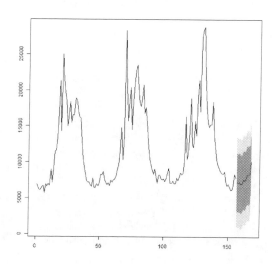

Fig. 2. Amount (Weight) of a Soft Cheese Product Sold in Germany from 01/2008 to 52/2010 including ARIMA-based Prognosis for 01/2011 to 12/2011

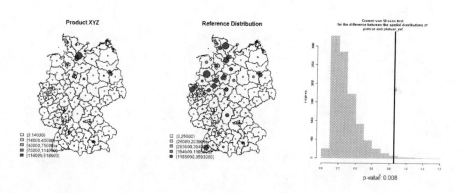

Fig. 3. Visualization of a statistical test to decide whether two distributions are significantly different

4   Conclusions

This research provides evidence that B2B data can be considered as supportive resources in dealing with foodborne crisis events. Depending on the availability of data (e.g. comparable data on commodity group "produce" are not available) this new resource might significantly support the work of risk assessors in Germany in food chain crisis investigations. To allow a seamless integration with epidemiological modelling tasks (which are crucial to understand the spreading of diseases itself) it is planned to integrate core functionalities of these workflows into the open-source spatiotemporal epidemiological modeler (STEM) software (www.eclipse.org/stem).

Acknowledgements. This work has been funded by the BMBF (13N11202) research grant.

References

1. Wilkinson, J.: The Food Processing Industry, Globalization and Developing Countries. In: The Transformation of Agri-Food Systems: Globalization, Supply Chains and Smallholder Farmers, pp. 87–108. Food & Agriculture Org., New York (2008)
2. Krause, D.O., Hendrick, S.: Zoonotic pathogens in the food chain. CABI, Wallingford (2010)
3. http://www.bfr.bund.de/cm/350/ehec-ausbruch-2011-aufklaerung-des-ausbruchs-entlang-der-lebensmittelkette.pdf
4. Michael, R.B., Nicolas, C., Fabian, D., Giuseppe, D.F., Thomas, R.G., Florian, G., Thorsten, M., Peter, O., Christoph, S., Bernd, W.: Knime: The Konstanz Information Miner (2006), http://www.knime.org
5. R Development Core Team. R: A language and environment for statistical computing (2008), http://www.r-project.org

Micro Aerial Vehicles in Disaster Assessment Operations – The Example of Cyprus 2011

Martin Frassl[1], Michael Lichtenstern[1],
Michael Angermann[1], and Giulio Gullotta[2]

[1] German Aerospace Center (DLR), Institute of Communications and Navigation,
Oberpfaffenhofen, Germany
[2] Federal Office of Civil Protection and Disaster Assistance (BBK), Bonn, Germany
{martin.frassl,m.lichtenstern,michael.angermann}@dlr.de,
giulio.gullotta@bbk.bund.de

Abstract. This paper describes the deployment of Micro Aerial Vehicles (MAVs) during a European Civil Protection Mechanism mission to Cyprus in July 2011. Extensive damages at an industrial structure were assessed and evaluated. The utilized aerial robotic platforms, operations and findings are described. This deployment is an example of an situation-adaptive usage of MAVs in response to a man-made disaster.

Keywords: disaster management, assessment, micro aerial vehicle, robotics.

1 Introduction

Robotic systems can explore areas a human cannot access, be it due to safety reasons or because of the robot's mobility (such as flying robots or small robots that crawl through debris). Micro Aerial Vehicles (MAVs) are increasingly discussed and developed for safety and security related applications. Equipped with sensors, such platforms can measure environmental quantities or show perspectives of an object which are not accessible from ground. Due to the small size of MAVs they can be used in dense urban structures or even inside buildings. On July 11th, 2011 a fatal explosion on the Cypriot "Evangelos Florakis" naval base caused 13 fatalities and injured more than 60 persons. The nearby Vasilikos Power Plant (VPP), which contributed nearly half of the energy needs of the Republic of Cyprus, was severely damaged, resulting in an immediate interruption of its power supply (Fig. 1). On July 13th the Cypriot government requested assistance through the European Civil Protection Mechanism (EUCP). On

Fig. 1. Structural damage at Vasilikos Power Plant after the blast

N. Aschenbruck et al. (Eds.): Future Security 2012, CCIS 318, pp. 475–479, 2012.
© Springer-Verlag Berlin Heidelberg 2012

July 16th, an EUCP team, consisting of disaster experts, structural and electrical engineers, was deployed to Cyprus. As many parts of the power plant's structures and buildings were inaccessible due to enduring danger of collapse and falling debris, Cyprus issued an additional request for technical experts with equipment to conduct low altitude aerial assessment of roofs, load-bearing primary structures and other unaccessible parts of the power plant. In response to this request the authors of this paper were deployed to Cyprus on July, 22nd and extended the EUCP team. In a series of rapid iterations with structural and electrical engineers several assessment flights on site were carried out on July, 26th, constituting the first time MAVs have been utilized in a European Civil Protection Mechanism mission [1].

2   Related Work

The utilization of hovering Micro Aerial Vehicles for civilian missions in dense urban environments is still experimental and rare in real disaster situations. To our knowledge the first deployment of aerial robots in the field took place after Hurricane Katrina in 2005. A rotary-wing iSENSYS IP-3 was used for imagery collection during the response and recovery phases. Based on the findings of this deployment a crew organization and a four-step operational protocol for close urban operations has been proposed by Murphy et al. [2]. The deployment of the same rotary-wing MAV after the collapse of the Berkman Plaza II building in 2007 in Jacksonville, Florida is documented in [3]. In this mission, the MAV had to be tethered to the ground due to legal issues, which resulted in an extended crew and additional cognitive load for the MAV operator. In [4] the first approach of a cooperative use of an MAV and an unmanned sea surface vehicle (USV) is described and challenges for such cooperations are discussed. In 2011 four Honeywell T-Hawk MAVs were deployed to the destroyed Fukushima Daiichi nuclear power plant in Japan. During several flights the T-Hawks were equipped with radiation sensors and cameras to gather videos and imagery [5].

3   Robotic Platforms

Two types of platforms were utilized for the aerial assessment on Cyprus, an AscTec Falcon and an AscTec Hummingbird. The Falcon is an electrically powered hovering platform with eight rotors, a total flying weight of 1920g, dimensions of about 800x850x160 mm, and an approximate flight time of 15 minutes. The system is manually remote controlled but provides good position stability in most outdoor situations using GPS, pressure and inertial sensors. It is equipped with a frame to stabilize a camera and allows to steer the camera's tilt independently from the platforms attitude, while the camera's pan is coupled to the yaw angle of the platform.

On this frame a Sony NEX-5 camera (E 16mm F2.8 lens, 4592x3056px image and 1920x1080px video resolution) is mounted (Fig. 5). A Hummingbird quadrotor was used for aerial assessment in areas with less free space, as the quadrotor

Fig. 2. Manual launch of a quadrotor   **Fig. 3.** Roof of the turbine hall

dimensions (about 540x540x90 mm) are about half the size of the Falcon's dimensions. The quadrotor is equipped with four rotors and achieves a total flight of approximately 15 minutes. A digital camera (2592x1944 pixel) was attached to the bottom (Fig. 2), and programmed to take images at a rate of 1 Hz.

4   Operations

A preflight assessment of the entire area was performed to familiarize the MAV team members with the environment. Focal areas were defined and safety issues pointed out. All assessment flights were performed under line of sight conditions. Live video was transmitted to the ground station and used by the pilot and in parallel by the camera operator on a separate larger display (Fig. 4). On this screen other EUCP team members also followed the video for immediate feedback on the flight plan. At all times the pilot had full control over the system and was able to override the camera operator's input. High resolution imagery/video was stored onboard and evaluated on ground in short breaks between the flights (Fig. 5). Analysis of each flight's data by structural engineers and assessment experts was immediately used for adjusting the flight plan of the subsequent flight.

Fig. 4. Team during the flight   **Fig. 5.** Discussion during flight breaks

5 Results and Findings

Onboard video and imagery (Fig. 3) provided valuable input for the civil engineers' findings and decisions about the structural integrity of the buildings. Additionally, GPS tracks and field notes have been collected for research purposes. One Human-Robot Interaction (HRI) problem in assessment flights in close urban structures is the limited depth perception of the human MAV operator. This problem was mitigated by adding a second person who was placed on a line of sight perpendicular to the pilot-vehicle axis and connected to the pilot via voice radio communications. This person provided additional depth information such as distance to structures and obstacles. This allowed for operations *close to* buildings but complex debris structures and insufficient position stability prevented safe flight *inside* buildings. Additional positioning sensors (ultrasonic, optical) are foreseen to facilitate this in the future.

6 Conclusions

During the first MAV deployment within the EU Civil Protection Mechanism two different types of Micro Aerial Vehicles helped to assess the situation in the Vasilikos power plant on Cyprus. Aerial imagery and videos served as immediate input to civil engineers and other experts. Tight integration of robotic platform operation and data analysis was a key success factor and enabled rapid adaptation of flight plans and sensor coverage. We believe that it is beneficial to involve MAVs as early as possible during a mission, as the aerial assessment results are valuable input for further assessment decisions. Manual operation of the MAVs under numerous geometric and safety constraints proved to be extremely exhausting for pilots. Pilot fatigue is likely to cause accidents and limits the operational endurance of MAV-based aerial assessments. Increased autonomy of MAVs could mitigate this problem. Furthermore, severe time constraints at a disaster site call for more rapid gathering of data. Therefore, we focus our research on utilizing multi-agent systems for future missions, to make use of parallelization and increase the temporal and spatial resolution of the observations. Robust communication and coordination algorithms as well as human-robotics interfaces with a focus on multi-agent systems serve this aim. In future missions this will allow to simultaneously control a number of agents in 3D-space, while maintaining continuous situation awareness of the state of the agents and the environment.

Acknowledgments. The research of this work is partially funded by the EU-Project SOCIETIES, co-funded by the European Commission within the 7th Framework Programme. Our mission to Cyprus was funded by the European Civil Protection Mechanism. The authors are indebted to all members of the EUCP team, the Monitoring and Information Center (MIC) in Brussels and the Cyprus Civil Defense (CCD) for their outstanding support during the mission.

References

1. European Commission: Humanitarian aid and civil protection - factsheet cyprus crisis (July 2011),
   http://ec.europa.eu/echo/files/aid/countries/Cyprus_factsheet.pdf
   (last accessed: June 24, 2012)
2. Murphy, R.R., Pratt, K.S., Burke, J.L.: Crew roles and operational protocols for rotary-wing micro-uavs in close urban environments. In: Proceedings of the 3rd ACM/IEEE International Conference on Human Robot Interaction, HRI 2008, pp. 73–80. ACM, New York (2008)
3. Pratt, K., Murphy, R., Burke, J., Craighead, J., Griffin, C., Stover, S.: Use of tethered small unmanned aerial system at berkman plaza ii collapse. In: IEEE International Workshop on Safety, Security and Rescue Robotics, SSRR 2008, pp. 134–139 (October 2008)
4. Murphy, R., Steimle, E., Griffin, C., Cullins, C., Hall, M., Pratt, K.: Cooperative use of unmanned sea surface and micro aerial vehicles at hurricane wilma. Journal of Field Robotics 25(3), 164–180 (2008)
5. Guizzo, E.: Robotic aerial vehicle captures dramatic footage of fukushima reactors (April 2011), http://spectrum.ieee.org/automaton/robotics/
   industrial-robots/robotic-aerial-vehicle-at-fukushima-reactors
   (last accessed: June 24, 2012)

Lighter-Than-Air UAVs for Surveillance and Environmental Monitoring

Michael Gerke, Ulrich Borgolte, Ivan Masár, František Jelenciak,
Pavol Bahnik, and Naef Al-Rashedi

FernUniversität in Hagen, Hagen, Germany
michael.gerke@fernuni-hagen.de

Abstract. This paper reports on the development of a computer
controlled airship for applications in surveillance and environmental monitoring. This covers the areas of crisis management and security situational awareness. Small airships are combining many features of planes
and rotorcrafts. They allow measurements very close to the scene, they
are able to carry even heavier payloads than comparable flight systems,
and they can move very slowly as well as close above ground. As no
dynamic force for lifting is necessary, on-board energy resources can be
completely applied to actuation, computer systems, and sensor equipment. Also, an airship possesses several inherent security features such
as usually small velocity, low weight, and a soft hull.

1 Introduction

While surveillance and data collection during security critical situations and also
monitoring of environmental conditions on the ground is quite common today
[1], there are many situations where additional information is required. Typical
application scenarios are panics in crowded areas, hazardous fires or explosions,
or guidance of rescue forces. To sense structures and persons on the ground,
a bird-eye's view is preferred [2]. Another example is the distribution of oil on
a water surface, which can be observed best from above [3]. Piloted airplanes
and helicopters are used since their invention for reconnaissance tasks. With the
improvement and miniaturization of sensors, space-based satellites are a major
source of information on environmental conditions [4]. But these systems are
limited with respect to availability, sensing coverage, data resolution, and long-
lasting observation. On the other hand, pilots exposed to radiation are very
limited in their length of stay.

What is needed for theses missions are heterogeneous flight systems consisting
of complementary devices. UAVs (unmanned aerial vehicles) overcome limitations based on the employment of pilots. Most of these systems are fixed-wing
aircrafts or rotorcrafts. Fixed-wing aircrafts are only ready for operation at a
certain minimum altitude above the ground for stable flight; also a minimum
velocity is necessary for aerodynamic lift. On the other hand, rotorcrafts are
less energy-efficient, resulting in less payload or shorter endurance. Therefore,

N. Aschenbruck et al. (Eds.): Future Security 2012, CCIS 318, pp. 480–483, 2012.

airships are an interesting option for long-endurance low-altitude sensing applications. These are based on a hull filled with a lifting gas allowing them to hover in the air by buoyancy compensating their weight and payload and operating with little thrust only. These Lighter-than-Air (LTA) flight systems can cruise at low speed and execute vertical take-off and landing, they 'float' through the air without engendering swirl and can stay close above the ground without applying an air-stream ('downwash') to the surface. Possible application areas in environmental monitoring are long-time surveillance of chemical or nuclear disasters, hazardous fires, sweeping of land mines [5], or search for trapped earthquake victims [6].

2   Hardware Design

The airship being developed at 'FernUniversität in Hagen' (Germany) is a blimp. Usually the filling gas of LTA systems is helium. Actual specifications are:

- 9 m length
- 2.3 m max. diameter
- 24 m^3 volume
- 20 kg mass without payload
- 5 kg max. payload
- 45 km/h max. velocity

This configuration allows operation as a UAV under the national law of Germany, where the upper limit is 25 kg mass.

The body of the airship resembles the classical 'cigar' shape. At its bottom side, two gondolas are attached. The main gondola contains batteries, electronics, and two main thrust motors. The second gondola incorporates additional payload (task specific sensors). The system is actuated by two DC motors. These motors can be vectored (tilted). For yaw motion, an additional small motor supports the aileron at the rear. Two pitch elevators laterally mounted at the upper tail end enable dynamic climbing and descending of the airship. Two packs of Lithium-Ferrite-Polymer type batteries are used for power supply.

The supervisory control system on the ground is a standard PC acting as base station. It is remotely connected to the on-board embedded computer via a wireless data link. As a backup solution, communication access via public network infrastructures is implemented.

3   Software Design

The software of the airship is strongly modular. Main components are modules for path planning, for flight control, and a data flow manager. The path planner is located in the base station, generating flight routes from high-level command inputs provided via user interface. The flight control module and data flow manager are calculated on board, they can operate the airship independently even if the data link is lost.

3.1   Airship Control

The airship control is based on a mathematical description of the LTA flight behavior [7]-[8]. The flight control system of the airship includes the 'autopilot' algorithms to assure trajectory following and control during flight, but also additional enhanced strategies for wind disturbance compensation. For stabilization during flight a roll-damping strategy is under development, which enables stabilization against undesired roll motion of the airship, which stifles monitoring the ground below.

3.2   Data and Communication

The main communication module is a data flow manager, which routes all data. Most of the airship's sensor data is related to its navigation, such as flight status information (such as velocity, acceleration, pose, and altitude). Additional data collected from application specific sensors are usually not analyzed on board. This information is routed to the base station and handed over to an application specific computer environment. At the time being, there is no separate channel for application sensors requiring high data rates (e.g. video).

The base station permanently sends pre-computed flight commands to the airship via wireless data link. In return, it receives status data from the airship. If any communication link is broken, the airship will try to use a redundant physical connection (e.g. UMTS) or will start a predefined emergency program if reconnection is impossible.

3.3   User Interface

During environmental monitoring, tools are expected to be nearly self-explanatory for the end-user (e.g. rescue forces). Thus the user interface of the UAV needs to be as simple as possible, and included into the operational environment of the user, with only little UAV-specific controls.

Core of the GUI is a topographic map or an aerial picture of the area of operation in order to define flight waypoints or areas to be monitored, and to display the current position of the UAV. Data collected from the application sensors can be integrated into the GUI visualization to update the environmental status. UAV status data (such as remaining battery capacity and height above ground) are embedded into the graphical display and simultaneously processed by the base station.

Incorporated are basic path planning features, which enable the airship to calculate optimal path trajectories, and at the same time consider time-variant hindrances in airspace. Airship control via GUI can always be overridden by remote teleoperation through personnel.

4   Surveillance and Environmental Monitoring

Some major classes of sensors for aerial monitoring can be identified: cameras (either photo or film cameras; sensitive to visible light, IR or UV; or multispectral cameras), scanning devices (e.g. RADAR, LIDAR), microwave sensors, and gas/particle sensors. In order to use these sensoric systems on-board of a UAV, some restrictions have to be considered: sensor weight, additional power supply and system stabilization during measurement.

Tests have been carried out on-board of our airship with different application sensors, e.g. cameras, laser scanners, and microwave radar. The flight system is open to any sensor payload which can be physically attached to the airship's gondola and fits to the weight restriction of approx. 5 kg. Sensor experiments under different environmental conditions proved the effectiveness of airship stabilization and flight control.

5 Conclusion

In this paper, first results of an airship control for autonomous flight manoeuvres with safety features have been presented. Various enhancements of airship control strategies are planned as future work, to reach a higher level of autonomy of the LTA flight system. Increasing the autonomy of our airship relieves any human tele-operator from flight control tasks and thus allows to concentrate on major mission tasks. These enhancements are focused on two main application aspects: to improve the LTA system's maneuverability and safety. It is intended to set-up automatic take-off and landing manoeuvres, and various emergency strategies like 'coming home'-procedures in case of the airship getting out of the range of teleoperation. Another aspect of future work is to increase the effective operating time of the airship by modification of the electrical actuation system into an advanced hybrid power system. This is an on-going development intended to provide to total flight time of more than 2 hours.

References

1. Fenger, J.: Urban Air Quality. Atmospheric Environment 33, 4877–4900 (1999)
2. Campbell, J.B.: Mapping the Land: Aerial Imagery for Land Use Information. Association of American Geographers (1983)
3. Oil Spill Monitoring Handbook. Prepared by Wardrop Consulting and the Cawthron Institute for the Australian Maritime Safety Authority (AMSA) and the Marine Safety Authority of New Zealand (MSA). Published by AMSA, Canberra (2003)
4. Szekielda, K.-H.: Satellite monitoring of the earth. John Wiley & Sons, Inc., Somerset, New Jersey (1988)
5. Meurer, H., et al.: An Emerging Remote Sensing Technology and its Potential Impact on Mine Action. In: Proc. International Symposium Humanitarian Demining, pp. 66–70 (2010)
6. Hada, Y., et al.: Information acquisition using intelligent sensor nodes and an autonomous blimp. In: Proc. SICE Annual Conference, pp. 988–991 (2008)
7. Gomes, V., Ramos, J.: Airship Dynamic Modelling for Autonomous Operation. In: Proc. IEEE Conference on Robotics and Automation (1998)
8. Gerke, M., Masár, I.: Modeling, sensorics and Control of a Robotic Airship. In: Proc. IASTED International Conference on Robotics and Apllications (2007)

Protection of Spaceborne Systems

Jan Eilers and Thomas Neff

German Aerospace Center, Oberpfaffenhofen, Germany
{Jan.Eilers,Thomas.Neff}@dlr.de

Abstract. As known, satellite systems operate in a harsh environment. Nowadays one of the main topics is space debris driven by different incidents. The Chinese ASAT-test in 2007 with the FENGYUN-1C weather satellite or the collision of the COSMO 2251 and an IRIDIUM 33 satellite in 2009 are examples of those incidents. But space debris is only one color of the huge spectrum of possible threats for spaceborne systems. If we want to protect our systems, we have to look at the big picture and try to determine the major impacts to tweak the most important threads with counter measurements and so to increase the protection level of spaceborne systems.

Keywords: Satellite protection, countermeasures, natural threats, man-made threats.

1   Introduction

Satellite systems can be seen in modern society's as a critical infrastructure. Most people don't be aware of this fact because spaceborne systems are used without knowing anything about the system behind, like navigation, communication and earth observation. Therefore it is crucial to point out the need to protect these systems. For strategic decisions it is necessary to take a look at the big picture of the space environment. There are many threats, which can be divided into different classes. We can talk about natural threats and man-made threats. The last one can further be subdivided in non-intentional and intentional threats.

Natural Threats: Natural threats are normally driven by the environment of space therefor we have the potential threats of temperature, vacuum, gravitation, near earth objects and also the space weather with an influence to the magnetic field, radiation and to the atmosphere resp. ionosphere. Furthermore a non-calculable system behavior could exist. For instance the movability of mechanical parts which work proper in the earth environment but due to the lack of an atmosphere the friction is too high and the mechanism stuck.

Non-intentional Man-Made Threats: Those threats came from the usage of the space environment by the mankind. Space Debris, constructional failures, the amount of spacecraft's which are controlled by several operators and the usage of the same frequencies where estimated in the study.

N. Aschenbruck et al. (Eds.): Future Security 2012, CCIS 318, pp. 484–487, 2012.

Intentional Man-Made Threats: The intentional man-made threats aim to destroy dam-age or temporarily disable a satellite. One theater is given in Figure 1, where some of these threats were identified like jamming, hacking, microwave or high frequency wea-pons, asymmetrical dangers, LASER, anti-satellite weapons, "killer satellites" and last but not least the high altitude nuclear detonation and its electromagnetic pulse.

Fig. 1. Man-Made Threats [1]

In general all those threats where described in detail in the main study. An example for construction failures is given in Table1.

Table 1. Types of failure [2]

Cause	%
Assigned	
Design	24.8
Environment	21.4
Operations	4.7
Random	
Parts	16.3
Quality	7.7
Other	6.3
Unknown	18.9

We see three major points for a system failure in this table: The design, the envi-ronment and unknowns, due to the fact that it is a piece of luck to determine the real reason for a satellite loss. As Donald Rumsfeld said "There are things we know that we know. There are known unknowns. That is to say there are things that we now know we don't know. But there are also unknown unknowns. There are things we do not know we don't know".

The question is "How is it possible to handle these threats?" To answer that an identification of given onboard protection possibilities would be useful. These are thermal control, redundancies, electromagnetic shielding, space weather forecast, Meteoroid Debris Protection Systems, de-orbiting, orbit maneuver to prevent collision with debris or other satellites, louver, communication strategies and encryption. Also there are a few possibilities to think about for the future like decoys, dummy satellites, algorithms to identify intruder, onboard laser weapons, constellation of many little satellites for one function, sensors to detect a threat, service satellites, reduce space debris, development of new energy systems and stealth techniques. Now it is necessary to combine the threats and the countermeasures. In a first step a group of space experts created a hazard classification listed in Table 2.

Table 2. Hazard Classification

Hazard Classification	description
Hazard Class 0	Fully operational, no damages
Hazard Class I	Minimum influence to operations, light damages, passive reversible disturbance, loss of redundancies, shorted lifetime
Hazard Class II	Influence to operations, mid damages active, reversible disturbance, loss of redundancies, shorted lifetime
Hazard Class III	Maximum influence to operations, heavy damages, irreversible disturbance, loss of redundancies, strong shorted lifetime
Hazard Class IV	System destroyed, non-operational

With this classification the group created tables for the natural, the non-intentional man-made and the intentional man-made threats. Each table consist a correlation between the single threat and the classification of this threat. Further an assumption of the probability for every threat has been made.

The next step is a correlation between the protection methods and the threats combined with a simple cost estimation model for each countermeasure and the probability for every single threat. The result can be figured out in Table 3.

2   Conclusion

Table 3 gives a good overview of all estimated threats and related protection methods. With this tool it is possible to react to different threat scenarios by changing the input variables and values. In this approach the matrix output based upon the feeding of values defined by experts at a specific time. Supported by Figure 2 it is easy to see that the measures of add-on sensors to detect threats, redundancies and additional system engineering increase the protection level of a space system best regarding cost and probability. It is also to consider that the other threats didn't disappear and the other countermeasures therefore don't lose its right to be adopted. With this figures it is easy to increase the system reliability with a small amount of money.

Table 3. Correlation matrix between countermeasures and threats

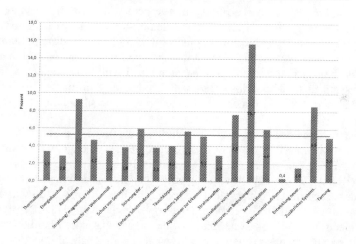

Fig. 2. Overall estimation of the countermeasures

References

[1] Space Technology Guide (US-DOD, Washington, Fiscal Year 2000/2001)
[2] Harland, D.M., Lorenz, R.D.: Space Systems Failures Disasters and Rescues of Satellites. In: Rockets and Space Probes. Springer (2005) ISBN 0-387-21519-0

CHICAGO – An Airborne Observation System for Security Applications

Hartmut Runge[1,*], Josef Kallo[2], Philipp Rathke[2], Thomas Stephan[2], Franz Kurz[1], Dominik Rosenbaum[1], and Oliver Meynberg[1]

[1] DLR, Remote Sensing Technology Institute, 82234 Wessling, Germany
[2] DLR, Institute of Technical Thermodynamics, 70569 Stuttgart, Germany
hartmut.runge@dlr.de

Abstract. The paper describes the layout of a new research aircraft for security applications. The typical applications for such an aircraft are outlined and the system requirements are derived. Furthermore, the performance of the system and a first mission is described.

Keywords: airborne, electric flying, fuel cells, digital camera, observation, security, mass events, traffic data.

1 Introduction

DLR has developed an airborne observation system with an array of cameras on a glider aircraft which acts as a research and demonstration platform for a variety of security applications. The project makes use of the know-how of different branches of DLR, especially remote sensing technology, aviation, fuel cells and communication. The goal is the observation of large areas combined with a near-real time on-board data processing and direct transmission of the derived information to the ground facilities. Furthermore, due to a circling of the aircraft a persistent monitoring of a site shall be achieved.

Participants of major events, festivals, religious ceremonies, sports events, ect. may be bothered from aircraft flyovers or the presence of police helicopter. From the DLR project "VABENE" a mature sensor system and data transmission facilities are available (Ref. 1). These have been adopted by the project designated "CHICAGO", which is described in this paper. Here we avoid the use of noisy and relatively large aircrafts but use a small and extremely quiet power glider named "DLR Antares H2". It has an electric propulsion system and is that small, that it can hardly be detected from the ground, when flying in a typical operational altitude of 1.000m. Furthermore, the team works on the integration of a fuel cell for energy storage, which will enlarge the range and flight time of the glider considerably. With this combination of sensor and unobtrusive as well agile platform several discreet surveillance applications in the security area can be covered.

---

[*] Corresponding author.

N. Aschenbruck et al. (Eds.): Future Security 2012, CCIS 318, pp. 488–492, 2012.

We are aiming at the following **applications**:

Crowd Monitoring

In order to ensure the safety of mass events monitoring of movement and density of the people in the venue is required. Typical operational areas are football arenas, Olympic Games and large public ceremonies. Ground based camera systems installed on masts will never provide a perspective as from an aircraft in high altitude! Furthermore, ground installations can be destroyed in a mass panic and real-time monitoring by video camera operators is tedious and tiring. Therefore, automated image processing on-board the aircraft shall deliver real time information about the crowd behavior.

Live Imagery from Security Hot Spots

Wild fires, road accidents, flooding, areas affected by an earthquake and spots with criminal activity require live observation. A data link to the operations center will enable immediate and adequate response. A geo-referenced live image from the scene will be of inestimable value for the rescuers, medical staff and the police.

Traffic Monitoring

After a catastrophe or terrorist attack common information services on the internet may not be accessible and it is necessary that the security forces have their own and independent means to gather import information. One essential is up-to-date traffic information to know which roads can still be used for evacuation or ambulances. In the course of the VABENE project algorithms have been developed which allow deriving the traffic status from a series of aerial images (Ref. 2 and 3). For this application the agility of Antares aircraft allows to follow exactly the stretch of a motorway.

Transport Observation

Here the glider checks a given route in order to detect any obstacles, such as traffic jams, accidents, fires, trees and rocks on roads, or, on railway tracks, so that the obstacles can be moved as quickly as possible, with drivers being warned and to prevent that high value transports, VIPs or ambulances get stuck in the traffic.

2   System Requirements

In general the observation system shall provide persistent surveillance for immediate situational awareness over a large area. It shall deliver continuous imagery of critical infrastructure like motorways, harbors, pipelines as well as power plants and power lines. Many applications require a quiet, unobtrusive aircraft which is difficult to detect from the ground.

Payload Requirements

- Lightweight and cost effective
- Use of high performance, commercial off-the-shelf and ruggedized cameras with high frame rate
- Geo-referencing of the images in near real time with an accuracy the range of 1 to 2m

- On-board data processing doe automatic ground motion tracking and speed measurement of cars
- High rate data link to send live images to the ground station
- Robust low rate data link for remote control and transmission of target coordinates

Aircraft Requirements

- High agility and ability to follow curved flight paths like roads, coasts and borders
- Wide range of possible air speeds, high acceleration
- Ability to circle in order to enable a persistent monitoring
- Long endurance by using highly efficient electric engines and fuel cells for energy storage
- Special aids for the pilot to facilitate the navigation along complex flight passes
- Low noise emission
- Low visibility from ground
- Cost effectiveness

3   The Antares DLR-H2 Power Glider

The Antares DLR-H2 is a power glider with electrical propulsion which serves as a flying test facility for payloads with security applications and for different energy storage concepts, including fuel cells. It is manufactured by Lange-Aviation, Zweibrücken, Germany (Fig. 1). For the accommodation of the additional systems the wings of the Antares DLR-H2 have been reinforced and equipped with mounting points for the attachment of wing pods. In the battery version each pod contains a pack of 72 high energy lithium-ion cells. Together with another 72 cells in the wings a battery capacity of 123Ah is available which lasts for nearly three hours of flight.

Fig. 1. Antares DLR-H2 glider aircraft with two wing pods

Being very compact the battery packs leave enough space for the additional integration of the CHICAGO payload in the aft section of the right wing pod. Alternatively the Antares DLR-H2 can be equipped with a fuel cell energy storage system consisting of the tank mounted on the right wing pod and the fuel cell system itself on the left wing pod. It provides 25kW of electrical power with voltages in the range of 190 to 270V which enables the plane to take off solely using fuel cell power. While the battery system can provide higher power and therefore permits highly dynamic manoeuvres, the fuel cell system provides much higher endurance, offering the possibility for longer missions of up to 5hours. The concept of hybridization allows for combining the advantages of both energy storage systems. Therefore, batteries on the wings are carried along in parallel to the fuel cells resulting in a propulsion system providing high power/dynamics and high energy/endurance. The highly efficient drive train consisting of power electronics, motor and propeller shows an efficiency of more than 90%.

For the surveillance of mass events is very important that the aircraft is hardly visible and audible from the ground. At typical mission flight altitudes in the range of 1.000m it has been proven that the aircraft isn´t detectable from the ground by its noise. Measurements showed a noise level of about 50 [dB (A)], which is the order of a quiet table conversation and not distinguishable from the background noise. Also visually the Antares is extremely difficult to notice. This is due to its extremely slim fuselage and white painting. Experiments have shown that also with a thermal camera it is impossible to detect the aircraft from the ground.

4   The Payload System

The first payload which was realized for the Antares consists mainly of an array of three high resolution cameras (front, rear and side view), an on-board computer and high data rate communication equipment. The C-band microwave data link has a downlink capacity of up to 54MBit/s, depending on the transmission range and data rate. A low data-rate UHF-link provides back-up communication with the ground station. The most expensive parts of the payload are the IMU (Inertial Measurement Unit) and SMU (Sensor Measurement Unit), which provide highly accurate measurements of position and orientation of the cameras and allow for a near real time geo-referencing of the images in the order of 1m. The total weight of the payload adds up to 27 kg.

For the first set-up off-the-shelf EOS 1Ds Mark III digital cameras with Distagon (2/35mm) and Makro-Planar (2/50mm) lenses have been used. These commercial cameras are ruggedized, relatively low cost, have high performance and can accommodate a wide variety of lenses from different manufactures. Two of the three cameras are nadir-looking and tilted with an inclination of 12.5° to the front and rear. When the aircraft is circling the side view camera is activated, which is mounted with a 31° roll offset angle. The circling mode enables a continuous monitoring of a security hot spot. The parameters for the different viewing angles, the Field Of View (FOV) of the stitched images and the ground coverage for different altitudes as well as the associated pixel size GSD (Ground Sampling Distance) can be found in Ref. 3. As an example the side looking camera covers at 1000m flight altitude a ground area of 716m x 1038m and achieves a GSD of 18,4cm. Other parameters can be obtained by the use of different lenses.

5   First Results

The CHICAGO system has already been used for fully automatic road traffic data extraction from image sequences. On May 19, 2012 the Antares aircraft with the CHICAGO payload was deployed for a first mass event, the Soccer Champions League Final at the Munich Allianz Arena. The aircraft was circling around the overall area from the subway station in the south, the Esplanade and the stadium itself at an altitude of 800m. The down looking cameras observed the traffic on the A9 and A99 motorways while the side looking camera took image sequences of the influx of the soccer fans from the subway station to the gates of the stadium. The high resolution images where transmitted in near-real time to the DLR facilities in Oberpfaffenhofen, which is 30km away. It has been shown, that the system offers a good platform for tryout of different security scenarios for the development of end-user applications.

References

1. Hohloch, M., Nippold, R., Kurz, F.: Weitblick für den Notfall. DLR Magazin 128, Band 11 (2010)
2. Rosenbaum, D., Leitloff, J., Kurz, F., Meynberg, O., Reize, T.: Real-Time Image Processing for Road Traffic Data Extraction from Aerial Images, In: Technical Commission VII Symposium 2010, Vienna (2010)
3. Kurz, F., et al.: Low-Cost Optical Camera Systems For Real-Time Mapping Applications. In: PFG 2012, vol. 2, pp. 159–176 (2012)

Analysis of Future Threats to Civil Aviation within the Project COPRA (Comprehensive European Approach to the Protection of Civil Aviation)

Julia Ziehm[1], Frank K.F. Radtke[1], and Tobias Leismann[2]

[1] Fraunhofer EMI, Efringen-Kirchen, Germany
[2] Fraunhofer EMI, Freiburg, Germany
{julia.ziehm,frank.radtke,tobias.leismann}@emi.fraunhofer.de

Abstract. In the last decades and after 9/11 more and more security technologies, regulations and processes have been implemented into the aviation security system without fully integrating them. This has led to a complex and time consuming system that cannot handle the expected increase of passengers in the next decades. COPRA aims to set up a research roadmap for a European perspective on short-, mid- and long-term aviation security concepts, standards and proliferation issues. In this contribution we present the overall approach of COPRA and the first fundamental step where we focus on the threat analysis to detect the threat situation and its evolution regarding new and emerging threats.

1   Introduction

Security in the aviation system has become a major topic in the last decades, especially after 9/11. The number of security measures and regulations is increasing steadily and represents a major impact on the aviation business and on those businesses that depend on fast transportation and increasing mobility.

Besides this fact, the number of air passengers and flights are expected to rise significantly (by a factor of two) within the next 15 years. The threat situation and risks to the aviation system develop continuously and newly arising threats, caused by the evolution of technologies and their proliferation, are hard to predict. Furthermore, new security measures and regulations lead to huge expenses and could cause problems regarding public acceptability due to privacy concerns. The current security system is close to its limits and cannot be adapted to the future challenges in a cost effective and sufficient way to overcome the continuous increase of terror attacks on the air transport system (Fig. 1).

The European airlines and airports are concerned about these high costs incurred by ever increasing security measures they have to comply with. Currently, security costs at European airports largely account for an average of 25% of their budget[1]. Therefore it is the foremost goal of the industry to overcome the current regulation-based security system.

---

[1] Source: Frost & Sullivan, 2008, European Airport Passenger Screening Market, M192-16.

N. Aschenbruck et al. (Eds.): Future Security 2012, CCIS 318, pp. 493–496, 2012.
© Springer-Verlag Berlin Heidelberg 2012

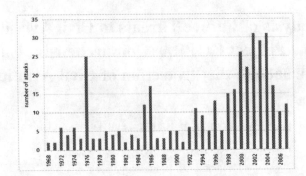

Fig. 1. Number of terrorist attacks on airports, worldwide by year. (source Fraunhofer EMI, Terrorist Event Database TED[2])

2   Project COPRA

To start a way towards interchanging this purely reactive paradigm by a comprehensive approach the project COPRA aims to devise a research roadmap. The project is funded by the 7th Framework Programme of the European Commission, Security Theme (Theme 10). It started in September 2011, ends in March 2013 and aims to answer the following two questions:

- How does the threat situation in civil aviation evolve in the future taking into account both existing and new technologies and their continuing development and proliferation?
- Which opportunities arise from the development and proliferation of new technologies and security procedures to overcome the current complex and expensive security situation to enable sustainable growth for the future?

COPRA consists of 5 work packages (WP) where each WP includes a workshop with more than 30 external experts from industry, research and governmental institutions to support the objectives of the WP and to add a broader view on the results.

3   Methodology and Results of the Threat Analysis

One of the first steps and basis for the following work packages is the threat analysis of WP2. The aim of the analysis is a catalogue of categorized and prioritized present and (new) future threats to the aviation system.

For the categorization we distinguished between three high level targets in the aviation system:

---

[2] U. Siebold, I. Häring, 2009, Terror Event Database and Analysis Software, Future Security 2009.

- <u>Aircrafts:</u> All threats relevant to an aircraft regarding the physical aircraft as well as the aircrafts on board systems (e.g. communication, IT).
- <u>Airport Infrastructure:</u> All threats having consequences for the physical infrastructure or people within it.
- <u>Auxiliary Infrastructure:</u> Threats (like cyber-attacks or EMP) relevant for IT-systems, air traffic control, scanning systems, power supply, etc.

Within this categorization we defined a sub-categorization of the threats to indicate their time relevance:

- <u>Known Threats:</u> Threat is widely known and the inherent risk is monitored.
- <u>Emerging Threats:</u> Threat is known to the air transport security specialists, monitored by appropriate intelligence bodies but no specific countermeasure is developed nor deployed.
- <u>New Threats:</u> Threat is identified, but not characterized and not publicly know or only known to experts (<1 year).

To collect the threats in these categories, sub-categories respectively, we set up a questionnaire (filled by the COPRA-partners) to not only collect the threats but to get detailed information regarding the destructive impact potential, costs of a threat technology, the availability and the timeframe of availability. As mentioned in section 2 a workshop with experts was held in the end to add a broader view and to validate the results.

In total 70 known, emerging and new threats were collected which were prioritized regarding likelihood (cost of threat technology, availability, timeframe of availability, refer to Table 1) and impact (direct destructive impact potential, indirect destructive impact potential, refer to Table 2).

The prioritization regarding likelihood and impact ranges from 1 (low likelihood, low impact respectively) to 5 (high likelihood, high impact respectively) and its sub-prioritization topics (cost, availability timeframe and direct and indirect impact) are linked to the questions in the questionnaire to ensure traceable results.

The final lists of high and low prioritized threats is not a ranking, as a misleading focus in the following WPs should be avoided. Therefore a broad list without prioritization numbers for each threat is provided.

Table 1. Likelihood prioritization table

Likelihood	5	4	3	2	1
Cost of threat technology	< 500 €	< 1000 €	< 10 000 €	< 100 000 €	> 100 000 €
Availability	Very easy to obtain, no special knowledge needed, only one person needed, available on public market	One or more persons needed, some technical proficiency needed, available on black market	Special knowledge and / or high level of expertise required, materials are scarce but freely available,	Requires expert having not widely spread knowledge, regulated materials	Hard to obtain (military), highly regulated materials, multiple Expert knowledge, group of people needed
Timeframe of availability	Immediately	Very short-term (weeks)	Short-term (within 3 years)	Mid-term (within 8 years)	Long-term (within 15 years)

Table 2. Impact prioritization table

Impact	5	4	3	2	1
	catastrophically	critical	severe	insignificant	negligible
Destructive impact potential (direct)	e.g. casualties (fatalities and injuries), complete destruction, long term contamination / breakdown, large impact area, loss of top secret information, ...	Recovery by changing system-components, casualties (mainly injuries), repair is possible, loss of secret information	Injuries (no fatalities), major repairs needed, short-term breakdown, recovery by reinstallation, loss of confidential information	recovery by rebooting a system, slight injuries, one backup (system), loss of restricted information	e.g. no harms, only small repairs, highly redundant, no contamination, small impact area, no classified information lost
Destructive impact potential (indirect)	e.g. people refuse to travel by plane, security regulations beyond operability, air traffic is no more profitable	security regulations with high impact on operability, severe reduction in profit and number of passengers,	Less people traveling, people travelling with fear, security regulations with impact on operability	security regulations with slight impact on operability, minor reduction of profit,	No changes in the security processes, no resonance, no effects for the future

Besides the lists the threats are illustrated in likelihood-impact-diagrams (L-I-diagram) to visualize the prioritization (refer to Fig. 2). Results are shown in the presentation.

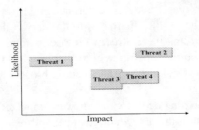

Fig. 2. Example of L-I-diagram to visualize the threat prioritization

4   Outlook

In the following work package (WP3) mitigating measures for each identified threat are collected, including existing technologies and processes but focusing on those that are under development or could be developed in the future. The collection includes the development, implementing and operational costs. Comprehensive concepts are depicted within the COPRA framework, including those under discussion within the aviation industry as well as new concepts under development in the research community. Concepts are analyzed regarding social acceptability, organizational as well as cost-benefit aspects. All results will be combined in a roadmap for a comprehensive European approach. This roadmap will give short-, mid- and long-term recommendations on future aviation security research as well as for the implementation of new and emerging aviation security concepts, security standards, proliferation issues and the development of new and emerging threats.

Acknowledgement. We are grateful to our colleagues from TNO (Netherlands), CEA (France), Airbus (France) and Fraport (Germany) for their valuable contribution to the threat analysis.

Cross-Organizational Preplanning in Emergency Management with IT-Supported Smart Checklists

Gertraud Peinel, Thomas Rose, and Alexander Wollert

Fraunhofer FIT, Schloss Birlinghoven, 53754 Sankt Augustin, Germany
{gertraud.peinel,alexander.wollert,
thomas.rose}@fit.fraunhofer.de

Abstract. Process management for rescue organizations and relief services is a vital asset in the context of disaster preparation and response. Major disasters require services provided by an ample range of organizations by nature. Hence, effective networking of these organizations for communication and collaboration is decisive. This networking requires proper preparation in terms of a pre-planning of activities inside and also across organizational boundaries. Thus, process modeling surfaces as natural candidate for such planning endeavors. Process models foster transparency inside and across organizations in first place. Moreover, formal representations of emergency procedures in terms of process models enable process designers to assess the quality of their processes. However, sole process management tools are far too complex for daily use by rescue forces. Hence, we developed a light-weighted variant: IT supported smart checklists. A checklist resembles a light-weight process representation with limited control flow patterns but full-fledged execution support in the future.

Keywords: Smart Checklists, Process Planning for Emergency Management.

1   Introduction

Several disasters in the recent past led to a change of mind-set in Germany, such as the power outage of Münster (lasting several days in winter 2005, with large quantities of snow and a temperature below zero Celsius), the Love Parade 2010 disaster at Duisburg, claiming the lives of 21 people, and 2011 a mass panic during a television event in the city of Oberhausen causing 60 young people being injured. Prior to these tragedies, silent admiration for security forces dominated. But these catastrophes raised some critical voices in public opinion complaining about poor planning and preparation performance, lack of transparency, and bad communication among security organizations and authorities during and prior to such events (improper strategic coordination). Moreover, insurance companies are clamoring an investigation of reasons and background of these incidents in order to find a scapegoat to hold liable. Hence, such events have to be prepared more thoroughly.

Typically, major events are prepared by considering some worst-case scenarios, e.g. a riot in front of the main station when leaving from the event. Such worst-case scenarios serve as basis for the planning of cross-organizational counter-measures for

N. Aschenbruck et al. (Eds.): Future Security 2012, CCIS 318, pp. 497–508, 2012.

very specific disasters. Yet, cross-organizational preparation also calls for a reconciliation of operational procedures of rescue organizations and relief services. Thus, planning of procedures calls for more attention in order to improve the provision of cross-organizational services in case of disasters.

Our research focuses on these planning processes for cross-organizational preparation, on how to create formalized plans for procedures and on how to share them between different emergency organizations to detect collisions and conflicts. Thus, we were heading out to design and create a collaborative planning support tool, which on the one hand supports user concepts and goals, and on the other hand formalizes plans in terms of models to enable an exchange and analysis similar to Business Process Modeling tools. An important prerequisite of our approach is that the solution should be usable by the experts of the emergency management domain itself. We do not favor a consulting approach where process modeling experts draft the models after interviewing domain experts. Thus, it has to be intuitive, easy to use, and follow closely already well-known software interfaces like Office software.

In this paper we discuss issues of shared pre-planning as preparation for emergencies. In particular, we present our concept of smart checklists and its implementation by an interactive tool. A prototype called Plan your actions - Tool (Plan-T) is introduced, which has already been evaluated by end users inside project InfoStrom [13], namely fire departments and public emergency response authorities of two counties in Germany. InfoStrom strives to improve communication and collaboration of organizations involved in crisis management in case of a wide-range and long-lasting power blackout.

This paper is organized as follows. The following section gives a summary of problems we identified during our research work. An overview of related work follows. Then, the concept of smart checklists as our main contribution is described. Section *Implementation* shows and declares our tool support Plan-T. The results of a first evaluation round with our end users are presented in section *Evaluation*. While the last section *Outlook & Conclusion* draws conclusions on our next steps and research work to do.

2   The Problem

Our research is founded in several projects with security organizations in order to investigate methods they currently employ for planning, and also technologies that could elevate the quality of their planning processes. In addition, we elicited their planning requirements and studied planning aids, which might be appropriate for emergency management organizations. Another research issue was to investigate supporting tools for on-site emergency management when plans were to follow.

We identified the following facts and problems:

- Security organizations like fire departments or police do currently not use any planning software for emergency management planning apart from Office documents with checklists and service regulations. Moreover their alarm and response procedures governed by regulations and by-laws are directly encoded in operational procedures of their control systems.

- Police as well as fire brigades both voiced their attitude, that
  - each disaster is unique, thus planning can only be done in a very abstract way, which is somehow senseless for preparation and for execution;
  - each disaster can be broken down into smaller events, for which they already have response measures;
  - pre-planning for rare and improbable events does not take place due to the reasons above, but also because of time and resource constraints;
  - pre-planning can also be covered by exercises of given topical scenarios serving as point of reference; such topical scenarios often relate to disasters that happened somewhere shortly before and which are now on everyone's agenda;
  - they are interested in the planning of other organizations to ease collaboration at the scene, but that they only need a summary of measures, information about organizational and command structure, and resources needed and used.
- Communication across security organizations is often compounded by different terminologies [1, 2]. Thus, misconceptions and diverging understandings are common during operations with different rescue forces: "intersections are weak points" [19].

Our first attempt has been the support of security organization with business process management (BPM) means for pre-planning, simulation, and execution. But due to the problems listed above and since BPM tools seem to be not the appropriate solution for this domain [3], we embarked on a new strategy that we we coined IT-enabled smart checklists. They are implemented in a tool called Plan-T (Plan your actions - Tool). As a side-effect, such checklists resemble their line of thinking and documentation. We will evaluate whether we will be able to encourage our security organization users to pre-plan large scale disasters with this tool, and whether exchange of such checklist plans between organizations will support understanding and ease communication.

3   Related Work

Several projects have tried at haphazard to apply process management means directly to standard operating procedures for emergency response: Many of these BPM approaches sought a partial automation of control flows for the execution of standard operating procedures [4-7]. Other approaches strived for seamless information flows by integrating information management and data streams in and between command centres [8-10] or between command centres and rescue units during a crisis [11-13]. All of them discovered in the course of their projects that the identification and capture of procedures of rescue organisations are essential for any research contribution that strives to improve the support of rescue workers and their organisations [14]. But, from our experience we draw the conclusion that business process management methods and tools cannot be directly applied for planning in the emergency management domain [3].

Specifically, we did not find any project investigating how users of this domain are able to model their procedures themselves, means to grasp, to abstract, and to

formally model their courses of action for pre-planning on their own. Our objective is
to support emergency experts in their modelling endeavours with a bespoke solution.

Taking also into account that regulations are mainly not detailed in a BPM similar
way, but by merely presenting tasks in flat sequential order [15], we investigated plan
authoring tools [16-18] mainly used in the military context. Moreover, we explored
checklists as proposed by [19, 20], that is, written guidelines that walk actors
"through the key steps in any complex procedure" [19]. Hence, our main research
question is now on how to support a collaborative planning taking into account different terminology, structures, and goals of emergency organizations, since collabora-
tions are the critical points [21-23]. The first result of our design and implementation
efforts, combining the approaches of process modelling, plan authoring, and checklists, will be presented in the following.

4   IT-Enabled Smart Checklists

Checklists are used in several areas, especially where the order, integrity, and completeness of work are of great importance for human lives, for instance in medical
care, aviation, construction, and military. Besides avoiding errors caused by boring
routines or by stress, checklists offer a solution to people with increasing complexity
of their responsibilities, as presented in [20]. Checklists are typically paper sheets
containing briefly defined tasks as crisp items in a more or less strict order with boxes
to be checked on each task to mark when accomplished. A checklist is created for a
specific role and summarizes all necessary tasks for a certain scenario.

Nowadays, checklists used in emergency management organizations are based on
Microsoft Word and Excel documents and their print-outs. But these Office documents are difficult to manage, analyze, maintain and to exchange. Also, tracking of
changes, updates of the spread paper documents, and the search for similarities and
conflicts are hardly to manage.

Our goal is that end users of the emergency management domain can create and
edit their checklists themselves in a brief and intuitive way while the system keeps
them formal for analysis and exchange. In [12] we made a proposal on how to characterize a task of a checklist formally and how a task can easily be described by attribut-
ing it with five capital W's: *Who* is doing *What* and *Where* with *What* and *Why*. A
"task" represents one item of a checklist.

Figure 1, the meta model of our checklist, shows that a plan (id est a checklist)
consists of tasks that is related to several entities, mainly (Organizational) Role - Unit,
Measure, Resource, Rule, and Event. A Measure and a Role are mandatory, since they
carry the core information about *What* has to be done and *Who* is doing it. All other
attributes are optional depending on the user's wish to detail. Resources can be Material or Machine -which gives the answer to the question with *What*- and a Path as
Where can be used as direction as well as a location being a resource (for example, for
the lineup of emergency vehicles and for evacuation and shelter places). Here we see
one of the most important conflict points, when several emergency organizations want
to occupy the same location.

Last but not least, it might be necessary to take down *Why* a task has to be done: with the Event attribute information about the circumstances and with the Rule attribute further hints on regulations can be stored. Thus, changes of regulations having impact on checklists can be traced.

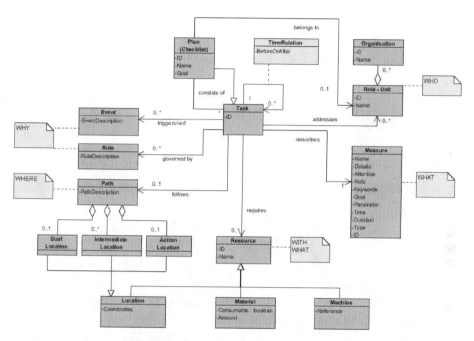

Fig. 1. Meta model of a Checklist of Plan-T

Concerning the smart factor we designed two concepts of support: 1) Change of terminology depending on organization of the user, and 2) Uncovering resource conflicts between several organizations planning the same scenario. The first concept is implemented by translating all organization specific terms in appropriate terms of the user logging in. This on-the-fly translation is based on editable glossaries, but we also support links to external information sources (like Wikis), or by showing images or referencing other related documents. The underlying glossaries can also be edited by users. For the second concept, the system exposes multi-allocations of resources or units by warning messages during editing or when instantiating. Also, we plan to implement the analysis of resource per time use and want the system then to propose other matching "free" resources. The implementation of this latter concept is still in an early phase and we are presenting in this paper only an outlook of what is planned.

5   Implementation

The Plan-T framework consists of three perspectives and a central editor (figure 2). The central editor is located on top of the forms of the perspectives.

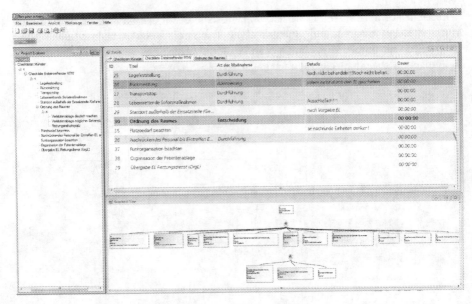

Fig. 2. Plan-T – Overview

Checklist View

This view contains checklists in a classic table style. It consists of items that are created and ordered linear. Attributes of an item (see figure 1) are assigned and presented in the respective columns in the table.

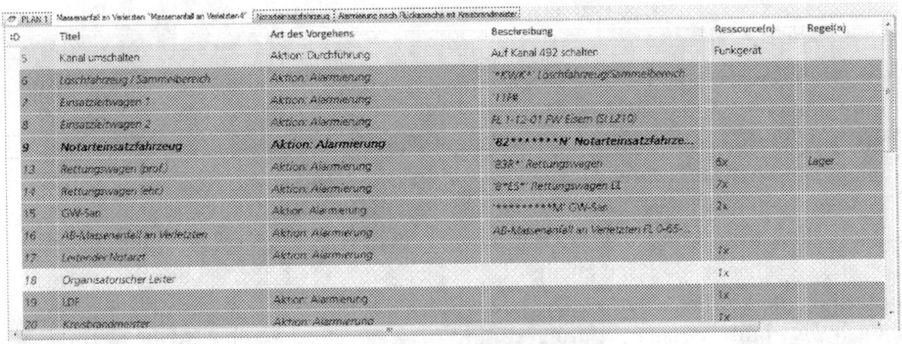

Fig. 3. Plan-T – Checklist View

The domain-specific terms adapt to the user's terminology by a switch of the domain. All columns containing no attribute are hidden to gain a better overview. Tasks in bold font style signal the availability of subtasks. Since these are separate checklists they can be displayed within another tab. Italic styled tasks highlight additional information to units or resources, for instance links to Wiki pages (see figure 3).

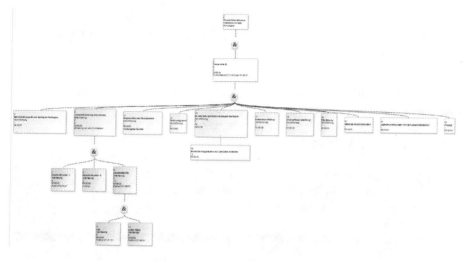

Fig. 4. Plan-T – Graphical View

Graphical View

In this view a checklist is represented only with its basic values and drawn as tree diagram to give an overview over the "big picture" and the hierarchical structure of a plan. Items can be created and deleted, too, but the attributes belong only to the checklist view. The focus lies on the presentation of tasks, subtasks and branches. The user can zoom into and out of the diagram to get more or less details (see figure. 4).

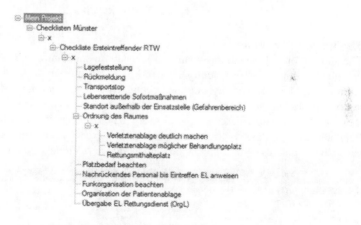

Fig. 5. Plan-T – Explorer View

Explorer View

In the Explorer view (figure 5) the focus lies on the visual presentation of the hierarchical structure of a checklist to support the overview, similar to the concept of the Graphical view.

Central Editor

In a central editor all functions are collected that are necessary to create new tasks with all attributes or to change them. All attributes from the model in Fig. 1 can be applied in different tabs:

- *Art der Maßnahme* (type of measure): Title and character of the measure.
- *Ereignis* (event): Event that triggers a measure.
- *Einheiten* (units): Unit(s) that are responsible for a measure.
- *Details* (details): Additional information, code, numbers or comments.
- *Vorgänger* (predecessor): Predecessor of a measure that indicates a sequence.
- *Dauer* (duration): Duration of a measure in minutes, hours and days.
- *Ressourcen* (resources): Locations, tools and material that are needed.
- *Regeln* (rules): Rules and regulations that justify a measure.

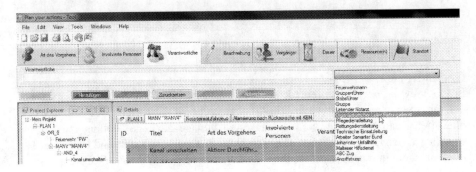

Fig. 6. Plan-T – Central Editor

Terminology Treatment

The application is fed with information of a database containing terms concerning terminologies of domains. Every entry in a task, e.g. its title or the content of one of its attributes, is checked word by word and compared to a glossary in the database. Depending on the domain of the user and the domain the plan was created in, the terms will be translated immediately based on the glossary. The database is meant to be managed by stakeholders. This database can also be filled with terms by importing glossaries. Editing can also be done inside the application with a Glossary Window (see figure 7).

Begriff	Info-Web-Link	Feuerwehr	Rettungsdienst	Behörde	Energieversorger
Feuerwehrmann	http://www.feuerwehrmann.de/	Feuerwehrmann	Feuerwehrmann	Feuerwehrmann	Feuerwehrmann
Gruppenführer	http://de.wikipedia.org/wiki/Gr...	GrFü	Gruppenführer	Gruppenführer	Gruppenführer
Stabsführer	http://en.wikipedia.org/wiki/St...	StFü	Stabsführer	Stabsführer	Stabsführer
Gruppe	http://de.wikipedia.org/wiki/Gr...	Gr	Gruppe	Gruppe	Gruppe
Leitender Notarzt	http://de.wikipedia.org/wiki/Le...	LNA	LNA	Leitender Notarzt	Leitender Notarzt
Organisatorischer Leiter Rettung...	http://de.wikipedia.org/wiki/Or...	OrgL	OLRD	Organisatorischer Leiter Rettun...	Organisatorischer Leiter Rettun
Pflegedienstleitung	http://de.wikipedia.org/wiki/Pfl...	PDL	PDL	Pflegedienstleitung	Pflegedienstleitung
Rettungsdienstleitung	http://www.brk-muenchen.de/...	RDL	RDL	Rettungsdienstleitung	Rettungsdienstleitung
Technische Einsatzleitung	http://www.tel-northeim.de/ind...	TEL	TEL	Technische Einsatzleitung	Technische Einsatzleitung
Arbeiter Samariter Bund	http://de.wikipedia.org/wiki/Ar...	ASB	ASB	Arbeiter Samariter Bund	Arbeiter Samariter Bund
Johanniter-Unfall-Hilfe	http://de.wikipedia.org/wiki/Jo...	JUH	JUH	Johanniter Unfallhilfe	Johanniter Unfallhilfe
Malteser Hilfsdienst	http://de.wikipedia.org/wiki/M...	MHD	MHD	Malteser Hilfsdienst	Malteser Hilfsdienst
ABC-Zug	http://de.wikipedia.org/wiki/A...	ABC-Zug	ABC-Zug	ABC-Zug	ABC-Zug
Angriffstrupp	http://de.wikipedia.org/wiki/Gr...	A-Trupp	Angriffstrupp	Angriffstrupp	Angriffstrupp
Atemschutzgeräteträger	http://de.wikipedia.org/wiki/At...	AGT	Atemschutzgeräteträger	Atemschutzgeräteträger	Atemschutzgeräteträger

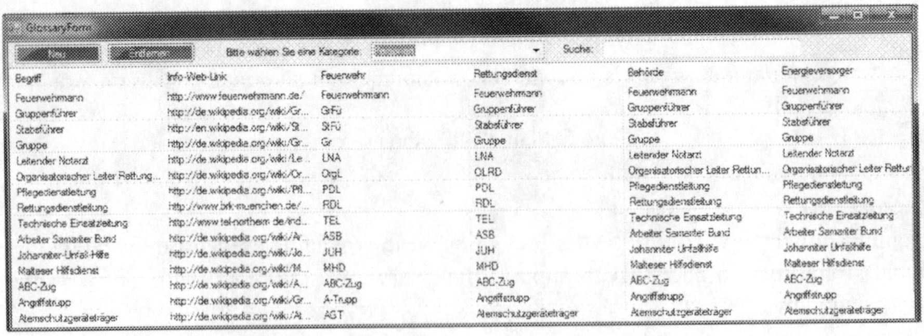

Fig. 7. Plan-T – Glossary Window

6   Evaluation

Our first evaluation rounds took place in the headquarters of crisis authorities of the county of Rhein-Erft and the county of Siegen-Wittgenstein by in total four presentations with several feedback rounds with around 20 experts of authorities (from fire brigades, police, and members of the local authority responsible for crises management). Especially the fire brigades are using checklists for their scenario planning and they are currently working with hundreds of Excel and Word documents describing these checklists. Their feedback and suggestions have been protocolled and its correctness signed.

To summarize their feedback to our presentation of Plan-T: They found our solution very instrumental, specifically for organizing and updating checklists. They consider it also as a management server for collaborative checklists. Some critical issues resulting in future work for us include:

- For future collaborative access, access and rights management must be stronger implemented: "who is allowed to change which parts of the checklists" must be pre-defined and strictly enforced.
- Then, based on this access management, versioning and the tracking of changes can be improved.
- Consequently, notifications of changes to other users have to be supported (in the sense of an information circulation slip).
- Sophisticated printing functions are desired – from an electronic version to a paper version to pick up: design of layout (specifically color highlighting) and export to PDF; as future prospect, a direct export to a mobile device on-site (see below).
- Exchange of information between organizations should also be supported by a semi-automatic "resume generator", summarizing the essential facts of procedures. They argued that individual steps of other teams might be less interesting than a short summary of time, resources, and quality of service(s) others can provide.

They also risked a view in the future and anticipated that such a system could also help directly in the response phase in situ. They named as example the tasks of an emergency physician on-site the place of emergency (in Germany, physicians are always accompanying ambulance men to the scene). They might use such a checklist on a tablet PC as an online medical guide, use it also for information from and to their assistants, and for information exchange from and to hospitals and command centers. In addition, post-processing could be supported, since such checklists can remind actors to describe any reasons for deviance from guidelines; which in turn can lead to better quality if learning effects take place.

Also, Plan-T was presented to representatives of the Federal Office of Civil Protection and Disaster Assistance (BBK). As content we populated Plan-T with their guide for crisis management in case of a power blackout [24], which we transferred from a comprehensive Word document with hundreds of tables to several electronic checklists in Plan-T. Their feedback was also very positive and a test usage in future crisis exercises was envisaged.

We plan to extend the evaluation by accompanying a workshop of our users in Rhein-Erft-Kreis in about three months where they want to re-plan the procedures of the mass causalities incident. Starting with the "old" plans filled in Plan-T we want to conduct them on using Plan-T and at the same time we aim at exposing usage problems.

7   Conclusion and Outlook

In this paper we have presented our approach to enhance the pre-planning of security organizations for emergency management scenarios. Main idea of Plan-T is the exchange of information about procedures and resources used to prevent conflicts of interests and collisions. Plan-T is still in an early development state. Besides the core features for plan capture and management, further services are required to embed Plan-T into organizational context. For example, a web interface is considered important for means of flexibility of use. However, a web interface with collaborative access immediately raises the question of organizational rights and privileges for updating existing plans. Sophisticated access policies are required.

While we currently only target the preparation and post-processing phases of emergency management, our users surprised us with the very progressive idea of using such a system also on scene for guidance and documentation. We will investigate these ideas by exploring mobile user interfaces and by implementing an export to such interfaces depending on the role of the user.

We will also gear our focus on the fundamental concepts of terminology provision. It still lacks a validated meta model and the integration of external ontologies to guarantee correct matching of terms. In addition, we think about a direct connection to command center software to gain access to resource lists in order to avoid a double maintenance of concepts. The analysis of the allocation of available resources per time has to be finalized too.

Our research prototype Plan-T has been evaluated with emergency management organizations and federal state authorities. All of them expressed their interest in using Plan-T for their emergency management preparation. Hence, we expect further fruitful feedback from them.

References

[1] Reuter, C., Pohl, P., Pipek, V.: Umgang mit Terminologien in inter-organisationaler Krisenkooperation-eine explorative Empirie. In: Mensch & Computer 2011. FachüBergreifende Konferenz für Interaktive und Kooperative Medien. überMEDIEN - ÜBERmorgen, pp. 171–180. Oldenbourg-Verlag, München (2011)
[2] Schaafstal, A.M., Johnston, J.H., Oser, R.L.: Training teams for emergency management. Computers in Human Behavior 17, 615–626 (2001)
[3] Peinel, G., Rose, T., Wollert, A.: The Myth of Business Process Modelling for Emergency Management Planning. In: 9th International Conference on Information Systems for Crisis Response and Management (ISCRAM), Vancouver, Canada (2012)

[4] Rüppel, U., Wagenknecht, A.: Improving emergency management by formal dynamic process-modelling. In: 24th Conference on Information Technology in Construction (2007)

[5] Khalilbeigi, M., Bradler, D., Schweizer, I., Probst, F., Steimle, J.: Towards Computer Support of Paper Workflows in Emergency Management. In: Proceedings of the 7th International ISCRAM Conference (2010)

[6] Paulheim, H., Döweling, S., Tso-Sutter, K., Probst, F., Ziegert, T.: Improving usability of integrated emergency response systems: the SoKNOS approach. In: Informatik 2009: Im Focus das Leben, Beiträge der 39, Jahrestagung der Gesellschaft für Informatik e.V (GI), September 28-October 10, pp. 1435–1449 (2009)

[7] Becker, T., Lee, B.-S., Koch, R.: Effiziente Entscheidungsunterstützung im Krisenfall durch interaktive Standard Operating Procedures. In: Workshop IT-Unterstützung von Einsatz- und Rettungskräften: Interdisziplinäre Anforderungsanalyse, Architekturen und Gestaltungskonzepte, Conference Software Engineering 2011, Karlsruhe, Germany (2011)

[8] Kittel, K., Sackmann, S.: Gaining Flexibility and Compliance in Rescue Processes with BPM. In: Sixth International Conference on Availability, Reliability and Security (ARES), pp. 639–644. IEEE (2011)

[9] Soini, J., Polancic, G.: Toward adaptable communication and enhanced collaboration in global crisis management using process modeling. In: Kocaoglu, D.F., Anderson, T.R., Daim, T.U. (eds.) Proceedings of PICMET 2010, Portland International Center for Management of Engineering and Technology, Technology Management for Global Economic Growth, Phuket, Thailand, pp. 981–990 (2010)

[10] Ziebermayr, T., Huber, J., Kollarits, S., Ortner, M.: A Proposal for the Application of Dynamic Workflows in Disaster Management: A Process Model Language Customized for Disaster Management. In: Proceedings of the 22 International Workshop on Database and Expert Systems Applications, pp. 284–288. IEEE (2011)

[11] de Leoni, M., Mecella, M.: Mobile process management through web services. In: 2010 IEEE International Conference on Services Computing (SCC), pp. 378–385. IEEE (2010)

[12] Franke, J., Charoy, F.: Design of a Collaborative Disaster Response Process Management System. In: International Conference on the Design of Cooperative Systems (COOP 2020), Aix-en-Provence, France (2010)

[13] Franke, J., Widera, A., Charoy, F., Hellingrath, B., Ulmer, C.: Reference Process Models and Systems for Inter-Organizational Ad-Hoc Coordination-Supply Chain Management in Humanitarian Operations. In: Proceedings of the 8th International ISCRAM Conference (2011)

[14] Kunze, C., Rodriguez, D., Shammas, L., Chandra-Sekaran, A., Weber, B.: Nutzung von Sensornetzwerken und mobilen Informationsgeräten für die Situationserfassung und die Prozessunterstützung bei Massenanfällen von Verletzten. GI Jahrestagung (2009)

[15] Harand, A., Peinel, G., Rose, T.: Process Structures in Crises Management. In: Future Security 2011. Fraunhofer Group for Defense and Security, Berlin (2011)

[16] Kim, J., Blythe, J.: Supporting plan authoring and analysis. In: Proceedings of the Intelligent User Interfaces Conference, p. 116. ACM (2003)

[17] Aitken, S.: An ontological account of action in processes and plans. Knowledge-Based Systems 18, 295–305 (2005)

[18] Leifler, O.: Combining technical and human-centered strategies for decision support in command and control: The ComPlan approach. In: Proceedings of the 5th International Conference on Information Systems for Crisis Response and Management (2008)

[19] Gawande, A.: The checklist manifesto: How to get things right. Profile Books (2010)

[20] Wucholt, F., Krüger, U., Kern, S.: Mobiles Checklisten-Support-System im Einsatzszenario einer Großschadenslage. In: Workshop zur IT-Unterstützung von Rettungskräften 2011 im Rahmen der Informatik 2011, vol. 41. Jahrestagung der Gesellschaft für Informatik, Berlin (2011)

[21] Jäger, B.: VFH in Wiesbaden, Studienort Gießen, (web page restructured) http://www.polizei.hessen.de/

[22] Lasogga, F., von Ameln, F.: Kooperation bei Großschadensereignissen. Gruppendynamik und Organisationsberatung 41, 157–176 (2010)

[23] Schafer, W.A., Carroll, J.M., Haynes, S.R., Abrams, S.: Emergency management planning as collaborative community work. Journal of Homeland Security and Emergency Management 5, 10 (2008)

[24] Grambs, S., Schultmann, F., Thiede, T.: Krisenmanagement Stromausfall Langfassung. In: Zusammenarbeit mit dem Innenministerium Baden-Württemberg (Hrsg.), und dem Bundesamt für Bevölkerungsschutz und Katastrophenhilfe (ed.), Heidelberg (2010)

Resilience: Approach, Definition and Building Policies

Leire Labaka, Josune Hernantes, Ana Laugé, and Jose M. Sarriegi

Tecnun - University of Navarra, Paseo Manuel Lardizabal 13, 20018 San Sebastian, Spain
{llabaka,jhernantes,alauge,jmsarriegi}@tecnun.es

Abstract. Advances in Critical Infrastructures (CIs) have increased the society's welfare but at the same time they have made us to be more dependent on CIs proper functioning. In light of this situation it is essential to create resilient systems in order to avoid a crisis occurrence or respond in the most rapid and effective way. Through an extensive literature review, two different perspectives regarding the resilience concept have been identified. Some authors define resilience as the capacity to respond to crises reactively, whereas some others extend this perspective by adding the proactive capacity to avoid the occurrence of a crisis. Finally, some principles to improve the resilience level of the organizations have been defined.

Keywords: Resilience, Crisis Management, High Reliability Organizations.

1 Introduction

The welfare of society has increased considerably due to advances in Critical Infrastructures (CIs) such as power sector, telecommunication sector, financial sector and health sector. But, at the same time, these improvements have made us to be more dependent on their proper functioning, becoming critical for our daily lives.

CIs capacity to prevent a crisis occurrence and respond effectively to adverse events depends highly on the system's resilience level. There are many definitions and perspectives about the resilience concept. The aim of this paper is to provide an extensive review about the resilience concept in the field of crisis management.

2 Resilience

Resilience has widely been used in different disciplines such as environmental science [1], engineering [2], psychology, organizational studies and economics. The term implies both the ability to adjust to "normal" or anticipated events and also to adapt to sudden shocks and unexpected events.

Resilience concept has also been widely used in the crisis management field. To better understand the definition of resilience in this context we should keep in mind the four phases of the crisis management [3], [4]: prevention, preparation, response and recovery.

In this field, there are mainly two different views regarding the scope of the resilience concept. Some authors understand resilience as only a post-crisis strategy that

N. Aschenbruck et al. (Eds.): Future Security 2012, CCIS 318, pp. 509–512, 2012.

helps coping with and minimizing disaster impacts whereas others expand this perspective by adding that resilience seeks not only to deal with the response and recovery but also to prevent crisis occurrence. Therefore, the second perspective understands resilience as a strategy to deal with both the pre-crisis and the post-crisis phases.

2.1   Resilience as a Post-crisis Strategy

Some authors propose that resilience only becomes visible after the triggering event when it serves to cope with its consequences. They believe that resilience does not assist in preventing a crisis occurrence but in responding rapidly and efficiently minimizing the consequences from crises.

Wildavsky [5], for instance, defines resilience as "the capacity to cope with unanticipated dangers after they have become manifest, learning to bounce back" but he does not provide any information about how to prevent a crisis.

Longstaff [6], however, apart from the resilience concept, defines resistance to refer to the proactive capacity of a system to avoid a crisis occurrence. He defines resilience as the "capacity of a system to absorb disturbance, undergo change, and still retain essentially the same function, structure, identity and feedbacks" and resistance as "the strategy that attempts to keep the danger away from the system in the first place". McEntire [7] also defines the same two concepts, resistance and resilience, to refer to the proactive and reactive response, respectively. Rose [8] and Mileti [9] reduce the scope of resilience to the post-disaster strategy and define mitigation as a pre-crisis strategy to prevent potential crises.

2.2   Resilience as Pre-crisis and Post-crisis Strategy

On the other hand, other authors expand the scope of resilience proposing that resilience not only helps once the triggering event has struck but also before its occurrence, avoiding or preventing it. Levenson et al. [10] argue that resilience should be understood not only as the ability to respond appropriately but also to avoid failures and losses. They define resilience as the ability of systems to prevent or adapt to changing conditions in order to maintain the system's property.

Bruneau et al. [11] extend the concept of resilience by defining it as the capacity of the system to reduce the probability of failure, to reduce the consequences from failure and to reduce the time needed to carry out all the response and recovery activities.

The United Nations International Strategy for Disaster Reduction (UNISDR) that aims to promote a common terminology for crisis management defines resilience as "the ability of a system, community or society exposed to hazards to resist, absorb, accommodate to and recover from the effects of a hazard in a timely and efficient manner, including through the preservation and restoration of its essential basic structures and functions". They understood resilience as a whole crisis lifecycle strategy.

Focusing on CIs, Kahan et al. [12] assume that resilience is the outcome result with the aim of limiting damage to infrastructure (resistance), mitigating the consequences (absorption) and reducing the recovery period to the pre-event state (restoration).

Despite the fact that failures could come from the dynamic instability of a system, the challenge in system safety is to understand and be able to foresee when the system may lose its dynamic stability by becoming unstable. Thus, resilience can be defined as the intrinsic ability of a system to adjust its functioning prior to or following changes and disturbances, so that it can sustain operations even after a major mishap or in the presence of continuous stress [13]. Westrum [14] refines this definition by describing the three major components of the resilience: foresee and avoid (prevent something bad from happening), cope with ongoing trouble (keep something bad from becoming worse), and repair after catastrophe (recover from something bad once it has happened).

3   Resilience Building

Although there is much information about the resilience concept; less information can be found about how systems can develop or increase their resilience level. High Reliability Organizations (HROs) are those organizations that have been successful in avoiding a crisis or responding to a crisis efficiently [15]. Their resilience level is high what makes them to be able to overcome warning signals and reduce the probability of failure. Their main principles are the following ones [16]:

- Preoccupation with failure: HROs are very preoccupied with failures and any little incident is analyzed in depth because they know that something could have severe consequences if several separate small errors happened to coincide.
- Reluctance to simplify: They know that the world they face is complex, unstable and unpredictable and simplification could lead to the non-detection of failures leading to a crisis occurrence. Therefore, they are reluctant to simplify processes.
- Sensitivity to operations: They make continuous adjustments that prevent errors from accumulating and enlarging.
- Commitment to resilience: HROs develop capabilities to detect, contain and bounce back from the inevitable errors by training and preparing personnel with deep and varied experience.
- Deference to expertise: HROs push decision making down to the people with the most expertise to make better decisions because they are the ones that more know about the problem.

4   Conclusions

In the field of crisis management there are basically two perspectives about the scope of the resilience concept. Some authors believe that resilience is the capacity to, once the crisis has occurred, absorb the impact, respond in the most effective way and quickly recover to the initial state. Others authors, however, state that resilience also helps to avoid a crisis occurrence.

Despite having a mature definition of resilience, there are many difficulties in putting this theoretical concept into practice. HROs have been the most significant approach in achieving this objective and they define a set of principles that organizations should take into account in order to increase their resilience level. These principles however, are still quite theoretical and some specific policies are needed.

References

1. Holling, C.: Resiliency and stability of ecological systems. Annual Review of Ecological Systems 4, 1–24 (1973)
2. Lecoze, J., Capo, S.: A Conceptual and Methodological Comparison with the Field of Child Resilience. In: Proceedings of 2th Synposium of Resilience Engineering (2006)
3. Drennan, L., McConnell, A.: Risk and Crisis Management in the Public Sector. Routledge, New York (2007)
4. Alexander, D.: Principles of Emergency Planning and Management. Oxford University Press, Oxford (2002)
5. Wildvasky, A.: Searching for Safety. Transactions Books, New York (1998)
6. Longstaff, P.H.: Security, Resilience, and Communication in Unpredictable Environments Such as Terrorism, Natural Disasters, and Complex Technology. Harvard University, Cambridge (2005)
7. McEntire, D.A.: Why vulnerability matters: Exploring the merit of an inclusive disaster reduction concept. Disaster Prevention and Management 14, 206–222 (2005)
8. Rose, A.: Defining and measuring economic resilience to disasters. Disaster Prevention and Management 13, 307–314 (2004)
9. Mileti, D.: Disasters by Design: A Reassessment of Natural Hazards in the United States. Joseph Henry Press, Washington, DC (1999)
10. Levenson, N., Dulac, N., Zipkin, D., Cutcher-Gershenfeld, J., Carroll, J., Barrett, B.: Engineering Resilience into Safety-Critical Systems. In: Hollnagel, E., Woods, D.D., Leveson, N. (eds.), pp. 95–123. Ashgate, New York (2006)
11. Bruneau, M., Chang, S., Eguchi, R., Lee, G., O'Rourke, T., Reinhorn, A., Shinozuka, M., Tierney, K., Wallace, W., von Winterfelt, D.: A framework to quantitatively assess and enhace seismic resilience of communities. Earthquake Spectra. 19, 733–752 (2003)
12. Kahan, J.H., Allen, A.C., George, J.K.: An Operational Framework for Resilience. Journal of Homeland Security and Emergency Management 6 (2009)
13. Hollnagel, E., Woods, D.D., Leveson, N.: Resilience Engineering: Concepts and Precepts. Ashgate (2006)
14. Westrum, R.: A Typology of Resilience Situations. In: Hollnagel, E., Woods, D.D., Leveson, N. (eds.), pp. 55–65. Ashgate (2006)
15. Roberts, K.H.: Some Characteristics of one type of High Reliability Organization. Organization Science 1, 160–176 (1990)
16. Weick, K.E., Sutcliffe, K.M.: Managing the Unexpected: resilient performance in an age of uncertainty. Jossey-Bass, San Francisco (2007)

User-Centered Elaboration of an Integrated Crisis Management Modeling and Simulation Solution

Johannes Sautter, Wolf Engelbach, and Sandra Frings

Fraunhofer IAO, Stuttgart, Germany
{prename.surname}@iao.fraunhofer.de

Abstract. Today a variety of models and simulation tools exist that support crisis management in specific situations. The FP7-funded project CRISMA aims at offering an integrated modeling and simulation platform especially for applications during short-term and long-term planning, training and debriefings after exercises and crisis situations. This paper briefly discusses similar approaches and motivates an intended user-centered design methodology towards a solution complying with high standards in task suitability and software ergonomics.

Keywords: Modeling, Simulation, Crisis Management, Decision Support, User-Centered Design, Usability Engineering.

1   Introduction

Adequate crisis management for large scale crisis scenarios includes proper preparation and planning, quick reaction upon these plans and reasonable decisions based on underlying resources and capability constraints. On strategic levels information shall be aggregated and visualized to support deciders. Simulation tools support "what-if" and forecast questions of strategic crisis response, training and preparation based on conceptual models [1]. Most applications of simulation in crisis management foresee the standalone use of a particular tool [2]. However, planners, trainers, crisis managers and first responders need to asses widespread aspects of a specific crisis situation [3]. Also it is inconvenient to train crisis response personnel on several software tools to be applied depending on crisis type or crisis phase.

The CRISMA project, which is funded under the European Community's Seventh Framework Programme FP7/2007-2013 (grant agreement no. 284552), intends to support crisis management experts and practitioners by a simulation-based decision-support system based on models that reflect the uncertainty in crisis situations. CRISMA stands for crisis management modeling tool and aims at modeling and simulation of crisis management for improved action and preparedness. Seventeen partners form the CRISMA consortium, led by VTT Technical Research Center of Finland (www.crismaproject.eu).

Under the project's overall vision challenges in the integration of various existing standalone simulation solutions, in the overall-coordination of software and requirements engineering and in focusing on end-user's needs towards an overall-system that complies with high criteria in task suitability and software ergonomics are awaited.

N. Aschenbruck et al. (Eds.): Future Security 2012, CCIS 318, pp. 513–516, 2012.

In this contribution, we concentrate on the third challenge. This paper briefly describes related work regarding simulation tools and their integration. Further Usability Engineering within the project is motivated and outlined, followed by an outlook and a conclusion.

2   Related Work

A model is "an abstract representation of a system or process" [4]. Simulation means "driving a model of a system with suitable inputs and observing the corresponding outputs" [1]. In order to support complex crisis management, a coupling of pre-existing models and simulations can be helpful, which requests sharing of data. The conceptual interoperability model by [5] classifies interoperability capabilities by seven levels from no interoperability (level 0) via technical, syntactic, semantic, pragmatic and dynamic to conceptual interoperability.

Federated simulation allows the coupling of existing simulation models and the distributed execution of simulation runs [6]. Relevant standards include IEEE 1278 (Distributed Interactive Simulation, DIS) and High Level Architecture for Modeling and Simulation (IEEE 1516, HLA), which defines an architectural framework. These and other standards are maintained by the Simulation Interoperability Standards Organization (SISO, www.sisostds.org).

Several simulation tools were developed and practically applied in research and industry to support various use cases in crisis management and civil protection, such as plume dispersion simulation and analysis models for vulnerabilities of critical infrastructures [2]. To address the aspect of integrating several standalone simulation models and tools, [3] propose the integrated emergency response framework (iERF). It uses a classification scheme following the three axes "disaster event", "entities of interest" ("population", "response agents") and "application" to be able to assess different aspects of emergency scenarios and to match simulation tools to the respective needs [3].

The DIESIS project, which deals with federated simulation for critical infrastructures modeling, proposes a middleware that enables semantic interoperability of the federate simulators, a systematic, service-oriented approach to set up and run such federations, and a scenario-based architecture concept for modeling and federated simulation [7]. The Integrated Modeling, Mapping, and Simulation (IMMS) Framework for Planning Exercises is a distributed software framework aiming at integrating "metadata, heuristic domain knowledge and a uniform interface" [8]. Its main contributions are simulation templates to organize models according to planning needs and a discovery process that enables users to find and run appropriate models and simulations. It proposes the distributed software architecture SUMMIT (Standard Unified Modeling and Mapping Integration Toolkit), separated by resource owners, end users and a specific model and template SDK [8].

3   Usability Engineering Methodology

Evaluations of current information systems in crisis response enlighten problems with inconsistent interaction models and challenges within user interaction [9]. The application domain of crisis management and civil protection is characterized by hard boundary conditions. First, interdisciplinary collaboration within crisis task forces leads to challenges in communication and terminology. Especially for time-critical crisis situations and due to diverse information system skills among end-users, both ease-of-use and ease-of-learning requirements occur.

Proper software ergonomics is only feasible through systematic and continuous application of user-centered methods within the software engineering process [10, 11]. A flexible framework to enhance a software engineering process model with respect to usability is provided by the Usability Engineering Reference Model [12]. Applied to the elaboration of the CRISMA system, enhancements for the requirements engineering phase are the following:

- Which **market and mission goals** should be addressed by the solution?
- Which **similar solutions/simulation tools** exist? Which **users and tasks** do they support? Where are they (currently/envisioned to be) applied?
- Which **additional users and tasks** could potentially be supported?
- Which social/organizational/technical/physical **environmental conditions** apply?
- Which **general design principles** shall be applied? Are there similar systems used by the same user group relying on certain interaction patterns?
- Which qualitative and quantitative **usability goals** can be derived?

When skipping to the software design phase, the following activities occur:

- **Workflow Reengineering:** Which tasks are currently processed by crisis management operators in another manner as they are envisioned to be performed with the new system? Re-description and evaluation of those tasks
- **Conceptual User-Interface-Model:** How do users currently represent coherencies in their mind (from analysis phase)? How are they envisioned to do so? Which GUI-metaphors and interaction concepts shall be applied?
- **User Interface Mockups,** variations and iterative walkthroughs
- **Detailed User-Interface Styleguide**

4   Conclusion and Outlook

Crisis management is happening in situations of limited information and in conditions of uncertainty. Existing modeling and simulation solutions integrated into an envisioned CRISMA system have the potential to enable deciders to assess effects of different actions in emergency training, debriefing and planning. Generic crisis scenario modeling and simulations facilitate the dealing with uncertainty for crisis managers.

In order to face challenges in interoperability, usability and continuous software engineering, a series of measures are planned within the project. Usability Engineering methods are intended to ensure a strong focus on the end users and their tasks. For instance a risk that should be avoided is that existing user interaction concepts of standalone simulation tools may hinder users to apply the system in their work environment.

Three initial project workshops within four months obtained early results regarding the simulation usage, relevant crisis scenarios and challenges in the coupling of existing simulation tools. Next steps are the definition of common requirements engineering methods and notations, the conceptual consolidation of existing usage scenarios of standalone tools and the systematic assessment of market and mission goals, user goals and user requirements.

Acknowledgement. We acknowledge valuable discussion with CRISMA project partners during the project start.

References

1. Dugdale, J., Bellamine-Ben Saoud, N., Pavard, B., Pallamin, N.: Simulation and Emergency Management, p. 229 (2009)
2. Jain, S., McLean, C.: Modeling, Simulation and Visualization for Emergency Response. Draft Report Released at Workshop on Modeling and Simulation for Emergency Response, Gaithersburg, MD (2003)
3. Jain, S., McLean, C.: A Framework for Modeling and Simulation for Emergency Response. In: Proceedings of the 2003 Winter Simulation Conference (2003)
4. Carson, J.S.: Introduction to Modeling and Simulation. In: Proceedings of the 2005 Winter Simulation Conference (2005)
5. Turnitsa, C.: Extending the Levels of Conceptual Interoperability Model. In: Proceedings IEEE Summer Computer Simulation Conference (2005)
6. Casalicchio, E., Galli, E., Tucci, S.: Federated Agent-based Modeling and Simulation Approach to Study Interdependencies in IT Critical Infrastructures, pp. 182–189 (2007)
7. Usov, A., Beyel, C., Rome, E., Beyer, U., Castorini, E., Palazzari, P., Tofani, A.: The DIESIS Approach to Semantically Interoperable Federated Critical Infrastructure Simulation. In: The Second International Conference on Advances in System Simulation: Proceedings, pp. 121–128. IEEE Computer Society, Los Alamitos (2010)
8. M. a. S. F. f. P. E. Integrated Modeling, Integrated Modeling, Mapping, and Simulation (IMMS) Framework for Planning Exercises, https://dhs-summit.net/files/IITSECFall2010_to_appear.pdf (March 05, 2012)
9. Landgren, J.: Critical Lessons Learned: Evaluation of Commercial Mobile Incident Support Systems. In: Löffler, J., Klann, M. (eds.) Mobile Response. LNCS, vol. 5424, pp. 122–129. Springer, Heidelberg (2009)
10. Jakob Nielsen, R.M.: Heuristic Evaluation of User Interfaces (1990), http://www.cs.panam.edu/~rfowler/csci6362/papers/13_Nielsen-Molich_1990_Heuristic-Evaluation-of-User-Interfaces_CHI.pdf
11. Shneiderman, B., Plaisant, C.: Designing the user interface: Strategies for effective human-computer interaction, 5th edn. Addison-Wesley, Boston (2010)
12. Metzker, E., Offergeld, M.: An Interdisciplinary Approach for Successfully Integrating Human-Centered Design Methods into Development Processes Practiced by Industrial Software Development Organizations. In: Reed Little, M., Nigay, L. (eds.) EHCI 2001. LNCS, vol. 2254, pp. 19–33. Springer, Heidelberg (2001)

Towards a Real-Time Situational Awareness System for Surveillance Applications in Unconstrained Environments

David Münch, Stefan Becker, Wolfgang Hübner, and Michael Arens

Fraunhofer IOSB, Gutleuthausstraße 1, 76275 Ettlingen, Germany
{david.muench,stefan.becker,wolfgang.huebner,
michael.arens}@iosb.fraunhofer.de

Abstract. Observing public spaces like car parks, airports, and train stations via video surveillance is an extremely tedious and error-prone activity for human operators. A generic real-time system is presented which closes the situational awareness loop from basic object detection, object tracking and conceptual situation recognition. The situation recognition is implemented as formal knowledge-based reasoning approach. In order to process information about objects in a scene a sophisticated multi-person tracker was integrated. The person tracking relies on local features. For person representation a generalized appearance codebook is used. The whole system is parallelized to gain real-time performance on ordinary hardware. The proposed system was evaluated on data reflecting a prototypical surveillance scenario and promises practical results.

Keywords: ISM-based tracking, situational awareness, real-time system.

1 Motivation

The presence of dozens of surveillance cameras and other sensors in an area of interest is the common application of video surveillance systems these days. The challenge that arises is the overload of visual information for human operators observing the area of interest. Consequently, the awareness of what is happening in each moment is not given after a short time of gazing into the monitors. That leads to the need of supporting the human operator with automatic situational awareness in all possibly occurring situations in that particular area of interest. Such an automatic situational awareness system has to deal with the whole processing chain from image acquisition, people and object detection, and high-level semantic video understanding. Additionally, the application requires real-time capabilities. In the following we present our steps towards an integrated real-time situational awareness system. In the section below a generic person tracking module is presented. Section 3 describes the high-level semantic video understanding module and the modifications to gain real-time. Experimental results are summarized in Section 4, and Section 5 concludes this paper.

schenbruck et al. (Eds.): Future Security 2012, CCIS 318, pp. 517–521, 2012.
ringer-Verlag Berlin Heidelberg 2012

2   Real-Time Person Tracking

The basis for the proposed system with a high-level semantic video understanding module is the detection and tracking of persons in an observed scene. Correctly determined person trajectories depending on a stable and consistent tracking which maintains person identities are the input for a further analysis. For detecting and tracking we use a speeded-up version of the approach described in [3,4] for the case of persons.

The key idea is that the Implicit Shape Model (ISM) [5], which is a trainable object detection approach that builds on local features (we picked SIFT [6]), is extended for tracking. During a training phase reoccurring features found in person sample images are clustered to prototypes. Together with a spatial distribution (encoding the position of features relatively to the person center) these prototypes can then be employed to detect persons. By integrating temporal information on the level of features contributing to a person hypothesis into the detection framework the approach is extended for tracking. To build feature correspondence and form the temporal information integration, actually present features are matched with predicted hypothesis features. This integrated information is used to build a joint Hough voting space (see [3],[4] for details). The tracking itself is done in the Hough voting space by performing a hypothesis-specific maxima search.

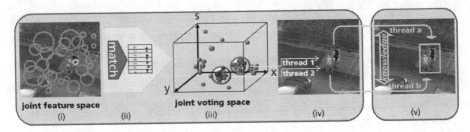

Fig. 1. Speeded-up person tracking. (i) Joint feature space: Green features are from the current image. Other colors are predicted features corresponding to known person hypotheses. (ii) Approximate feature matching to build the Hough voting space. (iii-iv) Parallelized mean-shift search for person tracking. Situation recognition (v) with agent-parallelized inference and knowledge sharing.

For the purpose to gain real-time performance three main steps are briefly introduced. One time consuming component consists of the extraction of SIFT features. Therefore we integrated an implementation of SIFT for GPU [10], which is able to achieve over 25 fps for an image with a 640 × 480 resolution. Furthermore, for the matching of features with codebook prototypes in high-dimensional descriptor space we use an approximate algorithm that provides large speedup with only minor loss in accuracy [7]. Exemplary one subcomponent – the mean-shift maxima search – should be mentioned where we added parallel program sequences. Not only this can be crucial for a large number of initial maxima but also it is appropriate, because the maxima search can start independent for every known hypothesis. Figure 1 illustrates the tracking approach with the integrated solutions to achieve real-time performance.

3   High-Level Semantic Video Understanding

A broad overview of semantic video understanding is given by [9]. The field can be roughly divided into direct methods, detecting situations directly on video features and into hierarchical methods consisting of several different architectural layers. First, there are studies relating on probabilistic graphical models like e.g. Bayesian networks, second, syntactical approaches like e.g. grammar-based methods and, third, description-based approaches. This work belongs to the latter ones. We extended and improved the high-level situation recognition system presented in [8]. It consists of three major parts, first the basic rules in fuzzy metric temporal logic (FMTL) modeling part of the basic physical laws of this world, second, situation graph trees (SGTs) exhaustively representing the knowledge about the expected situations of the current domain, and third, a situation recognition inference algorithm. The SGT-Editor, see [1], provides a framework dealing with SGTs, FMTL, and the situation recognition inference algorithm. Fortunately, all of the three are internally represented in FMTL. The theoretical complexity of FMTL is not promising – if at all – fast results. As in practice the amount of features used of FMTL and the relevant scope are far from exhausted, the whole system however reaches – with advanced parallelization techniques – impressive runtime performance beyond real-time.

The implementation is an agent-centered situation recognition process as FMTL inference engine which is available as efficient C application. This inference engine gets started as a separate thread, equipped with all the knowledge it needs to know, and is fed by requests returning the inferred situations. Simply parallelizing the inference engines per agent would not be sufficient, as the knowledge has to be shared, as the result of one agent may be needed as input for another agent's inference process. Thus we persistently link each agent with one inference engine thread. All concurrently running threads are sharing knowledge in every time step.

4   Experiments

The BEHAVE video dataset [2], see Figure 1 (v), is a dataset for multi-person situation recognition with over 90.000 frames corresponding to one hour of video. Kindly, the authors provide selected annotations both of persons and of ten different situations. Thus, this enables comparable evaluations on the results. The dataset was recorded with a static camera and the mapping from the image plane to the ground plane is provided, too.

We used a subset of this dataset to show that the proposed system works in -time on real data. The results of the recognized situations were successfully uated against the provided ground truth data which is available for the fol-ng situations: *InGroup, Approach, WalkTogether, Meet, Split, Ignore, Chase,*

Fight, *RunTogether*, and *Following*. Apart from the real-time capabilities, results concerning recognition rates are shown in Table 1. On ordinary hardware (Intel i7, 8GB Ram, NVIDIA GTX-580) the whole person detection and tracking is running at $7Hz$, situation recognition at least at $1Hz$ using the average value of seven frames.

Table 1. First qualitative results on the BEHAVE dataset (frames $24300-35,200$). The precision of the person tracking is near to 1 with recall about 0.8. On these tracking results with some missed non-tracked persons recall of the situation recognition is almost the same as for tracking but precision is lower due to some false positives arising from multiple hypothesis situation recognition.

Situation	precision	recall	comment
WalkTogether	0.6	0.7	similar to RunTogether
Approach	0.7	0.9	++
Split	0.6	0.8	+
InGroup	0.9	0.9	++

5 Conclusion

In this article, the modules for a real-time situational awareness system are integrated exemplarily and extended to achieve real-time performance on ordinary hardware. The contributions are reaching real-time performance on the one hand for the multi-person tracker and on the other hand for the situation recognition without forgetting integrating a whole working system. The experiments show that our system can deal with realistic scenarios and recognizes several – even competing – occurring situations. Future work to be done is both bidirectional handling of uncertainty and integrating the whole system into a user-friendly and easy to use prototype application.

References

1. Arens, M.: Repräsentation und Nutzung von Verhaltenswissen in der Bildfolgenauswertung. Dissertation, DISKI 287, Aka GmbH (2004)
2. Blunsden, S., Fisher, R.: The behave video dataset: ground truthed video for multi-person behavior classification. Annals of the BMVA 2010(4), 1–12 (2010)
3. Jüngling, K., Arens, M.: Pedestrian tracking in infrared from moving vehicles. In: 2010 IEEE Intelligent Vehicles Symposium (IV), pp. 470–477 (2010)
4. Jüngling, K., Arens, M.: Detection and tracking of objects with direct integratic of perception and expectation. In: ICCV Workshops, pp. 1129–1136 (2009)
5. Leibe, B., Leonardis, A., Schiele, B.: Robust object detection with interlea categorization and segmentation. IJCV 77(1-3), 259–289 (2008)
6. Lowe, D.G.: Distinctive image features from scale-invariant keypoints. IJCV 60 91–110 (2004)

7. Muja, M., Lowe, D.G.: Fast approximate nearest neighbors with automatic algorithm configuration. In: VISSAPP, pp. 331–340. INSTICC Press (2009)
8. Münch, D., IJsselmuiden, J., Arens, M., Stiefelhagen, R.: High-level situation recognition using fuzzy metric temporal logic, case studies in surveillance and smart environments. In: ICCV Workshops, pp. 882–889 (2011)
9. Ryoo, M., Grauman, K., Aggarwal, J.: A task-driven intelligent workspace system to provide guidance feedback. CVIU 114(5), 520–534 (2010)
10. Wu, C.: SiftGPU: A GPU implementation of scale invariant feature transform. SIFT (2007), http://cs.unc.edu/~ccwu/siftgpu

ISPS Port Risk Assessment:
Is the True Value in the Numbers or in the Process?

Gina Linkmann and Eric Holder

Fraunhofer FKIE, Neuenahrer Str. 20, Wachtberg, Germany

Abstract. Various activities to enhance security against terrorist threats were initiated in response to the 9/11 attacks. In 2004 the European Union released regulations based on the International Ship and Port Facility Security Code (ISPS Code) requiring ship owners, harbor operators as well as designated authorities to implement measures and procedures to prevent possible terrorist attacks or activities on port facilities and ships. VESPER^{PLUS}, a collaborative project funded by the German Federal Ministry of Education and Research, investigates security standards in the maritime domain. Among other activities, VESPER^{PLUS} reviews applicable risk assessment methodologies.

In this paper we review the ISPS risk analysis framework and its practical use for Port Facility Security Assessments (PFSA) and risk management activities. Our findings suggest that the numbers that are produced by most risk analyses methods are not as sure as the output may suggest, and therefore may not be the best base for preparing risk management activities. We propose that the process of conducting the risk analysis, rather than the numbers produced, holds the true value for understanding and prevention. The risk analysis methodology should be re-structured to capture the content of this process, considering additional options for collecting input, updates and insight from a wide range of experts, as well as for additional sharing of some of the output.

1 Overview of Port Risk Analysis as Required by the ISPS-Code

As defined by the International Maritime Organization, the ISPS code, "is a comprehensive set of measures to enhance the security of ships and port facilities, developed in response to the perceived threat to ships and port facilities in the wake of the 9/11 attacks in the United States." Enhancing the security of ships and ports is conceived as a risk management activity and in order to determine which security measures are required, a risk assessment must be conducted for each particular case (ship, port facility, objects therein, etc.). The code provides the standardized, consistent framework to be used to evaluate these risks. We examine the framework and its practical use for PFSAs and risk management activities.

Under the ISPS Framework [1] used for PFSA, "security risk is a function of threat of an attack coupled with the vulnerability of the target and the consequences an attack. The assessment must include the following components":

N. Aschenbruck et al. (Eds.): Future Security 2012, CCIS 318, pp. 522–525, 2012.
© Springer-Verlag Berlin Heidelberg 2012

- determination of the perceived **threat** to port installations and infrastructure (probability that a specific target will be attacked in a specific way during a specified period);
- identification of the potential **vulnerabilities** (probability that damage occurs, given a threat); and
- calculation of the **consequences** of incidents (magnitude and type of damage resulting from a successful terrorist attack) [2].

Although there are variations in the sub-factors and the algorithms used by different groups, the base formula to be used for analysis is therefore:

$$Risk = Threat * Vulnerability * Consequence \qquad (1)$$

During a PFSA these factors are then evaluated using a specific set of scenarios for various objects within the port facility.

2   Review of PFSA in Theory and Practice

Our analysis examines the ISPS risk analysis framework at the theoretical level, along with the challenges and problems experienced at various stages of putting the framework into practice. In this short paper we describe a priority sample of our preliminary results. The methods of analysis included a review of the literature for risk analysis overall, specific to terrorism risk, and specific to ISPS application; detailed evaluation of the risk analysis systems identified as relevant; and extensive observation, interviews (e.g., structured, unstructured), group discussion, and cognitive walk-through techniques with 8 risk analysts covering 3 major ports.

At the theoretical level, the central goal of any risk analysis process should be to generate enough knowledge to model the system, and subsystems, in sufficient detail to understand and evaluate the inherent risks. The results should be formatted and disseminated in a manner that supports informed decision-making for planning, response, or monitoring and preventive actions. The PFSA presents some special considerations. The formula (1) used in the ISPS-framework is adapted from risk assessment methods for technical systems where failures are unintended, but ISPS risk estimates must deal with terrorists' intended actions where targeting (and thus threat/ likelihood) considers consequences making them interdependent. Most models still treat likelihood and consequences independently. The ISPS code is strongly prevention focused, with the goal of detecting security threats and taking preventive measures against security incidents. In line with the preventative focus, the majority of the response activities in the case of an actual terrorist event are not covered by the ISPS scope and fall upon the local and state organizations. Therefore, the ISPS risk analysis framework must be examined primarily with a focus on its effectiveness for prevention. Evaluating the scope of the ISPS code is beyond the scope of this paper.

The stages of putting the framework into practice include collecting and entering the data, analyzing the data, and how results are captured and used. When completing analysis an individual or group will typically compute risk assessments for each "important" object within the port for each prescribed scenario by providing subjective estimates for threat (or at least likelihood), vulnerability, and consequences. There is very little validated data to base these estimates on and there is therefore inherently much variability and assumption underlying these estimates [2]. Changes in the specific formula, algorithms, guidance, and variable definitions can often produce significant variance in the outcome [3]. There can also be much variety in the experts used to collect this data (single person, group, panel of diverse port experts, etc.) and the background knowledge and perspective of these experts can significantly color the evaluation. Field expertise suggests incorporating a variety of perspectives in the process as one way to create a more robust view of port-specific risk [2].

There is a great deal of useful knowledge uncovered in the process of analyzing a port facility and making the calculations but much of this may be lost in a focus on the numbers. Current risk calculation methods often fail to capture the variability in the estimates or document the uncertainty involved at the time of analysis and retain this information when the results are disseminated as a report to other stakeholders, or if used for later activities. The judgments, assumptions, reasoning (e.g., description of the worst case used for estimates) and important distinctions between individual estimates can also be lost in the formula or tool leaving what might seem like a very precise estimate of risk, suitable for administrative review, but with little additional explanation of how the numbers were derived [4]. There is a risk that persons reviewing or updating the analysis, fail to appreciate the uncertainty in the numbers and/or understand the logic and assumptions underlying the original assessment. This creates the risk that persons viewing the final report only obtain part of the understanding.

The nature of the risk analysis process can also limit the accuracy and utility of the output. Threat, consequences, and vulnerability, and therefore the risk concept itself, are not static quantities. The PFSA is typically reviewed and updated once annually or at least once every five years. Producing a one-time estimate and developing a plan based solely on that single estimate is not conducive to effective risk management [3]. In practice port facilities adapt their risk management activities based on current events and circumstances (e.g., event-related crowds) but this information is not based on, or documented in, the PFSA. Including some of these port-specific scenarios could improve the process. Overall, in order to be useful the data on threat, consequences, and vulnerabilities that risk management decisions are based on needs to remain current and the process needs to support efficient and effective updating.

As noted above, the ISPS code is prevention focused, and the typical focus of a PFSA is, necessarily, very port specific. We argue that obtaining an accurate value of risk, and its subcomponents in the formula, on top of being unlikely is not required or extremely helpful to obtain the understanding required for effective prevention activities. The knowledge used by the analyst to think through the valuation process might be. The consequences must only be understood at a level that guides prevention activities, namely are there certain consequences that could be prevented, or removed altogether (e.g., defensive measures, changes in procedures or facilities) or certain object that require special attention due to their volatility (hazard presented). Similarly, no one truly knows, and the port personnel do not require, an exact value of threat. The port personnel must understand the nature of the threat at a level sufficient to determine likely tactics, access possibilities, and any distinguishing characteristics events that might reliably indicate a threat.

The vulnerabilities of the port, both for specific scenarios and overall, are the heart of prevention understanding. Despite this, not all models incorporate reductions, and other changes, in vulnerability based on preventive measures implemented (temporary or permanent). Models also have a difficulty including changes in terrorist targeting based on perceived target hardness and the factors responsible for the shifts. Risk perceptions and management activities are constantly changing but the PFSAs are not.

These are a few of the factors that influence people's ability to effectively complete a PFSA to produce valuable and usable results that truly support preventative, and possibly other, risk management activities.

3   Conclusion

Our review suggests the following considerations. The first is that the PFSA methodology needs to be designed to guide the analyst through the process and capture the logic, decision making, assumptions, and uncertainties of analysts, as they evaluate threats, vulnerabilities, and consequences for various scenarios. This may include reevaluating whether a numerical ranking system, based on uncertain estimates, is truly the best way to capture the analyses, especially to support the goal of prevention and hardening rather than ranking and comparison or allocation of resources. At a minimum, these factors need to be documented on any analysis worksheets used in order to support updating and review by other analysts. Consideration should also be given to including more of the logic and assumptions into the reports disseminated to other stakeholders. The second is to examine ways to better support the capture and presentation of the dynamic risk situation. This support may be related to opening the collaboration with other key port stakeholders, especially when it comes to sharing lessons learned (in practice or from exercises), new threat-related updates, and incorporating port-specific event scenarios and best practices in the PFSA. Increased collaboration can also include involving more expertise in the analysis process, as well as dissemination of filtered (but still useful) intelligence to relevant stakeholders. The second part of capturing the dynamic nature of the threat is to produce a process for updating that is not tied to a cumbersome and static capture of the situation.

References

1. Regulation (EC) No 725/2004 of the European Parliament and of the council of March 31, 2004 on enhancing ship and port facility security. Official Journal L 129 (April 29, 2004)
2. Willis, H., Morral, A., Kelley, T., Jamison, M.: Estimating Terrorism Risk. Rand Corporation, Santa Monica (2005)
   Clark, B., Ninic, D., Fidler, N.: Protecting America's Ports: Are we there yet? Research Report prepared by The California Maritime Academy (2007)
   Mueller, J., Stewart, M.G.: Terror, Security, and Money: Balancing the Risks, Benefits, and Costs of Homeland Security (2011)

Securing Area with Robots under BML Control

Thomas Remmersmann and Ulrich Schade

Fraunhofer FKIE, Neuenahrer Str. 20, 53343 Wachtberg, Germany
{thomas.remmersmann,ulrich.schade}@fkie.fraunhofer.de

Abstract. Securing larger areas with multi-robot systems is a challenging task when you want to have multiple robots controlled by only one person in an efficient way. One way to do this is to let the commanding person express high-level tasks and to build an intelligent multi-robot system (MRS) that can execute these high-level tasks and provide aggregated feedback to the commander. We implemented such an approach by using Battle Management Language for defining high-level tasks. In this paper we will show how tasks are disaggregated, scheduled and distributed among the robots of the MRS.

Keywords: securing area, MRS, multi-robot systems, C2 systems, BML, genetic algorithms, scheduling, planning.

1   Introduction

The reasons to secure large areas or borderlines by robots are manifold. It can decrease personnel costs, robots can handle multiple advanced sensors, and they can work in dangerous areas without human lives being risked. However, personnel costs can only be reduced if multiple robots can be controlled efficiently by one person and if the robots do the same jobs as human beings. Due to limitations of information processing power of a human, a group of robots cannot be led in the same way as a single robot. Whether we take a look at commanding structures used in the armed forces or in a business organization they all work similarly. The commander (boss) does not tell all fighters (employees) exactly what they have to do. Instead, he informs team leaders what their team should do in general and the team leaders tell their people on a somewhat less general level what they should do, and in the end, the fighters (workers) decide the best way to execute the tasks. We use this concept, the concept of mission command, for commanding multi-robot systems (MRS). This includes that orders are split into sequences of smaller tasks automatically and that feedback is aggregated and reported to the commander in the aggregated form. For expressing high level tasks we use Battle Management Language (BML) which is human-readable but also can be processed by systems automatically. Originally, BML was developed for interacting with units in simulation systems [1].

2   Related Work

Some work has been done in the area of controlling multiple robots under the constraint of keeping control on the workload. The unmanned systems in question were multiple tactical missiles [2] and heterogeneous UAVs [3].

N. Aschenbruck et al. (Eds.): Future Security 2012, CCIS 318, pp. 526–529, 2012.

Other related work focuses on *supervisory control* of multi-agent systems (MAS) [4]. The most basic approach here is the control-by-behavior approach: a set of basic behaviors is predefined and the operator selects one of them for each agent. However, this approach is not feasible for larger groups of agents. A more advanced approach is the control-by-policy approach: here global constraints or advice are given by the operator and corresponding actions are planned by the agents. A third is approach is the playbook metaphor: here a set of tactics, which can be parameterized, is known by the robots.

In our approach, we use task assignments formulated in the mission command style. The language is BML, which is an artificial, unambiguous, human-readable and automatically processable language. Originally, it was developed as an interoperability solution between C2 systems and simulations systems. BML allows the formulation of orders, requests, and reports. If, for example, C2Central wants Robot_Group_1 to recce Area_1 immediately, the corresponding BML order is

```
recce C2Central Robot_Group_1 at Area_1 start at now;
```

We developed a graphical user interface to allow intuitive generation of BML orders. First, a task's action is selected. Then the GUI shows which other elements are required for completing the task assignment. Robots (or MRSs) are selected from a list or from the map. Geographic elements such as areas also are defined on the map.

In [5], we discussed in detail how to command robots using BML. Fig. 1 presents photos from various demonstrations. As mentioned in [5], some orders are executed after breaking them down into suborders but suborders must be carefully synchronized. It is important which robot does what and when, so planning is needed. In addition, it is sometimes necessary to express strict conditions under which specific tasks need to be executed.

Fig. 1. Two groups of robots controlled using BML. (Left) A ground vehicle patrols a road and two drones accompany it scanning the surroundings. (Right) Three robots move in formation.

ch robot is allowed to execute only one task at a time and each subtask can only be cuted by one robot. According to [6] this is "single-task robot, single-robot task, e-extended assignment" (ST-SR-TA). Since the multiple-robot job scheduling lem is NP-hard [6] [7], it is not possible to find the optimal plan for complex tasks in an appropriate time. But it is possible to find a near-optimal solution using heuristics like genetic algorithms.

Genetic algorithms were developed by Holland [8]. The idea is to represent a solution as a string or chromosome and to do genetic operations on it to create "children", which hopefully represent better solutions. Solutions are rated by a fitness function. Solutions with a good fitness are kept, others are discarded. The genetic algorithm in our use decides the order of the tasks and though requires operations which solve ordering problems. The paper [9] gives a good overview of those operations. We used seven crossover operations (PMX, CX, OX1, OX2, POS, VR, AP) and six mutation operations (MO, DM, EM, ISM, SIM, IVM, SM), cf. [8][9] for details.

3   Disaggregation of the Tasks

In our work we combined the three MAS approaches mentioned in section 2. We started with high-level orders in a formal, human-readable language which included temporal constraints. We worked with a library of plans, similar to the playbook metaphor, according to which the high-level tasks are split up into basic tasks for the robots. This disaggregation depends on the properties of the MRS, constraints and additional parameters provided by the operator. Those basic tasks were scheduled and then executed at their assigned time by adjusting the behavior of the robot in question.

If, for example, a commander wants to secure a border while having only two drones with cameras available, it is not very efficient if those robots patrol the border together. However, if one of the drones has an infrared camera instead, team patrolling makes more sense. The drone with the camera can take high resolution pictures of those objects that emerge from the IR images.

We evaluated the process on test scenarios, e.g., an operator wants an MRS with three drones to reconnoiter an area. In our "playbook" there is an entry on how to

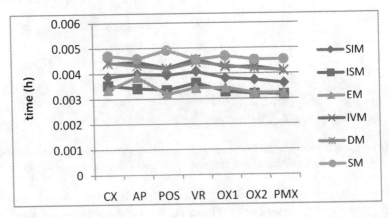

Fig. 2. Average time required by plans generated by pairs of crossover and mutation operato

recce an area: a grid is laid over the area and from each point of that grid a photo is to be taken. The scheduler, based on genetic algorithms, provides a plan including the necessary move tasks. Of course, a good approximation of the required time for each task is necessary to prevent re-planning. During execution the robots' behavior switches from "move to position" to "take a photo" according to the schedule. We tested with an area of which 5 x 5 (25) photos had to be taken by three drones and compared which crossover operator and mutation operator return the best results.

The result can be seen in Figure 2. It shows the average time a plan generated by a combination of one mutation and one crossover operator requires after 1000 generation with 80% crossover and 80% change of mutation. The graph shows that the mutation operator has much more influence on the results than the crossover operator. The best results are produced by the mutation operators ISM and EM. The best Crossover operators are OX2 and PMX.

4   Outlook

For future applications, more mechanism must be implemented. For example, the management of resources (like energy or tools) must be managed. In summary, however, the approach offers a way to control a multi-robot system effectively by a single controller.

References

1. Heffner, K., Brook, A., de Reus, N., Khimeche, L., Mevassvik, O.M., Pullen, M., Schade, U., Simonsen, J., Gomez-Veiga, R.: NATO MSG-048 C-BML Final Report Summary. In: 2010 Fall Simulation Interoperability Workshop, Orlando, FL (2010)
2. Cummings, M.L., Mitchell, P.J.: Operator scheduling strategies in supervisory control of multiple UAVs. Aerosp. Sci. Technol. 11(4), 339–348 (2007)
3. Nehme, C., Mekdeci, B., Crandall, J.W., Cumming, M.L.: The Impact of heterogeneity of operator performance in futuristic unmanned vehicle systems. Int. Command Control J. 2(2) (2008)
4. Coppin, G., Legras, F.: Autonomy Spectrum and Performance Perception Issues in Swarm Supervisory Control. Proceedings of the IEEE 100(3) (2012)
5. Remmersmann, T., Brüggemann, B., Frey, M.: Robots to the Ground. In: Concepts and Implementations for Innovative Military Communications and Information Technologies, pp. 61–68. Military University of Technology, Warsaw (2010) ISBN 978-83-61486-70-1
6. Gerkey, B.P., Matarić, M.J.: A formal analysis and taxonomy of task allocation in multi-robot systems. Intl. J. of Robotics Research 23(9), 939–954 (2004)
. Bruno, J.L., Coffman, E.G., Sethi, R.: Scheduling Independent Tasks To Reduce Mean Finishing Time. Communications of the ACM 17(7), 382–387 (1974)
   Holland, J.H.: Adaptation in Natural and Artificial Systems. The Univ. of Michigan Press, Ann Arbor (1975)
   ,arrañaga, P., Kuijpers, C., Murga, R., Yurramendi, Y.: Learning Bayesian network structures by searching for the best ordering with genetic algorithms. IEEE Transactions on System, Man and Cybernetics 26(4), 487–493 (1996)

Author Index